Prototyping Essentials with Axure

Second Edition

A comprehensive strategy and planning guide for the production of world-class UX artifacts such as annotated wireframes, immersive prototypes, and detailed documentation

Ezra Schwartz

Elizabeth Srail

BIRMINGHAM - MUMBAI

Prototyping Essentials with Axure

Second Edition

First Published: January 2012

Second Edition: May 2014

Production reference: 1200514

Published by Packt Publishing Ltd.
Livery Place
35 Livery Street
Birmingham B3 2PB, UK.

ISBN 978-1-84969-832-0

www.packtpub.com

Cover Image by Anna-Marie White (anna-mariewhite@sbcglobal.net)

Credits

Authors
Ezra Schwartz
Elizabeth Srail

Reviewers
Ben Judy
Sam Spicer
Jan Tomáš

Commissioning Editor
Martin Bell

Acquisition Editors
Sam Birch
Ellen Bishop
Wilson D'souza
Antony Lowe

Content Development Editor
Azharuddin Sheikh

Technical Editors
Pankaj Kadam
Rohit Kumar Singh
Ankita Jha

Project Coordinator
Venitha Cutinho

Copy Editors
Sarang Chari
Mradula Hegde
Sayanee Mukherjee
Deepa Nambiar
Karuna Narayanan
Alfida Paiva
Adithi Shetty
Stuti Srivastava

Proofreaders
Simran Bhogal
Mario Cecere
Ameesha Green
Sandra Hopper

Indexer
Hemangini Bari

Graphics
Sheetal Aute
Ronak Dhruv
Disha Haria
Yuvraj Mannari

Production Coordinator
Shantanu Zagade

Cover Work
Shantanu Zagade

Foreword

Axure RP 7 was one of the most significant product releases we've had to date. It reminded me a lot of Version 2, which was released in late 2003. In Version 2, we switched from an HTML-based editor to a diagram editor and laid the foundation for prototype generation. We were able to build upon Version 2 for the following 10 years to add milestones such as the dynamic panel, conditional logic, and shared projects. In Axure RP 7, we completely rearchitected the generated HTML with an eye towards the next 10 years of software and user experience design.

We've been lucky to work with thousands of customers over the years and listen to tens of thousands of feature requests and inquiries. Every request is tracked, reviewed, and categorized. It's been interesting to see patterns naturally emerge after each release, and this has helped us prioritize areas of focus for future releases. Our customers have given us a unique view into how many organizations are doing software design and development, and it's clear that user experience design has never been more important.

It's essential to be able to test and iterate quickly on ideas early in the design process. Once these ideas solidify, being able to truly experience the design as a designer, stakeholder, or user can be invaluable. I think Axure RP 7 takes a solid step forward in accomplishing these goals. The Shape widget in Axure RP 7 supports 17 events compared to only three events in Version 6.5. There is a new Repeater widget that is data-driven and supports sorting and filtering. We introduced Adaptive Views to apply different styles, positions, and sizes to the widgets based on the browser size.

AxShare has also been upgraded to give designers and developers much more flexibility. It is now possible to add custom JavaScript and HTML into hosted projects. This opens the door to hand-coded interactions and custom elements. It also makes it possible to integrate third-party solutions such as analytics and user testing. You can also assign a custom domain directly to a project.

There are currently over 80,000 licensed Axure RP customers, and we expect to reach over 100,000 this year. It's a great feeling when you can count people like Elizabeth and Ezra as customers and advocates. They are true leaders in the user experience and Axure communities. With the help of customers like them, we're confident the best is ahead.

Victor Hsu
Cofounder, Axure

About the Author

Ezra Schwartz helps organizations realize their strategic vision for a world-class user experience. As a principal experience architect, he holds lead positions in mission-critical projects for global corporations. An advisor to management and stakeholders, Ezra is an expert in transforming large-scale, data-driven systems into mobile-first, device/OS-agnostic UX frameworks.

Ezra enjoys solving the numerous challenges involved in complex systems, the organizations that build them, and the people who use them. He draws on his wealth of experience from projects in the financial, education, aviation, healthcare, telecom, publishing, research, manufacturing, and software industries. Ezra feels very fortunate to be practicing in a domain that affords him the opportunities to travel and associate with the exceptional cast of international experts he gets to collaborate with. He values mentoring and giving back to his professional and social communities.

Ezra is the founder and organizer of AxureWorld.org, a free community-driven international conference dedicated to UX prototyping. He talks regularly about UX at conferences and on his blog, `www.artandtech.com`.

Acknowledgments

This book is dedicated to my mother, Eda.

To Tsippi and Shlomo Bobbe.

To my wife, Orit, who gave me her full support despite me braking a promise to abstain from writing so soon after the previous book, and to my sons, Ben and Yoav, who, during the writing of *Axure RP 6 Prototyping Essentials*, were already smarter than me and now surpass me in height and strength as well. Some of the time that went to writing and editing was family time—their time.

To my family: Julia, Hillel and Eitan Gauchman, Hedva Schwartz, Ruth and Doron Blatt; and to my good friends: Lisa Comforty, Jim Carlton and Caroline Harney, Christine and Scott Marriott, and Ayelet. To Alon Fishbach, and Barbara Drapcho whose clarinet lessons taught me that in performing music, as opposed to most things in life, I cannot "wing it" and to Alan Brazil for his high-fives whenever we met on an early morning run.

To all the colleagues and friends who have contributed directly or indirectly to the writing of this book, I wish I could mention all of you. I would like to extend special thanks to Kalpana Aravabhumi, Sunni Barbera, Oren Beit-Arie, Kirk Billiter, Juli Boice, Janet Borggren, Martin Boso, Mary Burton, Gary Duvall, Richard Douglass, Mike Fleming, Chris Giesler, Jim Hobart, Victor Hsu, Allan Lawson, Ritch Macefield, Alice O'Brien, Kristin Richey, Julie Robertson, Iram Saiyad, Derik Schneider, Paul Sharer, Ginger Shepard, Sam Spicer, Andres Sulleiro, Arturo Ttovato, Kalyani Tumuluri, Zack Webb, Cord Woodruff, Donny Young, Maxine Zats, and Lynn Zealand for their tremendous support and encouragement.

I am tremendously grateful to my colleagues Sam Spicer, Ben Judy, and Jan Tomáš, the technical reviewers in this book, for their contribution. Their detailed, honest, knowledgeable, thoughtful, and generous comments helped make this a better book.

I would also like to acknowledge a few remarkable fellow practitioners who responded so generously to my request to share their expertise with the Axure community: Ildikó Balla, Adam Basey, Svetlin Denkov, Gary Duvall, Suresh Kandeeban, Ritch Macefield, Susan Grossman, and Shira Luk-Zilberman.
Thank you!

Last but not least, thanks to the people who are behind the scenes of this book. My sincere gratitude to the editors and staff at Packt Publishing, and especially Ellen Bishop, Venitha Cutinho, Wilson D'souza, Pankaj Kadam, and Azharuddin Sheikh for their guidance, tremendous patience, and continuous encouragement throughout this project. It has been a real pleasure collaborating with you on this book.

About the Author

Elizabeth Srail has been creating and leading designs since 2001, and throughout that time, she has learned that employing the lesson her parents taught her at a young age, which is to "put yourself in that person's shoes", is the key to a successful design. In an age where everyone is talking, mostly through social media, Elizabeth has been listening. She takes what she hears from the users and stakeholders, and removes or diminishes the problems these people face with designs that are thoughtful, easy-to-use, fun, and pretty. She employs that same lesson when managing others as well and believes that kindness is the greatest illustration of strength.

In addition, Elizabeth has guided large organizations by educating leaders on the nuances of the UX process and advising them on how best to implement this practice into their current delivery methodology.

Elizabeth started using Axure in 2008 and was happy that Axure allowed her to demonstrate her vision by creating interactivity without having to code and without having to use words to sell her designs; the design and experience spoke for themselves. She met Ezra in February 2009, and in the following years, they collaborated on how best to optimize Axure, often discussing and debating the evolution of the UX practice.

Elizabeth is a devoted practitioner and teacher of Ashtanga yoga. Practicing yoga has allowed her to be more creative and handle the stressors of work with poise.

Acknowledgments

First and foremost, I would like to thank my parents, Ruth and Ronald Srail, for understanding the tremendous responsibility of parenting and for doing everything they could to provide a safe, loving, and harmonious home for my sister and me.

I would like to thank my nephew who sat an entire Saturday with me while I edited chapters. My niece was smart and went to a birthday party, but I have to thank her as well. The two of you carry a sweetness that I hope you hold onto throughout your life.

I also want to thank my friends who had to listen to me stress over this book, especially my dear friends, Chris de Lizer and Abby Miller.

The majority of my Axure work has involved the use of Shared Projects, and thus, I like to call my colleagues and collaborators "Axure Roommates". I have been very lucky to share new Axure tricks with great roommates, and I made many friends along the way: Josh Barr, Katrina Benco, Teryn Cleary, Jacqui de Borja, Kathy Mirescu, Beth Roman, Rachel Siciliano, Laurie Tvedt, and Sarah Wallace. We worked on rather grueling projects, but we all dived in and did the best we could.

Victor Hsu and Paul Sharer spent many Tuesdays with Ezra and me to walk us through new features. They listened to our feedback when Axure 7 was in its pre-beta stages. Thank you for taking the time, even when you were faced with a major deadline!

Finally, many thanks to the editors and staff at Packt Publishing: Ellen Bishop, Venitha Cutinho, Pankaj Kadam, and Azharuddin Sheikh. Your support, tremendous patience, and hard work were always appreciated by Ezra and me throughout the writing and editing process. In addition, we had technical reviewers who provided very thoughtful and helpful feedback: Sam Spicer, Ben Judy, and Jan Tomáš.

About the Reviewers

Ben Judy takes tech from frustrating to fun. His passion is to understand the needs of people who use technology and design better systems that work well for humans.

He designed and built his first website in 1996. He began using Axure in 2006 to create rapid prototypes for all manner of digital projects with a user-centered design approach.

Ben has worked as a UX manager, contributor, contractor, and consultant with global Fortune 500 companies, family-owned small businesses, and small start-up ventures. Amid the complexity of collaborative software projects, Ben keeps his focus simple; it's all about the user experience!

Ben lives near Dallas, Texas, with his wife, Kristen, and daughters, Ashley and Emily—who keep him laughing and remind him of God's grace.

Sam Spicer is a digital design professional with 14 years of experience. Beginning with front-end development, Sam progressed through his MS in Human-Computer Interaction into the realm of Information Architecture in the early 2000s. Since then, he's contributed to, and has also led, redesigns and replatforms for international brands, ranging from e-commerce and financial services to the retail and food industry. When he's not geeking out on some obscure experience or technical thing, you can find him enjoying with his family, brewing beer, or otherwise getting into some sort of trouble.

Sincere thanks to Ezra for allowing me to contribute to this effort, which I've very much enjoyed and learned a great deal from. Also, of course, an incredible thank you to my wife, Nikki, for her support and partnership without which I'd never be able to get anything accomplished!

Jan Tomáš is the founder, consultant, and clown at CIRCUS DESIGN (`www.circusdesign.cz`). His specialization deals with user research and prototyping. He uses Axure RP on a daily basis for prototyping web and mobile applications to communicate his designs with developers, managers, and other stakeholders. Jan is also an active member of the User Experience community. He organizes meetings, called UX Circus Show (`www.uxcircus.cz`), every month to share knowledge and show that our work could be fun.

www.PacktPub.com

Support files, eBooks, discount offers, and more

You might want to visit www.PacktPub.com for support files and downloads related to your book.

Did you know that Packt offers eBook versions of every book published, with PDF and ePub files available? You can upgrade to the eBook version at www.PacktPub.com and as a print book customer, you are entitled to a discount on the eBook copy. Get in touch with us at service@packtpub.com for more details.

At www.PacktPub.com, you can also read a collection of free technical articles, sign up for a range of free newsletters and receive exclusive discounts and offers on Packt books and eBooks.

http://PacktLib.PacktPub.com

Do you need instant solutions to your IT questions? PacktLib is Packt's online digital book library. Here, you can access, read and search across Packt's entire library of books.

Why subscribe?

- Fully searchable across every book published by Packt
- Copy and paste, print and bookmark content
- On demand and accessible via web browser

Free access for Packt account holders

If you have an account with Packt at www.PacktPub.com, you can use this to access PacktLib today and view nine entirely free books. Simply use your login credentials for immediate access.

For all in the Axure community who approach design
with an open mind and open heart.

– Ezra Schwartz and Elizabeth Srail

Table of Contents

Preface

Designing the user experience has never been more exciting and prototyping it has never been more challenging. Prototyping is the single most cost-effective means to track usability problems before you begin investing in visual design or coding, and Axure RP 7 is the industry's foremost prototyping tool.

This detailed, practical primer on Axure 7.0 is a complete rewrite of the previous edition due to the numerous new features in Axure 7.0. The demand for skilled Axure professionals is high, and familiarity with Axure is an expected prerequisite for UX designers worldwide. Short on jargon and high on methods and best practices, packed with real-life scenarios and step-by-step guidance through hands-on examples, this book will help you integrate Axure into your UX workflow.

What this book covers

Chapter 1, Prototyping Fundamentals, covers the Axure option, project-level forecasting, a weighted checklist for UX projects, Axure construction strategy checklist, its usage in various project types, and tips for using Axure on large projects.

Chapter 2, Axure Basics – the User Interface, explains file formats and workspace. It also covers the wireframe, Sitemap, Masters, Widgets, Widget Interactions and Notes, Page Properties, and Widget Manager panes. It further explains adaptive views, repeater, Web Fonts, toolbar, and menu bar.

Chapter 3, Prototype Construction Basics, covers device/OS-agnostic frameworks, objectives and artifacts, naming and labeling conventions, requirements, use cases, flow diagrams, navigation, masters, dynamic panels, and visual effects.

Chapter 4, Creating Basic Interactions, covers Axure interactions, events, cases, and actions.

Chapter 5, Advanced Interactions, covers conditions, raised events, and variables.

Chapter 6, Widget Libraries, covers masters and widget libraries, built-in libraries, community libraries, creating your own widget library, managing libraries, and managing visual design patterns.

Chapter 7, Managing Prototype Change, covers change readiness checklist, estimating your work, rollbacks with Team Projects, custom styles, style painter, alignment with visual design, guides, and grids.

Chapter 8, UI Specifications, covers configuring page notes and annotation fields, annotation strategy, and configuring specifications generators.

Chapter 9, Collaboration, covers team projects, best practices for teams, and AxShare.

Appendix, Practitioners' Corner, discusses a survey that was conducted among Axure users, troubleshooting guidelines, and construction tutorials.

What you need for this book

To follow the demo project in this book and to experiment on your own, you will need the following:

- Axure 7 is available for Windows and Mac. To experiment with Axure's Team Project feature and with generating Word specifications, Axure 7 Pro is required. You can download a free, 30-day evaluation copy from `www.Axure.com`, and the company is very generous in extending the trial period. For latest list of system requirements to run Axure on either platform, check out Axure's website.
- For specifications, MS Word 2000 or newer for Windows and MS Word 2004 or newer for Mac.
- Chrome, in both platforms, is the recommended browser. Firefox is fine as well.

Who this book is for

This book is intended for:

- UX practitioners, business analysts, product managers, and others involved in UX projects
- Consultants or in-house staff who work for agencies and corporations
- Individual practitioners or UX team members
- UX practitioners who seek to deliver a higher value in a fraction of the time involved in wireframing and annotating with traditional techniques based on drawing tools

- UX practitioners who want to dramatically improve their productivity and skills with expertise in delivering rich, interactive prototypes and extensive specifications instead of static documents

The book assumes that the user has either little or no familiarity with Axure. Perhaps you are evaluating the tool for an upcoming project or are required to quickly get up to speed in a project you just joined.

The book assumes familiarity with the principles of the user-centered design methodology.

Conventions

In this book, you will find a number of styles of text that distinguish between different kinds of information. Here are some examples of these styles, and an explanation of their meaning.

Code words in text, database table names, folder names, filenames, file extensions, pathnames, dummy URLs, user input, and Twitter handles are shown as follows: "By default, the `.rp` files are stored into the `root Documents/Axure` folder."

New terms and **important words** are shown in bold. Words that you see on the screen, in menus or dialog boxes for example, appear in the text like this: "Once you have installed Axure and launched it, you are presented with the **Welcome to Axure RP Pro 7.0** window."

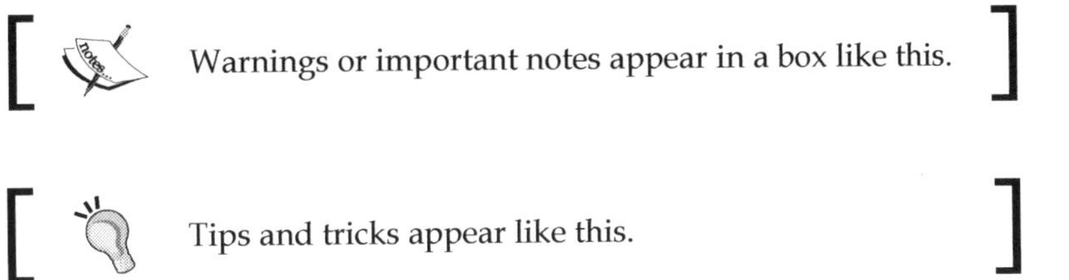

Warnings or important notes appear in a box like this.

Tips and tricks appear like this.

Reader feedback

Feedback from our readers is always welcome. Let us know what you think about this book—what you liked or may have disliked. Reader feedback is important for us to develop titles that you really get the most out of.

To send us general feedback, simply send an e-mail to `feedback@packtpub.com`, and mention the book title via the subject of your message.

If there is a topic that you have expertise in and you are interested in either writing or contributing to a book, see our author guide on `www.packtpub.com/authors`.

Customer support

Now that you are the proud owner of a Packt book, we have a number of things to help you to get the most from your purchase.

Downloading the example code

You can download the demo files for this book at `http://prototypingessentials.weebly.com`.

Errata

Although we have taken every care to ensure the accuracy of our content, mistakes do happen. If you find a mistake in one of our books—maybe a mistake in the text or the code—we would be grateful if you would report this to us. By doing so, you can save other readers from frustration and help us improve subsequent versions of this book. If you find any errata, please report them by visiting `http://www.packtpub.com/submit-errata`, selecting your book, clicking on the **errata submission form** link, and entering the details of your errata. Once your errata are verified, your submission will be accepted and the errata will be uploaded on our website, or added to any list of existing errata, under the Errata section of that title. Any existing errata can be viewed by selecting your title from `http://www.packtpub.com/support`.

Piracy

Piracy of copyright material on the Internet is an ongoing problem across all media. At Packt, we take the protection of our copyright and licenses very seriously. If you come across any illegal copies of our works, in any form, on the Internet, please provide us with the location address or website name immediately so that we can pursue a remedy.

Please contact us at `copyright@packtpub.com` with a link to the suspected pirated material.

We appreciate your help in protecting our authors, and our ability to bring you valuable content.

Questions

You can contact us at `questions@packtpub.com` if you are having a problem with any aspect of the book

1
Prototyping Fundamentals

"Come gather 'round people
Wherever you roam
And admit that the waters
Around you have grown
And accept it that soon
You'll be drenched to the bone
If your time to you
Is worth savin'
Then you better start swimmin'
Or you'll sink like a stone
For the times they are a-changin'."

– Bob Dylan, from The Times They Are A-Changin'

The Times They Are A-Changin'

There is good news and not-so-good news to report on the state of things since the publication of *Axure 6 Prototyping Essentials, Ezra Schwartz, Packt Publishing*. The good news is that Axure now has over 80,000 licensed copies in 126 countries, and over 1 million `.rp` files have been uploaded to AxShare in 2013 alone (including new versions of the same file). The not-so-good news is that **Responsive Web Design** (**RWD**), a development approach hatched by programmers for programmers, has swiped the rug under the brief autonomy that **User Experience** (**UX**) designers had, over the creation of rich, interactive HTML prototypes, which tools such as Axure afforded without writing a single line of code. In RWD, developers solved a serious problem that they had to deal with: how to effectively and efficiently deal with multiple display sizes with a single code base. For designers, however, it became a struggle to construct and document the interactive prototype for variable screen sizes even in Axure. Increasingly, the task of building the prototypes appeared to be shifting back to the developers.

What happened? A profound change in human-computer interaction is sweeping the world, leaving in its wake injured giants of hardware and software, who less than a decade ago, roamed undisturbed in an ecosystem dominated by Intel- and MS Windows-driven desktops and laptops. The trigger was squeezed on June 9, 2007, with the introduction of the iPhone and again on April 10, 2010, with the introduction of the iPad. Since then, iOS and Android devices moved to account for the majority of devices sold worldwide.

That the world is rapidly turning mobile or that Intel and Microsoft lost their dominance so quickly, is part of the transformations we are experiencing. For UX, it is rather the emotional attachment that owners develop with their devices, which drives their popularity. The devices facilitate experiences and connections with both the real and virtual worlds through the mashing of personal and social, work and leisure, content discovery and consumption, and entertainment and learning.

For decades, user interfaces were assembled out of a small and finite collection of beloved widgets tied to a small and finite set of mouse and keyboard interactions. These user interfaces were composed of a small and finite set of window types. The majority of these interfaces were delivered to displays that increased incrementally in size and resolution over time. Yet, it turned out that it is not so simple to slap together a bunch of widgets on the screen.

But the complexity of designing a good user interface just a few years ago, pales in comparison to the present state of chaos; the number and flavor of user interface widgets keeps exploding, as new means of interactions are being invented via fingers, gestures, voice, eyes, and most recently, our brain.

Anywhere-Anytime used to be a favorite marketing catchphrase in the '90s, but globalization and technology turned it into an Anywhere-Anytime-Any OS-Any Device reality. Organizations are scrambling to adjust to this reality and for some, it's a survival effort.

Designing acceptable and good experiences kept eluding the majority of software of all types, regardless of the investment. After several decades of a slow and uphill battle for recognition, business and engineering stakeholders are ceding to the emerging UX profession. This is because good UX drives down the overall life cycle costs, increases market share, and earns the user's satisfaction and loyalty. Simply said, a bad user experience is bad for business.

However, guess who else is scrambling these days? We are! Just as UX has earned a prime-time spot at the software development life-cycle table—prototyping the experience for a device-agnostic world, has been snatched again by front-end developers, who invented a practical technique to deal with the challenge. They came up with a practical approach, while in UX circles, people were still debating the merits of Visio and paper static prototyping.

We have a great deal of respect for front-end developers who, in our opinion, are UX's best partners in evolving exceptional user experiences. Gary DuVall, lead presentation layer architect, talks about the challenges of keeping up with the constantly shifting technologies, and how front-end developers can greatly help UX when developers and designers tightly collaborate. As an example, he mentioned a project he worked on that experienced serious challenges with tables in a responsive design. The research and experimentation lead by the presentation-layer team has yielded a feasible approach that allowed the designers to use it to great success and solve the design problem.

At the time of writing this book, RWD is the most practical, technical method to deliver OS and device-agnostic experience to the Web. This explains its rapid propagation if you are a developer, but for UX, there is a sense that designers are back where they were a decade or so ago: front-end developers create prototypes and designers are further removed from being able to experiment first-hand with interactivity.
The following diagram visualizes the two common models for UX prototyping:

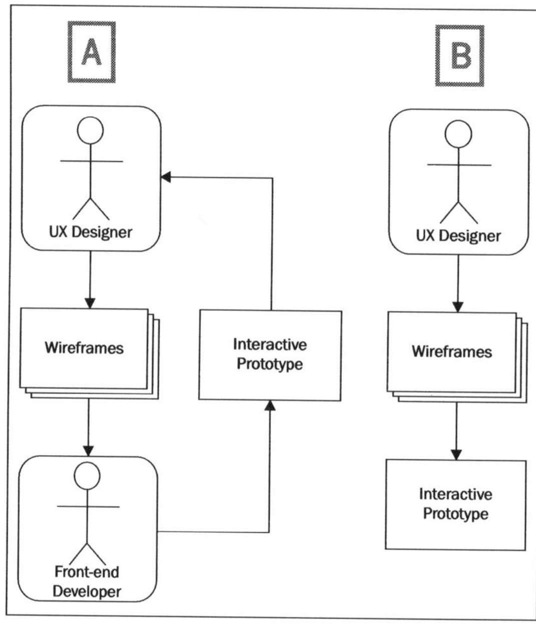

Image 1

- **Option A**: Complete dependency on front-end developers to express interactivity ideas and accept the risk of becoming marginalized. In this scenario (*Image 1*, **A**), UX creates static wireframes. The front-end developer turns them into HTML. The concern is not only around the waste of time and money this option can be, but also around issues that emerge in interpreting the dynamics of the interaction.
- **Option B**: You can become a coder yourself. You can learn HTML, CSS, and JavaScript, as it seems that there are no good UX tools to deal with RWD or are there?

It is common to find ads that look for a UX designer who can: plan and conduct user research, conceive and lead the design, create wireframes, build production grade html-css-javascript prototypes, and write detailed documentation. In other words, a one-person team that can do the work of several professionals, each with a specific expertise, but get paid as an individual. This, in our opinion, reflects how deeply UX is still misunderstood.

We believe that the primary focus of UX designers must be set on conceiving, experimenting with, and communicating UX. A tight collaboration with developers and a solid understanding of the technologies that drive modern software development, including HTML and CSS, is a must. UX practitioners should not be treated as a "jack of all trades" because they then become expert in none. Instead, UX designers need specialized and powerful tools to design UX.

The Axure Option

We propose a third option in which UX designers do not need to cede control over rapid prototyping to front-end developers nor become coders. While the learning curve of Axure 7 is somewhat more demanding, one can easily imagine and materialize contemporary UX firsthand. In Axure 7, you can evolve from a concept, to high-level wireframes, and then a detailed design in a responsive manner. If you are a current user, there are some new capabilities that will require you to drop familiar construction methods such as how you use dynamic panels.

Yet, and here we are talking from our experience; you will quickly adopt the new capabilities because they are built into and extend the familiar framework. If you are coding, Axure is surprisingly robust in its support for JavaScript and CSS. If you don't care much about this fact, you can still create amazing responsive simulations without having to code them.

> "*We shape our tools, and thereafter our tools shape us.*"
>
> – *Marshal McLuhan*

Marshal McLuhan's insight is especially intriguing in the context of tools that help us conceptualize and express the user experience. Our motivation to write this book has been shaped by personal experience with Axure. Early on, we were struck by the freedom to design, test, iterate, and present fully clickable interactive, and now, responsive, HTML prototypes of the experience we design. This is accomplished without a front-end developer and yet, our energy is focused on the user and the best UX instead of being thinned by struggling to learn a programming or authoring language.

Both Elizabeth and I share an experience that many other Axure users had. Within a few hours of launching Axure for the first time, we were able to create an interactive prototype without coding. Since that day, we have rarely used Visio as a wireframing tool. We also realized that in addition to being able to create interactive prototypes, Axure can help us deal with a major chore—creating and updating the user interface's UI specifications document.

If you ever created a specifications document in a traditional way using Visio, Word, or InDesign and a screen capture utility, you would know the drill—a tedious, time-consuming, and expensive process that involves adding footnote tags to Visio wireframes, taking screenshots of these wireframes, saving them, importing them to the specifications document, and finally, writing the relevant annotations.

However, iterative design is at the heart of the UX process, meaning that updates are frequent and sometimes substantial. And so you have to retake screen captures, name and save the image files, import the updated version to the document, and update the annotations. Sometimes, changes to wireframes require a cascading change in the order of annotations, which involves more work and potential errors. The process needs to be repeated for each updated wireframe. Multiply the time it takes by the number of modified wireframes in your project, and the magnitude of the effort becomes clear and daunting—a real drain of time, money, and energy which is bad for everyone involved in the project.

Axure's integrated specifications offered an innovative approach that had the potential to greatly reduce the manual process through automation. Axure numbers the annotations on the wireframes, takes the screenshots, and organizes the entire content in a customizable layout. While configuring the UI specifications document takes some experimentation, the effort pales in comparison to the manual process. Moreover, once you are happy with the way the specifications generator works, you no longer need to deal with it.

Since its introduction in Version 4.X, Axure's support for teams has evolved as an important enhancement that helped cement its adaptation among UX professionals. Any sizable project requires multiple UX resources, and collaboration is a critical prerequisite, which Axure addressed with its Shared (now known as Team) Projects feature.

Elizabeth and I share another experience with many users. As we started using Axure, we occasionally stumbled on technical issues or had questions we could not figure out. The company's responses were and continue to be prompt and detailed. Files sent for checkup are reviewed, the issues are explained, and bug fixes are promptly posted. This commitment and dedication to customer support has been, and continues to be, the reason for the loyalty Axure users have for the company.

Axure users also benefit from an incredibly helpful community of fellow users worldwide on Axure's discussion forum (refer to `http://www.axure.com/forum`). Typically, you can get a helpful response to your query within hours, and people are generous with sharing their expertise. Over time, as users gain some expertise with the tool, many enjoy being able to help others in the forum. Overall support is very important when a tool becomes critical in our work, because it has a direct impact on our livelihood. Support becomes a lifeline in times of crisis and the knowledge of that such a level of support exists plays a major role in wining user-based loyalty and tolerance.

Axure's value proposition continues to be strong and compelling, and its success in convincing clients and team members to approve or adopt it goes back to times when Axure was far less known among UX practitioners. This UX-centric integrated environment for wireframing, prototyping, UI specifications, and collaboration also carries a price tag. It is a small fraction of the cost and implementation complexities of enterprise tools.

A few years ago, some clients raised a concern about the ability to find UX resources who knew how to use Axure and some UX designers raised a concern about switching from tools they were very familiar with to a new tool. Despite the fact that these two concerns can potentially feed each other in a damaging loop, which makes it difficult to affect change, Axure has captured a dominant position in the UX industry despite numerous competitors.

External pressures also drive a change in attitudes and acceptance of the new competitor. Indeed, the growth of Axure's popularity among UX designers paralleled two important trends: the solidification of UX as an integrated part of the overall development process and technological advances that afforded the creation of rich user experiences. As more companies recognized the business value of modern user experience, budgets opened up and with them, the demand for UX professionals increased.

With this increase in demand came the pressures to deliver on time and budget, both often aggressive to absurdity. At a certain point, overly ambitious schedules create serious friction with the core principles of user-centered design, an inherently time-consuming methodology, which calls for contextual research, iterative design, and user validation. Many in the UX community realized that besides helping to produce world-class deliverables on a tight schedule, Axure is also helping UX stay profitable. This is because we can deliver a lot more value to our clients in less time, with less resources, and less sweat.

Profit is always important because at the end of the day, design agencies and independent consultants need to turn a profit in order to stay viable. In-house UX departments also need to increase productivity and reduce costs to help their company's bottom line. It is impossible to stay viable for long if you have to double and triple your workload just to keep up with the pressure of constant updates to a prototype and UI specifications. Axure helps maintain profitability because it is relatively easy to master and it affords substantial efficiencies through a clever use of customizable patterns, templates, and automation.

In conclusion, and reflecting back on McLuhan's observation mentioned earlier, Axure is a tool that has been shaped by UX designers over the course of over a decade. At the time of writing this edition of the book, it is widely used, with tens of thousands of licensed copies running worldwide on Mac and Windows, probably making Axure the de facto UX design tool in our industry.

In this chapter, we will introduce you to a simple planning and logistics methodology that will make your life easier while working on projects. We will cover the following topics:

- The *A Weighted Risk Checklist for UX Projects* section covers a diverse set of variables over which you have little control at the start of a project, will help you develop a predictive estimate of possible challenges and suggests actions you can take to turn lemons into lemonade
- The *Axure Construction Strategy Checklist* section helps define your approach to the construction of the Axure project file well before you even fire up the software
- To remind you that UX projects are a collaborative effort, the stakeholders' expectations list will help orient your position related to business, project management and engineering stakeholders, as well as other design and user experience practitioners

UX Prototyping by UX Designers

Our friend and a UX pro, Rich Macefield, told us about his amazing trip to Egypt, where, instead of joining the crowds at the Great Pyramids of Giza, he visited the site of smaller pyramids constructed around the 27th century BC. These pyramids are considered the prototypes of the famous structures. Back in the 15th century, Leon Battista Alberti described an event that took place in the first century BC. In his classic text, *On the Art of Building in Ten Books*, Alberti mentions that Julius Caesar "completely demolished a house on his estate in Nemi, because it did not totally meet with his approval." and continues to recommend "...the time-honored custom, practiced by the best builders, of preparing not only drawings and sketches, but also models of wood or any other material...".

One might think that, given his authority as the ruler of the Roman Empire, Julius Caesar was perhaps abusing his powers by acting in a capricious, short-tempered manner. We can also think about Caesar as a typical client, reacting somewhat badly to a design that did not meet his requirements and specifications.

Two millennia later, this is another way to think about the event that has an immediate relevance to us. The core of the problem is how to figure out what the client wants, and deliver a product that meets those expectations. This is a problem of communication, and UX designers face the challenge of resolving it satisfactorily on each project they work on. Often, the client might have a clear idea in their head of the exact way, the software should look and function. Sometimes the client has no idea of how the structure should look or function, but has a need to have it in place in order to fulfill a business requirement or some other pressing need.

From the early days of computer science, people found obvious parallels to physical architecture and borrowed from it liberally—terms and titles such as architect, build, configuration, and so on. Similarly, to architects and builders of physical structures, we need to create a functional product, and face the challenges of tracking tight budgets, adhering to schedules, and making our clients happy.

However, beyond borrowing terminology from architecture, aspects that relate to engineering and process rigor take much longer to implement. For example, the use of modeling for user interface and user experience design as we think about it today, came quite late to the development life cycle. This perhaps explains why a very high number of software or Web projects fare badly, but our cities are not littered by the ruins of collapsed buildings. Compare a large architecture project set to build a 100-storey skyscraper with a large enterprise software project. What are the odds that both will be fully up and running within a couple of years? The odds are very high for the skyscraper and far less for the software.

In other words, if we compare the rigor, efficiencies, and processes that translate a cardboard model and blueprints into a skyscraper with the typical chaos of software projects (perhaps with the exception of software for airplanes and such no-failure uses), we probably have some ways to go; it is an evolutionary process.

The truth is that of the billions of private residences, public buildings, and industrial structures that humans constructed on earth since moving out of caves, relatively few ever benefited from the design of an architect. Not that these are necessarily bad; in fact, many of the structures we see today evolved successfully over millennia. People build their own homes—individually or as a communal effort. Read Donald Harington's *The Architecture of the Arkansas Ozarks* for a wonderful account of such an evolutionary process.

Alberti further writes: "Having constructed those models, it will be possible to examine clearly and consider thoroughly relationship between the site and the surrounding district, the shape of the area, the number and order of parts of a building...It will also allow one to increase or decrease the size of those elements freely, to exchange them, and make new proposals and alterations until everything fits together well and meets with approval. Furthermore, it will provide a surer indication of the likely costs—which is not unimportant—by allowing one to calculate costs".

It is fascinating to translate Alberti's writings about modeling for buildings to UX prototyping for software. He is talking about the ability to articulate the layout, hierarchy, organization, and order of entities. He further talks about the ability to use the prototype for cost and effort estimation.

Another example of providing a client with wireframes and ensure its alignment with the client's needs is mentioned in the book, *Painting and Experience in 15th century Italy, Michael Baxandall, Oxford University Press*. Baxandall writes about the 15th century painter, Filippo Lippi. Back in 1457, Lippi was commissioned to paint a triptych for Giovanni di Cosimo de' Medici, the Italian banker and patron of the arts. In a letter to Giovanni, Filippo writes "...And to keep you informed, I send a drawing of how the triptych is made of wood, and with its height and breadth".

Prototyping Interaction

So it turns out that we did not quite invent the prototyping wheel after all. The value propositions, ROI calculations, and fancy technical terminology of prototyping have been around for a couple of millennia, if not more. There are however, several important differences that make prototyping rich user experience particularly challenging for UX practitioners.

In the past, structures did not involve dynamic interaction with the occupant nor did they need to shrink or expand at a whim. Buildings stood there, whether there was an occupant or not. However, we are entering an age when, as you enter a building, rooms could contextualize themselves instantly to reflect your preferences and perhaps even adjust physically to reconfigure the space to your specific needs.

When it comes to prototyping a rich user experience, the complications come from the need to demonstrate the following norms, among other things:

- **Scenarios**: The prototype needs to simulate the possible paths a user would have on any given screen and the system's appropriate responses of the actions that the user is taking. Often, the path could be conditional and take several steps to complete in a coherent and satisfactory way. The arsenal of interaction patterns that is available to UX designers today is significantly richer than what was available a decade ago.

- **Multiple screen sizes**: We must consider screen sizes, for example, small for smartphones, medium for tablets, large for desktops, and extra large for those large, high-definition screens. The user experience is influenced by the size of the screen, although the user might expect the same content and functionality regardless of the device in order to accomplish a task.
- **Prototyping in-page data refresh**: Back in the eighties, a prevalent workflow for a given task in client-server software involved hopping from one window to another. In the nineties, the common web navigation was hyperlinking from one page to another, facilitating a similar goal. These days, the need to negotiate multiple windows has been greatly diminished with asynchronous in-page data updates, but the complexities of prototyping in-page data refresh have increased.
- **Personalized experience based on login**: The prototype needs to simulate how the system will render for different users based on the entitlements. In the case of non-registered users, the site might display special offers to entice the user to register. A registered user may get information based on the preferences they have set in an earlier session and a paying user needs access to additional content based on their past activity on the site. Increasingly, we are asked to model all of these permutations.
- **Scalability and future scope**: Many applications are deployed in phases, making it possible for the business to prioritize its investment in the project based on strategic goals and practical, budgetary, and technical constraints. The prototype, which often begins as a full-fledged visionary concept, needs to be able to support *graceful degradation* or fall back on less-ambitious capabilities of the present and scale in the future.
- **Adaptability to localization**: In a global economy, a common requirement is to develop an application that can be easily localized to reflect the language and cultural preferences of the local demographics of its users. The prototype needs to demonstrate the ability to render in multiple languages.
- **Exception handling**: Following business rules helps dictate the logic that drives user-system interaction. One of the toughest requirements to prototype is how the application will respond when the rules for moving through an interaction path are subject to exceptions. For example, sales representatives want to increase the allowed discount on a product. Often, the demand for overrides surfaces late in the design process as a result of a push back from stakeholders who demand such capabilities.

Similar to architecture and construction, software is an evolving art and science. However, unlike construction, many of the tools and methodologies are evolving at such a rapid pace that it is very difficult to establish solid patterns of development. While physical architecture and construction evolved over centuries and stayed relevant for a long time, in technology, work created ten years ago is practically ancient and moot today.

Project-level Forecasting

"It is possible to fail in many ways... while to succeed is possible only in one way."

– Aristotle from the Nicomachean Ethics

Aristotle's observation predated by in some twenty-three hundred years Tolstoy's famous maxim that states:

"Happy families are all alike; every unhappy family is unhappy in its own way."

The idea is now encapsulated by the **Anna Karenina principle**, which, loosely speaking, describes an undertaking (say, UX project) in which an issue in any one of a number of factors dooms it to failure. Consequently, a successful undertaking (the same UX project) is the one where every major problem has been projected and avoided; this is our goal.

A Weighted Risk Checklist for UX Projects

Before you embark on a UX project, you should carefully consider several heuristics which will help you predict what lies ahead, how to take appropriate steps to take advantage of the potential opportunities, and how to avoid potential pitfalls. These heuristics share an important attribute—you have little or no control over them at the start of the project, but you may be able to affect change as things move along.

The checklist we propose has the following benefits:

- The factors in this checklist are generic and relevant to any UX project.
- The value of each factor can only be one of two possible options.
- Each option is weighted.
- In each option pair, the `Base` option's weight equals 1.
- The risks are not bad or good; it is just that, a risk of the project that will run over time and over budget because of complexities, churn, miscommunication, and other factors that are relevant to the risk.
- Before you engage in the project and start it, you should know the value for each factor.
- When you add up the numbers, the total score is a measure of your forecasted risk. The higher the number, the higher the risk.

The idea is not to prevent you from moving forward with the work. There are additional factors to consider when it comes to that. There is a risk in anything we do in life.

The Heuristics

The purpose of the following list is to get you ready and when possible, prepare. Feel free to modify—add or remove—items as you see fit to your personal circumstance. The key takeaway here is that you should have a list. It is a repeatable measure and tool that helps you identify patterns so that you can develop the best practices from one project to the next.

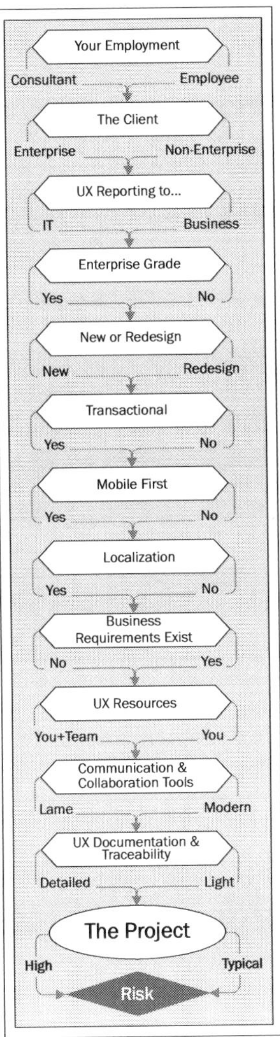

Image 2

#	Heuristic	Base	Wt	Higher Risk	Wt
1	Your Employment	Employee	1	Consultant	2
2	The Client	Non-Enterprise	1	Enterprise	2
3	UX Reporting to...	Business	1	Engineering	2
4	Enterprise Grade...	No	1	Yes	2
5	New Product or a Redesign	Redesign	1	New product	2
6	Transactional	No	1	Yes	3
7	Responsive	No	1	Yes	5
8	Localization	No	0	Yes	1
9	Business Requirements Exist	Yes	2	No	5
10	UX Resources	You	1	UX team	2
11	Communication & Collaboration Tools	G Docs and similar.	1	MS based	1-3
12	UX Documentation & Traceability	Light	1	Detailed	3-8
	Min Possible		12	Max Possible	30-37

The Score

When you sum up the items in the preceding table, you will end up with a score that is a predictor of what your scope will be. When you roll off the project, go over this list again and compare the prediction to the reality that you experienced. It is a good debriefing technique. The following table proposes a way to interpret the score:

Range	Prediction about your experience with the project
0-8	Green (lowest risk)
8-17	Yellow
18-23	Orange
24-37	Red (highest risk)

If you have some experience with previous projects, think about them, score them, and see to what degree the result fits your personal experience. We have tested this, and it seems to work quite well.

Note that a stormy prediction can also be a very rewarding professional and personal experience. Over the years, both Elizabeth and I had the opportunity to work on projects that were challenging and yet the reward of colleagues and friendships, the creativity, and satisfactions minimize the difficulties.

The following is an expanded review of the heuristics. Feel free to send us a note and share your personal insights.

Your Employment Type

The form of your engagement is at the core of your starting position in the project. While there are infinite variations given one's seniority and role, the two most common types of employment that frame your relationships with stakeholders can be your ability to influence things and the well-being of your emotional investment. The weighting of employment types is:

- You are a consultant of the company (Risk Weight = 2)
- You are an employee of the company (Risk Weight = 1)

Risk Factors for UX Consultants

The following are the risk factors for UX consultants:

- You probably don't really know anyone—who are real influencers and who are puffed pretenders—friends or foes of or office politics? How strong is your sponsor and how dependent are they on your success?
- You are an outsider and are being constantly evaluated at the start of the project. Trivial misunderstandings may get blown out of proportion. Some are hoping to see you make mistakes.
- You are not familiar with the culture and attitudes and need to be aware of the possible gaps in the expectations of how things get done.

Of course, being an employee does not shield you from significant challenges. If you are an employee, the preceding items may be relevant. However, for the purposes of this evaluation, we assume that employees are *insiders* and are better-positioned than consultants.

Opportunities

The following are some tips to find opportunities:

- Ask for an organization chart and explore the organization's intranet if it is accessible to you. Study it. Review the CC fields in your e-mail and match the names to the organization chart.
- Move as fast as possible to expand the circle of stakeholders who are aware of your existence by arranging short *discovery* meetings. Ask about their expectations and concerns and if relevant, continue to seek their input as the project moves along.

The Client

UX projects in large and small organizations are often challenging from a UX perspective due to the dynamics of influence and the need to handle stakeholders' power plays that may hijack important aspects of the design. The savvy to successfully oppose a dominant and powerful stakeholder comes naturally to few of us, but typically, it takes experience and courage. The sheer size of enterprise projects diminishes the influence of a single stakeholder over all. In a small company, any person on the project carries a significant influence just because there are far fewer competing voices. In both cases, we propose you read about group behavior in the context of social psychology to understand *group think* and other situations. Remember that in the end, you win some and you lose some. Weighting the options as follows:

- The customer is a large enterprise, a small company, or a startup (Risk Weight = 2)
- The customer is a mid-size company or organization (Risk Weight = 1)

Risk Factors

The following are a few risk factors that should be taken into consideration:

- The larger the organization, the higher the probability that one hand does not know or care about what the other hand is doing, thus leading to fragmentation and political power play
- The larger the organization, the slower things move due to added layers of hierarchy
- Busy decision makers may be too far removed from the project's nuts and bolts, making review meetings with them susceptible to major setbacks and blowouts due to miscommunication and misunderstandings
- Vertical silos are common in large organizations leading to misalignment and miscommunication around various aspects of the project's priorities, goals, and approach
- Small companies and startups can be chaotic and dominated by overloaded stakeholders with strong personalities

Opportunities

The following are some tips to find opportunities:

- In a large corporation/organization, you should master the operational mechanics, such as the phone system, reserving conference rooms, and online sessions, as fast as possible. You want to avoid a potential derailment of important meetings just because you could not figure out how to dial-in, reserve a room in advance, and so on. While this is an attitude you want to adopt in any setting, smaller organizations tend to be less formal and bound by procedure.
- Understand the organization, flow of work and responsibilities between departments, as well as governance structures that have impact on UX. Also make sure to understand processes such as change management and change control.

UX Reporting To...

It is rare that UX has complete organizational autonomy and influence, a situation that would be ideal. However, for most projects, UX is either sponsored by marketing, sales or other business functions or by the engineering department. Typically, UX projects are initiated by the business as part of a larger strategic goal. The closer the relationship with the business, the easier it is to affect alignment of the experience with these goals. The weighting for this category is:

- UX is reporting to Engineering (Risk Weight = 2)
- UX is reporting to Business (Risk Weight = 1)

Risk Factors

The following are a few risk factors that should be taken into consideration:

- Engineering sometimes lacks a complete or accurate insight into the entire set of strategic and tactical business objectives that drive the project.
- In many organizations, Engineering is focused on the maintenance and upkeep of software, which is an operational model that is radically different from the software development mode. As a result, you might find yourself trapped in what appears to be an unnecessarily slow and bureaucratic environment that is not optimal for rapid, iterative development.
- It seems that there is an infinite number of development methodologies and it is possible that unless you are with the same organization, you will have to adapt the UX process to whichever methodology is used in the project.

- Projects often start with an enthusiastic embrace of some methodology, such as a flavor of Agile, and degrade over time to a state of loose chaos.

Opportunities

The following are some tips to find opportunities:

- Since you typically have little control over whom you will report to at a given project, it is important to stay apolitical and avoid falling into the camp trap of assigning blame to one party or another. We are uniquely positioned to bridge differences of opinion as long as we communicate clearly and to the point.
- If you feel that the methodology enforced by engineering is compromising UX, make sure to understand the constraints that are at the root of the matter.
- It is possible to come up with recommendations and workarounds that while still a compromise, ends up working better overall.

Enterprise Grade

There are various definitions on the Web for the meaning of enterprise grade, and some include buzzwords such as "mission critical" and so on. Size matters! The larger the project, the higher the risks involved in a successful experience project. Enterprise-grade projects are notoriously challenging due to the need to deal with multiple tentacles of a complex organizational hierarchy. This hierarchy is often spread across coasts and continents, its culture, silos of power, and legacy constraints. The weighting of this category is:

- Enterprise-grade project (Risk Weight = 2)
- Non-Enterprise grade project (Risk Weight = 1)

Risk Factors

The following are a few risk factors that should be taken into consideration:

- An enterprise project means that UX is impacted in multiple dimensions such as scope and phasing, complexity, number of stakeholders involved, and resources.
- UX-specific dependencies are often not accounted for when the project road map and project plans are created. Omissions include no or insufficient time for adequate iterative review and revision cycles, prototype refactoring, digestion of usability testing results, and so on.

Opportunities

The following are some tips to find opportunities:

- It is sometimes difficult to remember, but every one wants to be part of a success. Recognize the forces of groups and social psychology that are in play and be a positive force in meetings. Be flexible when accepting critiques, yet firm in defense of the user experience.
- People are hesitant to voice their opinions even if they object to something. However, they need to hear alternatives. Try to be prepared with design options.
- As little as two voices, yours and another stakeholder's, in support of your idea can help you convince a larger group of your design direction despite stronger opposition. Always support your design with relevant arguments that stem from research, experience, public examples, and so on.

New Product or a Redesign

UX work typically involves a revamping of an existing product or the invention of a new one from scratch. It is the latter that is more problematic because only high-level concepts have been explored but not in great detail. Unfortunately, the devil, as the beaten phrase goes, is in those details. The weighting for this category is:

- The project is for a new product (Risk Weight = 2)
- This is a redesign project (Risk Weight = 1)

Risk Factors

The following are a few risk factors that should be taken into consideration:

- There is a lot that is unknown and will be in flux throughout the duration of a new product. Major changes might and will happen at unexpected times.
- Initial assumptions are likely to be blown away as the project evolves. Scope creep is endemic.
- Stakeholders who don't have a clear vision or true understanding of the work will introduce doubt, hesitance, and tangential alternatives that may derail aspects of the design and sometimes, the entire project.
- Redesigns too have their potential risks, especially when the there are high expectations for a contemporary, engaging user experience, which is greatly limited by the constraints of backend legacy technologies.

Opportunities

The following are some tips to find opportunities:

- It is rare to be involved in the creation of a brand new product. Take time to do the research and develop design principles and framework concepts that best fit the experience for your new product. The more solid and well-supported your approach is early on, the better your chance to place UX as a key player in the project.
- Design is critical when shaping the requirements, but it is hard to design with requirements that are being shaped and thus, often change. This is a typical conundrum. So, while it is extremely challenging to work in an environment that sometimes may feel like quicksand, remember that it is difficult for everyone on the project. UX can help by proposing rapid iteration on evolving concepts that help stakeholders arrive at the requirements.
- Despite the fast action, always present your work in an organized and prioritized way. Always tie your work products to your understanding of the importance and priority or requirements.

Transactional

Transactions mean that something is moving from a source (sender) to a target (receiver). The volume of transactions is a function of the number of sources and targets and the frequency of transmission. In addition to front-end experiences, a robust administrative interface must be provided as well, to facilitate the ability to deal with settings, business rules, and exceptions. Often, the administrator interface gets short changed at the start of the project because it is not customer facing, only to emerge as a massive, complex undertaking, once the work on the customer frontend winds down. The weighting for this category is:

- The project includes aspects of transaction management (Risk Weight = 3)
- No transactions are involved (Risk Weight = 1)

Risk Factors

The following are a few risk factors that should be taken into consideration:

- Transactional systems involve exception handling, which may complicate UX. Often, the business requirements have gaps in these areas.
- Prototyping transactional systems that needs to afford work with a lot of data is more time consuming; not only is it important to simulate screens that show many transactions—accuracy of simulated data is important. This means that we have to pay close attention to the flows and data transformations from one screen to another.

Opportunities

The following are some tips to find opportunities:

- Axure's new repeater has great potential in helping simulate transactional data
- Transactional application can provide you with opportunities to design very compelling work

Responsive

The term, "Mobile First", became popular in 2013 and is a strategic declaration that organizations make. In these declarations, they express their commitment to reaching their audience on tablets and smartphones, ahead of desktops. This can be accomplished in several ways, including OS native apps. However, the proliferation of operating systems and devices turns native apps into a very expensive proposition. Responsive Web Design levels the playing field by eliminating the cost associated with native apps. However, for UX, the risks and challenges are still significant, as the experience needs to be optimized to the display size. The weighting for this category is:

- Yes (higher risk, Weight = 5)
- No (typical risk, Weight = 1)

Risk Factors

The following are a few risk factors that should be taken into consideration:

- With RWD, you must have the design for all sizes ready at the same time. In other words, you cannot release a website that is only optimized for a smartphone and wait for the desktop view.
- Each breakpoint size requires an optimization such that the user gets the appropriate experience. Even when you are very efficient, it takes extra time to consider the various layouts across all sizes.
- Stakeholder meetings, user validation, usability testing, and of course, construction take more time because you need to go over multiple layouts.

Opportunities

The following are some tips to find opportunities:

- If you are new to RWD, this is the chance to learn!

- It is easier to affect change and help stakeholders empathize with users by reminding everyone to look at their phones. Because desktop and mobile experiences are so different, stakeholders, who may initially be oblivious to the quality of the user experience on a desktop, get your point immediately when smartphones and tablets are discussed.

Localization

When software needs to be translated to one or more languages, several layers of complexity are added to the project, both on the design and the implementation side. The weighting for this category is:

- Localization needed (Risk Weight = 1)
- No localization needed (Risk Weight = 0)

Risk Factors

The following are a few risk factors that should be taken into consideration:

- The design must support text directionality (left-right, right-left).
- The design must be flexible to support elegantly wider scripts, such as French and German.
- While the first two should be evident and simple for any professional UX designer, it is important to know about the customization and presentation of content as soon as possible due to cultural or business needs in a particular local, which may render key templates unusable and require extra work.
- There may be a need to factor in time for usability studies with users overseas. Time zones, holidays, and other issues may introduce unexpected delays in the execution of the testing program unless taken into consideration early on in the planning phase.

Business Requirements Exist

Unless you are totally new to UX and are facing your first project, some flavor of this heuristic is familiar. UX is supposed to follow business requirements. Without these requirements, the work is unfocused, with a high probability of going nowhere. The weighting for this category is:

- Requirements don't exist, are skeletal, and/or too general, or they are being developed (Risk Weight = 5)
- Well-developed requirements exist, and they are well written (Risk Weight = 2)

Risk Factors

The following are a few risk factors that should be taken into consideration:

- Writing good business requirements is a skill and also an effort that requires time. It is more common to find requirements that are vague, a compound of several requirements where some don't even fit together, and so on. UX often needs to drive the process of clarifying unclear or ambiguous requirements but the process can be slow and lengthy.
- It is common to get business requirements that try to dictate the user experience. You will have to educate and advocate for abstraction of the requirements from the specifics of UX. Your job will be to demonstrate how the requirements are fulfilled in detailed design.
- Another risk factor can be insufficient time in the project plan for creating the requirements, digesting them, and iterating their implementation in UX. The design is essentially due before or when the requirements are delivered.

Opportunities

The following are some tips to find opportunities:

- This is a tough spot to be in and we have been there numerous times. Therefore, if you don't understand the requirement, ask for a detailed explanation.
- Be organized. If requirements are not numbered, number them. If a bunch of requirements are lumped together in a single blob, break it apart. Everyone prefers order and organization over ambiguity and sloppiness. Make sure that you approach this in a diplomatic manner as part of the UX process and not as a critique of the person or group that created the requirements.

UX Resources

There is a famous saying that, "One woman can deliver a baby in nine months, but nine women can not deliver a baby in one month". For some, working alone is compelling for a variety of reasons. However, there is only so much we can do single handedly and the larger the project, the larger the UX team. While your role in the team depends on your experience, seniority, and several other factors, teamwork is not trivial. The weighting for this category is:

- You are part of a larger UX team on the project (Risk Weight = 2)
- You are the only dedicated UX resource on the project (Risk Weight = 1)

Risk Factors

The following are a few risk factors that should be taken into consideration:

- You don't know anyone on the team, and for some, adjusting to team work is difficult
- Skillsets, experience, and savvy can vary greatly
- The fact that not everyone on the team carries their weight, is not immediately apparent, and can explode just when the team is overflowed with stress and work
- It will require additional time and effort to align the work each team member contributes, and often, time and energy are very scarce

Opportunities

The following are some tips to find opportunities:

- Having a team has its own benefits. You get to learn, mentor, or be a peer of a colleague.
- There is a lot to learn from experiencing distributed work on multiple work streams and dealing with the complexity of managing and orchestrating timelines and efforts; they all merge at certain milestones.
- Extend your expertise in designing and applying global design patterns that will serve the entire team.

Communication and Collaboration Tools

This heuristic deals with the seemingly mundane software that is used to support the teams working on the project. In large budget projects, you will commonly find that critically important and highly collaborative documents, such as business requirements, are created in MS Word or Excel and distributed through a SharePoint repository. Wikis are also popular despite their being hideously convoluted and difficult to use. Similarly, UX work is expected to be created in a static wireframing tool such as Visio as opposed to Axure. The weighting for this category is:

- Excel, Word, Visio, SharePoint, and Wikis are the primary methods of documentation and content/project management (Risk Weight = 1-3)
- Collaborative software (not Wikis) is used (Risk Weight = 1)

Risk Factors

The following are a few risk factors that should be taken into consideration:

- Inefficient communication leads to miscommunication, mistakes, misunderstandings, and more serious problems.
- It is difficult to work collaboratively with multiple versions of documents floating around in e-mails. Referential integrity becomes a risk when work and review are done on the wrong/outdated copy of a document.
- Having to wait for another person or multiple people to finish work on a document is frustrating and time consuming.

Opportunities

The following are some tips to find opportunities:

- It can be very difficult to get the organization to adopt new tools such as Google Docs and similar ones, for a variety of reasons including concerns about security and confidentiality. Make sure that you follow the internal procedures and protocols.
- It may be possible to get the organization to let you use Google Docs or some other collaborative tool just for UX. This will be a good opportunity to facilitate reviews, both in person or remote.

UX Documentation and Traceability

In some circumstances, detailed specifications are acutely needed, when the coding is done overseas and the organization is contractually committed to providing as detailed instructions as possible to the developers who have only the documentation to support their work. However, even in this case and in most others, the general sentiment is that creating such detailed specifications is a massive and ineffective waste of time.

The demand for traceability is less common, so if you are expected to show specifically where each business requirement is fulfilled in UX, be aware that this can be a massive, complex undertaking.

The combination of having to provide both detailed specifications as well as traceability audits is severe in terms of time and resources and typically, not well accounted for. The weighting for this category is:

- Detailed specs and UX traceability are required (Risk Weight = 3-8)
- Light annotation and no traceability (Risk Weight = 0)

Risk Factors

The following are a few risk factors that should be taken into consideration:

- Writing specs takes a lot of time. If this time is not accounted for, you have a real problem.
- There is an expectation that the specifications will be delivered with the requirements. This is a sad but common paradox in which, although UX is being updated up to the last minute to accommodate new or changing requirements, the writing of the specification is supposed to happen automatically.
- Resist managing requirements in Axure at all costs (see the following *Opportunities* section for an exception).
- Although Traceability may look like a chore, it is in your best interest to have an efficient strategy to map each requirement to where it has been implemented in the design. Some clients may require such inventory as a condition for payment. However, even if they don't, it helps avoid complications due to the requirements that were forgotten during the design process and their unexpected reappearance breaks the design and requires change.

Opportunities

The following are some tips to find opportunities:

- Well in advance and as early as possible, engage all relevant stakeholders in an effort to develop the required annotation fields.
- Make sure that the metadata requirements are the minimum possible, because each added field will mean input in multiple places and have a compound impact on the time needed for writing the documentation.
- Also, collaborate on the format and organization of the specifications document so that you minimize the tweaking of the Word output after it has been generated.
- It may be possible to format an Excel spreadsheet in such a way that it could be used in a repeater, thus affording a close tie between requirements, diagrams, wireframes, and prototype. Handle these requirements with care because they constantly change, and you don't want to lose time constantly updating the Axure file.

Axure Construction Strategy Checklist

There is no need to reinvent the wheel on each and every UX project, but we keep doing this despite the fact that in principle, all projects share more things in common than are unique to them. Before you embark on a UX project involving Axure (or any prototyping tool, for that matter), you should carefully consider several factors that will help you predict what lies ahead, how to take an appropriate approach to take advantage of Axure's features, and how to avoid potential pitfalls downstream.

These considerations share an important attribute—you have quite a bit of control over them at the start of the project. The checklist is driven by the deliverables you are contracted for and are expected to deliver. Another benefit of this method is cumulative; as you complete the project, make sure that you review your original assumptions and decisions so that you can apply your learning in the next project.

The following table lists many of the important deliverables or work products for which Axure can be used. The items on the list are classified as opportunities and potential risks to be aware of. This is by no means an exhaustive list, and yet, we feel that you could plug in any items that are relevant to you.

#	Category	Deliverable/Work product	Notes
1	Diagrams	Discovery report	Opportunity
2	Diagrams	Personas/user types and tasks	Opportunity
3	Diagrams	Concept models	Opportunity
4	Diagrams	Use Case library	Opportunity
5	Diagrams	Task Flow library	Opportunity
6	Diagrams	Sitemap	Opportunity
7	Wireframes/prototype	A heuristic review of the current site	Opportunity
8	Wireframes	Wireframes	Opportunity
9	Wireframes /prototype	Pattern library	Opportunity
10	Wireframes /prototype	Vision prototype	Risk
11	Wireframes /prototype	Low fidelity prototype	Opportunity
12	Wireframes /prototype	High fidelity prototype	Risk
13	Wireframes /prototype	Usability testing prototype	Risk
14	Documentation	Light annotations (HTML)	Opportunity
15	Documentation	Detailed specifications (Word)	Risk

Showcasing Opportunities

The following is a list of ideas for adding even more value to your work:

- **Flows and diagrams**: Create and aggregate all your abstractions in Axure as opposed to creating them as discrete PDF documents in Visio or OmniGraffle. While Axure's diagramming capabilities are not very robust, what you lose in fine detailing of an individual diagram is gained by the mere fact that they are always available during design and stakeholders' meetings. We often find that while a significant amount of thought and effort is invested early on in understanding and documenting flows, they end up being buried somewhere on the network, quickly forgotten and never used. As part of the Axure file, these diagramming can stay in sync with the work as initial assumptions evolve.
- **A heuristic review of the current site**: One of the first steps before moving to design the new site is a detailed analysis of the existing software. Using Axure to reproduce highlights, insights, and reports of the *current state* is fast and easy. The benefits are substantial. You can dissect and analyze any aspect of the design in a structured way with the aid of custom annotation fields.
- **Pattern library**: Axure's support for the creation and management of widget libraries is ideal to help control the consistency of the interface and interaction across the application. Additionally, the construction of wireframes gets a significant productivity boost from reuse of these widgets and masters.
- **Interactive prototype**: The most effective tool that UX designers have in their arsenal is a simulation of the experience. Time and again, we have witnessed the impact of walking stakeholders and users through a clickable prototype. The speed with which such simulation can be placed in front of stakeholders and users for validation of initial concepts provides you with many opportunities to establish yourself. There is no need to have something flashy or complete as long as the presentation is not sloppy.
- **Documentation—light annotations**: Perhaps, it is the propagation of agile methodologies and a growing frustration with the expense and ineffectiveness of detailed documentation that is never accurate and nobody reads carefully; we are witnessing a general willingness by clients and stakeholders to accept benefits of **light** annotations—brief and contextual documentation that is generated with the HTML prototype. Instead of reading through hundreds of pages of a document, UX guidance, details, and descriptions are provided as companions to the visualization that, within itself, contributes greatly to the understanding of the application.

Considering Risks

Each of the following is a resource and time-consuming artifact in its own right. Often, you may produce several of these throughout a project. This affects the project's schedule and budget.

- **Vision prototype**: A vision prototype is a glamorous, early-stage artifact that is often used to sell the project to leaders and investors. It is more often than not an exercise in wishful thinking: significant changes happen when detailed design and requirement work begins. Beware of an expectation to use the vision prototype "as is" or an expectation to use it for generating Word specifications. Refactoring is often needed and depending on the complexity of the project, you might as well start from scratch.
- **High fidelity prototype**: The scope and depth of the prototyping effort should be determined early on so that you are not spending valuable time and energy on visualizing the entire application in great detail. A prototype, even if it is a high-fidelity depiction, is just a sample of the complete product.
- **Usability testing prototype**: Make sure that the construction of the prototype is guided by agreed-upon key flows that should be validated during usability testing. Focus first on the interaction that maintains data and context across the flows. Avoid the pressure and crisis of having to make significant changes in order to create appropriate flows in a short time.
- **Detailed specifications**: If you need to deliver such a document, make sure that you view the output early on and avoid a serious crisis if you wait until the end of the project to generate the Word specifications.

Practical Axure

Some colleagues of ours swear by Axure and claim to do everything with it. The rest of us typically fire it up when we are ready to wireframe. Frequent questions are when to use Axure and for what kinds of projects or tasks it is suitable. In the following sections, we discuss the aspects of Axure usage, which were motioned earlier, in more detail.

Small Projects

Often, initial conversations around a project begin with "we need a simple website, something very basic..." This later turns out to be not that simple or trivial at all. Ideally, you want to discover this before the contract is signed.

We are not sure what a simple website is, but we know one when we use one. The word "simple" is used on purpose, because a common understanding of "simple" tends to focus instinctively on the most prominent functionality—the number of pages involved. However, this can be a gravely misleading measure, and here is why:

- Modern web applications have a relatively small number of page templates, such as an overview, list, and details pages. Within each, however, the level of transformation and complexity can be significant, and this is typically hidden during early exploratory discussions.
- Content strategy is required to prioritize and organize content in a way that is appropriate for a device. This means that for any given screen, the content for a minimum three layouts should be considered. For some types of applications, the increase in complexity can be exponential to ensure the fidelity of multiple workflows and conditions across multiple screens.
- Another measure could be the number of audiences that the application will serve. Does it need to dynamically change content and functionality based on login? Are any types of registrations involved? Are there any transactions? If the answer to all these questions is *no* and what you are looking at is stringing a number of pages together with some global navigation, you are most likely looking at a simple project.

However, as we said, there are certain simple sites. Is Axure the right tool for such simple projects? One could argue that Axure is an overkill and that a tool such as PowerPoint or Keynote will be more productive because you can concentrate on the content and not lose energy on learning the prototyping tool. Additionally, the deployment of simple websites today is most successful with platforms such as WordPress or Squarespace. These enable a non-techie person to experiment and create a highly sophisticated website using prebuilt and easily customizable templates. For rapid visualization and brainstorming of ideas and approaches, using Axure on a simple site can help keep the project from unnecessary complications and help determine which technology and service to use.

Web Applications and Portals

This class of prototypes is probably the *meat and potatoes* for Axure use. While there are many portal platforms, corporations often require custom development and enhancements that meet their business needs. For many organizations, such projects are viewed as transformative and strategic and are significant financial investments. The following are some attributes that such projects have in common:

- To secure the approval and go-ahead from corporate leaders, the initial UX involvement may be limited to the creation of a highly polished vision prototype. The UX footprint may be small in terms of the actual resources involved but significant in terms of the impact on moving forward.
- The application involves multiple modules that oftentimes represent discrete organizational business units. It is common for these business units to be spread across the country or the world. Each business unit may have its own rules, requirements, and supporting technologies. These need to be streamlined and unified to make the integrated application work as envisioned.
- If you are tasked with creating a high-fidelity prototype, keep organizational complexity in mind. As much as possible, document your working assumptions, the guidance and feedback of various stakeholders, their priorities, and potential areas of friction.
- On the one hand, UX often enjoys a mandate to come up with an all-new, efficient, and great design. Then there comes the push-back and sometimes the blame: UX is too ambitious and risky and the UX team is ignorant of the constraints of legacy and business rules. The ability to walk the fine balance between pragmatic and aspirational is important, especially because UX rarely gets enough time to gain deep knowledge of the business. And so, we recommend that:
    - Don't assume anything. Ask as many questions as you need to clarify the terminology and processes you don't understand.
    - Point out, early on, the potential gaps and implementation risks. In Axure, annotate the risk field for relevant widgets and layout regions you are concerned about, and go over those items during the review sessions.
- You might truly say that more than just widgets and regions, the documentation of risks related to business rules, which may affect interfaces, is crucial too. We've mentioned that requirements should not necessarily be managed in Axure. However, are references to risk, embedded in the Axure annotations, appropriate? This is a chronic problem that deserves its own book. However, our answer is *no*. The main concern is that it quickly becomes impossible to track and update the requirements and the risks in Axure, and you end up adding to the confusion.
- To handle the complexity and specific needs of each module, developing such application requires a large team of business and technology stakeholders; a larger UX team is required as well.

- Start using a team project early on and communicate a lot with the team about establishing design patterns and other common elements. Balancing the flexibility of work streams and their ability to address unique needs with the overall consistency and integrity of the application is a major challenge, and we will discuss some strategies to address it later in the book.

Heuristic Evaluation

A heuristic analysis of the existing user interface (*current state*) is often one of the initial steps that UX designers perform at the inception of a redesign project. The outcome can help decision makers determine the scope, budget, and timelines for the project's *future state*, and also determine an opportunity to get the UX designer familiar with the application and its user-experience issues.

You can very rapidly create a mini replica of the actual application by placing and linking screen captures in Axure pages. Add more details, such as drop-down lists, form fields, and action buttons over the appropriate places in the screen captures, to create a hybrid of an image- and widget-based prototype. Add your comments in relevant annotation fields and generate an HTML prototype and a Word document, which you will use as you walk the stakeholders through the findings.

User Validation

A by-product of creating an interactive prototype in Axure is, of course, the fact that you have a tremendous instrument to use in various user validation activities, such as focus groups and **usability tests** (**UT**); this is a no-brainer. However, it is important to include the refactoring work necessary to use the prototype for such activities in the project's budget and timeline. This is especially important for complex applications that adjust the user interface based on the user login. Here are some points to keep in mind:

- Make sure that the scenarios planned for UT are actually built into the prototype. Making the prototype work for unplanned scenarios may involve considerable rework and modifications to the construction of the file.
- If the file is also intended to be used to create specifications, how will the tweaks and added interactions needed to make the prototype work for UT affect the generated specs?

- Does it make sense to duplicate the current file and have a dedicated file just for the purpose of UT? It really depends on where you are in terms of construction. The benefit of developing the file separately is that you can work quickly and tweak the construction without having to worry about the specifications or impacting other sections of the project. On the other hand, it means that any updates made to the production file will have to be updated in the UT file.

Deliverables – Prototypes and Specifications

Are you contracted or expected to deliver only an interactive prototype or the annotated specifications as well? The following list takes you through some important pointers to consider. Don't worry about Axure terms and functionalities you are not familiar with, since we will cover those later in the book.

- If specifications are in play, what are the expectations for the format and delivery of those specifications? Is it, for example, an exhaustive Word document or a light HTML-based annotated version of the prototype?
- Did you have an opportunity to discuss these flavors of documentation with the relevant stakeholders (typically the development team) or are the specifications mentioned casually and their scope only implied? If this is the case, you should get explicit clarifications as early as possible.
- Ask for an example of a previous specifications document used by the development team to get a sense of what is acceptable.
- If you are contracted to deliver an interactive prototype, what level of fidelity is expected? Interactivity means different things to different stakeholders. Their expectations are often shaped by past experiences, if any, with user experience projects.
- If the application needs to support different types of user roles based on login, are you expected to simulate the entire user experience for each of these roles or just for a primary role? This point alone can make or break a project because stakeholders may demand to see the differences in each role, while you have budgeted and scheduled the work for simulating only one.
- Knowing in advance that various sections within wireframes are global, that they will have to reflect user types, or have multiple states, implies the use of masters and dynamic panels to reduce wireframe redundancy and other construction inefficiencies. Use of masters also implies the possible use of Raised Events.

- Demonstrating how the interface renders for different user types or for different workflow paths is likely to involve the use of variables and functions, and as mentioned earlier—the use of masters, dynamic panels, and raised events. Knowing what is expected will help you acquire the Axure skills that you need in advance.
- Are you expected to simulate features such as type-ahead or is it enough to call out such behaviors in the annotations? It is not that difficult to build the simulation in Axure, but is there value, and more importantly, the time and budget allocated for constructing such common interactions?
- How much of the interface is expected to be prototyped, and how much can be just defined by static wireframes?
- Often, the conversations around the scope of work occur before the actual work has begun. It is a good idea to agree with stakeholders on the desired wireframes, the complexity of each wireframe, and priority of the wireframes and flows that will be simulated in detail and the ones that will be addressed as static wireframes.
- Is the plan to quickly deliver a high-fidelity vision prototype first and once the project gets a green light, use it for detailed design and specifications? If this is the case, keep in mind that refactoring—the need to rebuild sections of your Axure file—is likely to be required. There are several reasons for this:
    - To begin with, the work on a vision prototype tends to be a very high-level show off, with the best of all the possible-functionalities and features in the world. Often, there may not be enough time or details to validate that the proposed user experience can actually be supported by the underlying business processes or technology. When work on detailed design moves forward, many of the assumptions that were made for the vision need to be scaled back in order to meet the actual business requirements and technical constraints.
    - One particular pitfall to watch for has to do with administration screens. Most applications have some sort of administrative functionalities that range in capabilities, from allowing a super user to assign access permissions to other users to setting the values of a wide range of defaults and other parameters. As very few users will actually interact with this part of the application, it is often dismissed casually in early conversation, only to resurface deep within the project.

Create an inventory of all the modules and key screens of the application. With the relevant stakeholders, agree which screens are in scope of what treatment. This will be the blueprint for working on the prototype and for change management as a result of scope realignment.

Tips for Using Axure on Large-design Projects

The following are some tips that should help you get the most out of using Axure on a large project:

- Axure can promote, but not enforce, consistent design; ensuring a consistent design still requires a governance process
- It is critical to construct wireframes properly and consistently across all teams
- Create a naming convention for wireframes and dynamic panels; validate proper naming during governance reviews
- Agree on a common structure/organization of wireframes and enforce that organization across all teams
- Allow time to train new users on the finer points of using Axure
- At the beginning of the project, pilot a number of ways for using masters and dynamic panels and then settle on a common approach; validate the implementation during governance reviews
- Be sure to bake time into your project plan for maintenance of the Axure file
- Refactor the project file at strategic points, such as before major usability tests, or before resuming work on the file following major de-scoping or major design modifications. Other refactoring effort may be required:
    - Between the completion of wireframes and writing the specifications
    - After the completion of a release
- Plan on having one wireframe structure for prototypes and another for specifications

UX and Stakeholders' Perspectives

In his classic movie *Rashomon*, Akira Kurosawa unfolds the details of an event by telling the story from the perspectives of multiple characters, including a dead person. Each character, who was also a direct witness to the event, recounts the story by telling the narrative from their point of view. That same form of the event actually happened is undisputed, but as it happens, the stories, while similar in structure, end up contradicting each other.

User experience practitioners often find themselves in a Rashomon situation because of UX's unique position at the intersection of business, engineering, people, and systems. The success of the UX project rests on our ability to fuse the various entities in a coherent and elegant way.

Our colleague, Sam Spicer, often speaks of empathy being vital to the role of UX. Understanding the perspectives of the stakeholders we work with is important not only for arriving at a good design but also for a strong collaborative environment that can handle the stresses of constant change and fleeting schedules.

Leadership

Regardless of the organization's type or size, any successful commitment to high standards of user experience and satisfaction must be driven from the top down. Chief executives who take time to learn and understand the importance of UX are the most important sponsors of our work in the organization. The commitment will materialize in strategy, resources, and budgets. When such recognition comes from the very top, the tendency is to discount the value of UX because many of the deliverables are dismissed as soft and hard to measure.

Obviously, your interaction with the senior leadership is tied to variables such as your seniority, the organization size, and the project you are involved with. Still, the following situations are common:

- For small companies, the project is likely to be really important and top leadership will take a close interest in it, sometimes too close. A desire to direct or control the outcome and influence the design is not uncommon. Such circumstances may get you stuck between the project's leadership and the company leadership, which are often not the same group of individuals. Your Axure file can become an invaluable asset to all as a live document that captures key decisions around the experience. Consolidation of diagrams, flows, wireframes, and relevant documentation makes it possible and easy to access and present relevant support to a design decision.
- In a large organization, your contact with the senior leadership may be limited only to those who are directly leading the project because there are just way too many levels of hierarchy. Still, mission-critical projects are visible at the executive suite because the organization needs it to succeed and because it is expensive. Your work will be exposed to the scrutiny at the highest stratospheres of the organization. Regardless of your audience, it is important that the construction quality of your work is high, even when you are only experimenting with high-level concepts.

Project Management

Project managers are tasked with tracking the progress of projects and facilitate solutions that help resolve roadblocks along the way. In many projects, UX does not have the benefit of a dedicated project manager. This can lead to problems for medium and large projects, such as:

- If a project manager is not budgeted to the project, it is a good idea to raise this as a flag and take extra effort in developing a comprehensive, mid-level plan yourself
- If a project manger is budgeted, make sure to jointly review the entire project plan, ask questions, and flag dependencies such as where a projected UX effort has not been considered

For example, many plans do not account for the time it takes to refactor the Axure file from a vision prototype to detailed design prototype. Others don't take into account the time it takes to iterate and revise the prototype. Sometimes, the time it takes to arrange the logistics of usability tests such as recruiting is not considered. The more time spent early on with the project manager as the plan is being developed and revised, the better the project will track later on.

Engineering

One would not be blamed for thinking that developing the user experience and software development are complementary processes. However, as we often find out, there is a gap between UX and engineering. There are many reasons for the friction, but a fundamental means to resolve these is communication.

It is surprising to hear stories about large projects where the interaction designer and the developers only got together well after a splashy high-fidelity vision prototype, commissioned by the business side of the organization, has been used to drive the top management to move forward with the project.

The problem, from the perspective of the development team, is managing the expectations of the top leadership that the new application will have a close resemblance to the vision prototype and be in production in no time. If only life was so simple. Engineering leaders often express concerns that UX does not always take into account the constraints of available technology, impact of the new UX on performance, scarceness of development resources available to the organization, or the complexities involved in the accessibility and localization implementation of the new UX.

These concerns are often valid and true. With Axure, however, UX has a tool that helps improve communications via visualization of interactivity and integrated annotations. Conversations, analysis, estimation, and adjustments can start early on in the development life cycle and reduce the stress on the engineering team.

Visual Design

Visual design introduces some of the most daunting challenges for rapid prototyping projects and a hidden iceberg for Axure prototypes. Why? This is because of a gap, sometimes a serious one, that grows between the wireframe prototype and the visual design.

This gap poses both UX and development risks because of the need to reconcile between the two presentations of the same screens. Sooner or later, a refactoring of the Axure prototype will be needed, especially if the intent is to keep using the file throughout the entire life cycle of the product.

The two sets of wireframes are developed asynchronously. Normally, we start with Axure wireframing as rough conceptual sketches that evolve through rapid iteration. These wireframes address information architecture and actionable tasks and the layouts are often tentative. With Axure, we can enhance these rough ideas and evolve the concept as an interactive prototype that demonstrates the vision for navigation and interaction patterns.

All this work, however compelling, tends to be in grayscale without visual design. As user experience architects and designers, we want to isolate the feedback we obtain from stakeholders and potential users. The conventional wisdom is that adding visual design cues at such an early point is adding unnecessary noise to the feedback. This is because people's response to colors and layouts are both extremely subjective and strong, and the concern is that such feedback tends to push more substantive issues to the background.

It is impossible to separate the visual design from the user experience. This argument sounds especially compelling when it comes to the design of mobile apps, where beauty is inherent to the design of the user experience.

What often happens is that at some point in the UX process, visual design gets involved and the ugly duck emerges as a beautiful swan. Now, everyone needs to start looking at the two sets of the design (wireframes and the visuals). Often, the two sets will continue to evolve on separate tracks because while the work with the visual designer takes place, the work on finalizing the Axure wireframes for specifications continues.

Sometimes, UX designers do not fully appreciate the complexities and challenges that visual designers face. Busy and stressed by our own issues, it is tempting to dump on the visual designer a great deal of information, often not fully baked, and expect that the designer will get it somehow. However, it is often the case that the visual designer has very little time to dive into the depth of the application.

The bottom line is that since you will know when the visual design phase is planned, you should be able to build into the timeline time to refactor the prototype so that at some point, the approved visual design is reflected in the wireframes, prototype, and documentation.

The UX Perspectives

When individuals or organizations hire an architect, they are typically influenced by that person's body of work. However, they are also certain that as a certified architect, the person has formal educational and professional qualifications. The clients and contractors who work with an architect also have a formal understanding of the type of deliverables the architect needs to provide. There are also legal and other regulations the architect must abide by. After all, you would not take an uncertified architect to design a skyscraper or your home.

Hiring a qualified user experience practitioner, on the other hand, is somewhat like rolling the dice despite the fact that the project's scope and complexity makes it like a skyscraper in comparison. It is not quite clear to the client what exactly UX is. Unlike architecture, anyone can call themselves an experienced architect as there is no standard professional certification or accreditation that can serve as a lighthouse to help a client choose. However, this, by no means, is a fault of our discipline. Architecture has evolved over thousands of years, but the formalization of who is a qualified architect is a relatively modern development.

As in any profession, there is the level competency and mastery of the technical skills we bring to the table. For someone who is only versed and comfortable with wireframing in Visio, developing an interactive prototype in Visio will be a real challenge.

Of course, it is a lot easier to create such a prototype in Axure. However, should you embrace this tool? It is best to avoid heated tool-camp loyalty arguments, as the answer typically boils down to a strategic business and professional decision:

- Are you a single user? Perhaps an independent consultant or the single UX practitioner in an organization? In this case, you need to consider the cost of investing in the tool and the return on your investment.
- Think about the projects you have created so far with the tool/s you have. Is there a gap you need to fill?

- Axure is becoming a good skill to master. Will learning the tool open up new employment opportunities?
- What about the cloud-based services for which you pay a subscription? Certainly, it is a good idea to review the option. However, the thing to consider here is that many corporations may frown upon having their most strategic plans placed on some cloud. Moreover, firewalls and other security barriers may make it difficult for stakeholders to access the work.
- Are you a member of an interface design agency or an in-house design team?
- What are the challenges of running a shared Axure project?
- What kind of training is needed to level the team's prototyping skills?
- What are the project opportunities that open up with using shared projects, efficiency, savings, and increased profits in terms of reusing the widget libraries, masters, and generators?

The Axure Perspective

As users of software, we demand constant improvements. As professionals who are involved in the process of making software, we can be more sympathetic to the challenges and tradeoffs that Axure, the company, is facing:

- The more features and capabilities Axure supports (adaptive views, advanced interactions, logic, variables, functions, and so on), the more complex the tool becomes. In fact, we already find a demand in the market for specialized Axure prototypes, people who can take Axure to the max and create really powerful vision prototypes. Ironically, freeing ourselves from dependencies on developers and the ability to quickly and easily create an interactive prototype is exactly the goal that Axure sets out to tackle, being a tool for non-developers. So, how can the company balance these two extremes:
    - Prototypes versus specifications: The demand for high-fidelity vision prototypes is on the rise and is becoming a norm. The turn-around times for such prototypes is shrinking, and they are extremely influential in getting decision makers to give the green light to ambitious development projects. However, turning a vision prototype into a specification—a deliverable that is often contracted for—is most likely to require refactoring. This effort can be substantial and yet, often not planned for, budget or schedule wise. Clearly, there are some challenges around reducing the gap between prototype construction and specification generation. How will Axure try to address this in the future?

- The landscape of UX is rapidly changing. Apple, through iPhone and iPad and its ongoing quest to integrate iOS, its mobile operating system, with OS-X, its desktop operating system, is impacting the user experience in profound ways. As a result, the syntax of interaction patterns is evolving. New multifinger gestures are a good example. How will Axure support the creation of prototypes for the next generation of devices?

Summary

Our success as UX designers rests on our ability to synthesize and express the many diverse, often conflicting inputs, we gather from sources such as business and engineering stakeholders, user research, and data from analytics. At the end of the day, our goal is to find the pragmatic balance, opportunities, and innovation for the best user experience possible, regardless of the device or operating system that drives that device. To help us conceive, visualize, communicate, and document our vision, a specialized UX tool is invaluable.

Axure is considered by many to be the tool of choice for the UX industry worldwide because the company works hard to evolve the tool so that it supports the escalating demands on UX. The company listens closely to practitioners as it strives to balance a rich feature-set with complexity and cost, and has proven repeatedly that it is the right tool to help us in our demanding line of work.

The following chapters will introduce you to the wealth of features Axure offers in the context of real-life circumstances. As you read the book and get a better sense of how Axure might fit your needs, keep in mind that Axure is just a tool. There is no substitute to rigor, collaboration, and iteration to achieve a successful prototype that communicates our design for a product that will exceed the expectations of our clients and their users. The next chapter provides a comprehensive guide to Axure's user interface and various features.

2
Axure Basics – the User Interface

"People should not worry so much about what they do but rather about what they are. If they and their ways are good, then their deeds are radiant... for it is not our works which sanctify us but we who sanctify our works."

– Meister Eckhart

We rely on tools such as Axure to express our ideas and to hopefully push the creative envelope. As mentioned in the previous chapter, Axure has made a lot of positive changes in Version 7.0. Whether you are new to Axure or entering this new version as a seasoned Axure user, it is imperative that you take some time before you dive into it and discover its features and familiarize yourself with the nuances and capabilities. Axure is powerful, but remember that the work will only be as good as your attitude and commitment.

This chapter is designed to help you establish a solid familiarity with Axure Pro's concepts and rich capabilities. Axure 7 for Windows and OS X are fully compatible, so for the most part screenshots show the Mac OS. We will cover the following topics:

- Getting started
- Environment
- Widgets
- Masters
- Widget Interactions and Notes
- Style
- Widget Manager
- Prototype

Getting Started

Once you have installed Axure and launched it, you are presented with the **Welcome to Axure RP Pro 7.0** window as shown in the following screenshot:

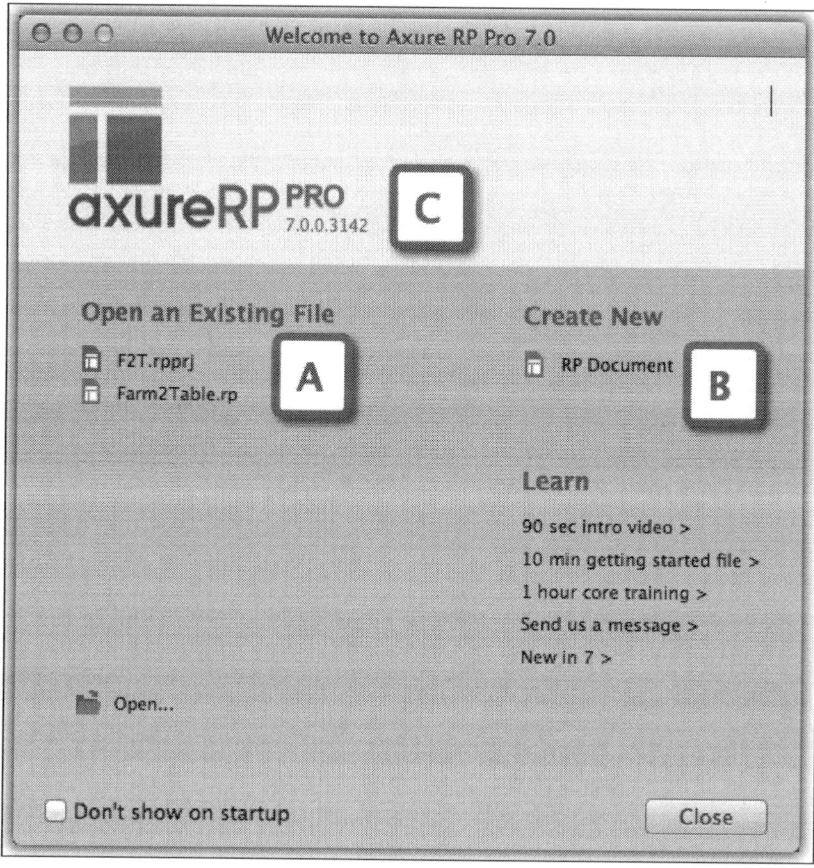

Image 1

The Welcome **to Axure RP Pro 7.0** splash window allows you to:

- Open recent files (*Image 1*, **A**).
- Create new RP files (**B**). An RP file is a local file, which we will discuss later in this chapter.

- See which version of Axure you are running (**C**). Typically, Axure releases several updates during a version's life cycle. If you are part of a team, it is recommended that all team members use the same version and point release. If you are upgrading from an earlier version of Axure, keep a backup copy of your files. Version 6 files opened and saved in Version 7 will not open back in Version 6. By default, Axure 7.0 performs a push release. Once it runs, you will be presented with the **Check for Updates** dialog, which is also available in the **Help** menu. You can either update to the newer version or decline it. Uncheck the **Check for updates when Axure RP starts** option (*Image 2*, **A**) to disable the auto-check, as shown in the following screenshot:

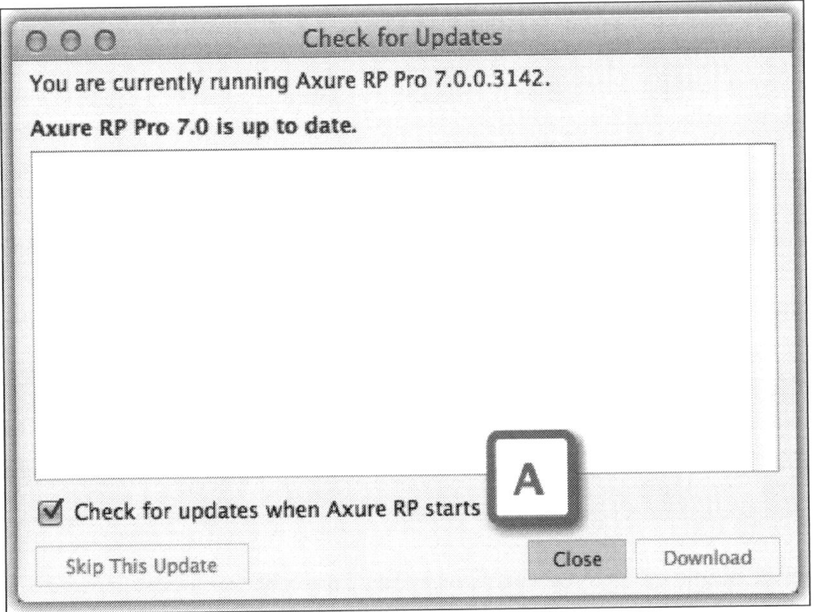

Image 2

On Windows, Axure allows you to run multiple instances of Axure with one open project per instance. The Mac version runs a single instance per Axure version (for example, Axure 7 and Axure 6.5 open at the same time), with multiple files opened per instance.

Axure File Formats

There are three modes of prototype development workflows:

- The first is focused on the needs of a single designer, who is the sole author of the prototype in Axure. Axure's RP file format is the default when you create a new Axure project. This file is essentially stored on your hard drive. By default, the `.rp` files are stored into the `root Documents/Axure` folder.
- The other workflow mode facilitates team collaboration, with built-in features such as controlled check-ins and check-outs and version control. Axure's RPPRJ file format offers so many benefits that a single practitioner should seriously consider using this mode as well. This feature is available only in the Axure Pro version.
- The last format is for custom widget libraries, and that format is a RPLIB format.

The RP File Format (Standalone Files)

By default, the RP file is stored as a single file on your local drive, for example, `My Project.rp`. This is identical to any other file-based application, such as Excel, Visio, or Word. You do not have to use the default storage location and can dictate the location for which you choose to save this RP file.

One of the challenges in UX projects is managing change. Rapid iteration is the essence of prototyping, and so the RP file you are working on will evolve from day to day. The need to revert to an older version—perhaps because you messed up something or for some other reason—is highly likely. This is impossible if you use the RP file (unless you keep a daily version of the file) and one of the reasons why we recommend making it using the team project format, which supports version control.

The RPPRJ File Format (Team Project)

This is the appropriate format for a team of UX designers who are collaborating on a UX project and desire version control. The feature is only available in the Axure Pro version. *Image 3* illustrates this model in which the project repository (**A**) is hosted on a remote server or a shared directory on the network. Several UX designers (**B**) and a business analyst (**C**) can access the file from their Mac or PC and collaborate on the construction and annotations. The ability to distribute work among multiple resources is very important, especially for large-enterprise projects. The topic of collaboration is discussed at length in *Chapter 9, Collaboration*.

The key features of this format are:

- Checkout/Checkin controls
- Ability to cancel checkouts, basically a form of undo, in case you mess up something in the wireframe and choose to start over
- Version control and the ability to restore previous versions

Team Projects

Team projects can be created from a new file or from an existing RP file.

Before you can create a team project, you must first have a project on a SVN server or on a network drive.

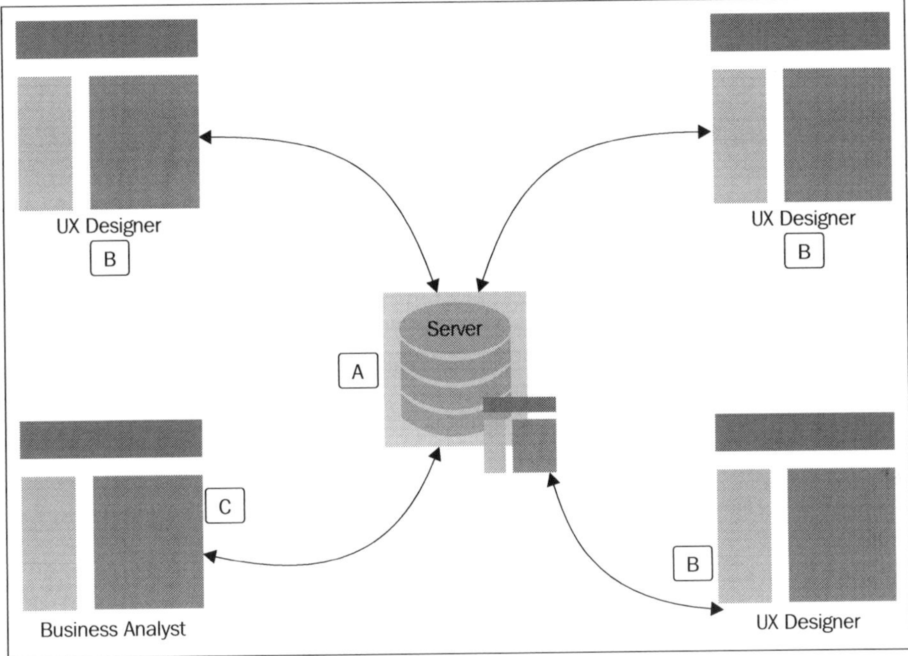

Image 3

Environment

Axure's workspace is straightforward, as seen in the following screenshot:

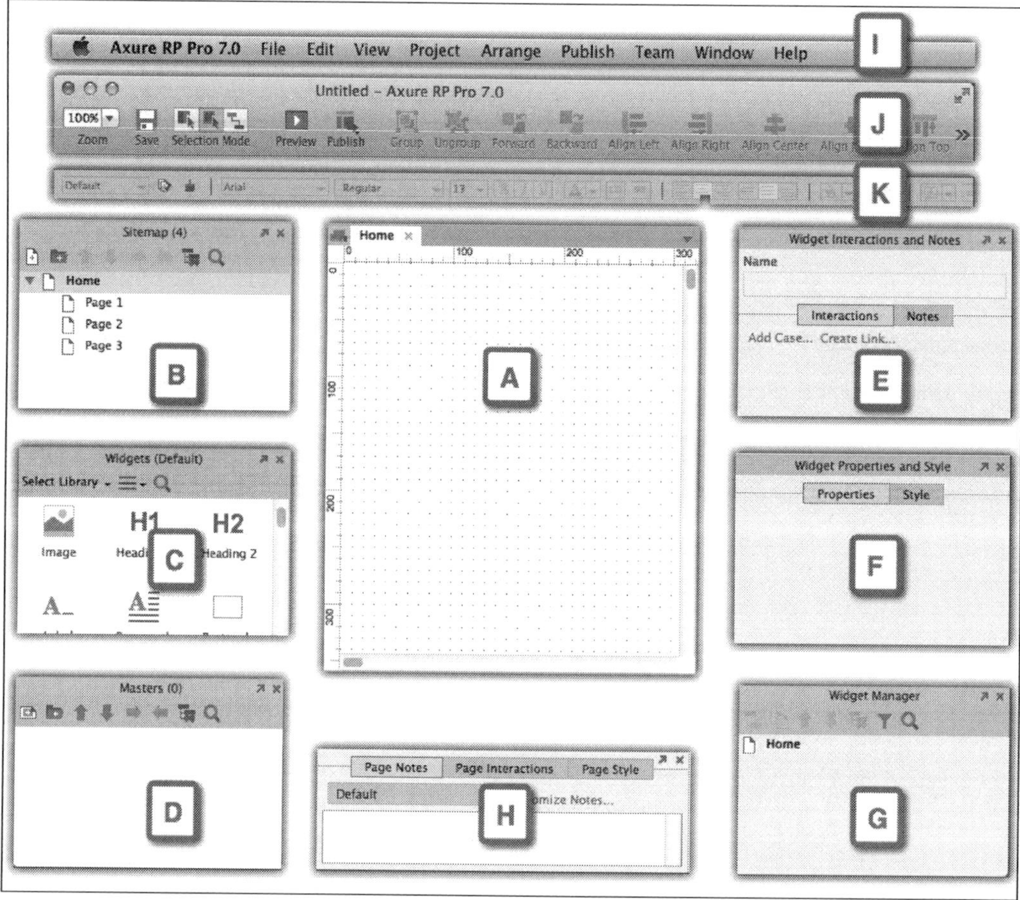

Image 4

Your main wireframing construction space is the wireframe pane (*Image 4*, **A**), which is at the center of the screen, flanked by supporting panes on the left and right, and at the bottom:

Left panes:

- The **Sitemap** pane (**B**)
- The **Widgets** pane (**C**)
- The **Masters** pane (**D**)

Right Panes:

- **Widget Interactions and Notes** (E)
- **Widget Properties and Style** (F)
- **Widget Manager** (G)

Bottom Pane:

- The Page Properties pane, which includes the **Page Notes**, **Page Interactions**, and **Page Style** tabs (H)

The menu bar (I) , toolbar (J), and the format bar (K) complete the composition at the top.

The preceding screenshot (*Image 4*) shows the Mac user interface. The Windows version is similar with the exception of the toolbar.

Customizing the Workspace

You have some control over the arrangement of the workspace, which includes:

- **Hide/Show individual panes**: Use the **View** menu option (*Image 5*, **A**) and click on the **Panes** option (**B**). You will see the panes listed. If you accidentally remove a pane, simply go here to show it again.

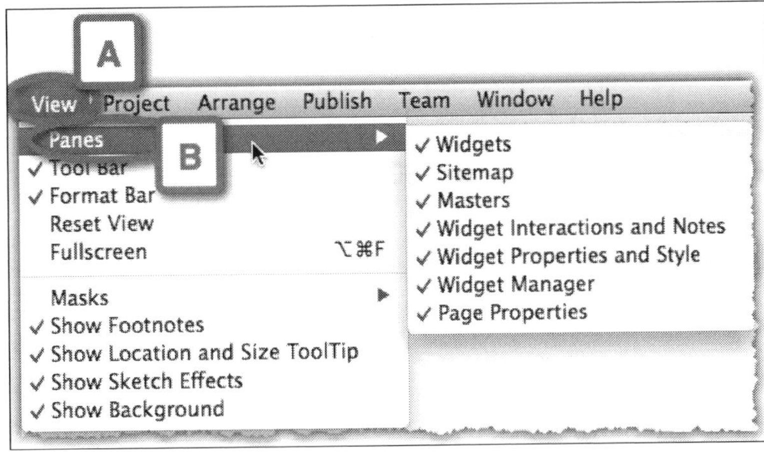

Image 5

- **Detach Panes**: The ability to detach panes and move them around is really handy to use as the items in the pane grow large or if you simply desire your working area to be larger. To detach the pane, click on the diagonal arrow (*Image 6*, **A**). To remove a pane from the view, click on the **X** icon.

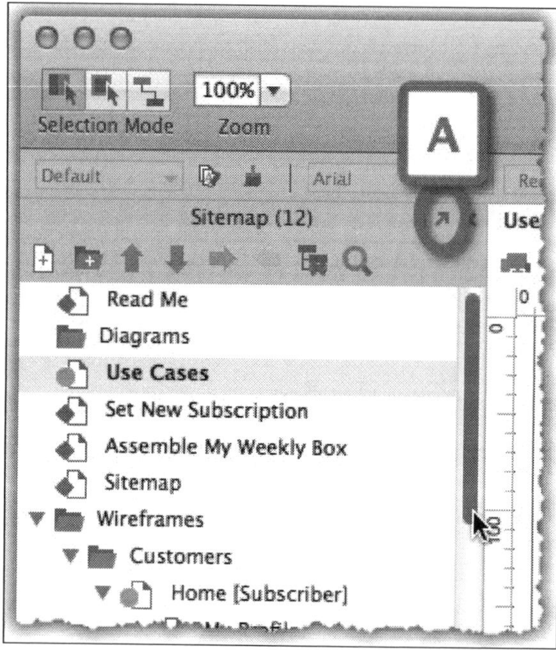

Image 6

You cannot change the default location of panes when they are in their docked state. For example, the **Sitemap** pane is always parked on the upper-left corner and cannot be placed in any other location.

The Sitemap Pane

The **Sitemap** pane is where the pages live, including wireframes and task flows. Pages are the highest-level elements in Axure. When you launch Axure, it opens a new, untitled document. The **Sitemap** pane of this new project has a default structure that includes a page called Home and three child pages beneath it. You do not have to keep or use these pages, but you can choose to use them as the foundation for your project.

In the **Sitemap** pane, you can:

- Create new pages (*Image 7*, **A**).
- (New!) Organize pages by creating a folder to house related wireframes (**B**).
- Change the order of pages (**C**) by moving them up and down using the arrows.
- Nest pages to reflect a page hierarchy by changing their nesting level (**D**). Note that by nesting one page under another, you are only creating a visual representation.
- Delete pages (**E**).
- Search pages (**F**). For very large projects with many nested or child pages, the search capability is a tremendous time saver. Click on the magnifying glass icon to toggle the visibility of the search field, which appears below the pane's rows of icons. Alternatively, right-click to view this functionality as well.

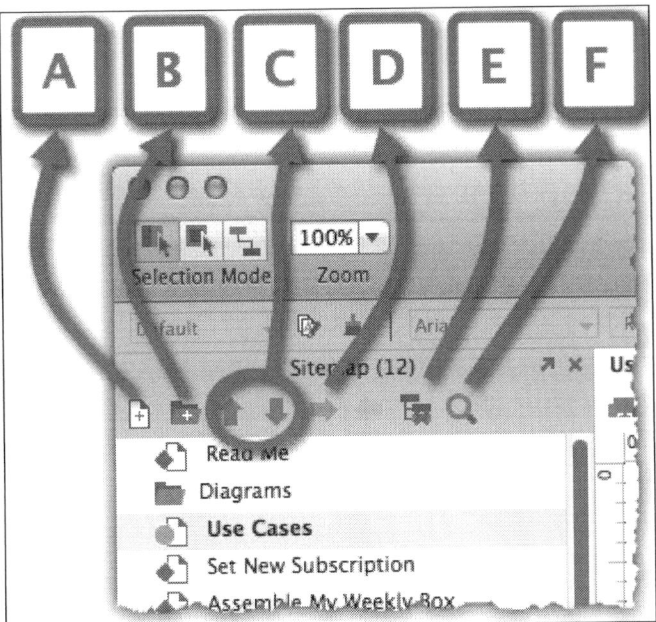

Image 7

The Widgets Pane

The widgets pane allows you to access Axure's built-in widgets collections, manage and organize imported third party widget libraries, or manage your own custom widgets collections. If you choose to use any of the flow widgets to create a task flow, sitemap, and so on, this is the pane that allows you to do so. We will explain that more in the *Flow Widgets* section. Just like many of the other panes, you can also search for widgets by clicking on the search icon.

This widgets pane, as shown in the following screenshot, is grouped into three categories: **Common**, **Forms**, and **Menus and Table**:

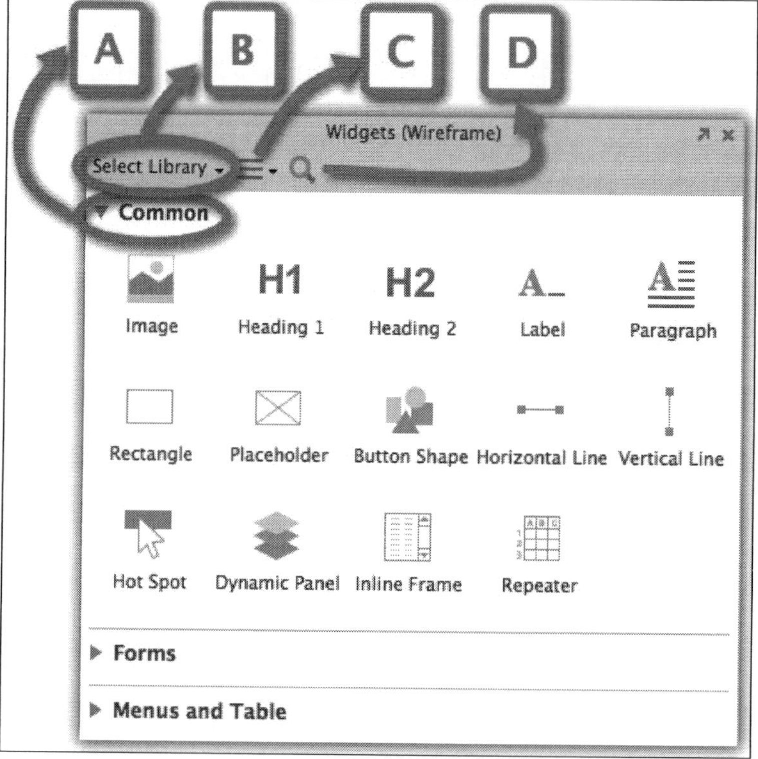

Image 8

- By default, the pane shows Axure's common set of wireframe widgets (*Image 8*, **A**).

- Use the **Select Library** drop-down menu (**B**) to switch between the default widget collection, the flow widgets, and any libraries you may have loaded into your Axure file (more about widget libraries, in *Chapter 6, Widget Libraries*).
- Use the **Options** menu (**C**) to manage custom widget libraries.
- To search for widgets use the magnifying glass (**D**).

Wireframe Widgets

A wireframe is composed of a set of widgets. Once you drag-and-drop a widget onto your wireframe, you can format it, annotate it, label it, and set an interaction to it.

Selecting a Widget Shape – Option 1

Drag a **Rectangle** widget onto your wire (*Image 9*, **A**). For round corners, click-and-drag the yellow triangle on the upper-left corner (**B**), or type a number into the **Corner Radius** field (**C**) under the **Fills, Lines, + Borders** section in the **Style** tab of the **Widget Properties and Style** pane

To change the widget's shape, click on the little grey circle (**D**) on the upper-right corner of the widget to see a graphical menu of shape options.

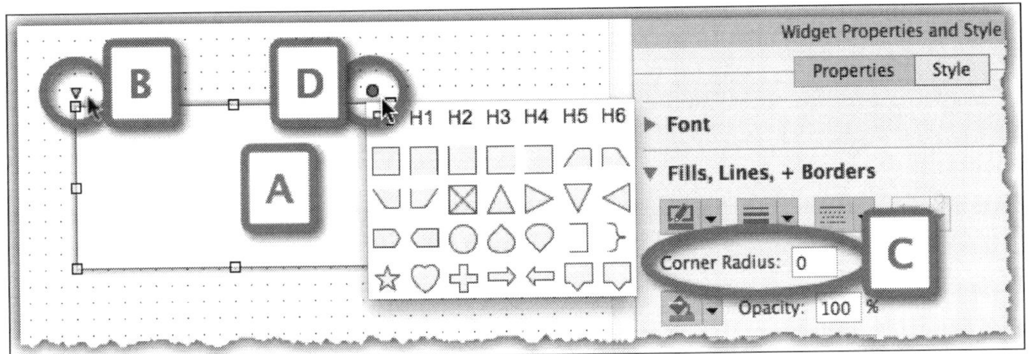

Image 9

Selecting a Widget Shape – Option 2

Alternatively, right-click on the widget and use the **Select Shape** option (*Image 10*, **A**) from the context menu to select a shape from the list (**B**).

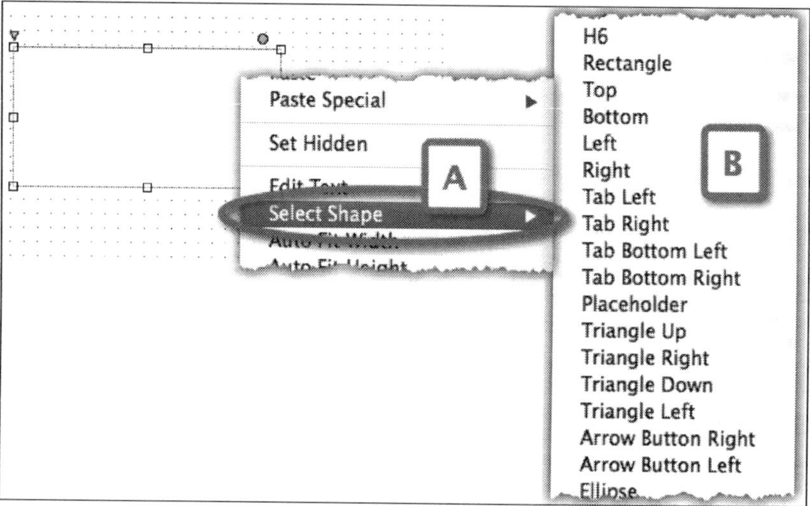

Image 10

Selecting a Widget Shape – Option 3

The third method to change a widget's shape is available in the **Properties** tab of the **Widget Properties and Style** pane. Click on the **Select Shape** drop-down (*Image 11*, **A**) and select the shape you want from the visual menu (**B**).

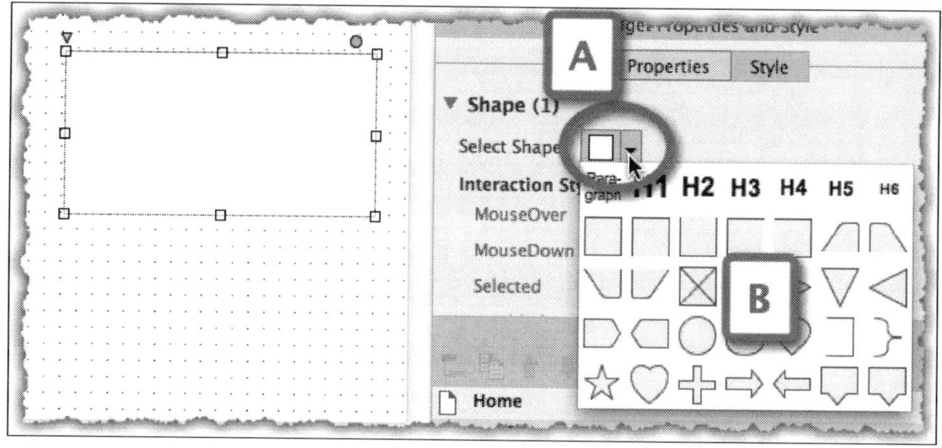

Image 11

Shapes – Highlights

The following are nice features that are in place for various widgets that we would like to highlight:

- Text widgets, such as Paragraph, Label, and Headers can be assigned a style on **MouseOver** and **MouseDown**, and for the widgets **Selected** or **Disabled** (*Image 12*, **A**) states.
- Shapes can be set to autofit height and width to be as wide and/or tall as the text in the shape (**B**). This is a new feature to Axure.
- The Paragraph widget contains the default Lorem Ipsum text (**C**), a nice timesaver introduced in Axure 7.

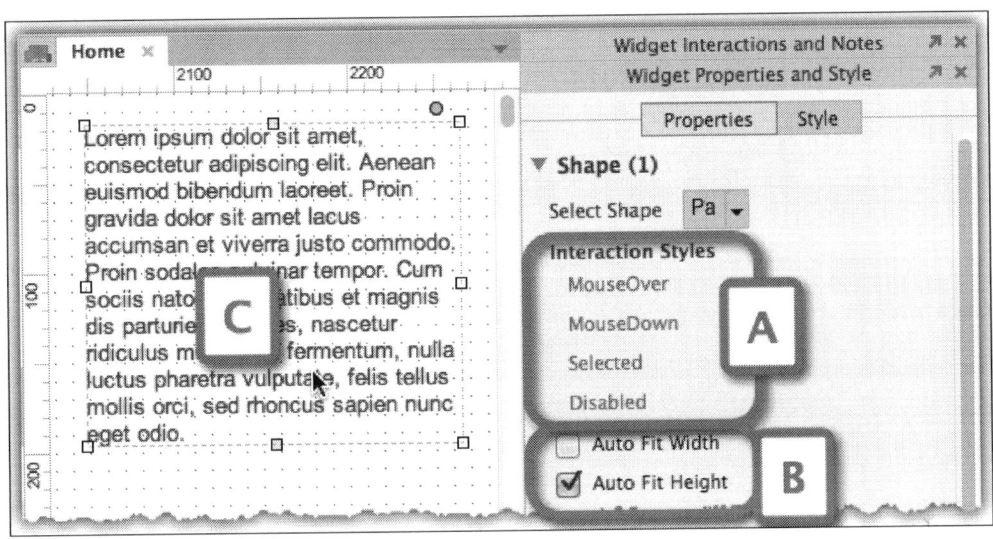

Image 12

Form Fields – Highlights (New!)

Form fields, too, gained some enhancements in Axure 7:

- Text fields (*Image 13*, **A**) located in the **Forms** section of the **Widgets** pane can be assigned a field type, such as e-mail, number, phone, URL, search, and so on (**B**).
- Text fields and text areas can be assigned a hint (**C**)—text that is displayed in the field and is dismissed when the user begins typing.

- The hint can be assigned a custom style with **Hint Style** (**D**). To preview the style, click and hold the rectangle on the upper-right corner of the widget (**D**).
- In another helpful enhancement, Droplist widgets can be assigned a custom height.

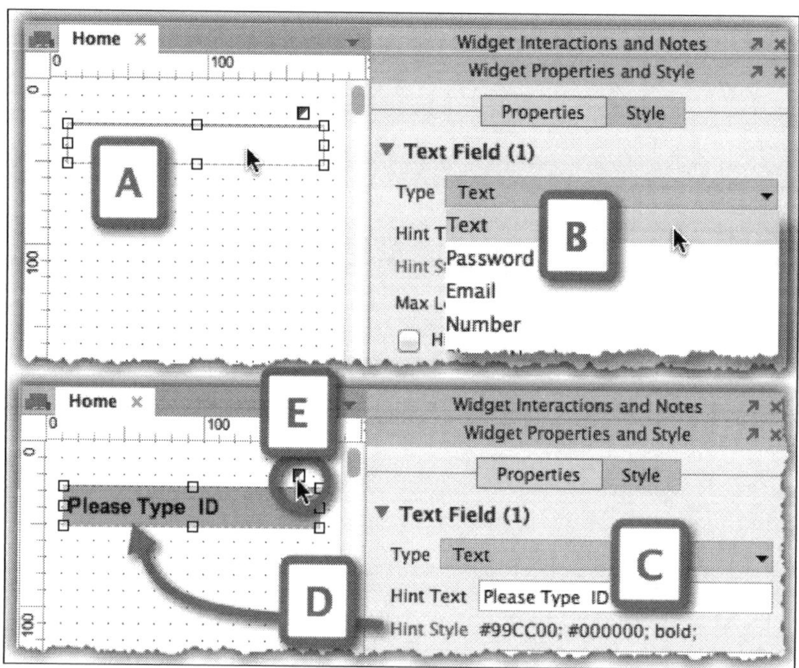

Image 13

Dynamic Panels – Highlights

This may be a new concept if you are new to Axure. *Chapter 4, Creating Basic Interactions*, discusses dynamic panels in detail, but it is worthwhile to introduce this widget type here. A dynamic panel is a container that holds other widgets that have multiple states. The dynamic panel allows you to shuffle between the states:

- Dynamic panels have an option to fit to content. In other words, the content will drive the size of the dynamic panel. This is checked by default.
- Dynamic panels can be set to 100 percent when generated in a browser. This is great for carousels and for sites/pages that have images as a background.

- If you are familiar with previous versions of Axure, you will find this enhancement very valuable. All widgets can now be set to hidden without having to create a dynamic panel! The following screenshot shows two of multiple ways to do this: using the context menu (*Image 14*, **A**) or by checking the **Hidden** box (**B**) in the **Style** section in the **Widget Properties and Style** pane, as shown in the following screenshot:

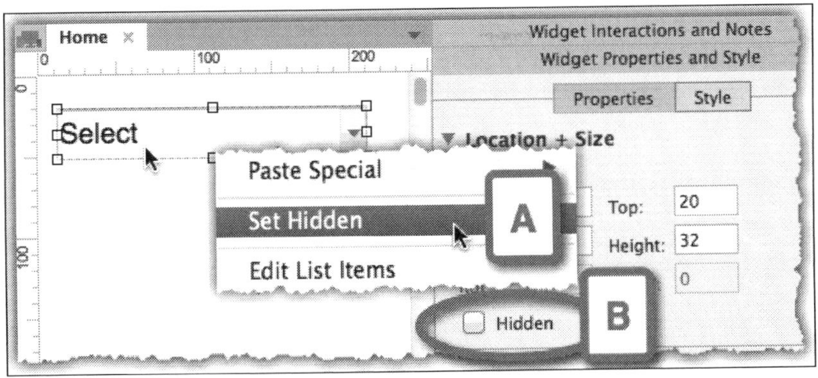

Image 14

The Repeater Widget (New!)

The repeater widget can be used to display repeating patterns of text, images, and links. Repeaters are good to use for the following UI patterns: product listing, contact information, and data tables such as recent transactions. The repeater widget can also be formatted. We discuss this powerful widget in more detail in the book and there is a great example of using it to simulate a **Type Ahead** search in *Appendix, Practitioners' Corner*.

Style

At its core, a wireframe is nothing but a framed rectangle with some boxes, interface controls, and text. It can work perfectly when sketched on a napkin or an index card, but this technique can get you only that far. With the evolution of user experience as an established discipline, there has been a shift towards higher fidelity. Now, this does not mean that the project/wireframe begins at high fidelity. In fact, we recommend maturing the wireframes as the project matures or evolves. Large and complex projects will allow the opportunity for the wireframes to become more high fidelity if the project team has a desire for it. However, we think it is important to allow the visual designers the opportunity to apply their creative stamp. Therefore, only small amounts of color are good to use in order to show hierarchy and importance.

The experience is determined as much by how the interface looks as by how it behaves. On the one hand, user experience designers want to keep the discussion subjective, focused on structure and flow. For this approach, sketchy styling can help enforce the tentative aspect of an emerging design. On the other hand, user experience designers have a vision or idea they want to communicate to the client. If your idea does not come across as thoughtful (low fidelity), it can be misconstrued as a half-baked idea and gets passed. Higher fidelity wireframes can help sell the designs to higher management. Lastly, some user experience designers are at a company where the brand guidelines are well established, so it may make sense to work with the assets at the wireframing stage.

Whatever are the stylistic expressions appropriate for your project and design philosophy, you can define the visual properties of widgets by using the **Style** tab.

Like the **Widget Properties and Style** tab, the **Style** tab is contextual to the selected widget. This tab is divided into the following five collapsible sections (*Image 15*, **A**):

- **Location + Size**
- **Base Style**
- **Font**
- **Fills, Lines, + Borders**
- **Alignment + Padding**

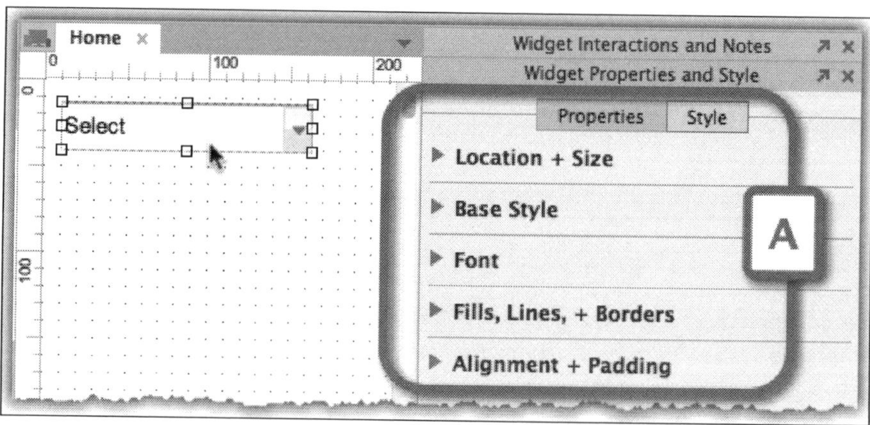

Image 15

Most of the formatting attributes that appear in this tab are also available through the **Format Bar** and the **Context Menu** (via right-click), but here you get a one-stop access to all of the formatting under a single tab.

Location and Size

The **Location + Size** section allows you to:

- Set the **Left** and **Top** position (*Image 16*, **A**)
- Set the size of the widget using the **Height** and **Width** (**B**)
- Rotation of a widget, and the text within the widget (**C**)
- Hide/show an individual widget (**D**)

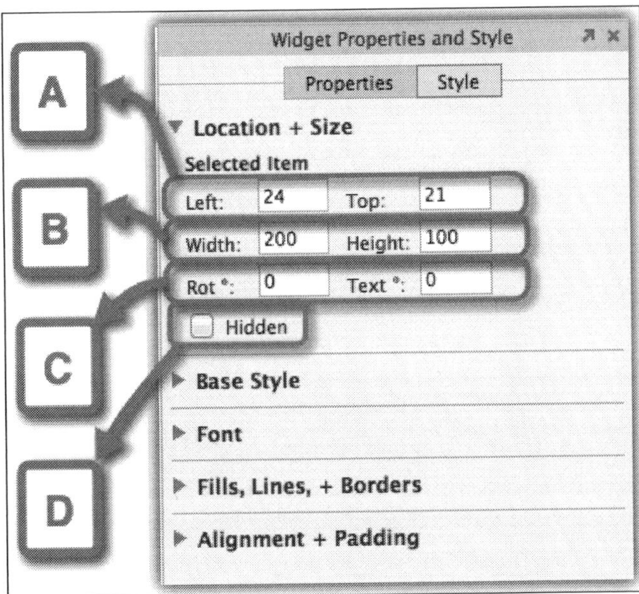

Image 16

Base Style

An Axure style is a collection of formatting attributes that can be applied to the shape and text components of a widget. Each widget type in Axure has a default style, which determines how it appears when added to a wireframe and when it is generated in the prototype.

There are two methods to modify the style of a widget:

- Manually change various attributes of a selected individual widget using the **Style** tab (shown in the previous image), **Format** bar, or the **Context** menu. This can become slow and repetitive when you want to apply a consistent look across a group of widgets.
- Apply/assign a style to a widget that can be assigned to multiple widgets or text elements. To do this, use **Widget Style Editor** to apply many updates at once. This will also ensure a consistent look across the wireframes.

The Style Editor – Default Styles

As we have mentioned, all widgets have a default style. Early on in a project, specific styles may not yet be applied. However, you and/or the team may want to modify the defaults styles to have a specific font or change the color of the text to be pewter rather than black.

Change the default style of a widget. In the **Style** section, click on the Widget Style Editor icon (*Image 17*, **A**) to bring the **Widget Style Editor** dialog.

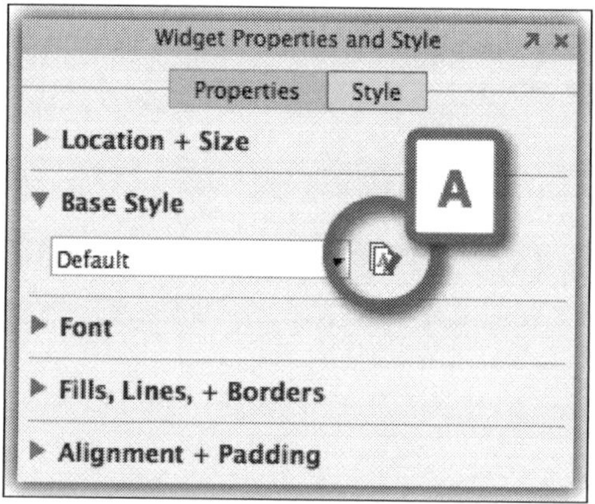

Image 17

The **Widget Defaults** tab (*Image 18*, **A**) in the **Widget Style Editor** window lists all the widgets and their default styles (**B**).

The defaults can be changed. In the example illustrated in *Image 18*, the defaults **Font**, **Typeface**, and **Font Color** of the **H1** widget were modified (**C**).

This means that when anyone on the team pulls in the **H1** widget, the new style will be applied.

In the Axure Pro version, additionally, the **Check Out** or **Check In** option and the status indicator (**D**) will be displayed.

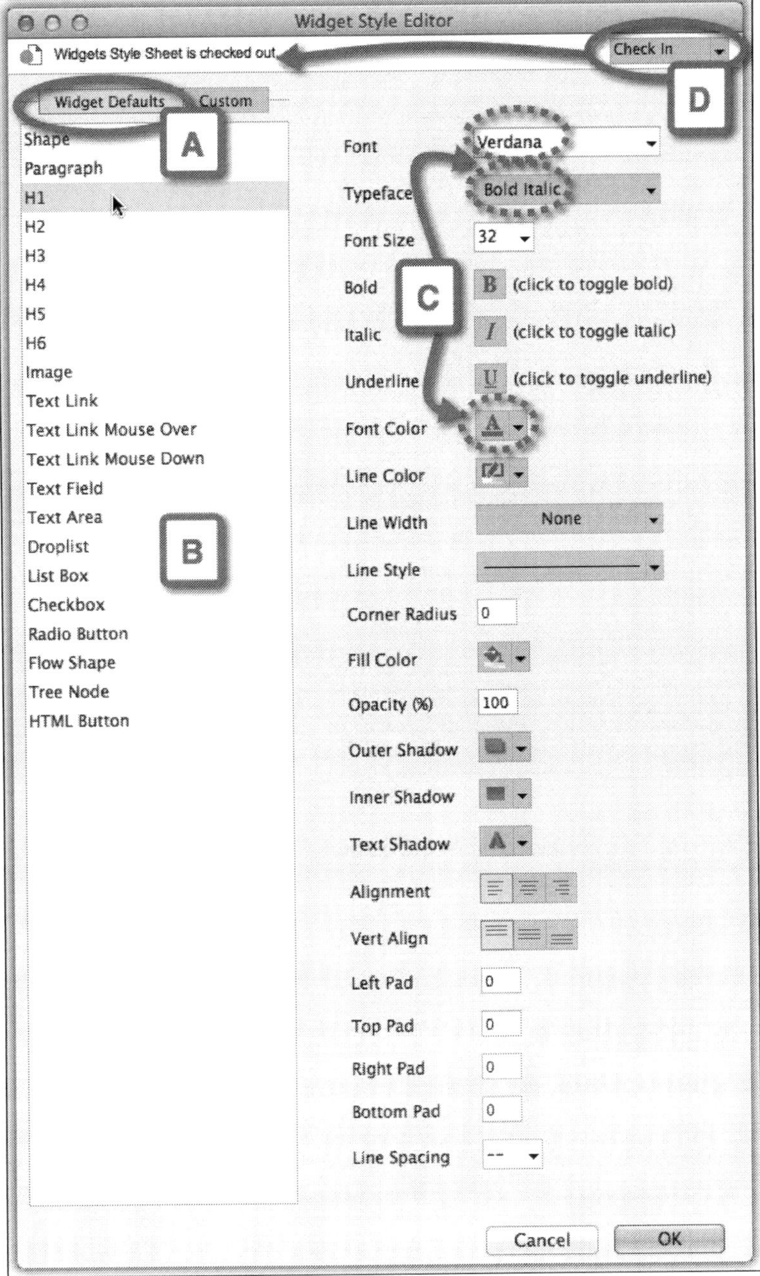

Image 18

The Style Editor Dialog – Custom Styles

Custom styles are an excellent tool to use once visual design patterns begin to evolve. Examples of elements that are good candidates for customization are: buttons (primary, secondary, tertiary), headers, background colors and textures for page sections, error messaging, and so on. Let's walk through creating a custom style:

1. In the Format bar, click on the Widget Style Editor icon (*Image 19*, **A**) to launch the **Widget Style Editor** dialog.
2. Alternatively, click on the widget style editor icon (**B**) in the **Style** section of the **Widget Properties and Style** pane.

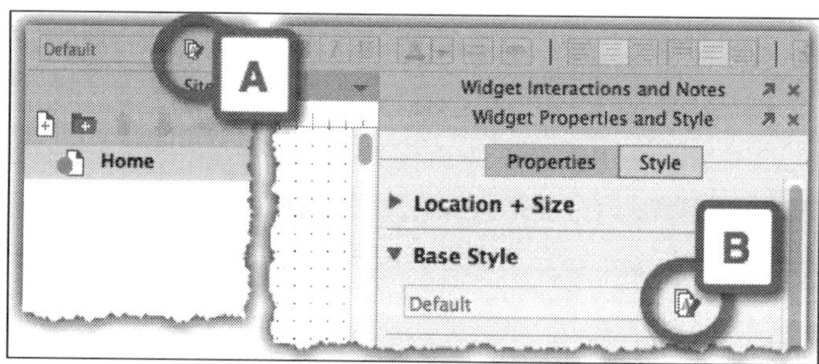

Image 19

3. In the **Widget Style Editor** window (*Image 20*, **A**) , click on the **Custom** tab (**B**) and create a new custom style by clicking on the green **Plus** sign (**C**).
4. Name the new custom style (**D**), and then modify the relevant properties you want for this style (**E**).

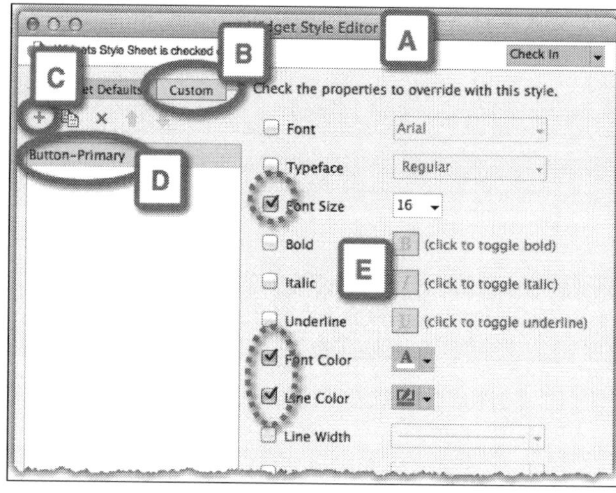

Image 20

5. Once added, custom styles can be immediately applied to any selected widget (*Image 21*, **A**) through the **Style** drop-down list on the Format bar (**B**) or in the **Style** section in the **Widget Properties and Style** pane (**C**).

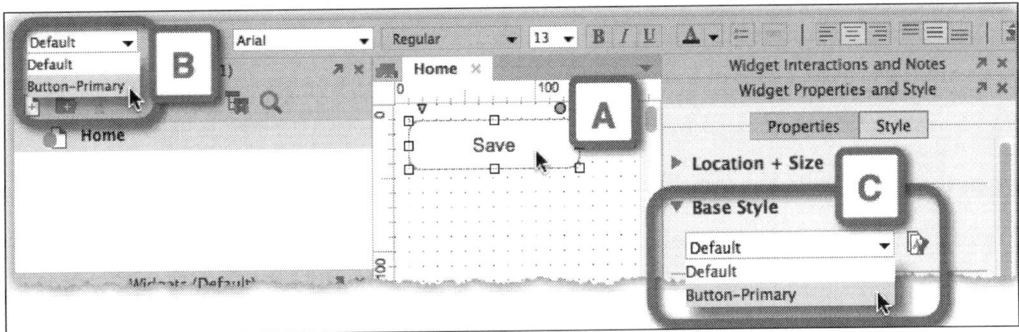

Image 21

It is a good idea to set up your styles at the start of a project and be diligent about assigning styles to your widgets and text (via the dropdown). That way, if there is a change in style down the road, the update will be easer to accommodate.

When naming the custom styles, be descriptive enough so that your colleagues understand where to use the style.

Font

In this section, you can modify the font attributes of a single widget or multiple selected widgets:

- Font family
- Font size
- Font styling, bold, italic, and underline
- Font color
- Toggle bullet list styling

The role of typography in your prototype cannot be underestimated. The typeface, its size, styling, color, and spacing can make a sea of difference in how your work will be perceived by stakeholders and end users. Axure supports Web Fonts which we will describe later in the book.

The following *Image 22* visualizes the **Font** section (**A**), which becomes active when a widget or multiple widgets are selected (**B**). Note that applying a font shadow is actually in the section **Fills, Lines, + Borders** (C).

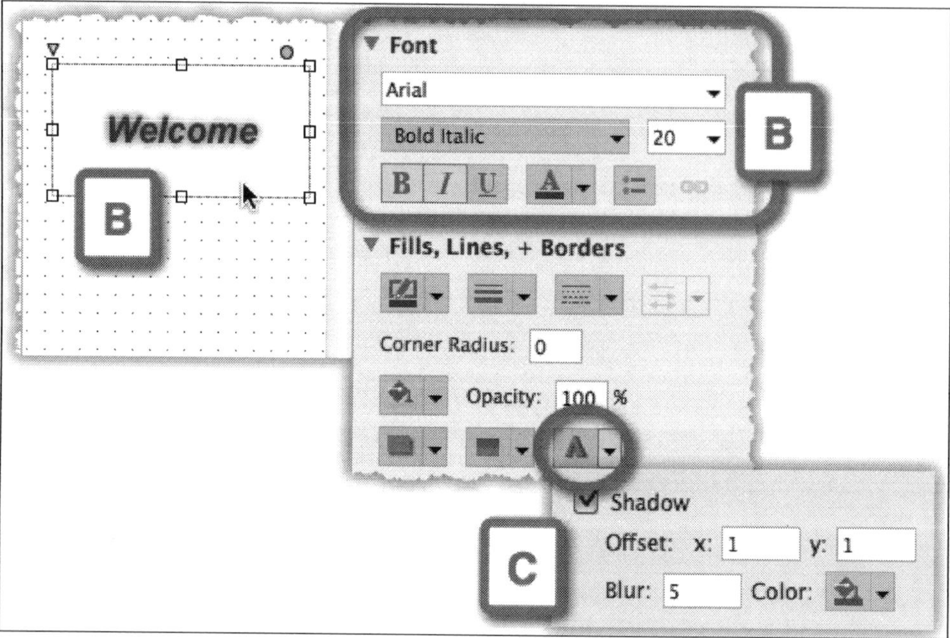

Image 22

Fills, Lines, + Borders

You can apply the following attributes to a single or multiple selected widgets:

- Set **Fill Color** (supports gradients and transparency/opacity)
- Set **Line Color** (supports gradients and transparency/opacity)
- Set **Line Width/Weight**
- Set **Line Pattern**, otherwise referred to as borders, (solid, dotted, and so on.)
- Set an **Outer Shadow** or **Inner Shadow** on a widget (new!)
- Set a **Text Shadow** (new!)
- Set the **Corner Radius** on a widget—a radius that rounds the corners. If you want a square button, set the radius equal to `0` (new!)

The following screenshot illustrates the use of the fills, lines, and borders functionality:

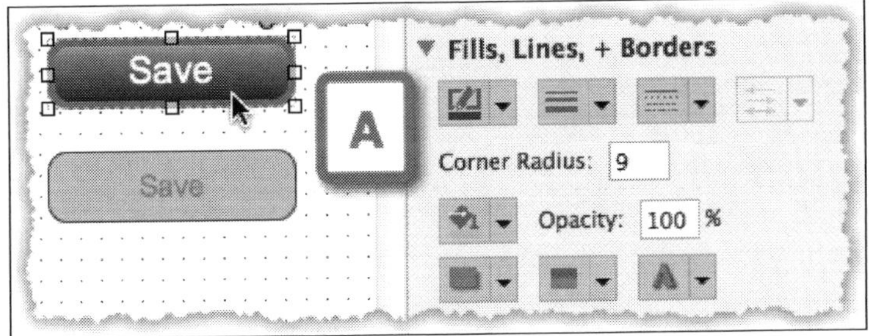

Image 23

Borders render within the dimensions of the widget for accurate dimensions.

Outer and Inner Shadow

Shadows can add some amazing richness to a design. The following *Image 24* shows a Rectangle widget (**A**) to which both an outer shadow (**B**) and inner shadow (**C**) have been applied. Clicking on the icons presents a menu with relevant settings (**D**).

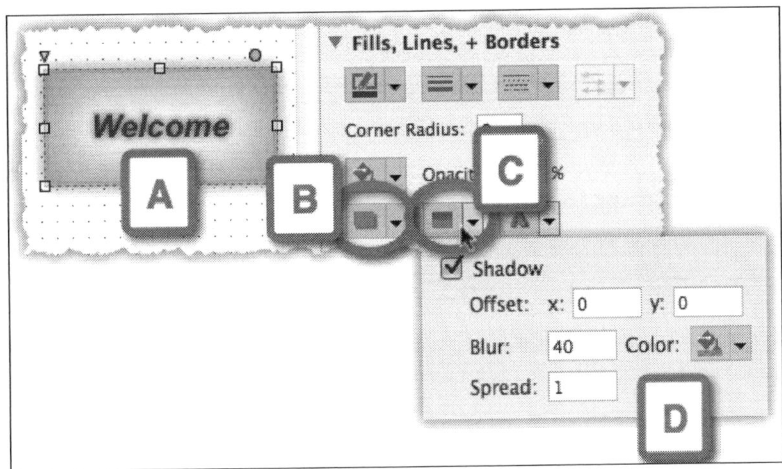

Image 24

One of the properties of the inner shadow (*Image 25*, **A**) is **Spread** (**B**), which provides an interesting combination of solids and shadow inner fills.

The default value for **Spread** is zero (**C**). A spread with a value 10 is visualized in (**D**), and with value 100, which appears as a solid fill, in (**E**).

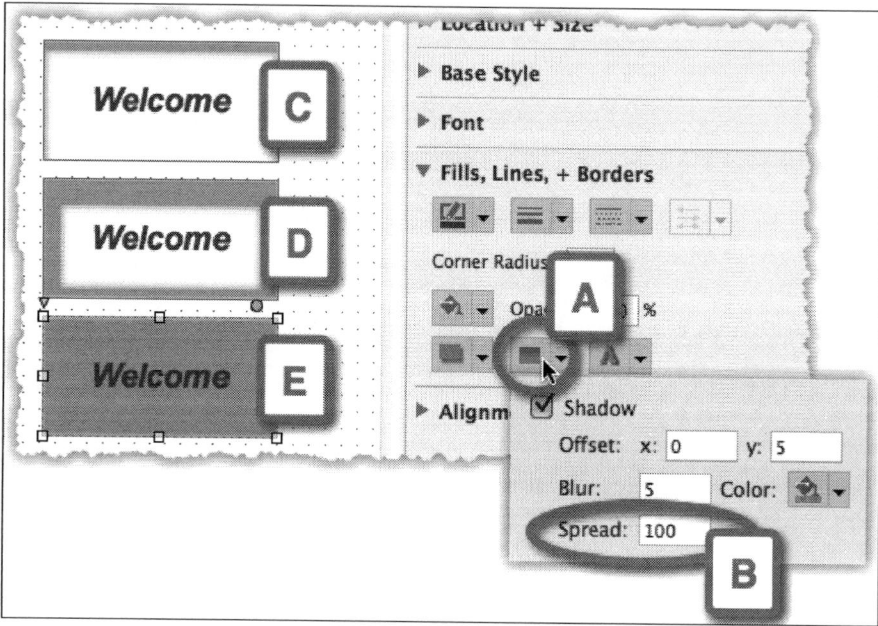

Image 25

Alignment + Padding

There are instances when it makes sense to add a widget and then place a label or header on top of it. However, oftentimes this is unnecessary because of the alignment and padding feature. This section is closely associated with the **Font** section in that it affords control over the text attributes in widgets. You can control:

- The horizontal and vertical alignment of text in relation to the widget:
    - Left, center, and right
    - Top, center, and bottom
- The left, top, right, and bottom padding of the text from the edge of a widget
- The line spacing of text lines in the widget

The following example demonstrates the value of the **Auto Width** and **Auto Height** options when applied to buttons:

1. Drag a **Rectangle** widget (*Image 26*, **A**) onto the wireframe pane. Right-click on the widget and select **Auto Fit Width** (**B**) from the context menu. After applying the autofit height, the widget shrinks to the size of the text (**C**).

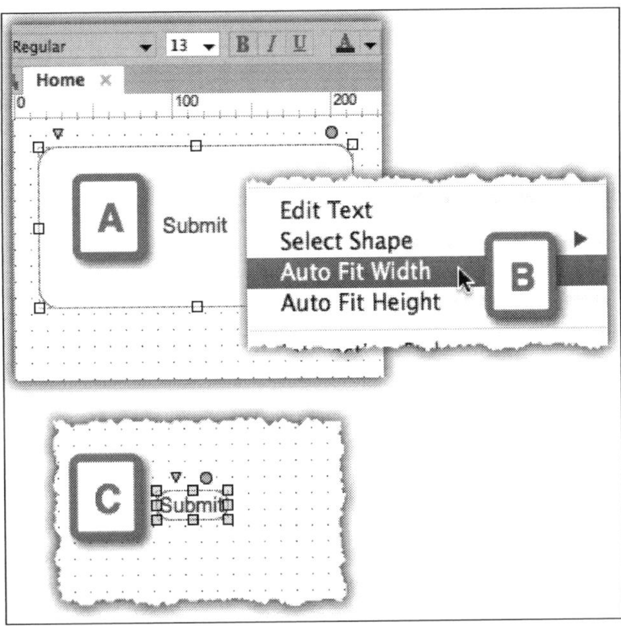

Image 26

2. As you apply padding (*Image 27*, **A**) to the button (**B**), its size expands to reflect only the padding. Add additional formatting as required.

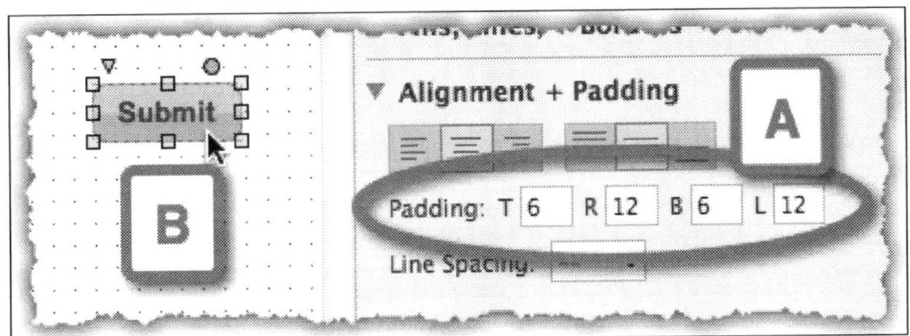

Image 27

3. Copy and paste the button created in step 1 (*Image 28*, **A**), and change the text on the new button (**B**) to a longer string. Despite the longer text, it does not wrap, but rather the button resizes with the text string while maintaining the padding.

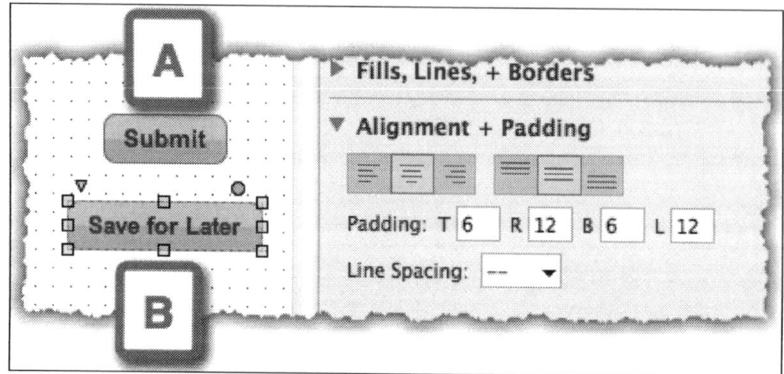

Image 28

This behavior is valuable especially when setting the value of text dynamically.

Line Spacing

This feature defines the height of each line, known as **line-height** in CSS, for those who have used Adobe Photoshop or Adobe Illustrator. This is a very handy feature.

The Design Area

Now that you understand how to use the widgets, let's put them to use. Simply put, the design area is your workspace where you build your wireframes. Each page (wireframe) opens in its own tab. There are four types of wireframe items that open in the design area:

- Pages, which can be managed and organized in the **Sitemap** pane
- Masters, which can be managed and organized in the **Masters** pane
- States of dynamic panels
- Repeater item/s

Tabs display the name of the opened wireframe (*Image 29*, **A**). You can change the order in which the tabs appear by clicking-and-dragging a tab to the left or right. The **Tabs** menu (**B**) lists all the open wireframes (**C**) and affords quick navigation between tabs when many are open. Finally, you can close an individual tab by clicking on the close icon (**D**).

The tabs open from left to right, which means that the page or master you opened most recently will be farthest to the left.

It is common to work with multiple open wireframes. Pretty quickly, you will find yourself flipping through the tabs in search of the wireframe you want to focus on next. To quickly clean up a cluttered design area, use **Close All Tabs** or **Close Other Tabs** (E).

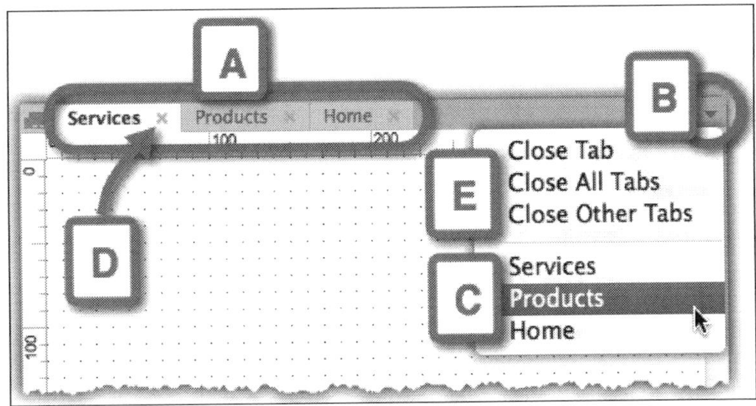

Image 29

Adaptive Views (New!)

Adaptive Views have been introduced in Axure 7 to help UX Designers who are on **Responsive Web Design (RWD)** projects. Adaptive Views define breakpoints, where you want your pages to switch to a different style or layout based on the size of a target screen.

In a non-responsive project, all the wireframes are designed with a particular target screen size in mind, such as a desktop or a smartphone, that adaptive views provide. Without adaptive views, creating specialized instances of the wireframes for a radically different screen size would involve a significant hit on productivity and turnaround speed as all wireframes would need to be recreated and fitted to the new target size. More significant changes to the functionality in one set of wireframes would need to be manually applied to the other set of wireframes. The more the size variations required, the more overwhelmingly difficult the task of maintaining all wireframes in sync.

Inheritance is the most importance concept behind adaptive views because it addresses to a great degree the productivity aspect of managing multiple sets of wireframes, each set optimized for a target screen size. In a nutshell, a widget in an adaptive view inherits properties such as its location, size, and style from its parent view. If you change the color of a button in a parent view, it will change the color of the button in the child view. If you change a button in the child view, it will not change that same button in the parent view. Axure also makes it possible to have the changes applied from a child view across all views.

Adding Adaptive Views

You begin, of course, with a single view whose wireframes are constructed with a target screen size in mind, such as desktop or smartphone (*Image 30*, **A**). This view is referred to as **Base**. To add views that correspond to other target sizes, click on the **Manage Adaptive Views** icon (**B**) or select **Adaptive Views** from the **Project** menu and the **Adaptive Views** window (C) will appear. To add a view, click on the plus icon (**D**). **Presets** (E) allows you to select the target display from the drop-down list (**F**). Repeat the process as required to establish additional adaptive views. Axure allows you to create custom display targets.

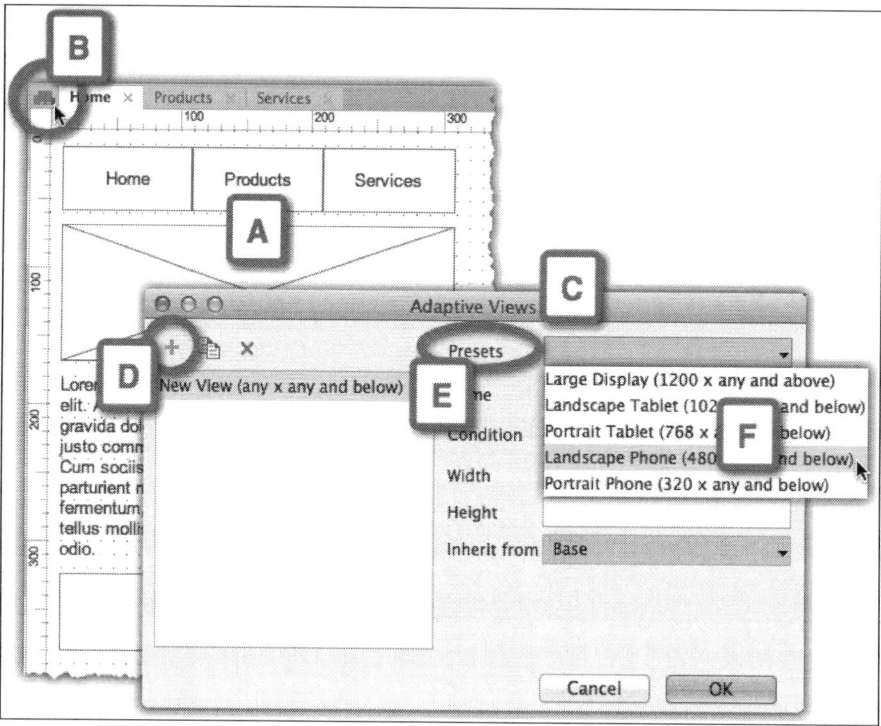

Image 30

Adaptive View Definitions

The **Adaptive Views** window has the following set of fields (*Image 31*, **A**):

- **Presets**: These are preconfigured device display sizes listed by width
- **Name**: This is the label for the view
- **Condition**: The condition determines the transition to the breakpoint
- **Width**: If you want to define a custom view, use this to declare the width
- **Height**: If you want to define a custom view, use this to declare the height
- **Inherit from**: This specifies the parent view of this view

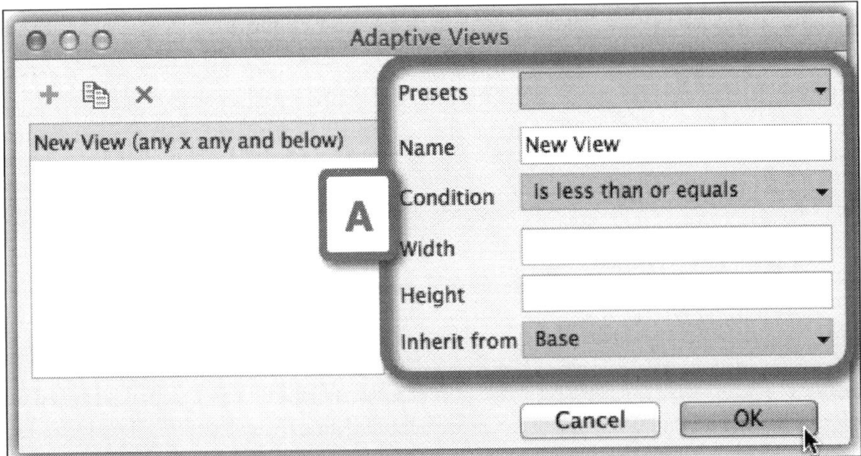

Image 31

The Page Properties Pane

This pane is where you go to document a page, set up page level interactions, and/or apply page-level styling. This pane is divided into the following three tabs:

- **Page Notes** (*Image 32*, **A**): For annotating pages and masters in the writing space that follows (**B**).
- **Page Interactions** (**C**): Creating cases is very similar to how you would create them for widgets (**D**). The three common interactions at page level are the **OnPageLoad**, **OnWindowResize**, and **OnWindowScroll**. Click on the **More Events** link (**E**) to choose additional options from the menu (**F**).

- **Page Style** (G): Apply formatting properties to pages.

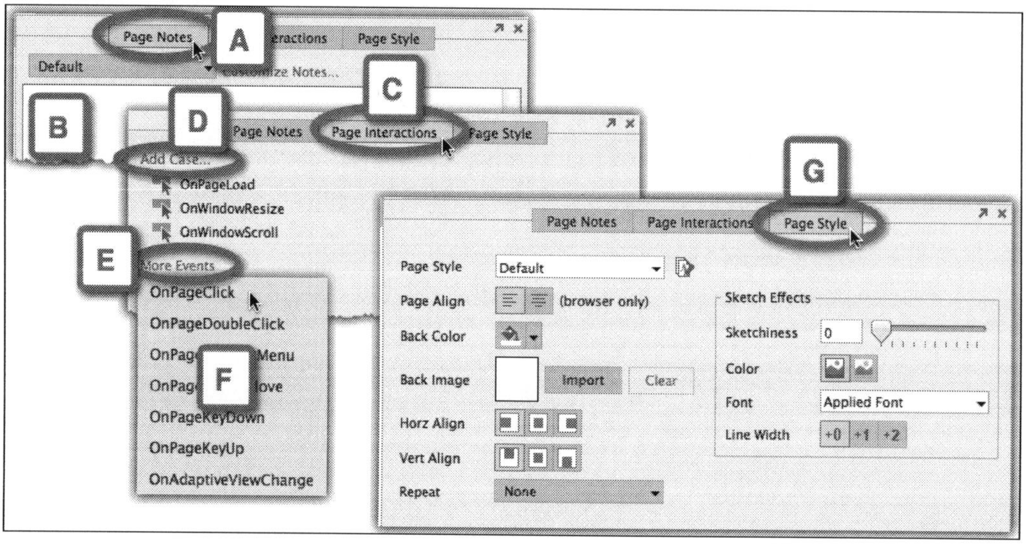

Image 32

Page Notes

Axure provides an integrated wireframing and annotation environment. The **Page Notes** tab is where you enter page level information, such as a description of wireframe, entry and exit points, container size, and so on. This feature is relevant for those who need to generate a UI specification document or HTML annotations to it and can be very useful as a means to communicate important information about the page to team members, or for a transition of work.

The text can be formatted in this section as well:

- Change the font and its color
- Make it bold, italic, and underline, by highlighting the section you want, and applying the style from the Format bar

You cannot change the font size, create bullets, or change paragraph alignment.

Once you generate the HTML prototype, your notes, including their formatting, will appear in the **Notes** tab, which is on the right-hand side of the **Sitemap** pane in the browser by default.

Manage Notes

Axure allows you to group notes in categories, which is important for clear and well-organized documentation. Still the default category can serve as a "catch-all" for page annotations.

The approach to adopt for your project depends on the complexity of the project, the documentation output (HTML versus Microsoft Word / PDF), and stakeholder expectations. It is a good idea to discuss and align expectations early to make sure that your documentation is satisfactory and to avoid nasty and/or costly surprises.

The benefit of using just a single notes field is obviously simplicity, at least for you. The drawback is that stakeholders may require varied content. In most projects you are addressing an audience that has specific interest in only part of your description. For example, developers might be interested in behavior patterns of the screen and other technical information, while the business team is looking for the fulfillment of the business requirements. If all your information is packed in a single field, readers will have to weed through information that is irrelevant to them.

Since Axure lets you segment page level notes into several note sections and allows you to control which notes to display to whom, it is a very viable option. Examples of such categories include:

- **Business Requirements Document** (**BRD**) references
- Accessibility (WAI/Section 508) notes
- UX description
- Exceptions, Personalization, or Localization notes
- Private team communication

You control:

- The titles of notes section
- Inclusion of the notes in the HTML prototype
- Including on the notes in the Microsoft Word / PDF specification documents
- Selection of which note to include in the output
- Note order

To create or rename a page-note category, clicking on the **Customize Notes...** link (*Image 33*, **A**) launches the **Page Notes Fields** window (**B**).

Add new page note categories by clicking on the **+** icon. You can modify this name as well. To delete a category, select it in the list and click on the **X** icon.

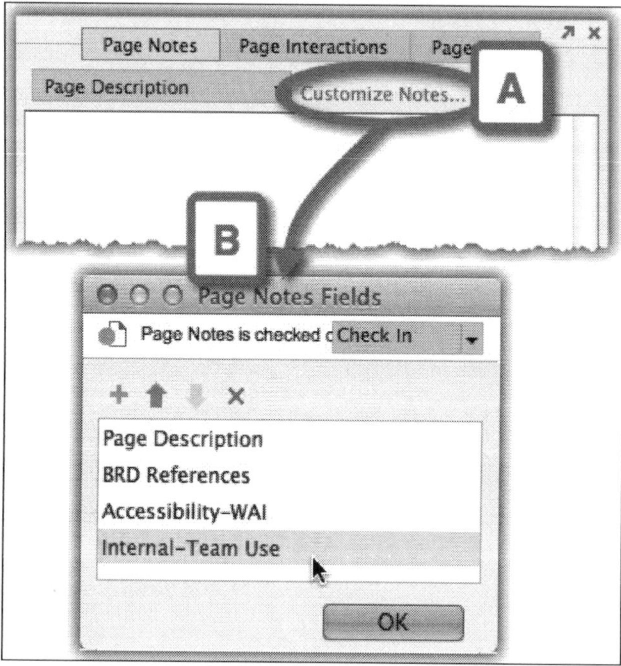

Image 33

In a team project, adding additional note categories impacts the entire team as they all see them and may be required to fill them—additional work that warrants discussing with your colleagues the workload impact before you begin adding additional categories.

Page Interactions

This tab allows the UX designer to dictate what to show on the page when the page is generated. This is an awesome feature because it affords an economy of construction. For example, instead of creating a unique page that visualizes how the page looks when a first-time visitor accesses it and another unique wireframe to show the page after the user logs in, you can use a single page with dynamic panels. Each state in the dynamic panels will correspond to a unique view.

Say you specify an **OnPageLoad** event that fires when the browser loads the page. The browser will then execute the actions that you specified for the event and will render either the visitor page or the registered user page. We will cover this technique later in *Chapter 4, Creating Basic Interactions*, and *Chapter 5, Advanced Interactions*.

Page Formatting

Page formatting can be applied only to pages, and not to masters or dynamic panel states. You can define the following attributes:

- Page alignment (left or centered) only applies to the browser
- Background color
- Background image, including horizontal and vertical alignment, and repetition
- Horizontal alignment
- Vertical alignment
- Repeat droplist
- Sketch effects (which are described in the next section)
- Font color, font text, and line width

You can save a combination of these attributes as a custom style and apply this custom style to other pages—a great time saver for ensuring consistency across pages.

Sketch Effects

There is an amazingly compelling quality to the human touch, and in the context of prototyping, Axure allows you to apply sketchy effects to your deliverable, which lends them a handmade feel.

Using the sketchy style during the early conceptualization phase can help you communicate to the stakeholders and reviewers the fact that they are looking at a conceptual wireframe or prototype. The following screenshot visualizes a wireframe with 0 percent sketchiness (*Image 34*, **A**) and the same one with 100 percent sketchiness (**B**).

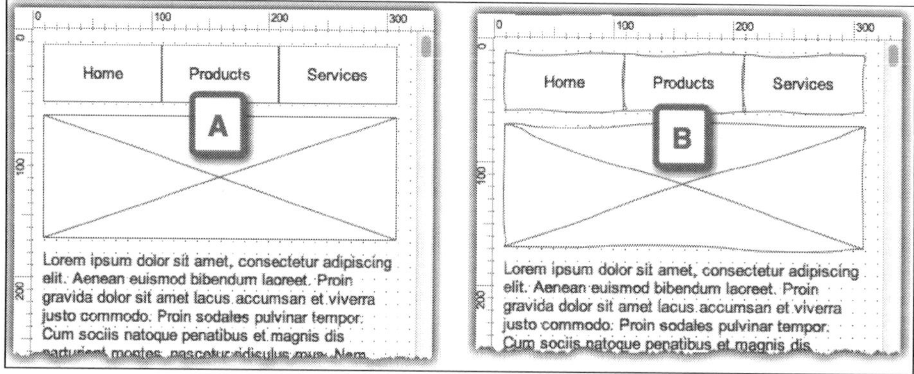

Image 34

Flow Widgets

Flow widgets are available in Axure 7 from the **Widgets** pane. To access the flow widgets, click on the **Select Library** menu (*Image 35*, **A**) and select the **Flow** option (**B**) to view the various widgets available in this built-in Axure library (**C**):

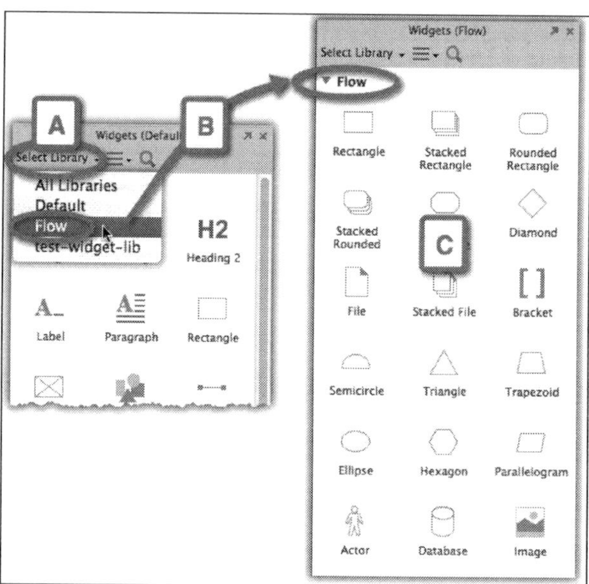

Image 35

Flow diagrams are interesting because they are an abstraction of a flow, an algorithm expressed not as a mathematical formula, but rather in concrete shapes, arrows, and text. The phrase, "A picture is worth a thousand words", illustrates a general problem with flow diagrams, however: Flow diagrams are often not very easy to understand, and some complex flow diagrams sometimes require "a thousand words" to explain exactly what is going on.

Whatever choices you make for creating flow diagrams for your project, Axure can help you put them together in a compelling way. In addition to the geometric shapes commonly used for diagramming, such as the diamond for decision points, there are specialized shapes such as database and bracket, and most importantly, the persona shape.

To use the connector line, click on the **Connector Mode** icon (*Image 36*, **A**) in the **Selection Mode** icon group, as shown in the following screenshot:

Image 36

The Widget Interactions and Notes Pane

This pane facilitates two major prototyping aspects: interactivity and documentation. The pane is contextual to a widget selection as it becomes active only when you have a single widget selected. Once a widget is selected, the widget properties pane allows you to define its behavior and attributes in the following two tabs:

- Interactions
- Notes

The Interactions Tab

The effectiveness of simulating interactivity in UX projects cannot be exaggerated. The reality is that most stakeholders have a hard time imagining how something might work, even when they are presented with a sequence of static wireframes.

Less than a decade ago, desktop and web software had lent themselves easily to a page-to-page sequencing because refreshing the entire page followed most actions. It was easy to model these types of interaction flows with static wireframes. Modern interfaces are remarkably dynamic; they respond to a growing array of direct user manipulation including auditory commands and they often have smooth, engaging visual animations and special effects. Data on various sections on the screen seamlessly and fluidly updates in the background, independent of other sections and without requiring a page refresh. This stuff is impossible to communicate successfully with static wireframes.

For example, think about communicating even the simple mouse-over interaction, where the user's mouse is hovering over a text. The styling changes from normal to bold and underlined. Its color changes from dark gray to blue. After two milliseconds, a small tooltip appears to the right of the hovered text. This is what you would have to say if you are using a static wireframe or you would show the two states. Additionally, you would have to mention that there is no mouseover in the mobile view and so on.

Now, imagine a stakeholder's meeting with high-level management to whom you want to communicate your vision of the design. The most trivial of interaction patterns requires so much explanation that it inevitably slows down the overall delivery of the experience you envision. Alternatively, you can use an Axure prototype to demonstrate the interaction by moving the mouse over the text: the experience is communicated *instantly*.

Interactions

Interactions are an Axure term for a set of instructions you define to add interactivity behaviors to the prototype. Interactions can be created in the Page Properties pane, and, widget and master level interactions can be created in the **Widget Interactions and Notes** pane.

In a nutshell, there are two things you have to remember about widget interactions:

- They are contextual to the selected widget
- Each interaction is a self-contained unit, which is made of three components:
    - **Event**: Each interaction is tied to a single event, for example, **onClick**
    - **Case**: Each event can have one-to-many cases
    - **Action**: Each case can have one-to-many actions

The actions available to any given widget may differ. We will discuss interactions in depth in *Chapter 4, Creating Basic Interactions*.

The Notes Tab

Notes fields capture attributes associated with a selected widget. Axure comes with a default set of fields, but most likely, you will end up with your own set—those that best fit the needs of your project. The fields come in four data type flavors:

- **Text fields**: Use these to capture attributes such as description, default value, and so on. This is the field we use most often.
- **Select list fields**: Use these for as many attributes as possible, to enforce consistency of values and to save time while annotating, for example, status, release version.
- **Number fields**: Use these when you want to enforce a numeric attribute. However, we failed to find a good use for it. For normal attributes, such as release or phase numbers, the **Select** list is probably more appropriate because of the set values. However, Number fields are available in case you desire to use them.
- **Date fields**: These are used for date-specific attributes. For example, you can create a field called last updated and update the value after each edit to the widget. This may sound like good and useful information to track, but remember that the update is manual. You will have to remember to make those updates for all widgets as you update them.

To customize the default notes fields, switch the **Widget Interactions and Notes** pane to the **Notes** tab (*Image 37*, **A**) and click on the **Customize** link (**B**).

The **Widgets Notes Fields and Sets** dialog (C) will open the **Fields** tab (**D**), which lists the build-in set of fields that come with Axure (**E**). These fields can be renamed, deleted, or used as is; it is up to you and the documentation requirements of the project.

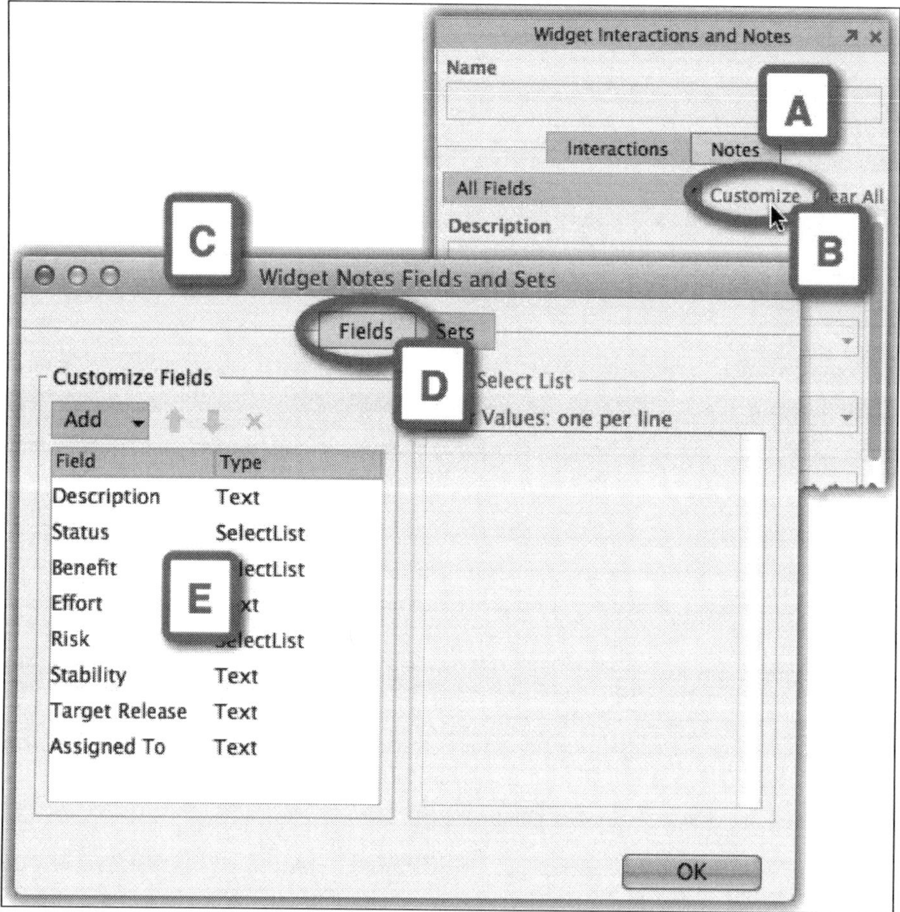

Image 37

Managing notes via the menu and icons set (*Image 38*, **A**) includes the ability to:

- Add a new custom field of the four possible field types.
- Set the order as you wish to view the notes.
- Remove any fields you do not wish to use. Axure will prompt you with a warning (**B**) when you try to reduce the risk of unintentionally deleting a field in which annotation have been created.

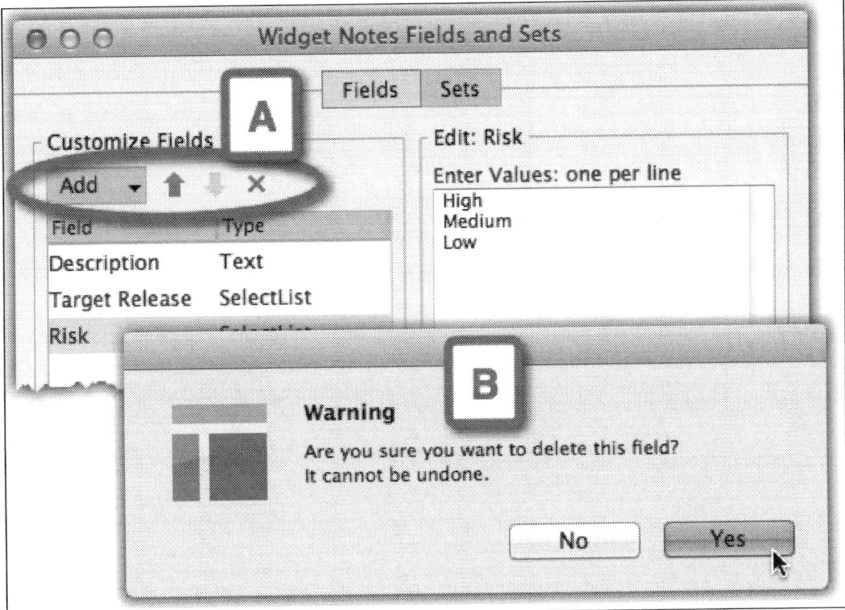

Image 38

Discuss the optimal set of fields with your colleagues and stakeholders. If the stakeholders have never worked with Axure before, they may have no idea of Axure's capabilities.

There is no limit that we are aware of, to the number of note fields you can have, but be practical. Remember that these are widget level fields and you will have tens, if not, hundreds of widgets in your project that might require some annotation. The more fields, the more effort to create and update the attribute data, especially as requirements are likely to change often and at the last minute.

Note Sets

Annotation fields can be grouped into sets. These are very useful when the project requires the use of many fields, and also when different types of users need to write annotations. Either way, instead of scrolling down a long, sometimes confusing list of fields, a smaller, more relevant set can be displayed.

Some uses of sets are:

- Organizing business-related fields in one set and development fields in another.
- In multi-release projects, organize by release-specific sets.
- With multiple workstreams, organize by workstream-specific and global sets.
- In multifunctional teams, organize by sets optimized for the requirements of the particular discipline. For example, BAs populate functional requirements in dedicated fields and designers in another set.

Configuring sets is easy once you have determined how to group the fields. In the following example (*Image 39*), one set of fields is grouped under **Mandatory**—fields that must be populated for each widget, and a group called **Optional** for the rest:

1. In the **Sets** tab (*Image 39*, **A**), click on the **+** icon (**B**) to add sets and name them (**C**).
2. Click on the set you want to define and from **Add** drop-down list (**D**), select the fields you want to associate with it from the complete list of fields (**E**).

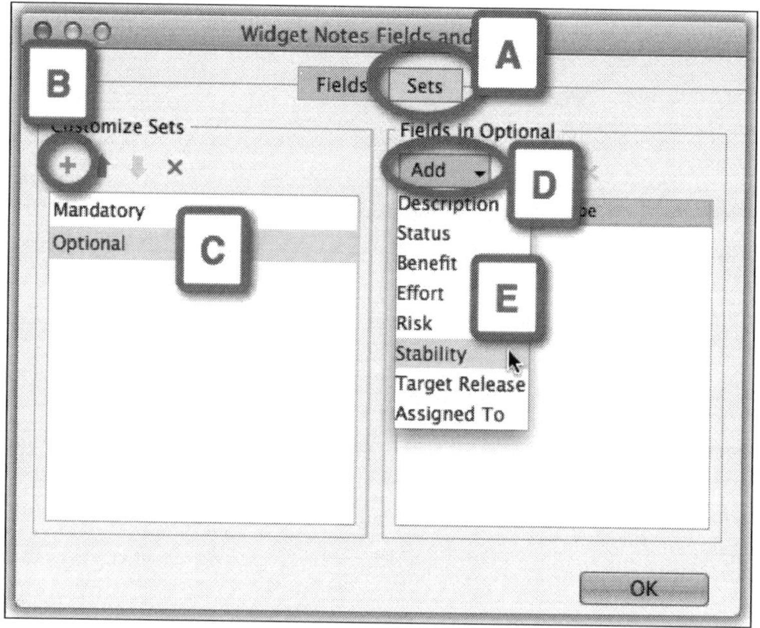

Image 39

3. Now, in addition to having the **All Fields** option, the drop-down list (*Image 40*, **B**) now includes the set. Picking a set will remove all other fields and displays in the **Widget Interactions and Notes** pane (**A**) only the fields in that set.

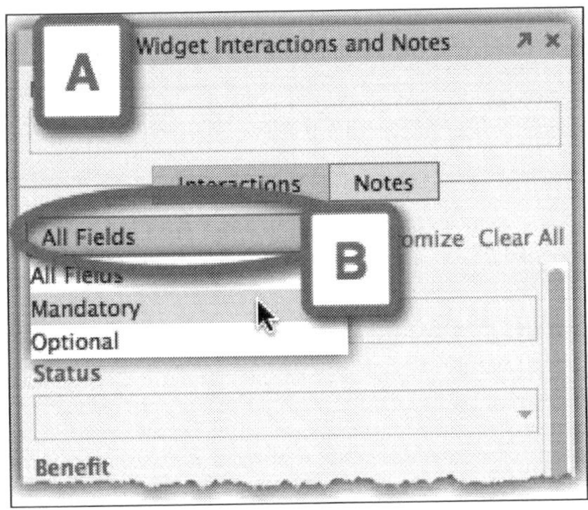

Image 40

Be mindful of entering annotations in the correct set. The sets are not contextual to the widgets, so switching between them is manual.

Grid and Guides

Grid and guides are standard features that we come to expect in any graphics software since they provide a visual aid for alignment and composition.

Setting Guides

To access these features, right-click anywhere in the design area. You can also launch it from the menu **Arrange | Grids and Guides**.

The **Grid and Guides** menu (*Image 41*, **A**) is divided into grid-related options (**B**), guides-related options (**C**), and the **Snap to Object** feature (**D**).

If you use your keyboard arrows to move/align widgets, deselect the **Snap to Object** option as the elements will not nudge.

To control the snapping vertical and horizontal tolerance of widgets, select the **Object Snap Settings...** from the menu, and switch to the **Object Snap** (E) tab in the **Grid Dialog** pop up (F).

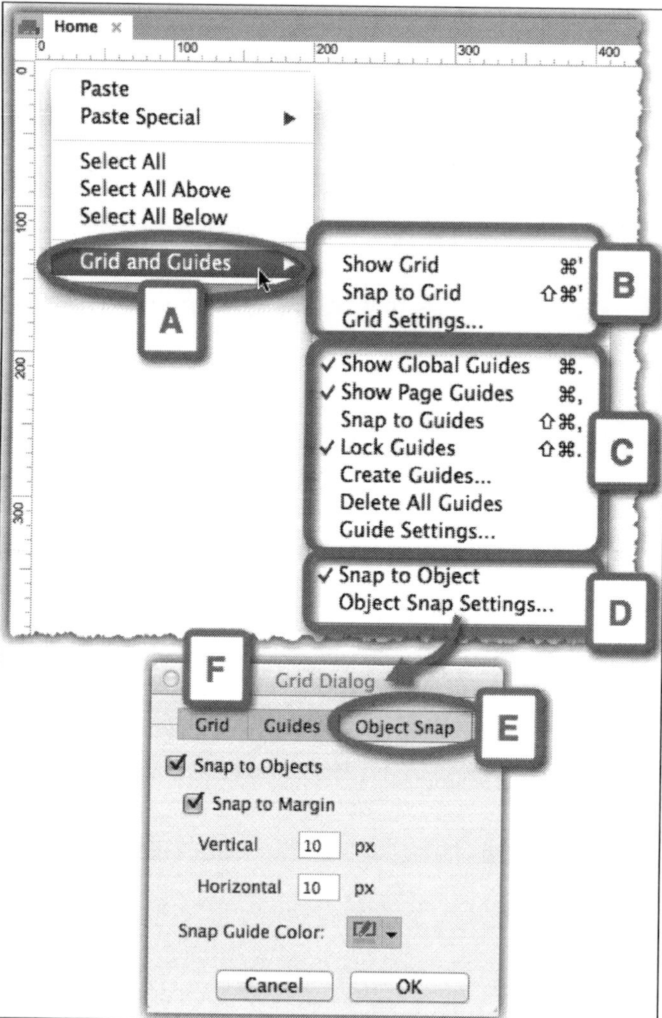

Image 41

The Masters Pane

As the name suggests, a master is a single wireframe that can be reused on other wireframes. When you edit the master wireframe, the change will instantly be applied to all the instances of this master, effectively updating all the wireframes where the master has been placed. There are several good reasons to incorporate masters into your prototype construction as much as possible:

- Manage consistency of design patterns across the user interface.
- Save yourself enormous amounts of time by updating to the master wireframe; Axure will reflect the change on all other relevant wireframes.
- Save more time, write your annotation once, and avoid extra work, redundancy, and errors in the UI Specifications document in the output.
- Reduce the size of your Axure file as masters reduce the redundancy of duplicated widgets.

Use the **Masters** pane to:

- Manage and organize the project's masters, including the option to add, delete, rename, group in folders, change order, and so on.
- Select a master for editing.
- Set the behavior of masters on the pages they are placed on.
- Add or remove masters from pages.
- View usage report and see if a master is actually used in your prototype or not.
- Search masters when you have many of them in your project file.

You can annotate a master at wireframe level. This is very important because Axure lets you assign different behaviors to the master instances across the prototype using **Raised Events**. In previous Axure versions, master annotation was limited to the master wireframe itself, making it difficult to document the different behaviors of its instances. Annotating the instance at the wireframe level solves this issue.

The following screenshot illustrates the **Masters** pane context menu (*Image 42*, **B**) when right-clicking on a master (**A**):

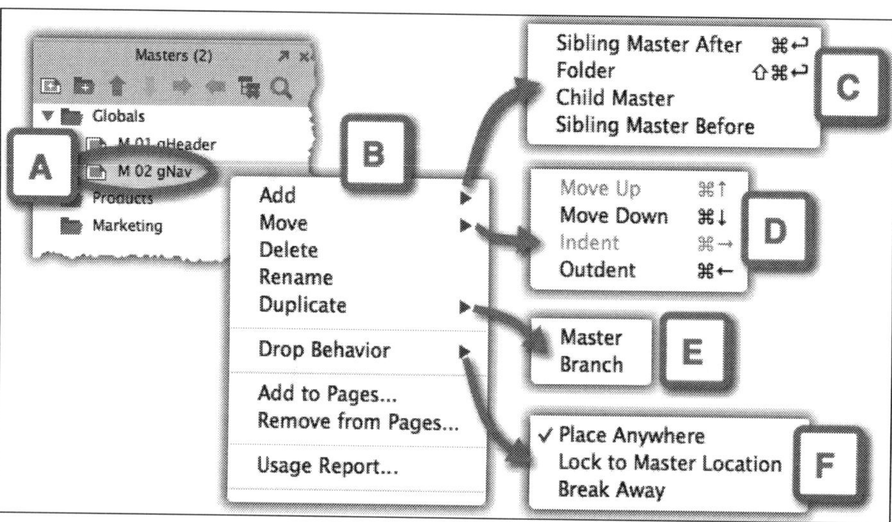

Image 42

The **Add** (C), **Move** (D), and **Duplicate** (E) submenus provide the expected options for managing folders and masters within the **Masters** pane. **The Drop Behavior** (F) provides controls over some settings of the master on the page. These settings are explained in the following sections.

Master Drop Behavior

This feature allows you to determine how to apply a master instance to a wireframe. The term, behavior, is somewhat confusing, but the actual options are straightforward and useful. Additionally, the visual appearance of the master is different:

- Place anywhere (*Image 43*, **A**)
- Lock to master location (**B**)
- Break away from master (**C**)

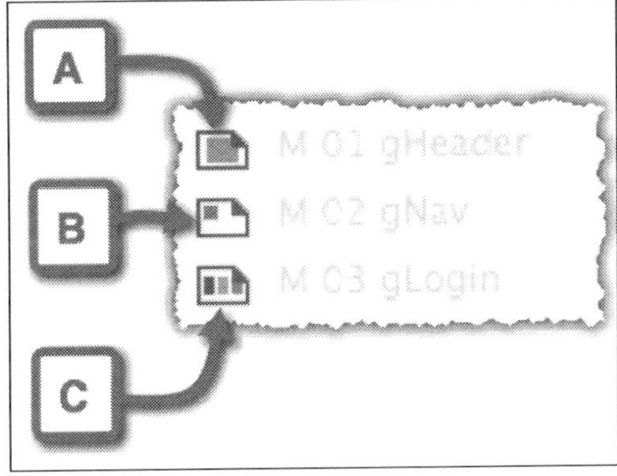

Image 43

These three options are explained in the following sections.

Place Anywhere

This is the default master behavior: place an instance of the master anywhere on a wireframe and across page, and the position of each instance (its *x* and *y* coordinates), will be preserved even after you edit the master wireframe. In other words, while the visual appearance of all instances of the master are identical, each instance is allowed to have its own position on the page.

Lock to Master Location

This option will maintain the *x* and *y* position of every instance exactly as it is in the master wireframe. For example, if the widget is at *x*=`10` and *y*=`10` in the master, that is where the instance will be positioned when you pull it into your wireframe page. The instance will stay locked to that position.

Break Away from Master

This option was known in earlier versions of Axure as the **Flatten** option, which breaks away an instance, cuts the cord, so to speak, between the master and the instance. From that point on, the instance is reduced to being a normal collection of widgets. Changes made to the master wireframe will not cascade to the disconnected instance.

Usage Report

Axure offers a useful feature, the masters **Usage Report**. Right-click on a master in the **Masters** pane and select **Usage Report** from the context menu. The **Master Usage Report** dialog lists all the pages and other masters where a particular master is used.

The Usage Report is incredibly handy:

- The list will help you identify if the master is used on wireframes created by other team members so you can contact them to discuss the changes
- The Usage Report allows you to understand the implication of the change if the design is already in development
- If you are trying to delete a master, it will not allow you because it is attached to a wireframe or is in a different master; run a Usage Report to find out where it is
- If the list is empty, it means that the master is not used anywhere and so is a candidate for deletion

The Widget Manager Pane

A wireframe is a collection of widgets, dynamic panels, and masters, although not all of these elements are necessarily used on all wireframes. The number of widgets on a wireframe can mushroom very quickly. Of course, you can visually scan the wireframe and try to identify a widget, but it is inefficient. To get to a widget in a dynamic panel, for example, you need to open the dynamic panel's state and hunt for the widget in its states. The Widget Manager helps you find or search widgets, and filter them; capabilities that greatly improve our work efficiency.

With the addition of Adaptive Views in Axure 7, inheritance makes it possible to use a single widget across all or some of the views while changing some aspects of the widget, so its appearance fits each view. Suppose you use three views, for desktop, tablet, and smartphone. Axure does not create three separate widgets. Instead, a single widget propagates to the views. If you decide that the widget is not needed on the smartphone view and delete it, it will be removed from all views. It thus becomes very important to know if a widget is on all or some of the views. The terms used for this in Axure are **placed** and **unplaced**. In all, the **Widget Manager** pane is an easily accessible interface for the complete inventory of widgets used, which is illustrated as follows:

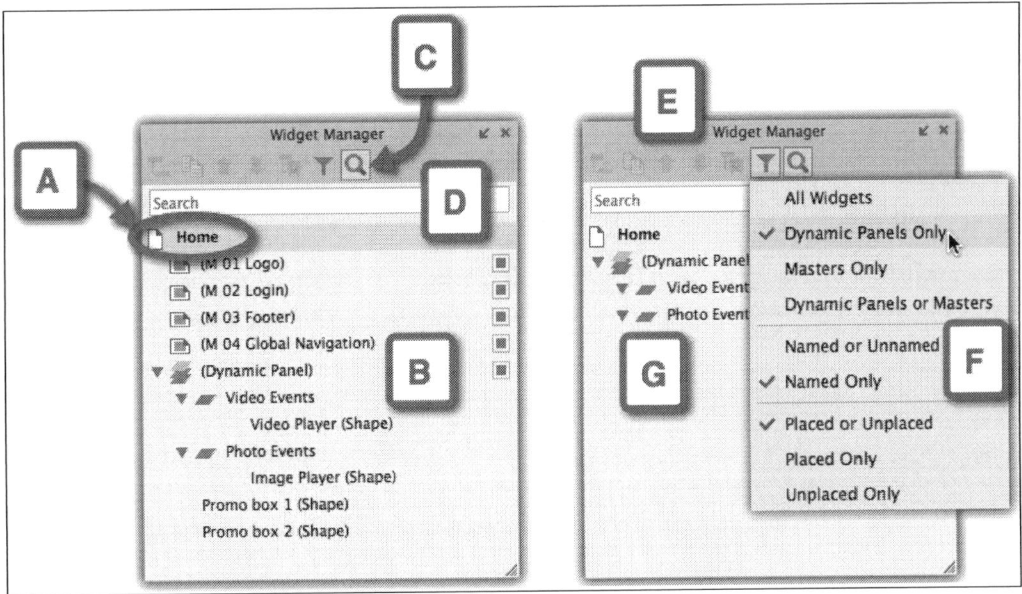

Image 44

In this example, we see the contents of some **Home** page wireframe (*Image 44*, **A**). Without actually seeing the wireframe itself, its entire inventory of widgets is listed in the pane (**B**). Masters, dynamic panels, and widgets are easily identified by their type.

Clicking on the **Search** icon (**C**) toggles the **Search** field (**D**), making it easy to look for labeled widgets.

Clicking on the **Filter** icon (**E**) displays a set of filters that helps isolate widgets by their type (**F**).

Widgets Manager Functionality

The functionality is contextual to the item that is selected in the list, which is illustrated as follows:

- Add a state to a dynamic panel (*Image 45*, **A**)
- Duplicate a dynamic panel's state (new!) (**B**)
- Move items up or down, depending on their position (**C**)
- Delete an item from the list, which also deletes it from the wireframe (**D**)
- Filter the Widget Manager list (**E**)
- Search the Widget Manager list (**F**)

- Previews the item upon hover (**G**) (new!)

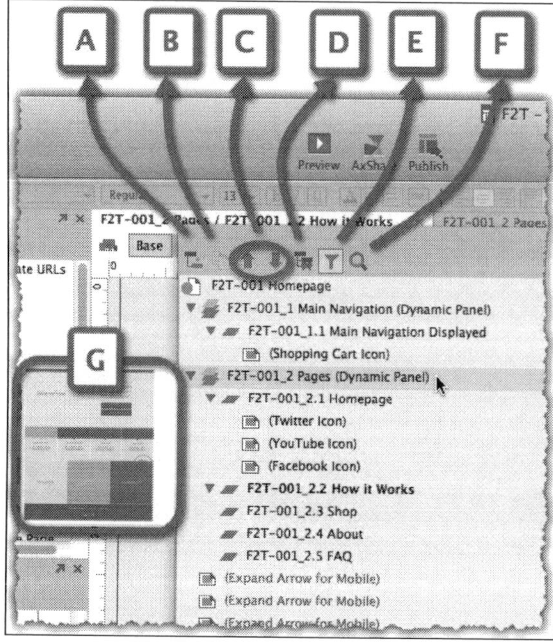

Image 45

Widgets Manager – Filter

To view the filter list, click on the funnel icon as shown in the following screenshot (*Image 46*, **A**):

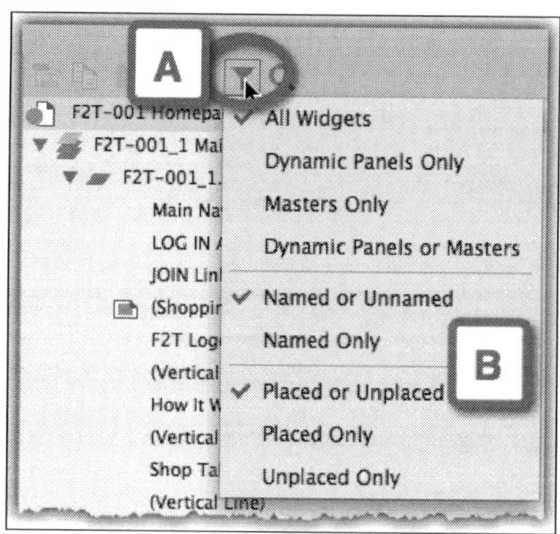

Image 46

You can apply filter using one of the following methods:

- **Filter by item**: Options are **All Widgets**, **Dynamic Panels Only**, **Masters Only**, and **Dynamic Panels or Masters**
- **Filter by name**: Options are **Named or Unnamed** and **Named Only**
- **Filter by place status**: Options are **Placed or Unplaced**, **Placed Only**, and **Unplaced Only**

Unplaced items are displayed in red, which insinuates that this is a bad thing. It is your choice whether or not you want to have the widget display, so don't worry about it. We prefer Axure put in red so that it will bring your attention to it and then you can decide what you choose to do with it.

Web Fonts Mappings (New!)

For many years, typography on the web was notoriously bad because only a very small set of fonts was guaranteed to load properly regardless of the browser, operating system, or device used. We are finally reaching a point where the technology is there to allow designers to harness the power and beauty of fonts in order to improve the user experience.

Axure's support of Web Fonts is a boon for projects that intend to take advantage of Google Fonts and other options.

How does this work? Axure's default font for widgets is Arial. If you assign a widget to a proprietary font you have installed on your computer, and publish the prototype to AxShare, stakeholders who don't have that font installed on their system will see a substitute their browser rendered for the proprietary font. If you assign the widget to a Web Font instead of a proprietary font, all viewers should see it rendered on their browsers.

The process for mapping fonts includes the following steps:

Step 1 – Assign/Tag the Font

In the **Widget Style Editor** pane, change the font associated with the widget type from the default Arial to some other font, demonstrated as follows:

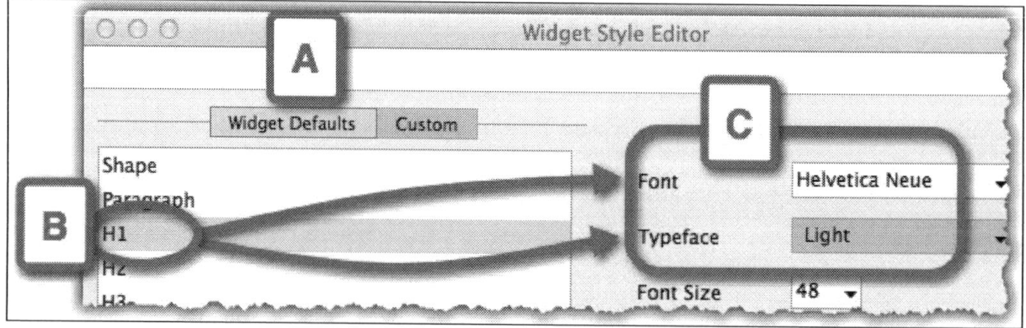

Image 47

In this example, we are modifying the **H1** element. In the **Widget Default** tab (*Image 47*, **A**), click on the **H1** widget (**B**) and change its **Font** to **Helvetica Neue** and **Typeface** to **Light** (C). Now, every **H1** widget will use the Helvetica Neue font with light typeface.

Step 2 – The Web Font

In this example, we chose to use a font called **Lato** (*Image 48*, **B**), from the Google Fonts library (**A**) `https://www.google.com/fonts#`. Perform the following steps to tell Axure where this font is:

1. From the list of styles, select **Normal 400** (C).
2. Note that in the actual Google interface, the selection of styles is much larger. Google provides code identifying this specific style's character set. The code is embedded in a URL (**D**). Copy this URL.

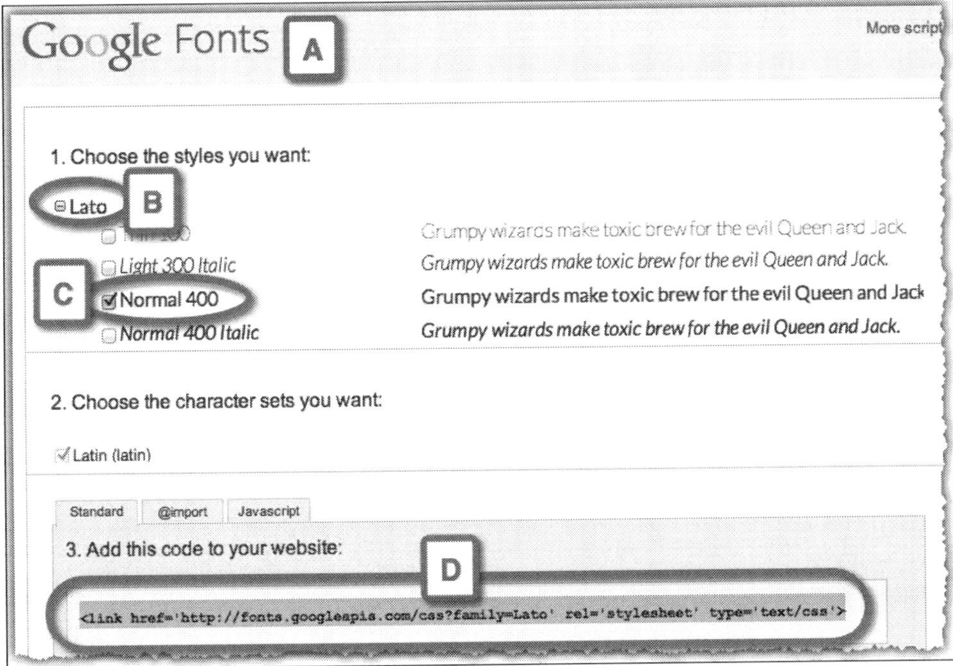

Image 48

Step 3 – Copy the Code into Axure

Perform the following steps to copy the code into Axure:

1. From the toolbar, click on the **Publish** icon and then click on the **Generate HTML Files...** option to launch the **Generate HTML** window (*Image 49*, **A**).
2. When you first use the **Web Fonts** section (**B**). Click on the **+** icon (**C**) to add the Lato front.
3. In the **Name** field (**D**), make sure to label the font clearly.

4. Paste the URL copied from Google Fonts into the **URL** field (**E**). Your first Web Font is now listed and referenced in your Axure file (**F**).

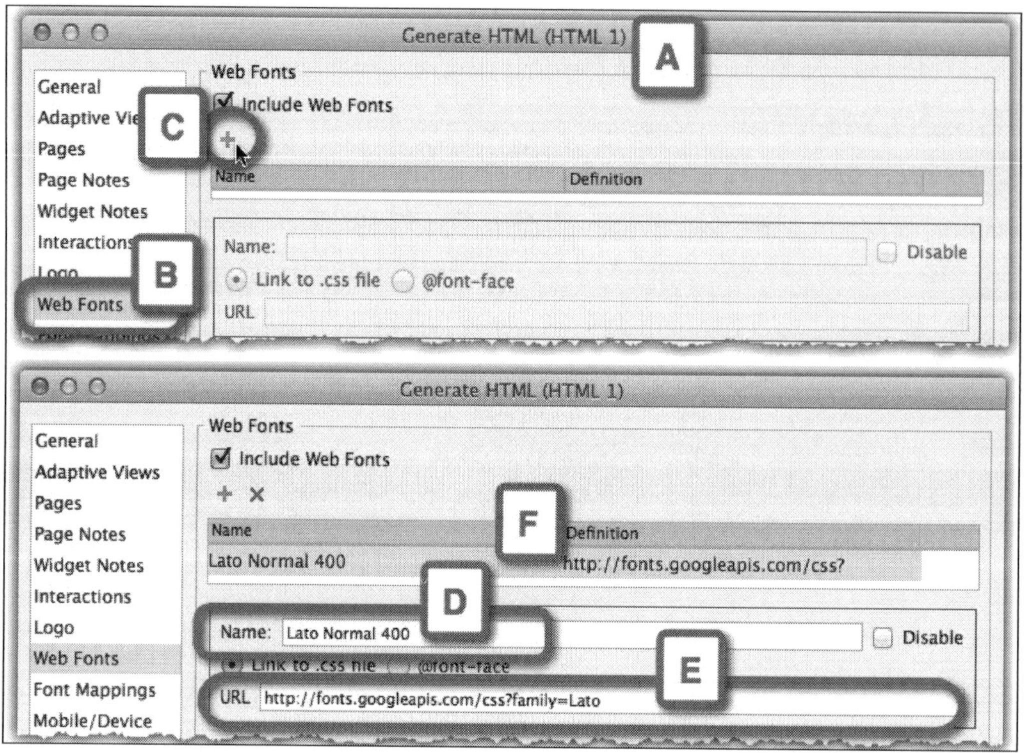

Image 49

[Keep *only* the http portion of the Google URL, that is, `http://fonts.googleapis.com/css?family=Lato`.]

5. In the **Font Mappings** tab (*Image 50*, **A**), use the **+** icon to create a new mapping.
6. In the left-hand side column, select the font you want to map from the drop-down list. You can also specify a typeface, such as Normal, Bold, or Italic (**B**). In our example, we have Helvetica Neue Regular.

7. In the right-hand side column, enter the **font-family**. If you unchecked **the Choose a specific typeface** option, add the font-weight and font-style (C). In our example, we have Lato, 400, normal.
8. When you generate the prototype, the web font will appear on all the widgets that use the font mapped to it.

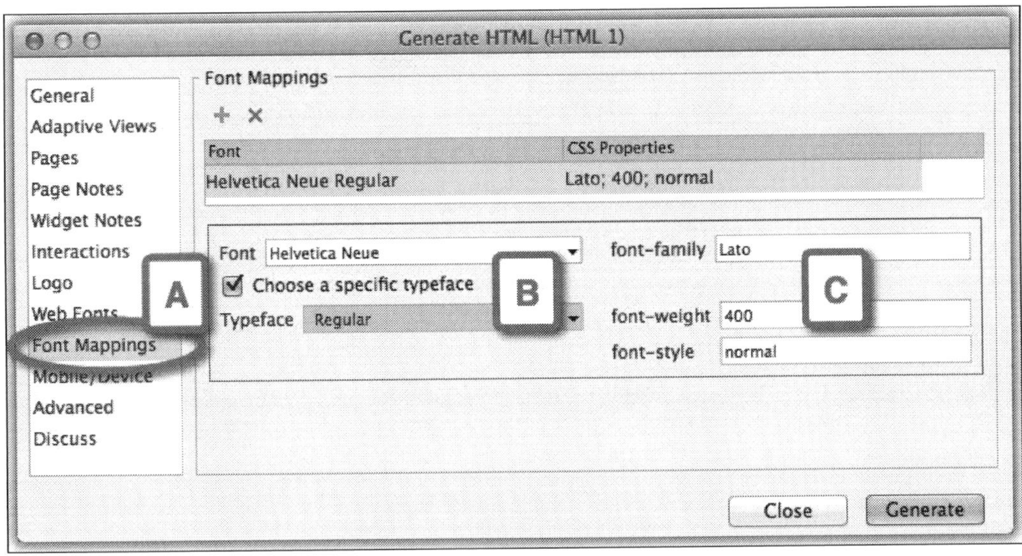

Image 50

The Toolbars and the Menu Bar

The main difference between Axure for Mac (*Image 51*, **A**) and Windows 7 (**F**) is caused by the way each operating system handles the menu bar and the toolbar. On the Mac, if the Axure window is too narrow to display all the functions, clicking a double right-arrow (**B**) displays the rest (**C**). To customize which items are displayed, right-clicking anywhere on the toolbar displays a context menu (**D**) from which the full options are available (**E**).

On Windows, the standard toolbars can be managed by clicking on the **View** menu (**G**) and by selecting the toolbars to display (**I**) from the **Toolbars** submenu (**H**).

The following screenshot visualizes the native treatment of Mac and Windows 7 of the menu bar and toolbars:

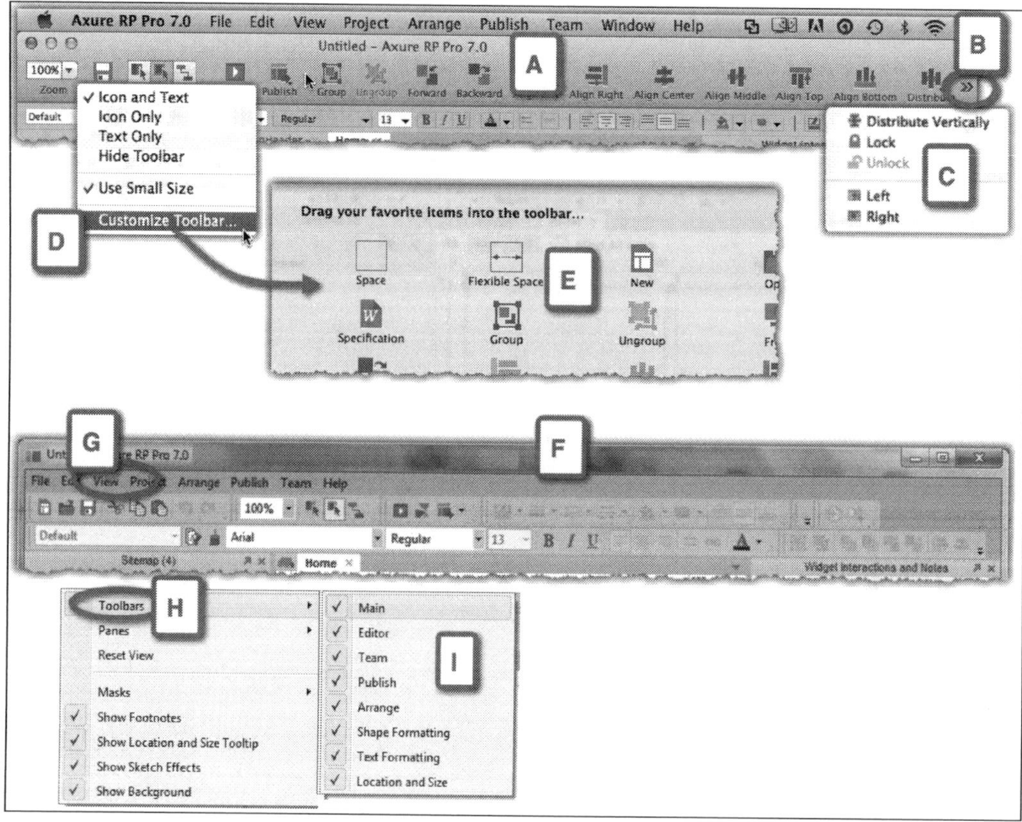

Image 51

The Generated Prototype

Within the generated HTML prototype, there is a toolbar under the **Sitemap** tab (*Image 52*, **A**) that allows you to do the following:

- Select the Adaptive View if your prototype is responsive (**B**)
- Toggle the display of footnotes (**C**)
- Highlight active elements (**D**)
- See the value of variables—this is really helpful for debugging (**E**)

- Generate live URLs for the prototype with various options related to the **Sitemap** pane (**F**)
- Search the sitemap (**G**)

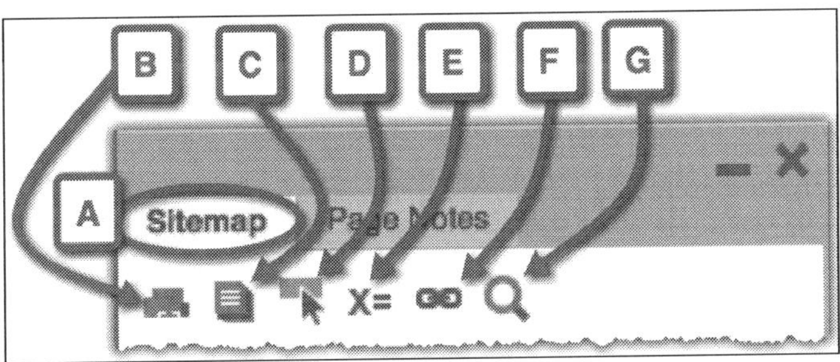

Image 52

Summary

If you are new to Axure, we hope that this chapter helped you to get familiarized with the tools' integrated environment and the capabilities. If you've been using Axure for a while, we hope that this review helped close a few gaps and inform you about some of the new and enhanced features. If you have not done so already, we highly recommend visiting Axure's website. It offers a wealth of videos and tutorials that will help you master the tool's rich feature set.

Many users, us included, were able to do productive work with Axure within hours from downloading the trial version (offered for a 30-day evaluation). If you plan to purchase Axure, we are confident that you will get a return on your investment very quickly. Finally, if Axure becomes your primary prototyping tool, the more you know about it, the more freedom you will have to express your ideas in a powerful and compelling way.

In the next chapter, we lay down the foundations for best practice prototyping construction. We cover the concepts of pages, masters, and dynamic panels, as well as the methods for constructing scalable and reusable wireframes.

3
Prototype Construction Basics

In the previous edition of the book, this chapter started with the following paragraph:

> *"User experience design is part art, part craftsmanship; the fusion of methodology and patterns with creative problem solving. The prototype plays a major role in the success of UX projects because it is simultaneously a concrete interactive preview of both the vision for and the actuality of the application being designed. For the UX designer, Axure offers the ability to deliver simulations of rich interactive user experience, quickly, iteratively, and without having to know programming."*

These statements still hold true and the only update here would be:

With the introduction of new features such as Adaptive Views and the Repeater widget, Axure 7 offers UX designers the ability to deliver interactive simulations of data-driven device/OS-agnostic user experience quickly, iteratively, and without having to know programming. If you know something about programming, Axure opens new and exciting possibilities.

Prior to Axure's ascent in the late 2000s, the cost of providing timely ("timely" is the operative word here) interactive prototyping was prohibitive for many organizations because most UX designers were not programmers, and were thus limited to producing static wireframes in Visio or similar tools. Skilled developers had to be engaged in order to convert the static wireframes into interactive JavaScript, dynamic HTML, or Flash simulations. Axure and other tools made it increasingly possible for designers to take control over simulating the interactive experience because no programming was required.

However, since the rapid adoption of RWD in 2012, we have seen a return to either using front-end developers to create prototypes or pressuring designers to master code.

Involving a developer—an intermediate—in the process of prototyping can be problematic because the process is slower, expensive, and inefficient. Interactive explorations that should help the designer shape the experience risk, turning into mini-development efforts, which require the UX designer to invest significant amounts of time to communicate interaction flows and the behavior of various widgets to the developer, and later help debug the simulation. It is harder to rapidly experiment with alternatives: once a prototype has been coded, it typically reflects outdated versions of static wireframes, because while coding was taking place, the wires were subject to one or more iteration cycles.

Adaptive Views is one of Axure 7's new features that is intended to help UX designers create very sophisticated, interactive, and responsive prototypes without having to code, or having to engage developers to create the simulation for them. With this power comes a need for strategies, methods, techniques, and best practices. Applying these consistently to prototype construction in Axure will help make the process more predictive for you, and reduce unpleasant fallout caused by mistakes that could have been avoided. There is no need to reinvent the wheel for each project.

In this chapter, we will cover the following topics:

- Alignment of UX principles with prototyping
    - Strategy: user-centered design meets business needs
    - Mobile first meets budget and timelines
- Communicating discovery
    - Constructing use case and task flow diagrams based on information gathered during discovery and from requirements
- Prototype construction (foundations)
    - Establishing a naming convention scheme
    - Basic wireframing aided by guides and grids
    - Masters and dynamic panels
    - Applying visual effects in response to mouse activity
    - Applying the sketch effect

The previous topics will be intertwined because the prototyping construction process is tightly coupled with the general practice of UX design, which is much broader than the prototype. Remember that the prototype is only a manifestation of the design—it is your primary communication artifact with your stakeholders.

Remember that in this book, we focus on prototyping strategy and construction, and not actual design. This is where you get into the picture!

Aligning UX with Prototyping Principles

Imagining the user experience and prototyping it are tightly coupled, but the skills and processes required for each do not necessarily correspond. The fundamental methodology for conceiving a successful experience involves planning, analysis, and synthesis of needs and constraints into a coherent and consistent interaction-design system. Translating this method into an actual prototype involves planning and hands-on use of Axure through rapid iterative cycles of review, validation, and revision.

As a UX designer, you want maximal control over the few things you do have control over, and such control is often a result of rigor and experience. Gaining a broad industry experience takes time, so there is value in adopting a rigorous approach, which can help even if your experience with a particular domain is limited. The following are a few simple, project-agnostic guiding principles to prototyping:

- Estimate, plan, and keep re-evaluating the prototyping and specifications effort. Rapid prototyping does not mean one needs to plunge into Axure and start wireframing immediately. Knowing where you are heading construction-wise will go a long way in helping you deliver on the experience, vision, schedule, and budget you committed to, and retain your sanity.
- Master the tools you are using, including Axure. The tools we master and the quality of our craftsmanship help shape our deliverables, and in turn increase the confidence of our clients and partners in our expertise and in the vision we help shape.
- Just because you can do it in Axure, does not mean you have to. Be strategic about the amount of low-level, high-fidelity details to which you are committing to.
- Be device/OS agnostic. Unless you are dealing with a truly device-dedicated unique project, make sure to come up with a device/OS-agnostic design. Axure 7 supports RWD.
- KISS: keep it simple, stupid. Surprisingly, this rule is not as simple to implement as it suggests, and more often than not, we tend to sink into unnecessary complexity before realizing it. Remember that simplicity and sophistication are not mutually exclusive, and your experience design and construction methods can be elegantly simple and sophisticated.

Throughout the book, we demonstrate the application of these principles in real-life scenarios using this main demonstration project or sample snippets, which you can view and download from **AxShare** (`http://share.axure.com/`). You will find that though many of the ideas and best practices are presented in the context of Axure, they are in fact tool agnostic and can help you in your work even if you use other prototyping tools.

Getting Started with Prototyping in Axure

The book's main demonstration project, **Farm2Table**, is meant to walk you through the major steps involved in the planning, construction, and iteration of a typical e-commerce site. The choice of this subject matter was driven primarily by the many opportunities to demonstrate numerous Axure features and techniques in the context of an application that conceptually should be familiar to all readers, either from their experience working on one or as consumers.

Size matters in projects, and yet, core activities such as discovery, user and application research, requirements gathering, iterative design, and usability testing are fundamental to user-centered design despite potentially profound difference in scale and complexity of the projects or culture differences between organizations.

This sample project is a much simplified, abbreviated version of what happens in reality, where the process involves rapid cycles of iterative design as we move through the following phases:

- Concept development
- High-level design
- Detailed design

Key Design Activities

The overall development process is not homogeneous, covering the entire spectrum from waterfall to agile. If you are a consultant, there is a high probability that engineering methodologies used in each engagement will turn out to be different from each other, sometimes drastically. Still, key design activities listed in the following table should take place as the project evolves, regardless of the development flavor of the day:

Factors	Concept development	High-level design	Detailed design
Activities	Discovery activities: • User research (personas, user types, roles, and task flows) • Competitive research • Stakeholder Interviews • Conceptual experience framework	• Design system for RWD • Content strategy • Experience framework • Key wireframes and interaction patterns	• Iterative design • Detailed wireframes • Documentation/ specifications
Things to keep in mind about your prototype	• Overall schedule (key milestones for what will be tested and when, refactoring or rebuilding the vision prototype from scratch) • Vision prototype • Understand expectations around scope of prototyping fidelity and documentation details	• Naming convention scheme • Prototype plan (what is going to be simulated for planned testing) • Experiment, socialize, and agree on documentation depth and output (light or heavy specs, Word, HTML, or both)	• Testing scenarios • Pragmatic interactivity

Any prototype should incorporate inputs from relevant users and stakeholders, and these inputs should inform the design approach, including:

- Vision and expectations from leadership
- Directives and prioritization from stakeholders
- User research insights
- Direct and indirect feedback from intended users
- Content strategy
- Business requirements
- Technical considerations
- Usability tests to validate the design

Assumptions and Disclaimers

Let's assume, for the purpose of this sample project, that you have already completed some of the initial project tasks, including some, but doubtfully all:

- Strategy sessions with various stakeholders in the company
- Contextual interviews with end users
- Establishment of a base line by conducting usability studies of the existing application
- Review of competitive and related applications
- Analysis and inventory of the current site's content
- Development of some of the IA, including high-level taxonomy and global navigation
- A prioritized list of key capabilities and features
- Development of personas and a matrix of user roles, their key tasks, and flows
- Tasks provided with and/or those that help develop high-level business requirements

With this solid understanding of the product and its intended users, you are ready to dive into Axure and unleash your creative energies.

Due to limitations of scope and format, this project does not deal with actual content, design, and the various RWD techniques, nor is it possible to discuss all UX artifacts and their permutations. Rather, we focus on methods and patterns that can be generalized and applied to your own work.

Objectives and Artifacts

In the early phases of the design process, we generate a number of UX artifacts that are important for establishing the overall user-experience framework of the software. From concept models to personas and use case diagrams to various task and interaction flows, these documents solidify a shared understanding across all stakeholder parties on the project. However, it is often the case that these artifacts are forgotten once wireframing and prototyping begins, and it is common to start drifting away from established understandings.

An important reason for the diminishing value of these artifacts is as simple as their availability as reference tools, or rather lack of availability. It is common to create these documents in diagramming tools such as Visio or OmniGraffle and save them—for sharing purposes—as PDF or PPT files. These discrete documents are often buried in a SharePoint-type repository or some Wiki, and they are difficult to retrieve. Thus, all the insights concentrated in them are forgotten.

We will demonstrate how to create and integrate these artifacts into your Axure file so that they are always a click away for easy reference. Integration of these artifacts with wireframes and the prototype creates a highly valuable communication and documentation package that UX contributes to the entire project team.

The following are some of the issues we will discuss next:

- Concept models and persona libraries.
- Use cases and flow diagrams as good examples of communication means used early on in the project when you are setting the conceptual framework for the wireframing and prototyping phase. It is an opportunity to discuss how Axure's diagramming capabilities feed the wireframing process.
- We will move to construction methods that feature masters and dynamic panels, and include some examples of iteration and feedback that will require a rework of our initial construction.
- As we dive into topics such as interactions, widget libraries, styling, and annotations, the demo project helps to visualize various concepts and construction methods, when applicable.
- Throughout, we consider various prototyping and specification activities in the context of the overall project plan, development methodologies, and effort and resources estimation.
- Finally, workflow-wise, we focus on a single UX designer that is a very common model for Axure practitioners worldwide and touch on team projects that are discussed in detail in *Chapter 9, Collaboration*; we will reference this project to demonstrate various team capabilities.

Naming Conventions, Labeling, and Unique IDs

It appears that humans have been in the business of naming things for quite some time. For example, in the book of Genesis, we find the following tale about Adam, the first man:

> "*...and whatever the man called every living creature, that was its name. The man gave names to all cattle, and to the birds of the air, and to every animal of the field;*"

Theology and religion aside, it is fascinating to observe that the first activity attributed to Adam is assigning names to things. Today, we call such activities tagging. When labeled, things and concepts can be explicitly referenced.

Names and labels are a good start, but unique IDs provide the ultimate referential integrity. For example, the ISBN number of this book makes it discoverable to both systems and humans. No translation is needed and ambiguity is eliminated. Without a solid system of reference—otherwise known as a naming convention—we risk chaos. Another old testament story, that of the Tower of Babylon, a large-scale construction project gone awry, is often cited as the quintessential example of massive failure due to communication breakdown occurring when multiple teams fail to adopt a single framework of reference.

Naming conventions are critical to any artifact that is produced in a software project in general, and to UX specifically. The benefits are significant, and it is not that difficult to come up with a consistent system or tweak the one we present here. Throughout this book, we repeatedly emphasize the importance of labeling widgets and using unique identification for pages, masters, and other elements. The following table shows arguments in favor:

Justification	Description
Reduce risk of miscommunication with stakeholders	Support explicit referencing with all stakeholders so that everyone is on the same page. For example, if engineering has a question about an element on a wireframe, it should be able to point it out explicitly, using its unique ID.
Making the Axure file easy to understand	Axure lets you access all widgets. However, if you don't label them (at least those that you use for interactions), it can be very time-consuming to create interactions, since all appear with a generic label.
Traceability	Support referential integrity when you need to show how and where the design aligns to requirements. Each requirement (with a unique ID) should be matched to a page, master, or other element, by its ID.

The Farm2Table Sample Project in a Nutshell

In this simulated project, we develop a website for a cooperative called Farm2Table, where local farmers sell their fresh organic produce to interested local consumers. In a nutshell, this is how the system operates:

- Each week, subscribers can make modifications to the content of the box of produce they purchased
- On Saturdays, the farmers deliver boxes to a central location in the served area
- Editorial content created by the cooperative, such as weekly recipes based on ingredients which are included in that week's box, help introduce subscribers to new ways to maximize the value of the produce they get, and try new things
- Finally, social features allow farmers and consumers get to know each other and strengthen the cooperative and overall community ties
- The principle of building on the strength of local communities supports the scaling concept of the cooperative business model, since the same system can be reproduced across the country

Interactive Concept Models

At some point in the discovery process, it becomes important to piece together the information collected through research activities and validate with stakeholders our understanding of the universe that makes up the foundations for the design. Concept models are useful when we want to communicate a high-level picture of the relationships between discrete entities.

A good example is the **Users Concept Model**, which is a diagram that identifies the key classes of users for whom unique features need to be developed in order to support their roles in the system. Typically, this would be a static diagram created in Visio or OmniGraffle.

Axure provides a set of **Flow** widgets that are perfect for creating this model right in the project file. The following diagram was created with Axure and is part of the sample file:

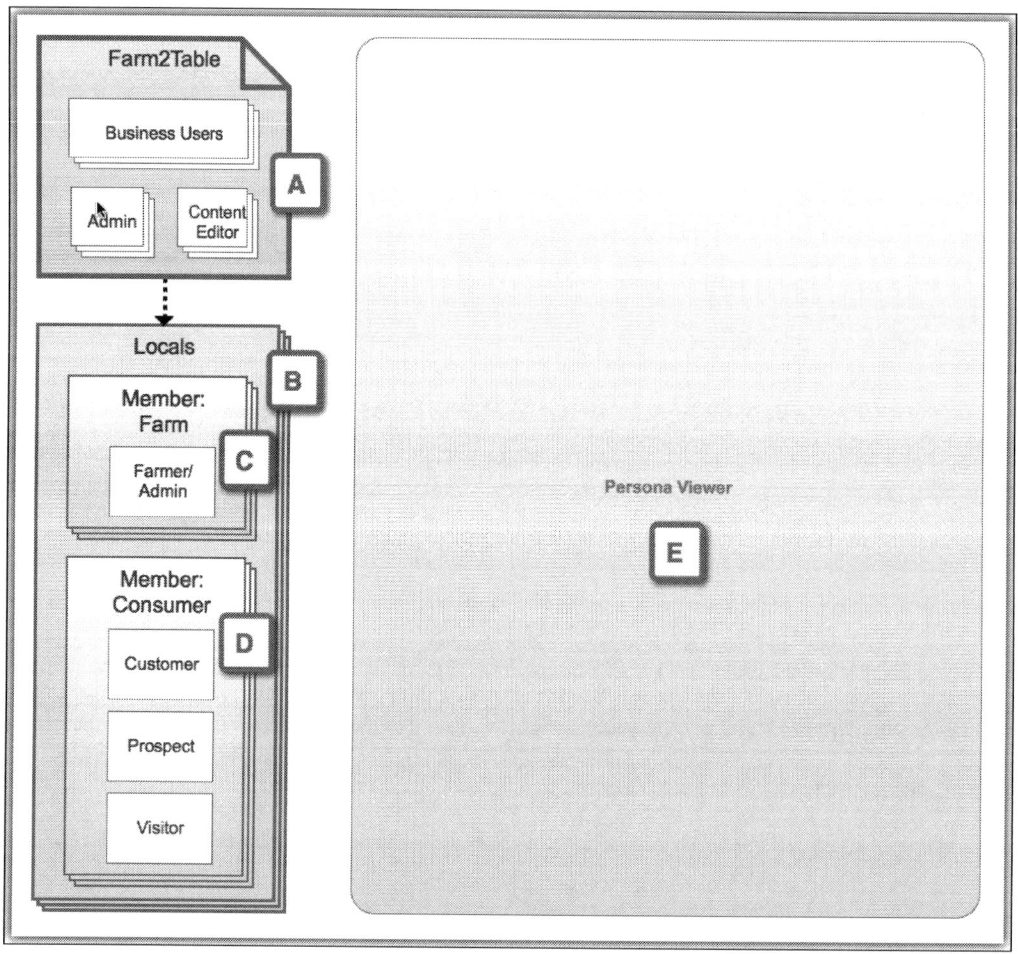

Diagram 1

In the Farm2Table project, we identify the following user types:

- Users who work for the cooperative Farm2Table (*Diagram 1*, **A**). These include:
    - Business users in management, accounting, sales, marketing, and so on
    - Administrative users who deal with support and maintenance
    - Editors and other staff who maintain the site's content

- In each area, or local, where Farm2Table operates (**B**), users are farmer-members in the cooperative (**C**). Farmers are very busy, especially during harvest season. They also don't have staff that can be dedicated to the site.
- In each area, or local, where Farm2Table operates, users are the consumers (D). Here we identify the following:
    - **Member-customer**: Individual who is a subscriber and is paying for the service.
    - **Non-member prospect**: Individual who upon visit to the site provided an e-mail and agreed to receive newsletters and other content.
    - **Non-member visitor**: Individual who visited the site but did not leave any e-mail address. Also, individuals who are part of the entire potential audience, for whom local, engaging content needs to be created to compel them to subscribe to the site.

The Axure Edge

The feature that makes this concept model stand out from anything created in Visio-type tools is the **Persona Viewer** box (*Diagram 1*, **E**). Imagine sitting in a stakeholders' meeting, discussing various tasks and user flows, being able to access this model, and instantly seeing the persona(s) developed for that type upon clicking each user type. Remember that concept models, other diagrams, and persona documents fade from the collective memory of the project team because they are not readily available as references, but this diagram as well as the persona profile could be created in the Axure file!

Keep this persona viewer in mind as you read this book, and at some point, try to create it yourself. In the actual demo file, we provide one approach to this, but see it as a future self exercise to create your own persona viewer.

On Capabilities and Requirements

The state of methodology for the creation of business requirements in the real world is disturbing. It is difficult, perhaps impossible, to find two projects that apply the same methodology, definition, and terminology to define what requirements mean, not to mention how to write them. Alas, the scope of this book greatly limits our discussion on this painful topic.

We will take a semi-happy path here. Based on discovery activities conducted so far, you should have, at a minimum, a list of high-level aspirations that provide a core set of guidelines and define the site. These aspirations are sometimes called capabilities. In some projects, the list of business requirements is handed to you, and in other projects, you play a key role in their development. Regardless, business requirements should not define the user experience. Rather, our contribution as UX designers is to translate the requirements into a world-class practical user experience.

There are many flavors of definitions and many passionate discussions about the terms listed in the following table. The table is meant to provide you with our pragmatic flavor in the context of this book. Most UX practitioners must maintain the flexibility of adjusting to the variability in terminology from one organization to another. To avoid unpleasant miscommunication, make sure you understand the specific use of terms as you start working on the project.

Term	Definition
Requirements	• A discrete statement that defines a business functionality • Each statement should cover a single functionality • Requirements should be classified under relevant headings such as business, user, system, and legal • Business requirements should not prescribe the UX. For example, the following is not acceptable: "The user should be able to select from a droplist one of the following items". The UX designer will determine the appropriate widget to be used here, droplist or whatever. • Do not use Axure to manage requirements
Use case	• A use case is a high-level graphical abstraction of an interaction between a user and the system • Use case diagrams should be created in Axure and linked to related flows and pages within the file
Scenario	• A scenario is a narrative that describes a likely path a user will take when performing a set of tasks in the system • The prototype should be designed to follow agreed-upon scenarios

Initial, High-level Requirements

It is not uncommon to get requirements in the form of a Word document which is a list of bullet points. That is, if you are lucky enough to get any requirements at all. As we repeat many times in this book, requirements are a dicey and complex problem. What we want to stress here is the need to number each individual requirement such that it can be uniquely identified.

The following sample is a set of requirements for the Farm2Table project. While we need these here in order to make sense of the sample prototype, remember that UX is not responsible for creating business requirements, and for good reasons that are beyond the scope of this section, the UX designer should resist the urge to define them. Still, we bring them here in order to underscore desirable attributes:

- Each requirement has a unique identifier (Column 1). The identifier follows a naming convention joining the prefix **BR** (**Business Requirement**), an associated capability, and a running number. The running number can support hundreds of requirements, which is important for large projects. The entire ID, when parsed, is meaningful to a human reader and can be sorted, grouped, and filtered when in a database or spreadsheet.
- The requirement text (Column 2) is atomic, meaning that it is limited to a single directive.
- The associated capability has a unique ID (Column 3). Naturally, the convention of this ID depends on the project.
- The associated capability (Column 4) helps group requirements in meaningful subsets. If the term capability is not used, the word category can be used instead, regardless of such an organizing element being necessary.

Home Page

The following table is a sample list of requirements for the home page, grouped by capabilities. The ID scheme proposed here is only meant to serve the needs of a scheme. It may or may not be relevant to the one used in your project. But there should be an identification scheme.

Requirement ID	Requirement	Capability ID	Capability
BR_C-01_001	All users—visitors and subscribers—should be able to see all the upcoming weekly offerings from local farmers.	C-01	Order Creation and Management
BR_C-01_002	The weekly offerings should be viewed by category (fruits, vegetables, and so on) or by farm.	C-01	Order Creation and Management
BR_C-01_003	All users should be able to add 10 different products from a single farm to the weekly box.	C-01	Order Creation and Management

Requirement ID	Requirement	Capability ID	Capability
BR_C-01_004	All users are free to select any combination that adds up to 10 items. For example, 10 units of onion, or 1 unit of each product type.	C-01	Order Creation and Management
BR_C-01_005	The quantity of individual items in each unit will be listed on each offering. For example, "4 yellow sweet onions".	C-01	Order Creation and Management
BR_C-01_006	The content of the weekly box should be visible and updated as the users add or remove items.	C-01	Order Creation and Management
BR_C-01_007	Only when the box is full (10 items) should the user be able to order it.	C-01	Order Creation and Management
BR_C-01_008	Users need to log in only when ordering their weekly box.	C-01	Order Creation and Management
BR_C-02_001	Premium users can add 12 items to an order.	C-02	Account Creation and Management
BR_C-03_001	All users should be able to access information about the farm and the farmer.	C-03	Social
BR-C-03_002	All subscribers can post reviews about farms and their offerings.	C-03	Social

Although it should not be your responsibility to write business requirements, we stress the following points:

- Working without any form of requirements is an invitation to disaster
- When you get the requirements, it is important to evaluate the quality and flag ambiguity, conflicts, contradictions, and other issues as early as possible
- The business is the ultimate owner of any requirements list, even if UX played an active role in helping generate them

Good requirements should be easily broken into short and unambiguous sentences with a syntax that includes the user, a user action, and the interaction outcome. In other words, each of these sentences becomes a use case. As already mentioned, use case methodology is beyond the scope of this book, but a wealth of information on this subject matter is available.

Axure and Requirement Management

Axure is not a requirement management system; it does not pretend to be one and should generally not be used as one. However, under certain conditions, Axure 7 becomes a viable alternative to Excel or Word documents. These conditions are as follows:

- Axure is deployed as a Team Project
- SVN is used
- A dedicated business analyst will be responsible for entering and maintaining the requirements in Axure
- The requirements are entered into a Repeater widget, essentially a spreadsheet
- The setup is piloted with a sample of real requirements

Looking ahead, the potential of integrating Axure with a requirement management system, or linking it to spreadsheets, introduces powerful benefits for a UX project done in Axure. This is because of the ability to efficiently maintain direct references to the latest version of the requirements that drive the project.

Use Cases

We could probably write an entire book only on use cases, as many such books exist. As with other artifacts, we highly recommend an alignment around the expectations from use case diagrams, at the start of the project. There are various interpretations as to what a use case diagram is, and there as several known methodologies for their creation, such as the **Unified Modeling Language** (**UML**).

It is often the case that business stakeholders and others who have a hard time understanding the diagrams. This is because use cases are abstractions of key processes that involve an actor (the user or the system) and some key business process. A good rule of thumb is to remember that the goal is not to create the perfect diagram, but rather one that can be understood without you having to walk stakeholders through it.

Out of the discovery phase and high-level requirements gathering in the Farm2Table demo project, it is possible to drive out the creation of the following use cases:

Use case ID	Use case name
UC-01	Setup a New Subscription [+Gift]
UC-02	Assemble My Weekly Box
UC-03	Suspend Delivery
UC-04	Set Repeat Box
UC-05	Review Farm/Produce Details
UC-06	Renew Subscription

The following are some useful guidelines to keep in mind when thinking about use cases and the prototype:

- Don't prototype stuff that does not correspond to a use case.
- Prototype high-priority use cases first.
- Each use case should have a primary and alternative scenario; negotiate which alternative, if any, needs to be prototyped.
- Label all use cases and stick to your convention. In this example, we use a straightforward UC prefix to denote the words use case.

Axure is an integrated wireframing, prototyping, and specifications system. It means that we can start developing the specifications document in parallel to the wireframing and prototyping effort. Diagrams are a good example of important documentation that can be created in Axure and generated in the Word specification document.

Use Case Diagram Page

The prototype is only a sample of the entire application. In most cases, it cannot simulate the various states and permutations that will occur to various users under various conditions.

This means that what gets prototyped must be pre-defined and agreed upon. A use case library built in Axure can provide the roadmap for aligning the expectation of stakeholders about the flows that will be submitted for review and testing. Along with other UX artifacts that you create in your Axure file, the effectiveness and value that you contribute to the projects is significantly improved.

Step 1 – Adding a Flow Page to the Sitemap

Occasionally, we meet Axure users who are surprised to learn about Axure's flow pages and diagramming capabilities.

When you launch Axure, it opens a blank new file with a **Home** page and three nested siblings (*Image 1*, **A**). We recommend keeping structure and flow pages, such as use case and flow diagrams, in a section above the wireframe pages.

Note that the order of pages in the **Sitemap** pane is the order in which those pages will appear in the HTML prototype and Word specification table of content. By placing structure and flow pages first, you control a logical narrative that provides high-level abstractions such as user flows, before moving into the actual wireframes and interaction. This will work well in early review meetings as you describe the prototype. Additionally, at a later stage, readers of the UX specification will be able to form a clear idea of the application by flowing the page progression.

In the **Sitemap** pane, navigate to **Add** | **Sibling Page Before** in the **Home** page (**B**).

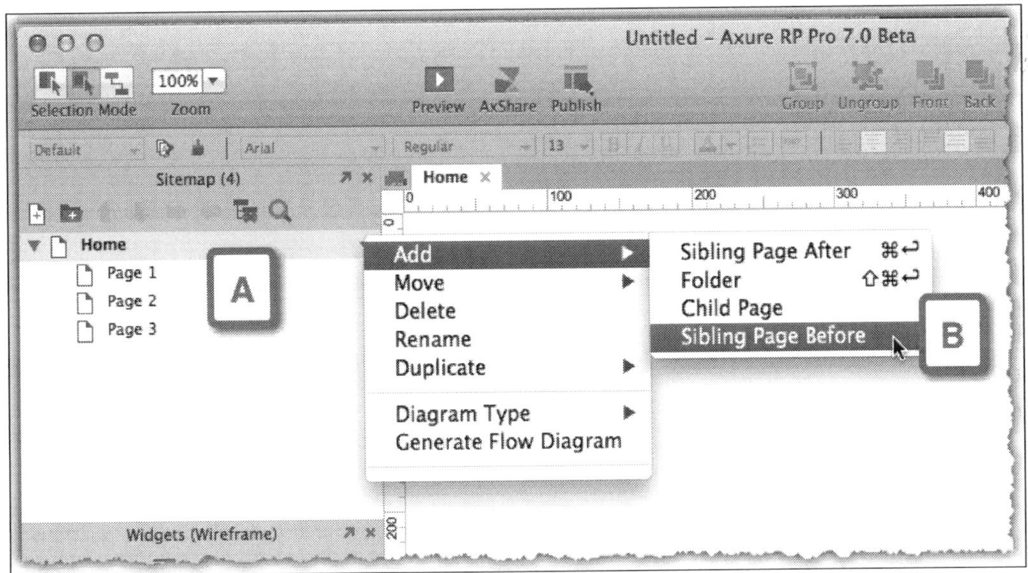

Image 1

Double-click on this new page to open it as a tab in the **Wireframe** tab. Next, rename the new page to `Use Cases` (*Image 2*, **A**). Axure provides a method to differentiate between wireframe pages and diagram pages: right-click and select the **Flow** option (**B**) from the **Diagram Type** contextual menu.

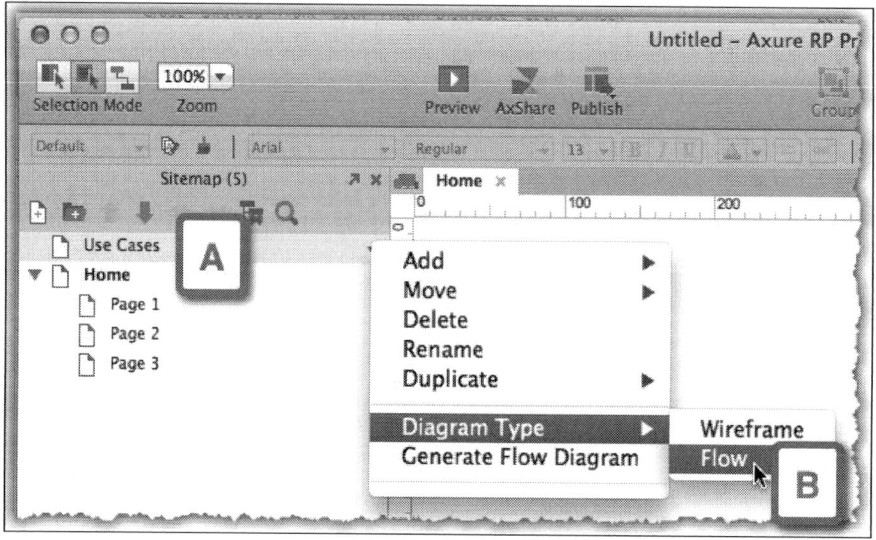

Image 2

Notice that the page icon (*Image 3*, **A**) has changed, making it easy to distinguish between wireframe and flow pages, as shown in the following screenshot:

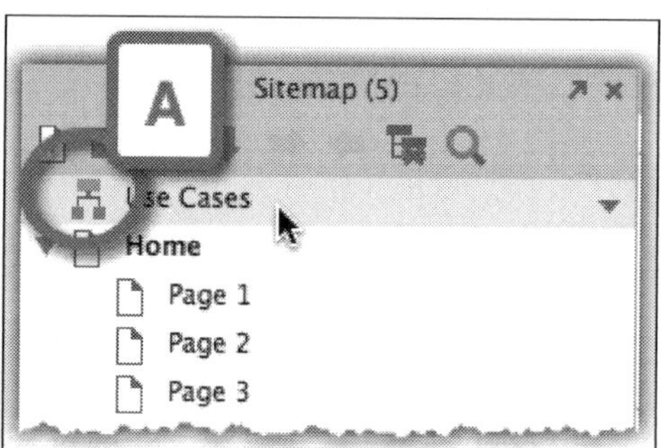

Image 3

Showing the Grid

Initially the grid—a helpful tool—may not be visible on the page and you would want to turn it on. You can do so by executing the following steps:

1. Right-click anywhere on the page area to display the context menu, and from there, select the **Show Grid** option (*Image 4*, **A**).
2. Alternatively, you can access the grid option from the **Arrange** menu. Finally, you can use the shortcut combination (Apple, Win) to toggle the grid display.

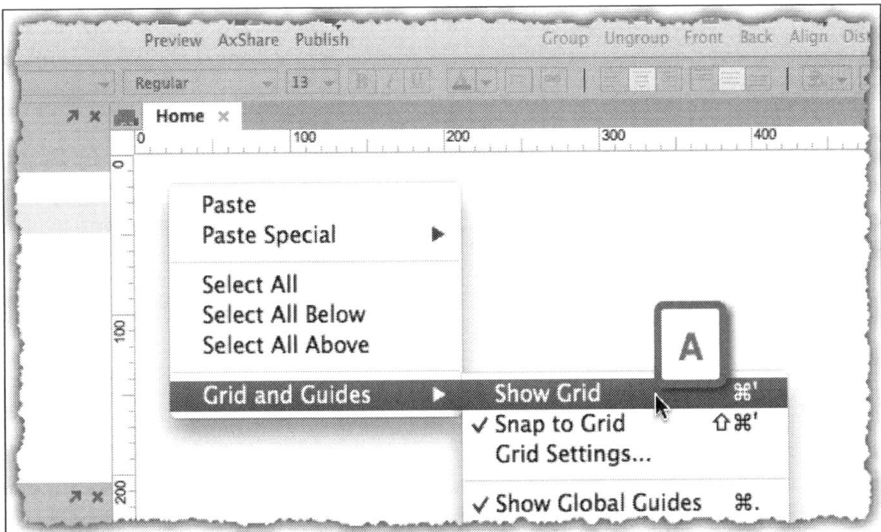

Image 4

Step 2 – Creating the Use Case Diagram

Next, perform the following steps to create the use case diagram:

1. Select the **Flow** widget library (*Image 5*, **A**) in the **Widgets** pane.
2. Drag out the **Actor** widget (**B**) to the page. This stick figure is the standard representation of users in UML and most diagramming methodologies.

3. Drag out an **Ellipse** widget and label it `Subscribe/Create Account` (**C**).
4. The **Ellipse** widget is the UML notation for use case. Continue to add and label ellipse widgets as needed, or copy them from the sample file.

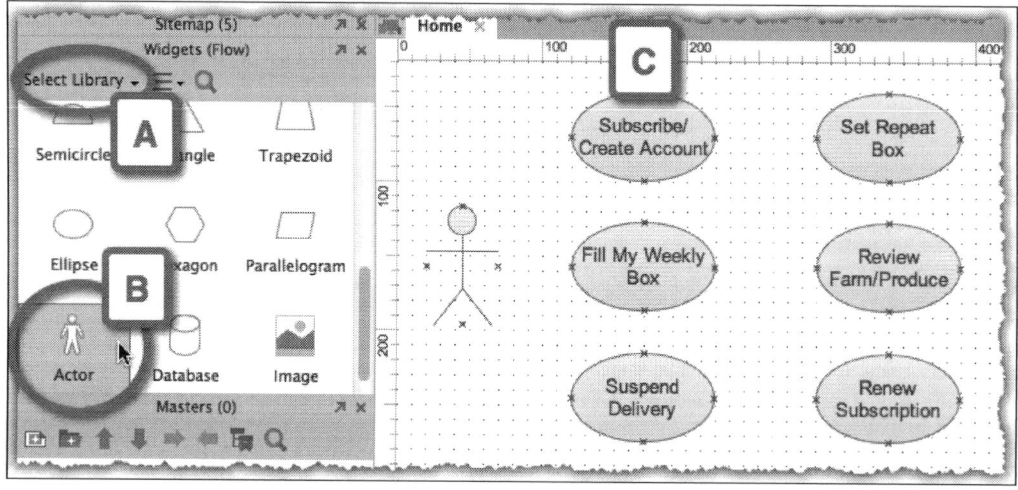

Image 5

Refine Diagram

To complete the use case diagram, we want to connect the actor widget to the use cases and organize the widgets nicely on the page for a polished presentation. Begin with the layout and organize the cases in a vertical order that follows a logical progression of possibilities.

In the following *Image 6*, we have shown a simplified visualization, which organizes the use cases under a shared background and only a single arrow connector is needed to associate the actor with these cases:

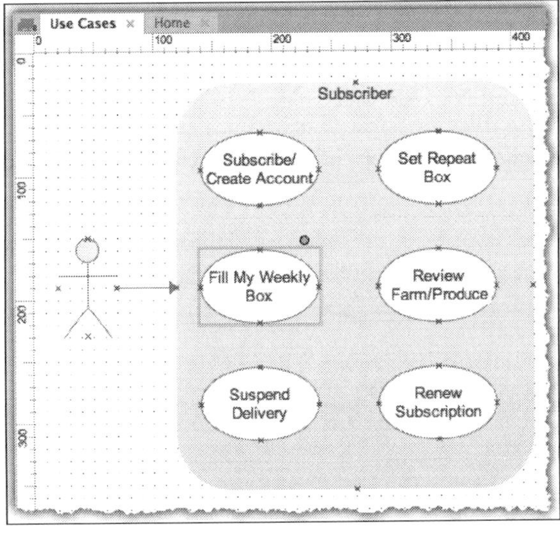

Image 6

Axure's Selection Modes

This is a great opportunity to get familiarized with Axure's three selection modes, which facilitate moving and arranging widgets on wireframe and flow pages. You can find the **Selection Mode** option on Axure's toolbar (*Image 7*, **A**) for the Windows version and (**B**) for the Mac version, as shown in the following screenshot:

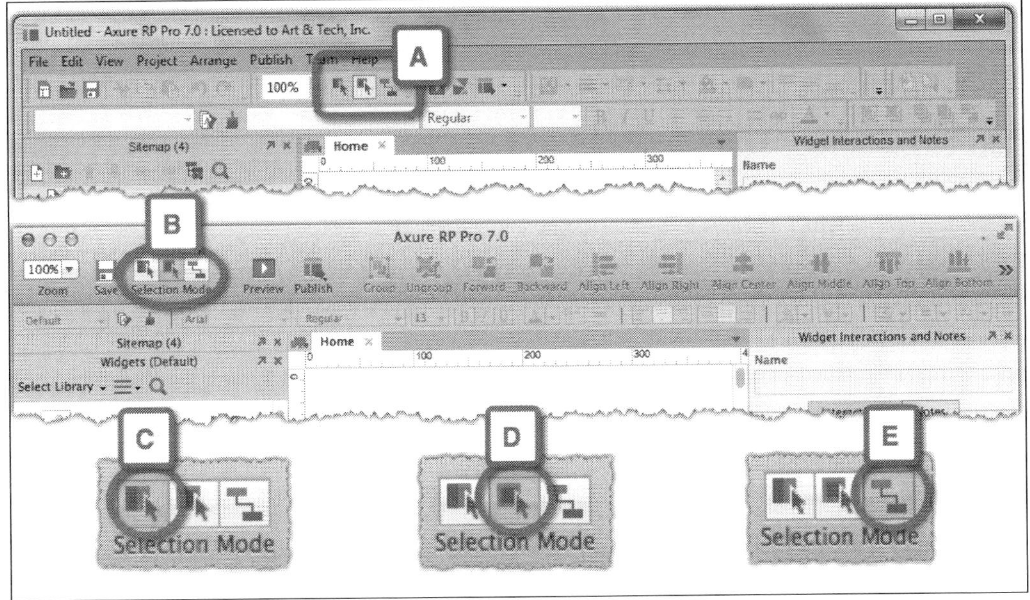

Image 7

The modes are described in the following table:

Select Intersected Mode	Select Contained Mode	Connector Mode
This is Axure's default mode (C). When you click-and-drag your mouse over the wireframe, all the widgets that are part of your selection area, even if they were only partially included in it, are selected.	In this mode (D), only widgets that are fully included in your selection are selected.	This mode (E) is most effective when you work with **Flow** widgets because it generates connector lines that you can use to hook up the various flow widgets in your diagrams.

Our personal preference is the **Select Contained Mode**, over the default **Select Intersected Mode**, because it provides precision by including only items fully encompassed by our selection, leaving out others that are in close proximity.

Working with Widgets

To organize widgets on a page, use the tools in the **Object** toolbar. *Image 8* shows the tools on the Mac version; the identical tools on the Windows version are shown as follows:

- Group and ungroup objects (*Image 8*, **A**)
- Move forward or backwards, top or bottom (**B**)
- Align objects left, right, and middle and top, bottom, and center (**C**)
- Distribute objects horizontally and vertically (**D**)
- Lock and unlock objects (**E**)

Image 8

Select a group of widgets in the use case page, illustrated in *Image 9*, and use the **Align** (*Image 9*, **A**) and **Distribute** (**B**) options on the toolbar to balance the cases on the page.

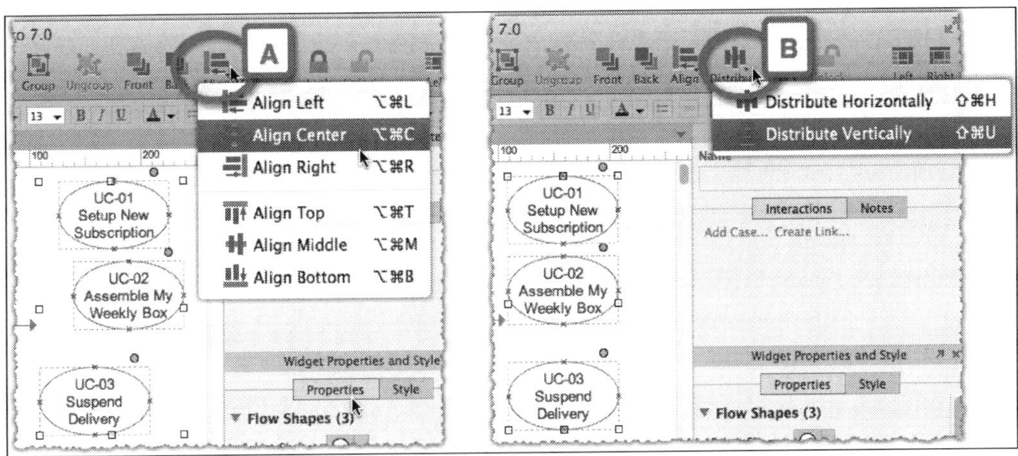

Image 9

With all the use cases vertically aligned and evenly distributed, group them together using the **Group** option on the toolbar. Select this group, and while holding the *Shift* key, select the actor widget. Use the **Align Middle** option to have the actor facing the use cases.

Next, switch to the **Connector** mode (*Image 7*, **E**) and draw lines from the actor widgets to each of the use cases. You should end up with a page that looks something like as shown in the following *Image 10*.

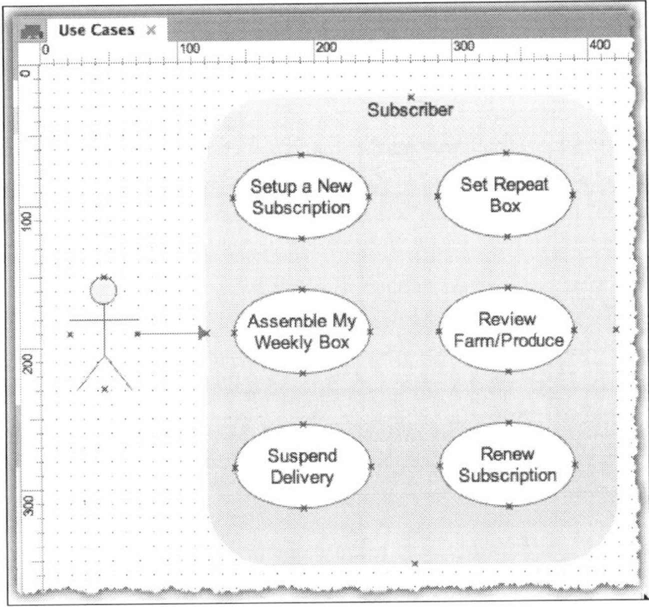

Image 10

Staying Organized with Sitemap Folders

The ability to group **Sitemap** pages in folders, high on the wish list of many users over the past few years, is one of those enhancements that seem minor, but provides significant convenience similar to folders in our e-mail client. Anything that helps us keep the Axure file organized and tidy is important.

Folders help keep the sitemap organized:

- Flow pages and wireframe pages can be kept separate (*Image 11*, **A**) as shown in the following screenshot:

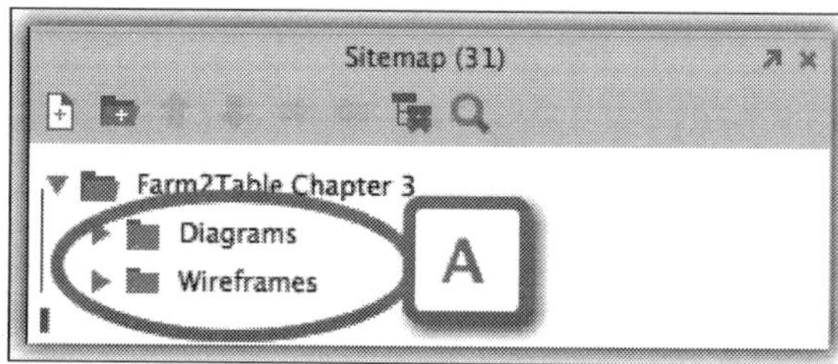

Image 11

- Reflect key domains of the project

In a team situation, avoid creating too many folders for each team member. In the Farm2Table prototype, the top-level folders are for **Diagrams** and **Wireframes** (*Image 12*, **A**) as shown in the following screenshot:

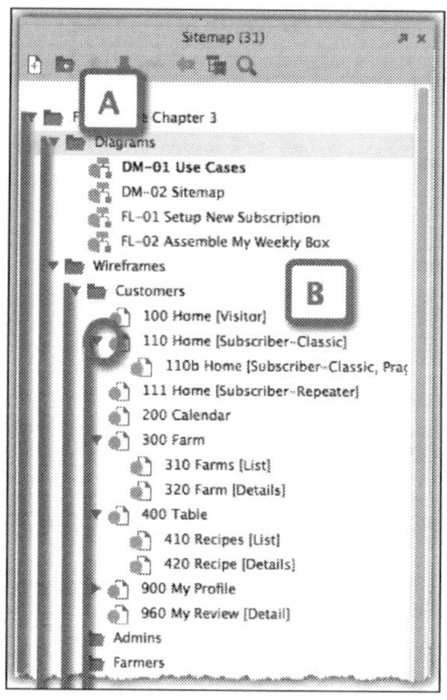

Image 12

Under **Wireframes**, there is a second level (**B**), breaking down the pages into the three key user types, as follows:

- **Customers**
- **Admins**
- **Farmers**

Within each category, pages can be nested further.

Saving the Project File

To paraphrase the joke on Chicago elections: save your work early and often. In our experience, Axure is very stable; if you share your painfully learned lessons from dealing with software in general, you will also develop the instinct to save your work frequently. In addition to the standard save, we recommend two strategies to support iterative design work. They are:

The RP Route

Use the **Save As...** command at the end of each day to create an archive of daily versions of your RP file. It is a good idea to use the **Save As...** command before making dramatic changes to key wireframes.

Here's why: your Axure file will evolve rapidly to incorporate tremendous amounts of detail, as you address increasingly finer requirements. Ideas that looked initially promising will not work as well as you thought. Feedback from stakeholders and users will require more changes, sometimes requiring that you backtrack to the previous version.

It is in your best interest to maintain an ongoing history of your Axure file. When you work on a standalone file (`.rp`), this means that you are responsible for managing the revision history. I am not talking about merely backing up your file here, which is a given.

For managing the history of revisions, a technique—or rather a behavior—that works for us is quite simple and easy to implement: at the end of each workday, save the file. Then, use the **Save As...** command to save the file in an **Archive** directory and append the date to the filename. The next day, open the file from the current directory. With this method, you will always be able to restore or find previous items and add them back to the current file, if needed.

The RPPRJ Route – Convert to Team Project

The design process is iterative—and rapidly so. It is hard to keep up, but you often regret that you made a change over some wireframe only to discover that the previous version was more compelling to stakeholders and users. What if there was a system that could automatically capture all your work and make it possible to restore to any previously saved version of your prototype?

Such a system is included with Axure and is primarily meant to support collaborative team work. However, who said that you cannot take advantage of its features, which include the ability to capture all of the above? We highly recommend this approach, which is described in detail in *Chapter 7, Managing Prototype Change*, over the standard RP standalone, with the exception of true throw-away fast explorations that are not meant to be saved and expanded.

Task Flow Diagram Pages

A prototype is tailored to visualize and demonstrate the user experience. Before we can develop the demonstration, we really need to nail down key user tasks which is, after all, the reason for the existence of the application. Since the scope of this book limits our discussion of the topic to the context of Axure, I will focus on the aspect of creating task flow diagrams.

Task flow diagrams are a model, an abstraction of the Ping-Pong exchange that makes up user-system interaction. These diagrams also play an important role in:

- Validating the sequence and logic of each task with business and technical stakeholders
- Developing an agreement on which flows and parts of flows should be prototyped, and to what level of fidelity

The diagrams should be shaped by explicit context, which is determined by a combination of inputs, including:

- What the system knows about the given user
- The options afforded to the user by the system
- The user's actions

While there are no set standards for UX flow diagrams, keep in mind that clarity, precision, and organization would help you during joint sessions with stakeholders.

Axure provides a one-stop shop for creating both flow diagrams and the wireframes that are associated with them. The ability to use a single application for modeling, simulating, and documenting the user experience gives us a powerful work environment.

Task Flow Diagrams (Sans Visio)

In a non-integrated world, you create, edit, and store your artifacts in dedicated software packages. Visio (PC) and OmniGraffle (Mac) were the tools of choice for many of us, frankly, because no tools were created primarily for UX. Both are good, general-purpose diagramming tools and many practitioners swear by them; they can do some amazing stuff. But let's get real: these are all static and single-user tools. In terms of workflow, there are costs and inefficiencies. The benefits of joining diagrams in Axure as opposed to spreading the IA across multiple tools are straightforward: all artifacts can be created in a single tool, organized within a project framework, be updated regularly in response to iterative design, and be linked.

Let's create a couple of task flow diagram pages, one for modeling the path of creating a new subscription and the other for the process of assembling the weekly box. In the **Sitemap** pane, add the two siblings below the **Use Cases** diagram page. Label the pages and use the **Diagram Type** menu to change their icons to mark them as flow pages.

Flow Diagram – New Subscription

To compose the diagram, you follow steps that are similar to those you would follow in Visio or Omni Graffle. But in creating the diagrams in Axure, you benefit from centralizing IA artifacts with the prototype and gain some benefits.

Compose the diagram (see sample file `FL-01`) with **Flow** widgets (*Image 13*, **A**). Use the **Connector mode** to draw connectors from one widget to another, and use the **Arrow Style** options to add directional arrowheads to the connectors.

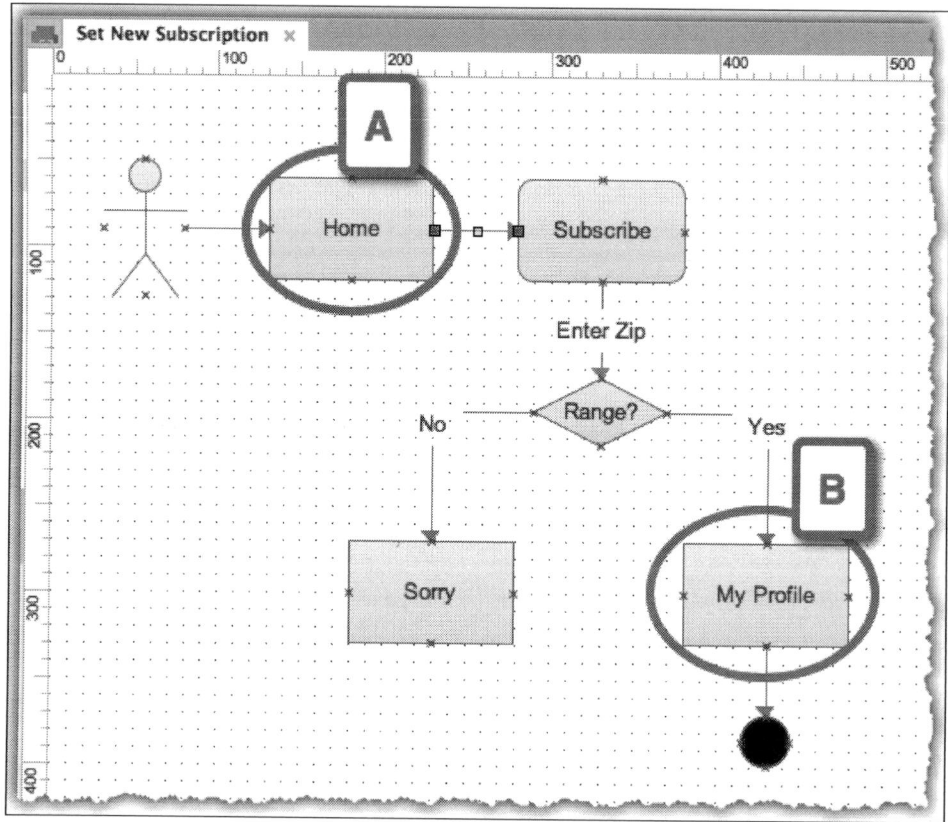

Image 13

It is a good idea to add a glossary using the **Wireframe** library widgets. But you can also drag pages from the **Sitemap** pane (FL-01B). Notice that the widget inherits its label from its parent page on the **Sitemap** pane. Also, note the document icon on the upper-left corner of the widget (*Image 14*, **B**). After you generate the HTML prototype, clicking on this widget will link to the actual pages.

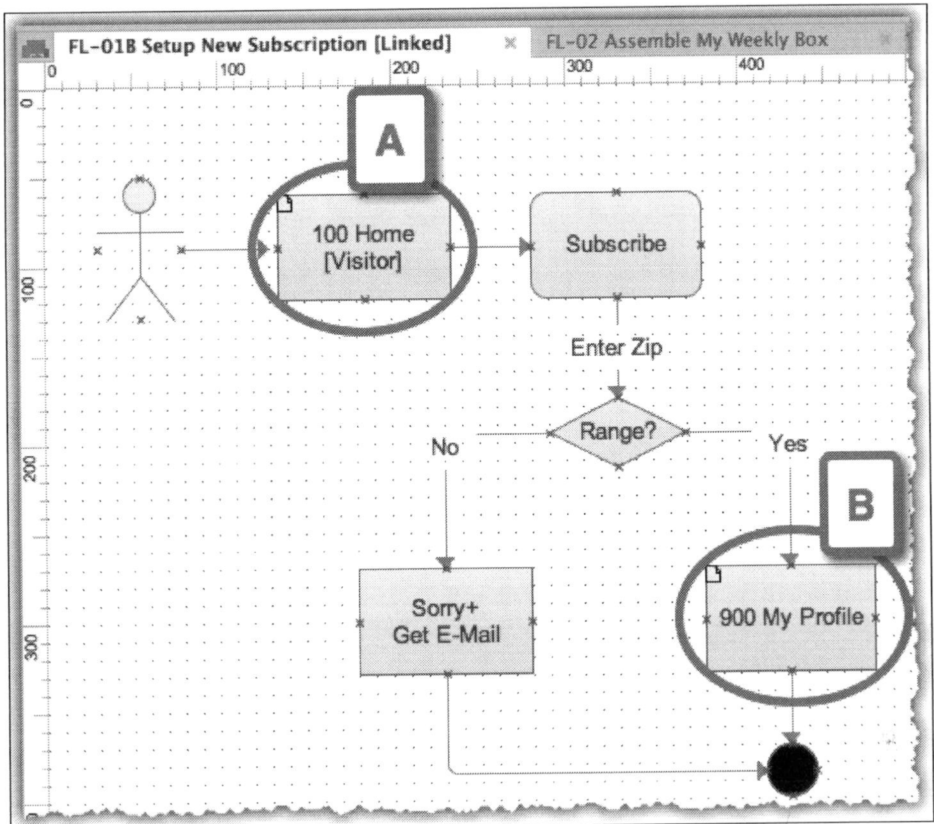

Image 14

Flow Diagram – Assemble My Weekly Box

Some of the initial requirements, as captured in *Image 15*, include:

- Ability to add/remove and edit the content of the box without having to log in
- Ability to log in only when done with the box and ready for a one-click order

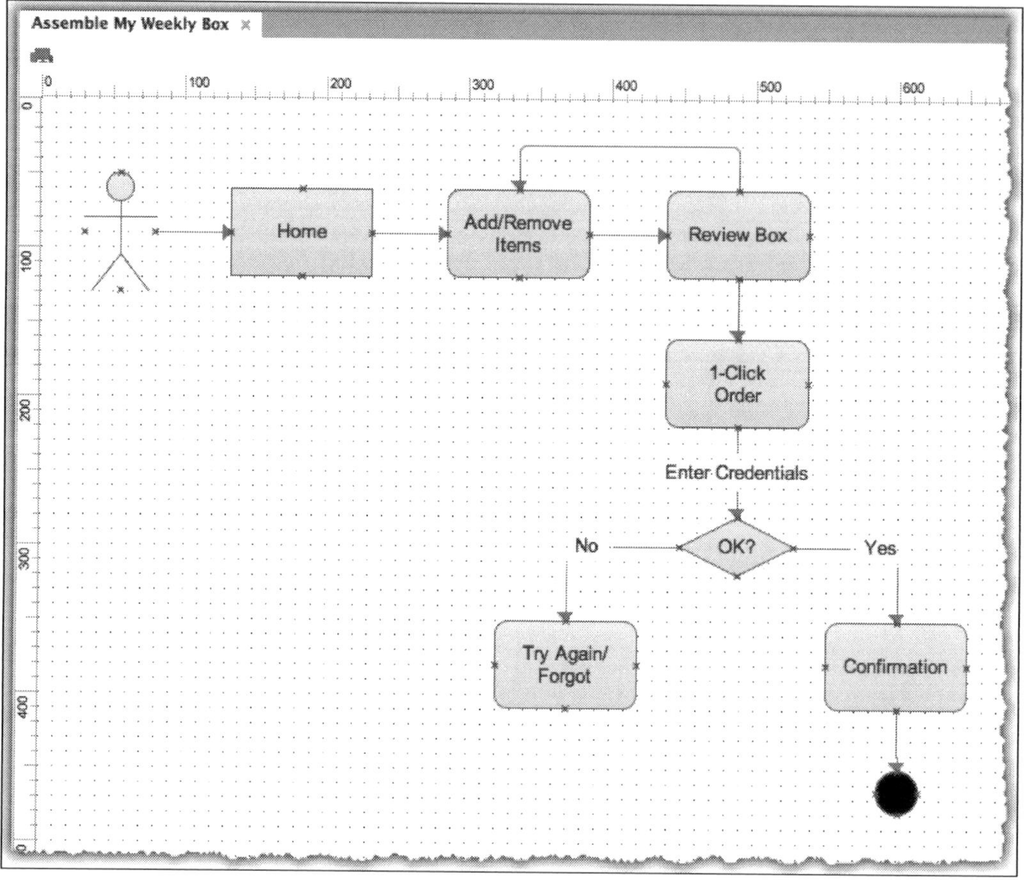

Image 15

As we mentioned earlier, when discussing use cases, it is desirable to align the diagrams that are in the Axure project with prioritized scenarios for usability testing. Also, focusing on the most important flows ensures that all stakeholders are clear on the scope of the prototyping effort.

Linking Use Cases to Flow Diagrams while Keeping Your Naming Conventions Intact

In addition to being able to create and store diagrams and wireframes within the same application, you can link Axure diagrams and wireframes to create a seamless transition from one to the other, with the help of the following steps:

1. Open the **Use Cases** page in the **Wireframe** pane.
2. Right-click on the use case **UC-01 Setup a New Subscription** (*Image 16*, **A**), and select the **Reference Page...** option (**B**) as shown in the following screenshot:

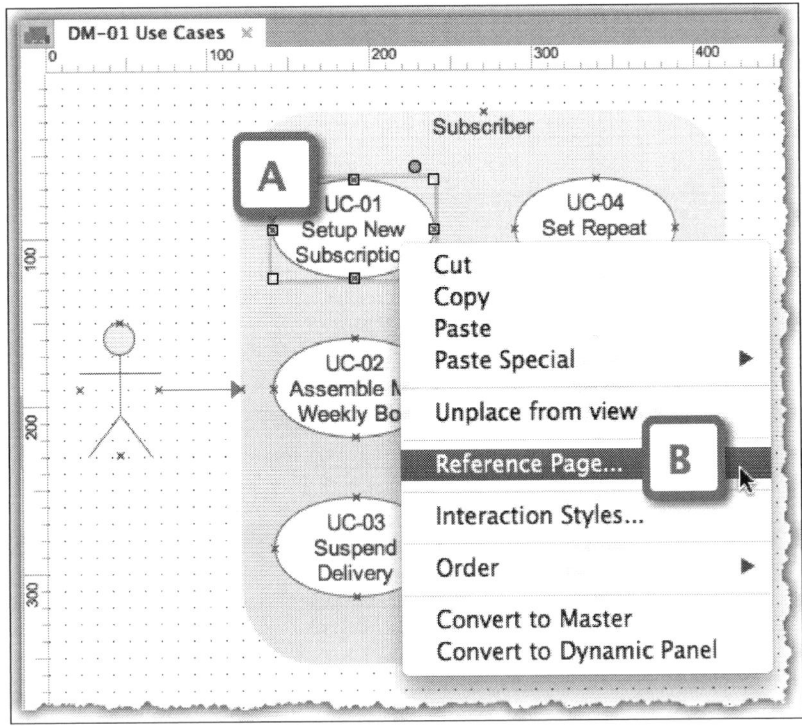

Image 16

3. The **Reference Page** popup (*Image 17*, **A**) lists all the pages in the **Sitemap** pane.

4. Select the page **FL-01 Setup New Subscription** (**B**) to link the use case to the page and close the popup, as shown in the following screenshot:

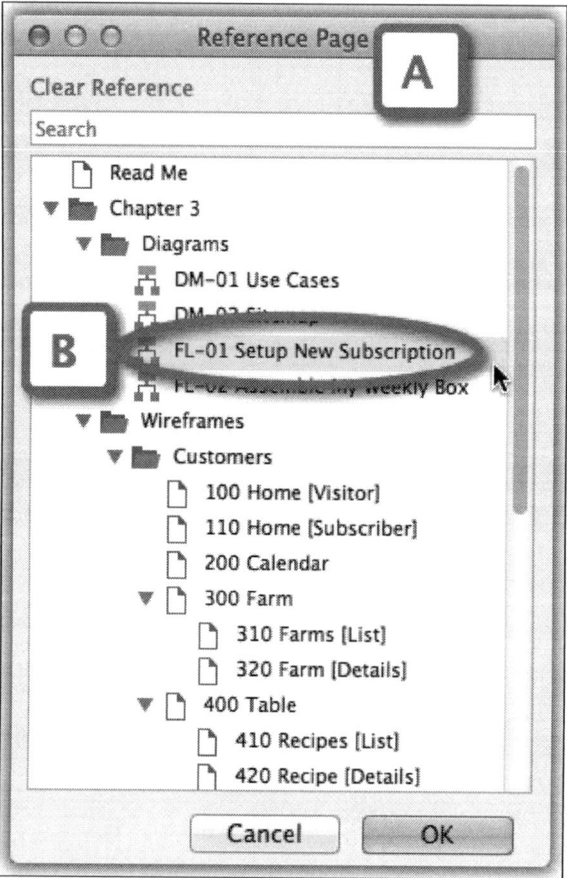

Image 17

5. Notice an unexpected change in the label of the use case: it is now showing the name of the page it is referencing (*Image 18*, **A**). This is a problem because you still want to be able to communicate with stakeholders about the use case independently from the referenced page. Also, you want to keep the ID of the use case permanent and not have it changed, in case you also change the ID of the page you are linking it to.

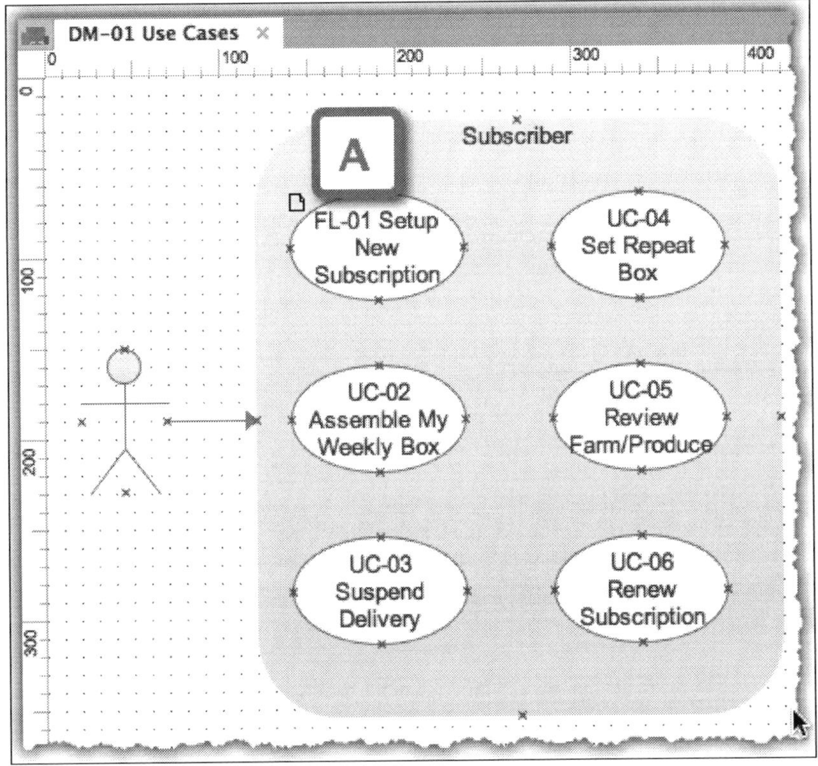

Image 18

6. To undo this, the fastest method is to just delete the shape and create a new one. Or, you can delete the **OnClick** case that Axure created.
7. With the correct ID showing, select the text on the widget (*Image 19*, **A**) and click on the **Link** icon on the toolbar (**B**) as shown in the following screenshot:

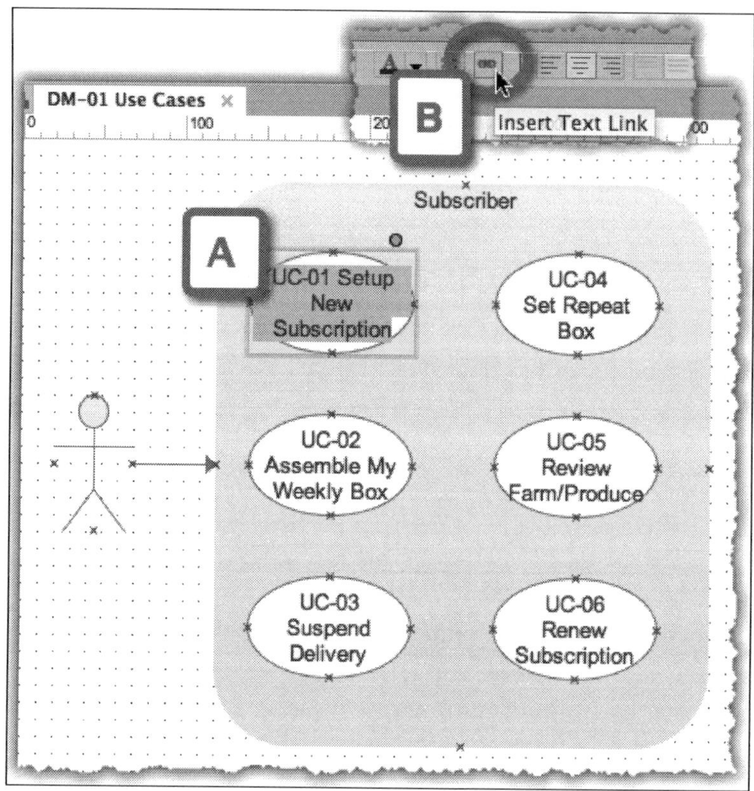

Image 19

8. From the **Link Properties** popup (*Image 20*, **A**), select the page you want to link to **FL-01 Setup New Subscription** from the list under the **Link to a page in this design** section (**B**) as shown in the following screenshot (*Image 20*):

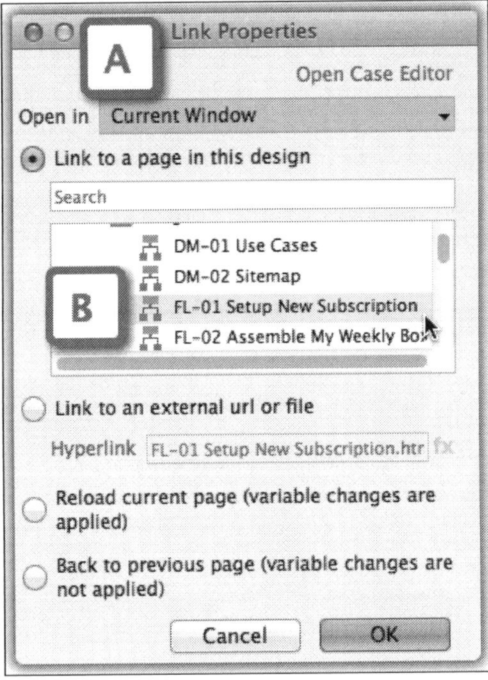

Image 20

9. Now the shape maintains its unique and permanent ID, and it is linking to the diagram flow page.

Generating an HTML Prototype

It is now time to generate your first HTML prototype, in order to review the work you have completed thus far. As your prototype advances, you will find yourself generating previews quite often, in order to validate that the HTML output works in the way you intended.

Generating the complete HTML prototype is accomplished from the **Publish** option, which is accessible either from the toolbar icon (*Image 21*, **A**) or from Axure's menu bar (**B**). The **Generate Prototype Files...** dialog (**C**) allows you to specify various settings that affect the output. However, at this early point, start with the **General** section (**D**) and let Axure know where to output the HTML prototype.

Use Axure's default for the destination folder, a directory labeled `Axure Prototypes` in your `Documents` folder. Alternatively, keep all your project work under the same directory, as described in *Chapter 2, Axure Basics – the User Interface*, which makes it easier to find all your project-related stuff, especially when you want to transport or back up your work.

Chrome or Firefox is the recommended browser, but you can specify your choice in the **Open With** section (D). Each time you generate the HTML prototype, it opens a new browser tab. It is a good idea to bookmark the page after the first time you generate the prototype, and from then on, use the **Do Not Open** option, to reduce to proliferation of open tabs in the browser. Just generate and refresh the page.

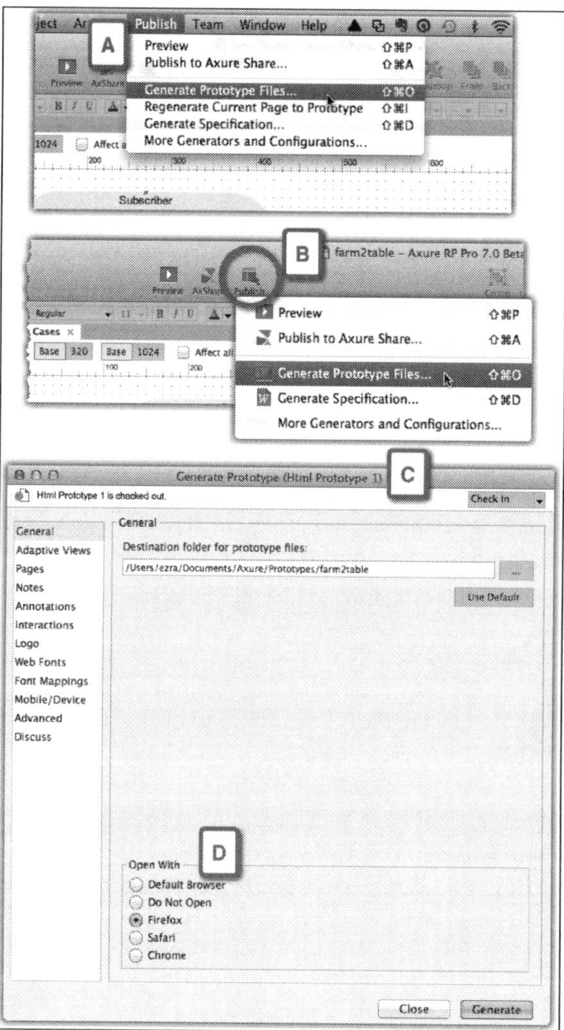

Image 21

Hit the **Prototype** icon to generate the HTML prototype. The screen is divided into the following two sections:

- On the left, a pane with two tabs, **Sitemap** and **Page Notes**. The **Sitemap** tab (*Image* 22, **A**) is selected by default.
- The main body, which displays the diagram or wireframe. The top page in the **Sitemap** tab is the default.

In our example, the **Use Cases** page (**B**) is selected in the **Sitemap** pane and displayed in the main section of the screen. In the main page, notice the little icon on the lower-right corner of the **Setup New Subscription** use case (**C**). Notice that the cursor changes, indicating an active link, which on click, loads the referenced **Setup New Subscription** diagram page in a new tab (**D**).

It is also possible to set up links from diagram shapes to their corresponding wireframes, as in the link to the actual wireframe of the **My Profile** page (E).

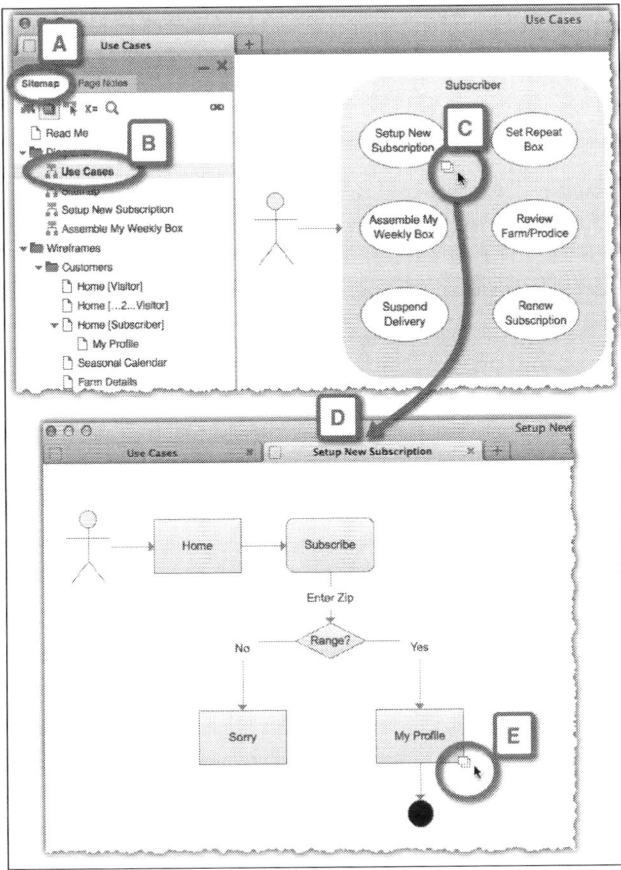

Image 22

To summarize what we've covered thus far:

- Creating use case diagrams
- Creating task flow diagrams
- Referencing and linking flow and wireframe pages from diagrams
- Generating an HTML prototype

Even an Axure novice can complete the activities we covered till now in 30 minutes or so and create a meaningful piece of work. As you continue to build the prototype, the underlying use cases and task flow will always be available for confirmation and validation.

The Sitemap Diagram

Another classic, basic, and very useful diagram is the Sitemap, which we can assemble by placing actual pages on the canvas, as shown here:

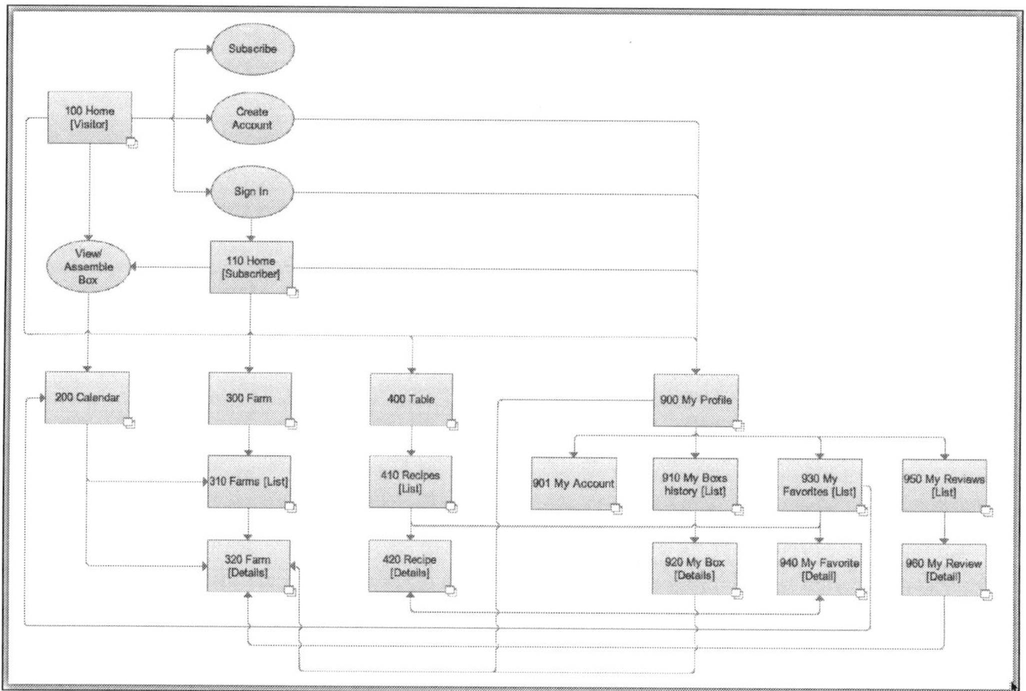

Image 23

The following list is a simple inventory of all key **Customer** pages in the Farm2Table site. Due to the limitation of this being a sample project and not a full-fledged project, we are not treating the farmers or admin pages here, which otherwise would be considered as well.

Notice that all pages have unique IDs in addition to names.

Axure Sitemap	**Customer**	
Page ID/Title	**Visitor**	**Logged in subscriber**
100 Home [Visitor]	Y	N
110 Home [Subscriber]	N	Y
200 Calendar	Y	Y
300 Farm [Main]	Y	Y
310 Farm List	Y	Y
320 Farm Details	Y	Y
400 Table [Main]	Y	Y
410 Recipes	Y	Y
420 Recipe [Details]	Y	Y
900 My Profile	N	X
901 My Account	N	X
910 My Box History [List]	N	X
920 My Box -[Detail]	N	X
930 My Favorites [List]	N	X
940 My Favorite [Detail]	N	X
950 My Reviews [List]	N	X
960 My Review [Detail]	N	X

Prototype to test: plan your prototype such that you create pages, page elements, and interactions that are part of a prioritized list of user flows that must be tested.

We will focus on developing the following pages:

- Homepage [Visitor, Subscriber not logged in]
- Home [Subscriber logged in]
- Profile (including My List, a feature that lets the user tag favorites items that can be used to automatically build a 1-click box)

- Seasonal Calendar
- Farm Detail
- Item Detail
- Recipes

A Device/OS-agnostic UI Framework

> *"Everything should have its place, and there should be a place for everything."*
>
> *– Various attributions*

The reality is that we must think and design devices/OSes agnostically. Smartwatches, smartglasses, smartphones, tablets, desktops, and large TV sets, all deliver a unique experience that should be optimized around the strengths and challenges their form-factor presents. A robust UI framework must provide a cohesive experience that can scale up—functionality wise—to accommodate new business capabilities; it also has to solve for a device-dependent experience. This is the catch, the challenge, and the opportunity.

It is difficult to optimize the design in such a way that regardless of the variability of device, its operating system, and screen size, the user experience will be optimal. The schedules, resources, and budget do not extend to comfortably accommodate all the work. Process issues, when all we had to worry about was the desktop experience, get exponentially worse.

There are conversations in our discipline around the best approach to develop an agnostic experience:

- **From small to big?**: Some maintain that we have to start with the smallest screen size, the smartphone, and work our way up. Others find it easier to start with a portrait view of a tablet; then, there are those who start with the desktop.

- **All or Subset?**: Some argue that there is only so much you can do on a small screen on the go and on limited bandwidth, and thus, smartphone content should be optimized for the device, and only a subset of all content and functionality should be offered there. Others maintain that with increasingly generous smartphone screens and the fact that they have become a primary work and pleasure platform for most users, the expectation is to have access to all content and all functionality regardless of the device used.

We will not take sides in these debates because changes are just too rapid. Instead, we will just point out that our experience has shown that it is more effective to validate content and functionality with stakeholders with wireframes and prototypes designed for a landscape desktop view, and show the smartphone and tablet experiences side-by-side.

It is easier for everyone to consider the entire set and then subtract, rather than working the other way round and figure out what is missing. Of course, a prioritization method for content and functionality is needed either way.

Still, we are talking about a design that does not become smaller or larger to accommodate the screen, but rather, a user interface system that transforms in response to the size of the screen. In order to develop such an interface system, we have to wireframe and prototype it first. For each screen, we have to wire, review, iterate, and test at least three versions, if not more, typically for desktop, tablet, and smartphone. The number of possible permutations is, of course, much higher.

Back in the Farm2Table project, with information gained from discovery activities and work done on the IA, it is time to develop rough wireframes that will guide the conceptual development phase of a user experience framework.

Before you dive into Axure's Adaptive Views feature, we recommend you first flesh-out the design in a fast and straightforward way. Whether you are new to Axure or a veteran user, this can be done without the Adaptive Views feature—just straightforward wireframing sketches.

If you choose to start the exploration and related discussions from desktop screens at landscape orientation (*Image 24*, **C**), it is useful to communicate to all that the importance and focus is on mobile first. When showing a comparative image of the layouts, start with the smartphone view (**A**), followed by the tablet portrait view (**B**), and close with the desktop view (**C**).

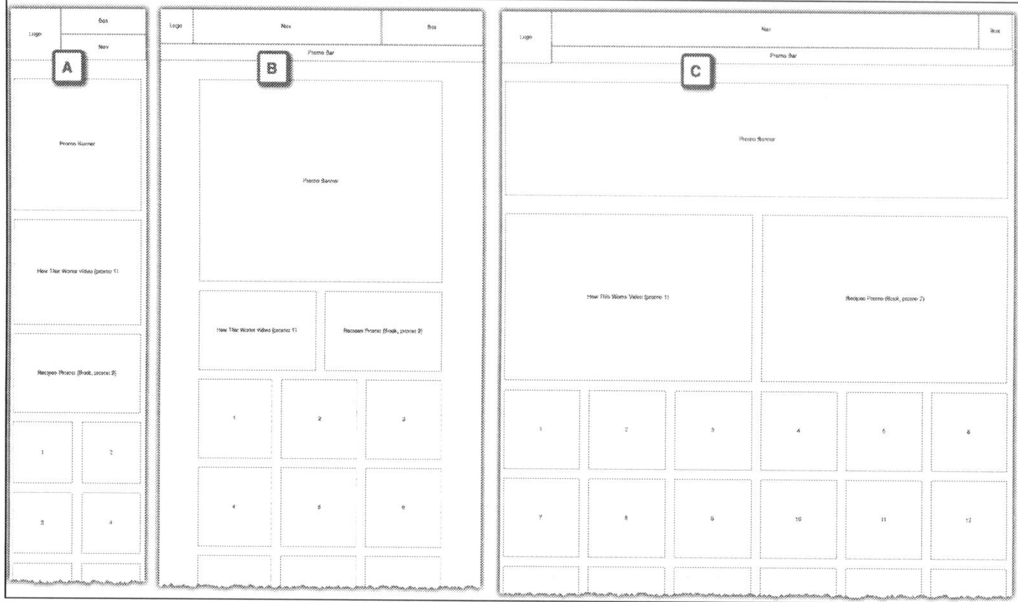

Image 24

RWD, Axure's Adaptive Views, and Base view

The world would be so boring without some semantic confusion, and so we are blessed with musings around topics such as the differences between Responsive Web Design and Adaptive Web Design. But for most non-technical people, and by that we mean many of the stakeholders you work with, the bottom line is an experience that transcends the device and its operating system. They want to see layouts for desktop, tablet, and mobile—in landscape and portrait orientation.

To create a prototype that simulates this behavior without coding it in HTML 5, CSS, and JavaScript, we use Axure's Adaptive Views capability.

Create your initial wireframe in the traditional landscape desktop view that is 1200 pixels wide. You organize all the elements that need to be there and you want to create additional views for narrower screens. The moment you add an adaptive view, the original 1200 pixel wide wireframe becomes the Base view, meaning that all the other views you create will inherit from it.

First Wireframe – Produce [Visitor, User Not Logged In]

Often, you might have a gut feeling about the general organization of the layout based on experience and familiarity with similar applications. You recognize the appropriateness of a particular pattern that could be applied, and since typically, the basic building blocks are elements such as header, footer, and body, they serve as the initial placeholders for deeper exploration.

The width of Axure's widgets is set in pixels and there is no option to set them as a percentage of the browser's window width. You cannot set the width of a widget to be 100 percent of the screen width, for instance. If you could, the widget's width would be elastic, making it resize to whatever the browser window width is. Therefore, it is important to decide what the wireframe's maximum width will be before placing widgets on the page. The decision can be simple if the target width is known. If the application is device agnostic, Adaptive Views addresses the issue. However, for each view, the width is fixed.

In the following example, we begin with a high-priority page, one most visitors will see: the **Produce** page as it is presented to visitors and subscribers who did not log in yet. Start the **Produce** page by outlining layout blocks with **Rectangle** widgets:

- Farm2Table Logo
- Global Navigation Bar
- Produce Box (Shopping Cart)
- Promo Banner
- How This Site Works Promo Box
- Recipes Promo Box
- Produce Items
- Footer

So, here are a couple of approaches to tackle the wireframe:

1: The quick and dirty approach	2: The device/OS-agnostic approach
This approach often does not bother with restrictions such as maximum width, widgets alignment, spacing, and other composition considerations. Widgets are placed on the pages quickly and tentatively, with a lot of copy and paste of similar widgets to speed up the construction. This approach can be compared to stream-of-consciousness writing, and for some, it is a great way to get ideas out.	This approach is based on the principle that small, upfront investment of time at the start of wireframe construction can pay off big-time later in the project. This means that you must pay attention to small details such as proportions, widget and text alignment, spacing, and so on.

A Quick but Structured Construction Approach

The third approach takes the advantages of both options listed in the previous table in that it affords rapid explorations, but anchors the work around an underlying grid structure. This supports conversion of the work to other sizes as it reduces throwaway work and expensive rework.

Keep in mind the mismatch between RWD's use of the term Grid and Axure's implementation of the same, called Guide. Regardless, the idea is to have a set of vertical lines establish the number of columns and their spacing on a layout. The following *Image 25* visualizes the screen:

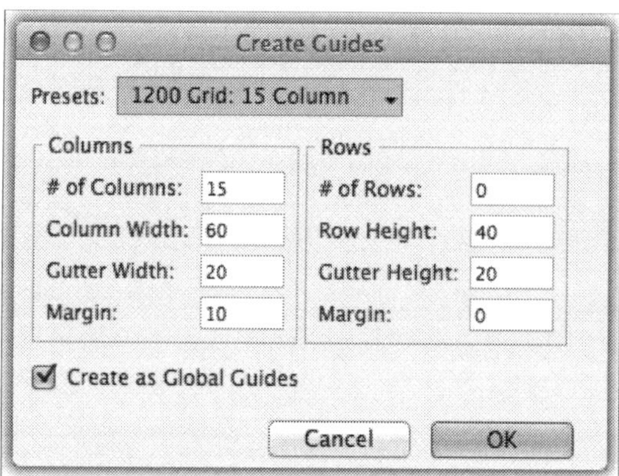

Image 25

Start by creating **Global Guides** for the Base view of the page. This is a 1200 pixel wide desktop, landscape-oriented layout. We use Axure's 1200 grid with 15 columns but you can modify and use the opportunity to create your own guides.

From the **Widgets** pane, drag over the **Rectangle** widgets that correspond to sections on the **Produce** page. Resize and organize them in the header, body, and footer areas. With Axure's **Zoom** feature (*Image 26*, **A**), you can adjust the display of the wireframe area to get a better sense of the entire composition: a useful feature when you want to move or resize wide objects.

Double-click on each widget to type in its label. Labeling widgets will be really important with Adaptive Views.

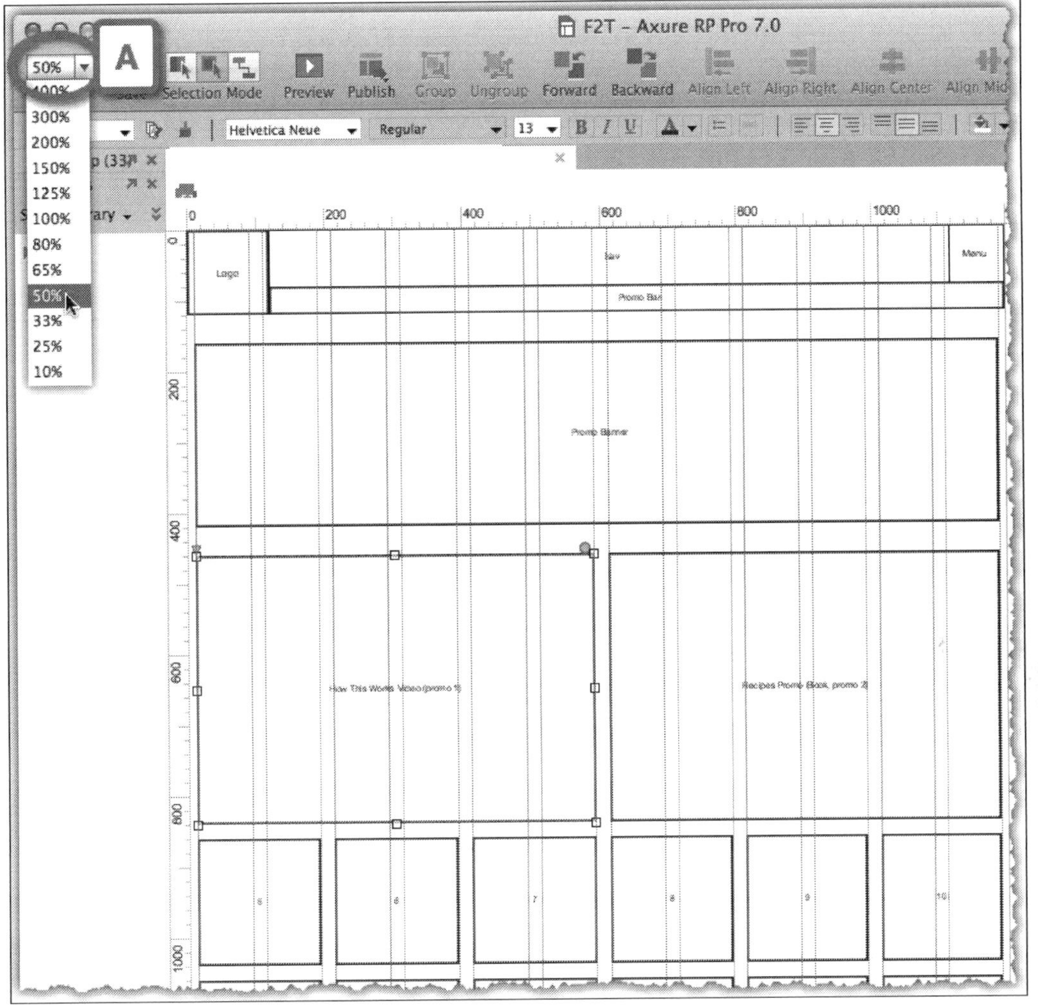

Image 26

Add other Views: Manually or with Adaptive Views?

With this simplistic, very high composition in place for view, duplicate this page and create related smartphone and tablet views. It may be a bit too early to use Axure's adaptive views at this point because all you need is a canvas for rapid consideration of all views. In other words, before you dive in to the specifics and get bogged down by having to manage adaptive views, develop your approach first.

Ok! So it is now time to move from big rectangles, which you could do in PowerPoint, to actual high-level definition of the various page elements. We want to focus our attention on high-level requirements and the information gathered so far. The following are some high-level, conceptual questions to develop:

- How is information organized and accessed on each screen in the case of Information Architecture?
- Where and how are key task flows initiated and ended?
- What are the main navigation systems?
- What common elements are shared across screens?
- How are common elements affected by a device size?

Getting Started with Masters and Dynamic Panels

Although we begin with a specific wireframe because we have to start somewhere, some global elements, such as header, footer, and navigation are shared across multiple pages. You could continue developing an element on a particular page and then copy and paste it wherever it is needed. But of course, now you will have to visit every page that uses this element each time you make a change and apply the updates. This is not an acceptable approach, although all of us probably ended up in such a situation at one project or another. It is a painful, slow, and expensive construction approach.

Global Elements as Masters

Some common elements of the UI framework, such as the header and footer, are natural candidates for consideration as global elements. Other modules typically include the login component, search and search results, help, and various alerts. Essentially, any element that repeats on multiple screens should be considered to be global. The global navigation is a natural global element since it repeats on most pages.

Axure Masters and Why to Use Them

Reuse, efficiency, productivity, edit one - update all! These are some of the benefits that immediately come to mind—that and the deep desire to avoid the pain mentioned previously.

Axure masters are not dumb rubber-stamps. Rather, they are powerful in that they can be assigned a behavior that is contextual to the page or element they are placed on. In *Chapter 5, Advanced Interactions*, we discuss masters in depth, but we will start using this powerful feature here.

The Global Navigation Bar

In most sites, this element appears in almost every page as it provides the user with an explicit indication to current position and available broad options. It provides a macro orientation:

- Where am I in the context of this site?
- What are the main sections of this site?
- Where can I find the content I'm looking for?

To construct the global navigation, perform the following steps:

1. Drag over and place a **Label** widget in the global navigation area. In Axure 7, it is no longer necessary to user rectangle widgets as a workaround to create rollover and other visual effects.
2. Change the text to `Home` and also label the widget `Home`.
3. Add additional labels for Calendar, Farm, Table, Contact Us, About, and FAQ. And finally, it should look similar to the following screenshot:

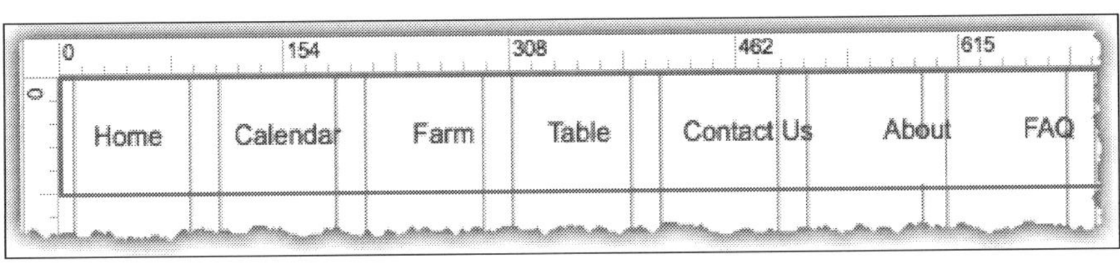

Image 27

Adding Wireframe Pages

At this point, add main category pages to correspond to the tabs in the global navigation:

- 110 Home (Subscriber)
- 200 Calendar
- 300 Farm
- 400 Table
- 900 Contact Us
- 910 About
- 920 FAQ

We have two options to continue from here:

Quick and dirty	Masters: A "Front-Loading" investment
Use the "quick and dirty" method to simply duplicate the **Produce** page, rename it, and adjust the widgets on each duplicated page. The drawback is that changes to repeating elements, such as the global navigation, will have to be applied manually to all wireframes. This approach is fast initially, but costly in the long run.	Use the somewhat slower but structured method of converting all the repeating elements on the home page into masters, then duplicating it to create the category pages. The masters will be reused, thus saving time in the long run, and ensuring construction consistency across pages. Since masters have adaptive views, they will work well later on. For a refresher on adaptive views, see *Chapter 2, Axure Basics – the User Interface*. This is the approach which will be demonstrated next.

Creating Your First Master

We are going to demonstrate the second approach, using masters. Masters are components of the user interface that appear on multiple pages. When you edit the master, all its instances in the prototype are immediately updated. A twist that Axure has added to masters is that while the look and feel of a master is identical wherever you use it, its behavior can be tailored to fit the context in which it is used. We discuss this feature, called **Raised Event**, in *Chapter 5, Advanced Interactions*.

So, our first master that we will create using the following steps will be the global navigation bar:

1. In the **Wireframes** pane switch of the **Home** page, select the group of widgets that make up the global navigation bar (*Image 28*, **A**).
2. Right-click anywhere within the selection, and in the contextual menu, select the **Convert to Master** option (**B**) from the **Arrange** menu.
3. Axure will prompt you with the **Convert To Master** dialog (C).
4. Make sure to re-label the master, replacing the default and generic `New Master 1` with something meaningful, and hit the **Continue** button. We will discuss naming convention strategies in *Chapter 4, Creating Basic Interactions*.
5. Leave the **Place Anywhere** option selected.

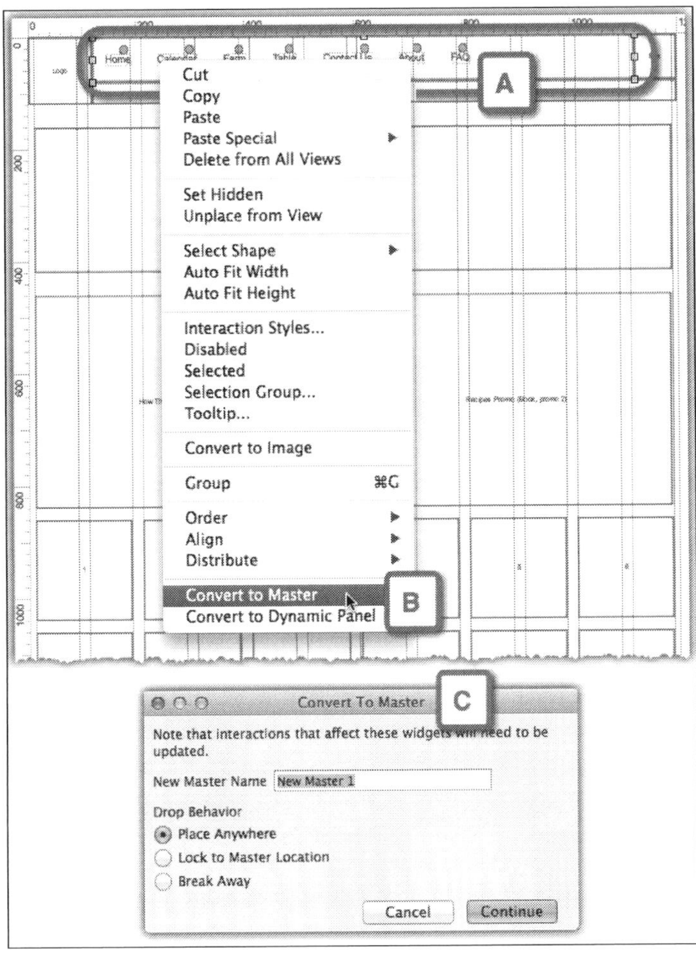

Image 28

Note that you can undo this action and revert the master to its original state by selecting the **Undo** option from the **Edit** menu.

Start the name of each master with an M. For example, `M Global Nav`. The prefix will make it easier for you to identify which open wireframes are masters.

You will immediately notice a change in the way the navigation bar looks: the entire block now has a pink shade (*Image 29*, **A**), which helps you distinguish masters from other widgets. The new master appears in the **Masters** pane (*Image 29*, **B**). Keep in mind that the **Masters** pane is not contextual to a specific wireframe. Rather, it is the repository of all the masters you have in your project file. The **Widget Manager** pane is contextual to the edited wireframe page.

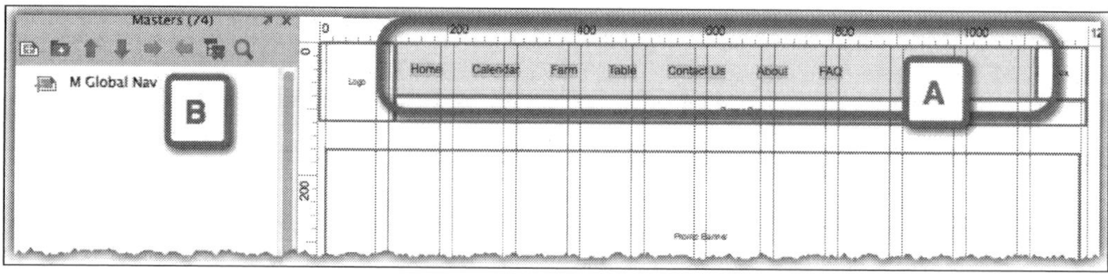

Image 29

In the **Produce** page, continue to create masters out of the Header and Footer blocks, since these elements too will appear on every page.

Masters from scratch

You can also create new masters without converting existing widgets by using the **Add Master** option in the **Masters** pane. This is a good option when you know in advance that the widget will be used as a master.

Basic Interactions

It is a lot of fun to get these interactions going. That is why we are using Axure, right? So indeed, it is so simple to get the global navigation to link to other pages that we start with interactions in this chapter.

In the **M-Global Nav** master, click on the **Calendar** button (*Image 30*, **A**), and from the **Interactions** widgets and **Notes** section, double-click on the **OnClick** interaction (**B**) to bring up the **Case Editor** window. There, select the **Open Link** action (**C**) from the first column, and in the third column select the target page, in this case **Calendar** (**D**). That's it.

Use the **Preview** button to view the page in the browser and enjoy the ease with which you were able to create the link.

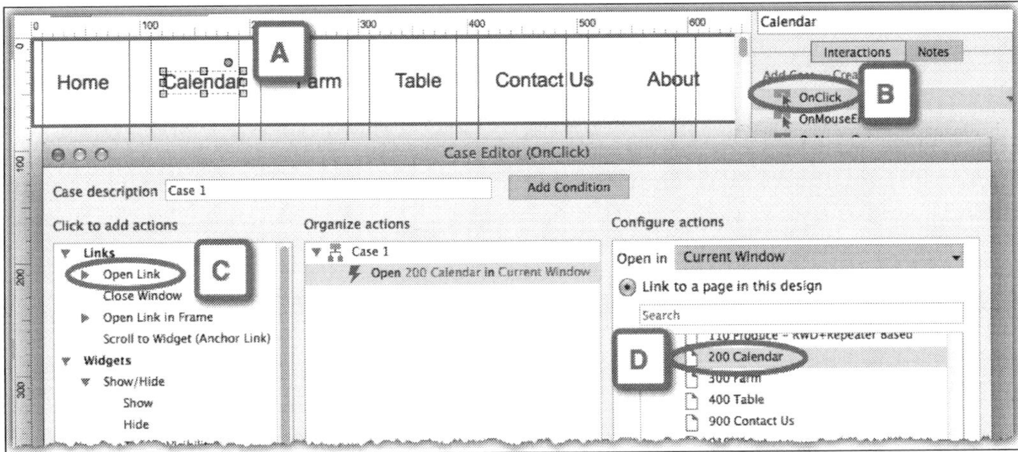

Image 30

Dynamic Panels to the Rescue

For the Farm2Table global navigation, we have chosen a simple, text-based design. But what if your design calls for something more elaborate?

For example, the global navigation is designed using tab widgets in such a way that the shape of the active tab clearly indicates to the user the page they are on. The implication of this design decision is that the global navigation needs to have four states, each with the active section tab. However, you have only one master, and it will always show the **Home** page tab as active.

Yes, it is possible to avoid this predicament—just have all buttons look identical, and change their fill and outline colors—but this is not what you want for the design.

This is the first example of a construction situation in which Axure's dynamic panels come into play. We provide a deep-dive into dynamic panels in *Chapter 4, Creating Basic Interactions*.

In the sample page, **DP Example** (use the Search feature in the **Sitepmap** pane to find it), open the global nav master, select all widgets, right-click, and select the **Convert to Dynamic Panel** option from the context menu (*Image 31*, **A**), as shown in the following screenshot:

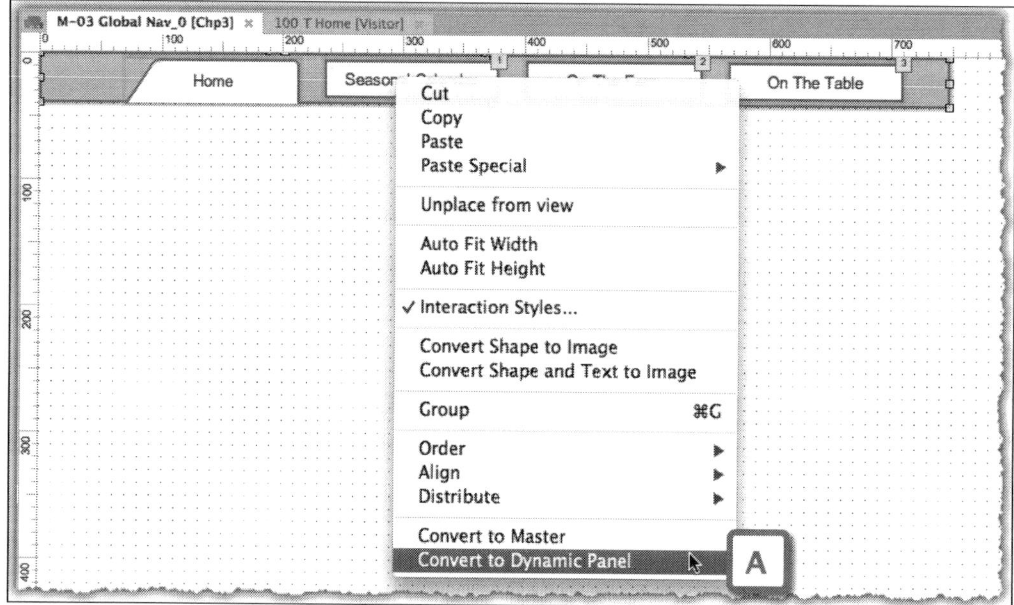

Image 31

You have just created a container that will hold the four states of the global nav. Once you close the dialog box, notice the changes in the master wireframe. The rectangle and navigation widgets now appear as a single box with a light-blue mask (**A**), which is how Axure helps you visually distinguish dynamic panels from other widgets.

The **Dynamic Panel State Manager** (*Image 32*, **B**) dialog appears when you double-click on the dynamic panel. Now is the time to relabel it to something meaningful, such as `DP Global Nav`. We recommend using a prefix such as DP (acronym for dynamic panel) to help identify dynamic panels by their label. Finally, the node nested under the dynamic panel is of its initial state, which is labeled with the default `State 1`. Relabel the state to `Home`.

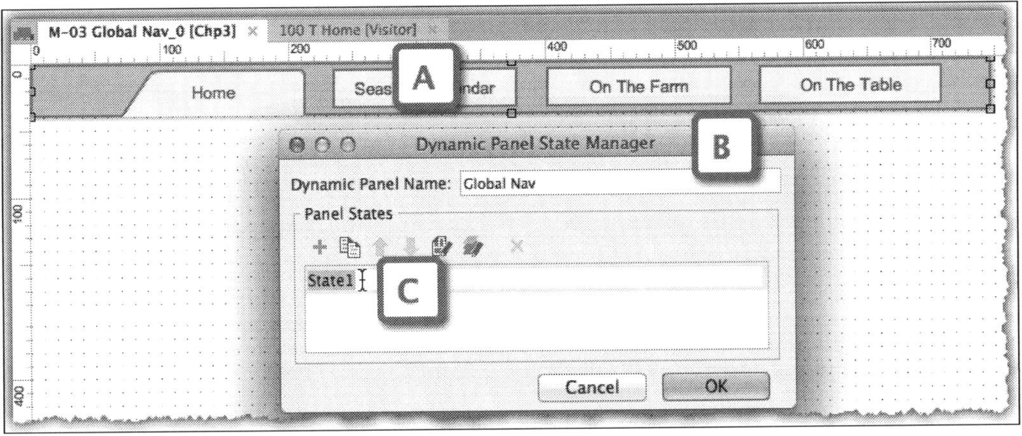

Image 32

Since adding the additional three states is self-explanatory, do this to complete this phase of the example.

New dynamic panel from scratch

You can also create a new dynamic panel by dragging over a dynamic panel widget to the wireframe. Double-click to edit, and the first state will open in a new tab in the **Wireframes** pane. Add widgets to this blank wireframe. This is a good option, if you know in advance that the component you are going to wireframe needs to be a dynamic panel.

States Construction in a Dynamic Panel

The following *Image 33* shows the dynamic panel (**A**) and the wireframes that make up its four states (**B** through **E**).

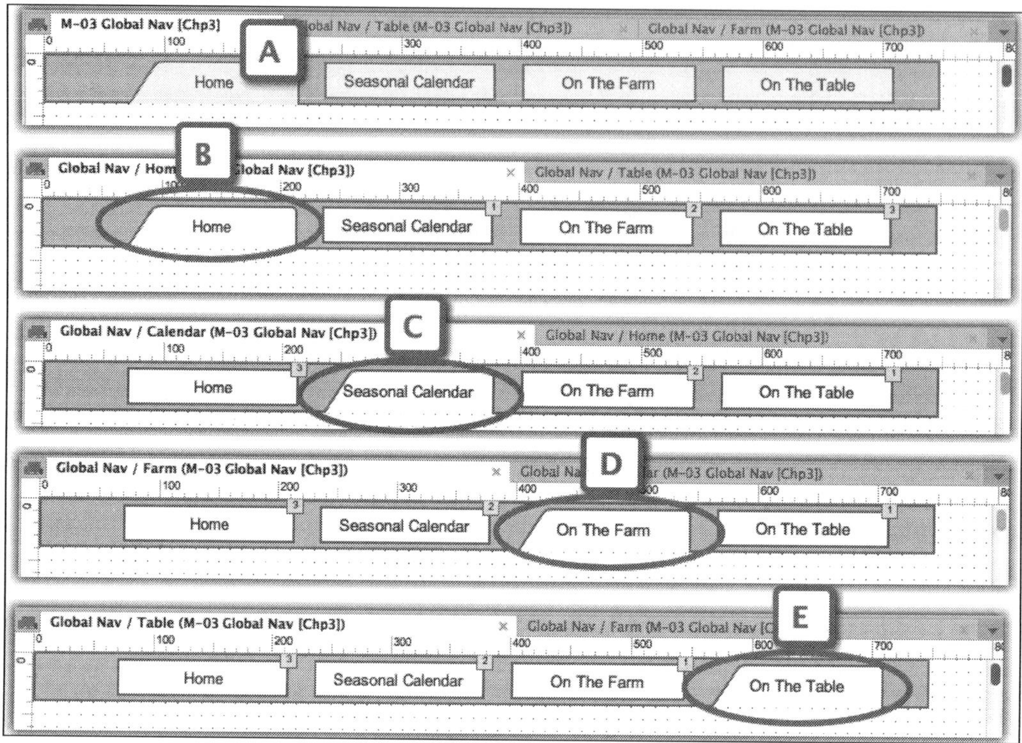

Image 33

In our example, the overall size and structure of the states is uniform, with the exception of the active tab (**B** through **E**). In other cases, each state of the dynamic panel may have different physical properties; we will go through such an example at a later point.

Automatically Resizing a Dynamic Panel and Associated States

In the previous version of Axure, you had to make sure to manually adjust the size of the dynamic panel such that it would accommodate its largest state. The dimensions of the dynamic panel were fixed, and thus, areas of a state that extended beyond the panel's boundary would not be visible. In Axure 7, **Fit to Content** solves this issue. The following screenshot shows the **Fit to Content** option (*Image 34*), which resizes a dynamic panel to fit the dimensions of the largest state:

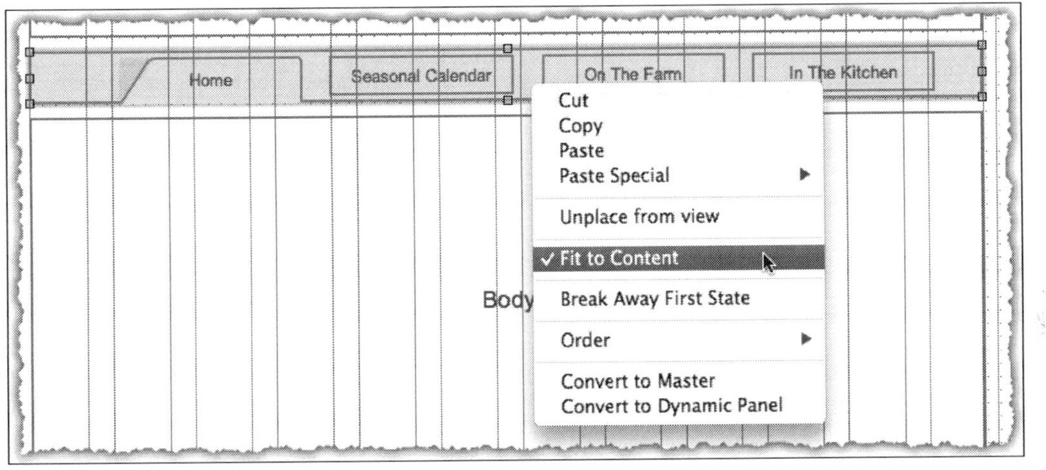

Image 34

Adding Visual Effects

Next, we want to enhance the user experience and provide visual effects in response to user actions. For example, when a user hovers over a tab in the global navigation bar, the tab should change its appearance. With Axure, you can create such effects effortlessly, which we will demonstrate on Farm2Table's **Global Nav** bar.

The **Set Interaction Styles** dialog (*Image 35*, **A**), provides a one-stop place to create and apply dedicated visual treatments to four states that reflect the widget's appearance in the listed conditions (**B**):

- **MouseOver**
- **MouseDown**
- **Selected**
- **Disabled**

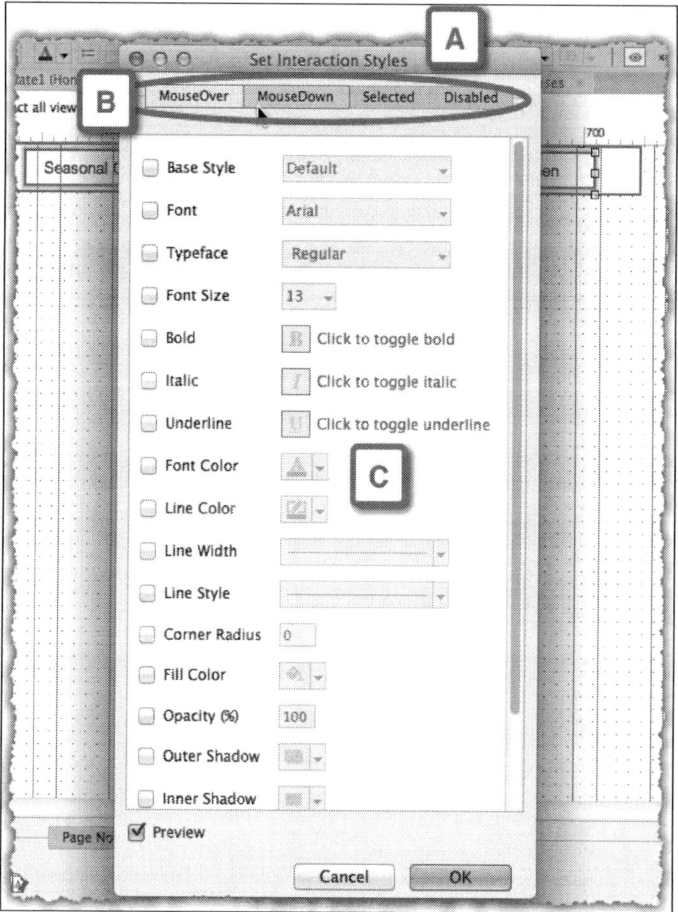

Image 35

The dialog contains various visual properties. You can also use a custom style by checking the first checkbox **Base Style**, and select the **Custom** style from there. We will discuss this important capability later.

There is still no way to link an actual CSS file.

Adding Sketch Effects

If you like to begin your design process for a project by sketching exploratory wireframes on paper or an iPad, you can achieve a similar tentative look by using Axure's **Sketch Effects** feature, which has been introduced in Version 6.

For early iterations of the prototype, this kind of treatment might help communicate to stakeholders that we are still looking at initial concepts. The effect can be applied on a page-by-page basis or to all pages as a global style. Sketchiness affects the entire wireframe, not only the selected widgets in a wireframe. The good news is that this effect can be easily removed at any time. Experiment with the **Sketchiness** slider to find the level that works for you. The following *Image 36* shows the before and after stages of the effect being applied to the page:

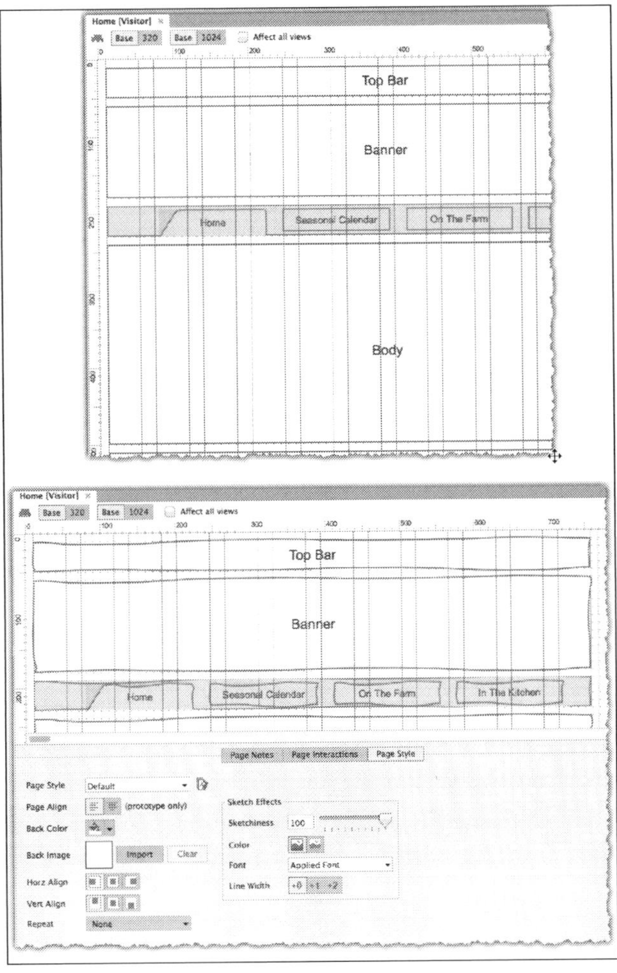

Image 36

Summary

This chapter laid out the foundation for the project's interactive prototype and proposed a structured, pragmatic, yet requirements-driven approach to wireframe construction. Taking advantage of Axure's unified wireframing and specifications environment, we covered:

- Constructing various artifacts such as concept models, personas, use case, and task flow diagrams based on information gathered throughout discovery and requirements activities
- Basic wireframing aided by guides and grids
- Wireframe construction with masters and dynamic panels
- The importance of labeling of widgets, naming conventions, masters, and dynamic panel states
- Applying visual effects in response to mouse activity
- Applying the sketch effect

You were introduced to Farm2Table, the book's demonstration project, and in a series of activities, created an initial set of diagrams and wireframes that included the use of wireframe and flow widgets, masters, and dynamic panels.

The next chapter will introduce you to Axure interactivity fundamentals such as interactions, cases, events, and actions. We will also discuss naming conventions and wireframe construction strategies.

4

Creating Basic Interactions

"Learning is not attained by chance, it must be sought for with ardor and diligence."

– Abigail Adams

We joke that Elizabeth is a true designer in the sense that her right brain will be on fire when she approaches her work, so shifting to logic is tricky for her. Despite this, she has been able to build rather sophisticated prototypes. So, while Axure 7 supports the creation of highly advanced rapid prototypes, the key to success for someone who does not have pseudo code running easily through their mind is: approaching interactivity with an open mind, writing down in plain language what the desired interaction should be, and the willingness to seek help from a colleague, online tutorial, or this book.

In this chapter, we cover the basics of Axure interaction and some of the simple-yet-powerful features that empower non-programmers to develop high-fidelity, clickable UX prototypes.

The basic model of creating interactivity in an Axure prototype involves four hierarchical building blocks: **Interactions**, **Events**, **Cases**, and **Actions**. Interactions are triggered by events, which cause cases to execute actions. These four topics are the focus of this chapter.

Axure Interactions

Client expectations of a good user experience continue to rise, and it is clear that we are in the midst of an enormous transition in software design. This, along with the spread of **Responsive Web Design** (**RWD**), has placed UX front and center of the web design process. Early in that process is the need to "sell" your vision of the user experience to stakeholders and you have a better chance of success if they have to be engaged as early as possible, starting at the wireframe level. There is less tolerance and satisfaction with static annotated wireframes, which requires an effort on the part of stakeholders to imagine the fluidity of the expected functionality.

Axure enables designers to rapidly simulate highly engaging user experiences that can be reviewed and tested on target devices as static wireframes are transformed into dynamic prototypes. In this chapter, we focus on how to make the transition from static to interactive, using simple, yet wickedly effective interactions.

Interactions are Axure's term for the building blocks that turn static wireframes into clickable, interactive HTML prototypes. Axure shields us from the complexities of coding by providing a simple, wizard-like interface for defining instructions and logic in English. Each time we generate the HTML prototype, Axure converts the interactions into real code (JavaScript, HTML, and CSS), which a web browser can understand. Note however, that this code is not production grade code.

Each Axure interaction is composed, in essence, of three basic units of information—when, where, and what:

- **When does an interaction happen?**: The Axure terminology for "when" is events, and some examples for discrete events include:
  - When the page is loaded in the browser.
  - When a user clicks on a widget, such as a button.
  - When the user tabs out of a form field.

  A list of events can be seen on the **Interactions** tab in the **Widget Interactions and Notes** pane on the right-hand side of the screen. You will also find the related list of events under the **Page Interactions** tab, which is located under your main workspace.

- **Where can we find the interaction?**: An interaction is attached either to a widget, such as a rectangle, radio button, or drop-down list; a page; or a master wireframe. You create widget interactions using the options in the **Widget Properties** pane, and page and master interactions using the options in the **Page Properties** pane. These are called cases. A single event can have one or more cases.
- **What should happen?**: The Axure terminology for "what", is actions. Actions define the outcome of the interaction. For example, when a page loads, you can instruct Axure on how the page should behave and what it will display when it is first rendered on the screen. More examples of this could be when the user clicks on a button, it will link to another page; when the user tabs out of a form field, the input will be validated and an error message. Ensure that all of the actions you want to include for that case or scenario are in the same case.

Multiple cases

Sometimes, an event could have alternative paths, each with its own case(s). The determination of which path to trigger is controlled with conditional logic which we will cover later in this chapter, and more extensively, in *Chapter 5, Advanced Interactions*.

Axure Events

In general, Axure interactions are triggered by two types of events, which are as follows:

- Page and master level events which can be triggered automatically, such as when the page is loaded in the browser, or as a result of a user action, such as scrolling.
- When a user directly interacts with a widget on the page. These interactions are typically triggered directly by the user, such as clicking on a button, or as a result of a user action which causes a number of events to follow.

Page-level Events

Think about this concept as a staging setup, an orchestration of actions that takes place behind the scenes and is executed as the page gets rendered in the browser. Moreover, it is a setup to which you can apply conditional logic and variables, and deliver a contextual rendering of the page. In short, events, which can be applied to pages and on masters, will likely become one of your frequently used methods to control your prototype.

Keep in mind that the order in which the interactions you build into the prototype will be executed by the browser. The following *Image 1* screenshot illustrates the **OnPageLoad** event as an example:

1. The browser gets a request to load a page (*Image 1*, **A**), either because it is the first time you launch the prototype or as a result of navigation from one prototype page to another.
2. The browser first checks for **OnPageLoad** interactions. An **OnPageLoad** event (**B**) may be associated with the loading page (**C**), a master used on the page (**D**), or both.

3. If **OnPageLoad** exists, the browser first evaluates page-level interactions, and then master-level interactions. As we will see in *Chapter 5, Advanced Interactions*, the benefits of this order of operations is that you can set the value of a variable on the page's **OnPageLoad** interaction and pass that variable to the master's **OnPageLoad** interaction. It sounds a bit complicated, perhaps.
4. If the **OnPageLoad** interaction includes condition(s) (**E**), the browser will evaluate the logic and execute the appropriate action (**F** and/or **G**). Otherwise, if the **OnPageLoad** event does not include a condition, the browser will execute the interaction (**H**).
5. The requested page is rendered (**I**) per the interaction.

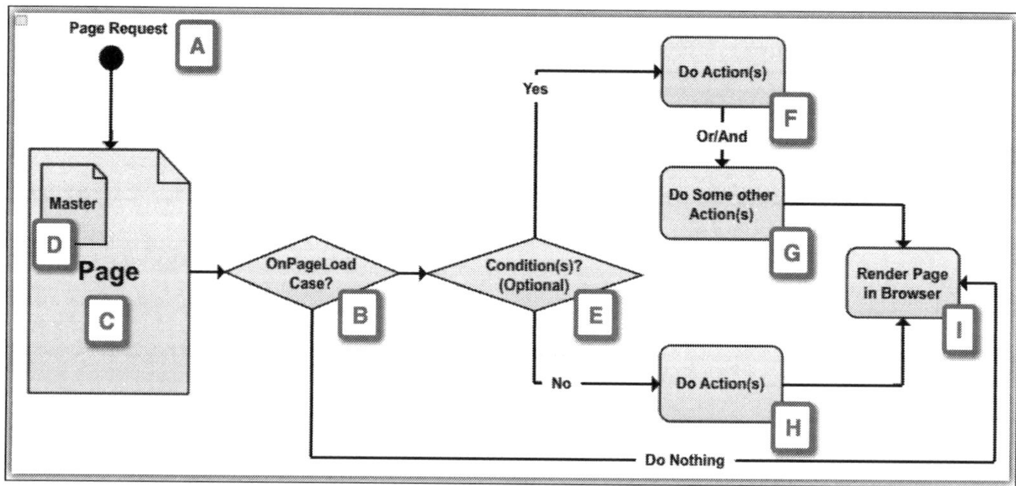

Image 1

The following table lists the events offered at a page level:

Event names	Definition
OnPageLoad	This event will trigger assigned action(s) that will impact how the page is initially rendered after it loads.
OnWindowResize	This event will trigger assigned action(s) when a browser is resized.
OnWindowScroll	This event will trigger assigned action(s) when the user scrolls the browser window.
OnPageClick	This event will trigger assigned action(s) when the user clicks on any empty part of the page (not clicking on any widget).

Event names	Definition
OnPageDoubleClick	This event will trigger assigned action(s) when the user double-clicks on any empty part of the page (not clicking on any widget).
OnContextMenu	This event will trigger assigned action(s) when the user right-clicks any empty a part of the page (not clicking on any widget).
OnMouseMove	This event will trigger assigned action(s) when the mouse pointer is moved anywhere on the page.
OnPageKeyUp	This event will trigger assigned action(s) when a pressed key is released.
OnPageKeyDown	This event will trigger assigned action(s) when a key is pressed.
OnAdaptiveViewChange	This event will trigger assigned action(s) on a switch from on adaptive view to another.

Widget-level Events

The **OnClick** event, whether using a mouse or tapping a finger, is one of the fundamental triggers of modern user-computer interactions. In Axure, this action is one of the several actions you can associate with a widget.

The following *Image 2* screenshot illustrates how widget-level events are processed:

1. The user interacts with a widget by initiating an event (*Image 2*, **A**), such as **OnClick**, which is associated with that widget (**B**).
2. The type of widget (Button, Checkbox, and so on) constrains the possible response the user can expect (**D**). For example, before clicking on a button, the user may move the mouse over it and the visual appearance of the button will change in response to the **OnMouseEnter** event. Axure includes events that can also handle mobile devices, the use of fingers, as means of enabling the user's direct manipulation of the interface.
3. The browser will check if conditional logic is tied to the widget event (**E**). For example, you may have created an interaction in which a rollover event will display different states of a dynamic panel based on some variable. The browser will evaluate the condition and execute the action(s) (**F** and/or **G**).
4. If no conditions exist, the browser will execute the action(s) associated with the widget (**H**).

5. Based on the actions tied to the event, the browser will update the screen or load some other screen (**I**).

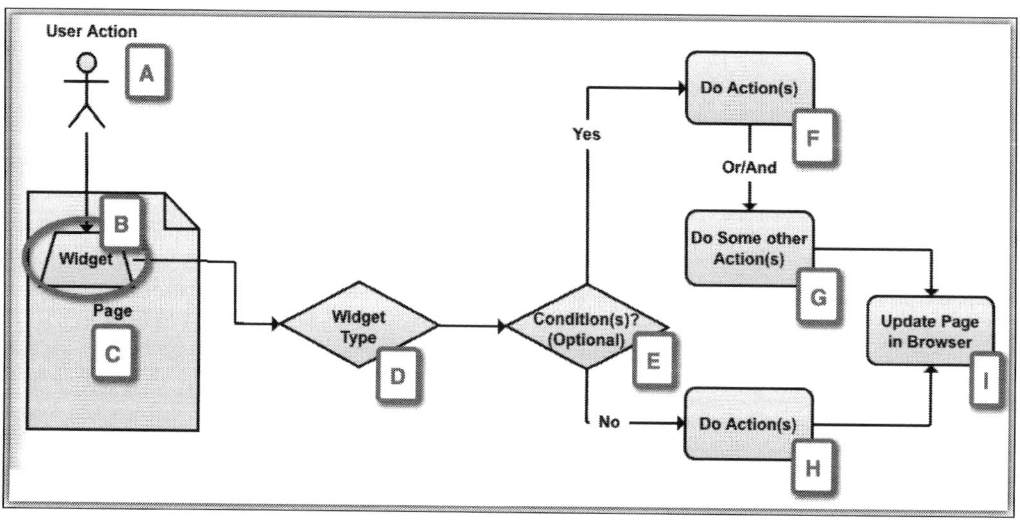

Image 2

The following table lists Axure's inventory of events which can be applied to widgets and dynamic panels. Each widget has its own set of possible actions:

Event names	Dynamic panels	Definition
OnClick		The user clicks on an element.
OnPanelStateChange	X	Dynamic panels may have multiple states and this event can be used to trigger action(s) when a dynamic panel changes states.
OnDragStart	X	This event pinpoints the moment the user begins to drag a dynamic panel.
OnDrag	X	This event spans the duration of the dynamic panel being dragged.
OnDragDrop	X	This event pinpoints the moment the user finished dragging the dynamic panel. This could be an opportunity to validate that, for example, the user placed the widget in the right place.
OnSwipeLeft	X	The event will trigger assigned action(s) when the user swipes from right to left.
OnSwipeRight	X	The event will trigger assigned action(s) when the user swipes from left to right.

Event names	Dynamic panels	Definition
OnSwipeUp	X	The event will trigger assigned action(s) when the user swipes upwards.
OnSwipeDown	X	The event will trigger assigned action(s) when the user swipes downwards.
OnDoubleClick		The event will trigger assigned action(s) when the user double-clicks on an element.
OnContextMenu		The event will trigger assigned action(s) when the user right-clicks on an element.
OnMouseDown		The event will trigger assigned action(s) when the user clicks on the element but has yet to release the mouse button.
OnMouseUp		The event will trigger assigned action(s) on the release of the mouse button.
OnMouseMove		The event will trigger assigned action(s) when the user moves the cursor.
OnMouseEnter		The event will trigger assigned action(s) when the cursor is moved over an element
OnMouseOut		The event will trigger assigned action(s) when the cursor is moved away from an element.
OnMouseHover		The event will trigger assigned action(s) when the cursor is placed over an element. This is great for custom tooltips.
OnLongClick		This is great to use on a touchscreen. Use this when a user clicks on the element and holds it.
OnKeyDown		The event will trigger assigned action(s) as the user presses a key on the keyboard. It can be attached to any widget, but the action is only sent to the widget that has focus.
OnKeyUp		The event will trigger assigned action(s) as the user releases a pressed key on the keyboard.
OnMove		The event will trigger assigned action(s) when the referenced widget moves.
OnShow		The event will trigger assigned action(s) when the visibility state of the referenced widget changes to **Show**.

Event names	Dynamic panels	Definition
OnHide		The event will trigger assigned action(s) when the visibility state of the referenced widget changes to **Show**.
OnScroll	X	The event will trigger assigned action(s) when the user is scrolling. Good to use in conjunction with the Pin to Browser feature.
OnResize	X	The event will trigger assigned action(s) when it detects that referenced panel has been resized.
OnLoad	X	The dynamic panel is initiated when a page is loaded.
OnFocus		The event will trigger assigned action(s) when the widget comes into focus.
OnLostFocus		The event will trigger assigned action(s) when the widget loses focus.
OnSelectionChange		This event is only applicable to drop-down lists and is typically used with a condition: *when selected option of X, show this*. Use this when you want a selection option to trigger action(s) that will change something on the wireframe.
OnCheckedChange		This event is only applicable to radio buttons and textboxes. Use this when you want a selection option to trigger action(s) that will change something on the wireframe.

Axure Cases

You are familiar with cases from modeling and diagraming the user experience. Cases are abstractions of interaction flows the user has with an application. Each case encapsulates a discrete path the user can take. Typically, we are asked to prototype the primary case and often, alternative paths which are either contextual to the user or to some other conditions that may cause the same task to have variable flows. Multiple cases of the same task infer some conditional logic that impacts which path of the task will have to be followed.

Axure cases are a way to build alternate paths for the same task. In all of the examples we constructed so far, we encountered cases as part of the process of creating interaction. However, other than labeling the case in a meaningful way, we had no real use for cases. That is because our interactions so far involved single cases and no conditions were involved. In the Axure vocabulary, the term "Case" references the way to build a single path or multiple paths for each event.

The following *Image 3* diagram illustrates the structure of an Axure **interaction**, and where the **case** fits in:

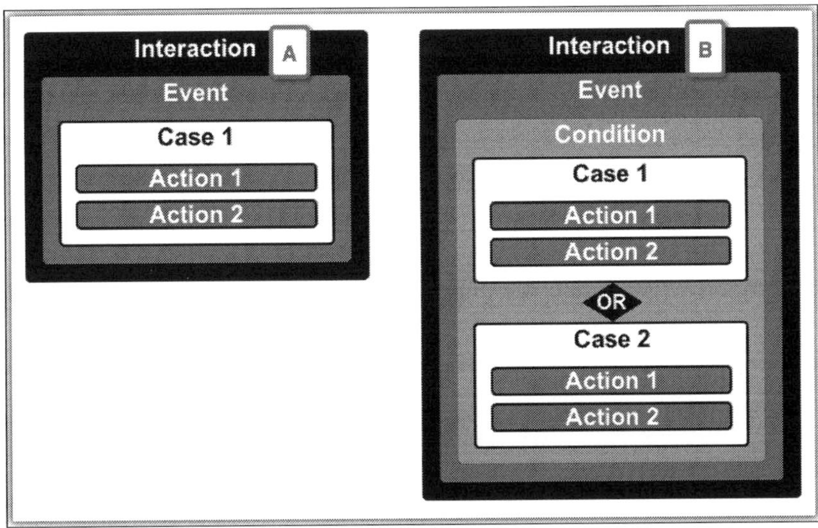

Image 3

Cases are typically used in one of the following two ways, in both page and master OnPageLoad events or in widget events.

- A single case with one or more actions (*Image 3*, **A**) per single interaction event. No conditional logic is involved.
- Multiple cases, each with one or more actions (**B**) per single interaction event. Conditional logic is used or manual selection of the prototype determines the execution of the interaction.

To conclude this topic, an Axure case is basically a container of actions and it is the construct that makes it possible for us to simulate alternate interaction paths. The higher the fidelity of the prototype, the higher the number of multi-case interactions.

Axure Actions

As described above, an Axure **case** is an organizational unit for one or more actions triggered by an **event**. In turn, each case includes a minimum of one **action**. The action is an instruction to the browser to do something. It is Axure's method to shield its users from having to code these instructions.

Axure currently supports the following actions, which are organized into six groups:

- Links
- Widgets
- Dynamic Panels
- Variables
- Repeaters
- Miscellaneous

Variables, raised events, and repeaters actions will be discussed in the *Chapter 5, Advanced Interactions*.

The following table lists all the actions currently available in Axure 7. Their functionality is for the most part self explanatory.

Categories	Sub categories	Actions
Link Actions	Open Links	Current Window
		New Window/Tab
		Popup Window
		Parent Window
Link Actions	-	Close Window
Link Actions	Open Link in Frame	Inline Frame
		Parent Frame
Link Actions	-	Scroll to Widget (Anchor Link)
Widgets Actions	Show/Hide	Show
		Hide
		Toggle Visibility
Widgets Actions	-	Set Text

Categories	Sub categories	Actions
Widgets Actions	-	Set Image
Widgets Actions	Set Selected/Checked	Selected
		Not Selected
		Toggle Selected
Widgets Actions	-	Set Selected List Option
Widgets Actions	Enable/Disable	Enable
		Disable
Widgets Actions	-	Move
Widgets Actions	Bring to Front/Back	Bring to Front
		Send to Back
Widgets Actions	-	Focus
Widgets Actions	Expand/Collapse Tree Node	Expand Tree Node
		Collapse Tree Node
Dynamic Panels	-	Set Panel State
		Set Panel Size
Variables	-	Set Variable Value
Repeaters	-	Add Sort
		Remove Sort
		Add Filter
		Remove Filter
		Set Current Page
		Set Item per Page
Repeaters	Datasets	Datasets
		Add Rows
		Mark Rows
		Unmark Rows
		Update Rows
		Delete Rows
Miscellaneous Actions	-	Wait
		Other
		Raise Event [Applies only to widgets in masters)

Things to Keep in Mind

The following are a few points to remember as you read through the chapter:

- An Axure **interaction** is a container that includes an **event** with a minimum of one **case** and each case has a minimum of one **action**.
- Multiple cases associated with an event provide a way to simulate multiple possible paths of response to that event.
- Remember that just because you can, does not mean you have to. Prioritize the creation of interactions by assessing the value the interaction provides to your ability to accurately communicate the desired experience to stakeholders, developers, and users.
- Focus on primary interaction flows first and then the alternatives. Seriously scrutinize the desire to deal with edge cases. In the end, the more complex the prototype, that more effort is involved in responding to changes.

Widgets, Events, and Context

Each of Axure's built-in widgets can be assigned to an interaction, but no single widget can perform all possible actions. This is a good thing because most user interface widgets have inherent, well-established constraints. For example, a radio button can be selected or deselected, enabled or disabled, and in or out of focus. Therefore, Axure events and widgets are contextual. We feel that the best way to internalize which actions are associated with a widget is to drag each widget to the **Wireframes** pane, and while it is selected, switch to the **Interactions** tab in the **Widgets Interactions and Notes** pane where the possible actions will be visible.

Note that you don't have to create interactions to enable some widgets for interaction. Form input widgets such as text fields, radio buttons, or drop-down lists will respond to the user without any interactions although no follow-up action will take place. For example, the user will be able to type in a text field, but actions such as evaluating the contents of the field or actions once the user exits the field will not happen unless you create the appropriate interactions. Other widgets, such as rectangle or image widgets, without an interaction will appear as part of a static image when the wireframe is rendered in the browser.

Labeling

Labeling is extremely important and necessary when it comes to interactions. Some may think that the newly added **This Widget** feature may remove the best practice to label widgets and dynamic panels, but we believe it to still be important for the following reasons:

- The **This Widget** feature is actually a development coding trick, a useful timesaving shortcut. But while it is a best practice for developers to comment code so that other developers can understand it, Axure, does not have a commenting feature yet and so labeling plays an important role in helping you and colleagues understand the logic set up in the file.
- The **This Widget** option can be used when the interaction is directly created for a selected widget. In this one case, it is possible not to label the widget. However, it is often the case when you want to impact the widget indirectly, as a result of some other event on some other widget, the label becomes invaluable in being able to reference the widget.
- You may have to produce a UI specification for review and a unique identifier will be necessary for meaningful reference and documentation.

The following screenshot shows **This Widget** (*Image 4*, **A**) listed among the list of all widgets in the **Configure actions** column (**B**):

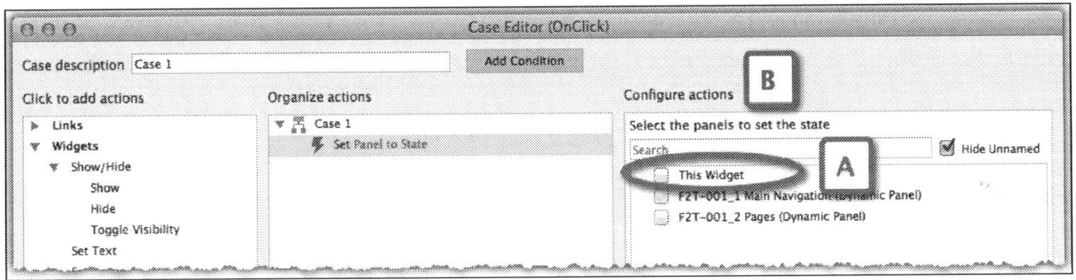

Image 4

The following examples demonstrate how simple interactions can transform an otherwise static slideshow of wireframes into a more engaging prototype. There are many ways to construct the following examples and our focus was on simplicity and utility—something that a novice user could adopt immediately. You can follow the example by taking a quick-and-dirty approach: create a new file and construct the wireframes at a very low fidelity which allows you to create the interaction. Alternatively, use the project demo files for a more elaborate approach.

Example 1 – Controlling Styles

A trivial user experience requirement is that the global navigation object will clearly communicate to the user which page they are on. Our basic objective in this example is that when a page loads, the global navigation bar will change to reflect the selected page. When broken into basics statements, an interaction can be described as follows:

- **When**: A page loads
- **Where**: Global Navigation
- **What**: Reflect which page is presented
- **Condition**: No

What's interesting about this and most requirements is that there are many ways to execute the "What" component. The active tab can be larger, it can have a different color than the other tabs, its label can have a font in bold and different color, and so on. While there are well-accepted UX conventions, creativity and innovation are at the core of what UX designers contribute to the process.

Because the interaction patterns of the application you are designing will be tied to your interpretation of requirements and to the application's visual design style guide, Axure's interactions are much like Lego blocks: you mix and match standard pieces and end up with a unique creation.

The interactions we describe in the example address user **orientation** by making the navigation bar reflect visually which page the user is on:

- Display the **Home** tab in its "selected" state when the page loads.
- Clicking on any of the other navigation tabs will switch the body's dynamic panel to a corresponding state and display the clicked tab on the navigation bar, in its "selected" state.

The **Homepage** (*Image 5*, **A**) body section (**B**) is constructed as a dynamic panel composed of fives states (**C**), each corresponding to an item in the main navigation bar. The navigation bar is not part of the dynamic panel and is positioned above it. With this approach, clicking on any of the buttons on the navigation bar (except the one that is in its selected mode), will trigger a switch to the appropriate state and show the button's selected mode.

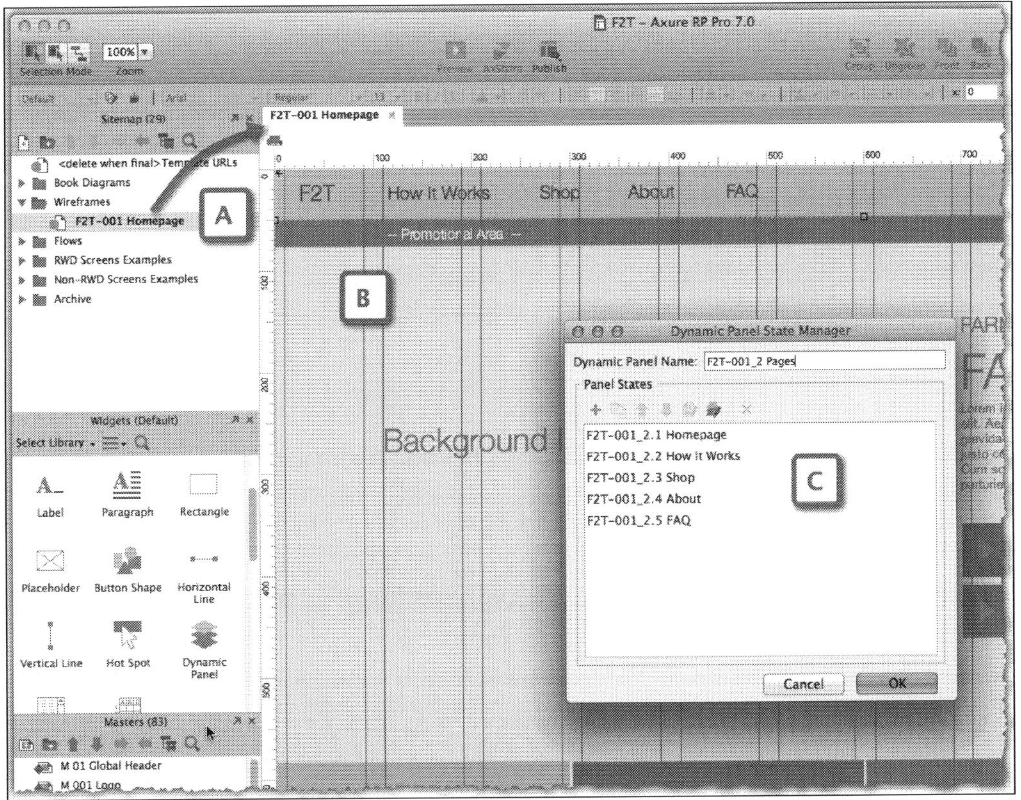

Image 5

Step 1 – Navigation Bar Setup

Start by setting the selected and normal style for these states of your main navigation:

1. Select a widget on the bar in this example, it is **How It Works** (*Image 6*, **A**).
2. In the **Widget Properties and Style**, click on the **Selected** link (**B**).
3. The style editor opens. In this example, the text color different from the widget's default state will indicate its selected state. Check the **Font Color** checkbox and click on its drop-down arrow (**C**).
4. Type in `008D7E`, or select a swatch you like, and click on **OK** to dismiss the window.

5. Repeat for each tab or copy and paste the Home link for each main navigation element and change the text. Make sure to label each one so it is unique.

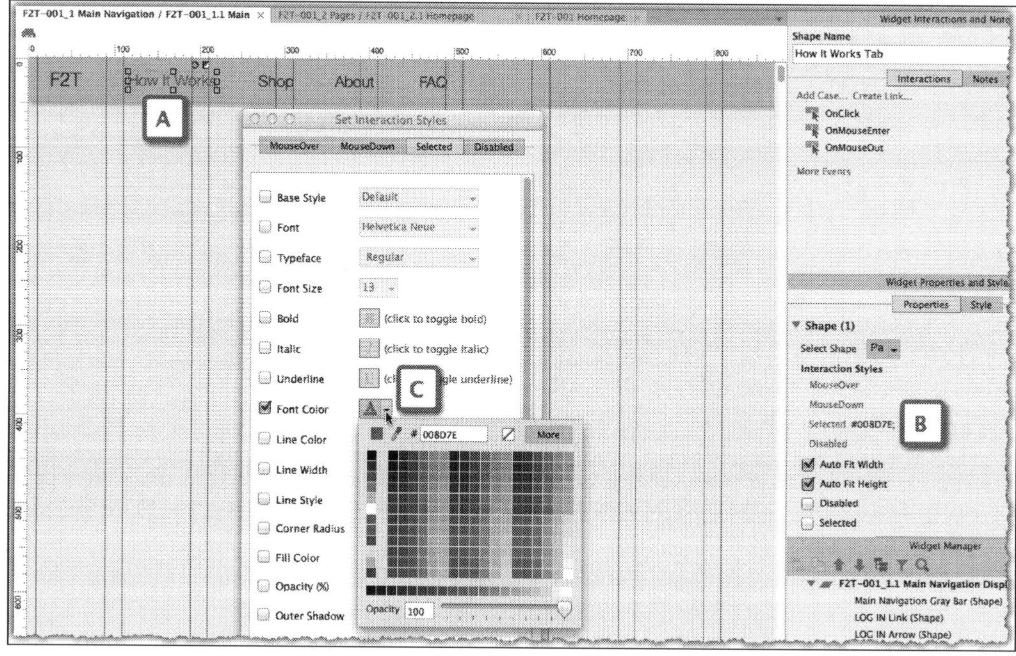

Image 6

Step 2 – Setting the Navigation to Reflect the Current Page

Global navigation should always let the user know which page they are on and which other major destinations on the site are available. The visual style of the selected navigation button is typically the indicator to the page the user is on. Upon clicking another button on the navigation, it assumes the selected style as the content of the page changes. We want to simulate this behavior here. The example is limited to the **Home** and **How It Works** widgets, but the method applies to all.

The interaction should accomplish the following:

1. When the user clicks on the **How It Works** widget:
   - The content of the body section will show the content of **How It Works**
   - Setting the **How It Works** tab to its selected state and visual style

   Therefore, this will be one case that has two actions.

2. In the **Widget Interactions and Notes** panel, click on the **Interactions** tab.
3. Double-click on the **OnClick** event, which will open the **Case Editor** window.
4. In the **Click to add actions** pane, click on **Selected** (*Image 7*, **A**).
5. In the **Configure actions** column, check the **How it Works** tab (**B**).
6. Set the **Home** link's selected state value to **true** (**C**) and all of the other tabs to **false** (**D**).

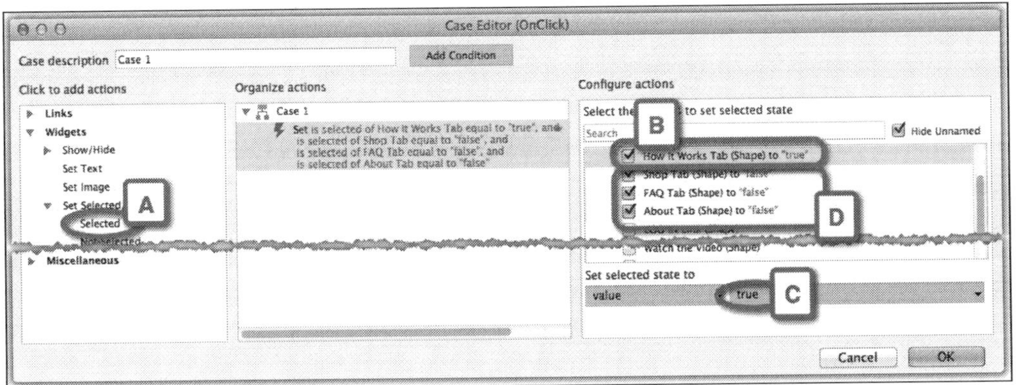

Image 7

Stay in the **Case Editor** window because you have one more action to add—clicking the navigation button should change the content of the body section:

1. In the **Click to add actions** pane, click on **Set Panel State** (*Image 8*, **A**).
2. In the **Configure actions** pane, choose the dynamic panel (**B**).
3. From the drop menu **Select the state** (**C**), choose the relevant state, which in our example is **How It Works** in this example (**D**).

4. Name the case, if you have not done it so far (**E**), and close the **Case Editor** window.

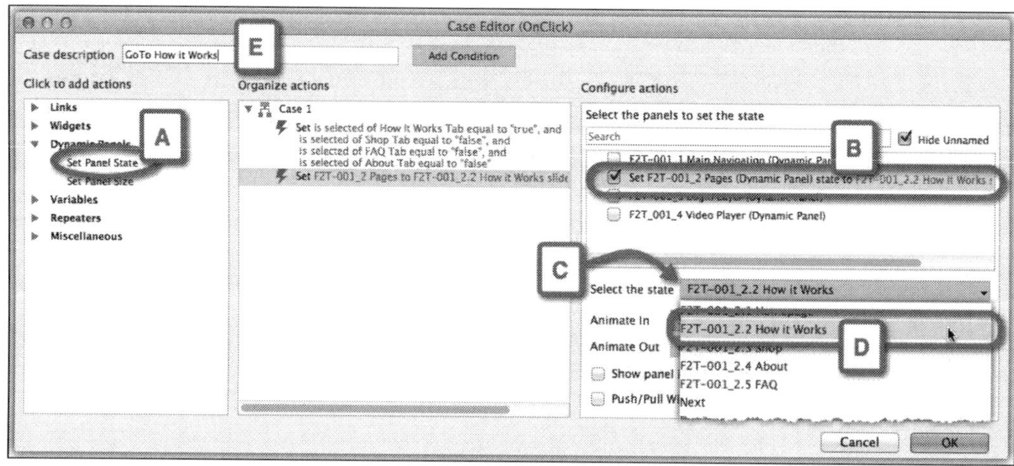

Image 8

Step 3 – Setting the Remaining Tabs

Setting up the other tabs is easy because it is possible to repurpose the case we have created earlier and use it for the other buttons on the navigation bar, with the relevant tweaks, of course. This is where Axure's **Copy Case** feature can be used. With the **How it Works** widget selected in the navigation bar:

1. Hover over the **How it Works** case (*Image 9*, **A**)
2. Right-click and select **Copy** from the context menu (**B**).

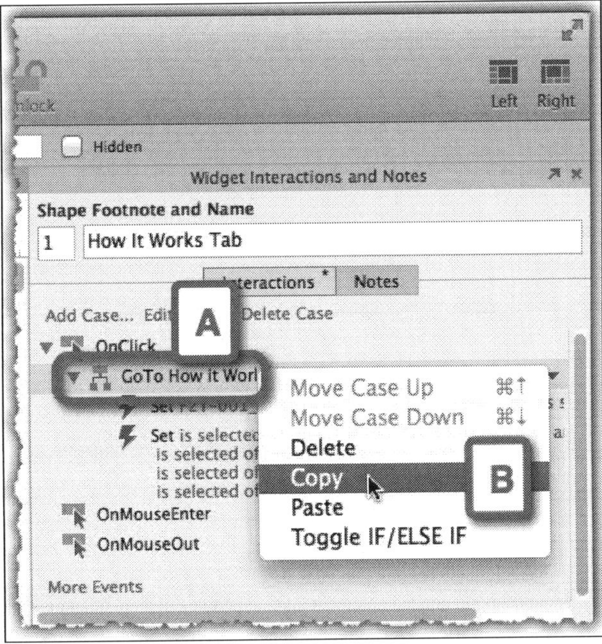

Image 9

3. Click on the **Shop** widget in the navigation bar, so it is active in the **Widget Interactions and Notes** pane (*Image 10*, **A**).
4. Hover over the **OnClick** event (**B**), right-click and choose the **Paste** option (**C**) from the context menu.

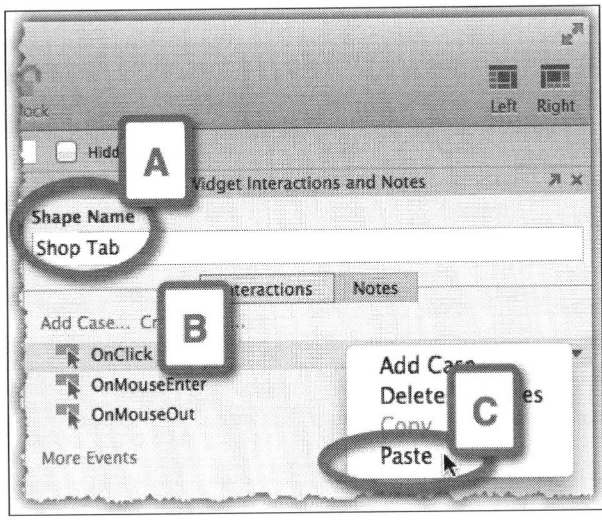

Image 10

To tweak the pasted case so that it now works for the **Shop** tab:

1. Open the **Case Editor** window by clicking on the case.
2. Change value for **Shop** to **true** and **How It Works** to **false** (*Image 11*, **A**).

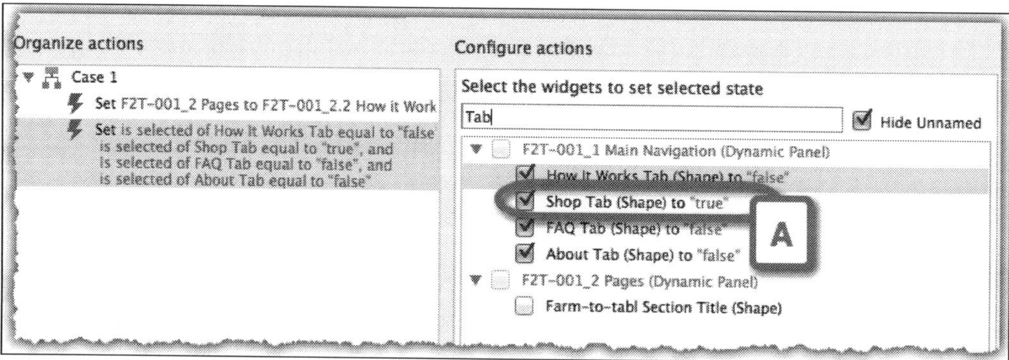

Image 11

Also, modify the target state that will show on the screen when **Shop** is clicked in the navigation bar:

1. Change the value of the **Select the state** drop-down list to **Shop** (*Image 12*, **A**).
2. Close **Case Editor**.

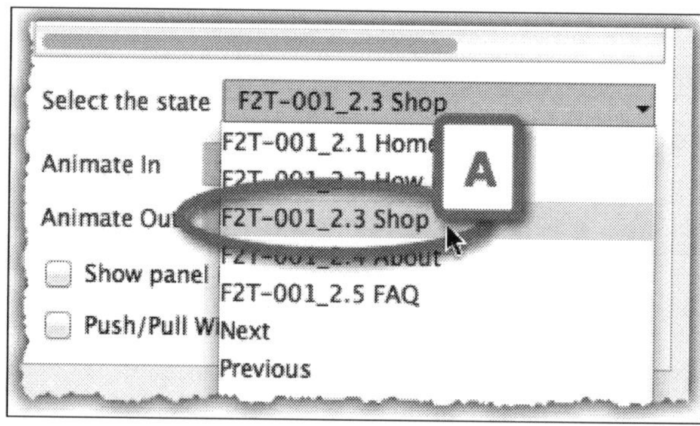

Image 12

Example 2 – Hide and Show

A typical login control includes username and password fields and a few options such as "forgot password?". It is not necessary to display this section on the page at all times. Instead, the section can be invoked by a much smaller element, such as a button, which we will cover in this example.

Construction Strategy

Let's begin with the approach to the construction:

- Position the **LOG IN** widget on the right end of the global navigation bar.
- Design the login section, then convert it to a dynamic panel which is hidden by default. You could later add a state that handles the "forgot password?" option to the dynamic panel.
- Finally, add the interaction on the login button which, when pressed, will make the login section visible.

Step 1 – Assigning Styles to the LOG IN Tab

Click on the **LOG IN** widget and in the **Widget Properties and Style** pane proceed to click on the **Selected** link (*Image 13*, **A**), which will launch the **Set Interaction Styles** window. The following settings should be applied:

1. Set the text to `bold` (**B**).
2. Set the **Font Color** to `#008184` (**C**).
3. Set the **Fill Color** to `#F3F3F3` (**D**).

4. Close the window.

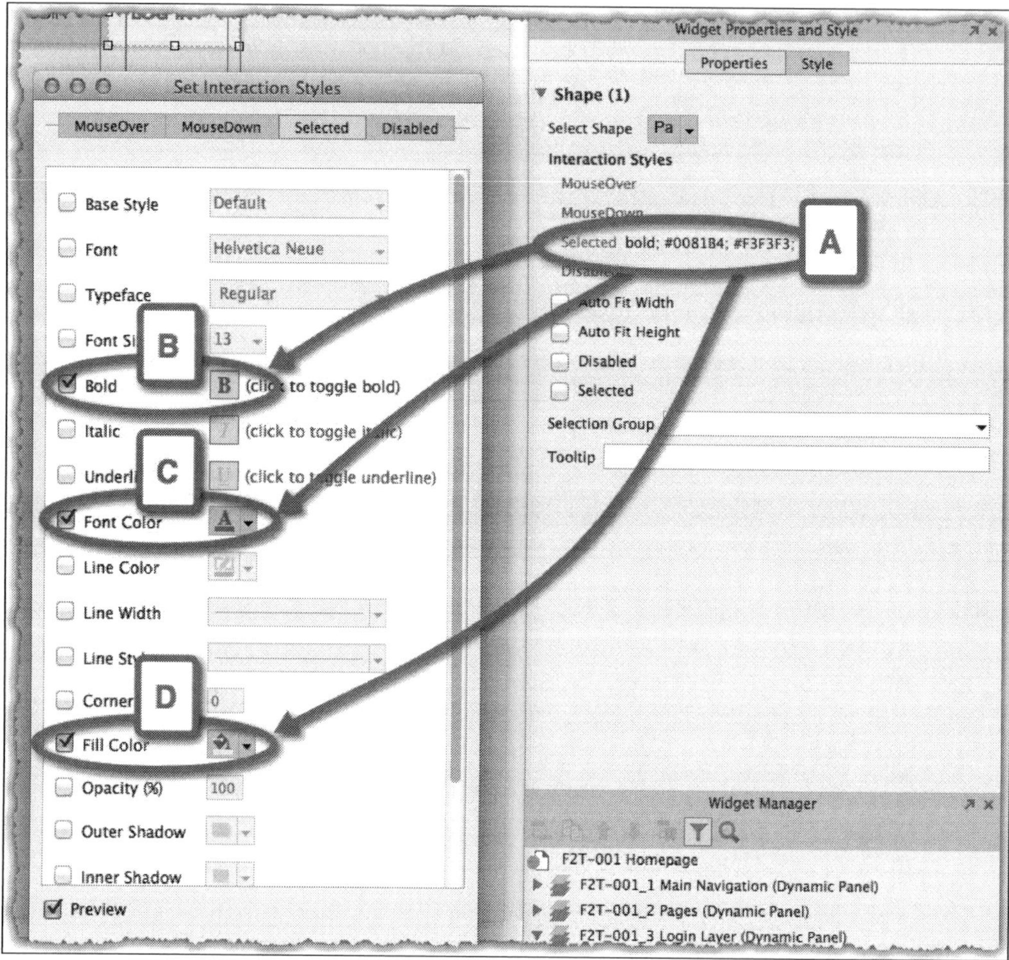

Image 13

Step 2 – Creating the Login Layer

To create the login layer, carry out the following steps:

1. The login section here is a small area which fits the username and password fields and a couple of options. You can work on this on a blank page and later copy the section to the homepage.

2. Once you have it designed, select all the widgets that make up the section (*Image 14*, **A**), right-click on it and choose the **Convert to Dynamic Panel** option (**B**) from the context menu.

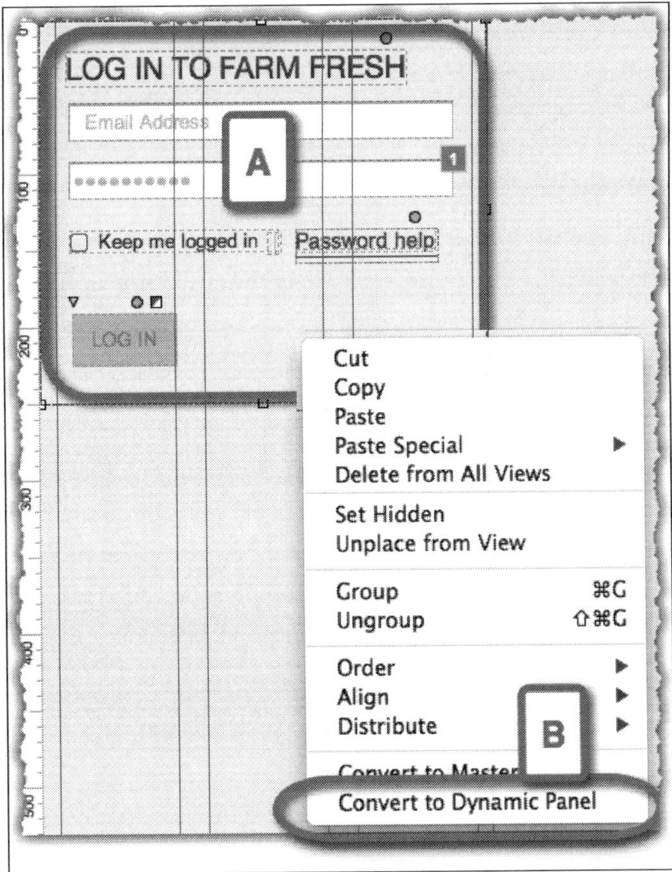

Image 14

3. Name the dynamic panel and its first state.
4. Position the dynamic panel just below the Login widget on the navigation bar.
5. Optionally, add a second state that helps the user reset their password. Typically, an e-mail field, reset password, cancel buttons, and some verbiage are all that's required.
6. Set the dynamic panel to **Hidden**.
7. Optionally, right-click on the panel and from the context menu, click on **Order** and select the **Send to Back** option.

By default, the first state of a dynamic panel is visible, which can make it difficult to assess how other states will appear on the page. Use the **Move Up** button on the **Widget Manager** pane to promote the state you are working on to the top of the state stack. When done, remember to restore the order of layers so that the correct state is on top.

To make sure that the page always loads with the correct state on top, create an **OnPageLoad** interaction using the **Set Panel State** action, specifying the desired state.

Step 3 – Show or Hide the Login Panel

With the widgets in place, we move to create the interactions. In this example, the **LOG IN** button on the navigation bar should operate as a toggle. When the user clicks on it:

- If the panel is hidden, it should become visible
- If it is already visible, it will become hidden

This is a very simple example. Our first step will be to create the logic to show the layer if it is not visible.

1. Click to select the **LOG IN** widget on the navigation bar.
2. In the **Widgets Interactions and Notes** pane's **Interactions** tab, create an **OnClick** event to launch the **Case Editor** window.
3. In the **Click to add actions** column, select the **Toggle Visibility** action (*Image 15*, **A**).
4. Select the **Login** dynamic panel in the **Configure actions** column (**B**).
5. Name the case in the **Case description** field (**C**).

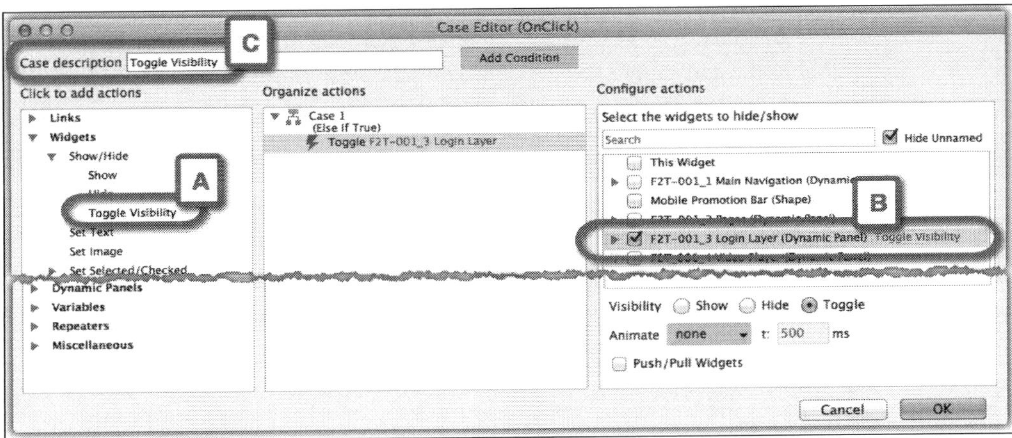

Image 15

Preview and test the interaction by clicking on the **LOGIN** button (*Image 16*, **A**). The panel (**B**) should become visible one the first click, hidden on the next.

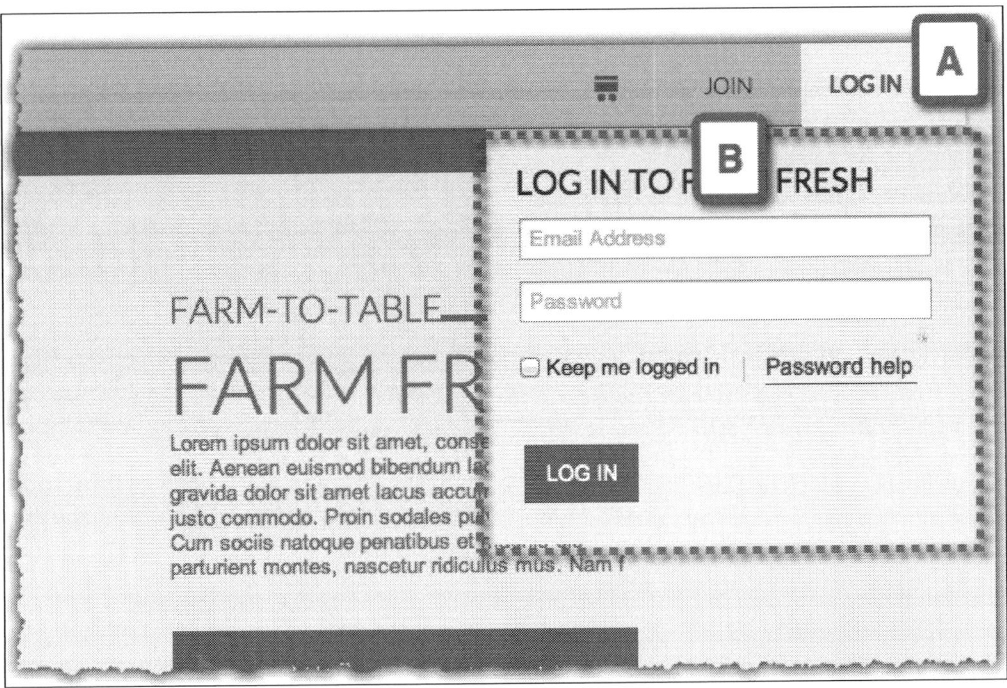

Image 16

Example 3 – Utility Actions

Sometimes we use actions that are not specifically relevant to the prototype but rather to support a more convenient construction. We call these "Utility" actions. In this example, we demonstrate how to apply the **Move** action to a lightbox widget so that we can keep it to the side of the main wireframe and move it to its appropriate location when the HTML prototype is generated. This technique helps de-clutter the working area, especially on busy screens.

Step 1 – the Lightbox Widget

As part of the promotional materials in the Farm2Table project, there is a video lightbox (*Image 17*, **A**) which is triggered when the user clicks on the **WATCH THE VIDEO** button (**B**). While the intent is to display the lightbox horizontally-centered and minimize possible vertical scroll, during construction it is more convenient to keep this large widget on another part of the canvas, so it is not in the way of accessing other widgets. While we could use the **Arrange** feature to send the lightbox to the back and bring it to the front when needed, it can be annoying. So we "park" the lightbox below the main wireframe area, at a vertical position of 1400 pixel on the *y* axis.

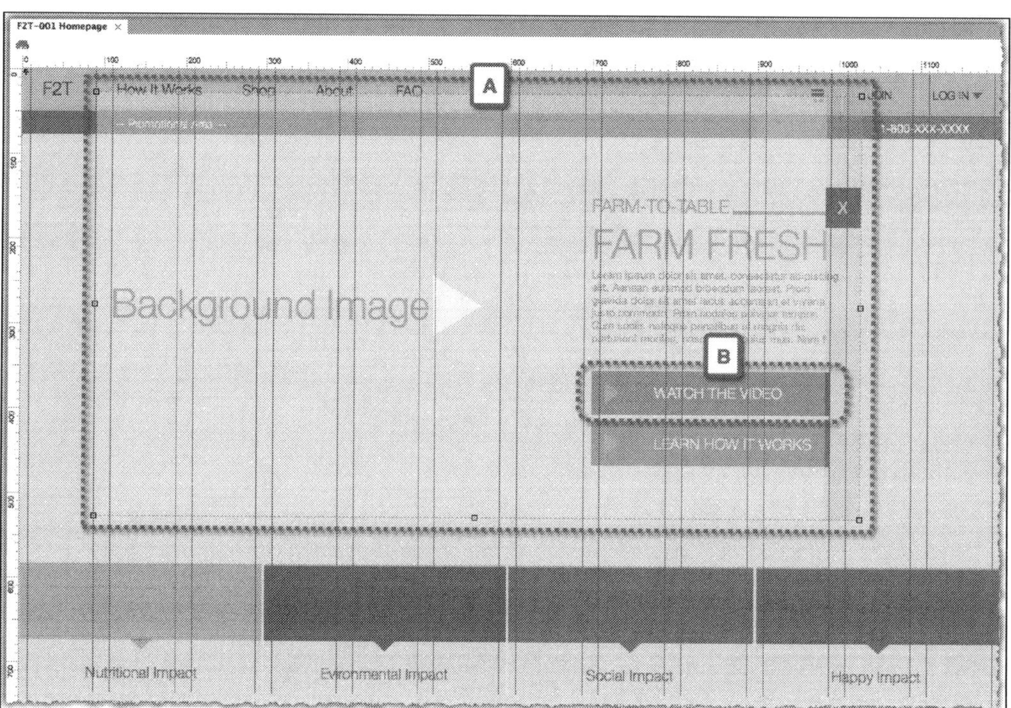

Image 17

The interaction that we plan to build for the **WATCH THE VIDEO** button will thus have to include the **Move** action, which in this case, serves as a mere "utility" action. The actions are as follows:

- Show the lightbox
- Move the lightbox
- Bring to front

Step 2 – Interaction

Click to select the **WATCH THE VIDEO** button and create an **OnClick** event for it. To set the **Show** action:

1. Select the **Show** action in the **Click to add actions** column.
2. Choose the lightbox widget in the **Configure actions** column (*Image 18*, **A**).
3. Set **Visibility** to **Show**.
4. Axure 7 has a new feature that allows you to choose the **treat as lightbox** option (**B**), which automatically grays-out the area outside of the lightbox—a fantastic time-saving enhancement.

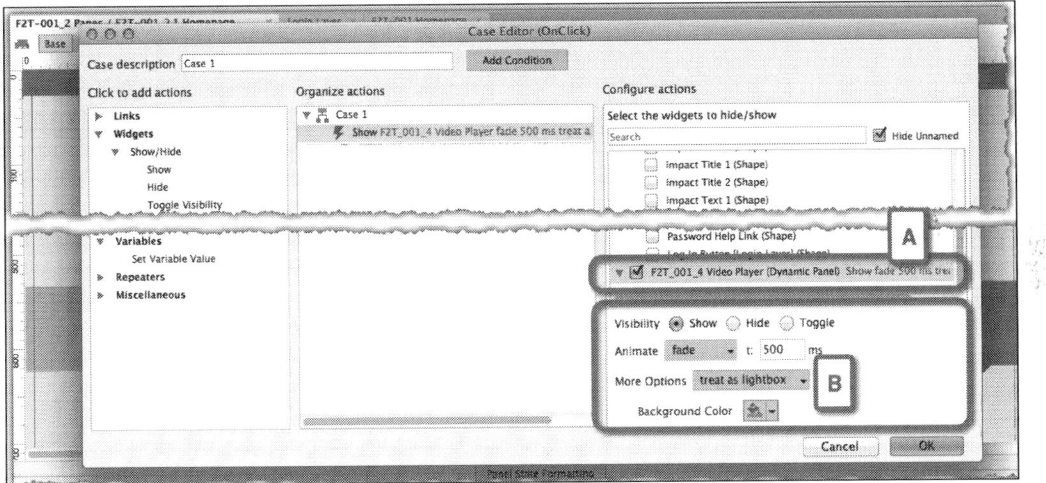

Image 18

Next, we want to reposition the lightbox from its "parking" space in the wireframe to its appropriate place on the screen:

1. Select the **Move** action (*Image 19*, **A**).
2. Choose the lightbox (**B**).
3. In the **Move** option, set the *y* axis to `-1381` (**C**). The minus in front of the value means that the widget will move up.

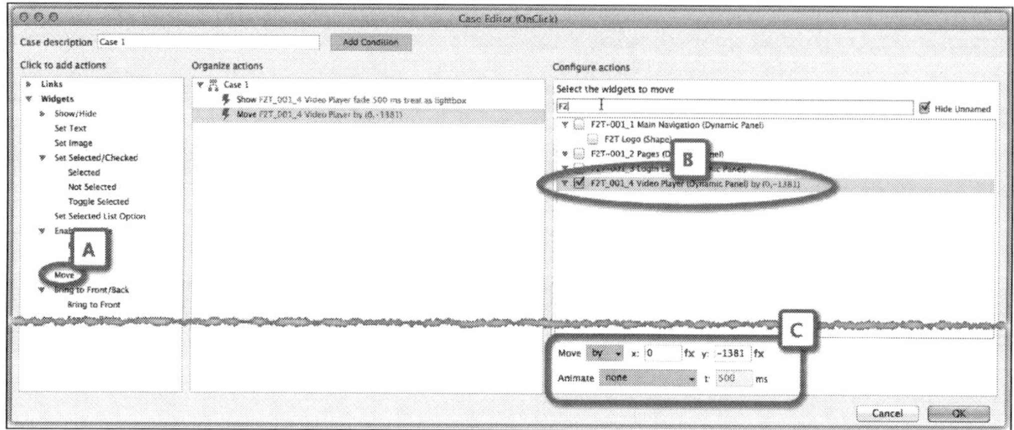

Image 19

Finally, add the action **Bring to Front**, which will ensure that the lightbox is not obscured by some other widget. As an extra credit, devise the reverse interaction that will hide the lightbox, and move it back to its "parking" position on the canvas. The following *Image 20* screenshot shows interaction in action:

Image 20

Summary

In this chapter, we covered the fundamental aspects of Axure interactions. Interactions can be associated with pages, masters, and contextually, with widgets. It is up to you to determine which elements in a prototype should be interactive and to what level of fidelity the interactions should mimic the planned application. As a rule of thumb, focus on your deliverables and on the value that each interaction can provide to make the prototype communicate better your intention for the user experience.

If you are expected to deliver a specifications document, the higher the fidelity and complexity of your interactions, the more difficult it gets to generate a clear and easy-to-digest UI specifications document. Start experimenting very early with the output of your prototype as a Word document. Final words to conclude this chapter—label widget and interaction elements in your wireframes!

In the next chapter, we will cover more advanced aspects of Axure interactions such as conditional logic, variables, raised event, to name a few. Don't let the word "Advanced" scare you off —the investment in learning some of the more intricate aspects of interactions and wireframe constructions will help you create really compelling high-fidelity prototypes.

5
Advanced Interactions

Axure, the company, does a unique balancing act with Axure, the software, on how to reconcile two opposing philosophical and practical approaches to their product, which are as follows:

- A designer-centric approach to rapid, interactive prototyping, which minimizes the need for coding knowledge that many designers lack
- A developer-centric approach that relies heavily on coding

The first approach appeals to an audience that represents a significant part of the UX community: practitioners who flock to Axure precisely because Axure is a tool that provides designers with an invaluable, hands-on opportunity to conceptualize and shape the user experience and an opportunity to create and communicate interactive design without a prerequisite to code HTML, CSS, and JavaScript or through an intermediary front-end developer.

Experience prototypes are multidimensional and temporal, a composition of organization and flow that can only be arrived at by the iterative process of a user-centered design. The closer UX architects and designers are to exploring the user engagement, the better the experience we design. The speed and relative ease with which Axure helps us conceptualize, validate, and iterate the prototype and gain approval is invaluable. Naturally, the fact that Axure offers more capabilities and more sophisticated options sets the bar for what constitutes a high-fidelity simulation. The bar is being raised by front-end developers' coding-responsive HTML prototypes. So, Axure 7 represents the most advanced and powerful UX-centric tool ever made available.

This leads us to the second approach. Implementing advanced features such as support for responsive is not trivial. However, there is a cost associated with the added power because the product becomes more complex. The learning curve necessary to gain expertise gets steeper as proficiency in logic, variables, and function—knowledge that we established earlier, many of us don't possess—becomes a prerequisite to unlock the potential embedded in the new functionality.

In recent years, we have seen the emergence of Axure developers—people with significant coding skills who discovered a niche in the industry—as they can gain all the benefits of Axure by adding their coding skills to harness more advanced features of Axure. However, does this put the majority of UX practitioners in a frustrating bind? Are we moving back to a time where we did not have direct control over our design because we had to hand it over to a developer?
The answer is a categorical *no*.

Don't let the word "advanced" scare you away from this chapter! We will cover a set of features such as raised events, conditional logic, and variables. We will also introduce terminology associated with programming and suggest complexity. It is understandable if you are not interested in, or are intimidated by the prospect of coding and wish to avoid using this set of Axure features as long as possible; however, you should not!

First, it is possible to create sophisticated prototypes without coding in Axure 7. By now, you are familiar with Axure's interactions and the Case Editor features, which require you to only select from a contextual selection of options and construct interaction simply by pointing and clicking and thus the only typing required is labeling. You will find a similar, easy-to-use interface when you use a feature such as the condition builder or when you simulate drag-and-drop interactions.

Secondly, consider some of the terminologies and methods we use in interaction design. For example, we use algorithms, pseudo code, and branching logic to determine use cases, scenarios, and how functionality responds to user interaction under certain conditions. Axure makes it fairly easy to model the logic we need in order to visualize branching paths in the interactive prototype.

Finally, not only will you maximize your investment in Axure, you will also enhance your own professional skills and have an opportunity to express your creativity. Similar to languages, the greater your vocabulary, the more expressive and persuasive your communication. It is the same with professional tools; like any professional tool, Axure, more than anything else, is an enabler for your creativity.

Conditions

When you incorporate conditional logic into your prototype, you save yourself from a great deal of overhead work because you can reuse patterns in multiple ways as you simulate conditional interactions and the branching of flows.

Let's face it. We use logic all the time, even if the results are not always logical, and in computer science and interaction design, conditional logic is necessary to accommodate a variety of business rules, situations, and exceptions. Yet, there still appears to be a general reluctance when it comes to dealing with direct use of logic among non-programmers who use software. A good example of this is the so-called *advanced* search feature that is common to library catalogs and most of the search engines, including Google, as shown in the following screenshot (*Image 1*, **A**):

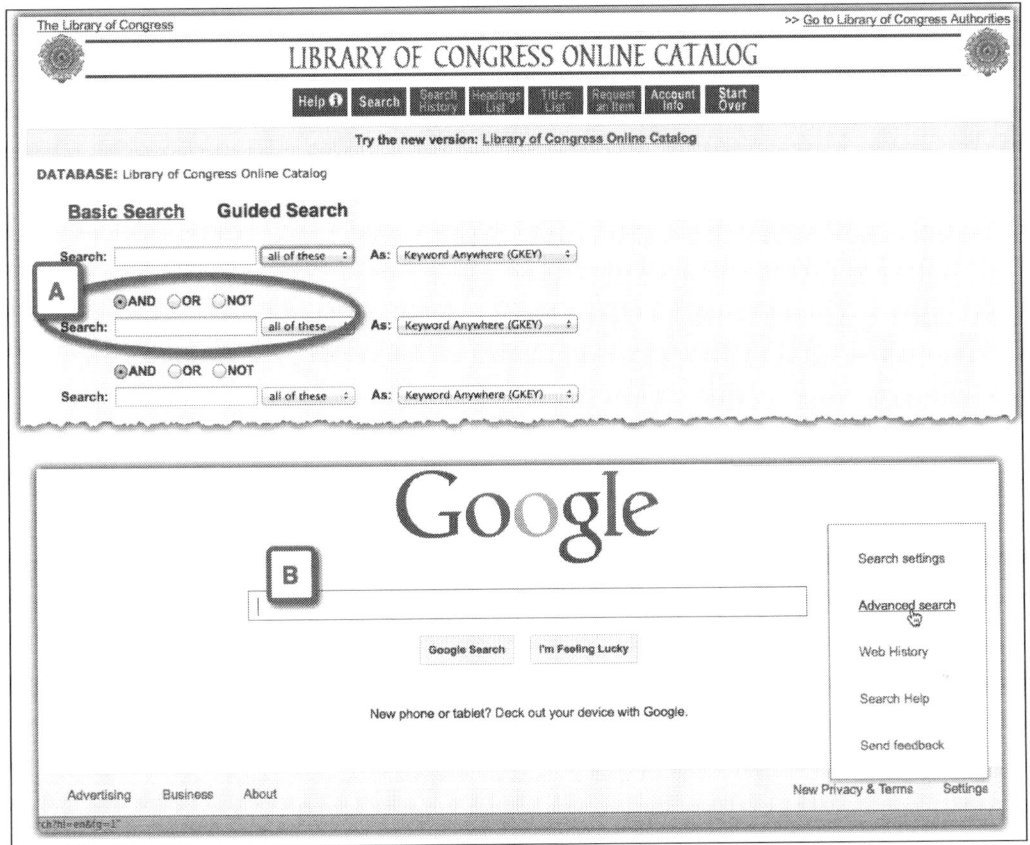

Image 1

When was the last time you actually used the advanced search, if ever? Google's concept of a single search field and no operators (**B**) was revolutionary and daring in the early 2000s. Since then, it has become the standard search interface, much to the surprise of librarians and other information workers who "owned" the space of search back in the day. However, these people were trained, experienced, and comfortable with structuring search queries, which are essentially logical statements with operators where a true evaluation typically results in a found set.

IF-THEN-ELSE

About 2,300 years ago, in ancient Greece, Aristotle invented logic, a formal discipline of abstract reasoning, which enabled the digital world we live in today. Among other features, logic makes it possible to form statements that can be evaluated to be TRUE or FALSE. Based on this evaluation, the exact path of an action can be determined with minimal details.

A Basic Set

The following logic table shows an example that relates to the Farm2Table project:

Evaluation	Statement A	Statement B	Statement C
IF condition	The user has a premium subscription.	The user has a regular subscription.	The user has no subscription.
If this condition is true, do this action	The user can make a weekly order of produce, grown by farms in the cooperative.	The user can order from a single farm in the cooperative.	The user cannot order anything.
ELSE (if this condition is not true)	Evaluate the next statement.	Evaluate the next statement.	If the statements A and B are FALSE, then the statement C must be TRUE.

Notice the following aspects:

- The subject of the preceding statements is the user.
- We don't need to know anything about the user other than whether they have a subscription and if they do, what type of subscription.
- We don't need to know anything about the farms involved, where they are, the content of the weekly order, and so on.
- At any given moment the evaluation is performed, only one of the statements can be evaluated to be TRUE.
- The word ELSE connects the IF statements and provides an automation rule for decision-making. If a statement is FALSE, move to the next one until you get to a TRUE statement and the evaluation stops.

- The word ELSE connects the statements that help us define the relationships between a subscription level and benefits associated with it.
- One of the statements must be TRUE.

We can generalize the specific example from the preceding table as the generalized abstraction:

IF the condition A associated with k and m is met (it is evaluated to TRUE)
THEN do X (and stop)

ELSE

IF the condition B associated with k and m is met
THEN do Y (and stop)

ELSE

IF the condition C associated with k and m is met
THEN do Z (end of the statement set)

The following table groups the ingredients of the preceding abstraction:

Conditions	Entities	Actions
Condition A = the user has a premium subscription	k = user	X = allow the user to order from any farm
Condition B = the user has a regular subscription	m = subscription	Y= allow the user to order from one farm
Condition C = the user has no subscription		Z = don't allow the user to order from any farm

The IF-THEN-ELSE statement is the most common logic device utilized throughout the process of design to help capture the impact of various rules on the behavior and interaction patterns of system and user. In the prototype construction phase, while adding interactions to static wireframes, think of it as the strings you pull to make a puppet move according to a script.

How Statements Relate to Each Other

In the previous example, there is a strong correlation between the entities in the statement set and the rules that guide the system towards the correct interaction. The following logic table shows another such example:

Evaluations	Statement A	Statement B	Statement C
IF condition	The user has a premium subscription.	An item in the user's weekly box becomes unavailable.	All the ingredients for a recipe are offered in the weekly calendar.
If condition is TRUE, THEN	The user can order the weekly produce from multiple farms in the cooperative.	The farm will substitute that item.	All the ingredients for a recipe are offered in the weekly calendar.
ELSE (If the condition is not TRUE)	Evaluate the next statement.	Evaluate the next statement.	If the statements A and B are FALSE, then the statement C must be TRUE.

While the individual statements that make up the entire preceding set can be evaluated as TRUE or FALSE, they are not related to each other and consequently it is difficult to see the logical thread that binds this to some consistent cause-and-effect pattern of interaction. When troubleshooting the IF-THEN-ELSE logic statements, make sure that it is possible to follow the set of statements to a meaningful actionable pattern.

AND and OR

One last topic before we move to Axure is that statements are connected with the logical operators, AND and OR. These are used to connect two or more sentences to create meaningful compound statements. A compound statement is used when multiple situations need to be evaluated in order to determine which action to take. To understand better, see the following logic table:

IF	AND (IF)	AND (IF)	AND (IF)	THEN
An item in the user's weekly box becomes unavailable.	The user has a standard subscription.	The user has set up a substitution list.	A substitute item is available at the user's home farm.	The farm will substitute the item with the substitute.

In the previous example, the word AND is used to connect the set of statements such that for a specific action to take place, all of the statements must evaluate to TRUE or Yes.

As you can see, conditions can quickly become complex, but the nature of business rules is often complex and multiple issues need to be looked at in order to determine the appropriate course of action.

The following table organizes the same set of rules, but they are stated in a different manner:

IF	OR (IF)	OR (IF)	OR (IF)	THEN
An item in the user's weekly box becomes unavailable.	The user has a standard subscription.	The user has set up a substitution list.	A substitute item is available at the user's home farm.	The farm will substitute the unavailable item with the substitute.

The result here will be very different. All of the statements in the first set need to be TRUE for the farm to send a substitute, whereas only one of the three statements, no matter which one, needs to be TRUE for the farm to take the same action.

This kind of decision-making is actually very natural to UX designers because we use a similar logic approach to model task and interaction flows based on business rules and other factors. When we create a conditional interaction, we reflect the flow's logic in the prototype.

Write it down first

If you need to use logic but you don't have much experience with the syntax or the prototype needs to respond to a complex set of rules, it is a good idea to first write down the logic on paper and make sure you are getting the correct outcome as you read the conditions.

Sandbox Files for Learning and Experimenting

Often, the most effective way to figure things out is by experimentation. In the course of prototyping, you will find yourself wondering how some Axure feature works or wanting to explore a new interaction. This is where the sandboxing technique can help, which is as follows:

- Create a new/blank Axure file on your desktop, work through your explorations on this file, and then apply your learning to the project file. In the sandbox file, you don't have to worry about breaking any of your previous work and can instead focus only on the mechanics of the feature you are trying to figure out. The technique will also keep your production file size small and free of experimentation wireframes.
- Alternatively, if you want to use specific elements from a **Team Project** file, export it to a standard RP format and explore locally on that copy.

Guided Example – Conditions

As you will see in the example, Axure makes it very easy to apply conditional logic to a prototype. We will use a sandbox file to explore the feature and then apply the learning to the `Farm2Table` project file.

The following diagram shows the typical flow for a successful approach to deal with conditions and interactivity:

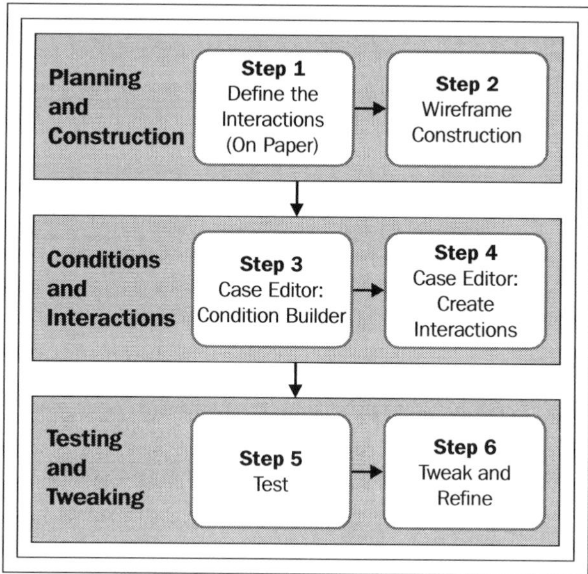

Image 2

Step 1 – Defining the Interaction

This example simulates a common e-commerce pattern of a product details screen. The user can choose from a list of properties, in this case, the color and size of a t-shirt. Typically, there is a dependency between the selections the user makes such as when a desired color is out of stock in a needed size.

This is the perfect opportunity to use Axure's conditional logic features. As we established in *Chapter 4, Creating Basic Interactions*, the first step is to define the desired interaction. Now that conditional logic is involved, it is important to spell out the logic of the interaction you want to create:

- **When**: When the user changes the color selection of a t-shirt.
- **Where**: The **Color** drop-down list widget.
- **What**: Change the state of the image dynamic panel, the text on the product header, and the values in the **Size** drop-down list.
- **Conditions**: When the page loads, the product name will be **Green T-Shirt**, the image will be of the green t-shirt, and the value of the **Color** drop-down list will be **Green**. The default value for the **Size** drop-down list will be **Select** and all the size options will be available.

  When the user selects the value in the **Color** drop-down list, they can do one of the following:

  - Change the state of the image dynamic panel and show the shirt of the selected color.
  - Change the values in the **Size** drop-down list to simulate that some sizes are not available.
  - Change the product name in the header to reflect the selected color.

The last point of the preceding bullet list specifies the **default state** of the page, that is, default values when the page loads. When you plan interactions that involve conditions, always make sure to establish the default state as the starting condition.

Step 2 – Wireframe Construction

The new Preview feature of Axure 7 is awesome in that it affords us an instant way to evaluate the looks and interactions on a page. However, it is also a good idea to prepare a sandbox in case you need to have multiple pages and generate a quick sample.

Create a blank directory on your desktop and label it `Axure Sandbox`. Create a new Axure file, label it `If-Then-Sandbox`, and save it in the `Axure Sandbox` directory.

Next, create a wireframe with the necessary widgets. While the sample file we created is slightly more involved because we used photos of colored shirts, sandbox files should be quick-and-dirty affairs where plain-colored rectangles could easily substitute fancy photos. Your wireframe should include the following widgets:

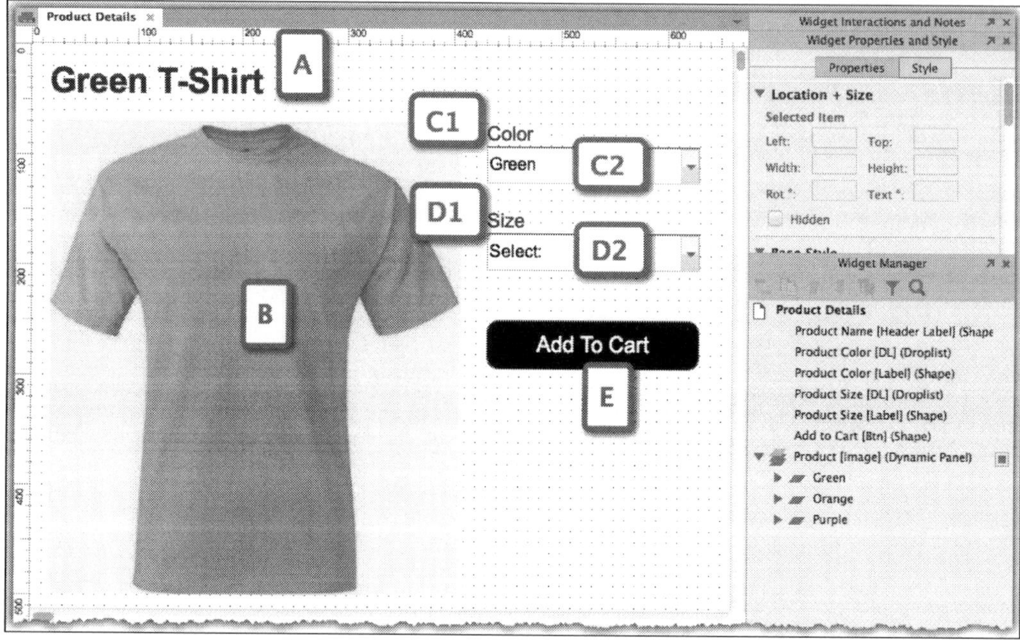

Image 3

- The product name label (*Image 3*, **A**); optional for your own sandbox
- A dynamic panel with three states (**B**), each with an image rectangle widget of the corresponding color— green, orange, and purple
- The **Color** drop-down list (**C2**) and its label (**C1**)
- The **Size** drop-down list (**D2**) and its label (**D1**)
- The **Add to Cart** button (E)

Step 3 – Setting the First Condition

When you start with interactions, having the flow preplanned helps in both creating the wireframe and adding the interaction. Now that we've covered both of them in *Step 1 – Defining the Interaction* and *Step 2 – Wireframe Construction*, let's set the conditional logic for the interaction to be as follows:

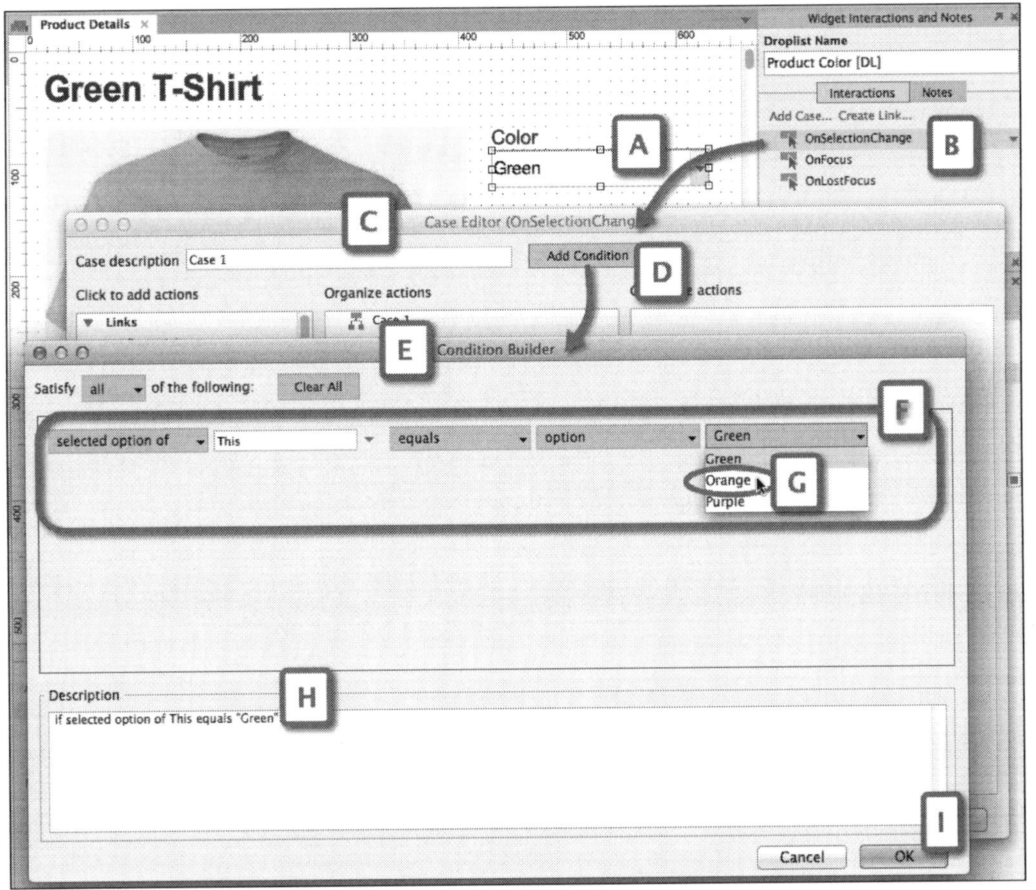

Image 4

1. Click on the **Color** drop-down list widget to select it (*Image 4*, **A**) and then double-click on the **OnSelectionChange** (**B**) in the **Interactions** tab.
2. In the **Case Editor** window (**C**) that pops up, click on the **Add Condition** button (**D**).
3. In the **Condition Builder** dialog that appears (**E**), create a condition that responds to the selected value in the drop-down list. The condition row (**F**) is repeated in as a plain language sentence in the description section (**K**).
4. In our example, the condition checks whether the value of the drop-down list equals "Orange" (**G**).

When done setting the first row, click on the **OK** button (**I**) to close the dialog.

When you create conditions, always make sure to account for all the possible cases that are applicable to the interaction.

Step 4 – Adding an Interaction to the Condition

Next, create the action that is triggered when the condition is met. In the initial case, when the value of the drop-down list is **Green**, various widgets on the screen, such as the image of the t-shirt, reflect that selection. Now, you might ask yourself, "the screen already reflects the green choice, why check for it?"

This is because, once the user selects a value from the **Color** drop-down list that is different from the default value **Green**, the widget will change to reflect that new choice. At that point, the user should be able to select the **Green** value again, which is why we provide the condition and actions to show how to update the screen to the **Green** choice. This is illustrated as follows:

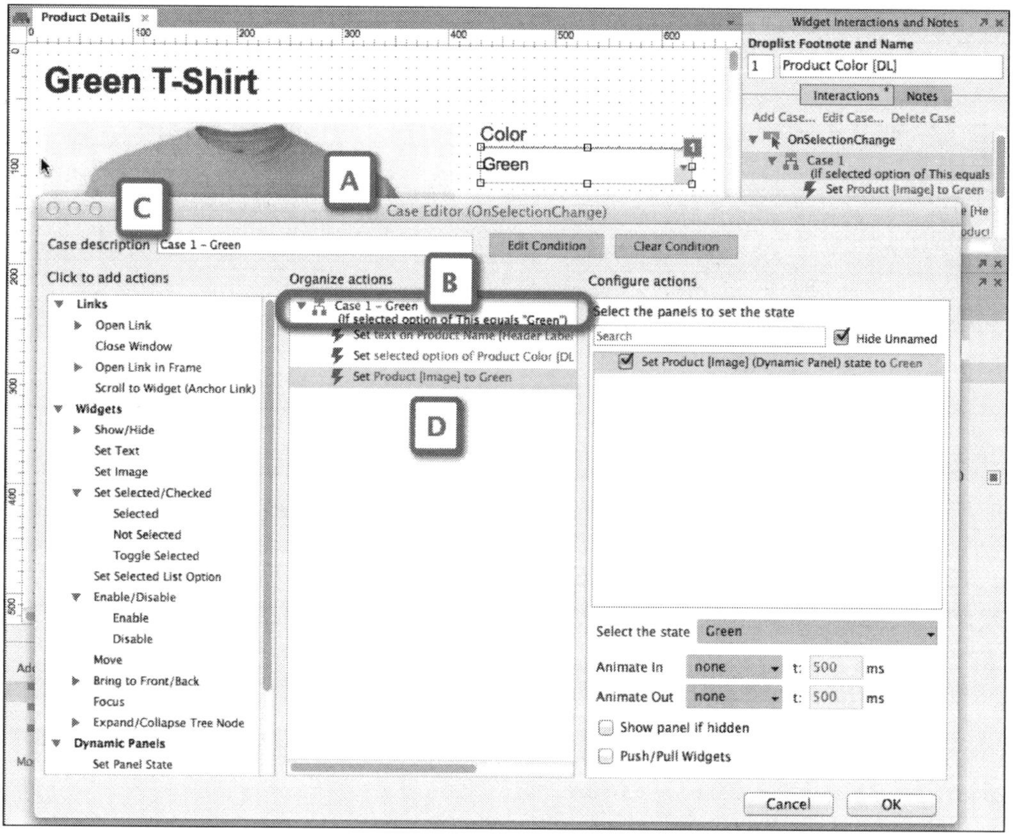

Image 5

In the **Case Editor** window (*Image 5*, **A**), the first condition you just created appears in the **Organize actions** column (**B**).

We recommend that you make a habit of labeling your cases (**C**). It takes less than five seconds and is a good investment.

Now, configure the actions **Set Text**, **Set Panel State**, and **Set Selected List Option** to reflect the **Green** selection (**D**).

However, there is no action that can take care of changing the values of the **Size** drop-down list!

It is common to start work on conditional interactions and find that the wireframe needs more work. Over time, and with experience, you will forecast such needs early.

Click on **OK** to close the **Case Editor** window. Convert the **Size** drop-down list into a dynamic panel, duplicate and re-label the states, and change the values in each drop-down list to simulate that not all sizes are available in orange and purple.

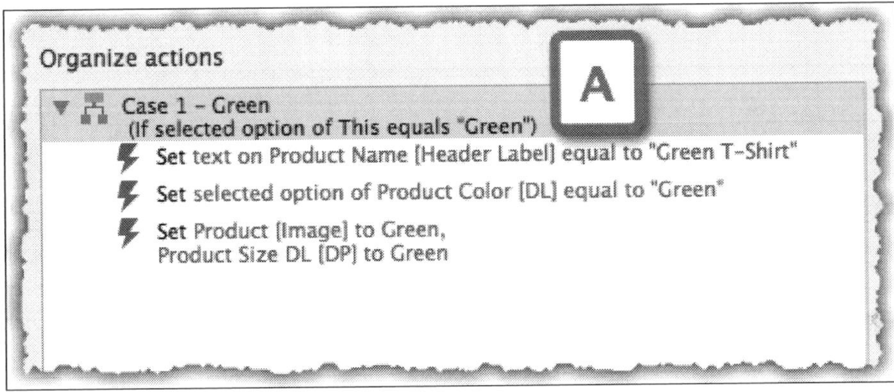

Image 6

With the tweak to the **Size** drop-down list done, return to the **Case 1 - Green** case (*Image 6*, **A**) and add it to the **Set Panel State** action.

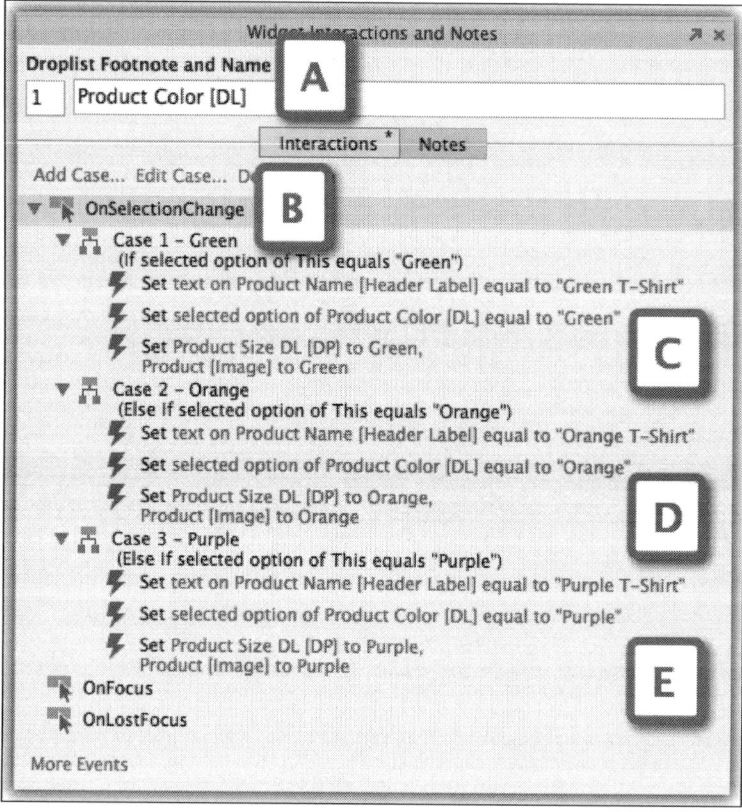

Image 7

Copy and paste to duplicate and modify the action and the condition.

Note about testing

Typically, you want to test an interaction before duplicating it. In this example, however, as the first condition-interaction pair is the default state, testing will not work until you add at least another case.

The completed conditional set for the **Color** drop-down list (*Image 7*, **A**) should have three cases (**C**, **D**, and **E**) attached to the **OnSelectionChange** interaction (**B**).

> **Label widgets, interactions, and cases**
>
> When you review the sample Axure file, notice that all relevant widgets, cases, and conditions were labeled. You may have created your own sample file without bothering to label and probably noticed that it can become tricky to identify the correct widgets you want to control. Labeling is a chore, but it is a minor one relative to the value gained from a clear, well-identified file.

Step 5 – Testing the Interaction

At this point the construction should be complete, but it must be tested to verify that the interaction works as intended:

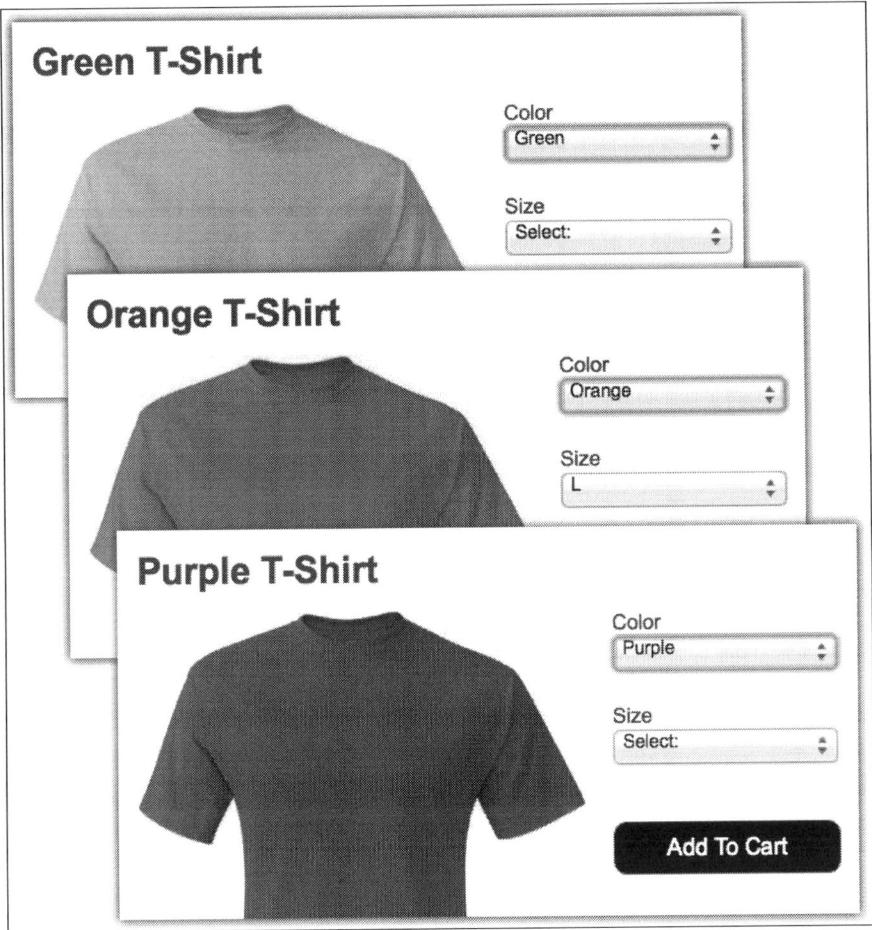

Image 8

Generate the HTML prototype or use the Preview feature. As you switch from one color t-shirt to another, the header label, image, and size selections should change as planned (as shown in *Image 8*).

There are chances that while changing the value in the **Color** drop-down list, the details do not change at all or the wrong information is displayed.

Troubleshooting of such problems can be done as follows:

- The actual interaction logic in this example is quite simple, so the culprit is highly likely to be attributed to a copy-and-paste issue, such as values not changed correctly.

Step 6 – Tweak and Iterate

Once the basic conditional interactions are functioning as planned, it is tempting to enhance the fidelity of the prototype. For example, disabling the **Add to Cart** button until the user selects a shirt size. Generally, breaking the construction of interactions into autonomic units makes the entire process more efficient and troubleshooting becomes easier.

The Condition Builder in Detail

This is where the brain of our prototype lives. Each condition occupies a row in the builder. Many of the columns in the condition are composed of contextual drop-down lists, which make it easy to pick the appropriate value needed for the task. This is essentially a combinatorial system with nearly endless possibilities to control an interaction. In this section, we will take a deep dive into the builder.

Each condition row is composed of five drop-down lists that form an equation in which we compare the first two drop-down lists to the last two drop-down lists. The following screenshot illustrates how the segments are assembled in the builder:

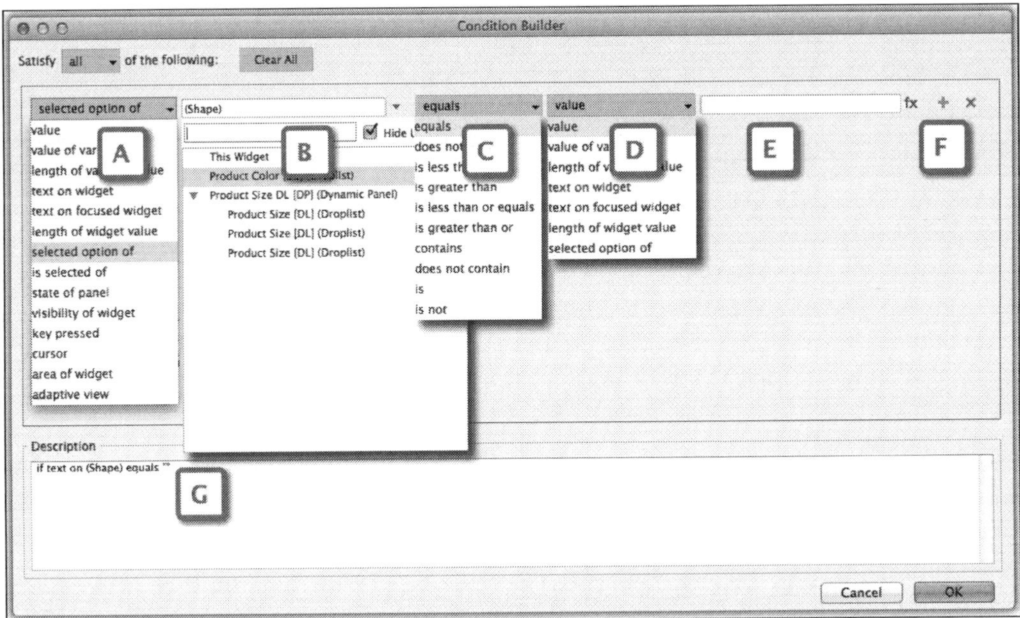

Image 9

The following table provides the breakdown of each field in the condition builder with reference to the preceding screenshot:

A	B	C	D	E	F and G
selected option of is one of the fourteen choices in this drop-down list. The selection made here impacts the other drop-down lists.	The choice in the first drop-down list narrows the options of this drop-down list to droplists and listbox widgets.	The third drop-down list is where we determine how to evaluate choices in the first two drop-down lists (that is, **A** and **B**) to choices in the next two drop-down lists (that is, **D** and **E**). In addition to the **equals** option, there are nine more options to construct the evaluation.	In the fourth drop-down list, we specify what type of value is being evaluated.	The last drop-down list is contextual to the selection we make in the previous drop-down list (that is, **D**).	Add new conditional rows or remove existing rows using the controls at the end of each row (**F**). The **Description** section (**G**) is automatically generated by Axure to reiterate the condition in plain text.

Guided Example – Higher Fidelity with Multiple Conditions

Actual applications often evaluate multiple conditions against business rules before determining which action to take, for example, contextual rendering of a screen based on the user login and other parameters. The **Condition Builder** window is a significant time saver because with relatively few wireframes, mostly variations within dynamic panel states, it is possible to create multiple conditions and simulate sophisticated interactions.

As mentioned throughout this book, doing something just because it is possible is nice, but a better approach is to limit the more complex parts of the prototype to agreed-upon flows. The prototype cannot simulate the entire product, and so the effort should focus on types of interaction that you want to validate in usability testing.

Step 1 – Define the Interaction and Desired Fidelity

The following figure shows subscription flow that defines a single condition evaluation:

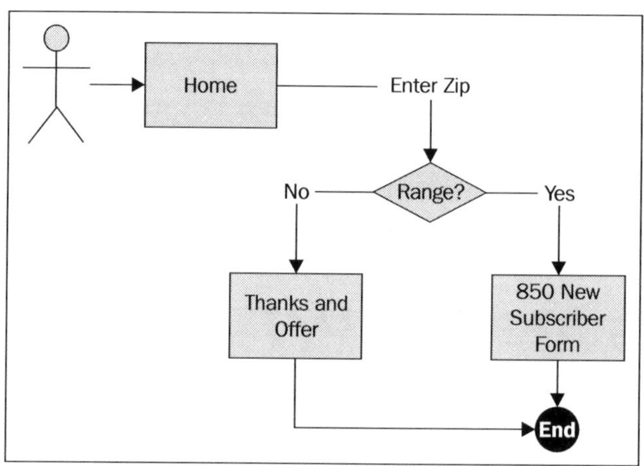

Image 10

If the visitor's zip code is within the range of service, move on to a subscription form. Otherwise, thank the visitor and let them know whether and when the service will become available in their area. Also, provide the user with an opportunity to provide an e-mail address for a notification when the service is available in their area.

We will start the prototype with this basic level and advance from there.

From Low to High

The iteration process is evolutionary, and we do not expect the design to dramatically change in each iteration. Rather, foundations and principles established early provide the necessary structural support. Things that don't work, however, should be reevaluated and dropped, if needed. The following image gives a tongue-in-cheek illustration of the iterative process:

Image 11

The simplest and crudest prototype will have a zip code field that accepts any type of input and any number of characters, which means that no validation of any sort will be performed. The **Submit** button is always active and links to the next step even if the zip code field is empty. This is essentially a static wireframe.

From there, prototypes get more and more advanced in simulating an experience that is governed by business rules and the interaction quality we design for it.

For starters, we have a couple of choices, which are as follows:

- The user enters the zip string and clicks on the **Join** button. The string will be evaluated then, and if it is an invalid entry, the user will be messaged to reenter the zip string.
- As the user types in the zip, we only evaluate an input of 5 digits. Why 5 digits? Because this is the basic zipcode standard in the USA. In this case, a message is displayed if the zip is not a digit and is hidden when the typo is fixed. The **Join** button only becomes active when all five digits have been typed.

In this example, we will use the **Condition Builder** window to create the second option and the first step is to define the desired interaction. As with all interactions that involve the conditional logic, this is the opportunity to spell out the logic:

- **When**: When the user inputs the zip code
- **Where**: In the **Zip Code** field
- **What**: Validate the zip code while typing. Alert the user if there is an issue or switch the user to the new account page
- **Conditions**: On entry, the **Zip Code** field is empty and the **Join** button is disabled

The following table is an aid that helps organize and group conditions according to triggers that fire their evaluation:

#	Evaluated condition(s)	Action(s)	Evaluation trigger
1	If the user types in a non-numeric character.	The **Join** button remains disabled and a message alerts the user to fix the input.	After each keystroke
2	If the user enters less or more than five digits.	The **Join** button remains disabled.	After each keystroke
3	If the user's input equals five digits and they match our range.	Activate the **Join** button.	After all digits were typed
4	If the zip code is not within the range.	A **Thank You** message is displayed; the user can submit an e-mail address for a notification that will be sent when the service becomes available at the desired zip code.	After all digits were typed

The Evaluation trigger column in the preceding table is very useful as an organizational and planning tool to determine which Axure event to use for the interactions. In this example, it makes more sense to start with evaluating the conditions after each keystroke and then the entire typed string.

Step 2 – Wireframe Construction

For this example, we will use a standalone RP file. A similar but not identical set of widgets is provided in the `Farm2Table` project file on the homepage wireframe (#100). You are invited to create the interaction there as well, as an additional opportunity to practice.

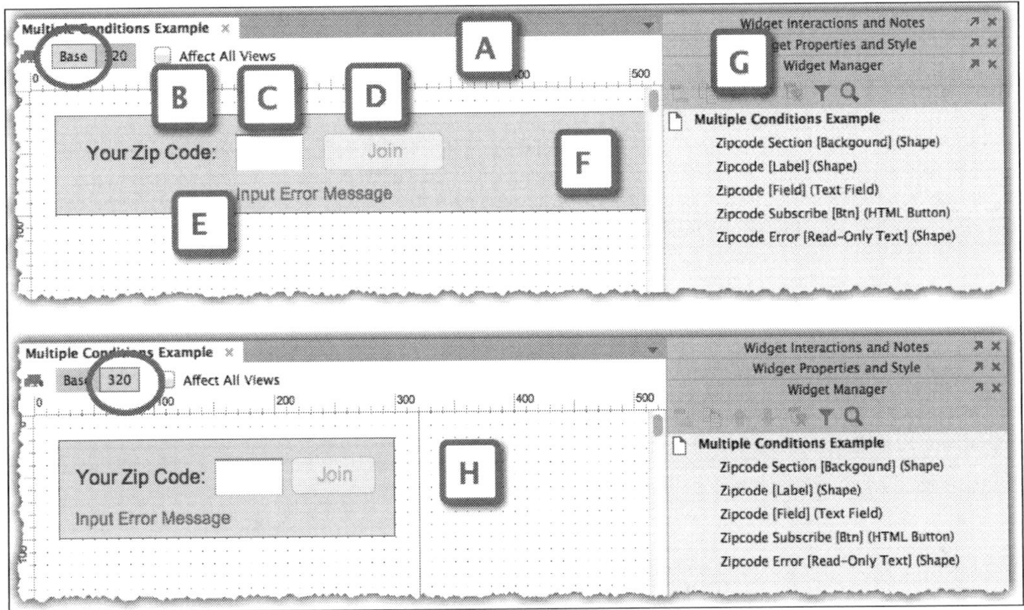

Image 12

To make the example further relevant, we use Axure's Adaptive Views feature although it limits the example to a desktop base view (*Image 12*, **A**) and vertical (portrait) orientation for smartphone (**H**).

Start by placing the widgets in the base view and then create the smartphone version.

The widgets are:

- A label widget **Your Zip Code** (**B**)
- A text field widget for the zip code (**C**)
- A button widget that is disabled **Join** (**D**)
- A (hidden by default) label widget for error messages (**E**)
- An optional rectangle widget to frame the other widgets (**F**)

Again, as demonstrated in the file, we recommend that you label the widgets as you go.

Step 3 – Evaluating Conditions

Let's start with the first couple of conditional requirements that need to be evaluated:

#	Evaluated conditions	When	Actions
1	If the user types in a non-numeric character.	After each keystroke	The **Join** button remains disabled and a message alerts the user to fix the input.
2	If the user enters less than five digits.	After each keystroke	The **Join** button remains disabled.

Divide and Conquer – Part 1

While the preceding conditions are evaluated after each keystroke, they don't yield the exact same response and so each must be evaluated separately.

Let's begin with the first condition, which is as follows:

#	Evaluated condition	When	Action
1	If the user types in a non-numeric character.	After each keystroke	The **Join** button remains disabled and a message alerts the user to fix the input.

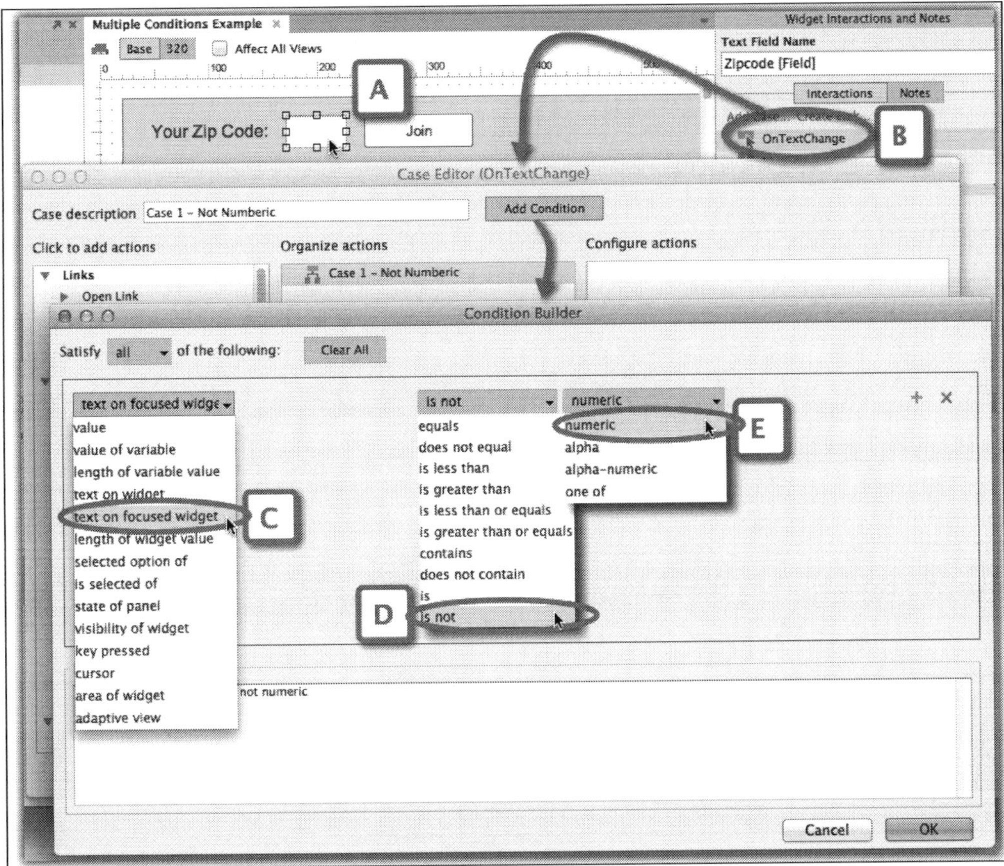

Image 13

All the interaction cases are associated with the selected zip code field (*Image 13*, **A**), and the first condition, which we immediately label as `Case 1- Not Numeric`, will use the **OnTextChange** event (**B**).

In the left-most columns of the **Condition Builder** window, options that can work are **text on widget** and **text on focused widget**. The latter (**C**) is the one we want because it eliminates the next drop-down list in the builder and the need to specify which widget we mean.

Next, select **is not** (**D**) because we want to alert the user if they type a non-numeric value, which is why we select **numeric** from the final column (**E**).

Close the **Condition builder** window and add the following associated actions:

- Set the text in the error field to something similar to `Numbers only, please`.
- Make this hidden widget visible.

The next step is to preview the interaction to validate that it is working.

Counter Conditions

Occasionally, we need to add interactions that were not part of the initial set. Specific to our example, we need to show what happens when the user fixes the error by deleting the letter and typing the number. The counter action essentially serves to reset the action(s) triggered by the initial condition. The following is an example:

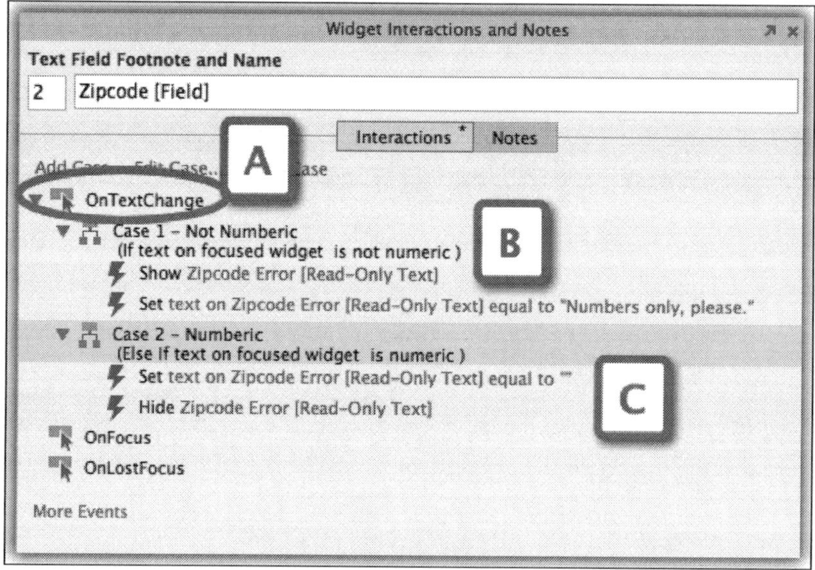

Image 14

1. Duplicate the first case and relabel it `Case 2 - Numeric`.
2. Change the condition evaluation to `is numeric`.
3. Add an action to clear out the text in the error widget to `""` (that is, empty).
4. Add an action that hides the message widget.

Now, there are two cases under the **OnTextChange** action (*Image 14*, **A**). **Case 1 - Not Numeric** (**B**) alerts the user in the case of typing in a letter instead of a number, and **Case 2 - Numeric** (**C**) clears the warning after the user fixes the issue.

Divide and Conquer – Part 2

We are now ready to address the second condition, which is as follows:

#	Evaluated condition	When	Action
2	If the user enters less or more than five digits.	After each keystroke	The **Join** button remains disabled.

Checking for the number of digits in the field is also associated with the third condition, which is as follows:

#	Evaluated condition	When	Action
3	If the user's input equals five digits and they match our range.	After all digits were typed.	Activate the **Join** button

There is some redundancy here that we can eliminate. The **Join** button is disabled by default. It will change the state to `enabled` when its length equals 5. In other words, we only need to address the third condition and it will take care of the second condition.

There is a normal tendency to dive into an interaction in an ad hoc manner. The value of planning ahead is the potential to reduce the work and complexity. Generally, the less interaction you need to isolate and debug, the better. The following is an example:

This initially looks like an easy one:

1. Add a case to the **OnTextChange** action and label it `Case 3 - length is 5`.
2. Add a condition that checks the length of the input into the zip code field.
3. Add an action to enable the **Join** button.
4. Preview the interactions.

Although showing and hiding the error message works as before, typing in five digits does not activate the **Join** button. This is not working! What is going on?

Toggle IF/ELSE IF and Order of Execution

The following is an example of how Axure and most software handle the processing of conditional logic sets:

IF

This condition is **TRUE**, do something

(and stop the evaluation)

ELSE IF

Another condition is **TRUE**, do something

(and stop the evaluation)

ELSE IF

Another condition is **TRUE**, do something

(and stop the evaluation).

In our example, as the user types into the field, each keystroke is being evaluated as a letter (alphabet) or number and the evaluation essentially pauses until the next keystroke. This is a binary situation; the character must be one and as a result the third evaluation that checks for the length of the string never gets evaluated.

Instinctively, you might think of shuffling things around and making the length of the string the first condition to be evaluated. Try it. Indeed, once you type in five numbers, the **Join** button becomes active. Alas, if the fifth character the user typed was a letter, the **Join** button still becomes active and the error alert will not be displayed. Now you know that it is because the evaluation stopped after the keystroke was evaluated for length.

To keep the third case associated with the **OnTextChange** action, Axure provides a method that makes it possible to disassociate it from the previous two actions, as visualized in the following example:

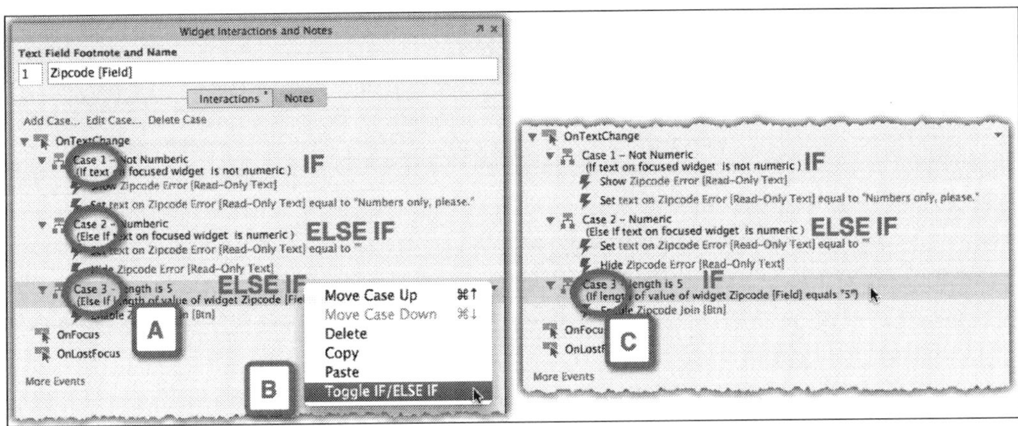

Image 15

In our example, Axure scans the interaction from top to bottom and treats the three cases as a single set of cases: **IF**, **ELSE IF**, and **ELSE IF** (*Image 15*, **A**).

Right-click on **Case 3 - length is 5** and from the context menu, select the last option **Toggle IF/ELSE IF** (**B**). Now, Axure scans through the three cases very differently. It will start with the first two cases, evaluate for IF and ELSE IF. It will stop when the character entered is a letter or a number. It will then start a separate evaluation for the length of the string, which is only an IF and is not associated with the other case.

Satisfy ALL or ANY

You probably recall your parents telling you that you can have dessert IF you finish your broccoli AND IF you behave well at the table. This is an example of satisfying ALL conditions. Now, you probably figured out that if you negotiate, behave well but don't finish the broccoli, your parents' hearts would melt and you will get the dessert. It was sufficient to satisfy ANY of the conditions and that is how you learned about the difference between ALL and ANY.

Back to Axure and our example. We are ready to deal with the second part of the third condition, which is visualized in image 16, and is as follows:

#	Evaluated condition	When	Action
3	If the user's input equals five digits (*Image 16*, A) AND they match our range (B).	After all digits were typed.	Activate the **Join** button

Jointly both the parts activate the **Join** button. We will add condition rows that look for a match with the specific zip codes. For the purpose of prototyping and validation in usability tests, it is sufficient to use a small number of zip codes.

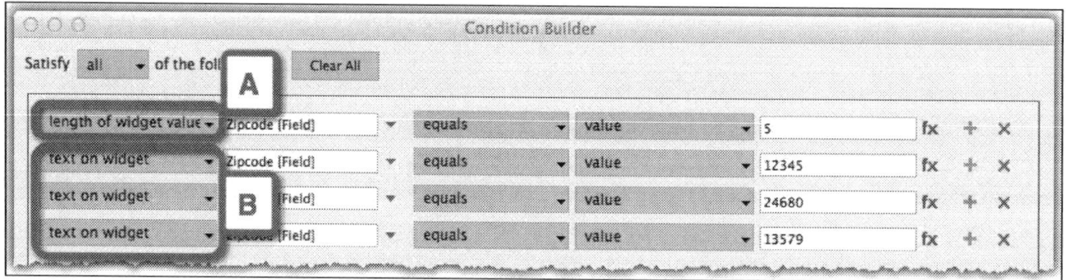

Image 16

In the condition builder for this case, we now have four rows. The first row was created earlier and looks for a string with length of 5. The other three look for a value that matches those entered.

When we test this, it does not work! Why?

When multiple conditional statements need to be evaluated in a single conditional block, in addition to the **Toggle IF/ELSE IF** option, you must also pay special attention to the value you want in the **Condition Builder** window's **Satisfy** drop-down list (*Image 17*, **A**), which has only two values, **all** and **any**. The following screenshot shows these two options in the **Satisfy** drop-down list:

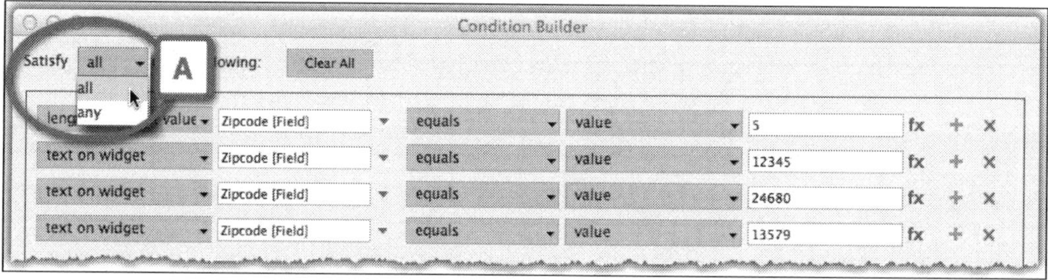

Image 17

By default, the **all** option of the **Satisfy** drop-down list is fine if you have a single condition in the **Condition Builder** window. With two or more conditions, it becomes critical that this drop-down list is set to the correct value. To help you create the condition, the drop-down list is set as part of a sentence. Always read the entire sentence when you are considering the option to be set. It will be one of the following:

- Satisfy ALL of the following. (Eat your broccoli AND behave well.)
- Satisfy ANY of the following. (Eat your broccoli OR behave well.)

Is this going to solve our current problem?

Choosing **all** seems to be correct because the **Join** button can be activated only when five digits are entered and they match a certain predefined value. Alas, it does not work because it wants the zip code field to match three different values simultaneously, which of course is impossible.

If we change the setting on the **Condition Builder** window to **any**, we will also get into trouble because the **Join** button will get activated as soon as there are five digits in the field, which is enough to satisfy the **any** processing.

Negative Thinking

There are, of course, several ways to accomplish what we discuss in this example, but one of our primary goals is to introduce you to issues that you will encounter throughout the process of building conditional interactions and the approaches to resolve them. The solution here involves just a bit of mental exercise, as is explained in the following example:

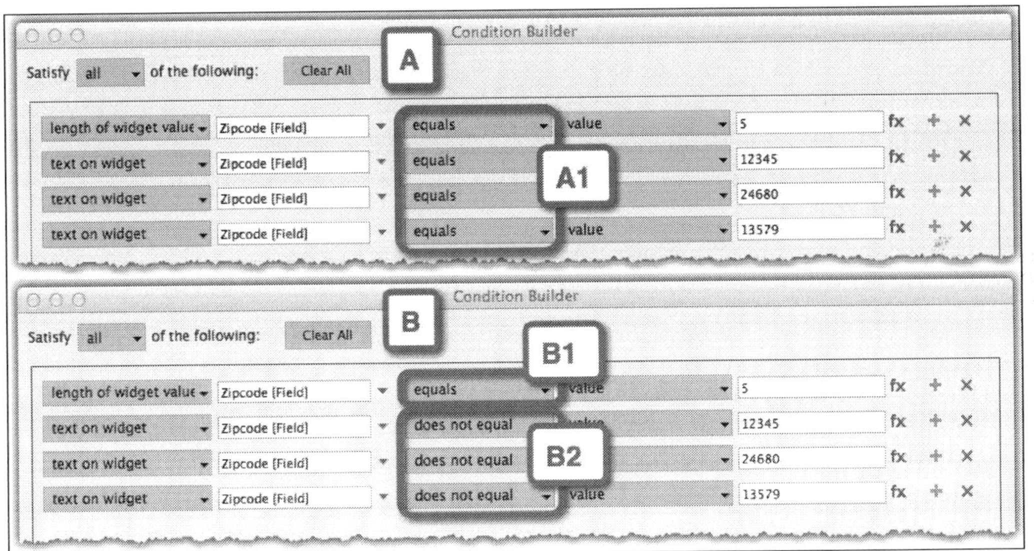

Image 18

Although in our initial approach (*Image 18*, **A**), we created a set of four rows in the **Condition Builder** window (**A1**) in a modified approach (**B**), they can be thought of as two groupings, which are as follows:

- The first row checks for the length of the string in the zip code field (**B1**)
- The next three rows check for the validity of the entered zip code (**B2**)

The three conditional rows associated with the second group can be set to **does not equal** instead of **equals** as we initially created. We keep the selection in the **Satisfy** drop-down list to **all**. Let's compare how Axure processes in both **A** and **B** approaches:

	Approach A		Approach B	
Row	**Evaluate**	**Processing**	**Evaluate**	**Processing**
1	The length of the zip code field must be **equal** to 5	Even if this is TRUE, each of the other rows must be TRUE.	The length of the zip code field must be **equal** to 5.	Even if this is TRUE, each of the other rows must be TRUE.
2	The value of the zip code must be **equal** to the first predefined value.	Even if this is TRUE, each of the other rows must be TRUE.	The value of the zip code must **not** be **equal** to the first predefined value.	Even if this is TRUE, each of the other rows must be TRUE.
3	The value of the zip code must be equal to the second predefined value.	Even if this is TRUE, each of the other rows must be TRUE.	The value of the zip code must **not** be **equal** to the second predefined value.	Even if this is TRUE, each of the other rows must be TRUE.
4	The value of the zip code must be equal to the third predefined value.	Even if this is TRUE, each of the other rows must be TRUE.	The value of the zip code must **not** be **equal** to the third predefined value.	Even if this is TRUE, each of the other rows must be TRUE.
Conclusion	Obviously, it is impossible that the zip code field will be equal to the values of the second, third, and fourth rows simultaneously. The evaluation will never be TRUE regardless of the zip code values. It is logically wrong and the **Join** button will never become active whether we create an associated action that enables it or an action that disables it.		It is possible that the second, third, and fourth rows will evaluate to TRUE and it is possible to satisfy all conditions. In other words, as long as the entered zip code does not match any of those listed in the conditional rows, the **Join** button will stay disabled.	

With approach B, we can take a step further and actually remove the first row. It is not necessary to maintain the button disabled unless the correct zip code is entered. An evaluation of the entered zip to the predefined values cannot happen unless it has five digits!

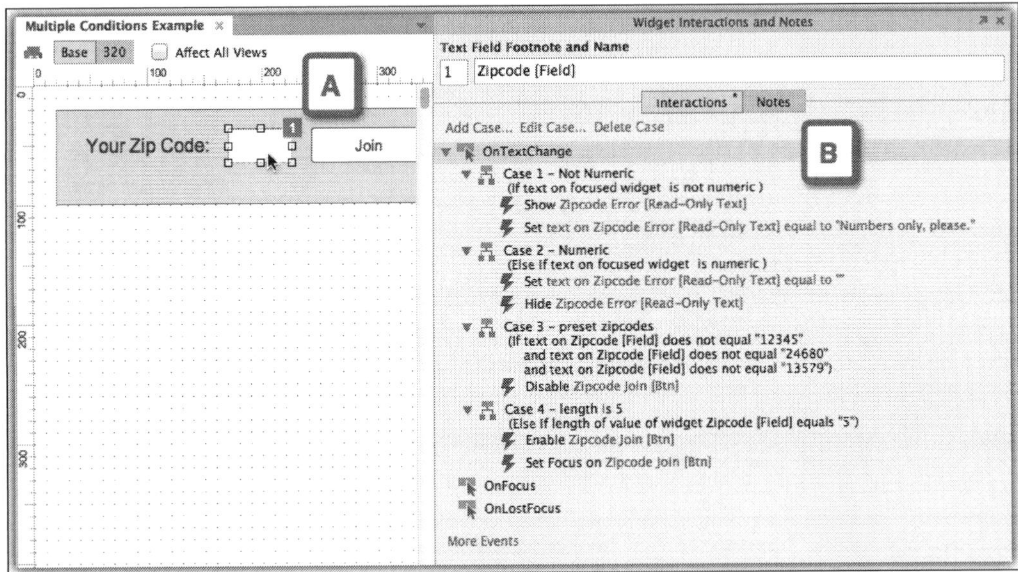

Image 19

We finalize the work by adding a fourth case, which finally enables the **Join** button if the length of the zip code field (*Image 19*, **A**) equals 5. Combined, the four cases take care of validation, messaging, and branching of the flow according to the rules stated at the start of the construction process.

More Than Meets the Eye

To reduce overall interface complexity and visual load, Axure 7 surfaces key actions in the **Widget Interactions and Notes** pane and others are accessible via the somewhat easy-to-neglect **More Events** link (*Image 20*, **A**). It is possible to assign various cases to multiple actions. The entire inventory of actions is available through the context menu (**B**).

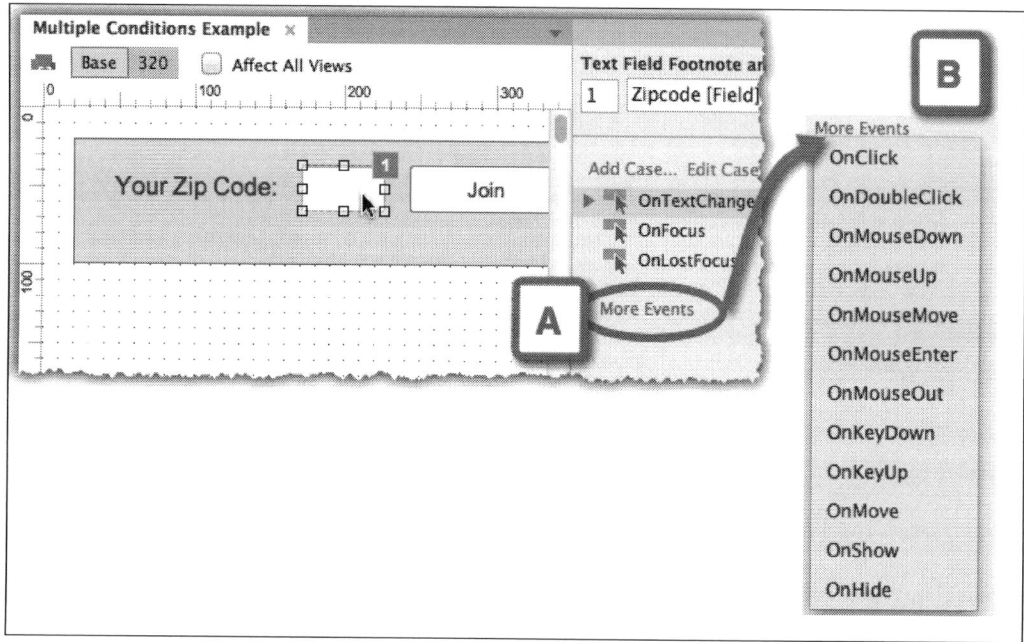

Image 20

Time Estimation for Conditional Work

Even if you are familiar and experienced with logic and with Axure's **Condition Builder**, not to mention if this is a new territory for you, make sure to cushion your construction time estimates. You might get an unpleasant surprise after spending several frustrating hours trying to get some conditional interaction to work just to find that it was a simple logical slip. As the previous example demonstrated, there may be multiple ways to construct conditions and logical statements. The more complex the logic, the more opportunities there are to slip and thus more time is required to rethink, organize, and iterate.

Troubleshooting Conditions

As much as many interactions and conditions are easy to set up in Axure, We can guarantee that there will be cases where your interaction will not work as expected. The following are some basic troubleshooting ideas:

- The most common culprit—a simple copy-and-paste issue—might explain the inexplicable behavior of a widget. The problematic widget may have inherited the interactions and conditions of the original widget. Clean up as needed.
- Are you evaluating the correct widget? Axure presents all the widgets that are placed on the page (or master). The list can be very long and so picking the wrong widget is understandable. If you are having a hard time finding the widget, relabel it temporarily as `XYZ`, which will make it much easier to spot. Remember to restore to the original label after you fix the interaction.
- Take a moment to write down the conditional logic and review it against what you have in Axure. Make sure to review it in order. Sometimes just writing the logic, especially if it is complex, makes it easier to spot the problem in Axure.
- Check the **Satisfy** drop-down list if you have multiple conditions. Depending on how you want the logic to work, the setting may be wrong.

Raised Events

Can a tiger change its stripes? Can an Axure master change its size or shape from one page to another? The answer to both is, unfortunately, no. However, you can control the behavior of a master so that each of its instances, across multiple pages, will have a different behavior for the same event. Axure's Raised Events feature greatly extends the usefulness of masters and once you learn this feature (it's easy, we promise), you will find yourself using it often.

The following are important points to remember about raised events:

- Raised events can be created only for widgets that are on masters
- A master may have multiple numbers of raised events
- Creating a raised event is a two-step process:
    1. Create the raised event on the master.
    2. Place the master on the page and click to select the master. Create the interaction for the raised event.

Why do we need raised events? The bottom-line answer is context and reuse. The explanation for this is as follows:

- Masters would be of very limited use for an interactive prototype if there was no way to allow the master with different behaviors based on the page the master is placed.
- When a master is placed on a page, it is not possible to edit or assign interactions to any of the master's widgets directly. The master's wireframe has to be edited separately. Raised events afford a way to create an interaction on a wireframe, which can be applied to widgets within masters without editing the master.

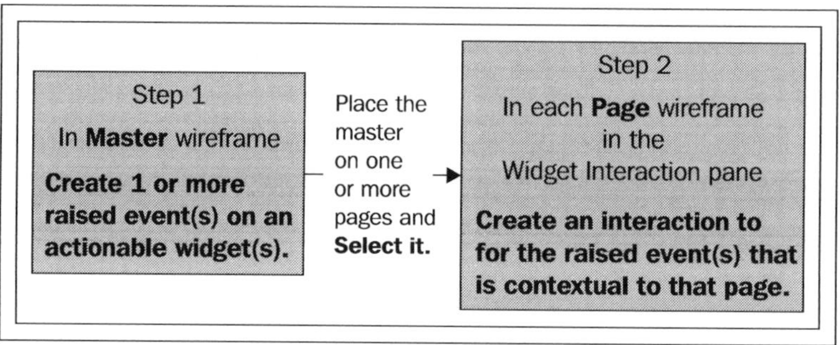

Image 21

Guided Example

This example is meant to help you understand the idea of raised events and how useful this feature is. We feel that it is easier to consider a construction strategy that maximizes the use of masters in your prototype when you have the power and flexibility of Raised Events.

In this example, we demonstrate how a single master placed on three different pages can trigger, with Raised Events, different actions based on which page they are placed. This will be impossible without the Raised Event feature because inherently the master must perform identically on each page.

See the raised event's example RP file for reference and try to implement the Raised Events feature on the `Farm2Table` project file using the master **M 100 RE Item** and page **200 - Produce**.

Step 1 – Creating a Raised Event on the Master

Masters maintain their visual consistency wherever they are used, allow a single point of documentation, and are critical in applying a particular design system across an application. When taking the build-as-you-go, ad hoc construction approach (which is normal), our wireframes are littered with redundant widgets across pages. Each needs to be labeled, sometimes documented, and styled consistently. This is inefficient and more troubling and can lead to UX defects during development.

In this example, we use a basic widget (a button) to demonstrate a powerful and surprisingly easy Axure feature. We will return to it when we discuss widget libraries and custom styles, so consider Raised Events as a strategic feature that adds significant power to your prototype.

The following are the steps to create a raised event on the master:

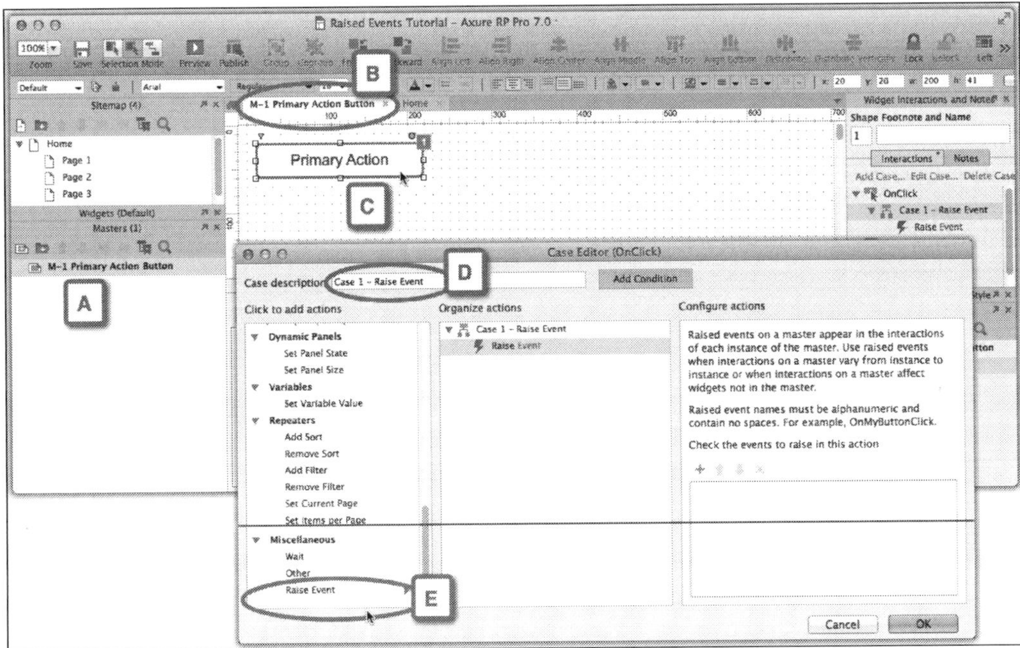

Image 22

1. Create a new RP file, save it as `Raised Events Tutorial`. Don't bother with the default set of pages in the **Sitemap** pane; keep them as is.
2. Create a master and label it `M-1 Primary Action Button` (*Image 22*, **A**). Double-click to open it for editing (**B**).
3. Use a rectangle shape to create a button. Label it `Primary Action` (**C**).

4. Create an interaction case for the **OnClick** action. Label it `Case 1 - Raise Event` (**D**).
5. From the list of actions in the **Case Editor** window, select the last item, **Raise Event** (**E**), which is found under the **Miscellaneous** category.

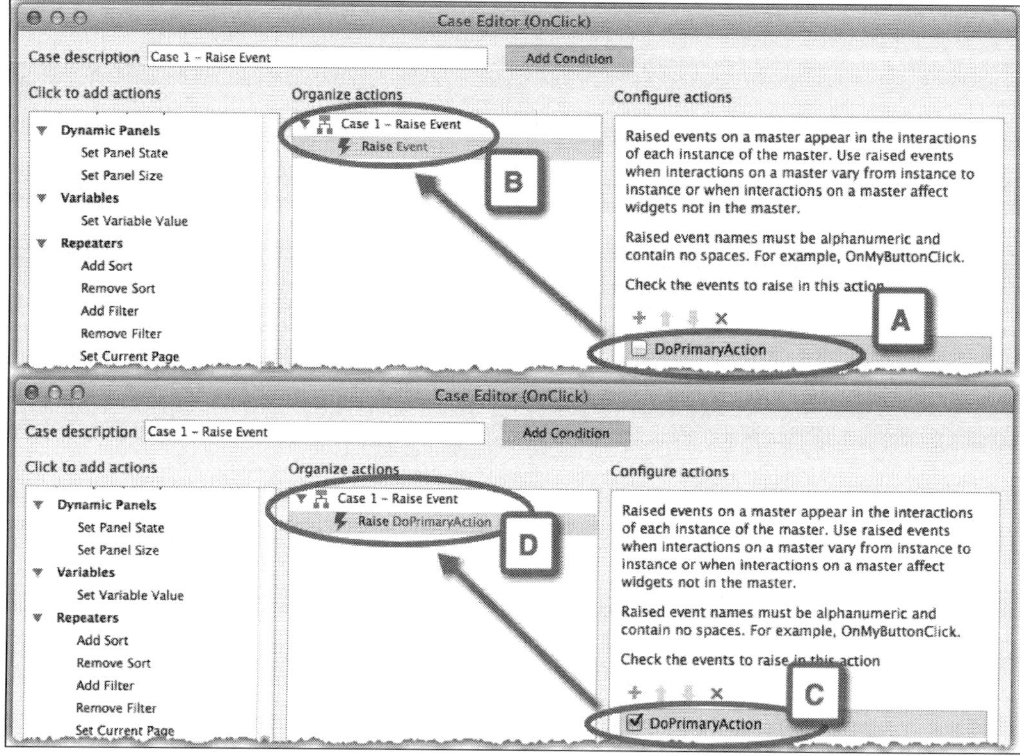

Image 23

6. In the **Configure actions** column (*Image 23*, **A**), click on the **+** icon to add a raised event and label it `DoPrimaryAction` (**B**).

Important

Notice the checkbox to the left of the newly labeled raised event (Which must be alphanumeric only and without spaces). It is not selected (*Image 23*, **A**). In the **Organize actions** column of the **Case Editor** window, the action appears as a generic, unassigned **Raise Event** (**B**). Select the checkbox for this raised event (**C**) and now the action is associated (**D**).

Congratulations on creating your first raised event! You can create multiple raised events for each master. The next step is to get the raised event to do some work for us.

Troubleshooting raised events

The first thing to check if a raised event does not work is to make sure that the checkbox next to the raised event name in the **Case Editor** window (*Image 23*, **C**) is indeed selected!

Step 2 – Applying an Interaction to Raised Events on a Page

Here is the cool and powerful aspect of raised events and the time invested in understanding raised events will finally pay off. As masters are meant to be reused and placed on multiple pages, the list of raised events will be exposed on each page, including on the wireframe pages of other masters. On each page, you can create different interactions for the same raised event. This is how the same master can have different behaviors on different pages.

Wireframe Construction

On the **Home** page, our master will toggle the visibility of a widget:

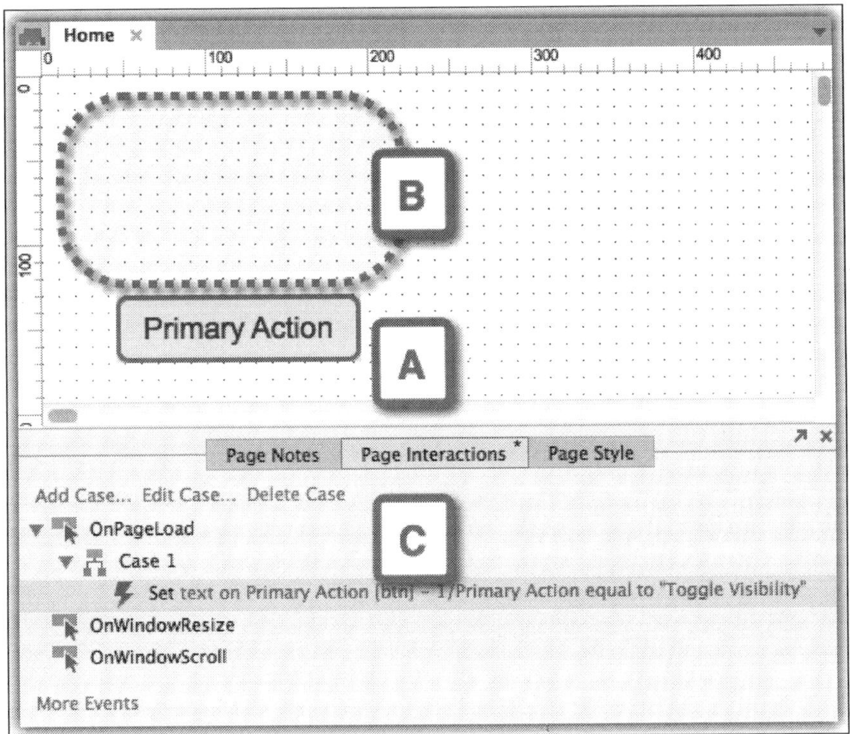

Image 24

1. Open the **Home** page to edit and drag the following:
   - An instance of the master (*Image 24*, **A**). Label it `Primary Action [Btn] - 1`.
   - A rectangle widget. Label the widget `Widget 1` and set it to **Hidden** (**B**).
2. Switch to the **Page Interactions** tab and add a case to the **OnPageLoad** action that sets the text of the master to **Toggle Visibility** (**C**).
3. Now, preview the page.

Binding the Raised Event with an Action

In this step, we will connect the raised event that was created on the master to a specific action for this page.

Essentially, raised events are handles that you attach to a master so that you can access it on the page. While the name of the raised event does not change from page to page and from one instance of the master to another, the action you assign it to does.

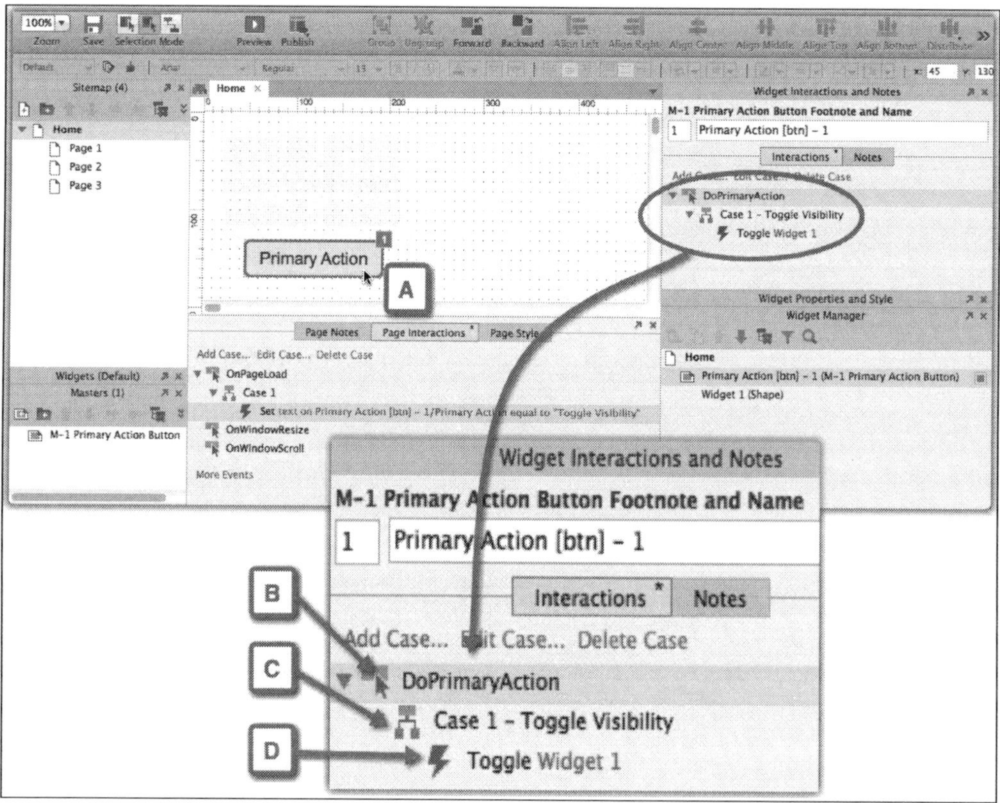

Image 25

When you click to select the master (*Image 25*, **A**), the raised event **DoPrimaryAction** (**B**) appears in the **Interactions** tab of the **Widget Interactions and Notes** pane.

Now, create a case and label it `Case 1 - Toggle Visibility` (**C**) and assign it the **Toggle** action for the widget. Preview the interaction.

Same Master but Different Behaviors

You get the idea. As you drag additional instances of the master to the same page or place the master on other pages, the raised event you created for the master will become visible and at that point, you can assign it different actions. In the example file, the master is placed on each page in the prototype, sometimes multiple instances, and each does something unique. The advantages are as follows:

- The visual properties of the master are maintained everywhere
- The master can be documented as a pattern
- Each instance of the master can be documented for its unique behavior

Amplifying Raised Events in Nested Masters

It is common to nest one master within the wireframe of another master. The raised events of the nested master, however, will not be exposed when the enclosing master is placed on page wireframes. Ezra coined the term "Amplified" raised events several years ago to describe the following three-step technique to solve the issue:

1. Create a raised event *X* in master *A*, and place an instance of master *A* in the wireframe of master *B*.
2. In the wireframe of master *B*, select master *A* and create an interaction for the exposed action X. This interaction too will use a raise event action. Label this raised event `Amplify X`.
3. Place master *B* on the wireframe of page *N*, and select master *B* to expose the action Amplify X. Now, you can create the action under Amplify X, which will actually be what you want master *A* to do.

The following example will illustrate the concept.

Construction

We want to include the **M-1 Primary Action Button** master in another master and use the **DoPrimaryAction** raised event associated with it, so perform the following steps:

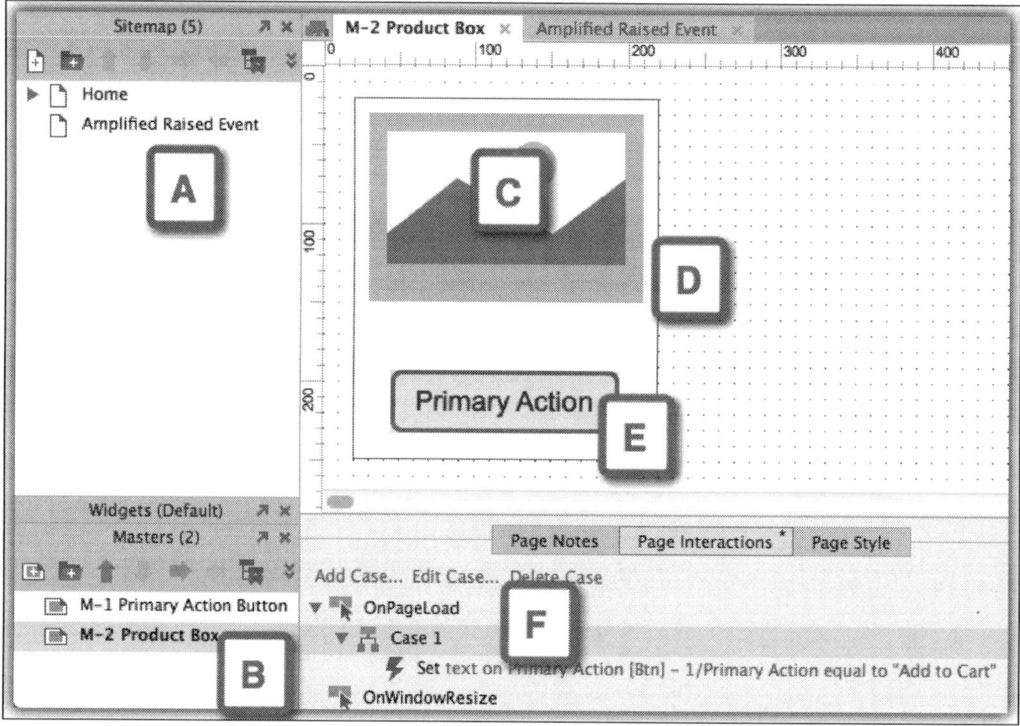

Image 26

1. Add a new page to the **Sitemap** pane and label it `Amplified Raised Event` (*Image 26*, **A**).
2. Add a new master, label it `M-2 Product Box` (**B**), and open it for editing.
3. There, frame an Image widget (C) with a Rectangle widget (D) and add the first master, that is, **M-1 Primary Action Button** (E), to form a product thumbnail component.
4. In the master wireframe, add an **OnPageLoad** interaction which sets the label of the **Primary Action** button to **Add to Cart** (F).

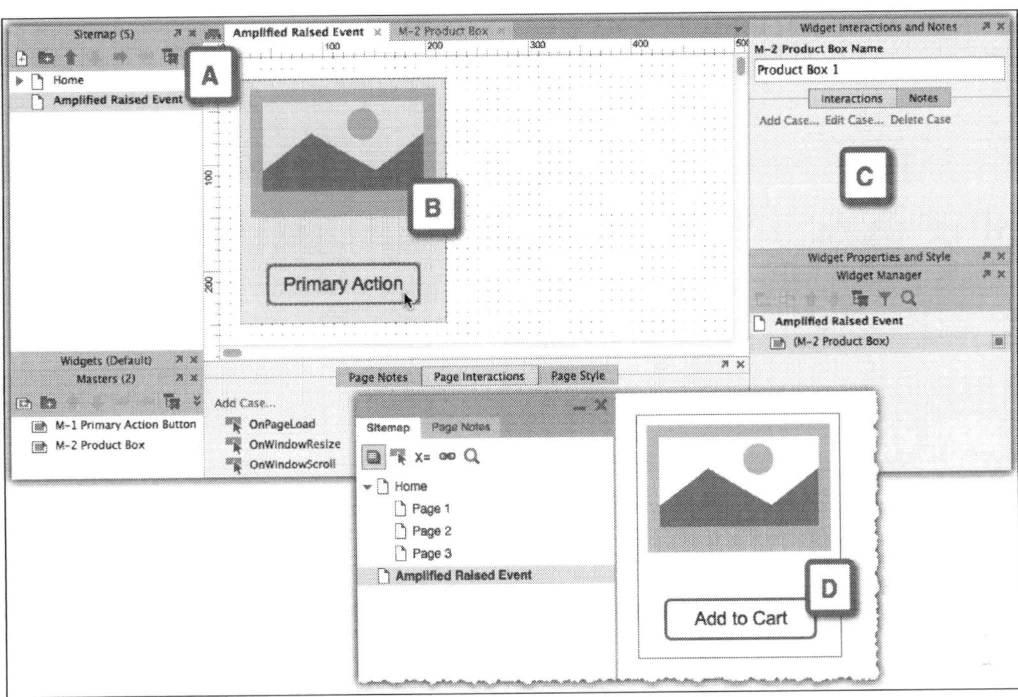

Image 27

5. Now, open the **Amplified Raised Event** page (*Image 27*, **A**), place the **M-2 Product Box** master on it, and label it `Product Box 1` (**B**).

   The **M-2 Product Box** is a nested master inside the **M-1 Primary Action Button** master; the **Primary Action** widget button is nested in **M-2 Product Box**. However, when you click on the **M-2 Product Box** master, nothing shows up in the action list in the **Interactions** tab of the **Widget Interaction and Notes** pane (**C**).

   The raised event that is embedded in **M-1 Primary Action Button** is not exposed to the page that uses **M-2 Product Box**.

6. Preview the page. The **OnPageLoad** interaction that you created for **M-2 Product Box** is working fine—the label of **M-2 Product Box** changes as planned to **Add to Cart** (**D**).

Amplifying a Raised Event

The following steps will help you amplify a raised event:

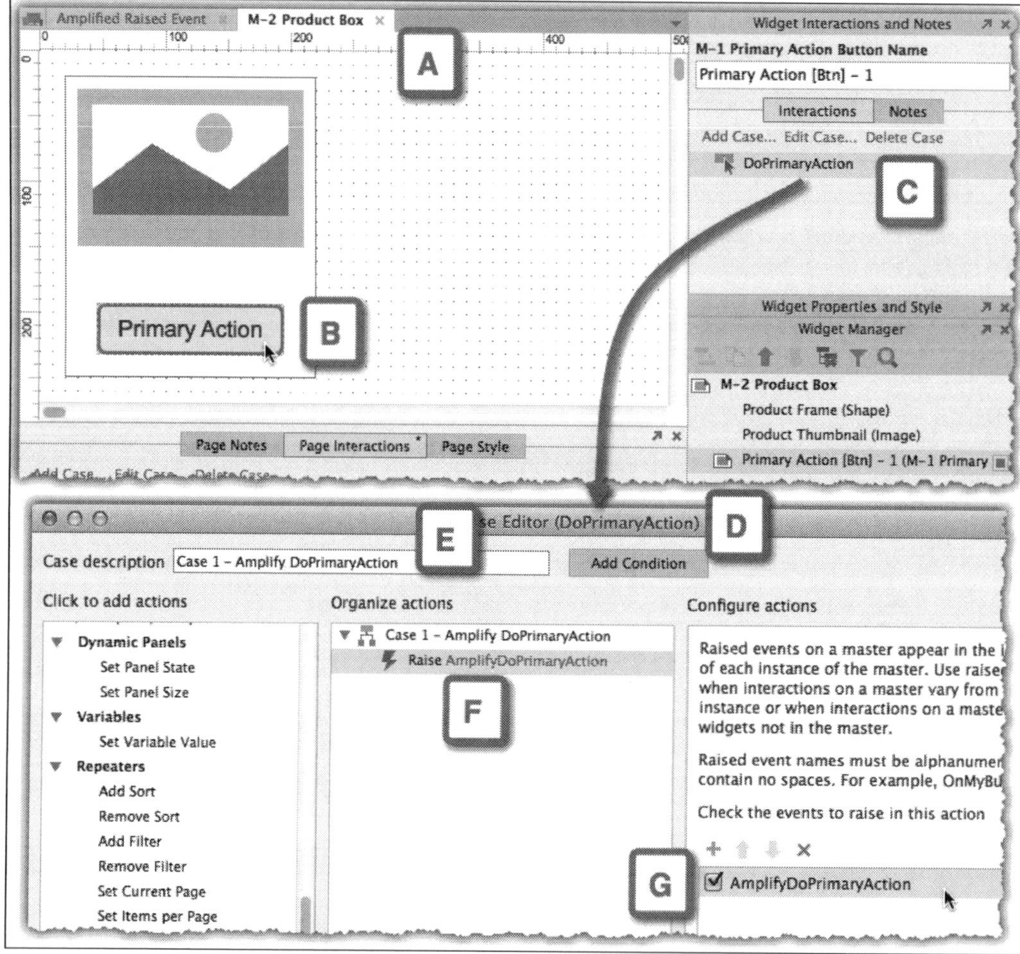

Image 28

1. Open the **M-2 Product Box** master for editing (*Image 28*, **A**), and select the nested master of the **Primary Action** button (**B**).
2. That master's raised event **DoPrimaryAction** is visible in the **Interaction** tab of the **Widget Interactions and Notes** pane (**C**). In the **Case Editor** window (**D**), create a case for this action and label it `Case 1 - Amplify DoPrimaryAction` (**E**).
3. This case (**F**) too is a raised event. Label it `AmplifyDoPrimaryAction` and remember to select the checkbox (**G**).

Completion

With the amplified raised event added to the nesting master **M-2 Product Box**, we return to the **Amplify Raised Event** page (*Image 29*, **A**).

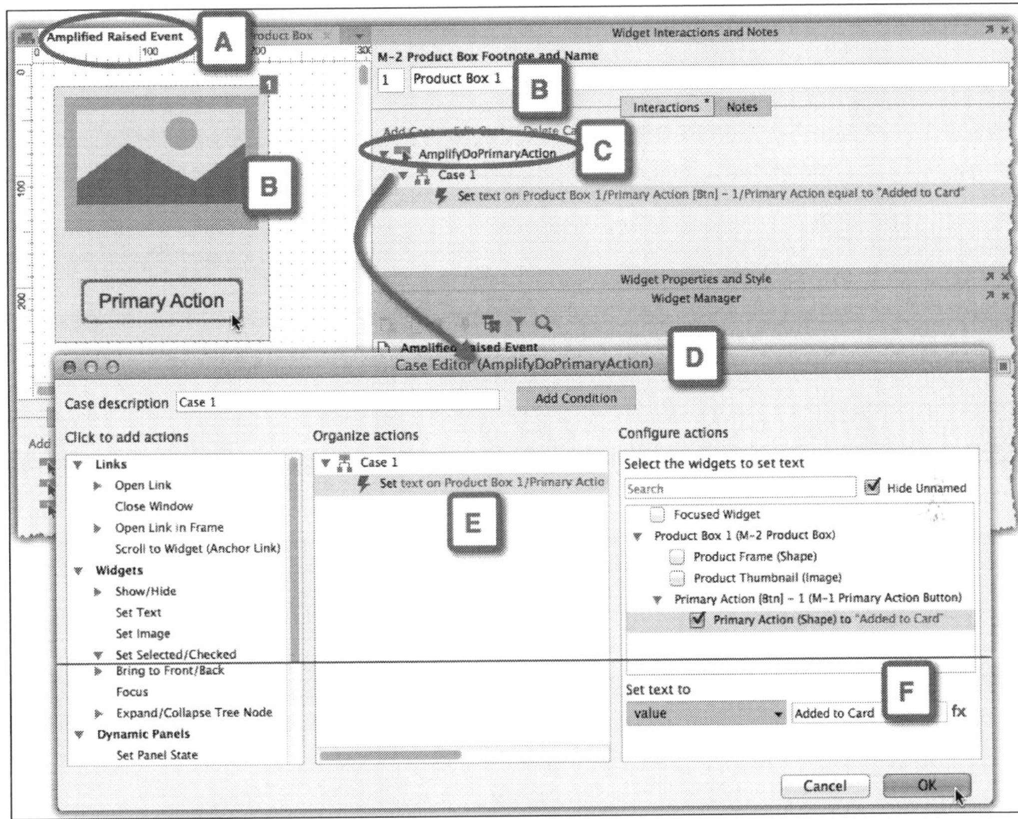

Image 29

Now, clicking anywhere on the **M-2 Product Box** master (**B**) exposes the **AmplifyDoPrimaryAction** action in the **Interactions** tab of the **Widget Interactions and Notes** pane (C).

Although, this action is tied to a raised event in the **M-2 Product Box** master, it is tied to the raised event of the **M-1 Primary Action Button** master. The action you add to it on the page should be related to the behavior of the button.

At this point, adding an interaction in the **Case Editor** window (D) is straightforward. In our example, clicking on the button only triggers a **Set Text** action (E), which changes its label to **Added to Cart** (F). However, this could be whatever is needed.

To conclude the raised events topic, we want to reemphasize the tremendous usefulness of this feature to the construction of high-fidelity prototypes. While masters help us enforce visual consistency and reduce the number-redundant wireframes, raised events help assign contextual behaviors to those masters.

Variables

About two thousand years ago, the Greek philosopher Epictetus said that:

> "*The materials of action are variable, but the use we make of them should be constant.*"

The ancient Greeks loved deep concepts like atoms, so it is not surprising that they invented information architecture and the notion of separating a reference to data from the actual data it contains. Wikipedia has a good definition for a variable. In the context of computer science, it is a symbolic name given to some known or unknown quantity or information for the purpose of allowing the name to be used independently of the information it represents.

We use variables all the time. When we think (or perhaps, prefer not to think) about our account balance, the term "account balance" is the name for a variable. The actual amount of the balance changes, but our way to reference it does not have to. As Epictetus said, the variable is constant, only its value changes.

In addition to storing data, variables are used to pass this data around from one event that sets their value to another event that consumes that value. As a result, variables are very useful when you have conditional logic because it is possible to check the value of a variable in order to determine which path to take.

We can also control the scope in which variables can be used:

- Local variables are limited to a certain function in a certain area of the application and are not available to other functions in other areas of the same application.
- Global variables are visible or available to all functions across the entire application.

A simplified analogy is human memory. We are equipped with a working or short-term memory. It is a limited storage capacity that enables us to complete specific tasks; for example, it helps us remember that we put water to boil or where we left our phone. There is no need to store this information after the activity ended and the information is replaced by new transient information. We also have long-term memory, which enables us to retrieve information on demand, long after its acquisition.

Guided Example – Tracking Items in a Shopping Cart

Keeping track of stuff is very useful and this functionality is common in many applications, from the number of unread e-mails in an inbox to the number of items in a shopping cart. In this counting example, we cover fundamental principles of working with variables, conditional logic, and Axure's environment for using them.

Step 1 – Defining the Interaction

We will start with a very basic counter. The user is presented with a page of products; each product includes an action button, which when clicked does the following:

- Advances the counter of items in the shopping cart by 1
- Changes the button label from **Add to Cart** to **Remove from Cart**

Step 2 – Constructing the Interaction

We need a page with a few products and a representation of a shopping cart with a counter. As items are added or removed from the cart, the counter will keep track of the number of items in the cart, described as follows:

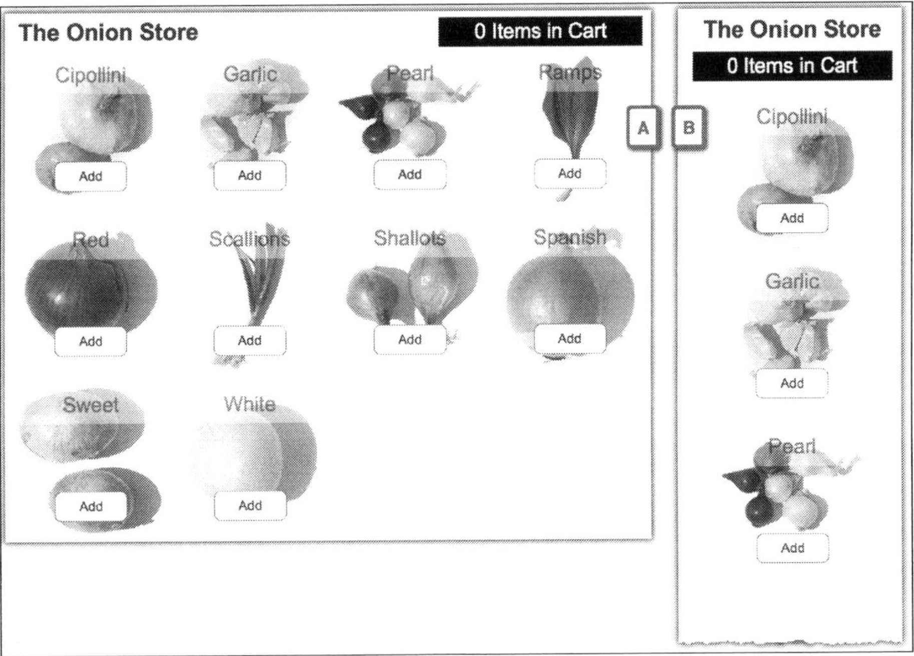

Image 30

Your own file does not have to be fancy; the use of Adaptive Views is immaterial to variables.

However, if you want to take the opportunity and practice your Repeater and Adaptive Views skills, all the resources are in the Variables tutorial file. Here we use only the **Base** (*Image 30*, **A**) and smartphone-vertical views (**B**).

Start a new RP file and save it as `Variables Tutorial`.

Rename the **Home** page as `The Onion Store` and delete the other auto-generated pages from the **Sitemap** pane.

The Repeater Wireframe

The repeater wireframe (*Image 31*, **A**) consists of three widgets:

- A semitransparent rectangle labeled **Onion Name** that displays the onion's name (**B**)
- An Image widget labeled **Onion Image** to show a thumbnail of the onion (**C**)
- A Rounded Rectangle widget labeled **Add** (**D**)

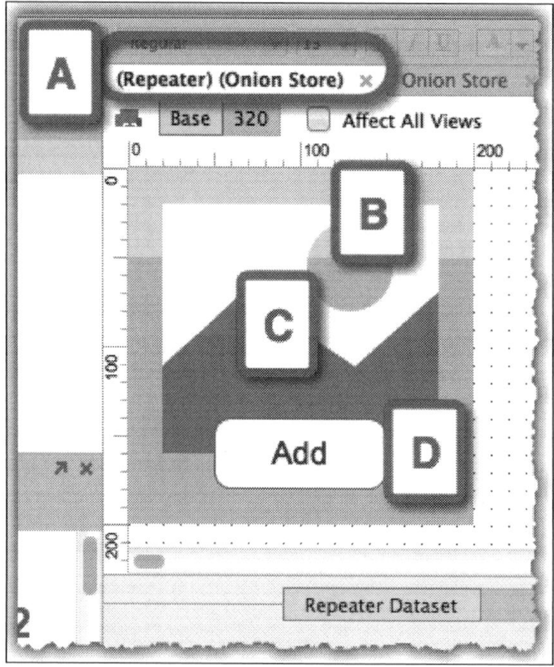

Image 31

The Repeater Dataset

There are only three columns in the table, which are as follows:

- The row number, which is not used for display, but is good to have for reference (*Image 32*, **A**).
- Names of onions (**B**).
- The third column consists of images of onions (**C**). Left-click on the cell in this column and from the context menu, select **Import Image...** (**D**).

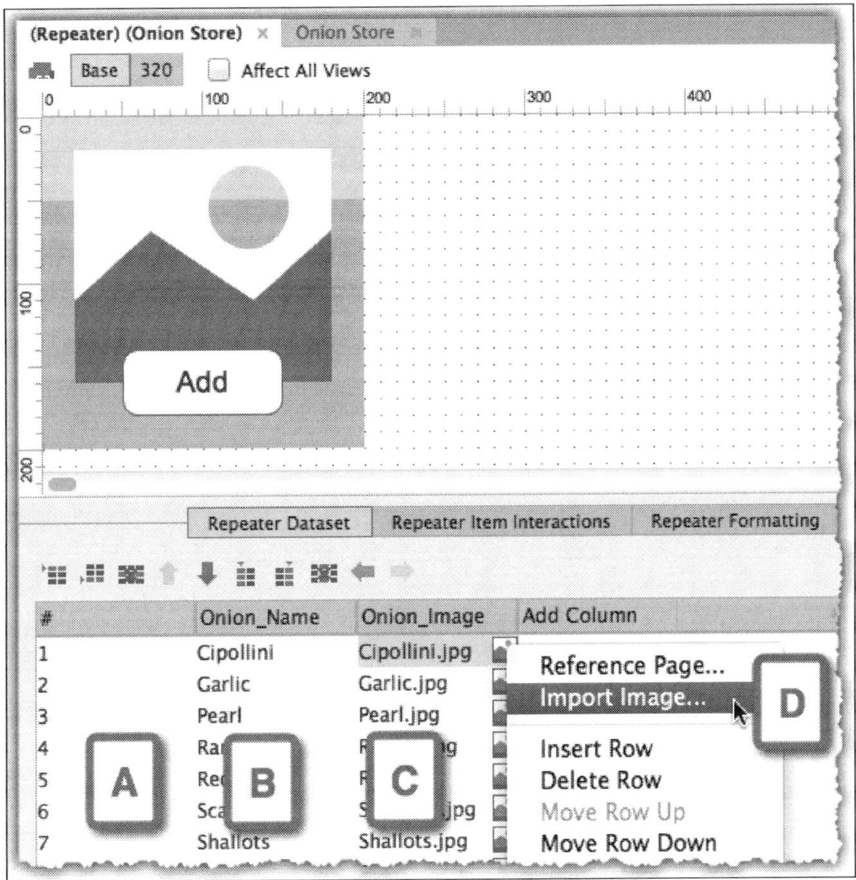

Image 32

Repeater Item Interactions

The dataset populates repeater items on the **OnItemLoad** event (*Image 33*, **A**).

Create a case to populate the repeater and label it `Case 1 - Populate Repeater` (**B**).

The two actions we need are (**C**):

- **Set Text**: This action populates the **Onion Name** widget with values from the **Onion_Name** dataset column
- **Set Image**: This action places the image in the **Onion_Image** dataset column

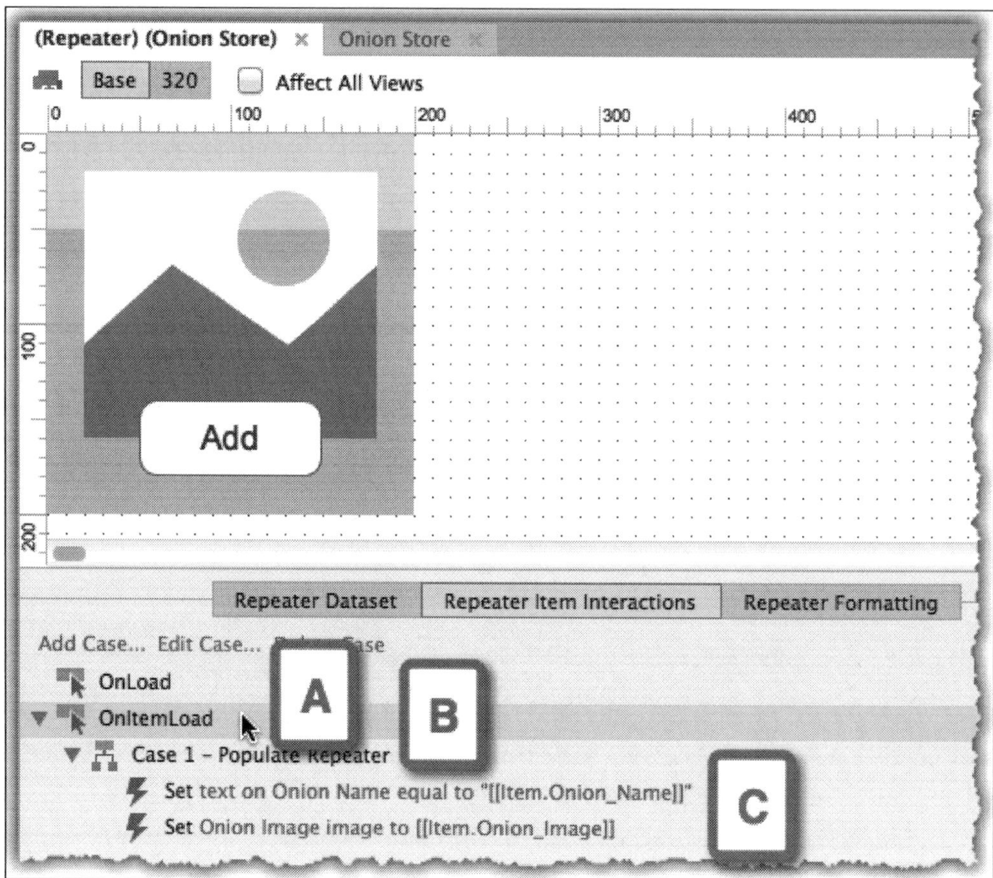

Image 33

Repeater Formatting

Finally, the organization of repeater items on the page for **Base** (*Image 34*, **A**) and a **320** smartphone views (**B**) is given as follows:

- **Layout**: Select the **Horizontal** option for both views, **Wrap (Grid)** of **4** items per row for **Base**, and **1** for **320** (**C**).
- **Item Background**: Do not select anything here for both views (**D**).
- **Pagination**: Do not select anything here for both views (**E**).
- **Spacing**: Enter spacing as `20` px for both row and column for both views.

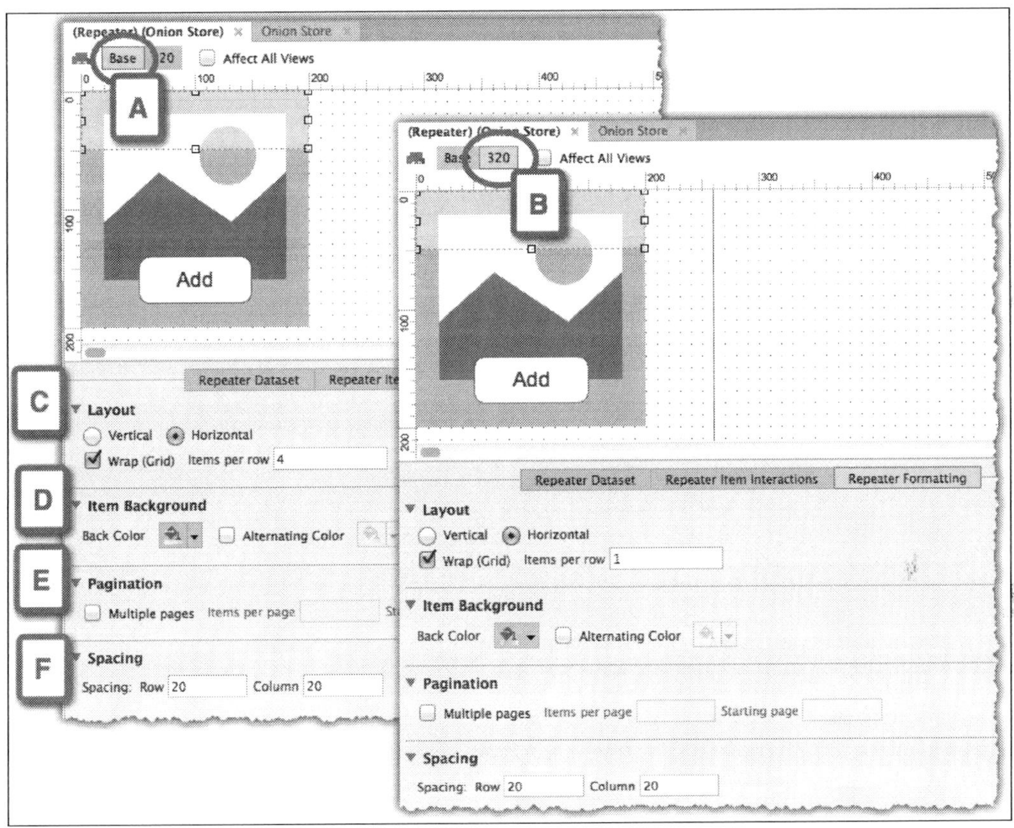

Image 34

Step 3 – Introducing Variables

Personalized and contextual user experience is a core tenant of modern applications. Therefore, it is highly probable that you will be expected to prototype such adaptability in your projects.

Without variables, prototyping interactions that are contextual to user actions, the data on the screen, and accurately mirrors the actual behavior—is very difficult. For years, UX practitioners have resorted (and some still do) to using very tight scripts and hard-coded wireframes to demonstrate such interactions. This method subjected stakeholders and usability-test participants to lengthy explanations about the envisioned behavior and exertion of mental energies to imagine the interface, rather than interacting with it.

With Axure 7, the use of variables and their incorporation with cases that involve conditional logic is easy and powerful. As we continue with our example, note that planning is still the key to efficient prototyping.

Identifying Needed Variable(s)

Start by writing down what needs to happen when the user clicks on the **Add** button of any item in the body:

- The user should be able to click on any item in any order
- Clicking on the **Add** button adds to the counter of items in the cart
- The label of the **Add** button changes to **Remove** when the item is added
- Clicking on the **Remove** button subtracts from the counter of items in the box

We need a variable to store the number of items in the cart. The following are the points we know and can control about the variable:

- The variable name. We are going to label it `cartCounter`.
- Its default value. In this case, the default value is 0.
- We will probably want to place the cart or the number of items in the cart on multiple pages. This means that the variable should be accessible across the application. Such a variable is called a **global variable**, which we will cover later in this chapter.

Adding Variables to the Prototype

The typical opportunities to create global variables are:

- While you are creating an interaction triggered by a widget.
- While you are creating a page interaction.

Creating and Managing the Variables

In all cases, the **Global Variables** dialog will appear (*Image 35*, **A**) as shown in the following screenshot:

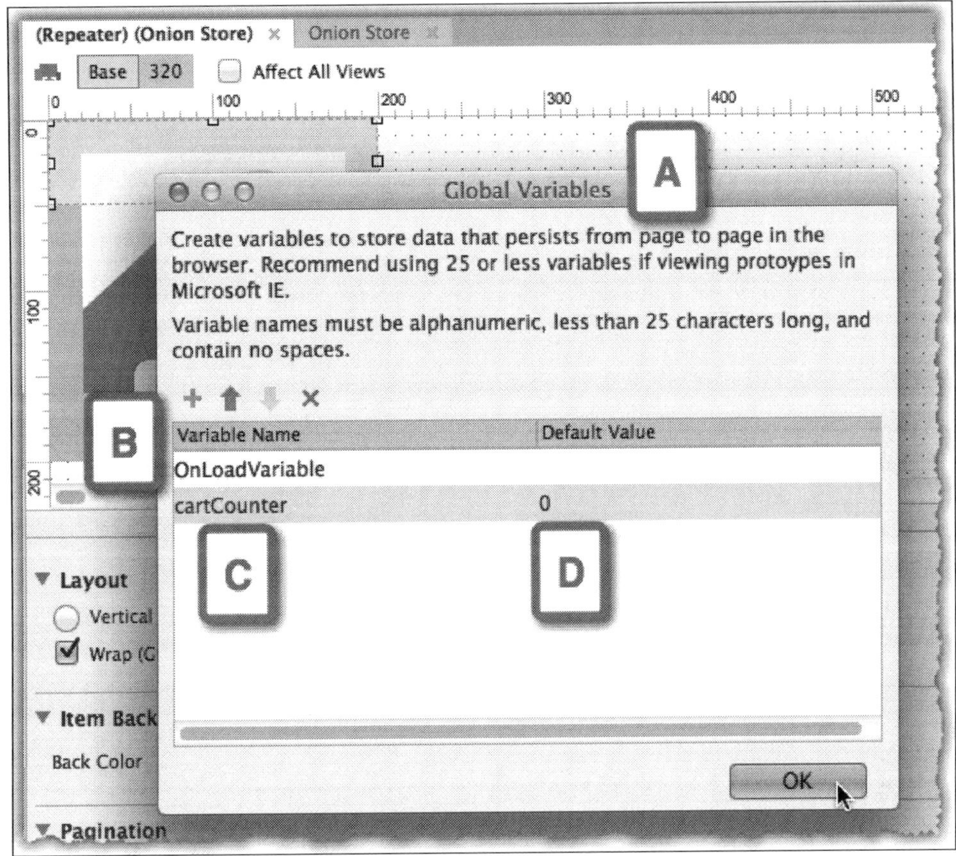

Image 35

This is where you manage the inventory of variables in the prototype. The built-in variable, **OnLoadVariable**, is available for use by default (**B**). Adding and removing variables is trivial, but you need to follow Axure's naming rules while naming variables; these rules are as follows:

- Must be alphanumeric
- Must have less than 25 characters
- Must not contain any spaces

Variables are listed in the table, with their names (**C**) and default values (**D**), both of which can be edited inline in the row.

Getting Variables to Work – Step 1

Perform the following steps:

1. Switch to edit the repeater wireframe (*Image 36*, **A**) and select the **Add** button (**B**).
2. Create an interaction for the **OnClick** event (**C**).
3. In the **Case Editor** window, label it `Case 1- Add an Item` (**D**).
4. Select the **Set Variable Value** action (**E**) and in the column **Configure actions**, keep the default, **value**, in the drop-down list **Set variable to** (**F**).

The value of the variable should be its existing value plus 1.

5. To identify the variable and create the formula, click on the function button **fx** (**G**).

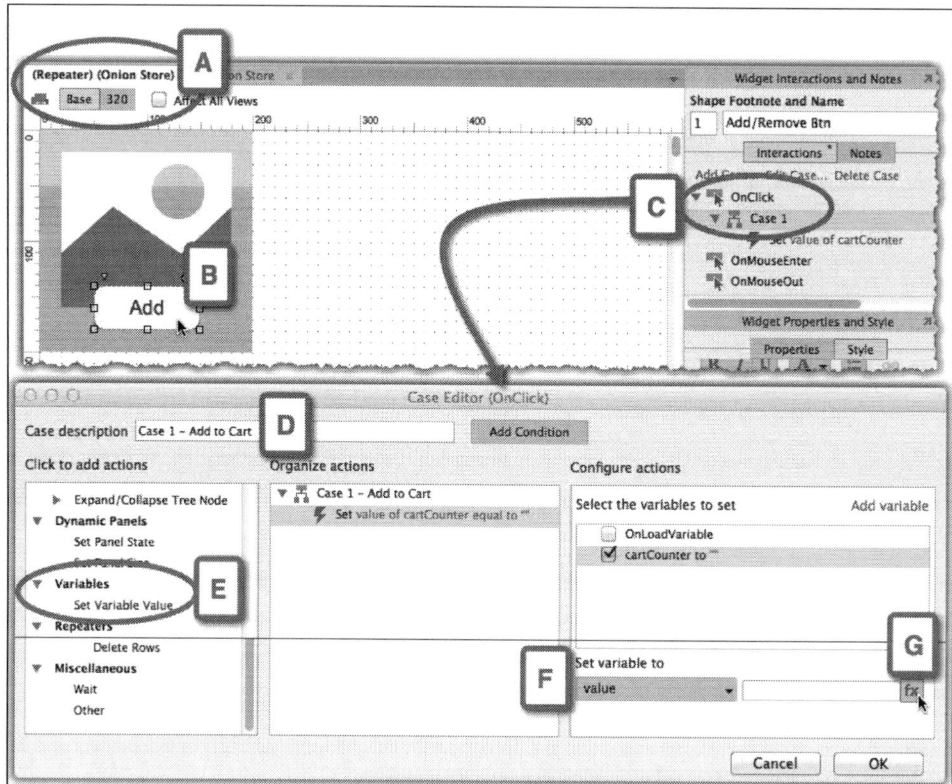

Image 36

Getting Variables to Work – Step 2

The **Edit Text** dialog (*Image 37*, **A**) launches when clicked on **fx** as shown in the following screenshot:

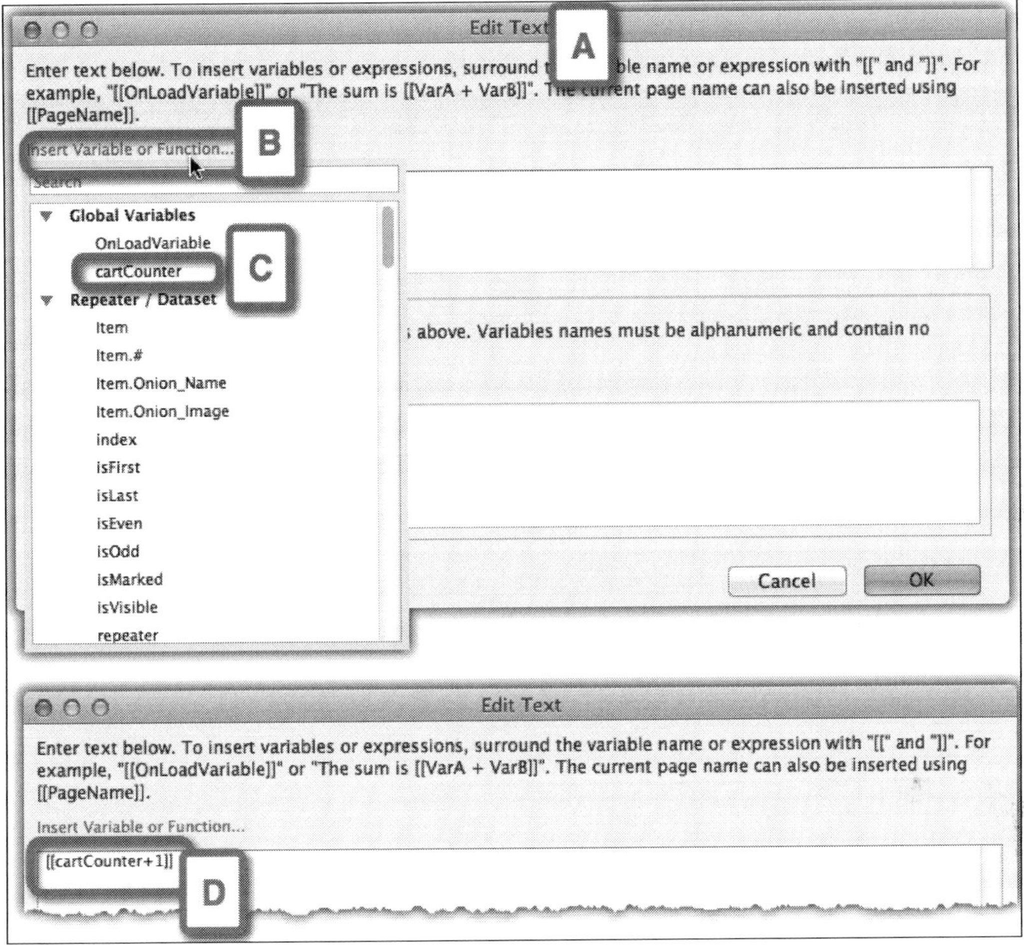

Image 37

Click on the **Insert Variable or Function...** link (**B**) and then click on **cartCounter** (**C**) from the functions drop-down list.

The variable initially appears between two square brackets like **[[cartCounter]]**. The final calculation should look like **[[cartCounter+1]]** (**D**).

Getting Variables to Work – Step 3 (Preview)

Preview the page. Click on the **X=** icon on the **Sitemap** bar (*Image 38*, **A**) to view the variables pop-up, which lists all the variables on the page and their values (**B**).

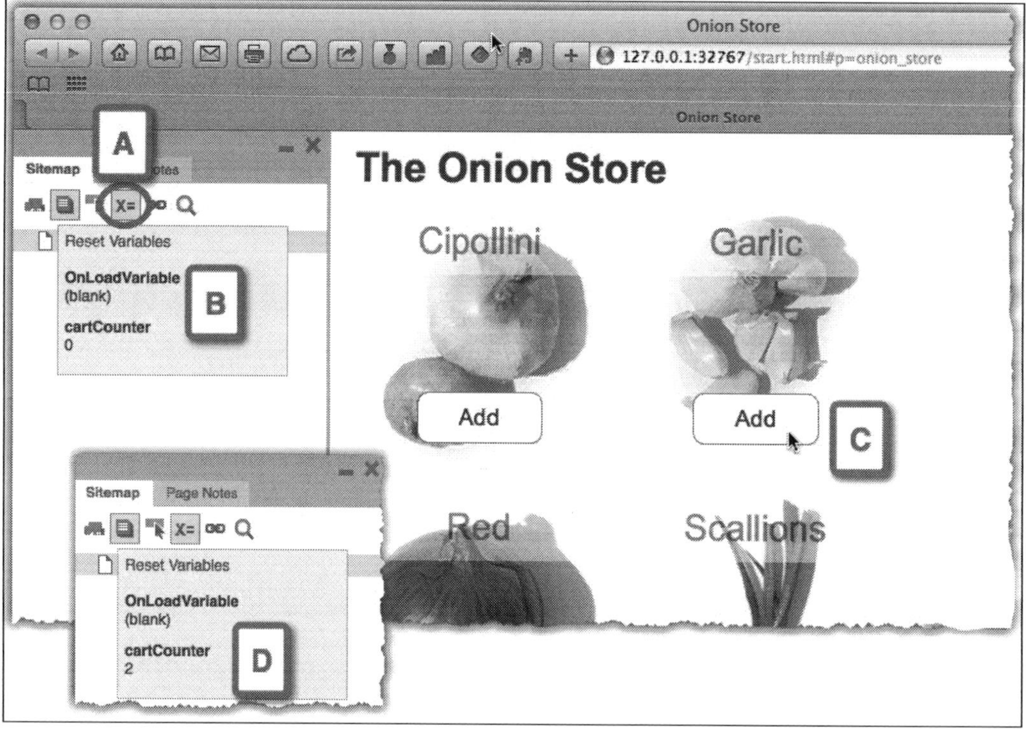

Image 38

The initial value of cartCounter is 0. Now, as you click any of the products on the page, in any order, the counter will advance (**D**).

> When you troubleshoot interactions involving variables, always use this pop-up to see whether the variable value is changing as expected.

Finishing the Interaction

To complete the work, we have to do the following:

- Display the value of the **cartCounter** variable on the shopping cart widget
- Change the text on the **Add** button to `Remove`
- Change the behavior of the button such that it subtracts 1 from the variable

With the button wired to advance the value of the variable (*Image 39*, **A**), adding a second **Set Text** (**B**) action takes care of changing the text of the button to `Remove` (**C**) and reflecting the variable value on the counter (**D**).

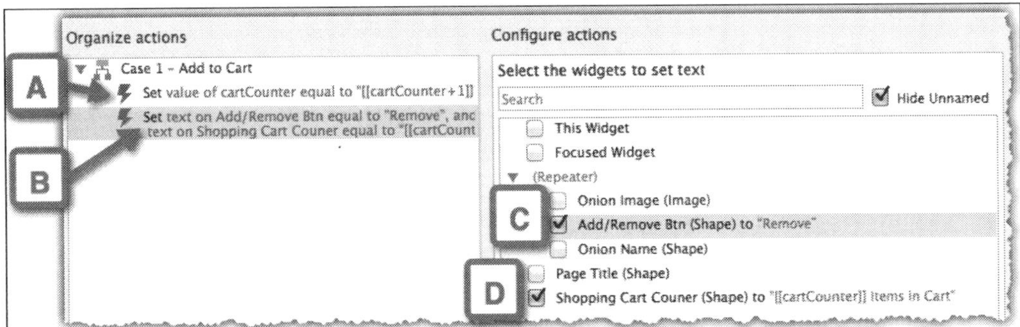

Image 39

Preview the wireframe and you will see how the **Add** label changes to **Remove** after the first click. You will also see that the shopping cart shows the new value correctly.

However, if you continue to click on the **Remove** button (*Image 40*, **A**), the text will not revert to Add and the total number of items in the cart will continue to advance by 1 with each click on the **Remove** button (**B**).

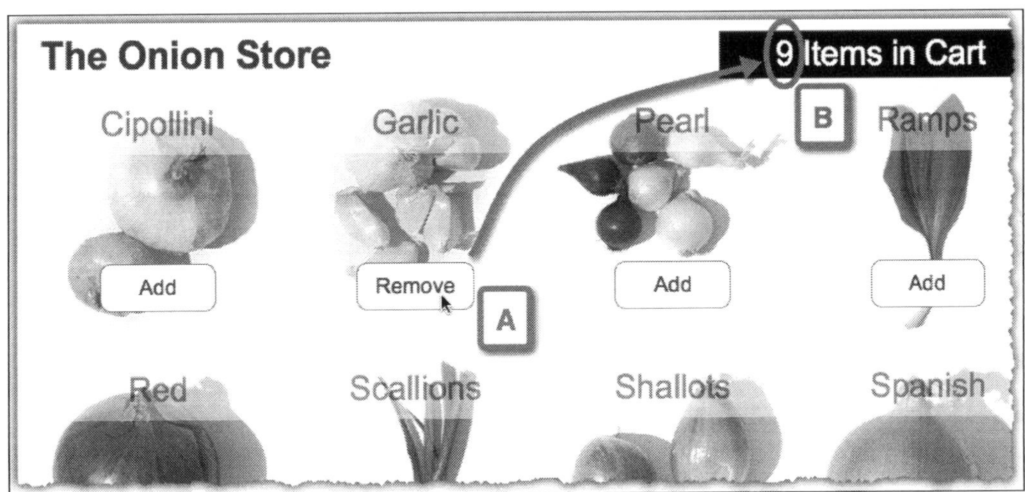

Image 40

To actually get the buttons to work, we need to use conditional logic.

Here is how to think about the first condition:

IF the text of the button is equal to "Add" (*Image 41*, **A**), THEN perform Case 1 (**B**).

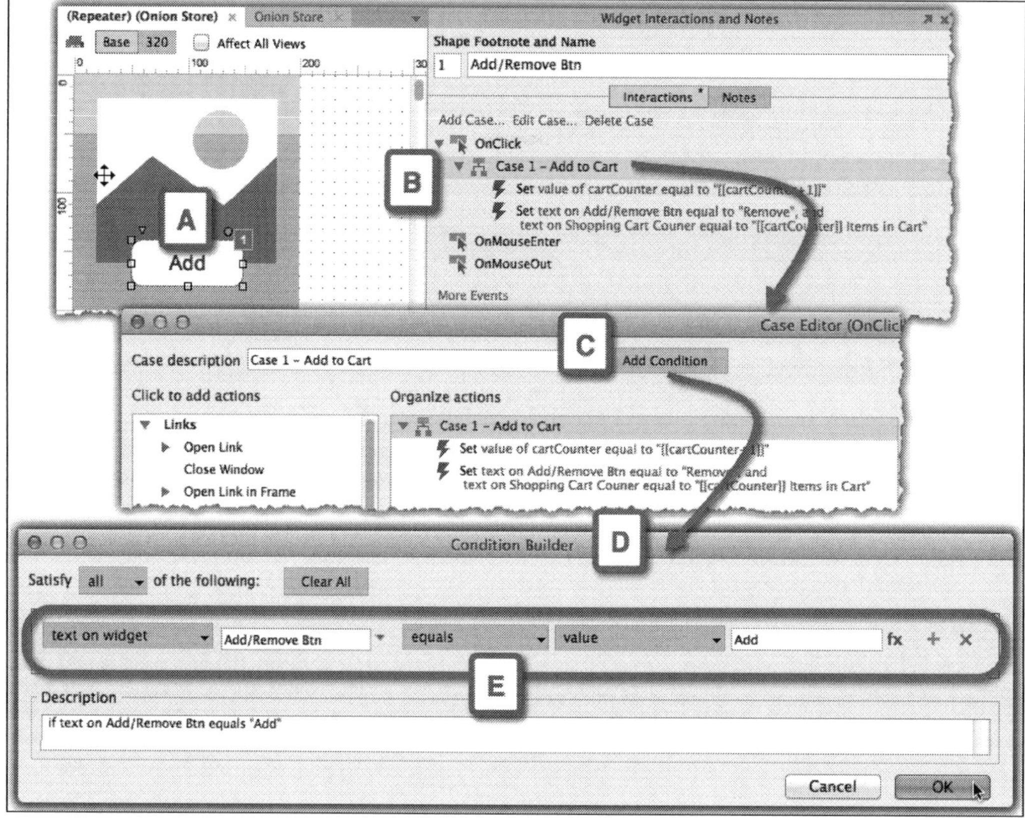

Image 41

In the **Case Editor** window, click on the **Add Condition** button (C) to bring the **Condition Builder** window (D), and compose the condition row here (E).

Finally, duplicate the **Case 1- Add to Cart** case and relabel it to `Case 2 - Remove from Cart` (*Image 42*, **A**), as shown in the following screenshot:

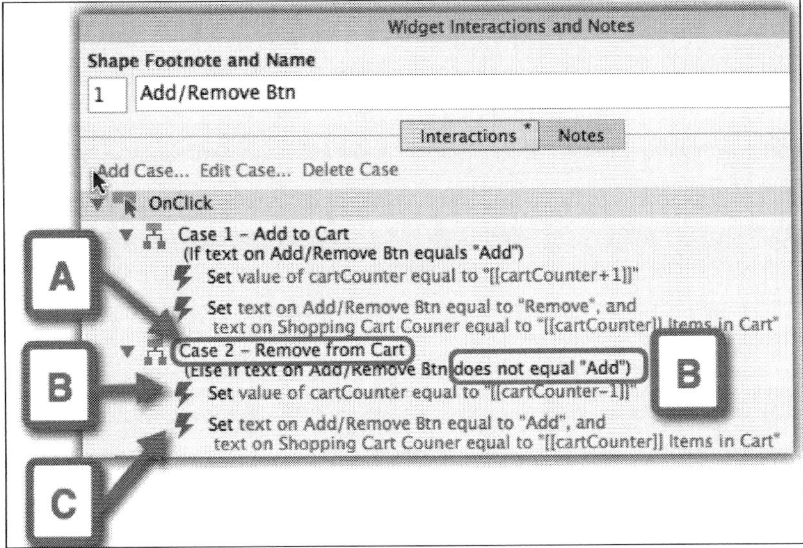

Image 42

This case just does the opposite of Case 1. Remember to do the following:

- Change the condition
- Change the value of the variable so that with each click, 1 is subtracted (**B**)
- The text on the button changes back to **Add** (C)

Points to Remember about Variables

Debugging interactions is unavoidable and can be extremely time consuming. Axure 7 introduces important aids to efficiently deal with the debugging process:

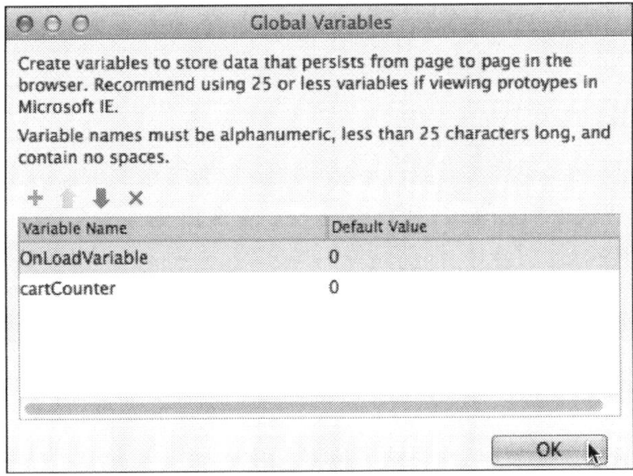

Image 43

The **Global Variables** window (*Image 43*) provides a one-stop destination to view all the global variables in the project and their default values. Initialing variables (in other words, setting a default) is very important. So, remember this while creating a variable. When the prototype loads, the variable will be set to that value and will provide you with a base from which you can follow the changes in the variable throughout the interaction.

When you generate the HTML prototype with **Sitemap**, one of the new options is the button **X=** (*Image 44*, **A**), which displays the variable viewer pop-up (**B**).

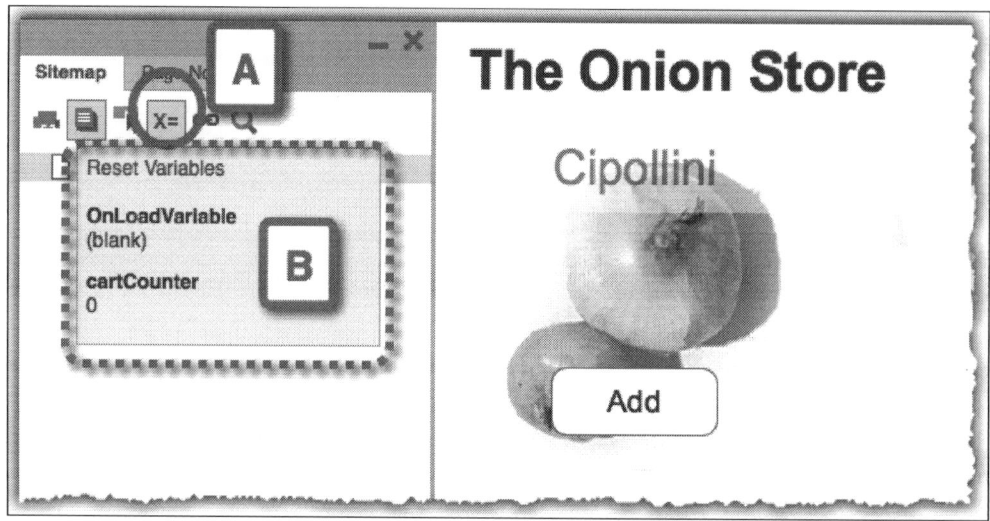

Image 44

As you step through the interaction, you can observe your variables in real time. Pinpointing an interaction bug is easier because you can identify the exact spot where the variable value does not match the value you expected.

[Think about your variables as a herd of sheep. You want to know their condition at all times. Maintain a list of the variables you use in the file, their possible values, and the resulting path based on the value. One method is to keep such a list in Axure as a dedicated page on the **Sitemap** pane. This is especially beneficial in shared project files because all team members can easily share and learn about the variables used in the file.]

This concludes the guided example on variables. While on paper the process may appear long and complex, it is, in actuality, quite fast and straightforward. Many of the steps mentioned here are basic and take seconds to perform. The key for success with this type of advanced interaction is to think through the entire flow. Remember what it is that you are trying to simulate and be practical about it.

Variable Types

Axure supported variables in the previous versions, but Axure 7 has some significant enhancements that improve the practical use of variables in your prototype and open up new possibilities to create high-fidelity prototypes. Axure offers three types of variables: global variables, special variables, and local variables.

Global Variables

As their name suggests, global variables, once set, are available to any page throughout the browser session. In other words, they will expire only when you close your browser tab or window.

Axure's Built-in Variable

Axure comes with one built-in global variable labeled, by default, `OnLoadVariable`. This variable is ready for you to modify. Rename as needed and set a default value. You can, of course, use it to track stuff when a page loads.

Create Your Own Variables

Axure supports unlimited variables, but like everything good in life, there are some limits. If you are using Internet Explorer to test and socialize your prototype, Axure recommends limiting the prototype to a maximum of 25 variables. In practice, 25 variables can satisfy a great number of advanced prototyping.

If you use any of the other browsers for viewing HTML prototypes, the sky is the limit if you want to use variables to the max. Variables are passed via a URL and as an example, the limit of the Firefox URL is 64,000 characters. In other words, when you add up the characters that make up the names of your variables and their values, the sum total should be 64,000 or lower. So, while there is a limit, 64,000 characters should be more than enough. In any case, the phrase "less is more" applies to variables as well.

Special Variables

Displaying the current day, date, or page name in the prototype is a valuable capability and another welcome enhancement to Axure 7. Like other topics discussed in this chapter, don't let the terminology hold you from using this function. Think about special variables as the Insert feature in Microsoft Word. You can insert today's date into a document or display the page number in the footer. Similarly, Axure provides a form of built-in access to useful parameters you can incorporate into the prototype when relevant.

Currently, these built-in variables include attributes of the current day or the name of the current page. Most likely, items such as current time and others' attributes will be added to Axure in the future. The following is a list of the special variables offered in Axure 7:

Variable name	Description	Example in editor	Result in prototype
PageName	Name of the current page as it appears in the **Sitemap** pane.	This is the [[PageName]] page.	This is the Home page.
Day	The numeric value of the current day. The value will be within the range of 1 to 31.	Today is day [[Day]] of the month.	Today is day 17 of the month.
Month	The numeric value of the current month. The value will be within the range of 1 to 12.	This is month [[Month]] of the year.	This is month 5 of the year.
MonthName	The name value of the current month.	This month is [[MonthName]].	This month is May.
DayOfWeek	The name value of the current day.	Today is [[DayOfWeek]].	Today is Friday.
Year	The current year. It will consist of 4 digits.	The year is [[Year]]	The year is 2011.
GenDay	The numeric value of the day in which the prototype was generated. The value will be within the range of 1 to 7.	Generated on day [[GenDay]].	Generated on day 3.

Variable name	Description	Example in editor	Result in prototype
GenMonth	The numeric value of the month in which the prototype was generated. The value will be within the range of 1 to 12.	Generated in month [[GenMonth]].	Generated in month 8.
GenMonthName	The name value of the month in which the prototype was generated.	Generated in [[GenMonthName]].	Generated in January.
GenDayOfWeek	The name value of the week in which the prototype was generated.	Generated on [[GenDayOfWeek]].	Generated on Tuesday.
GenYear	The year in which the prototype was generated.	Generated in [[GenYear]].	Generated in 2011.

Usage Examples

Here are some examples of combinations you can make with variables:

In the editor	Result in prototype
Today is [[DayOfWeek]], [[MonthName]] [[Day]] [[Year]]	Today is Thursday, August 21 2011
Prototype generated on [[GenMonth]]/[[GenDay]]/[[GenYear]]	Prototype generated on 12/28/2011

Local Variables and Functions

Both of these features are new to Axure 7 and add a significant boost to our ability to create sophisticated interactive prototypes. However, a serious discussion of these topics is beyond the scope of this book and a short explanation of how these features work can be more confusing than helpful.

Naming Variables

Axure variables have basic naming rules. A variable name must meet the following conditions:

- It should be alphanumeric
- It should be less than 25 characters long
- It should not contain spaces

Here are some best practice suggestions to keep in mind:

- As you cannot use spaces and are limited to alphanumeric characters, use the CamelCase convention, which makes it easy to parse words within the variable string. Basically, you need to capitalize the first character in each word. For example, use "WishListCount" instead of "wishlistcount".
- Use descriptive names so that you or others who work on the file will understand what the variable stands for. Avoid names such as Var1, Var2, and so on, because we can guarantee that within days or weeks you yourself will not remember what these names stand for.
- If you are working on a shared project file, each team member should add their initials at the end of the variable name in the upper case. For example, "WishListCountES". Note the potential for redundant variables as each designer creates their own version of the same variable. This is an example of a collaboration process issue, which we will discuss in *Chapter 9, Collaboration*.

Pros and Cons of Using Variables

Be strategic! Always keep in mind the phrase, "Just because I can, does not mean I should". In the previous sections of this topic, we discussed many of the aspects involved in using variables and the value of integrating them into the prototype. If you plan to use variables extensively, it is important to understand how interactions in general and variables in particular will affect your work, and in the case of a team, everyone who is using the file.

Axure makes it fairly easy to figure out the construction of a prototype and the interactions involved. Events, cases, and conditions are presented in a natural language that shields you from the obscurities of programming language code. As long as you label your widgets in a meaningful way, any Axure user should be able to open up your file and understand how you wired it.

However, it is difficult to infer computations and the use of variables that you yourself did not create. You might need a few minutes to remind yourself what is going on in the file if you open it after several weeks or months. It is not uncommon to forget which variable value is meant to trigger which path and so on. Our advice is to document key interactions and variable assignments. For example, create a folder in the sitemap and label it `For Internal Use`. Here, create a page where you can describe interactions and the expected changes in variable values. Such a page can be included when generating the Word specifications document to communicate the logic to developers and others.

The use of variables enables you to gain considerable construction efficiencies. Instead of redundant instances that show variations of a page, you may use just one page or master and manipulate its layout with variables.

Summary

In this chapter, we covered a set of Axure functionalities that are responsible for creating truly engaging, high-fidelity interactive prototypes. Conditions, raised events, and variables extend our ability to move beyond the basics of navigating from one wireframe to another. We can also create relevant context in response to inputs.

The use of these capabilities, while not too complicated, does require a higher level of discipline and focus. This is not coding, yet conditional logic and variables involve formal evaluation of multiple possibilities and things can quickly get complicated. As long as you document the values of variables, and the possible actions that should take place given each value, you should be able to reduce interactions that don't work and save time on debugging.

Finally, don't hesitate to experiment and try interactions that may help you to better communicate your vision of the experience to stakeholders and users.

In the next chapter, we are going to cover widget libraries—an important Axure feature that is essential for managing and sharing the global design patterns of your project.

6
Widget Libraries

"Time is money."

– Benjamin Franklin

An Axure widget library is basically a collection of custom widgets that are stored in a special file format called **RPLIB**. These collections greatly extend Axure's built-in widget libraries; you can create these collections yourself or download a library made by others.

If you are not color-blind, Axure's `.rplib` library files (*Image 1*, **A**) can be visually distinguished from standard `.rp` Axure files (**B**) by the color of their icons. There are additional differences which we will discuss later in the chapter.

Axure's widget libraries are all about efficiency, consistency, and sharing because they provide a method for distribution and reuse. As such, they save time and reduce costs by eliminating needless redoing of assets created by yourself or others. Additionally, they help maintain the consistency of design patterns across a UX project or across a portfolio of UX projects.

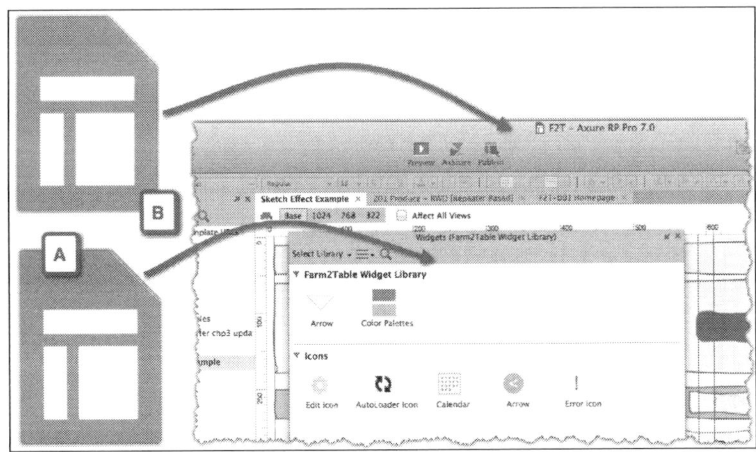

Image 1

As UX designers, we are tasked with delivering a compelling user experience that meets business requirements, technical constraints, and user expectations. The process typically moves very quickly from high-level conceptual sketches to detailed designs, from static diagrams to clickable simulations of interaction flows. Consequently, we have to:

- Produce many wireframes quickly
- Manage consistency of design patterns across the existing and new wireframes

The way to accomplish these demands successfully is through reuse. "Prefab" is at the heart of the construction industry, as well as in software development: the practice of using ready-made widgets saves the time of having to create those from scratch. In addition, we can manage the consistency of design patterns by propagating changes made to the pattern library to the project files that use it.

Before we dive deeper into widget libraries, it is important to have a brief discussion on design patterns because the concept is a deeply grounded principle across disciplines, from arts to engineering to computer science. The use of patterns in UX design is commonplace and complements the paradigm of object-oriented programming and application development. Within the user experience context, a pattern is a template for an application-agnostic group of widgets, which solves a specific interaction requirement in a generalized way.

Patterns are considered a very good thing in principle, but can be difficult to apply in practice. Everyone seems to agree that the adoption of patterns within an application and cross-applications improves skill transference, reduces the learning curve, and yields a superior user experience overall. Yet millions of users still have to put up with significant inconsistencies brought to bear by operating systems. To the decades-long battle between generations of Microsoft Windows and Apple OS, we now have to deal with inconsistencies among mobile platforms such as Google's Android, Apple's iOS, and others. To make things worse, the move to applications in a Cloud often translates to interaction patterns that are inconsistent with patterns of desktop applications, not to mention the patterns based on gestures, voice, and motion.

There is little we can do about cross-platform consistencies; and one could argue that the impact of such inconsistencies is relatively minor, because few users switch regularly between operating systems. This is not the real issue. The example underscores the fundamental problem with trying to leverage too much on any particular set of design patterns, because the rate of change is too high.

While the effectiveness of patterns depends on uniformity and consistent application, it is important to preserve openness to constant refinement, adaptation, and new patterns, and to avoid becoming dogmatic and enslaved to existing patterns.

Some examples of interaction categories where patterns play an important role include:

- Navigation
- Data Entry
- Grids and Lists
- Search
- Message and Error handling
- Shopping
- Sign-In/Out and Authentication

Don't enforce or lock into a pattern library too early in the design process. Remember that your ultimate goal is to design an application, not a pattern library.

This chapter is designed to walk you through the functionality of widget libraries. It will also help you determine the best approach for you and your team with regards to the creation of design patterns. We will cover the following topics:

- When to use a widget library
- Library types
- How to create your own custom library
- The pros and cons of using a widget library
- The pros and cons of using masters as a library

When to Use a Widget Library

If you are starting a brand new project and do not have any previous patterns you wish to use, explore the already created widget libraries especially if you are designing a mobile/responsive site, as there are many already produced mobile patterns available to UX designers. The following is a list of scenarios applicable for widget libraries:

- You want to create a widget library and share it with other UX designers.
- You want a repository of approved widgets for subsequent practitioners in your organization to use.

- You are on a large enterprise-wide project and want to share your patterns across the different product lines or projects.
- One person manages/updates the widget library. On larger teams, this may become an issue as the person responsible for updating may become a bottleneck.

Library Types

There are a few different libraries available for you to use and we will discuss each one in the forthcoming sections.

Axure's Built-in Libraries

Widget libraries are accessible from the **Widgets** pane. Axure includes two built-in libraries, which provide the basic building blocks for developing an extended user experience vocabulary. The built-in libraries cannot be altered, which means that it is not possible to add or remove widgets from these collections. It is quite possible to prototype an entire application, even a complex one, utilizing only a portion of these built-in widgets:

- Accessible from the **Widgets** pane, there are roughly 25 widgets in the **Wireframe** library.
- There are currently 17 unique flow widgets, which are meant to be used for diagram construction. Included in this library as well, is the Image widget. It is available in both libraries.

The mechanics of the **Widget** pane are described in more detail in *Chapter 2, Axure Basics – the User Interface*.

Axure and Community Libraries

In addition to the built-in libraries, Axure's website provides links to a growing number of widget libraries. Many libraries have been posted by UX practitioners for fellow UX practitioners. We include a description of one such library, written by its author, Marc-Oliver Gern, in *Appendix, Practitioners' Corner*.

The generosity of people within the UX profession is fantastic! The types of widgets you will find in the community libraries include iPhone, iPad and OS X user interface components, Android, Windows 7, various icons and social media elements, and much more!

Most of these community libraries are free of charge despite the substantial amount of thought and labor that was invested in creating them.

> To access the community libraries, visit `http://www.axure.com/community/widget-libraries`.

Of course, when you develop your own cool widget library, make sure that it is listed on the Axure site!

Submitting a Widget Library

Axure has very clear instructions on their website, but they are listed as follows to save you some time. This list is from Axure's website and here are the suggestions they request you to follow so that your library is approved and posted for the community to enjoy:

- Made in the current version of Axure (v7)
- Created using native Axure widgets rather than images
- Widget formatting controlled by Custom Widget Styles
- Utilizes interactive elements when necessary
- Widgets are organized into folders
- Library is saved as a RPLIB file

Your library must have a page on your website or AxShare with screenshots, a description, and a link to download.

> To submit the library, e-mail Axure at `contactus@axure.com` with your attached library and a link to your description/download page.
>
> Not all widget libraries will be approved and some may go through an editing process. Once approved, Axure will upload your listing to our widget library page.

Create Your Own Widget Library

Axure makes it very easy to create, manage, and distribute your own widget libraries, which is great because there are several circumstances for which extending Axure's built-in widgets is beneficial:

- You collaborate on a project with other UX designers and need to ensure consistency and efficiency throughout the file.
- You find yourself spending too much time repurposing parts of existing wireframes in new wireframes.
- You design user interfaces for applications that share an interface framework.
- You want to share with the world a set of widgets, which you think would benefit others in their prototyping projects.

How to Create a Widget Library

In this example, we will establish a widget library for the purpose of supporting consistency of design patterns in a prototype, in this case, for the book's demonstration project, Farm2Table.

Step 1 – Creating the Library File

Although the file-format of Axure's widget libraries is different than that of project files, and libraries are independent of the project files that are linked to them, the process of creating a new library requires you to begin with a new or existing RP file, as illustrated in the following *Image* 2 screenshot:

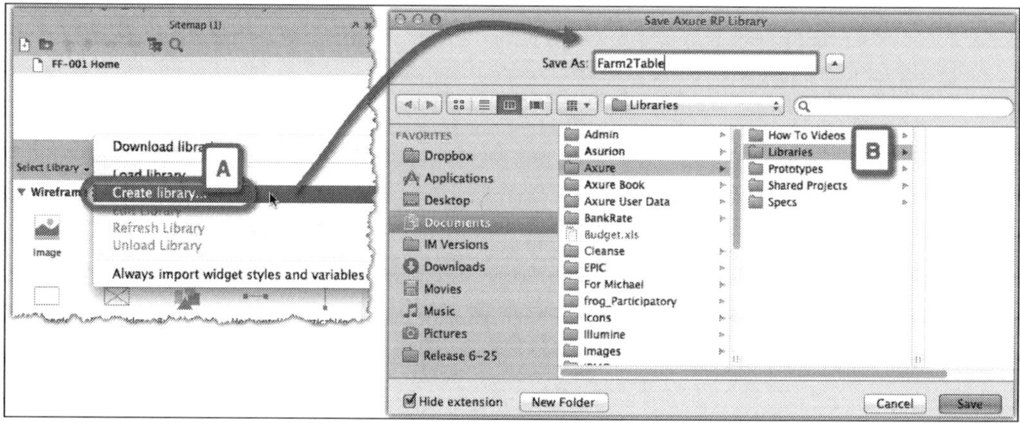

Image 2

Perform the following steps to create a library file:

1. Create a new or open an existing Axure RP file. From the droplist in the **Widgets** pane, select the **Create library...** option (*Image 2*, **A**).
2. Save the library to any destination you want.
3. The library file opens and you can begin to build it out.

> The prototype that you created the widget library from will automatically have a link to the newly created widget library (**B**).

A few things to note about the widget library user interface:

- The **Widget Library** pane (*Image 3*, **A**) replaces the **Sitemap** pane.
- The **Widget Properties** tab (**B**) and **Widget Notes** tab (**C**) replaces the **Page Properties**, **Page Interactions**, and **Page Style** tabs.
- The **Share** menu is not part of the RPLIB file format. This means that a widget library file cannot be converted into a Shared Project file. This poses some challenges for teams who share libraries.

With the widget library file ready, we can move to creating some widgets.

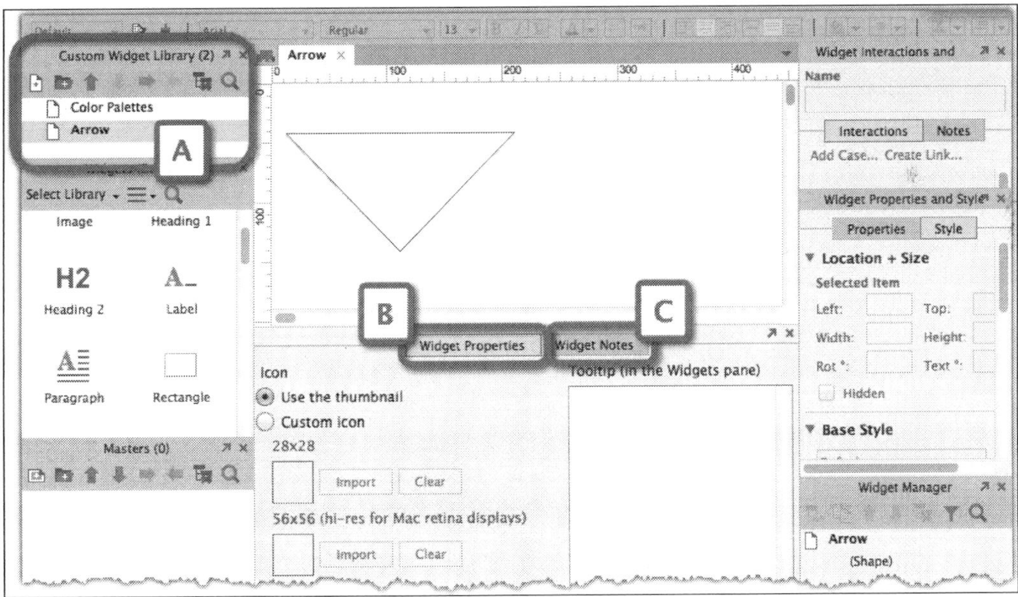

Image 3

Step 2 – Creating a Custom Widget

This is very straight forward. Click on the **Add Widget** icon (*Image 4*, **A**), and within that page, add your widget.

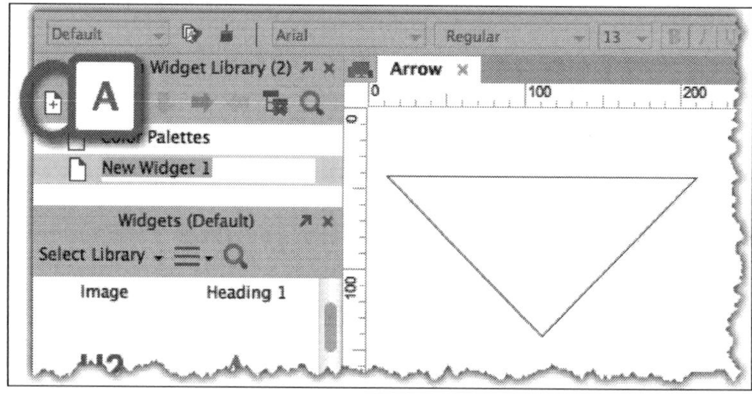

Image 4

In the **Widget Properties** tab, label the new widget (*Image 5*, **A**) and its tooltip (**B**). Organizations that use widget libraries gain the efficiency in their content strategy by managing consistency of language across all applications.

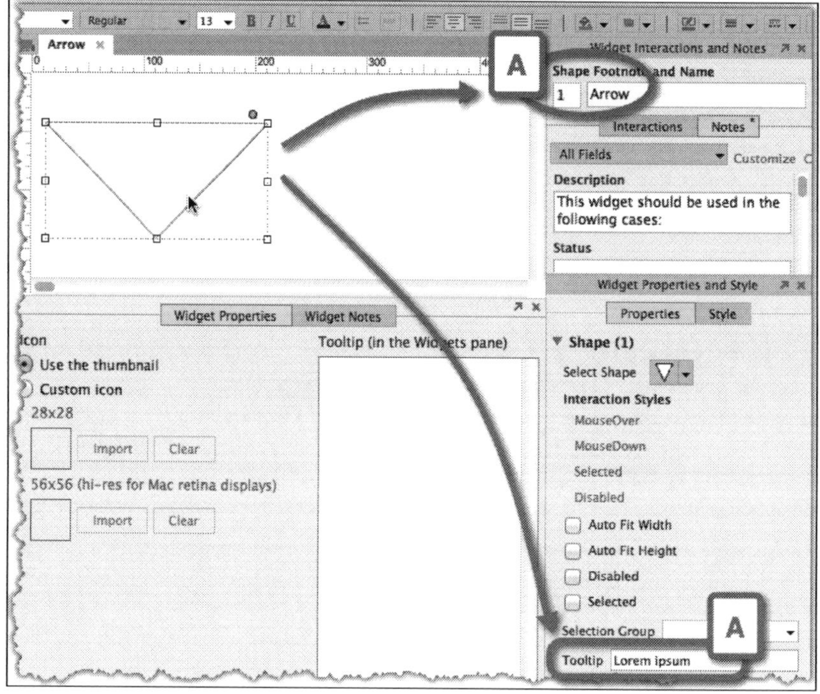

Image 5

Click on **Widget Style Editor** (*Image 6*, **A**) to launch it. There, click on the **Custom** tab, create a new custom style, and label it (**B**). Apply the style you want (**C**) and close the style editor. Special consideration should be given to naming widgets uniformly and in a non-specific way, such as a unique number, as the context of use for the widget, might change depending on the file it will be used in.

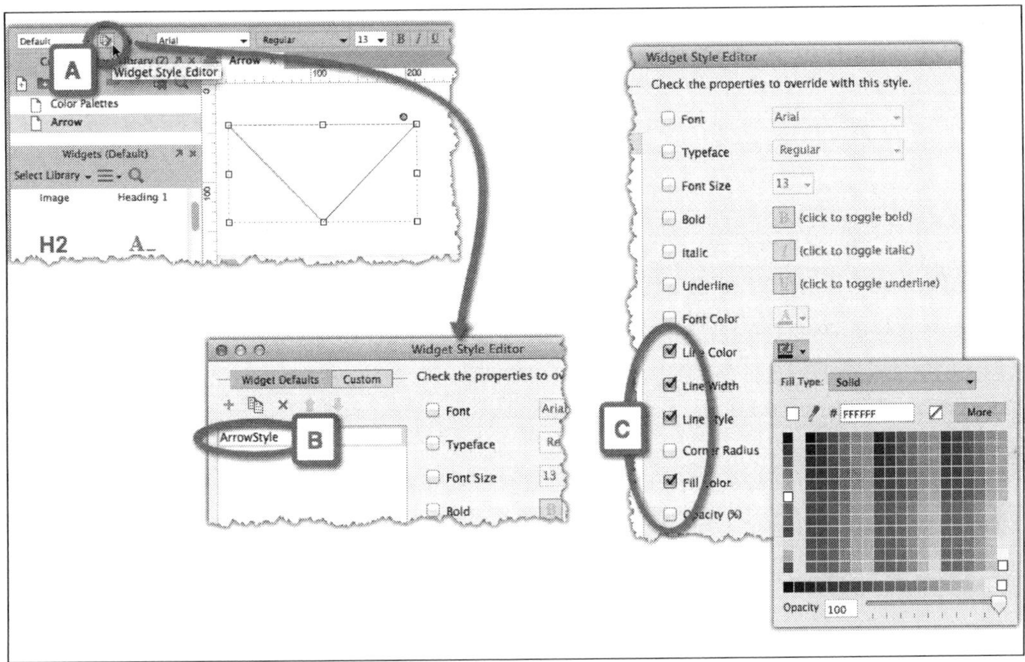

Image 6

Voilà! Congratulations, you have now created a custom widget.

Step 3 – Refreshing a Library in the Project File

The project file you used in Step 1, is automatically linked to the new widget library. However, as you add or modify the widgets in the library, you need to trigger an update whenever you want the latest changes to the library to be reflected in the project file. The following *Image 7* illustrates the state of the project file's **Widget Pane** before and after the update. From the **Options** menu (**A**), select the **Refresh Library** option (**B**). All the changes are reflected in the file (**C**).

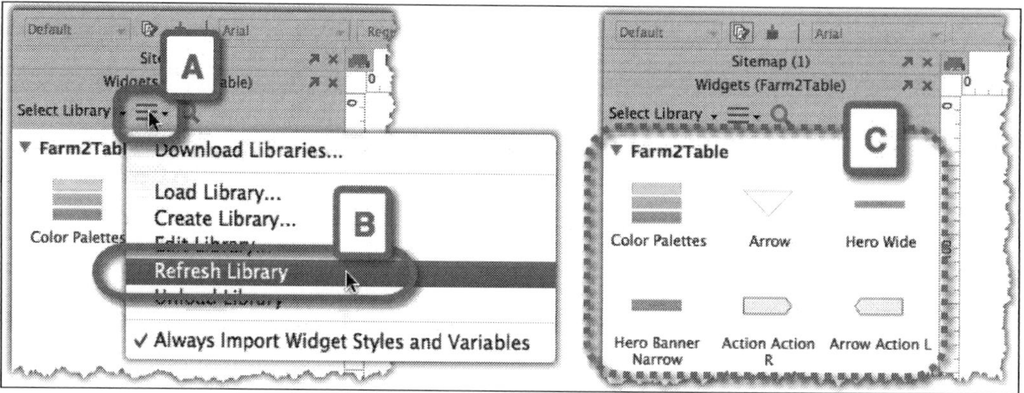

Image 7

[From now on, when making changes to the widget library file, we need to remember to refresh the library in the project file in order to reflect those changes.]

Managing Widget Libraries

You just created your first widget library, or perhaps you also downloaded a few community libraries. Now you are ready to use them in your prototype file. The **Widgets** pane is the hub for all activities related to widget libraries. Using the libraries droplist in the **Widgets** pane, you can initiate the following tasks:

- **Load Library...**
- **Create Library...**
- **Edit library...**
- **Refresh Library**
- **Unload Library**

When you want to use a custom widget from one of your loaded libraries, drag it over just as you would do with the built-in widgets. If the widget includes variables or a custom style, the **Import Wizard** dialog would flag such dependencies. If you want to create your own interactions or avoid importing styles that are incompatible with your project, use the **Cancel** button to import only the widgets or click on the **Finish** button to import the entire package.

Once you drag an instance of the widget into your wireframe, that instance is no longer associated with its original widget library, a behavior similar to that of Axure's built-in widgets and **break-away** masters. Thus, updates and changes made to widgets in the widget library are not applied to any of the instances of these widgets in your project file even after you refresh the library.

To track wireframes that use custom widgets, as well as the placed custom widgets themselves, add a new annotation field to your collection of widget-level notes in the project file. When you drag a custom widget from a library, write the name of the widget in the field. If you use multiple custom libraries, add the name of the library.

Remember that the widget library is a discrete file, completely unaware of and separated from your project file. When you add more widgets to the library, make improvements and modifications to the existing widgets, or download an updated version of a library you downloaded from the web, these changes are not automatically reflected in the **Widget Library** pane of your project file until you use the **Refresh** option. Once more, the widgets that are already placed on wireframes will not be updated, so you will need to update those instances.

Masters or External Widget Libraries?

Widget libraries are a great distribution vehicle for sharing your coolest widgets with the world. However, when it comes to managing a pattern library for a large project or an entire application suite, we need to consider the following two options:

- **Option A**: Store the project's patterns (Widgets and/or Masters) in an external RPLIB widget library and load it into the project file.
- **Option B**: Store the project's patterns as a collection of masters within a shared project file.

There are pros and cons to both approaches and depending on the circumstances of your project, you should determine which type of widget collection is appropriate for your particular needs.

Using RPLIB

The following is a list of pros and cons of using a widget library file.

Pros

- The library can be used simultaneously in multiple projects. Updates to a single library file will become available to all the projects upon refreshing the library.
- The library can become the organization's ever-evolving repository of record for standards, UX design styles, and patterns.
- For UX consultants, a personal library of patterns that are used often can become an invaluable time-saving tool.
- In a team situation, one can easily distribute the library file to team members.

Cons

- In a team situation, there arises the need to notify team members that new updates are available so that they know to refresh their link to the library.
- In a team situation, the owner of the library might make changes to widgets without taking into account the impact such a change might have on the wireframes of another team member.
- In a team situation, only a single user can make updates to the library at any given time. In large, high-velocity projects, this may become a bottleneck to the workflow because modifications to patterns are needed at a much faster rate.
- Updates to widgets do not apply to widgets used in the project. Change management of the prototype may require a significant amount of rework if the wireframes are constructed of non-master custom widgets.

Using Masters in an RP or RPPRJ file

We think the biggest benefits of using masters as a widget library are for shared projects. If you are updating masters on your local RP file, your colleagues will not be able to benefit. The following is a list of pros and cons of using a master as a widget library.

Pros

- Updates to pattern widgets are immediately applied across all wireframes where the masters are used.
- In a team situation, a designer who is about to change a custom widget pattern can first check where the master is used and discuss the potential implications with team members who are using the master in their wireframes.
- No need to refresh an external widget library.
- A smoother update workflow because the pattern library is built into the project file.
- In shared project files, multiple designers can own and update their custom widget masters. This parallel workflow works well for large, high-velocity projects.

Cons

- Widget patterns tend to be project specific, so it may be more challenging to consider a more generalized construction of patterns.
- Sharing with other prototype files has potentially serious limitations. The project file has to be made available to the importing user. If that user is working on another version of Axure, the masters may not import correctly.
- Difficult to evolve the patterns over time and across multiple projects, especially when the specific project file in which the masters were created, is no longer in use.

When to Begin Creating Patterns

As you can see, the steps involved in the creation of a widget library are pretty straight forward, so let's move to some best practices. In the past, we have seen many designers so focused on creating the coolest designs, that they forget to pause and see whether there are any new patterns emerging in their evolving project, often ending up with a fragmented design. This can pose many problems in the long run. The two most obvious problems are: poor usability of the site and longer development time because the developers are creating many unique elements. To avoid this, keep taking pauses while designing to check it. When you do and you find a pattern, add it to your widget library. At the very beginning of a project, it is obviously too early to have patterns unless you choose to begin with patterns from a previous project or use one of the many wonderful libraries that are out there.

> Our own behavioral pattern has been to start creating patterns once the direction of the design has been chosen. We work on very large-scale projects that tend to have many designers. So once we are clear as to the direction, we begin to create high-level patterns. As the project becomes more detailed, the patterns become more concrete or detailed.

The following is a list of the patterns we create right before the detail design process begins:

- Table styles
- Button styles (primary, secondary, and tertiary)
- Form elements
- Label styles (title case versus sentence case and placement of the label)
- Prototype style guide. For example, section background colors: while we design in gray scale, specific shade values should be used consistently across patterns in order to maintain visual coherence and quality.
- Any unique design elements for this particular design. For example, in the Farm2Table concept, we would place the image placeholder widget and the social media utility in the lightbox along with the lightbox itself in the pattern library.
- Of course, we would also have an icon library.

As you can see in the next screenshot, a pattern folder and an icon folder have been created:

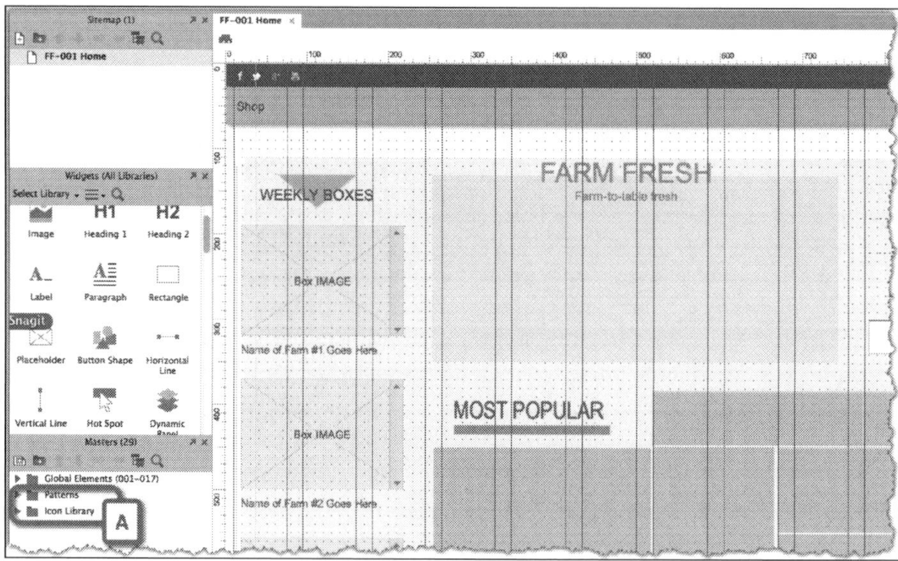

Image 8

Wireframe Global Patterns

We think it is important to document and design the following global patterns. We think it is good to get the client to think about these things and we guarantee the development team will ask at some point in the project. It is best to be thinking about these throughout the detail design process. In order to achieve this, we meet as a team to decide how we wish to solve issues such as error handling. We continue to check in with each other to ensure that our decided patterns continue to work as the design evolves. Each project may drive a unique set of global elements, but here is a checklist we use to ensure that we have tried to cover everything. Of course, we are not perfect and developers always think of something the team has missed!

- What is displayed when data is loading
- User input error handling (user input error)
- System error handling (system errors such as the system is down)
- Data display rules (this can be amounts, whole numbers, zeroes, and so on)
- Sorting rules
- Table patterns (document this once so that you don't have to document it throughout your design)
- Any form element behaviors
- Basic page rules and any rules for lightboxes

Summary

Widget libraries help extend Axure's built-in collection of widgets and share custom widgets with others, for free or a fee. The libraries available for download from Axure's website and elsewhere save you significant time and effort if you need to prototype for OS-specific mobile devices, popular social networks, and other commonly used elements. Additionally, widget libraries help develop, evolve, and enforce the global pattern library for a project or an entire suite of applications. In other words, they offer a strategy to manage and propagate change, which is the topic of our next chapter.

7
Managing Prototype Change

"Nothing endures but change."

– Heraclitus

Many UX projects are subject to two opposing change agents, which often place the design effort, sometimes the entire project as well, at risk. On one hand, good UX places a premium on multiple iteration cycles of design, review, validation, and revision, because these are likely to yield successful results. The process is inherently slow, can be costly, and involves constant change to the prototype. On the other hand, there are ambitious business plans, aggressive schedules, changing requirements, and limited budgets coupled with shifting priorities and scope. Typically, UX loses in this conflict.

Additionally, there is a dimension of change associated with our design tool. As we shift from sketches and high-level wireframes to a detailed design and interactivity, we are constantly developing the Axure file. New pages, repeaters, masters, and dynamic panels are added rapidly and wired with new interactions. It is tempting to use time-saving shortcuts such as copy and paste in order to quickly create alternative scenarios and possible dynamic panel states, instead of taking a longer path of thinking about the construction of masters and their reuse. It is also normal to keep the previous versions of wireframes in case we might need them at a later point. Before you know it, you are looking at a fairly bloated Axure file. It may take longer to generate the HTML prototype, not to mention finding the latest version of a wireframe.

In this chapter, we will look at Axure's features and construction strategies for dealing with prototype changes in a productive and efficient manner. The topics that we will cover include the following:

- Change readiness checklist
- Development methodologies, UX, and change
- Estimating Axure work effort
- Change and effective prototype construction

From a Vision to Reality

UX projects tend to follow an unfortunate yet predictable path. We begin with a project launch fuelled by excitement, high aspirations, and a bucketful of ambitious strategic goals. We follow with an intense, stimulating, high-level conceptual exploration phase, in search of a "killer" user experience. The outcome is a polished, high-fidelity vision that is presented to decision makers, who justifiably are impressed and excited, and they bless the ambitious project with the "green" light. They allocate a meager budget and issue a directive for delivery to be done "yesterday". Now, your polished high-fidelity prototype needs to address the details of low-level requirements, technical constraints, and pragmatic compromises that need to be made in order to meet the timeline and budget.

Perhaps this description is bleaker than what you have personally experienced in your projects; we truly hope this is the case. However, the numbers talk for themselves; let's compare the *2013 IT Project Success Rates* survey by Scott W. Ambler with the 2010 version that was mentioned in the previous edition of this book (refer to `http://www.ambysoft.com/surveys/success2010.html` and `http://www.ambysoft.com/surveys/success2013.html`):

Status	2010	2013
Successful	About 55 percent	About 60 percent
Challenged	About 32 percent	About 30 percent
Failed	About 13 percent	About 10 percent

Ambler breaks down the projects by paradigms such as **Lean**, **Agile**, and others, which we aggregated here. It is good to see a trend of improvement, but ask yourself: "What if only 60 percent of medical procedures were successful?", "What if 10 percent of skyscrapers collapsed and 30 percent of those finally erected were problematic?" These numbers are totally unacceptable, and yet, here we are.

Ambler compares other dimensions of software development paradigms, and on the scale of -10 to +10, he reports the highest performance on the following parameters:

- **Product quality**: Less than 5
- **Stakeholder value**: Less than 6
- **ROI**: About 6
- **Time/Schedule**: Less than 6

In other words, the results are really poor on all counts.

Despite the critical importance of UX to the success of products, it often still plays a small role in dictating and governing the budgets and schedules of the projects.

Regardless, by adopting commonsense practices for managing changes and utilizing the appropriate Axure features, we increase the value of UX in the project by maintaining a high quality and responsiveness to the ongoing change. We also improve the quality of our own life by reducing the stress and overtime that typically accompany a massive last-minute change.

The Change-readiness Checklist

The following are generalized and repeatable key steps that will help you and your stakeholders deal successfully, at least from a UX perspective, with the most permanent aspect of any project you will be involved with, that is, change. The common thread across this theme is the idea of upfront investment and foundation setting early on. In other words, to be able to deal effectively with change downstream, you must be prepared before your journey begins, and focus specifically on the following:

- Expectation settings
- Alignment on estimation and plans
- Construction strategies

Expectations, Paradigms, and Change

Regardless of your formal employment status, be it that of a consultant or an in-house resource, there are two issues that you need to address before the project officially launches:

- What exactly are you expected to deliver?
- What strategy should you choose for construction in Axure?

Answering the first question is often very tricky because it is difficult to make exact quantitative statements on the effort. However, it is possible to make educated estimates. While the answer to the first question underscores the relationships and agreements between you (UX) and the project's stakeholders, the answer to the second question affects your ability to deliver successfully on the agreements made.

An agreement on the granularity of detail that is expected from UX artifacts and deliverables is critical, because mismatched expectations are likely to result in a blunder and, often, a scramble to meet deadlines with significantly more work than planned.

Before reaching an agreement, you need to estimate the requested work in order to develop a reasonable estimate of time and budget. There is a tendency to come up with overly optimistic estimates, and here are some of the reasons for this:

- You are bidding on the project and want to be ahead of the competition
- Lack of prior experience in developing an application for a specific domain
- Lack of experience due to distortion of scale. An approach that worked in a small startup project may backfire in a large enterprise project
- Lack of familiarity with the culture of the particular client or organization
- Lack of experience with all of the previously mentioned reasons; typically, newly minted college graduates entering the workforce suffer from this
- You are a born optimist, and at the start of each new project, you hope that this time things will be better

Regardless, bad estimates will put the entire project at risk and affect your well-being. There is a high probability that you might find yourself working impossible, crazy hours just to keep up with an endless stream of demands and changes that you did not estimate for, but stakeholders expect you should deliver. This situation is not uncommon, yet it can be avoided, or at least minimized.

The larger the organization and the project, the less visibility you have due to layers of management, departmental silos, and office politics and strife, which often slow things down.

In this and other situations, consider three dimensions that will help you develop a reasonable estimate of the UX effort from an Axure perspective so that you can handle change with more ease:

- The software development model of the project
- The expected granularity level of the prototype
- The expected detailed level of the UI documentation—from light annotation to highly detailed specifications document(s)

These are generic dimensions, and are independent of your personal experience, the project domain, and other variables. They are all about expectations, and if you know at the start what is expected and in what context, then the budget, schedule, and the quality of deliverables can be in alignment with the project.

UX and Software Development Models

In an unscientific survey, we approached some colleagues in the UX community and asked if they can define the following development paradigms that Ambler lists in the survey mentioned earlier in this chapter:

- Lean
- Agile
- Iterative
- Ad-hoc
- Traditional

Are you clear about these models and can you define each of them? Not surprisingly, practitioners' definitions appear to reflect their own experiences, and there is a general frustration with the ambiguity and vast variability surrounding the paradigms.

Traditionally, UX has been weak on the smooth integration with development methodologies, often because these methodologies typically neglect to fully understand the UX process. Often, UX is brought in by the business side of the organization and is imposed on engineering, which may be set on internal methodologies and processes that are not aligned with those that the UX team expects to follow.

Make it a high priority to do the following:

- Get familiarized with the prevalent development methods in general and with the development flavor of your project, in particular
- Seek alignment of UX and engineering around methods, processes, artifacts, and deliverables

In our personal experience, and one that many of our colleagues share, we have yet to find a project that matches elegantly (and sometimes remotely) with any of the aspirational definitions for these models. We typically find a methodological blend, one that evolves and sometimes deteriorates as the project progresses. An extensive review of the entire landscape of popular development methodologies is well beyond the scope of this book, but we want to present a couple of them that are common on the spectrum.

Traditional (Waterfall)

Just a few years ago, an acceptable practice was to estimate the UX effort based on the number of wireframes needed to visualize a set of screens and user flows that was agreed upon. The common development model followed a fairly linear path known as **Waterfall**, in which requirements were first developed, followed by software and interface design activities, software build, testing, and release. After its first release, the software would continue to evolve through cycles of incremental enhancements until the end of its life cycle.

The traditional waterfall model did not require much collaboration or iteration, and it contributed greatly to the creation of a **silo** mentality in which businesses and development teams worked in relative isolation, and sometimes with hostility towards each other. The process called for each group to focus on its part of the project and hand over its deliverables to the next team.

It roughly looked (and highly simplified) something like this: The business team would spend a year on developing the complete business requirements for the product and hand the document over to the development team. That team would then spend another year on developing the application, and once complete, present it to the business team. The gaps between the expectations of the business and the development would often be substantial, although on paper, most requirements were being fulfilled. So basically, the organization would spend two or more years of substantial investment in the product and end up with a flop. Each group would blame the other due to the lack of shared accountability and ownership of the entire process.

UX often had little or no input in the planning phase. With little understanding of the UX process, business, and development, the stakeholders would make assumptions about how the interface should be designed based on their understanding of what users want. Little was done to validate these assumptions with the real users.

A minor benefit of UX was the relative ease of planning and estimating the user interface effort because so much of planning was done up front. Of course, once work started on the UX (design), the actual deliverables almost always deviated from the original estimate. However, keeping track of the changes was relatively easy as long as you and the stakeholders on the project established a clear change control process.

Agile

The Agile model shares fundamental values and principles with the well-established UX approach to User Centered Design. In fact, the first value listed on the "Agile Manifesto" (refer to `www.agilemanifesto.org`) is "*Individual and interactions over processes and tool*". Although the word *individual* referred to here is a member of the project team and not the end user that UX has in mind, this is a value that any UX practitioner would subscribe to.

The Agile software development model is highly collaborative and iterative and follows these key phases: requirements, architecture and design, development, testing, and feedback. Without iteration and emphasis on delivering a working software, these phases may remind you of the waterfall model. Instead of establishing both high- and low-level requirements before development begins, as is the case with the traditional waterfall model, Agile considers requirements in a flexible way, that supports rapid adaptations and changes as the iterative process unfolds.

From a UX perspective, there are some pitfalls to keep in mind. To start, Agile is fraught with technical jargon and terminology such as Scrum, Sprint, Timebox, Backlog, Burn Down, Team Velocity, Planning Poker, DOD, and on and on. Fortunately, there are also plenty of good resources online that can help you sort things out.

Jargon-heavy practices are always problematic because there is an increased risk of communication failure due to misinterpretations of key terminology. Always remember to not take anything for granted and make sure that you and those in charge of the Agile process are on the same page regarding the definition of various Agile terms. Down the road, this can reduce the risk of problems that occur due to inconsistent application of the same term by yourself and other team members.

If you are not familiar with the meaning of a term, don't hesitate to ask. If you are embarrassed to ask or worried that not being familiar with terminology will have a negative impact on how others in the team perceive your competence, research the term first and then discuss.

Agile Flavors

There are several agile methodologies that share the basic principles of the agile model, but they differ on implementation and sometimes also on terminology and practice. These methodologies include Scrum, **Extreme Programming** (**XP**), crystal, **Dynamic Systems Development Method** (**DSDM**), **Feature-Driven Development** (**FDD**), and **Lean** software development.

The profusion of methodologies and their associated jargon can be daunting for UX professionals who, in general, tend not to be well-versed in the arcana of developers. Agile is practiced in many flavors, and the differences between the implementation nuances of the model at various organizations can be substantial. Make sure to get a solid understanding of the particular Agile flavor that is planned, or is being practiced on your project, as early as possible. Your previous experience with Agile may lead you to assumptions about the process that may be irrelevant. Remember that you are part of a larger interdisciplinary team, so don't make assumptions and don't be shy about asking for clarifications.

Sometimes, the project plan has been outlined by the development team well before UX joined the project, a situation that is not uncommon when UX is outsourced. This plan may not take the full impact of specialized UX tasks into consideration. For example, a usability-testing activity may be included, but none or few of the activities that support the effort are accounted for, such as allowing enough time for recruitment, creating the scripts, and preparing the Axure file to match the tested scenarios. Reviewing the plan and ensuring that you are comfortable with it is important.

Estimating Axure Work

Keeping the development methodology aside, estimating your work, and more importantly, the budget that should be allocated to it, is a constant challenge. Due to the complexity of modern applications and the demands of RWD, agreements on the number of wireframes and the number of revisions are no longer realistic or practical as a basis for triggering change orders. With Axure, the boundary between static wireframes and highly interactive prototypes is blurry, compared to an interactive prototype coded by a front-end developer. Consequently, if you are a consultant, your risk of losing money, perhaps ending up working for less than the federal minimal wage, is real. We are not joking, and if you've been around the block for a while, you are not smiling.

The main problem we have in UX when it comes to valuating our work is the ambiguity most people have about our deliverables and the effort involved in producing them.

What appears to be a simple question, "What is a wireframe?" is not trivial when it comes to being paid for producing one. Let's use a home page to illustrate the situation, as all sites will have one. Only a few years ago, a home page would be considered as a single wireframe for the purpose of estimating and delivery. Today, we are likely to produce:

- A set of at least three layouts (for example, a desktop, tablet, and smartphone) corresponding to a responsive design system for the site

  Should this set be counted, for the purpose of estimating the budget, timeline, and resources, as a single wireframe or as multiple wireframes?

- Contextual variations targeting various user types such as visitors and signed-in users

  Should this set be counted, for the purpose of estimating the budget, timeline, and resources, as a single wireframe or as multiple wireframes?

On top of that, the page is no longer a collection of simplistic boxes but rather a composite of widgets, repeaters, masters, and dynamic panels that represent any number of common services and shared components:

- Each master is an independent wireframe and is potentially made of widgets, dynamic panels, and perhaps repeaters and other masters

  Masters are a powerful, time- and money-saving, Axure-specific feature, but should each master be considered a unique wireframe, or should we consider only pages in the Sitemap pane?

- Each dynamic panel is a set of unique states that are sometimes composed of additional nested dynamic panels and masters

  Dynamic panels are a powerful and useful Axure-specific feature, but should each state of a dynamic panel be considered as a unique wireframe?

- The wireframes also include a collection of interactions that enable the prototype
- Finally, the icing on the cake is adding the notes for the purpose of generating the necessary documentation of this compound wireframe/prototype

In other words, we can significantly pack more power and value into Axure wireframes, compared to what a traditional static type of wireframe can provide, but the time-and budget-estimating model should factor in your planned construction approach, complexity, and approval workflow.

Where Does Time Go?

The typical project schedule includes a built-in fallacy that equates blocks of eight hours per day to eight hours of productive work. For some reason, everyone buys into this nonsense despite knowing better. Additionally, most project plans fail to account adequately, or altogether, the following:

- **Analysis and synthesis time**: UX is often about creative problem-solving and developing a successful framework for a challenging project. This requires time. Time is necessary to digest the information that you collect during discovery and requirement development, analyze and synthesize the materials, and emerge with a concept or an approach. In short, you need time to think, and thinking takes time. Unfortunately, most project plans don't include thinking time.
- **Exploration and iteration**: Unfortunate as it is, these activities also take time. It is rare to hit the appropriate solution at the first draft. Often, several options need to be developed and explored, and the winning solution will emerge through such explorations and discussions. This is a time-consuming process, time that is also not fully accounted for in plans, if at all.

To be clear, we recognize that the clock is ticking and the pressure of time-to-market or other reasons that drive the project are extremely important. We are not suggesting a leisurely wandering-in-the-park-and-smell-the-flowers type of activity. Rather, we are looking at an up-front investment of time and resources that will pay off later as a cohesive framework, which will have sufficient opportunity to hatch, so make sure to fight for this time if needed.

- **Meetings**: UX is "face-time heavy", meaning that face-to-face meetings with stakeholders and team members will consume a significant portion of your day. At some point of the project, meetings can account for over 50 percent of your weekly schedule, for example, during the development and review of business requirements.
- **Elaboration**: Despite Axure's efficiencies and ease of use, wireframing and interactions take time, especially if you are modeling multiple use cases, conditional flows, and exceptions. You will be generating the HTML prototype frequently, reworking masters, states, and so on. This is time consuming.

- **Snags**: Sometimes, you will unexpectedly get stuck in a wireframe or interaction. You may have to reconstruct a wireframe that was previously considered finished, as a result of a required change. Don't assume that each Axure session will go absolutely smooth and fast.
- **Communication**: Phone calls and conference calls, responding and writing e-mails, creating presentations, and reading and creating support documentation are activities that will quickly add up to a substantial amount of time spent daily on project-related work, which you cannot postpone much.
- **Downtime**: We are not machines yet, although in some projects, you may feel the expectation to act like one. Taking food, coffee, and washroom breaks are fortunately still allowed and should be encouraged because productivity, creativity, and motivation suffer as a result of work pressures. Taking a break every 50 minutes or so is also encouraged in order to rest your eyes, stretch, and improve your circulation. Finally, even a quick visit to the washroom can potentially sink half an hour spent listening to a colleague's stories.
- **Health issues and personal emergencies**: We all get ill at some point or another. Flu, allergies, and other normal, seasonal maladies will require us to take a few days off from work in order to recover, not to mention avoiding the entire office catching your bugs.

There are no absolute answers to estimate both the amount of Axure work needed, such as wireframing and interaction, or the amount of real time it will take to produce. However, you can apply common sense and experience to any of the following formulas:

- **The optimist formula leaves only four hours of actual work a day**: Eight hours a day (100%) minus four hours (25% meetings and communications + 15% other project-related stuff + 10% downtime = 50%). In other words, plan for productive work of about four hours a day.
- **The realist formula leaves only two hours of actual work a day**: Eight hours a day (100%) minus 6 hours (40% meetings and communications + 20% other project-related stuff + 10 % downtime + 10% buffer = 80%). In other words, plan to work productively for about two hours of prototyping work.

This is why you will most likely find yourself at some point working well over eight-hour days, including weekends, and sometimes through holidays. If your experience does not agree with our description here, please let us know! What we hear so far seems to corroborate a general experience.

Account for Responsive Web Design (RWD)

RWD must be factored into estimates for obvious reasons. However, as you probably know from experience, depending on obviousness or common sense is not a reliable method as nothing should be left for change. The following are some of the elementary activities to be added to the estimate:

- Develop a device-agnostic design system
- Content and functionality strategies per layout
- Learning and experimenting with Axure's adaptive layouts feature
- Iteration cycles that consider the layout, functionality, and behavior of multiple layouts per your responsive system
- Scenario construction, debugging, and testing of the prototype across multiple devices

These are time-consuming activities, and moreover, changes to scope and functionality need to cascade across all layouts. It is difficult to have a generalized estimate without accounting for experience with responsive design as well as experience with Axure. As a rule of thumb, however, doubling your time and resource estimates is legitimate.

Account for Refactoring an Axure File

Refactoring is the process of restructuring an Axure file without changing the appearance of wireframes or the behavior of the prototype.

The first phase of most UX projects can be considered as the "honeymoon" phase, which typically yields what is sometimes referred to as a "vision" or "proof of concept" prototype. The honeymoon period is characterized by the following attributes:

- **Excitement**: It is a period of exploration during which you have an opportunity to understand the goals of the project and develop and validate a concept with stakeholders and end users.
- **Team building and familiarization**: Like the honeymoon of a newly married couple, everyone is on their best behavior, but some cracks may open here and there. If you are a consultant, you may also start getting a sense of internal politics. If you are an internal resource, you may already know many team members and be familiar with internal politics, which in turn might help you make quick assessments about the level of collaboration you can expect from others.

- **High-level requirements**: For their honeymoon, people often travel to some remote and romantic destination such as Paris, for example, or some Tropical Island. It is an opportunity to be away from the grind of daily routine. Similarly, the vision prototype is a high-level concept built to address strategic, high-level goals. You can explore and propose cool user interactions, highly efficient contextual presentations of information and user flows, and so on. Your work is unencumbered by the constraints of low-level business and technical requirements.

Typically, the transition from a concept to a detailed design will be impacted by the artifacts and deliverables you created and the expectations around the level of detail and elaboration in the preceding phases. This is when the vision prototype often needs to be refactored. Why?

In the vision prototype, you articulate a high-level UI framework, navigation, and layouts of the application, without having a good grasp of the nitty-gritties of business rules and other strategic or technical constraints. Naturally, your goal is to impress the team with your ideas and your abilities, and Axure is the right tool to iterate at a rapid-fire pace on conceptual wireframes and highly interactive prototypes.

You do your best to move with the flow and integrate all feedback and requests for modifications that stakeholders throw at you—"It would be nice if we could do such and such...", and you can mock it up before the sentence is finished and get stakeholders excited about the result. This is normal and good but all the while you typically do the following:

- Don't label or annotate anything
- Duplicate pages and widgets instead of creating and using masters
- Don't use Axure's custom styles feature to control the visual appearance of widgets—it appears to be faster to do it manually
- Don't pay too much attention to spaces and alignment of widgets, and don't use guides or think too much about proportional relations between elements

You move fast doing whatever you need to do to get an impressive concept out. When stakeholders and management embrace that concept, there is often a misperception that you are almost done!

The reality is that shifting to a detailed design of the vision prototype will have to adapt quickly to detailed requirements, business rules, pragmatic prioritization of scope, and technical constraints:

- Wireframes will have to communicate with stakeholders through annotations or detailed specifications using words and not just visuals. Labeling and notes will be required.
- Use of masters and/or a widget library becomes critical to ensure consistent construction, modification, and documentation of wireframes.
- Use of Axure's custom styles to implement consistently and cascade modifications of an approved visual guide design and branding guides.
- The prototype will have to be modified to support a prioritized set of primary and alternate scenarios for validation and usability testing.

More on Expectation Alignment

Generally, people only have a vague understanding of the essence of the work UX designers do. Stakeholders and other people from other disciplines who are working on the project consume our artifacts and deliverables, but they often greatly underestimate the amount of effort that was invested into producing them; this is a problem for UX.

You will gain substantial cooperation and understanding after you explain the work process, the value of using Axure, and the amount of work you need to do in order to create those great interactions and contextual flows. Most people get that and will begin taking into account the leg time that UX requires. The following are a couple of examples:

- **Prototype granularity**: The prototype will be consumed by everyone involved in the project. What level of granularity is expected from the prototype? Stakeholders may not realize that the more granular the prototype, the more effort has to be invested in managing it through iterations. The guiding principle for low-level interactivity should be its value to understanding the user experience and its use in usability testing as a part of an agreed-upon set of primary and alternative scenarios.
- **Specifications**: The primary audience for UI specifications is the development team. Stakeholders might incorrectly focus on the ease with which it is possible to generate specs in Axure with a click of a button, and not be aware of the following:

 - The tedious effort of writing the content that goes into the annotation fields.
 - The manual cleanup process that might be needed after the raw specification document has been generated.
 - The extra time needed to digest, review, and comment on various adaptive flows. More meetings are needed, and meetings will be longer due to the need to go over smartphone, tablet, and desktop views.

Construction for Change

The words "iteration" and "change" trigger different emotions. Iteration suggests a planned and consistent movement towards improvement, as in an evolutionary process, where more depth, detail, and fidelity yield a final outcome that is close to the original vision. It is a process. Change is a transition from one state to another, sometimes expected, and often unpredictable, a disruptive departure from the previous state, blunt and sudden. It seems to catch us by surprise, despite being a predictable reaction to dissatisfaction with the current state of things or to some unpredictable events. Evidence shows that there is a higher chance of achieving a vision through rapid iteration than through "change".

Paradoxically, what often happens in UX-heavy projects is that an iteration ends up getting a bad rap; it is too slow and too expensive. On the other hand, constant change in strategy, requirements, and people is accepted as a normal state of things. Perhaps it's because "change management" evolved into a thriving global business and "iteration management" is mostly mentioned in the obscure context of Agile development. A search in Amazon yields over 90,000 results with "change management" but zero for "iteration management".

In the context of change and developing UX in Axure, we focus on a set of features that support swiping and cascading change to wireframes and prototypes. We suggest that you approach the construction of the file keeping in mind that changes will disrupt and sometimes overturn the outcome of your iterative work. The expectations will be for a fast turnaround and you should be prepared.

Cascade Change and Rollback Change

In most projects, we typically encounter two types of change: one that involves going back and restoring an older version and one that involves changing an existing element across the board and advancing it to the next level of iteration (refer to *Image 1*).

We highly recommend a construction strategy that embraces change from the get-go, a strategy that takes advantage of several Axure features when creating wireframes and prototyping. It is a small, upfront investment that affords both the agility to reverse course and to implement new ongoing modifications.

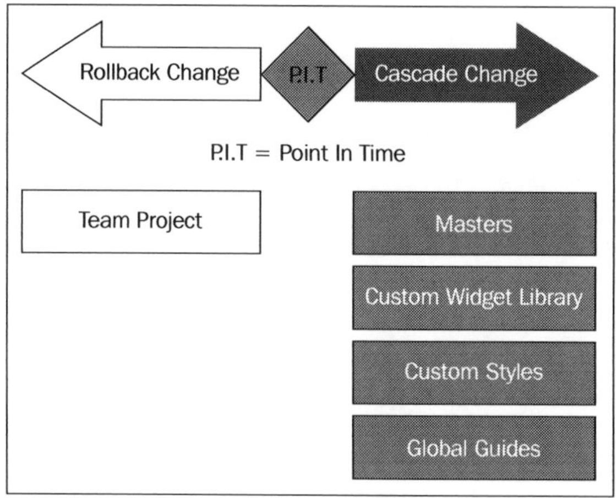

Image 1

Rollback Change with Team Project

Reversing course by reverting to a previous version of an entire page or some global element, sort of an *undo*, is a common occurrence, and the ability to support it is important. The reasons behind such changes may range from functionality descoping, a need for simplification due to time or budget crunch, to change in requirements. The first item on the construction-for-change list is the Axure environment itself. Even if you are the only person who will use Axure on the project, we highly recommend that you set your file as a team project and not as the default standalone RP file.

The ability to go back and restore the project to any point in its history is invaluable to iterative work. Often, there is a point where you are not satisfied with a wireframe or interaction, but you worry that it may be too much work to redo everything if your improved approach is not accepted. In other words, the cost associated with change seems too high. With a team project, you have the confidence that restoring will be easier. The following screenshot takes us through the use of the history browser:

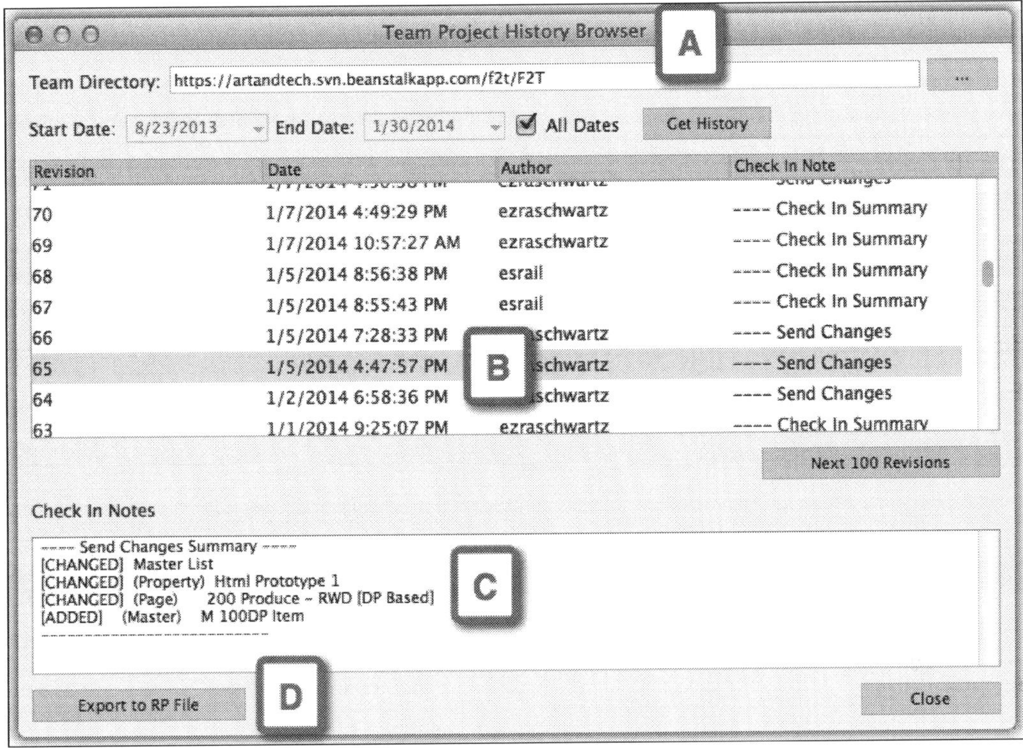

Image 2

The **Team Project History Browser** (*Image 2*, **A**) is the main conduit for pointing and restoring a previous version. By selecting any point in the span of the file's life (**B**), it is possible to identify the elements that were modified (**C**) and restore that complete version as an RP file. To read all about the team project, refer to *Chapter 9, Collaboration*.

Cascade Change with Masters and Libraries

Visual consistency is a fundamental principle of good software design and an attribute that can significantly help with managing change. Of course, not all screens in a given software will have the same layout. Rather, a level of visual coherence can guarantee a consistent experience across the application.

It is a common practice to develop pages as templates, for the following reasons:

- **Advantage to you as a UX designer**: Since we often need to create multiple versions of the same page in order to visualize variations, leverage design patterns across instances of the same screen to simplify construction of your Axure prototype and specifications.
- **Advantage to the development team**: Developers typically think about templates and code reuse, efficiency and reuse being native to programming. Developers will instantly understand and appreciate your approach of templates in the design. Discuss the structure of templates with the developers to align your modular approach to the coded modular approach.

The concept of page templates is very similar to that of masters, except that templates are not a built-in Axure feature. They are a choice of construction method you choose to use. In this section, we discuss several Axure features that lend themselves to the creation, use, and modification of Axure templates.

Cascade Change with Custom Styles

The widget style editor affords global control over the visual properties of a widget type. In other words, it is Axure's user-friendly way to apply **Cascading Style Sheet** (CSS) properties to widgets, with the exception of widget height and width.

Note the following items:

- Not all the widgets that appear in the **Widgets** pane are listed in the style editor. That's because some widgets, such as the dynamic panel, don't really have independent visual properties of their own.
- The **Rectangle**, **Placeholder**, and **Button Shape** widgets are referenced as a **Button Shape** widget in the style editor, so changes to the default of that style are applied to these three widgets.

Widget Properties' Cheat Sheets

The following tables aggregate properties that can be set per widget. Familiarity with the applicability of properties to the various widgets is useful when you plan the implementation of your visual design.

Also note that there are properties that can be applied to a shape as a custom style only when you create the widget for the first time. Changing the property later will not change the widgets that have already been styled with this custom style.

Consider the bold property for example. Suppose you create a style with a particular fill and line color, and the font is bold. When you drag a **Rectangle** widget and apply the custom style to it, the text in the widget will be bold. However, if at some point you change the custom style so that the color of the background is a different color and the text is not bold, all the widgets that you already styled with this custom style will have the new fill color, but the text in them will stay bold.

The properties can be clustered in three general categories such as font, shape, and alignment/spacing. They are listed as follows.

Font Properties

Font properties are supported by all widgets:

- Font
- Typeface
- Font size
- Bold
- Italic
- Underline
- Font color

Shape Properties

These properties can be applied to some widgets, but not to others, as listed in the following table:

Widgets	**Line color**	**Line width**	**Line style**	**Corner radius**	**Fill color**	**Opacity (%)**	**Outer shadow**	**Inner shadow**	**Text shadow**
Shape	Y	Y	Y	Y	Y	Y	Y	Y	Y
Paragraph	Y	Y	Y	Y	Y	Y	Y	Y	Y
H1 to H6	Y	Y	Y	Y	Y	Y	Y	Y	Y
Image	Y	Y	Y	Y		Y	Y		Y
Text link									
Text link Mouse Over									

Widgets	Line color	Line width	Line style	Corner radius	Fill color	Opacity (%)	Outer shadow	Inner shadow	Text shadow
Text link mouse down									
Text field					Y				
Text area					Y				
Droplist									
List box									
Checkbox									
Radio button									
Flow shape	Y	Y	Y		Y	Y	Y	Y	Y
Tree node	Y	Y	Y		Y				Y
HTML button									

Alignment and Spacing Properties

The following table shows the support for various alignment and spacing properties for widgets:

Widgets	Alignment	Vert Align	L-T-R-B Pad	Line spacing
Shape	Y	Y	Y	Y
Paragraph	Y	Y	Y	Y
H1 to H6	Y	Y	Y	Y
Image	Y	Y	Y	Y
Text Link				
Text Link Mouse Over				
Text Link Mouse Down				
Text Field	Y			
Text Area	Y			
Droplist				
List Box				
Checkbox	Y	Y		
Radio Button	Y	Y		
Flow Shape				
Tree Node				
HTML Button	Y			

Default Widget Styles

When you start a new Axure file, all the widgets have an out-of-the-box default style. By tweaking the default style of widgets in your project file, you can save time and enforce consistency across all your wireframes. The changes you make will be immediately applied across the entire file to all the widgets for which you modified the default style, with the exception of widgets to which you assigned a custom style.

Each time you drag a **Rectangle** widget (*Image 3*, **A**) onto the wireframes pane, its visual properties are to be preset to the default setting. These include setting black line and white fill, the font as **Arial**, size **13**, and so on. In the toolbar, click on the widget style editor icon (**B**) to launch the **Widget Style Editor** dialog (**C**).

Widgets that can be controlled by the editor are listed on the left-hand column, under the **Widget Defaults** tab (**D**). When you click on any of the widgets on the list, you can see its visual properties. Modifications that you make to these properties will be applied to all the widgets of this type across the entire prototype. For example, if you change the font, font size, background, and fill colors (**E**) of a Shape widget, the new settings will apply to the Rectangle, Placeholder, and Button widgets across all your wireframes in this file.

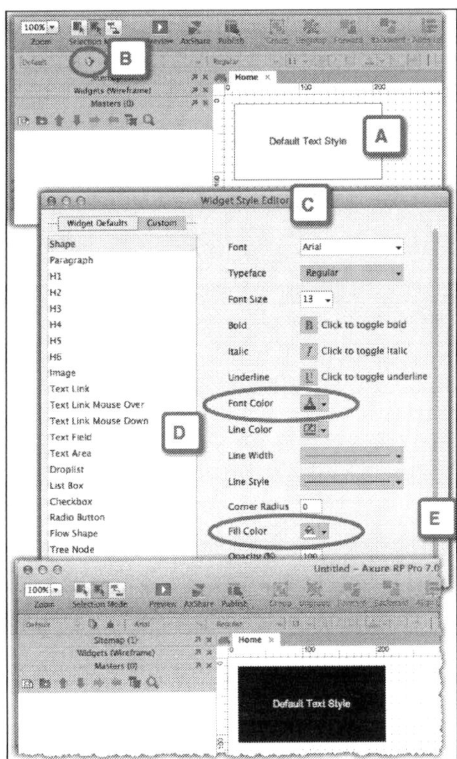

Image 3

> If you change the font family of one widget from **Arial** to **Verdana**, for example, make sure to apply the same properties to all the widgets listed in the editor. If you don't, the result might be an inconsistent mix of typefaces on various widgets. Also, make sure to review all your wireframes as some fonts are wider than others, and undesirable text wrapping may occur.

Local Changes with Style Painter

The style painter is a common feature in drawing and painting applications. With a single click, it allows you to apply the visual properties from one widget to other widgets.

For example, suppose there is a dialog box with a primary-action button and four secondary-action buttons. Initially, all the buttons share the default style of the Rectangle widget and all look the same. You want to style the action buttons in a way that distinguishes the primary button from the secondary one. The following are the steps:

1. Start by applying the desired visual properties to the primary-action button (*Image 4*, **A**) and the secondary-action buttons (**B**).
2. With the newly styled button selected (**C**), click on the Style Painter icon on the toolbar (**D**).
3. The **Style Painter** dialog (**E**) appears. Click on the **Copy** button (**F**). Don't close the dialog box yet. It will float above the work area, but you will be able to make selections on the wireframe.
4. Select the three unformatted secondary buttons (**G**) and click on the **Apply** button (**H**) in the **Style Painter** dialog. The desired style will be applied to the selected buttons.

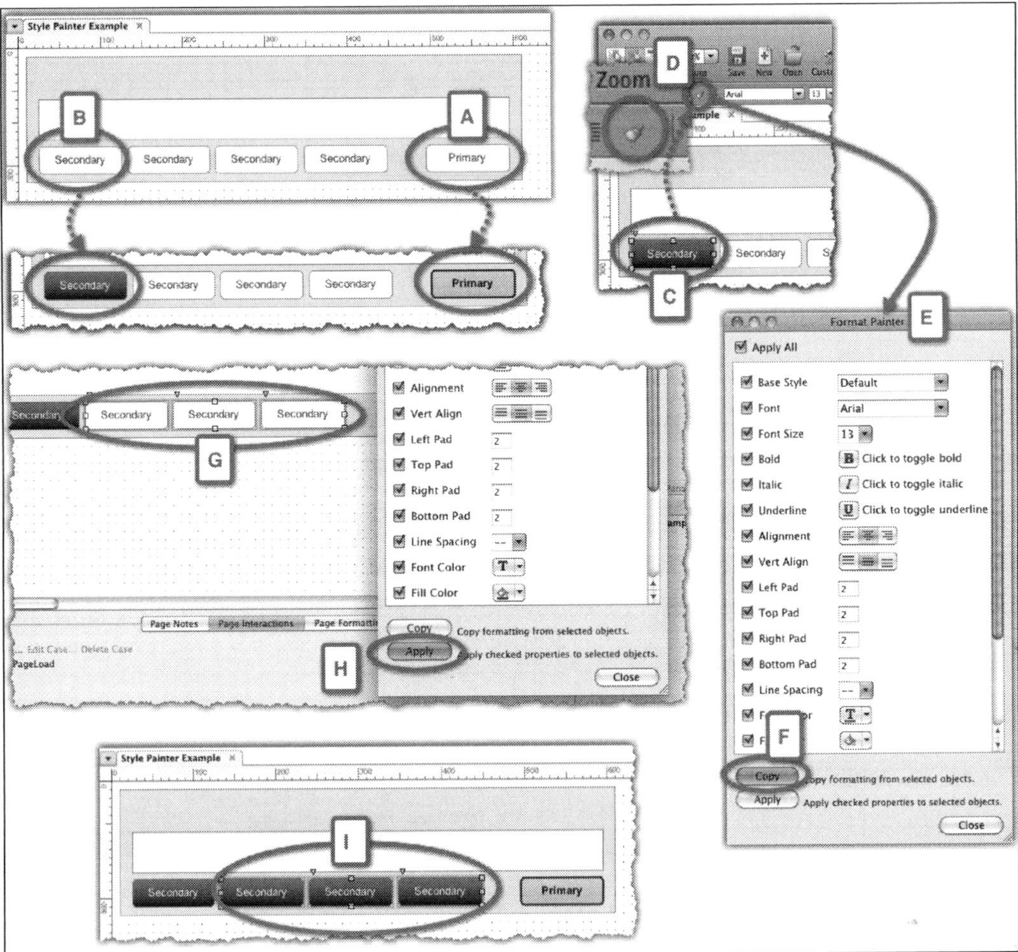

Image 4

Easy and fast, the style painter helps you maintain visual consistency across widgets. It is a real time-saver when you have to apply a set of visual properties that includes gradients, from a widget on one page to widgets on other pages. This is especially convenient in cases where using copy and paste to replace unformatted widgets with formatted ones is not a productive option.

There are a number of drawbacks in using the style painter as a systematic method for implementing style changes, which are as follows:

- You must apply the desired style to all like-widgets across all wireframes, which can be time consuming, especially if the style needs to be changed as a result of feedback.
- Even when minor style changes are required, for example, changing one of the gradient values used for the fill of primary action-buttons, the task of changing it is still time consuming because you have to go through the entire file and make the changes.
- It can be difficult to differentiate between widgets that have been updated and those that were not. Pressing the **Apply** button will be fast, but the rest is not.
- If you had started to apply the change to some widgets and had to stop for some reason, you may have a hard time figuring out which widgets have already been modified, and may have to go through the entire file again and make sure that all the widgets are updated.

Additionally, you cannot apply the painter styles, such as MouseOver, Selected, and so on, to other button states. The style painter is a welcome addition to Axure's widget-editing capabilities. It is great when creating quick drafts because it greatly reduces tedious repetitive formatting steps. However, when it comes to maintaining the consistency of an application's style guide, consider the approach we propose in the following section.

If you are using the style painter often, it is a good clue that you actually need to convert the same-styled widgets into a custom widget or a master.

Alignment with the Project Style Guide and CSS

The following technique promises to provide substantial efficiencies and speed in our ability to adjust wireframes and prototypes to the visual design. Axure does not yet support explicit integration of the CSS files, but hopefully, we will see this in coming versions.

Have a Style Guide?

A style guide is an extensive document that is typically produced by the visual designer on the project. For a large project, the style guide helps those who are responsible for governance and quality control with the primary tool to compare approved design specifications with what has been coded. A typical guide should cover the following aspects of the visual design:

- Branding Guidelines:
    - **The color palette**: This lists the HEX values of all the major colors, including gradients
    - **Application logo**: This includes all the allowed instances and sizes of the logo on various pages and display rules
- Design Elements:
    - **Typography**: This lists the fonts and the styling of fonts across the applications
    - **Graphics**: This lists the rules and styling for buttons and icons, including size, order, margin, and padding
- Structural Elements:
    - This covers the styling and sizing rules for data grid tables, windows, light boxes, alert, message and error boxes, and finally, forms

The style guide should be the document of record for anything related to visual design. The style guide is accompanied with a CSS style sheet that translates many of the properties' sheets, which translate many of the properties listed in the guide, into the CSS classes and IDs.

Some elements that are listed in the style guide, such as the details of the page anatomy, may also be covered in your UX documentation. Make sure to synchronize with the visual designer about the names and labels of various elements to avoid conflicting references.

Axure Custom Styles

Currently, Axure does not support explicit CSS integration either in the form of linking with external CSS files or by creating the CSS internally, but it is getting close. We have covered a number of methods that are available to quickly modify the visual style of widgets. We found that using the **Style Painter** or default widget styles have their limitations when you have to reflect the latest visual design in your prototype.

However, Axure custom styles are getting close to emulating the usage and behavior of CSS. While the implementation is not perfect, you can still gain substantial efficiencies in the change process and maintenance of the widgets' styles, and the ability to conform to the project's style guide and some of its CSS.

The following screenshot illustrates the use of custom styles to apply a primary and secondary look and feel to the buttons, including a default state (**A** and **C**) and rollover states (**B** and **D**). The details are provided in the following section.

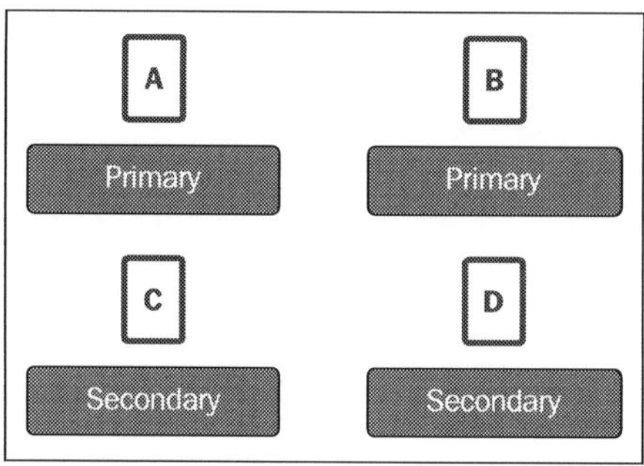

Image 5

The following table is a section of a typical style guide as it would pertain to the buttons in *Image 5*. It looks very different from a CSS file, which will be handed over to the developers. Typically, the style guide is an artifact that is delivered by the visual designer and is not created in Axure. With the new repeater widget, it is now conceivable to create the style guide in the Axure file. The possibility is not covered in this book, but we would love to hear about successful implementations.

Widget	State	Style guide	Image 5
Primary Button	Default	Fill gradation: Hex#: FF6600 bottom to Hex#: FFCC00 top Border width: 1px Border color: 99000 Corner radius: 8 Font family: Arial Font style: Normal Font weight: Normal Font size: 16px Color: Hex#: FFFFFF Text align: Center Padding left, right: 12 px Padding top, bottom: 6 px	**A**

Widget	State	Style guide	Image 5
Primary Button	Rollover	Fill gradation: Hex#: FFCC00 bottom, to Hex#: FF6600 top Border width: 1px Border color: FF0000 Corner radius = 8 Font family: Arial Font style: Normal Font weight: Bold Font size: 16px Color: FFFFFF Text align: Center Padding left, right: 12 px Padding top, bottom: 6 px	**B**
Secondary Button	Default	Height = 32 px Fill gradation: Hex#: FF9900 bottom, to Hex#: FFCC99 top Border width: 1px Border color: 99000 Font family: Arial Font style: Normal Font weight: Normal Font size: 14px Color: FFFFFF Text align: Center Padding left, right: 12 px Padding top, bottom: 6 px	**C**
Secondary Button	Rollover	Fill gradation: Hex#: FF6600 bottom, to Hex#: FFCC00 top. Border width: 1px Border color: FF0000 Font family: Arial Font style: Normal Font weight: Bold Font size: 14px Color: FFFFFF Text align: Center Padding left, right: 12 px Padding top, bottom: 6 px	**D**

The benefits of a style guide, as a communication method, over a CSS document are as follows:

- Style guides are a lot easier for non-developers to read, in comparison. Reading a CSS document is like reading code. Not a complicated code for some, perhaps, but class and ID names can be very obscure, and there may be other properties that typical UX designers may not be familiar with.
- Often, the CSS document will not be available for quite some time. While the style guide is created and handed over by the visual designer, a developer typically converts it into working CSS. This activity may take place later in the development process.

Without custom styles, managing styles is still possible. In the context of the buttons in the previous example:

- **Method A**: Create the buttons in the project's widget library. Whenever a primary or secondary instance of a button is needed, drag it over to a wireframe.
- **Method B**: Construct each button as a master within your prototype file. To use, drag the master over to a wireframe and flatten it in order to modify the text or size.

When it comes to managing changes of the visual design in your prototype, a major drawback of both these approaches is that once applied to a wireframe, you can no longer make a global change in any of the buttons' visual properties. You will need to go over each wireframe and apply the changes manually, which is a tedious and time-consuming process.

With Axure's **Custom Style** feature, it is possible to capture the visual properties of all the elements listed in the project's style guide, as custom styles, and from then on, use only these styles. Most importantly, this is useful in masters, as flattening masters will not remove the widget's link to the custom style. Consequently, updating the custom style will instantly update the master, its instances, and its flattened instances.

The following steps illustrate a simple example of the application of a custom style to a master, in this case, a button widget:

1. In a sandbox, create a master and label it `M Primary Button`.
2. Open the **Primary Button** master and create a button with a height of `32` pixels (*Image 6*, **A**).
3. Type the label `Primary` on the button and that's it for now as far as styling the master goes.

4. Click on the widget style editor icon on the toolbar (**B**) to open the **Widget Style Editor** dialog (**C**), and switch to the **Custom** tab on the left-hand pane (**D**). Initially, this column will be empty.
5. Click on the add icon to create your first custom style and label it. You can use spaces and other characters to separate the words in the name of a custom style; we recommend getting used to maintaining compatibility with CSS naming guidelines.
6. To apply the custom styles to the widget, click on the drop-down list (**E**) to the left of the widget's style editor icon. This drop-down list now lists the new style you just added. Select this value, and see your widget change to that style! As an alternate path, you can use the **Widgets Properties** pane, and switch to the formatting tab where the Style drop-down list also appears in the **Style** tab.
7. Repeat the process for secondary and other classes of buttons or widgets.

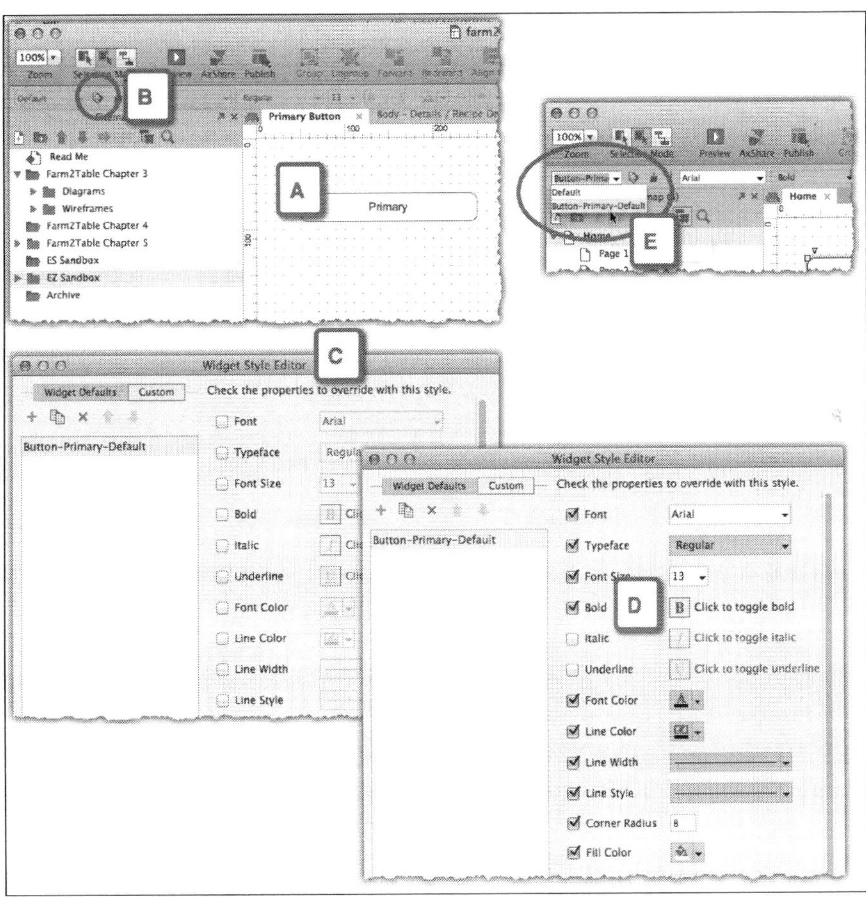

Image 6

If you have the project's CSS document and you understand it, you can use the class name used there. Otherwise, keep in mind the W3C's CSS 2.1 guidelines:

"In CSS, identifiers (including element names, classes, and IDs in selectors) can contain only the characters [a-zA-Z0-9] and ISO 10646 characters U+00A0 and higher, plus the hyphen (-) and the underscore (_); they cannot start with a digit, two hyphens, or a hyphen followed by a digit."

Please refer to `http://www.w3.org/TR/CSS21/syndata.html` for more information.

Axure Style Editor Versus CSS

The style properties listed in the Widget Style Editor dialog box match the properties in your style guide as well as the standard CSS syntax:

Axure Widget Style Editor	**Style guide/CSS syntax**
Font	Font-Family
Font Size	Font-Size
Bold	Font-Weight
Italic	Font-Style
Underline	Text-Decoration
Alignment	Text-Align
Vert Align	Vertical-Align
Left Pad	Padding-Left
Top Pad	Padding-Top
Right Pad	Padding-Right
Bottom Pad	Padding-Bottom
Line Spacing	Line-Height
Font Color	Color
Fill Color	Background-Color
Line Color	Border-Color
Line Width	Border-Width
Line Style	Border-Style

Continue to add the other styles and expand the custom styles library. As long as you style your widget using custom styles, you will be able to respond to changes in the style guide very quickly.

In fact, you could start your custom style library fairly early in the design process; a grayscale set of custom styles is a common use case. You can enjoy the benefits of visual consistency while you are working with this temporary grayscale palette. When the actual style guide is provided, updating the grayscale styles to reflect the actual design can save days of tedious manual updates.

Impact of Alignment of the Prototype with Visual Design

Should the prototype be aligned with the application's visual design? The benefits are substantial:

- Stakeholders and participants in usability testing can provide valuable response to the overall look and feel of the proposed user experience. Responding to change is inherent in user experience prototyping projects.
- Reduce confusion during development; the developers can easily see, in both the HTML prototype and the Word specifications, what they are supposed to code.

The second item is actually very important. When the prototype is kept at its basic grayscale and low-fidelity design, there is a need to manage two different types of wireframes:

- The wireframes of record, which are wireframes created in our Axure prototype.
- Visual design wireframes, typically created in Photoshop, which are delivered by the visual designer. These often reflect an older version of the Axure wireframes, which the visual designer used as a frame of reference for creating the visual design.

The problem is that it is very confusing for stakeholders and especially developers who need to figure out how to deal with these two different sets of wireframes. Everyone gravitates to the flushed-out visual design, and the grayscale work starts to get discounted and criticized for being outdated. The pressure to reconcile the wireframes and generate a prototype that has the target look falls on you and often sooner than you hoped. The desire to incorporate the new visual design is compelling and will be difficult to resist. Only through the use of techniques such as custom styles and masters can the effort be manageable, and even then, time for refactoring is necessary.

How do we get to two sets of wireframes?

- Typically, the conception process begins before visual design is engaged. In the early stages of the project, the focus is on to getting the basics right: the information architecture, global and process navigation, high-level functionality, critical task flows, and so on. By the time visual design is added, it is typically built as a skin on grayscale-based wireframes that are continuously used for iteration and testing.
- Some designers strongly feel that visual design is premature in the early stages and can often unnecessarily shift discussions from matters of substance to superficial topics of colors and graphics.

Alignment with Existing Visual Design

The following are situations in which you are restricted to an established design pattern:

- Comply with the look and feel of other applications produced by the company
- Be consistent with the branding guidelines of a corporation

The application you are asked to design can be new or a functionality enhancement of an existing application. The user experience you develop may represent a departure from the company's existing or legacy assets, but the visual design must match.

You may have access to the master files of the visual assets in the form of Photoshop, Illustrator, or PNG files. However, all you have to work with are often the graphics that are used on an existing site or application. These you can extract and modify for use in your own prototype.

With Axure, it is possible to use an exceptionally fast method to create, extend, and manage interactive prototypes that are based on an existing application. The following example demonstrates how to use screen captures of an existing site to create a custom widget library that becomes the source of building blocks that are required to design an extension to an existing application.

The following steps illustrate the example, which is based on the home page of `www.packtpub.com`:

1. Take screen captures of the existing interface. The PNG format is the best.
2. In Axure, use the **Slice Image** option to carve out repeating visual patterns. You can also refine the various widgets in an image-editing tool such as Fireworks or Photoshop, or a screen capture tool such as Snagit.
3. Create a widget library and add all the graphic assets.
4. You can now rebuild pages based on the existing look and feel and experiment with incremental changes to various patterns by replacing a graphic slice with a widget-based wireframe in the master.

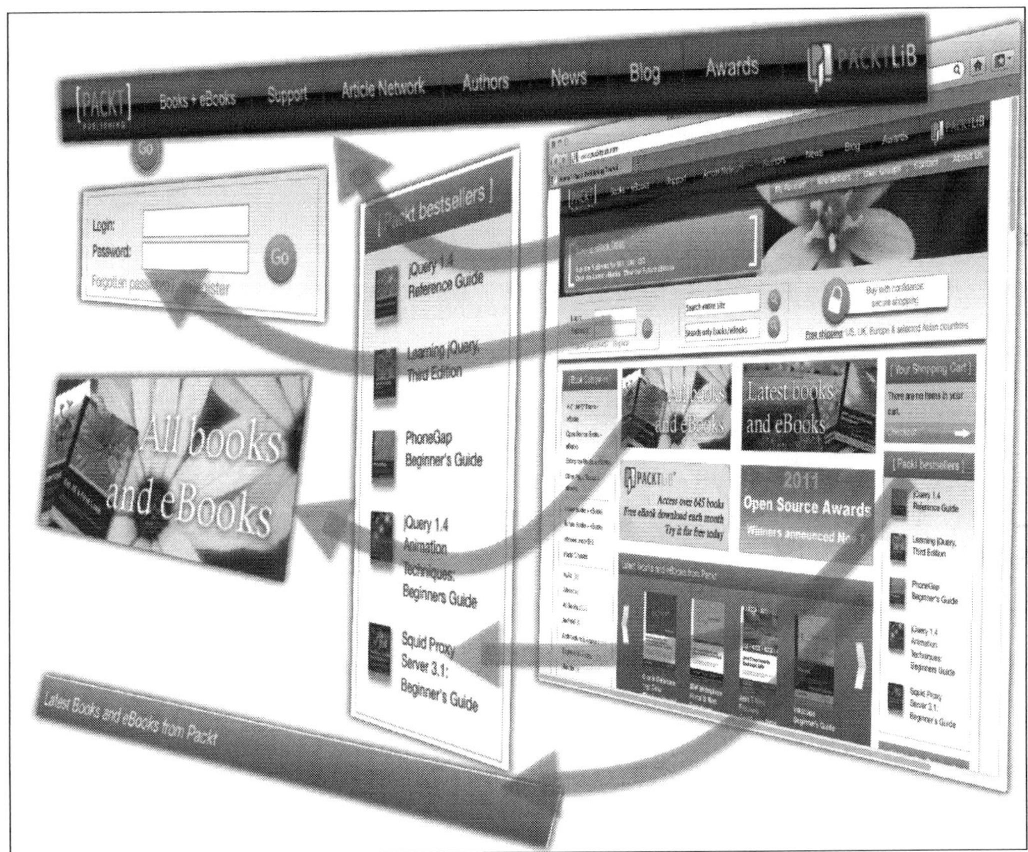

Image 7

The Page Style Editor

With the **Page Style Editor** dialog box, you can create custom page-level styles, which you can apply to a specific page in your prototype. The key benefits of this feature are as follows:

- Consistency across all pages that share similar properties.
- Ability to change wireframes quickly and efficiently during the detailed design phase. When changes to any of the page style's properties are called for, you only need to make the modification once to the custom page style.

We touched upon the **Page Style Editor** dialog box earlier in the book, in the context of the **Sketch Effect** feature. However, there are additional properties you can control, which, in a manner that is similar to the properties listed in the **Widget Style Editor** dialog box, map to CSS properties. Axure shields you from having to know CSS, its terminologies, and syntax, but understanding the mapping can be useful when you discuss visual design with developers and designers.

Axure Page Style Editor	CSS
Page Align	Margin and Padding
Back Color	background-color
Back Image	background-image
Back Image—Import	background-attachment
Horz Align	background-position
Vert Align	background-position
Repeat	background-repeat

Finally, note that page styles do not impact widget styles, but there is one exception: if you use the **Sketch Effects** feature, the sketchiness value will be applied to the widgets on the page. The widgets will retain all their standard or custom properties, but will appear sketchy.

Guides

The construction quality of the wireframes that make up the prototype is important because the recognition of such quality, or lack of recognition is instant. Stakeholders are unconsciously and consciously sensitive to the presentation quality of the wireframes and prototype. Make no mistakes as first impressions matter even if you are showing the first of many drafts of what will eventually morph into a high-fidelity prototype.

Quality is often expressed in small details, such as proper alignment, order, proportion, and the composition balance of the elements of the page. It is well worth the minor time investment of neatly organizing widgets on the page from the start instead of overlooking the positioning of widgets "because it is only a draft".

With Axure, it is possible to move beyond the casual use of guides as a temporary alignment aid. You can also take advantage of guides as scaffoldings that support the consistency of layouts and patterns across multiple pages of your prototype. Axure supports both global guides and page-level guides.

Global Guides

Axure's global guides are what most people who deal with RWD actually refer to as The Grid—an unfortunate terminology misalignment between Axure and the world.

The global grid is a construct that affects the entire design framework, and the idea that the contents of a page can be organized in a consistent, flexible, and proportional arrangement of columns is ancient. The overall effect helps create good page layouts that are pleasing to the eye because the width of all content elements and their span is based on the same ratio. If you consider the guide early in the design process, you are likely to gain efficiencies of construction because the width of widgets will be set to a standard ratio, allowing you the flexibility to mix and match widgets across pages.

Describing the grid concept and variations in RWD is beyond the scope of this book, but Axure's global guides is a feature that lets you generate a grid system based on a predefined number of columns that are applied to a page, and helps you arrange content in blocks that span any combination of the columns for that grid. Note the unfortunate terminology mix-up here; Axure has decided to use the term "guide" to refer to what is commonly referenced by all RWD frameworks as a grid.

Axure comes loaded with two global guide presets based on a 960 and 1200 grids. However, as RWD frameworks such as Twitter Bootstrap and ZURB Foundation are becoming mainstream, you are likely to create a grid that will be an approximation of the grid used by your development team. This is really important, so make sure to discuss the appropriate approach before you begin with a detailed design.

We are often asked to review Axure files and are always surprised to find that the pages do not conform to any global guides. As a result, it is difficult to develop a unified, widget library that can be repurposed across several pages. The width of widgets varies, and as a result, swapping, adding, and modularizing pages becomes a time-consuming task.

Global guides are important even if you are not designing with adaptive views, and are critical if you do.

Page Guides

Guides are also available on a page level. In addition to the global guides, which are created as a set, you can add individual vertical or horizontal rules by dragging them over from the horizontal and vertical ruler bars, similar to Fireworks, Photoshop, and other tools. The use of page guides is typically casual and probably more common than the use of global guides. Often, you just want a visual aid to help you with the organization of widgets on the page. The ability to control the guides per page provides additional flexibility for page-level design.

To apply page-level guides to other pages, copy and paste the guides from page to page. Unfortunately, you cannot save the local guides for reuse on other pages, and we hope such functionality will be added at some point.

The most common use of guides, however, is casual. Typically, the guide is needed to align objects across a horizontal or vertical line. Most users of drawing and painting applications are familiar with the convention of creating guides by dragging them over from the vertical or horizontal rulers.

To add a horizontal guide to the page, click on the horizontal ruler and drag down to the page area. A thin green line will appear. The Y coordinate will be displayed to assist with exact positioning (*Image 8*, **A**).

To remove a guide, you can either click and drag it out of the page (**B**) or right-click on it and use the **Delete** option from the context menu.

To lock a guide to the page, right-click and select the **Lock** option from the context menu (**C**).

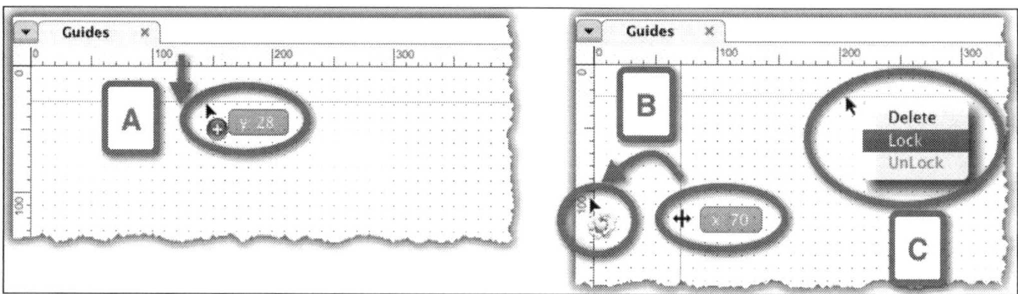

Image 8

Grid

We have noted that Axure's terminology conflicts with common RWD terminology, and so Axure's guides are RWD's grids. Axure's grid, on the other hand, is a visual tool that helps with the organization of wireframe layouts and is common to most drawing and illustration software. The grid is an infinite pattern of horizontal and vertical lines that are set to a predefined interval and are a part of the page background in the editing mode. However, they are not visible in the generated prototype or Word specifications screenshots.

The grid is perhaps a trivial and little-noticed feature of Axure, and many users don't bother to display it or change the default "out-of-the-box" settings. However, you can improve the construction quality of your wireframes by taking advantage of the grid to align widgets across a horizontal or vertical axis.

Customizing the Grid

You can customize the Axure grid using the **Grid Settings** option, which you can access from the **Grid and Guides** option in the **Arrange** tab from the wireframe's menu. Alternatively, you can right-click anywhere within an empty space in the wireframe area. You can also toggle the visibility of the grid. Axure also lets you toggle the **Snap** feature, which makes the grid lines function like a magnet; as you drag a widget across a wireframe, it snaps to the closest grid line. The following screenshot illustrates the process of customizing the grid:

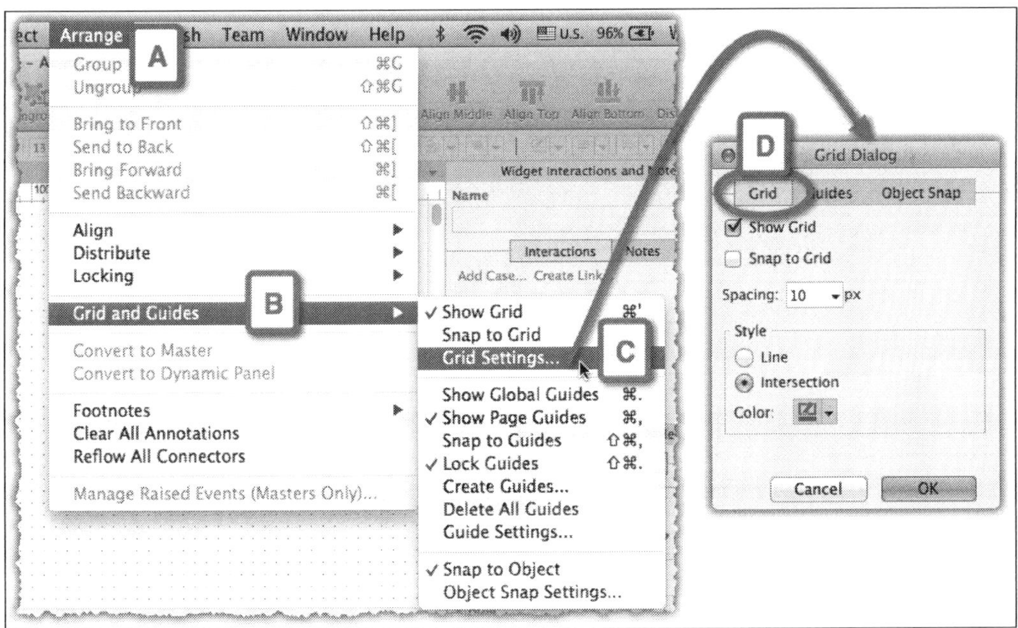

Image 9

From the **Arrange** menu (*Image 9*, **A**), select the **Grid and Guide** option (**B**), and then select the **Grid Setting...** option (**C**).

The **Grid Dialog** opens on the **Grid** tab (**D**). The default Axure grid is set to a 10-pixel spacing with **Intersection** style.

If you switch the grid style to **Line**, keep in mind that it might be difficult to distinguish between grid lines and guide lines. As always, experiment with the options and settle for what you are most comfortable with.

Summary

In this chapter, we discussed the challenges that UX practitioners face while managing predictable and unpredictable changes to the prototype. Many of these challenges have nothing to do with Axure, but fall squarely on the realities of software development. And of course, change in the form of constant iteration for the purpose of optimizing the user experience is inherent to UX. Consequently, it is in our best interest to figure out how to avoid the most tedious and time-consuming chores that typically involve tweaking the layout and visual design.

Axure provides a number of features that support changes on a global level. Some are common to many applications, such as the find and replace feature that is used for modifying text strings in the prototype. The powerful and still evolving **Custom Styles** feature provides dramatic time- and effort-saving in maintaining the consistency of visual design patterns across the prototype as do the use of masters, raised events, and "central-command" interactions.

The key to successful change management is, however, in expectations management. Assume that stakeholders need to be educated about the effort involved in requesting UX work because they are not familiar with the practice. Your ability to estimate the overall scope of effort and level of wireframing, prototyping, refactoring, and specification efforts should be combined with your ability to educate and articulate what's involved in your work.

In the next chapter, we will discuss the workflows involved in the creation of the UI specifications document, a process that begins with alignment of expectations around the document, the output format, and so on.

8

UI Specifications

"Great things are done by a series of small things brought together."

– Vincent Van Gogh

The UI specifications document is a communications tool; it is written in a formal way in which the UX designers prescribe to the developers the desired behavior of the user interface. If you need to deliver such a document, your takeaways from this chapter should be:

- When scoping the project, determine the deliverable; is it the prototype with annotations, a Word/PDF document, or both? The answer you receive will have a direct impact on your approach to Axure and thus, on your estimates.
- Understand your audience by learning what their expectations are from this deliverable.
- If it is a Word/PDF document, show the development samples and gain approval on the format and scope of the specifications as early in the project as possible.
- Communication with the development team is vital to success. No matter how much they want you to document, walking the team through the design and soliciting feedback will aid success.

The tendency to postpone dealing with the specifications until later in the project is natural. The specifications are typically the last major deliverable for UX and more pressing tasks on the designer's plate tend to take priority. On many projects, Axure is still a new concept and thus many development teams have no idea what they may need or want. Therefore, they are unwilling to discuss this topic at the start of the project.

Axure provides an integrated specification creation and output environment. This feature addresses the iceberg nature of specifications heads-on: it significantly reduces the labor and time involved in updating and producing the UI specifications artifact. In other words, it translates to real value for UX designers who use the tool. This capability has been prominent on Axure's long list of groundbreaking features since the product's release back in 2004 and helped propel its popularity within the UX industry.

Axure has streamlined the design and documentation process, but many of us still struggle with Axure's output of the file, as it can be difficult to consume. This chapter will provide you with some useful tips to address this and other issues.

If your project is **Responsive Web Design** (**RWD**), we highly recommend that you use a prototype as part of the deliverable. We will discuss some best approaches we have found for a RWD UI specification later in this chapter.

This chapter is designed to help you deliver a UI specification that is useful and well received by the stakeholders receiving the document. We will cover the following topics:

- Importance of collaboration
- Global specifications
- Creating and customizing a UI specification document
- Generating a UI specification document

Importance of Collaboration

At the end of the day, developers must translate the design artifacts (prototype, UI specification, or both) into a fully functional application. The UI specifications document binds the visualizations we have created throughout the project—the wireframes and prototype—with the technical details of the user interface.

The following are well-worn truisms that illustrate why the interactive prototype and the UI specifications document complement each other so well:

- The first is that "no one reads anymore". Typical software projects generate an obscene amount of internal documents. For those who are not responsible for authoring, you are expected to review and comment on mounds and mounds of documentation. When crunch time sets in, even the best-intentioned team member will find it impossible to review the document carefully.

- It is much easier for UX designers to express their ideas by just showing the stakeholders what you mean. Words can be powerful, but this is one instance where words cannot truly express what we hope to achieve.
- As UX designers, we have a unique relationship with product managers. The product manager comes to the project with a lot of historical knowledge, but they usually have no idea how their user-base interacts with their product. If we are lucky enough to conduct user research, we approach the design phase with a lot of knowledge on the users' mental model. Merging/leveraging each person's knowledge will lead to a much better product.

Creating concepts early in the design process and collaborating with the product manager throughout the process can be very effective; let's hope the product manger respects what we do and does not try to force a design.

UX designers, whether consultants or in-house resources, should remember that one of the most important factors for the success of UX involves building solid relationships with all stakeholders on the project. Fostering these relationships early on does not mean that the team will not face adversity, but a spirit of collaboration and communication leads to trust and helps avoid problems down the road. One often-overlooked relationship is the development team and as they are the primary consumer of the UI specifications, try to build that relationship as early in the project as possible so that if conflicts arise, the willingness to work together will be established.

Aligning Expectations

The development team is typically the primary target audience for the UI specifications document. To be successful with this deliverable, you many need to push to have this discussion early. As mentioned earlier in the chapter, the developers may not know what they want and/or may not find this conversation useful if they are new to Axure. The following are a few suggestions to ensure alignment:

- Meet the development team very early on in the project to explicitly discuss the UI specifications document.
- Ask to see an example of specifications the development team has been using for other projects, but don't be surprised if you do not receive any.
- Demo Axure's specifications features to the development team. There is a high probability that the tool will be an exotic unknown to the team, which may lead to initial resistance to Axure if the team is used to working with Visio/Word documents.

- Whatever hesitations the developers may originally have, it is likely that education and review of the various possibilities to generate specifications will help you build a compelling case.
- Discuss with the team the attributes and level of detail they would like to see. Schedule a follow-up meeting in which you will present a draft of the specifications that includes the agreed-upon fields an tweak as needed.
- Come to an agreement on the appropriate deliverables to document topics such as business rules, date requirements, and any style-guide elements.

The UI Specifications

As mentioned at the start of this chapter, Axure provides an integrated and configurable specification capture and output environment. However, by no means should you assume that the process of creating the specifications involves filling in the annotation fields and hitting the **Generate** button. You will get a document for sure, but it may not be something you want to hand over to your development partners.

A good specifications document should provide a high-level description of the user experience across the entire application, continue to cover the structure and behavior of the application's various screens, and conclude with the behavior of various widgets down to button-level elements. In other words, the document's underlying structure should be composed of the following:

- Global aspects of the application, using the Word template that is part of the specification generator
- Page-level description, using page notes
- Widget-level descriptions, using field annotations

The following sections will describe in detail how to customize the various elements to best fit the document you want to generate for your project.

Global Specifications

There is a great deal of interaction behaviors and display rules that apply across the application. The UI specifications should have a section that covers these conventions. This will save the UX designer/team time by documenting these global conventions in a single place. It will also help the stakeholders (from development, product, and so on) digest the information, and it will ensure one more level of quality as the team knows what type of pattern has been established. The following are suggestions to consider when writing the globals. Not all the following items may be relevant to any given project, but this is a good checklist to use as a start:

- Introduction, which conveys the purpose and target audience, that is, what this document is and for whom is it written
- Guidelines and principles, which includes the specifications of the following items:
    - Screen resolution
    - Devices support
    - Date and time display rules
    - Browser support
    - Performance, that is, the acceptable response time for various interactions from a UX perspective
    - Messaging display, which includes the specifications of the following fields:
        - User errors
        - System errors
        - User filtered the dataset to the point where there are no results
    - Confirmations
    - Alerts
    - User assistance and guidance
    - Handling of user access, permissions, and security
    - User customization features
    - Localization features
    - Accessibility requirements
- Interface layouts
- Table patterns
- Key patterns (samples), which includes the specifications of the following fields:
    - Windows and dialogs
    - Notifications such as the following:
        - Error messages
        - Warning messages
        - Confirmation messages
        - Informational messages

    - Miscellaneous may include the specifications of the following fields:
        - Calendars
        - Button patterns
        - Icon patterns
        - Sign in
- Abbreviated glossary of the Axure terminology where you define, in simple terms, what masters, dynamic panels, and widgets are
- Document control, which includes the specifications of the following fields:
    - Document versioning
    - Related documents (such as the visual design guide)
    - Reviewers' list
    - Approvers' list

We have seen over the years that the global specifications are an often undervalued and ignored section, mainly due to the fact that the reviewers do not realize how much valuable information is in the globals and also most likely due to the fact that project timelines do not allow enough time to review. The value is usually seen when developers start asking questions and we point them to the globals for the answers. In order to get stakeholders to pay attention to this section, we recommend requesting signoff on this section. In other words, do not lump it in with the wireframe signoff.

Generators and Outputs – Specifications and Prototypes

Before we dive into the details of capturing the project's global specifications, let's clarify the relationship between Axure's generators, specifications, and the prototype. The following screenshot helps illustrate the concepts:

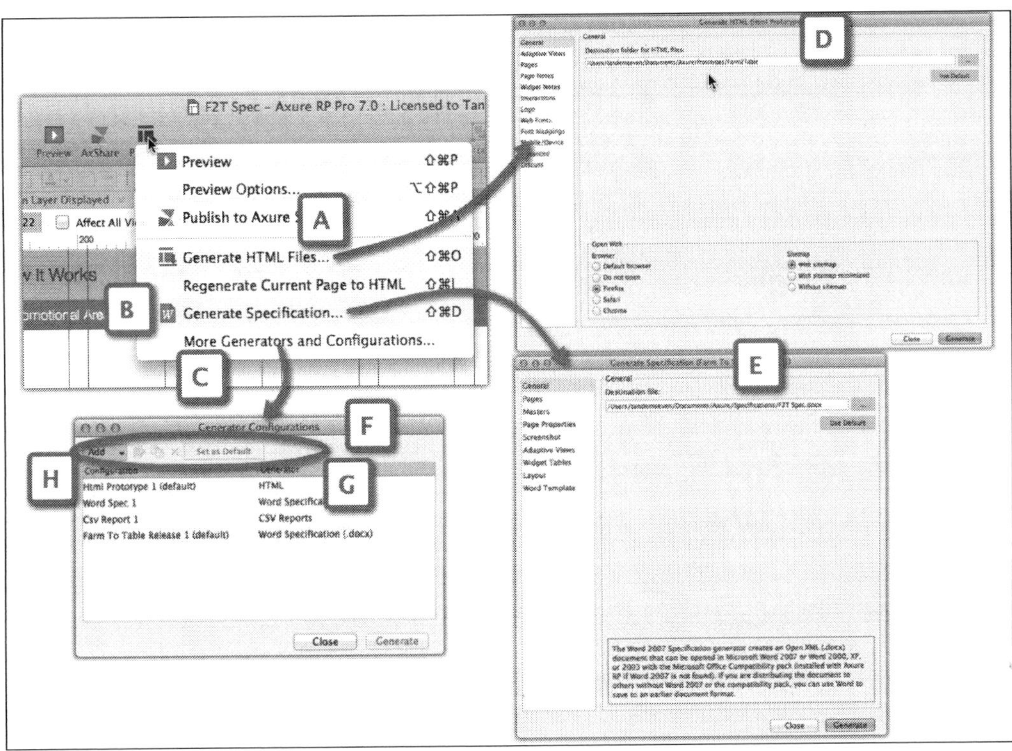

Image 1

The preceding screenshot shows the menu where you can output your work. The following list further defines this menu:

- **Prototype**: Always refers to an *HTML output* of your Axure file. Whenever you click on the **Generate HTML Files...** option (*Image 1*, **A**) in the **Publish** menu, you are presented with the **Generate HTML** dialog (**D**). In the dialog, you can specify various options of the default HTML output generator. You can create multiple HTML outputs, which is useful to break apart a large project into sections that generate faster.

  The HTML prototype generates the contents of the pages in your sitemap in Safari, Chrome, or Firefox.

- **Specification**: This always refers to a formatted *Word output* of the Axure file. Whenever you click on the **Generate Specification...** option (**B**) in the **Publish** menu, you are presented with the **Generate Specification** dialog (**E**). In this dialog, you determine the format and output options of the default Word output generator. Similar to the HTML output, you can create multiple Word generators. For example, you can divide a large project into smaller specification chapters that correspond to application modules.

- **Generators**: Axure provides three output options: HTML, Word, and CSV. Out of the box, Axure comes with one generator of each type. When you click on the **More Generators and Configurations...** option (C) in the **Publish** menu, you are presented with the **Generator Configuration** dialog (**F**), which lists all the generators you currently have in your project file (**G**). Here, you can manage your generator collection (**H**). The following are some of the actions that you can perform using the options listed in this dialog:
    - Create new generators in one of the output formats
    - Edit a generator
    - Duplicate an existing generator
    - Delete generators
    - Set the default generator for the HTML and Word outputs

Why would you need multiple generators? Consider the following examples:

- You may want to generate an HTML version with the footnotes visible and another with the footnotes hidden. When you meet stakeholders, you can have both versions available, allowing you to easily switch between one that is visually clean and the other that provides descriptive details about various elements of the interface.
- For large projects, you may want to generate the HTML only of a subset of pages, the ones you are currently working on in order to speed up the HTML generation.
- For large projects, you may want to divide the Word output into chapters, each corresponding to a workstream or an application module. This works well when there are different stakeholders and development teams for each module or workstream. Each can review and respond to the relevant portion of the specifications.

As opposed to the HTML output, for the specifications to be meaningful, you need to annotate the wireframes: pages, masters, dynamic panels, and widgets. This means that the effort involved in generating specifications extends beyond the configuration of a generator.

Customizing the Word Specifications Generator

Let's start with the first Word generator for the project. Although you can use the provided generator, we recommend creating a dedicated generator; leave this one for experimentations. Refer to *Image 2* to follow the flow:

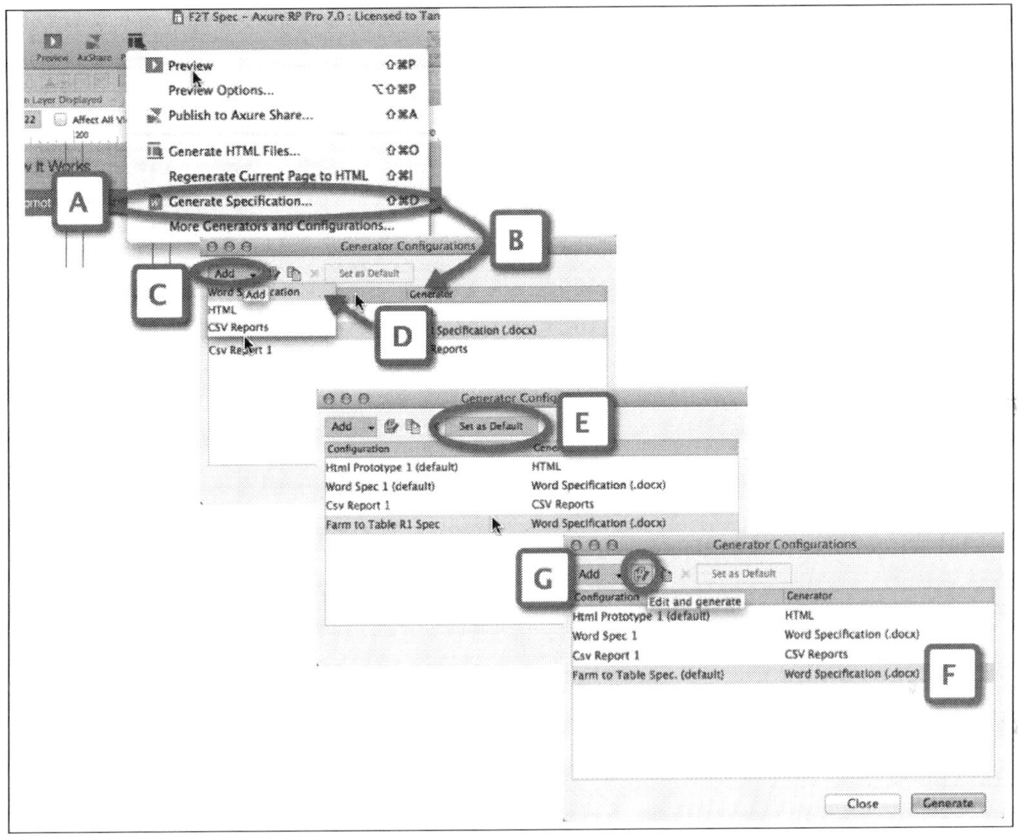

Image 2

The following steps will help you customize the Word specifications generator:

1. Click on the **Publish** menu and then the **Generate Specification...** option (*Image* 2, **A**).
2. In the **Generator Configuration** dialog (**B**), select the **Word Specification** option (**D**) from the **Add** drop-down list (**C**).
3. Rename the new generator with an appropriate name.

4. Click on the **Set as Default** button (E); the default generator is the one that is launched when you click on the **Generate Specification...** option in the **Publish** menu. Refer to the preceding screenshot (F) for the newly added Word specification, which is now the default.
5. Now, you can click on the **Edit and generate** icon (G), which will launch the **Generate Prototype** dialog. Here, you will set the various properties that determine the final output of the Word specification. We will cover this dialog in detail later in this chapter.

Now that you understand the relationship between generators and specifications and have a Word generator waiting to be configured, it is time to dive into the mechanics of capturing the specifications.

Page Notes

Axure's page notes provide the mechanics to capture the page-level description and other specifications. This is the place to provide the following details:

- High-level overview of the page
- Page entry points
- What the user can accomplish on this page (actionable items)
- Important user experience principles
- Key interface components

Out of the box, Axure provides a single-page notes field named **Default**, which you probably should rename. You can add additional note fields, which will help you provide an organizational structure to the page note section in the specification. For example, you can consider adding notes to discuss key business requirements that are addressed by this page, functional specifications, localization and personalization notes, and so on.

Although the section is named Page Notes, you can use it for pages and masters.

The page note categories you create in the file are available to all pages, although this does not mean that you have to fill all the notes sections on all pages. To customize the notes section, refer to *Image 3*, which illustrates this process:

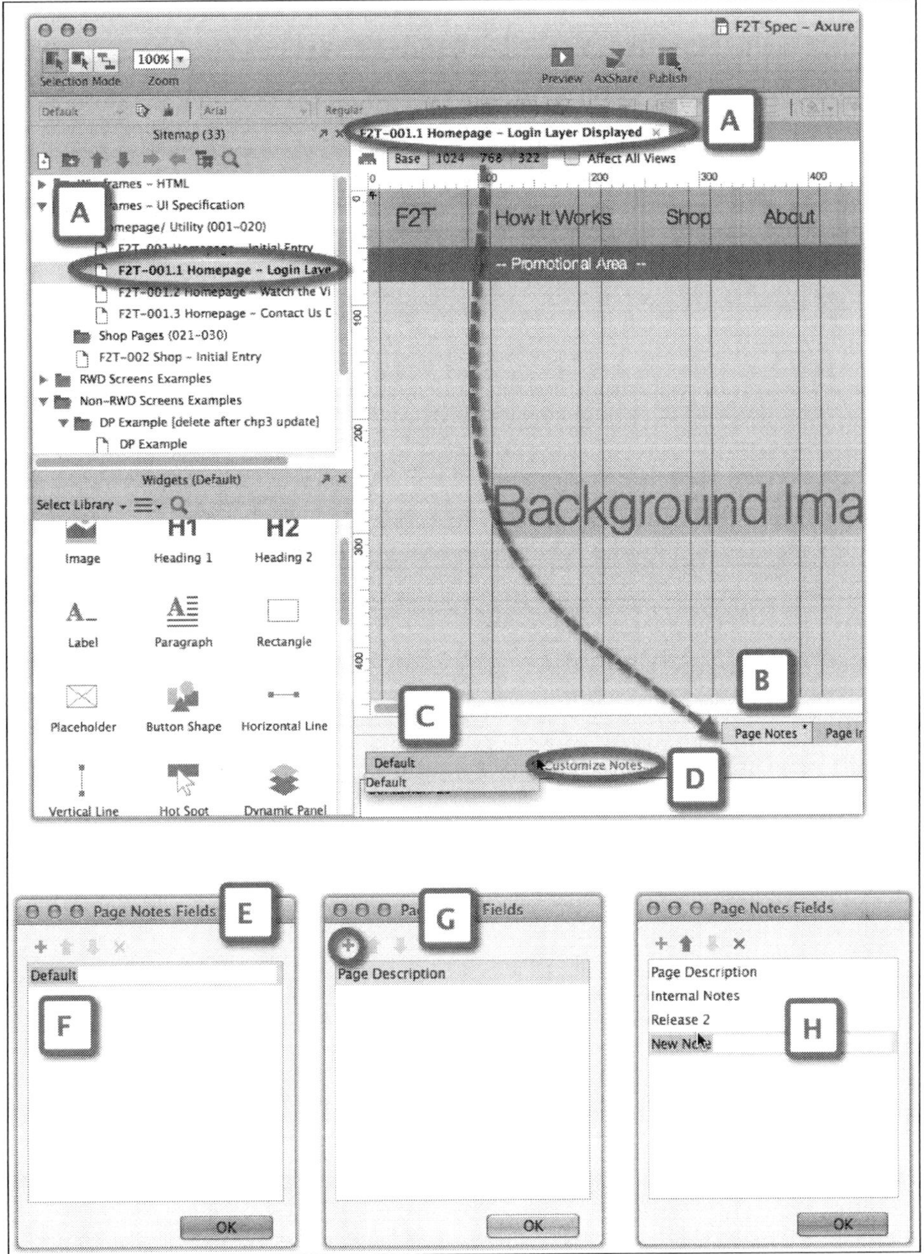

Image 3

1. Open the page for editing (*Image 3*, **A**) on the **Wireframes** pane.
2. Click on the **Page Notes** tab (**B**) in the Page Properties pane. You will see the **Default** note field (**C**) listed in the drop-down list.

3. A good reason to rename this field is that you will have an option to use the note name as a header in the specification document. Obviously, to the reader, the word "Default" will be somewhat vague.
4. To rename the note field, click on the **Customize Notes...** link (**D**).
5. In the **Page Notes** dialog (**E**) that appears, click on the first item (**F**) and type in the name of the new note field, for example, `Page Description`.
6. To add additional note fields, click on the Add icon (**G**).
7. It is a good idea to add a note field for your personal use (**H**)—a place to capture issues, ideas, or questions for stakeholders and so on. You can generate a version of the specification that has only this field, which will provide you with a good issue management system.
8. Close the **Page Notes Fields** dialog when you are done adding the fields you need. You can always tweak this section, although once you have started to capture information, be careful about deleting note fields.
9. From this point on, the renamed and new fields are listed in the drop-down list. Switch between fields using the drop-down list.

One Note Section Versus Many

One question often discussed by UX design teams is, "Is it better to have one single, yet large annotation field or a variety of discreet, topical annotation fields?". When discussing this topic with colleagues, there seems to be an agreement that a lot depends on the nature of the project. As a result, there is no right or wrong answer here. However, evaluate your needs and approach in light of the following:

- Some developers are interested in very detailed specifications, while others want to focus only on the absolutely necessary details.
- The specifications may be used by a remote team, often overseas, and the developers will interpret your words verbatim, while in an agile environment, the developers might barely read anything.
- In some projects, the specifications are also going to be consumed and signed off by business analysts, business stakeholders, and other non-developers. Understand what they are looking to get from the documentation and tailor note field content for this audience. This will help in getting their approval.
- With multiple note fields, it is likely that you will make mistakes! Also, forgetting to switch note fields will result in typing notes in the wrong notes field, which is a common mistake.
- Gather feedback once the development teams have begun using the UI specifications. You may find that developers gloss over this section. If this is the case, ask them where this type of information should be.

Annotation Fields

Every element on a wireframe was placed there for some reason; you started with a blank canvas after all. Someone, probably a developer, will need to translate the wireframe to live code.

In the UI specifications document, you are expected to provide both descriptive and prescriptive information about any widget in a wireframe. Axure takes care of many of the most labor-intensive tasks and delivers significant time savings. Still, you can expect to spend a significant amount of time on the specifications.

After establishing your page notes, it is time to configure the annotation fields. Across the UX industry, there is no standard for the UI specifications document. The deliverable's format and depth of coverage depends on the UX practitioner, the tools used to generate the document and special requests from the development team.

Axure comes with a set of nine annotation fields. You will want to rename or remove some of these fields. You can easily add your own fields and customize both their label and type. Annotation field types are as follows:

- Text
- Select List
- Number
- Date

Each UX project may be vastly different, but one can argue that across the board, there are generalized properties that can be, and are, applicable to any interface project. Naturally, as a discipline, UX is rapidly evolving and we need to address new interaction methods such as gestures, haptic feedback, and other factors.

This evolution is likely to expand the type of information that has to be captured in the specifications, and consequently, the annotation fields needed to capture and communicate such information to developers. The following are the steps to customize your annotations:

1. From the **Project** menu (*Image 4*, **A**), select the **Widget Note Fields and Sets ...** option (**B**).
2. The **Widget Note Fields and Sets** window (**C**) will appear, listing Axure's out-of-the-box fields in the **Customize Fields** column (**D**).
3. To rename a field (**E**), click on it and type a new label. While you can change the label of the annotation field, you will not be able to change its type.
4. If the field happens to be a Select List type field, the current values are listed in the left-hand side column (**F**), for example, **Edit: Status** in the next screenshot. You can easily modify, add, and remove values by typing in that area (**G**).

5. Use the controls above the list of fields (**H**) to add new annotation fields of various types, reorder them in the list, and delete fields. We highly recommend that you delete fields you don't plan to use in order to avoid confusion such as entering content in such fields by mistake.

We recommend that you start working with each delivery team to determine what type of information should belong in the annotation field. It is also best to start with a small number of fields.

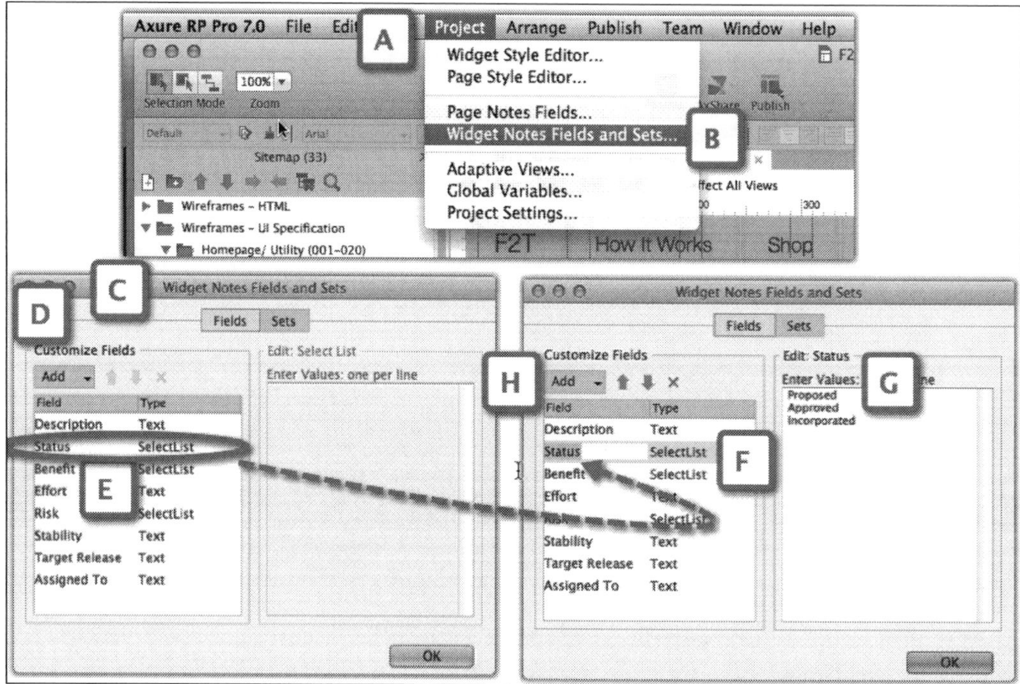

Image 4

Annotation Views

Annotation views is a feature that allows you to group your annotation fields. This is useful if you have a long list of fields and want to organize them in smaller groups. For example, you may decide, together with your development team stakeholders, that a subset of fields are mandatory and the rest are optional. By setting your **Annotation** tab to the mandatory view, the much shorter list of fields will be easier to scan as you go over your widgets and ensure that all mandatory information has been captured.

Generating Specifications

As mentioned throughout this chapter, it is important to experiment and test the output of the specifications early and often.

You control all the output properties of the specification document in the **Generate Specification** window. The window is divided into eight sections. When you are done tweaking them, click on the **Generate** button. Axure will launch Microsoft Word, which will open with the specification document ready for your review and edit.

The General Section

The following screenshot illustrates the first section, **General**, in the specifications configuration window (*Image 5*, **A**):

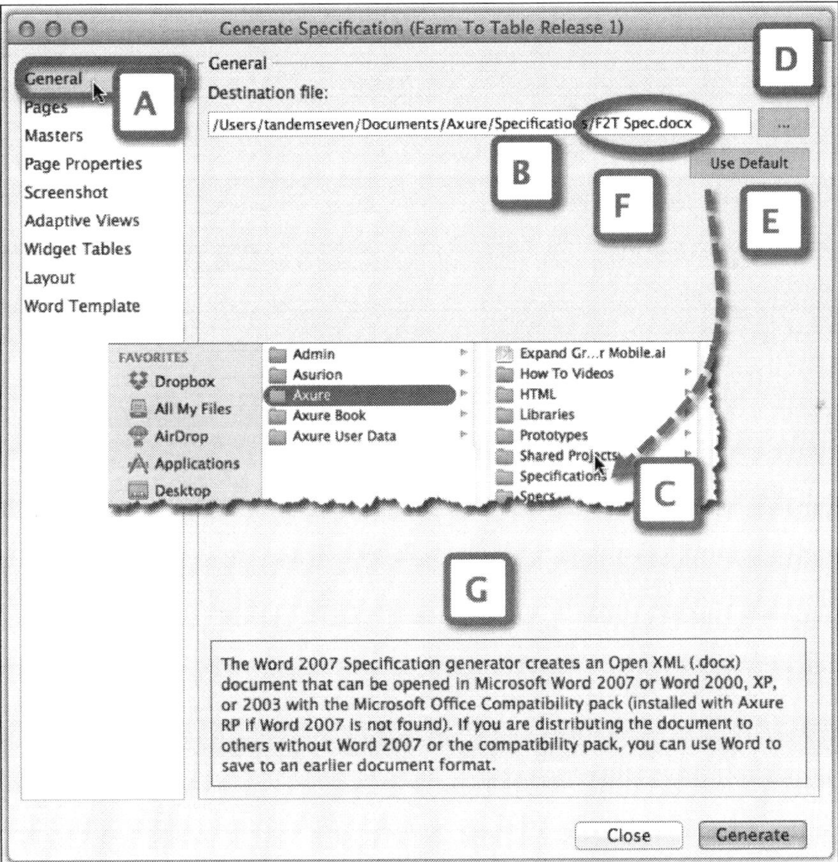

Image 5

In this first section, you instruct Axure about two things, which are as follows:

- **Where you want to create the generated specifications**: By default, the path (**B**) shown in the preceding screenshot leads to the **Specifications** directory (**C**) that is created when you install Axure. For Windows users, the directory name is `My Axure RP specifications`, and it is located under the `My Documents` folder or in the `Documents` folder on the Mac. Click on the ellipsis button (**D**) to change the path to your own destination, for example, if you want to store the document in a special folder you have for all your project's files. You can always use the default by clicking on the **Use Default** button (**E**).
- **The name of the specifications document**: By default, it is the name of your Axure prototype file. You can modify the last segment of the path (**F**) as needed.

The Pages Section

In the **Pages** section (*Image 6,* **A**), you select pages from the prototype's sitemap which will appear in the specifications as illustrated in the following screenshot:

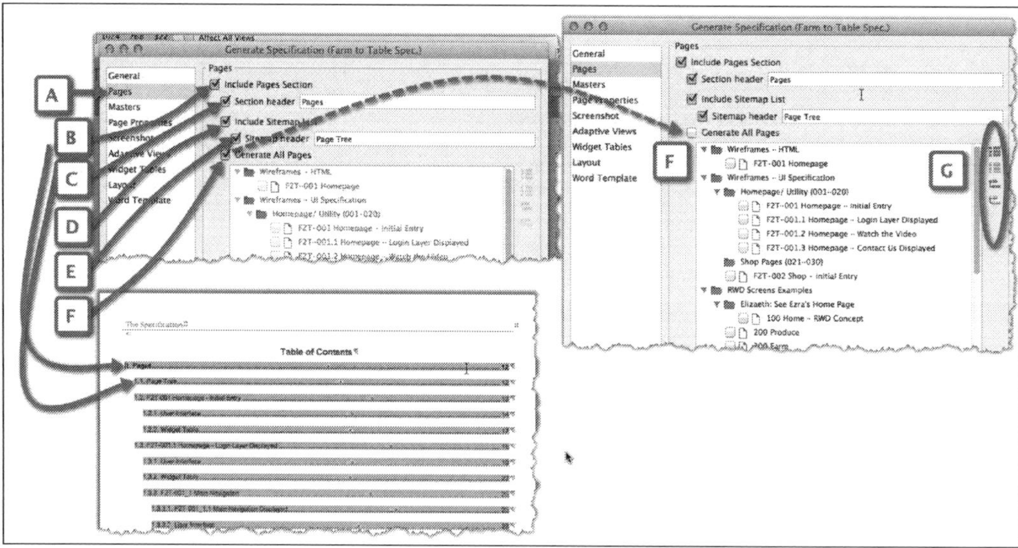

Image 6

The following table illustrates each option of the **Pages** section:

Options	Description
Include Pages Section (B)	This option supersedes the rest of the options below. If you uncheck this option, none of the pages in the sitemap will be generated.
Section header (C)	You can customize the name of the **Pages** section. For example, instead of Pages, you may want to call the label Screens. If you check this option, don't leave it blank. This label will appear in the table of contents of the generated specifications.
Include Sitemap List (D)	If you check this option, Axure will include a list of all the pages in your project's sitemap. Keep in mind that if you choose to generate some of the pages, the list will still show all of them, which may be confusing to the reader.
Sitemap header (E)	You can relabel the default sitemap header from Page Tree to Application Screens, for example. If you check this option, don't leave it blank. Your custom label or the default will appear in the generated Word document.
Generate All Pages (F)	By default, this option is checked. As mentioned earlier, it is most likely that you will want to uncheck it. The ability to segment pages is extremely useful. Not only can you have precision and select just the relevant screen you want to include in the specifications, but it also opens up the possibilities to generate chapters and sections that are tailored for specific audiences. In a large project, each workstream can generate its own set of specifications. This option is useful in large projects with many pages and subpages where Axure can control all the pages and subpages with the options **Check All**, **Uncheck All**, **Check All Children**, and **Uncheck All Children** (G).

The Masters Section

In the **Masters** section (*Image 7*, **A**), as illustrated in the following screenshot, you select which masters from the prototype's sitemap will appear in the specifications and how they will appear:

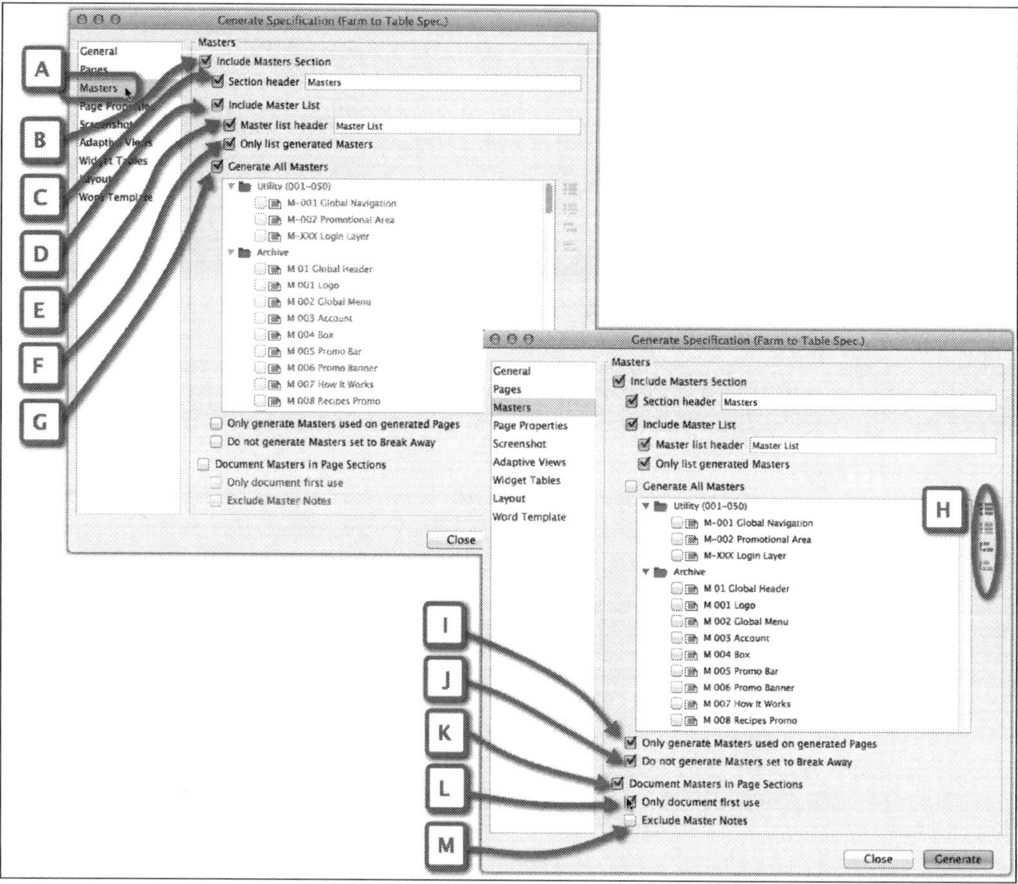

Image 7

The following table illustrates each option of the **Masters** section:

Options	Description
Include Masters Section (B)	This option supersedes the rest of the options below. If you uncheck this option, none of the masters in the prototype will be generated. To clarify, the masters will still appear in wireframes, but there will not be a special section for them in the specifications document. This can be useful if you want to create, for example, a PowerPoint presentation showing only key screens of the applications. Instead of manually taking screen captures of each from the HTML prototype, you can generate a specification of only the pages you need and exclude the masters. All the screenshots you need for the presentation will be automatically generated faster.
Section header (C)	You can customize the name of the masters section. For example, instead of the default Masters, a term which might be foreign to readers not familiar with Axure's terminology, you may want to call the label Reusable UI elements. Even if you stay with Masters, don't leave it blank, as the label will appear in the table of contents of the generated specifications.
Include Master List (D)	If you check this option, Axure will include a list of all the masters in your project.
Master list Header (E)	You can, for example, relabel the default master list header from Page Tree to List of Reusable Components. If you check this option, don't leave it blank. Your custom label or the default will appear in the generated Word document.
Only list generated Masters (F)	By default, this option is checked and we recommend leaving it checked— there is little value in listing items that do not appear in the document.
	This option is useful in large projects with many masters where Axure can control all the masters with the options **Check All**, **Uncheck All**, **Check All Children**, and **Uncheck All Children (H)**.
Generate All Masters (G)	By default, this option is checked, and if kept checked, it will generate all the masters in your file. You should consider unchecking it, especially if you are tweaking which pages will be generated. Typically, your file may include old versions of pages and masters, various design candidates, and even work in progress; there can actually be quite a few things you would want to keep out of the specifications.
Only generate Masters used on generated Pages (I)	By default, this option is not selected, but we recommend that you consider checking it, especially if you are generating only a subset of pages. Remember, masters are not independent elements; they are reused in one or more pages. If a master does not appear in the pages that are generated in the specifications, it will make little sense.

<table>
<tr><th>Options</th><th>Description</th></tr>
<tr><td>Do not generate Masters Set As Custom Widgets (J)</td><td>Masters that are set as custom widgets are typically intended to be modified once they are placed on the page. This means that a master set as a custom widget will not actually be easily recognizable as such, on the page. As a result, it will not be very valuable to the developers and will most likely create some confusion.</td></tr>
<tr><td>Document Masters in Page Section (K)</td><td>By default, Axure generates the Masters section after the Pages section. The table of contents will look similar to the following:

Page Section
  Page 1
  Page 2
  Page n
Masters Section
  Master 1
  Master 2
  Master n

This means that a developer working on a particular page needs to jump from the Pages section to the Masters section and locate a master mentioned in the page section, which can be inconvenient and sometimes confusing, as not all the elements associated with a single page are in one place.

By checking this option, Axure will generate the page with its associated master(s).

The table of content will look similar to the following:

Page Section
  Page 1
    Master 1
    Master 2
  Page 2
    Master 1
    Master n
  Page n
    Master 1
    Master 2
    Master n

This organization packages all the information about a screen in one section.</td></tr>
</table>

Options	Description
Only document first use (L)	If you checked the previous option, one immediate downside will be a redundancy of masters. Basically, each master will repeat on each page it is used on. Depending on the size and the project and the construction of your prototype, this redundancy may translate to hundreds of extra pages in your specification document, and we are not exaggerating here. So, the option to generate only the first instance of a master under the first page it is used on can be a tremendous space saver. However, it does end up intensifying the original problem of spreading masters in the document because this arrangement forces the reader to potentially hunt for masters all over the document.
Exclude Master Notes (M)	Similar to pages, you can add notes to masters. This is a very useful feature, especially if the master is a large, composite component that can benefit from its own set of notes. However, you do have an option to exclude those notes.

The Page Properties Section

In the **Pages** section, you selected which pages from the sitemap will be generated in the specifications. In the **Page Properties** section (*Image 8*, **A**), you are offered a wealth of 14 options to configure page information. These options will apply to all the pages in the sitemap as illustrated in the following screenshot:

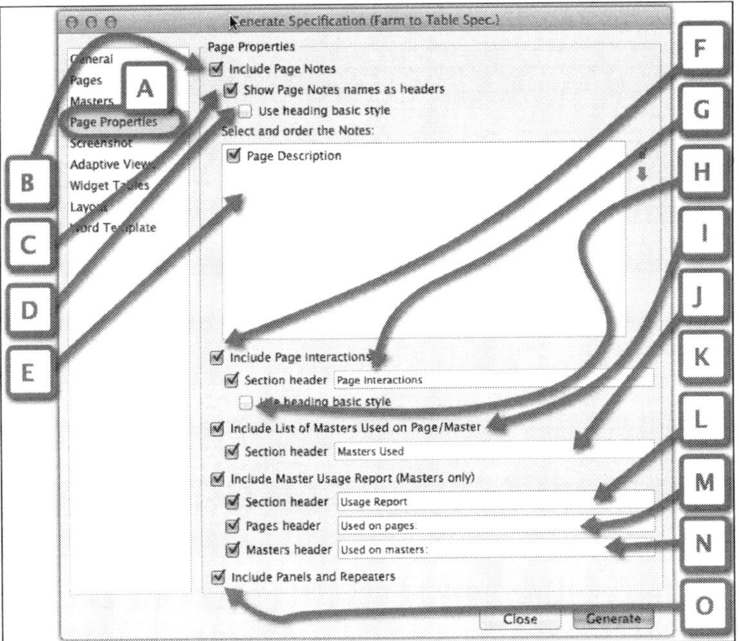

Image 8

Options	Description
Include Page Notes (B)	With this option selected, page notes will be generated for each of the pages.
Show Page Notes names as headers (C)	As discussed earlier in the book, you can create multiple note fields. With this option selected, these note names will appear as headers and the content of the notes below.
Use heading basic style (D)	If you checked the previous option, this option will become active. If it is unchecked, the style Heading 3 will be applied, giving page notes significant prominence. If you select this checkbox, the basic heading will be Heading 5, which is gray, with a smaller font, making notes less prominent.
Select and order the Notes (E)	This option allows you to govern the order in which the page notes will be generated within each page.
Include Page Interactions (F)	With this option selected, OnPageLoad interactions will be generated.
Section header (G)	If you do choose to include page interactions, you can use the default section header or relabel it.
Use heading basic style (H)	Similar to **Use heading basic style (D)**, you have the option of making the interaction section more or less prominent.
Include List of Masters Used on Page/Master (I)	Lists the masters used for the associated wireframe.
Section header (J)	If you check the preceding option, you can modify the default label.
Include Master Usage Report (Masters only) (K)	Each master will have a listing of all its instances across the entire prototype. This can be incredibly helpful.
Section header (L)	This is similar to **Section header (G)**.
Pages header (M)	This is similar to **Section header**.
Masters header (N)	This is similar to **Section header**.
Include Panels and Repeaters (O)	If you are using a dynamic panel in your prototype, you are likely to want this option checked in order to expose the various states associated with those dynamic panels.

The Screenshot Section

This is one of the great timesaving features involved in producing the UI specifications document—automatic generation of all wireframes' screenshots. This means that each time you generate a fresh version of the specifications, your screen captures are up to date! Not only that, but the annotation footnotes will be created as well. The following screenshot will help you understand the different options provided in this section:

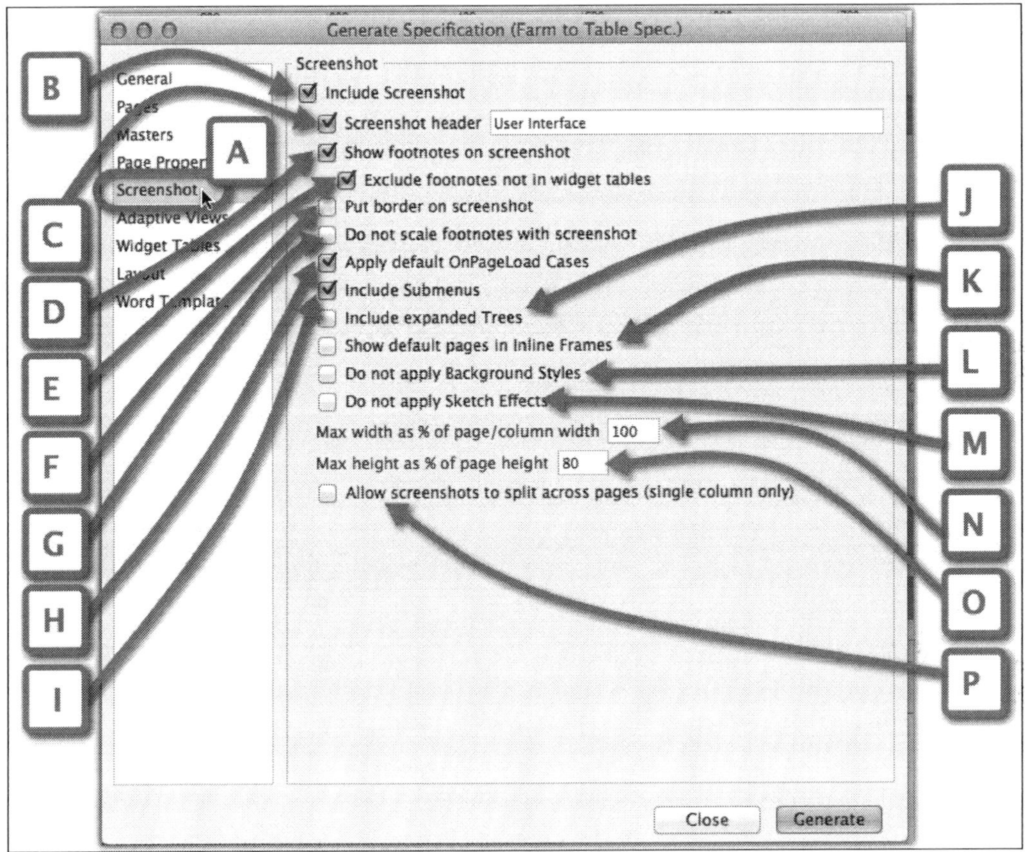

Image 9

The following table illustrates each option of *Image 9*:

Options	Description
Include Screenshot (B)	This option supersedes the rest of the options below. If you uncheck this option, none of the screenshots in the prototype will be generated. It is difficult to think about a situation in which you might not want to include screenshots.
Screenshot header (C)	You can modify the label of this section, for example, change the default Screenshot to `Wireframe`.
Show footnotes on screenshot (D)	With this option selected, the screenshots will include the little blue numbered footnotes that reference annotated elements on the wireframe. You are most likely to want this option selected for the specifications document. However, if you need to generate a set of wireframes to include in a PowerPoint presentation, the footnotes option can be skipped.
Exclude footnotes not in widget tables (E)	We will discuss widget tables in the **Widget Tables** section, which comes up next. Basically, the idea is that you may have more annotation fields in your Axure file than fields that you want to display in your document. You organize the fields in a widget table(s). With this option checked, footnotes that are associated with fields that are not part of the widget tables will not be generated. For example, you may have a field to capture internal issues, questions, and other miscellaneous details. Typing content in this field will create a footnote on the wireframe. However, as you are not going to include this field in the widget table(s), you don't want the footnote to appear; this option takes care of the situation.
Put border on screenshot (F)	This option does exactly what it claims. However, you may want to consider whether you need to use it. It might confuse the developer to think that perhaps the border is a part of the wireframe as visually it might be difficult to distinguish the Axure added border from a frame around the widget. Something to keep in mind.
Do not scale footnotes with screenshot (G)	With this option, the size of the yellow footnotes stays constant.
Apply default OnPageLoad Cases (H)	This may be an important option to check. There are many circumstances where the rendering of the page depends on the execution of the OnPageLoad event. The interactions are triggered not only when the HTML prototype renders in the browser, but also when the specification is being generated.

Options	Description
Include Submenu (I)	This option will generate screenshots of expanded menus if you use Axure's menu widgets in your prototype.
Include expanded Trees (J)	This option will generate screenshots of expanded trees if you use Axure's Tree widgets in your prototype.
Show default pages in inline Frames (K)	This is an incredibly important option to check if you load pages inside iFrames on other pages. It will ensure that the entire wireframe, the parent page as well as the page that is targeted for the iFrame, is generated.
Do not apply Background Styles (L)	If you use a background effect for the prototype, for example, a background color, you can have these removed from the screenshot output.
Do not apply Sketch Effects (M)	This is just what it means; while you can maintain the option of sketch effects on your prototype, you can choose to remove them from the output.
Max width as % of page/ column width (N)	This option provides a measure of control over the width of the screenshot, in relation to the output page. For example, 60 percent of a width of 7.5 inches, for a letter-sized page set to portrait (with half-inch margins to the left and right), we generate a screenshot that is 4.5 inches wide, leaving a 3 inch space for annotation information. Keep in mind that in a typical project, the variation between wireframes is significant and you'll want to experiment and ensure the quality of the output.
Max height as % of page height (O)	This is similar to the previous option, but this option controls the maximum height of the screenshot. This is useful for long, scrolling screens. Keep in mind that in a typical project, the variation between wireframes is significant and you'll want to experiment and ensure the quality of the output.
Allow screenshots to split across pages (single column only)	This option can be useful for very tall screenshots. If you limit the height of the image so that it fits onto the page, you will, by default, also reduce its width, potentially making it difficult to identify details.

Adaptive Views

The **Adaptive Views** section is only relevant if you are using adaptive views for your project. This section is straightforward, as you can simply choose which views you want to include in your specifications document. The **Adaptive Views** section is shown in the following screenshot:

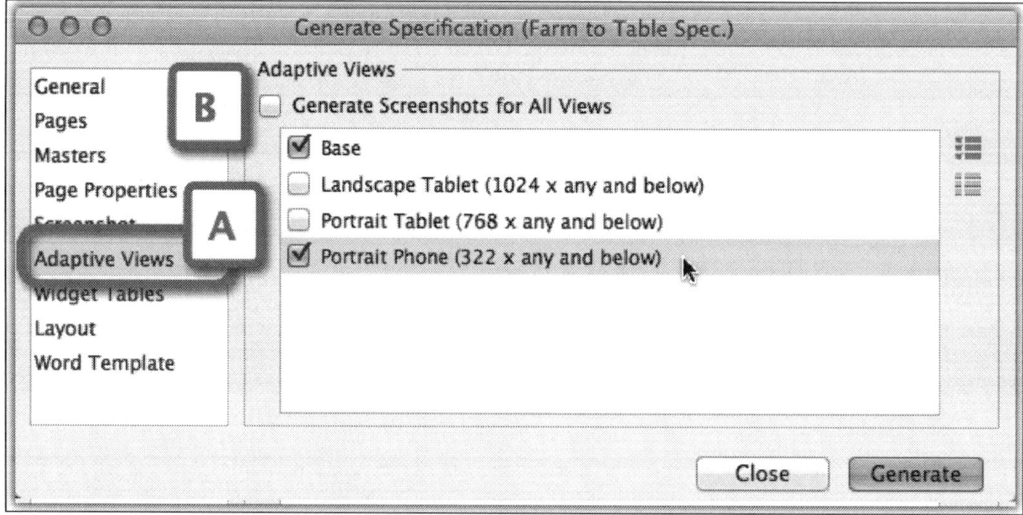

Image 10

The following table illustrates the option in the **Adaptive Views** section *(Image 10)*:

Option	Description
Generate Screenshots for All Views (B)	If you uncheck this option, you must choose which views to display. In this example, only two of the views are displayed. We feel it only makes sense to include the views that have a great enough difference in layout.

When generating a specification document that contains adaptive views, only display the views that are actually unique. In *Image 10*, just the base view and mobile (phone) view are included in the specifications, as the other two sizes are not that different from the base view. In any case, remember to discuss the options with the relevant stakeholders.

The Widget Tables Section

In the hierarchy of Axure annotations, **Page Note** fields can be described as the "macro" level of the specs: a configurable space that allows you to discuss an entire page and provide the UX an overview and context. The **Widget Annotation** fields are the "micro" option, allowing you to capture the UX properties of widget-level controls.

The **Widget Tables** section (*Image 11*, **A**) provides you with a number of controls that help you organize the presentation of widget annotations in the specifications document as illustrated in *Image 11*:

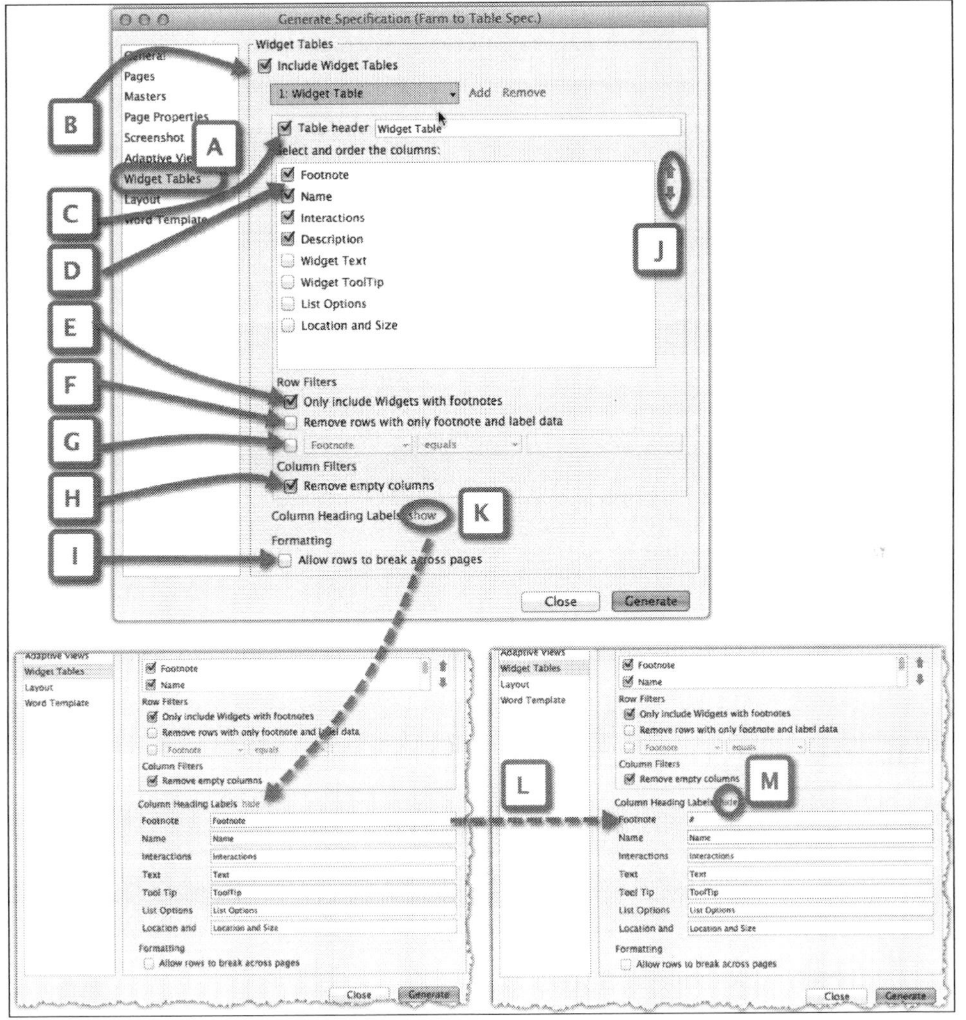

Image 11

The following table illustrates each option in the **Widget Tables** section:

Option	Description
Include Widget Tables (**B**)	This option supersedes the rest of the options below. If unchecked, none of the widget annotations will be generated. Axure lets you create any number of widget tables. Click on the **Add** link to add a widget table.
Table header (**C**)	You can change the label of this section. For example, if you add an additional table, the first can be labeled `Mandatory Annotations` (**K**) and the second table `Optional Annotations` (**M**). You can switch between the tables using the widget table drop-down list (**L**).
Select and order the columns (**D** and **J**)	All the widget annotation fields in your file are listed here. Each field is a column in the table. Obviously, the higher the number of fields, the narrower each table column is. Axure provides an easy and powerful method to avoid the problem by allowing you to associate fields with multiple tables. As a result, each table has fewer, wider columns, and the result is readable and clear. You can control the order of the columns within each table, which will be their order in the widget tables.
Only include Widgets with footnotes (**E**)	This option will reduce unnecessary clutter from the specification, listing only widgets that actually have footnotes.
Remove rows with only footnotes and label data (**F**)	This is a great space-saving option that will filter out widgets that have footnotes, but have no actual annotations.
Filter annotations (**G**)	This option allows you to filter a specific annotation field if its value is equal to, does not equal, contains, does not contain, is one of, or is not one of, some other value. By applying the filter, you can control at a very granular level and filter which annotations to include in the generated specifications. For example, if you track releases, this feature will help you output a specifications that only deals with a specific release.
Remove empty columns (**H**)	Another space saver that helps produce a more compact document.
Column Heading Label (**K**)	This option allows you to name the column headers. As you can see in this example, Footnote was renamed to # (**L**). Click on **Hide** (**M**) to collapse this section.
Allow rows to break across pages (**I**)	This is a self-explanatory option: although you want to discuss with the developers, they may prefer to see the entire row in one place and avoid a potential error in case the developer missed the continued row.

The Layout Section

The **Layout** section (*Image 12*, **A**) provides additional controls over the page layout of the specifications document as illustrated in the following screenshot:

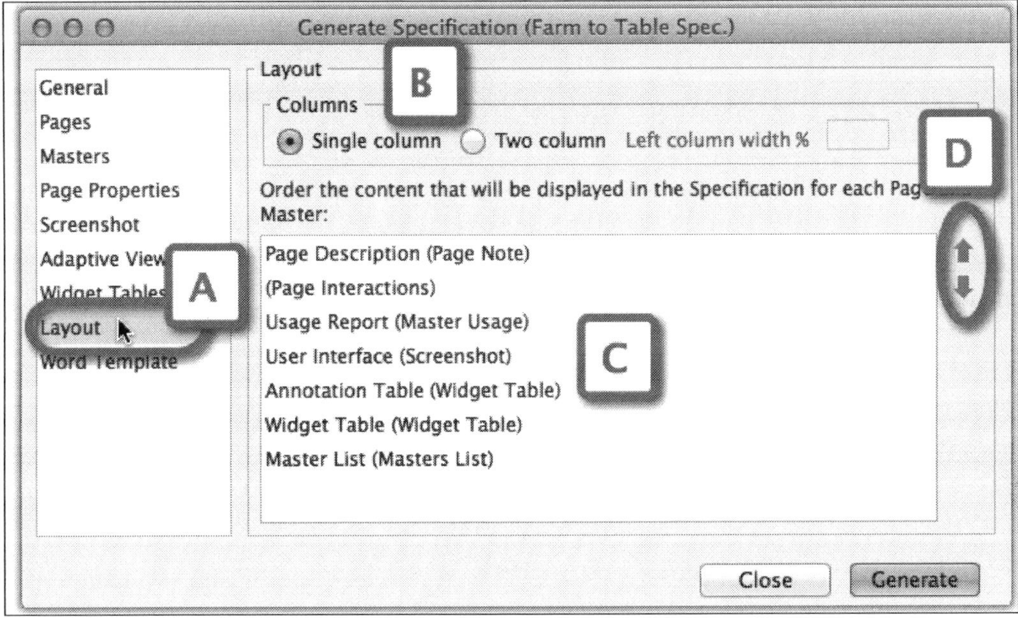

Image 12

The following table illustrates each option in the **Layout** section (*Image 12*):

Option	Description
Columns (B)	You have a choice of a single-column or two-column layout. Keep in mind that in a two-column layout, the screenshots may be too small for an application page. However, if these are specifications for an iPhone app, for example, this may be a perfect, compact format.
Order the content that will be displayed in the Specification for each Page and Master (C)	You can set the order of appearance of major content sections in the specification. Use the up and down arrows (**D**) to organize the sections.

The Word Template Section

Last but not least is the **Word Template** section (*Image 13*, **A**). When you click on the **Generate** button on this dialog, Axure gets a Word template to open with all the content organized as per your selection in the previous sections. This panel provides you with access to edit the Word template, import a template, or create one on your own, as illustrated in the following screenshot:

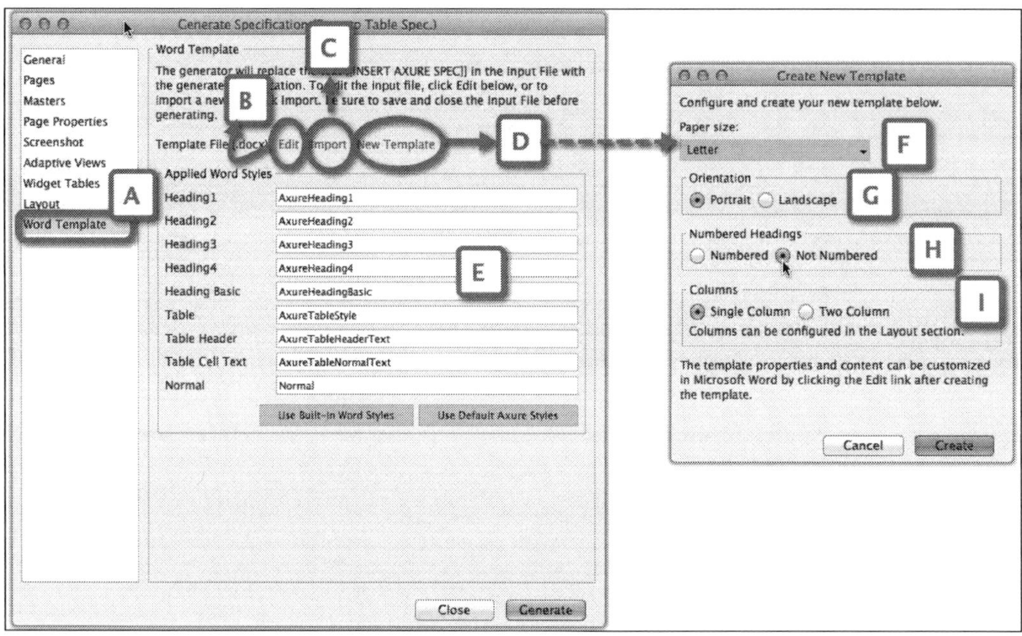

Image 13

The following table illustrates each option in the **Word Template** section (*Image 13*):

Option	Description
Edit (B)	This option allows you to edit the template you are using.
Import (C)	This allows you to import an already formatted template from your computer.
New Template (D)	This is the one we have used most often in our experience with Axure. In fact, set this up as early as you can.
Applied Word Styles (E)	You can modify the default style names if you want. You also have the option to use Word's built-in styles instead. You will have to experiment and determine which you like better. Refer to *Image 15* for some further explanation on this.
Paper size (F)	This lets you choose between U.S. formats such as **Legal**, **Letter**, **Ledger**, and the international **A4** format.

Option	Description
Orientation (G)	This lets you choose between the **Portrait** and **Landscape** orientations.
Numbered Headings (H)	We recommend that you choose **Not Numbered** if you have been numbering your wireframes and dynamic panels. This numbering will be sufficient and gives you more control.
Columns (I)	This lets you choose between one or two columns page layout.

Formatting-applied Word Styles

As a designer, it is very probable that you will want to format the headers to your liking, so it is worthwhile to mention how to actually do that! The following are the steps to format headers:

1. Once you have the customized Word template, click on the **Edit** link (*Image 13*, **B**).
2. The Word template will open. Highlight the heading you want to change to see which style is assigned to it as shown in the following *Image 14* screenshot:

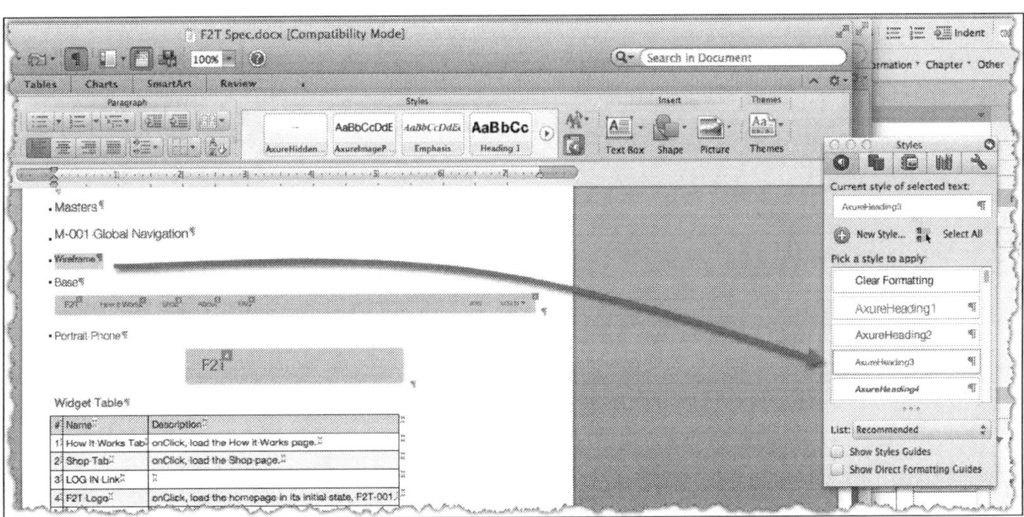

Image 14

3. Now, navigate to **Format** | **Style**; this is shown in *Image 15*:

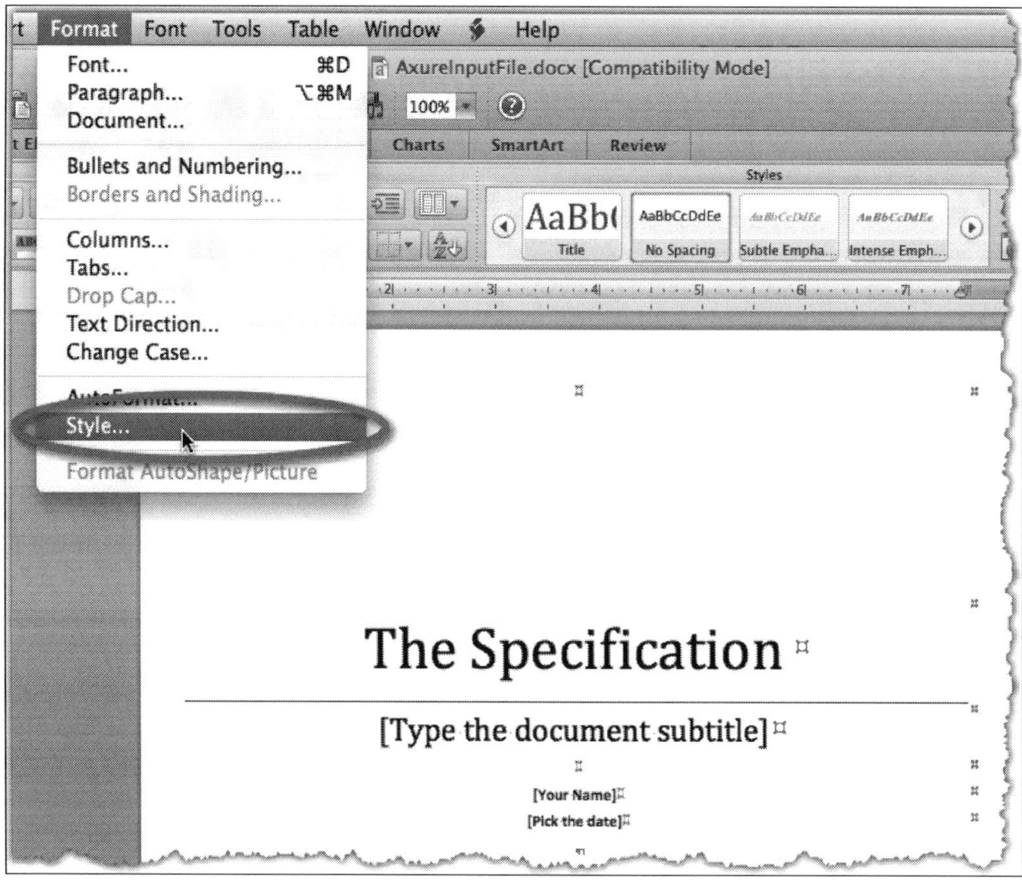

Image 15

4. Now in the **Style** window, click on the **Modify...** button and in the **Modify Style** window, you can update the formatting (**B**), as shown in the following screenshot:

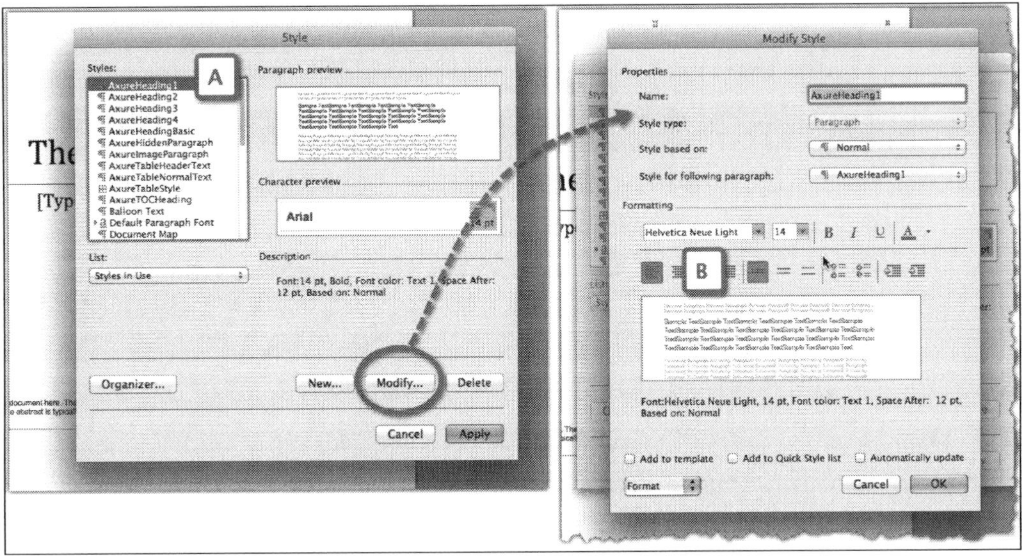

Image 16

Quick Tips to Improve the Layout

At the time of writing this book, Axure is by far the most effective and efficient tool. Having said that, our observation by talking to many in the community is that the Word UI specification document should be generated in a manner that is easy to read. The following is a list of things we have found over the years that have helped:

- Go light on dynamic panels.
- For each different scenario that you have to show, for example, the initial state of the home page and then how the home page looks when the login layer is opened, have a wireframe for each.
- In order to keep your layout organized, make each widget on the page a master. That master may have different states and you can utilize the OnPageLoad event to set the correct state that you want to display for that scenario.
- The smaller your master, the more flexibility you will have to drag-and-drop elements onto a wireframe to display what you wish.

- Remember that your labels are headers in your Word document. Do not be vague and label something `Widget 2`. This will make no sense to your reader.
- Number all of your wireframes, dynamic panels, and masters and do not use Word's default numbering system because you numbered them yourself. The Word numbering system is duplicative and will cause confusion.
- After you generate, take 5-10 minutes to clean up the document. You will most likely have to delete extra spaces.
- For RWD projects, the HTML prototype is the best way to go. If you have to generate a UI Word specification, only include the views that have a variance in design and behavior. All the preceding tips also apply to RWD projects.

Let's first look at a sitemap for a UI Word specification (*Image 17*, **A**) and for an HTML output (**B**), as shown in the following screenshot. The UI Word specification (**A**) is what we call a flat file, which is very similar to our *pre-Axure* days. Don't worry, this is efficient because you will have masters for everything and simply use the OnPageLoad event. The HTML output (**B**) is the exact same design, but as it is an HTML file, all of the scenarios in the UI Word specification (**A**) are simply dynamic panels in the HTML output (**B**).

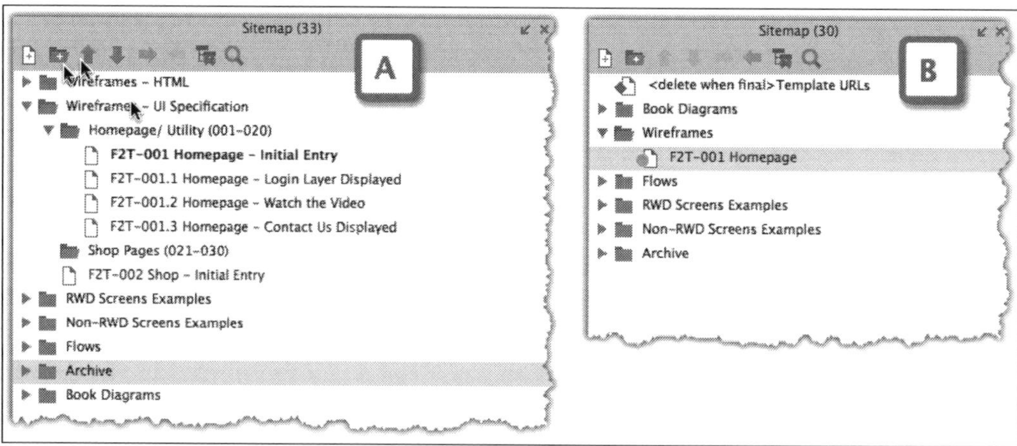

Image 17

Setting up the Wireframe with OnPageLoad

This concept may hurt your brain at first, but you will catch on quickly; we promise!

The following screenshot shows F2T-001 home page's initial entry on the left-hand side (*Image 18*, **A**). Notice the soft pink elements, which mean these are all masters. F2T-001.1 home page on the right-hand side shows the login layer displayed (**B**). All that was done here was we dragged-and-dropped the master onto a wireframe. Then, **OnPageLoad**, we set action to **Show** (**C**).

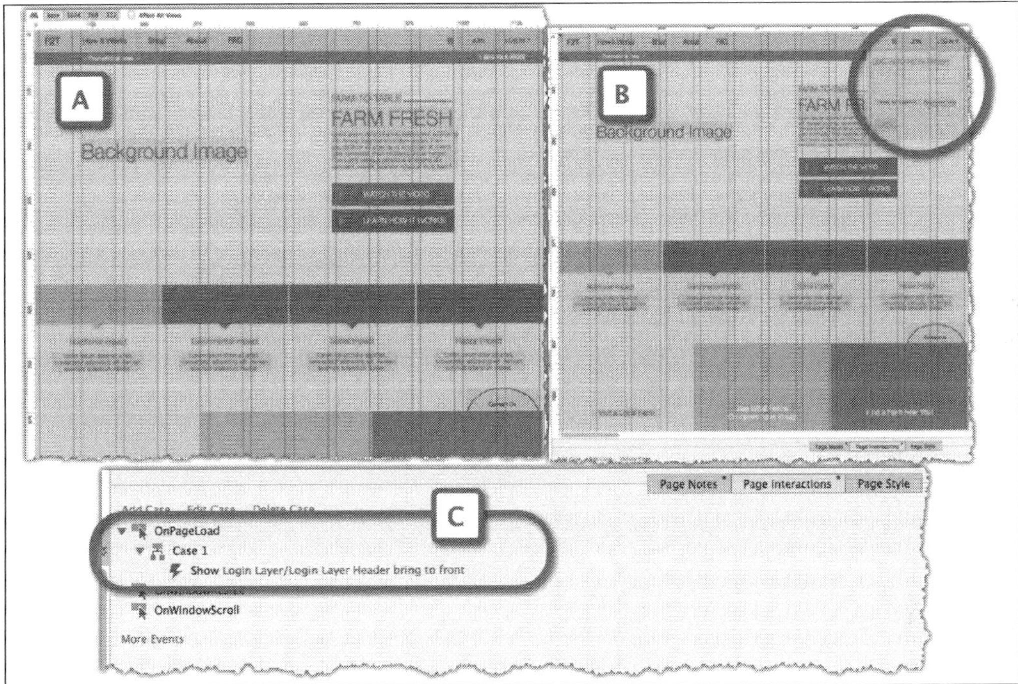

Image 18

Summary

Regardless of the tool you are using, generating UI specifications is a complicated affair. However, if you take the time to construct your file correctly, create global patterns and document them, and set up a template that works for the stakeholders, it will not be that bad. Remember to start the review process early and plan for it when creating a project plan.

The final chapter of the book will discuss the importance of teamwork and collaboration.

9
Collaboration

For this new edition of the book, we looked to refresh the quote by Henry Ford that was used in the previous edition:

> "*Coming together is the beginning, staying together is progress and working together is success.*"

But it turns out that Ford's quote is still very relevant for this new edition. Many aspects of team collaboration, such as uniformity in the quality of wireframes or proficiency levels, are taken for granted and often with little consideration to the nuts and bolts involved with setting up the appropriate conditions for success. In this chapter, we will explore Axure's collaboration feature set (available only in the Axure Pro version), appropriately renamed in Version 7 as **Team Projects**, as it relates to the three challenge dimensions in Ford's quote, which are as follows:

- "Coming together" relates to planning and training
- "Staying together" relates to communication and synchronization
- "Working together" relates to individuals and culture

Thus, while teamwork continues to be an acute pain point for UX teams, we feel that the combination of Axure 7 Team Project's features, adoption of best practices and awareness of potential pitfalls, can end up with a recipe for successful collaboration, which you can use repeatedly and with consistent results.

There are many reasons for difficulties. To begin with, a project has to be of a certain size and complexity to warrant the extended investment an organization will have to make in a UX team. Each UX designer is usually assigned to one or several workstreams or modules, each with its dedicated business, engineering, and other stakeholders. Then, add the constraints of tight schedule and budget, and you'll end up in a fast-paced environment with many asynchronously moving parts; you may be working in such an environment right now.

For a UX team that is using a traditional file-centric tool such as Word or Visio, an immediate concern is keeping wireframes or any artifacts for that matter in sync. Some of the challenges are:

- Only one person can edit the file at any given time, which means that each designer works on a separate file.
- To get a sense of the entire application, constant consolidation of the individual files is necessary.
- The larger the team and the more accelerated the project velocity, the harder it is to manage the consistency of interaction patterns and widgets across the files each designer is working on.

The UX team faces a similar challenge of collecting feedback from stakeholders. A common practice has each UX workstream create PowerPoint or Word documents of the latest wireframes, add some verbiage describing the interactions, and send them out to stakeholders for written feedback. There are several drawbacks here, stated as follows:

- Stakeholders need to respond to a static presentation of a dynamic interface
- Redundant, extra effort for the team, to create stakeholder presentations
- A challenge to consolidate the feedback from multiple stakeholders
- A challenge to share the feedback with the other UX workstreams on a timely and on-going basis

Axure 7 Pro supports two forms of collaboration, which help address major difficulties in all the areas mentioned earlier:

- The Team Projects format enables a team of UX designers and others, such as business analysts, to collaborate on the same project file
- The Discussion tab in the HTML prototype facilitates review by a stakeholder who can add comments for each page on the sitemap

Like other important Axure features, these capabilities translate to significant time and effort savings for the UX team and the entire project. For a UX team that is considering a prototyping tool that supports a collaborative environment, there are a few other "industrial strength" options at the price point and maturity offered by Axure. The Team Projects feature, known to users of previous versions as Shared Projects, has been around since Version 4.5 released in 2008. It is stable, reliable, and is being continuously refined.

Note the discussion around the use of Axure's axureShare cloud platform and the enablement of the Discussion feature later on in the project. It is an option integrated into the HTML prototype, where the entire team and stakeholders can share feedback and response to wireframe.

Collaboration still continues to pose significant challenges because such is the nature of this process: any project with many simultaneously, asynchronously moving parts is inherently a complex process to manage. This chapter focuses on Axure's collaboration features and the methods that will help you keep the UX team, stakeholders, and prototype in sync.

In this chapter, we will cover:

- The Team Projects environment
- Setting up a team project
- The Team menu
- Managing a team project
- Best practices for Team Projects
- axureShare

Team Projects (Pro Version Only)

When you save an Axure file for the first time, it will be saved as an `.rp` file by default, Axure's standalone format, which is just like a Word or Visio document that allows only a single person to access and work on it at any given time.

Axure's Team Projects (formally known as Shared Projects) feature seems to suggest obvious support for collaboration, but it is the versioning capability that also makes it compelling to single practitioners.

Understanding the Team Projects Environment

Axure's Team Projects environment is straightforward. The next diagram depicts a typical setup. The master prototype file is on an SVN server or in a shared directory (*Image 1*, **A**). Each team member (**B**) may be using a Mac or Windows machine and needs Axure 7. Each team member can check out the following elements:

- Pages
- Masters

- Annotation fields
- Global variables
- Page style sheet
- Widget styles
- Generators

To edit files that are on the shared repository, team members check out a desired element (**C**). If other team members attempt to check out the same item, Axure prompts them that the file is already checked out. Once done editing, team members check in the element (**D**) and it clears for editing by others.

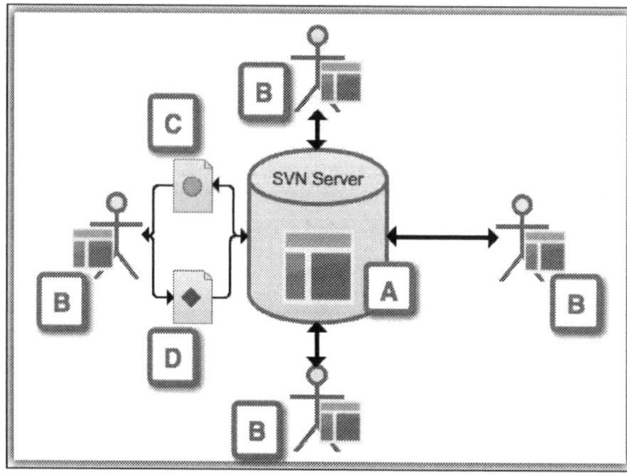

Image 1

Understanding the Check Out/In Status

The following table lists the Team Projects's check out/in statuses:

Status	Description	Icon
Checked In	The element is available for check out to all team members. However, the status indicates only what the local copy 'knows'. When you actually try to check out the file, Axure will let you know if it is available or not.	Blue diamond.

Status	Description	Icon
Checked Out	The element is checked out to you. The local copy of other team members will still display the file as checked in.	Green circle. The person who has the element checked out will see an indicator—in the form of an icon or a label—mark its status. The local copies of the other team members will show that the element is checked in, until they attempt to check the item out.
New	When you add a new element, it is first created in your local Axure project file. Once you check it in, other members of the team will be able to see or use it.	Green plus sign. The icon is applicable to pages and masters. It appears only on the local copy of the person who created it. Other elements may not have an indicator.
Conflict	The element on your local Axure project file conflicts with a version of the same element on the master project file on the server or shared directory.	Red rectangle
Unsafely Checked Out	You checked out an element despite being warned that it has been checked out by another team member. You or the other person will lose the work you did, once you attempt to check in the file to the repository.	Orange triangle

Setting Up a Shared Repository

The process of setting up the Team Projects environment is like following a recipe. You need to prepare some ingredients in advance so that you don't get stuck half way through. In this case, you need to have the location of the repository. As mentioned earlier, the repository can be stored on:

- A shared network drive
- A dedicated SVN server hosted on a company server
- An SVN hosting service such as Beanstalk or Unfuddle

Either way, you will have an address that will point to that repository location and with the location available, you are ready to proceed.

Security and backup

Some organizations forbid putting anything outside of their secured environment, so using an SVN host may not be an option. Additionally, whether your team's plan calls for the use of an SVN hosting service, the organization's own dedicated SVN server, or space on a shared directory, make sure to get a clear understanding of the support, such as regular backup and restore, that will be provided.

The following is the process of setting up a shared repository, which can be based on an RP file that gets converted to serving as a team project. Any Axure RP file can be converted.

1. With the file open in Axure, select the **Create Team Project from Current File...** option (*Image 2*, **B**) from the **Team** menu (**A**).

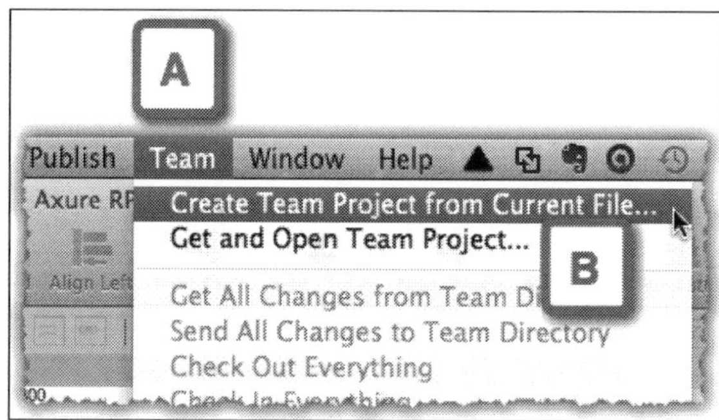

Image 2

2. The **Create Team Project** window (*Image 3*, **A**) will open, offering a wizard-type flow that will walk you through the steps of creating the shared repository.

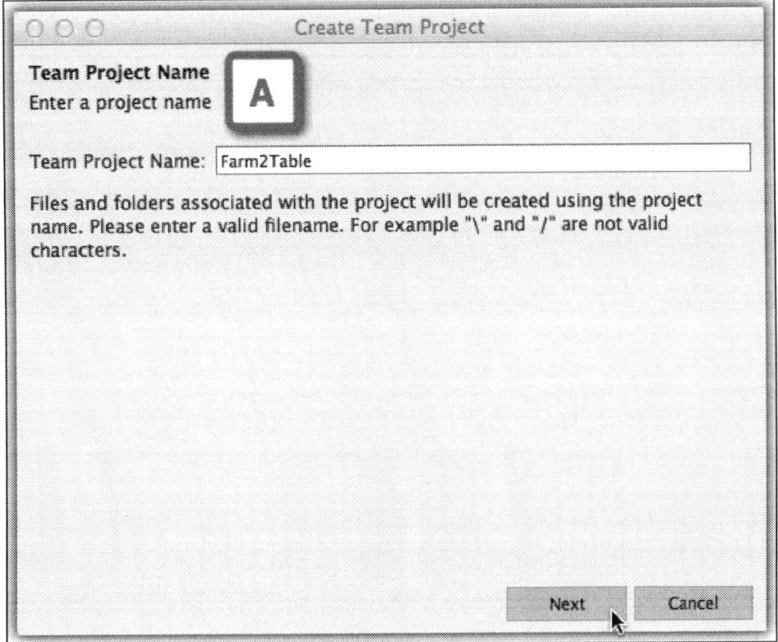

Image 3

3. Name the project in the **Team Projects Name** field. Pay attention to the disclaimer: **Files and folders associated with the project will be created using the project name. Please enter a valid filename. For example "\" and "/" are not valid characters**.

> Our recommendation is to keep the project name short, and use a hyphen to separate multiple words, for example, My-Great-Project, or CamelCase. The name MyGreatProject is later used in a URL, so we want to avoid spaces.

4. Click on the **Next** button to continue.

The **Team Projects Directory** step (*Image 4*, **A**) is where you point Axure to the location of the shared repository. This screen includes the following instructions:

- **This directory is commonly on a network drive where others can access the Team Projects.**

  Ex: /Volumes/Public/OurSharedDirectory

- **The Team Project Directory will be created on this directory with the project name.**

  Ex: /Volumes/Public/OurSharedDirectory/ProjectName

- **The Team Directory can also be a URL for an SVN directory. An SVN server must already be configured. Ex: http://svn.myserver.com/OurSharedDirectory/**

  Ex: svn://www.myserver.com/OurSharedDirectory/

Due to recent compatibility issues with Beanstalk, at the time of going to print, Axure recommends the services of Unfuddle. We do not endorse any vendor, and the use of a vendor in images is meant to provide realistic fidelity.

- **Team directories or project names with special characters may not work properly.**

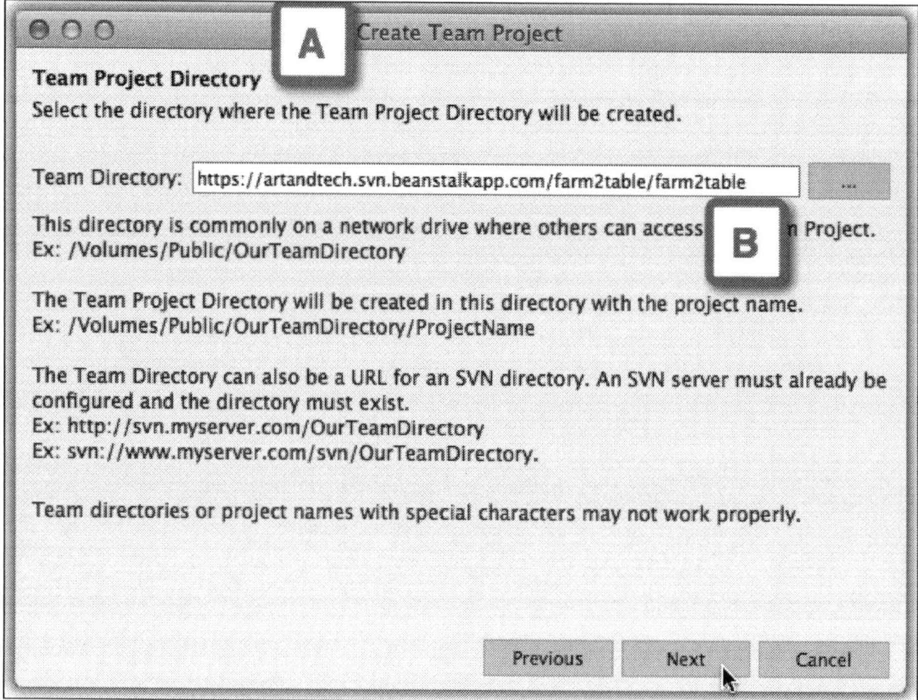

Image 4

You can either paste the address you prepared into the **Team Directory** field (**B**), or use the ellipsis button to the right of the field to navigate to the shared directory on the organization's network.

Before clicking on the **Next** button, make sure you have spelled the project name correctly because the typos will stay with the file throughout the life of the project. You can return to the previous screen and make the correction, if needed.

After you click on the **Next** button, Axure will prompt you if there is a problem with the information you provided. You'll have to validate that the path you have is correct. If you are dependent on someone else for validating the information, it is a good idea to do this setup during a time when that person is available.

Axure then asks you to point to the local directory for the team project (*Image 5*, **A**), which is where the local copy of the repository will be created on your hard drive. By default, Axure offers to store it in the directory labeled `Team Projects` in the `Axure` directory (**B**), but it is up to you where to store it.

Image 5

As shown in the following screenshot, Axure will offer to create the local directory for you, if needed (*Image 6*, **A**):

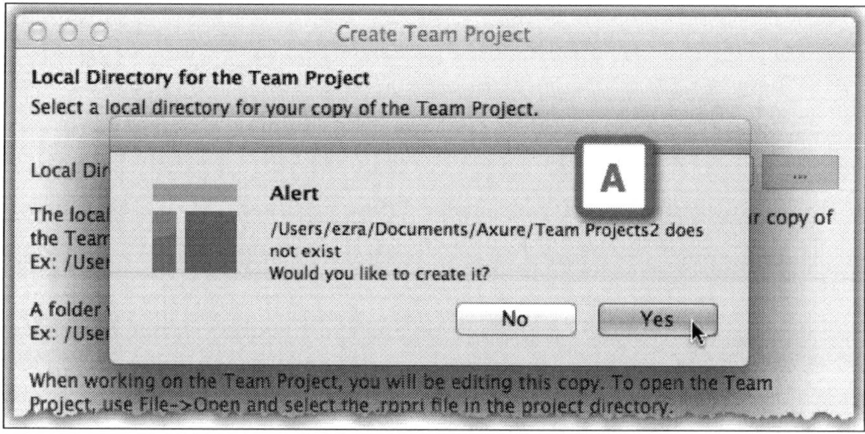

Image 6

Axure will prompt you with a **Success** confirmation upon completion of the process (*Image 7*, **A**), as shown in the following screenshot:

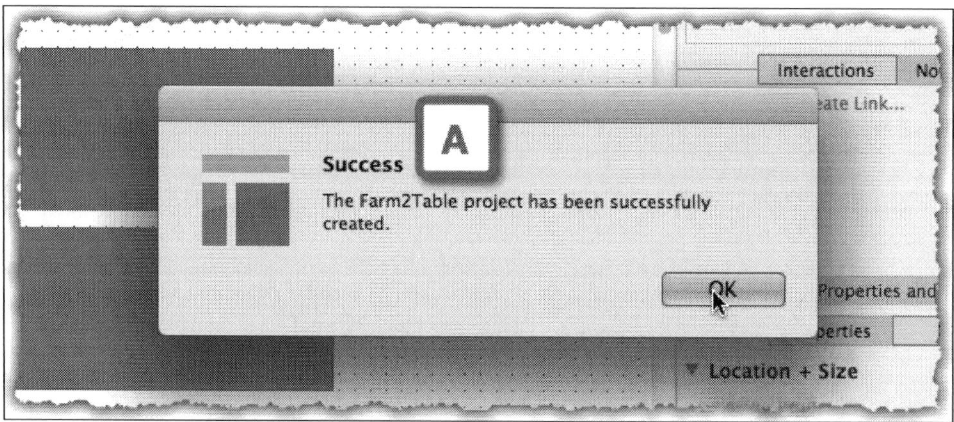

Image 7

When you look in the local directory, you'll find that Axure has created two items, which are as follows:

- The RPPRJ file, for example, `farm2table.rpprj` (*Image 8*, **A**)
- The directory `DO_NOT_EDIT` (**B**), which, as it clearly states, you should not mess with

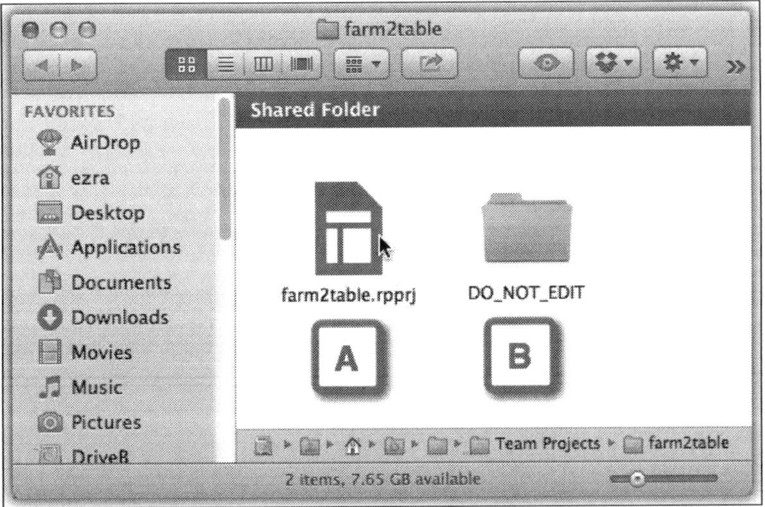

Image 8

Congratulations! The local copy of your team project is ready for you to use. The following are the steps that you should perform next:

- Make sure to distribute the link to the shared directory to all your team members.
- Have the link, as well as the username and password of the SVN server, readily available; this enables you to access the server the first time a team member attempts to load the file.

If you have been using a standalone version of the project, you will find the most prominent visual differences on the **Sitemap** pane (*Image 9*, **A**) and the **Masters** pane (**B**):

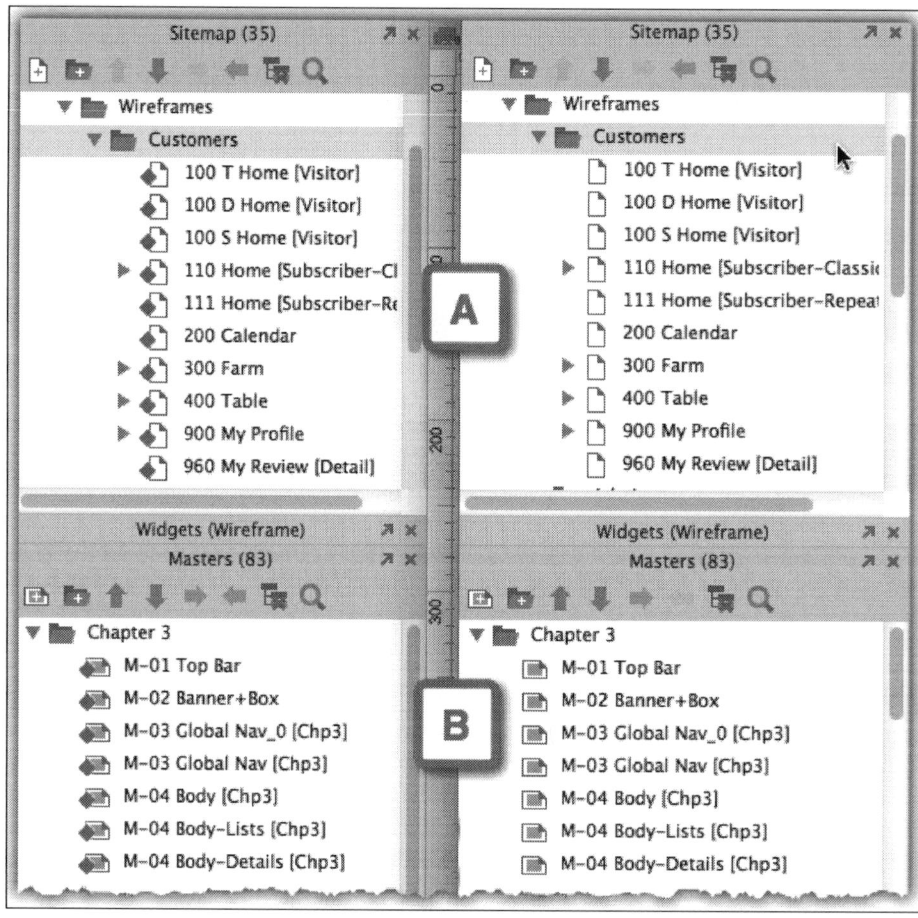

Image 9

In the team projects's RPPRJ file, the icons for pages and masters include a status indicator. This indicator reflects the state of the element on your local copy of the project, not its status on the server.

Another difference between a standalone RP file and a team projects file is the directories and files that make up a team project. Like the quintessential forbidden castle door in a fairy tale, the mysteriously labeled folder `DO_NOT_EDIT` might be attracting your attention. It is actually not a bad idea to take a quick glance to satisfy your natural curiosity.

The following screenshot illustrates the local copy of the repository, which has been created in the `Team Projects` directory—a subdirectory located inside Axure's main directory:

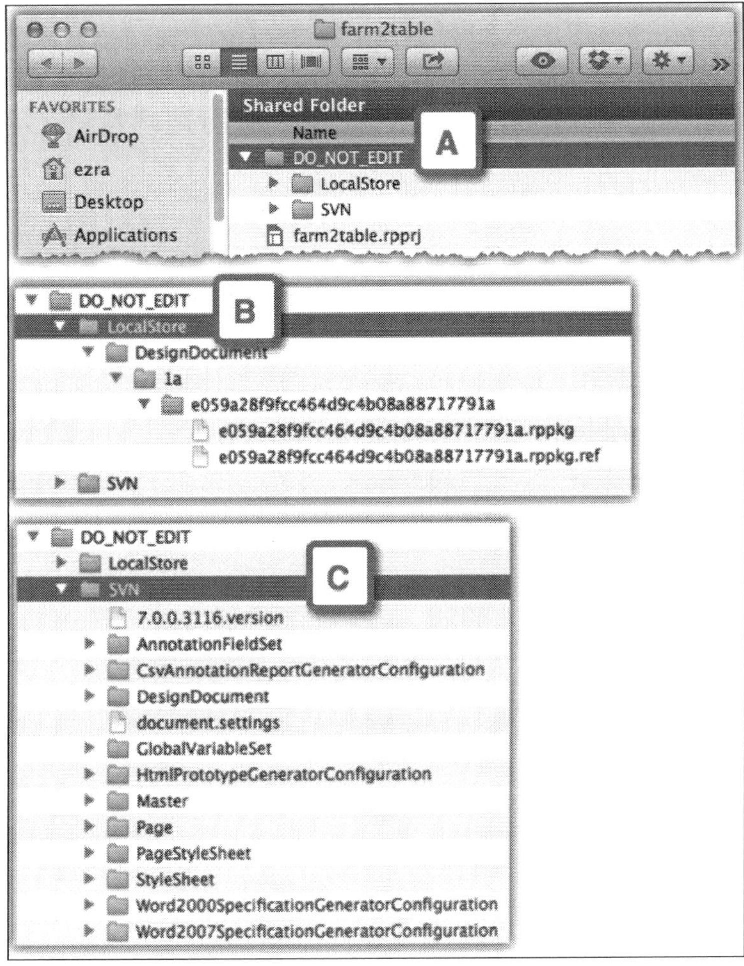

Image 10

Your project has a dedicated folder within the `Team Projects` directory, and as mentioned earlier, there are two items in its root level: the RPPRJ file and the `DO_NOT_EDIT` folder (*Image 10*, **A**). The `DO_NOT_EDIT` directory has the following two folders:

- `LocalStore` (**B**), which contains a small set of files used by Axure
- `SVN` (**C**), which contains all the project files used in communications with the SVN server. The size of this directory will grow as the projects advance.

If the name `DO_NOT_EDIT` is not clear enough, we will reiterate. Manually manipulating the content of these files is not advisable because there is a risk that the Axure file will get corrupted.

If you did not set up the Team Projects environment yourself or if you have to recreate the local copy of the project for some reason, you will need to create your local copy of the project by accessing the shared repository, which we will discuss in next section.

Loading from a Shared Repository

Before you start, make sure to have:

- The path to the shared repository on the server
- The username and password if the file is hosted on an SVN server

It is highly recommended that the person who is responsible for setting the shared repository makes this information readily available to the team and is also available to help with the setup, if needed. On your part, make sure to save this information for future use.

You should either have a path to a network directory or a URL to an SVN server that looks something like this: `https://company.svn.unfuddle.com/farm2table/farm2table`.

From the **Team** menu (*Image 11*, **A**), select the **Get and Open Team Project...** option (**B**) as shown in the following screenshot:

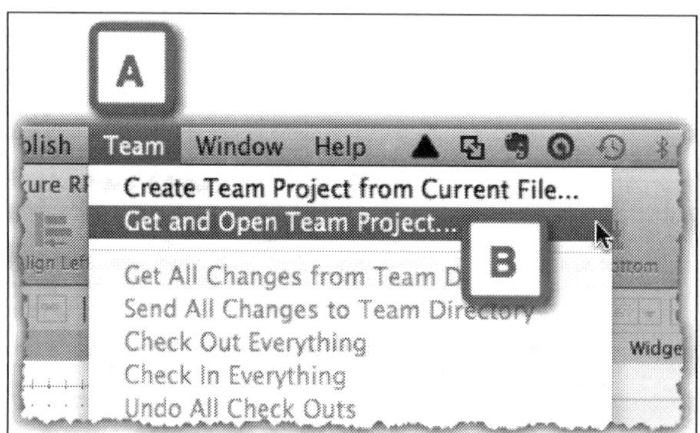

Image 11

Axure will present the **Get Team Project** dialog box (*Image 12*, **A**) as shown in the following screenshot:

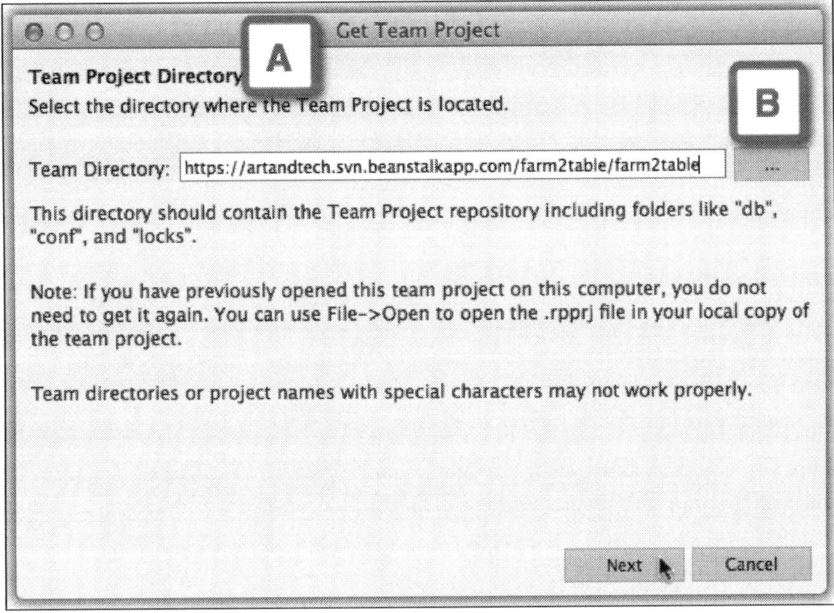

Image 12

The **Team Directory** field (**B**) is where you either paste the URL, a path such as the example we discussed earlier or use the ellipsis button to navigate within the network to the destination.

The dialog has the following instructional text, which is useful to keep in mind:

- **This directory should contain the Team Project repository including folders like "db", "conf", and "locks".**
- **Note: If you have previously opened this team project on this computer, you do not need to get it again. You can use File->Open to open the .rpprj file in your local copy of the team project.**
- **Team directories or project names with special characters may not work properly.**

Pointing to the local directory is the next step (*Image 13*, **A**) where you tell Axure to create a local copy of the repository. By default, Axure offers to store it in the directory labelled `Team Projects` in the `Axure` directory (**B**), but you can certainly point to another destination using the ellipsis button.

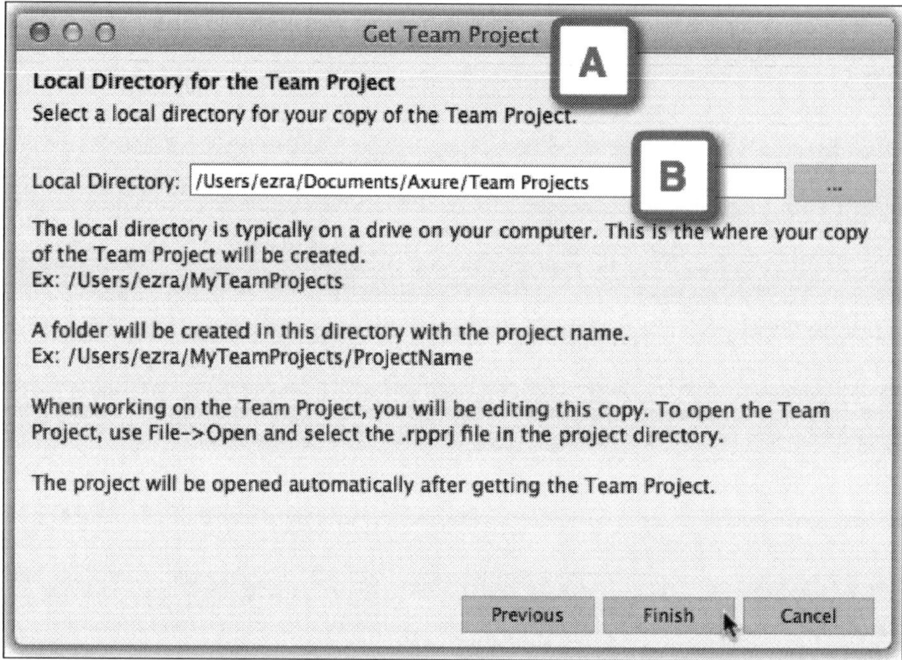

Image 13

After clicking on the **Finish** button, Axure will download all the necessary files from the server or network directory to the destination folder you indicated earlier. Depending on your network connection speed and the size of the file, this might take few seconds to a couple of minutes.

The shared file will open and you can start working. Remember to access the file on a day-to-day basis. You can use the **Open Recent** option from the **File** menu, or the **Welcome Screen...** option located under the **Help** menu. If for some reason you forgot where the file is located, use the file search option to look for the `.rpprj` string in the filename.

The Team Menu

Once you have the local copy of the project, you will be using the **Team** menu constantly. You and the entire team should have a solid understanding of the various menu options.

Creating and Loading

You typically have to use the following options only once per project:

Menu options	Description
Create Team Project from Current file...	Use this option if you want to create a team project file out of the current file. This option is only active when you have the `RP` file open.
Get and Open Team Project...	Use this option to create a local copy of a team project file. If you are also the person responsible for creating the team project, you can skip this step because a local copy will be created for you when you create the shared file.

Updating the Entire File

The following set of options apply batch-like functionality to updates, check outs and check ins:

Menu options	Description
Get All Changes from Team Directory	This option will update your local copy of the project file with all the latest changes that were made by other team members. Make a habit of getting all changes first every time you start working on the file and repeat it a few times during the day.
Send All Changes to Team Directory	This option will update the shared repository with all the new changes you have made since the last time you sent your changes. Consider this option as a form of saving your work. Although you can and should use the **Save** option to save your work to the local copy of the project, sending your updates will ensure that if something happens to the local copy, most of your work will be on the server. Note that the files you are working on are still checked out to you. The trade off is that when you send your changes to the shared directory, you can no longer undo them by undoing the check out.

Menu options	Description
Check Out Everything	This option will check the *entire* project for you—a highly unadvisable action. Fortunately, Axure will prompt you with a warning, as shown in the following screenshot: 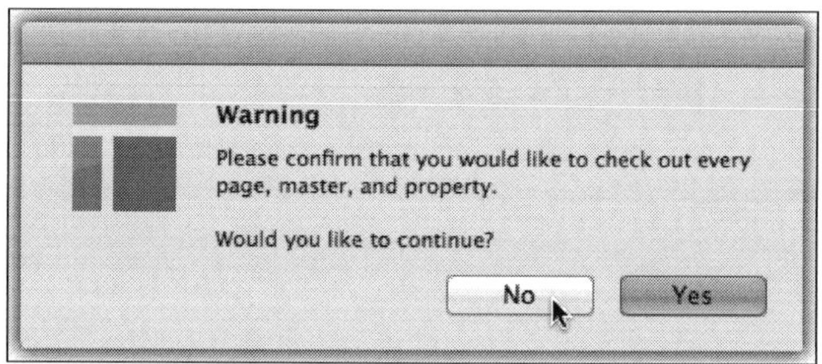 Image 14 If you do manage to somehow check out the entire project, check it back as soon as possible because the rest of the team obviously will not be able to safely check out any of the assets.
Check In Everything	This option will check in everything you have checked out. Develop the habit to use this option at the end of the day. This ensures that you have nothing checked out and that other team members can check out files in case you are out of the office.
Undo All Check Outs	This is a great option to help you undo undesirable work and revert the effected items back to their state before you check them out. For example, you check out a page and a few masters with the intention of further developing the prototype. Things fall apart and you realize that the best bet is to start over. Now, you were saving your work in the meantime, so you cannot undo the local copy. However, if you did not send changes, you can undo the check out.

Updating Single Page or Master

The following set of options allows you to deal with a single element at a time:

Menu options	Description
Get Changes from Team Directory	This option applies only to a selected page or master. New to Version 7, the name of the active page tab appears in the menu. If you right-click on a page in the **Sitemap** pane, the command in the context menu will not have the page name.
Send Changes to Team Directory	This option applies only to a selected page or master.

Menu options	Description
Check Out	This option applies only to a selected page or master.
Check In	This option applies only to a selected page or master.
Undo Check Out	This option applies only to a selected page or master.

Managing Team Projects

In a Team Projects architecture, each team member has a copy of the project on their computer. During the course of a day's work, each team member will create new elements, check out files, and generally modify the project. These changes will not be reflected in the shared repository until the team member sends all changes to the server or checks in all their checked out elements.

While you can tell if a page is checked out to you, you cannot tell if a page is actually available for check out or if it has been checked out by another team member, by looking at the sitemap. This applies not only to pages, but to all the elements that are controlled by the shared repository.

The **Manage Team Projects** console provides all team members with a real-time view of the availability status of the elements that are managed by the system. This view spares you from the hassle of attempting to check out an element that is checked out to another team member.

Let's walk through a normal use scenario.

Check Out/In Use Case – Team Member A

After doing some work on a couple of pages, it is time to send all changes to the shared repository using the **Send All Changes to Team Directory** option (*Image 15*, **B**) in the **Team** menu (**A**), as shown in the following screenshot:

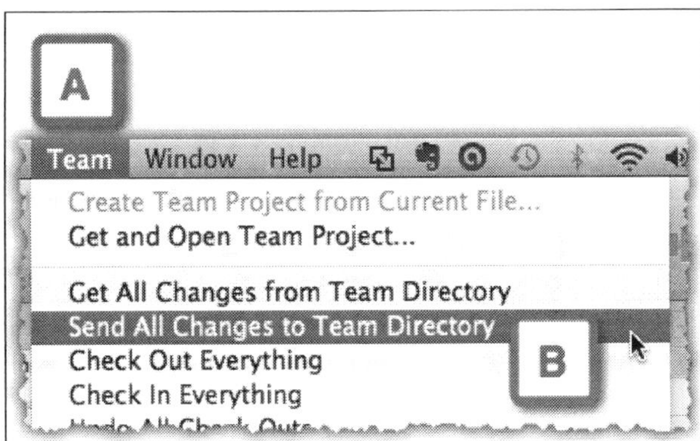

Image 15

Team member A is presented with the **Send Changes** dialog (*Image 16*, **A**), listing the elements that are going to be updated on the server in the top pane (**B**) and a field to enter what these changes were in the **Change Notes** pane (**C**). Upon clicking on **OK**, the updates will be sent to the shared repository.

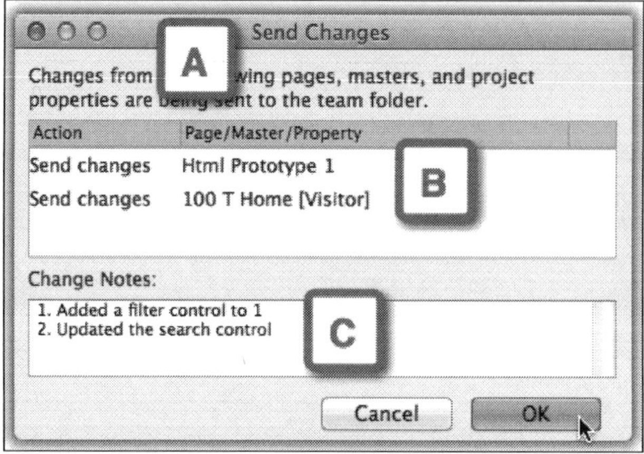

Image 16

Check Out/In Use Case – Team Member B

Switch to team member B, who also wants to check out the same page that team member A has checked out. To this user, the page appears available for check out on the **Sitemap** pane. To see if the page is available, the user chooses to use the **Manage Team Project...** option (*Image 17*, **B**) from the **Team** menu (**A**), as shown in the following screenshot:

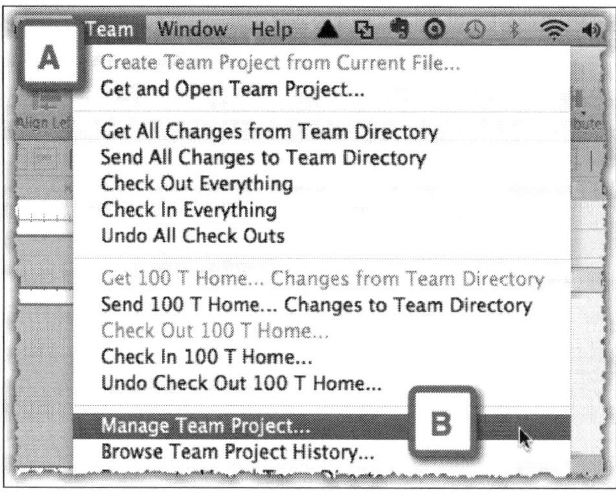

Image 17

The **Manage Team Project** dialog (*Image 18*, **A**) is presented. The top section of the dialog indicates the path to the shared directory and includes the instruction: **Click Refresh to retrieve the current status of the pages, masters, and document properties in the team project. Right click on an item or selection to check in, check out, and get the latest changes. Click the column header to sort by the column**. Indeed, notice that the main table area (**B**) is empty initially.

Upon clicking on the **Refresh** button (**C**), the table area is populated with the list of all pages, masters, and design documents in real time.

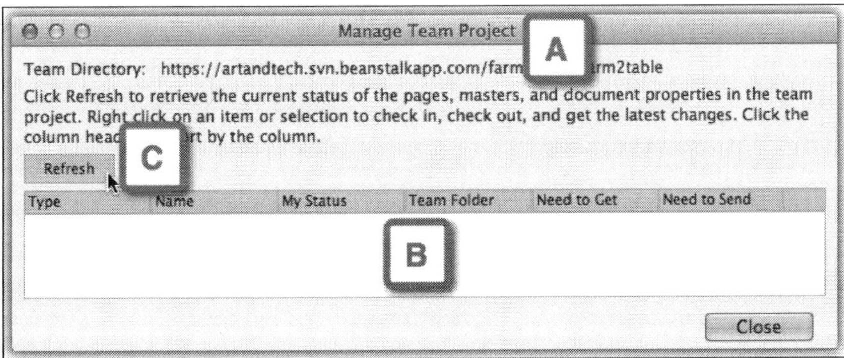

Image 18

Column headers in the window's table area (*Image 19*, **A**) are sortable, making it easy to quickly find out which pages are checked out and to whom.

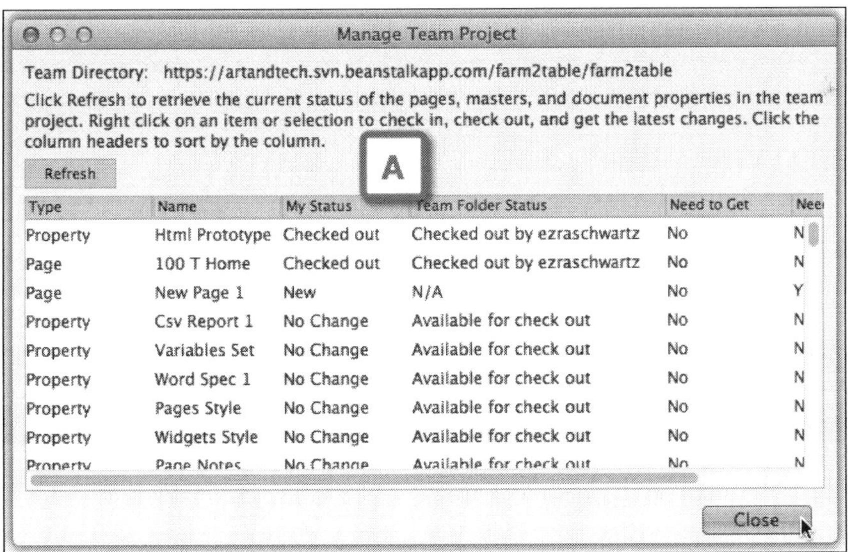

Image 19

Team members can easily coordinate their check outs. Right-clicking on the row presents a contextual menu listing available actions.

Dismiss this dialog by clicking on the **Close** button. It is a good idea to get into the habit of using the **Manage Team Projects** console before trying to check out pages that are the responsibility of other team members.

Browse Team Projects History...

Axure's Team Projects feature provides a team or an individual with additional invaluable features, which are as follows:

- The risk of lost work is significantly reduced. As long as the SVN server or the shared network directory where you host your project are regularly and reliably backed up, you can restore any previous version of the project from day one. It is not possible to exaggerate the importance of this capability and the peace of mind that comes with it.
- Gain the precious ability to step back in time and access earlier iterations of the prototype. When you consider the realities of a large and fast-paced project, you realize that the need to revert to an earlier version of some pattern is likely to occur. One of the most challenging aspects of iterative design is having an effective way to revert to or compare to an earlier version of the application.

The system maintains complete version control throughout the file's lifecycle. Each time a team member sends changes or checks in their work, a new version is added to the log. Each version, precisely identified with a unique revision number and the date of its capture, can be exported into a fully functional RP file, which reflects its condition at the moment the version was created. Items from that RP file can be imported back into the main project as needed.

Barring a catastrophic failure of the SVN server or a shared directory that has not been backed up properly, as long as the shared repository is available, you can access practically any restore point in the project, illustrated as follows:

1. From the **Team** menu, select the **Browse Team Projects History...** option (*Image 20*, **A**) as shown in the following screenshot:

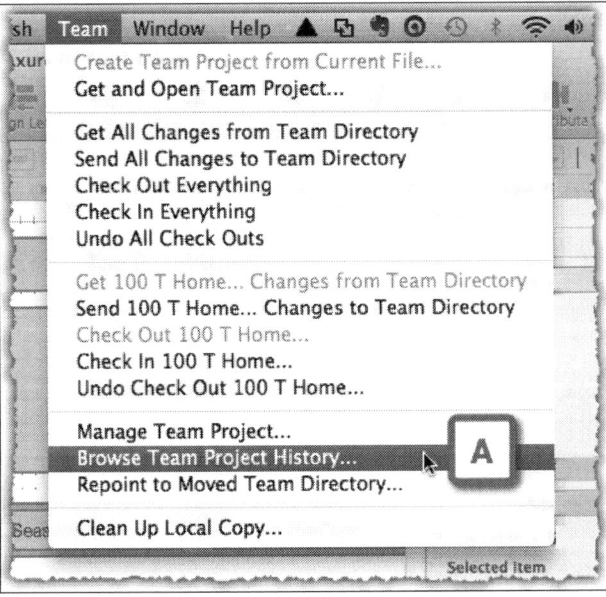

Image 20

2. The **Team Projects History Browser** dialog (*Image 21*, **A**) appears. The top field **Team Directory** points to the shared repository.

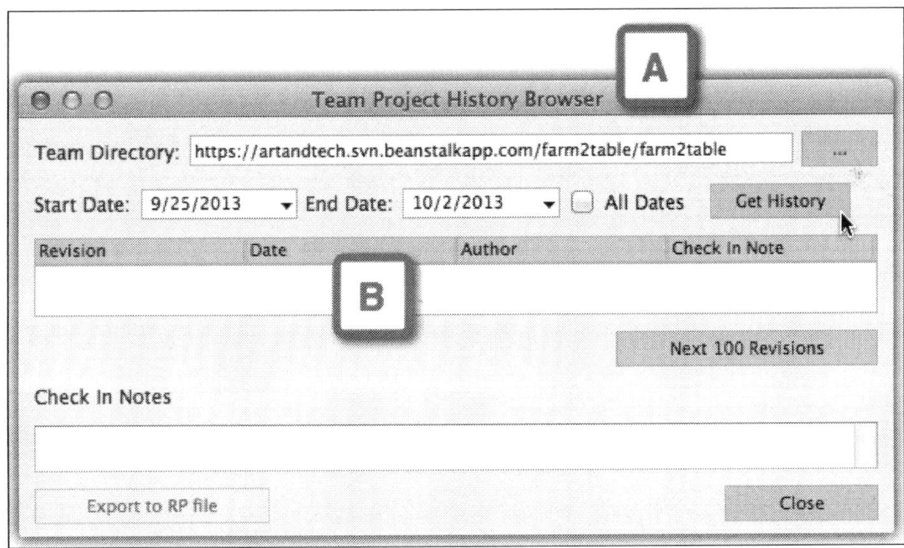

Image 21

3. Depending on the size of the team and the point in time that you want to recover relative to the start date of the file, the list of all versions can be overwhelmingly long. To narrow down the list to the set of potential versions that correspond to the date and time you are looking for, use the **Start Date** and **End Date** calendar controls (*Image 22*, **A**). By default, the start and end dates are set to capture the last seven days worth of work.

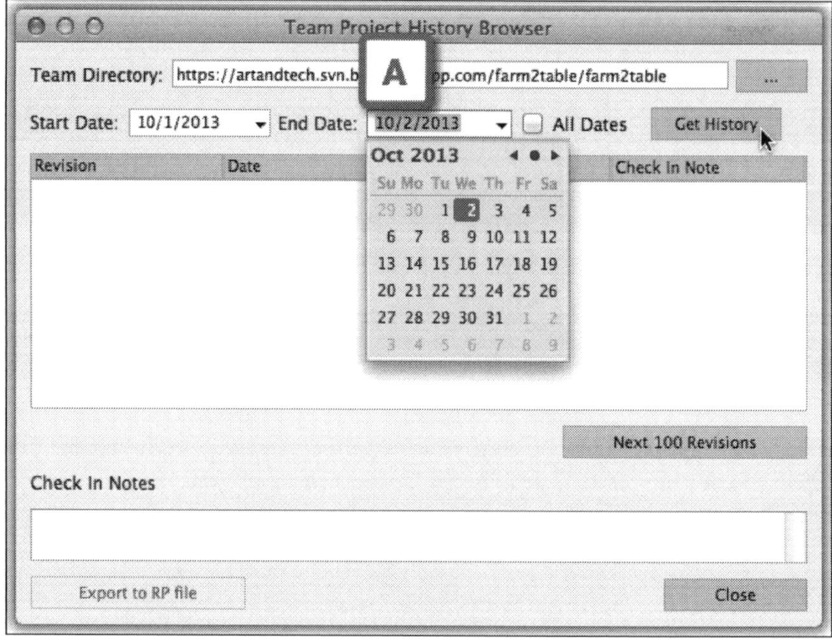

Image 22

4. If you want to override the calendar pickers, you have an option to retrieve the list of all versions by checking the **All Dates** checkbox. Click on the **Get History** button to continue.
5. Within seconds, the table area (*Image 23*, **A**) gets populated by a list of versions, with each row representing a fully functional restore point of the Axure file. Each row can be sorted by one of the version's attributes, including **Revision number**, **Date**, **Author**, and **Check In Note**.

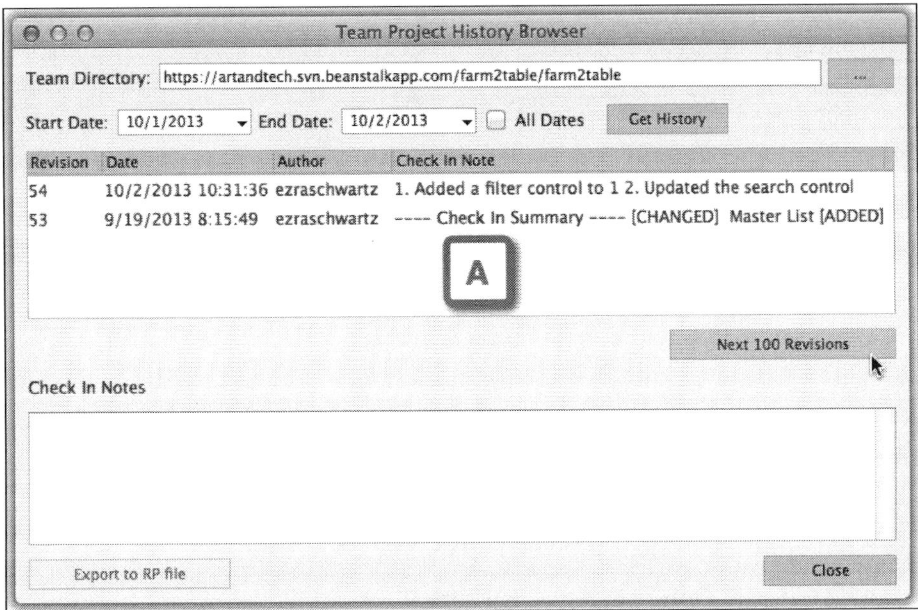

Image 23

6. Identify in the list the version that is most likely to contain the last good version of the item or items you are looking to restore. Normally, you will see several versions for each day. Since the revision number is serial, the highest revision number corresponds to the last update for that date.

When you click on a row, all the activity that has been automatically recorded by Axure, will be displayed in the **Check In Notes** pane. This information is incredibly valuable because typically, you will be looking to restore a particular page or master.

Now comes the truly fantastic part. If you identified the revision, use the **Export to RP file** button and Axure will prompt you to save the file on your drive. Within a few seconds, you'll be able to open a fully functional, standalone Axure file (in the `.rp` format)—a snapshot of the entire project corresponding to the time and date of that revision. Now, you can find the element you were looking for and import it into the current share project file if you want.

However, if this ends up not being the snapshot you need, continue exploring until you find it. If more versions are available, the **Next 100 Revisions** button will be active. Use the **Close** button to dismiss this window when you are done.

A side benefit of the history browser is that there is no need to keep old versions of pages and masters in the active **Sitemap** and **Masters** panes, especially since the constant additions and updates by multiple team members tend to greatly bloat the working environment. As the project moves deeper into detailed design, it is beneficial to do regular audits with team members, discard pages that are no longer relevant and discard masters that are not used on any pages. The result will be a leaner file that generates faster as both HTML prototype and Word specifications document. As we discussed, all the previous work can be easily restored, if needed.

Repoint to Moved Shared Directory...

Occasionally, there is a need to move the shared directory from its location on the network drive. As long as the repository has been moved in its entirety, this is a safe operation. All team members can continue to use their local copy of the file, but point towards the new location of the shared repository.

The following steps will help you if there is a need to move the shared repository:

1. Coordinate the move with the entire team. Ideally, pick a date and time that will minimize the impact on the team's schedule. Try to avoid proximity to major deadlines.
2. Make sure that team members are aware of the planned move. Clearly communicate to all that the shared repository will not be available at the set timeframe.
3. At a set time, before the move, all team members should use the **Check In Everything** option.
4. After the move, provide all team members with the updated path.
5. Each team member will repoint to the new location by using the **Repoint to Moved Team Directory...** option in the **Team** menu and entering the provided URL into the **Team Directory** field (**B**).

Image 24

Clean Up Local Copy... and Dealing with a Working Copy Locked Alert

Sometimes, for some unknown reasons, bad stuff happens. With Axure, such events are extremely rare. However, suppose you are attempting to check in your work and you get the error message **Working Copy Locked**. As explained by Axure, the message **A variety of things can cause "Working Copy Locked" errors. These include virus scanners and losing connection to the server or a computer failure during a previous operation** as shown in the following screenshot:

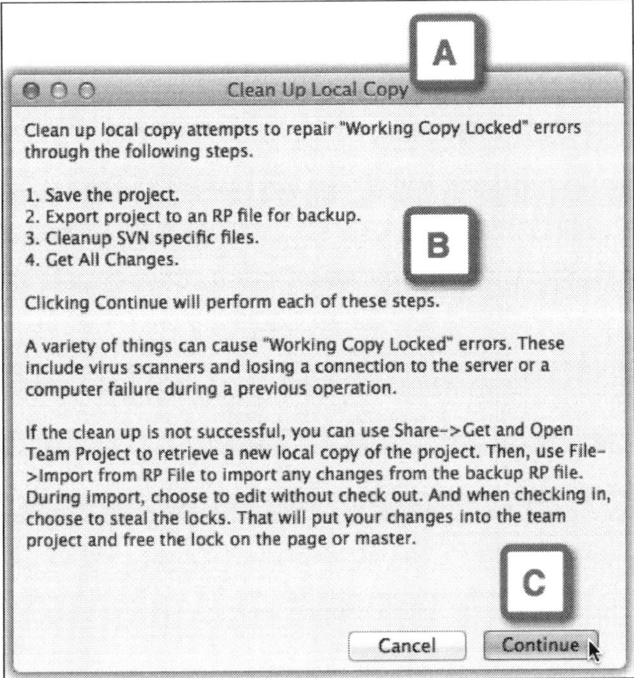

Image 25

Execute the following steps in the event of a Working Copy Locked error (typically occurs when you try to check in something):

1. Select the **Clean Up Local Copy...** from the **Team** menu
2. Axure will attempt to repair the problem, as described in the **Clean Up Local Copy** dialog (**A**), a process which includes the following steps (**B**):
    1. Save the project. (You have to do this.)
    2. Export the project to an RP file for backup. (You have to do this.)
    3. Clean up SVN-specific files. (Axure does this.)
    4. Get all changes. (Axure does this.)

From our personal experience and that of some of our colleagues, we can attest to the fact that this feature seems to work just fine and you are able to send your work to the server.

Best Practices for the UX Axure Teamwork

Teams are complicated. The number of variables that determine a teams' makeup and workings can be wildly different, making meaningful comparison difficult. However, as the famous proverb goes, "For every problem, there is an opportunity". In this section, we are not attempting to resolve the challenge, but rather, isolate the most fundamental team attributes.

Attributes of the UX Team

The following are the attributes to evaluate your potential challenges and opportunities for your team:

- **Team size**: How big is the UX team? Obviously, two people are a team, but the larger the number of UX designers involved in a project, the harder it is to keep everyone on the same page. Larger teams are likely to break into multiple workstreams that tend to form silos of concentrated isolation, so there is also the challenge of cross-workstream communications.
- **Location**: Are all team members sharing the same physical office space? Is everyone on the same floor and in close proximity? Are people spread across the corporate campus or across multiple cities? Are some team members working remote from their home-offices? Are team members spread across the globe?
- **Knowledge of project's domain**: Some team members may have previous project experience with and exposure to the application's domain. Other team members are new to the domain and its nuances. This can be an issue with expert systems.
- **UX experience and expertise**: Some team members may be UX veterans with established track record, but also with a set preference for how they are used to having things done. Other team members may have a different take. Junior members may have significantly less experience with UX work and may lack the ability to foresee potential problems and estimated workload and confidence when presenting to stakeholders.

- **Axure expertise**: Veteran team members are likely to have years of power-use skills with tools like Visio, but little Axure knowledge, perhaps even some resistance. Some team members will be totally new to the tools, while a few may have significant Axure experience. Additionally, some veteran Axure users may not be familiar with the new features of Axure 7, such as adaptive views and the Responder widget.
- **Individual personalities**: This section is impossible to cover in a few sentences. However, the normal mix of extroverts, introverts, assertive, shy, outgoing, reserved, blunt, self-starters, strong work ethic, lazy, overly polite, alpha and beta types, and so on can turn a team dynamic into a soap opera.
- **Cultural influences**: In some cultures, it is not polite to behave in an assertive way around team members of higher seniority. This might be mistakenly interpreted by one from an all-are-equal culture as timidness, hesitation, or lack of confidence. Team members might find the attitude and manners of others to be rude and inappropriate, leading to tension and hostile relations. The combinations are as diverse as the world we live in.

Regular and effective communication is the fundamental ingredient for successful teamwork, yet it is easier said than done. This is especially true with virtual teams of individuals who work remotely from their homes and on-site teams spread across several geographical locations. That said, all too often, colleagues who share a cubicle, fail to exchange meaningful information despite their physical proximity. The following are a few practices to consider for your team:

- As much as possible, it is important to allocate time for staff development. Ensure that all team members are at a level of Axure proficiency that makes them not only productive but good enough to avoid loss of work due to basic errors that might mess up the Team Project file. As we know, such calamities tend to happen just before a major deadline.
- Team members should understand how to work with Team Projects. All should be comfortable with the various options under the **Team** menu, and with the difference between options such as **Get All Changes from Team Directory** and **Get Changes from Team Directory**, for example.
- New team members should have an on-boarding deep-dive session with a knowledgeable team member to cover the structure of the site. In large, intense projects, new members are often thrown into the cold waters of a Team Projects file to sink or swim because the team is at the height of some crunch. Disoriented and under pressure to get up to speed as soon as possible, the incoming member can be easily lost in the intricacies, and depart from the set approach.

- All team members should participate in a weekly status meeting that covers the structure of the sitemap, variables (since these are global and limited), and other important changes. Use web sharing to view the file and make sure that team members understand how other members constructed their wireframes.
- Despite looming deadlines, it is important to be careful and pay attention before checking in and out. A few seconds of concentration can save hours of lost work.
- Team members should avoid unsafe checkouts; this is critical. There are few and clear reasons for breaking this rule, more so when the person who has the elements checked out, is going to be away for some time.
- Before you begin work on a page, make sure to get all changes from the shared directory; this will ensure you have the latest copy.
- Start your work session by getting all changes. Continue to update your file frequently throughout the day.
- When done editing a page or master you checked out, check it in so that it will be available for other team members.
- Check out only what's needed for your design work and check in as soon as you are done. Then, check out the next chunk you are going to work on. Avoid hogging files you are not working on and are still checked out from.
- If possible, structure the sitemap and masters in sections such that team members can work on chunks of the file in parallel. Agree on unique page and master IDs and a naming convention to help team members access the right files.
- Make sure that the shared file is backed up regularly.

axureShare – Axure's Cloud Solution for Sharing

axureShare, formally known as AxShare, has been around for a number of years now, and it is the foundation to an Axure cloud-based hosting service for your HTML prototypes.

Axure keeps adding features and capabilities to this valuable service, so despite our efforts to update this section as late as possible in the production process, some stuff might have changed by the time you read this.

Please make sure to visit the website for the latest updates. A couple of updates that are of high value to consultants and agencies are as follows:

- Use and manage custom domains, that is, ensure the ability to point your domain to `share.axure.com`
- Brand the client experience

axureShare is currently hosted on the Amazon Web Services cloud platform, which is quite reliable and secure as far as cloud environments go.

Due to time and space limitation, we will not cover the entire set of capabilities of axureShare here, but focus on its collaboration capabilities, which are as follows:

- Host your prototypes of axureShare and share them with stakeholders
- Enable the use of the Discussion feature in the HTML prototype to generate off-line discussion among stakeholders and the UX team

You can link to axureShare from `Axure.com` or directly, `share.axure.com`. The following are the screenshots of axureShare webpages before (*Image 26*) and after (*Image 27*) logging in:

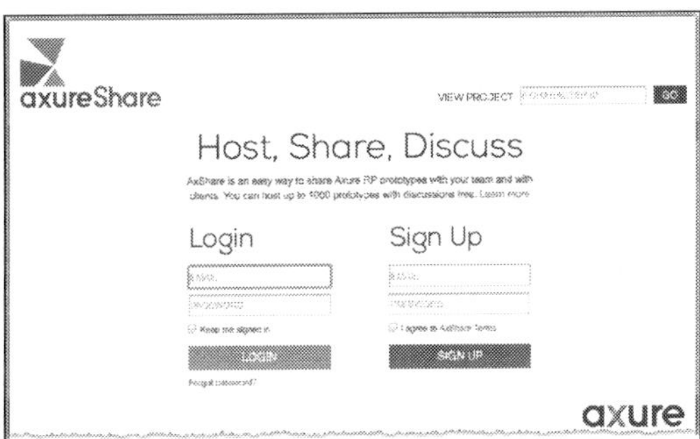

Image 26

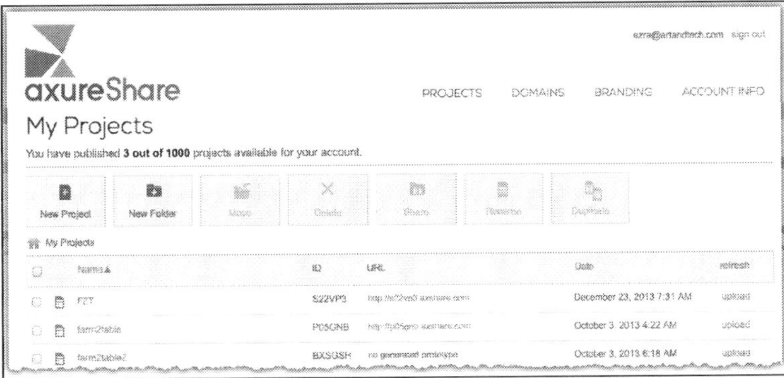

Image 27

Creating an axureShare Account

To take advantage of Axure, you need to create an account. As of May 2014, axureShare is totally free. An account allows you to upload up to 1000 (yes, one thousand) projects and the size limit for each project can be 100 MB. This is quite awesomely generous: Axure has eliminated a tiered subscription strategy it had experimented with and refunded those who held paid accounts. The current free plan—the only axureShare plan—is like the discontinued Enterprise plan, but with an additional 500 projects that you can upload.

Feedback from Stakeholders – the Discussion Tab

Only a few years ago, the means of collecting feedback from stakeholders about a proposed user experience was very limited, because it was rare to actually have an interactive prototype available for review on a regular basis. Axure helped revolutionize the way user experience is expressed by replacing static wireframe presentations with compelling interactive simulations. However, for a while, methods for collecting feedback were few and somewhat limited.

Normally, you gather stakeholders in a meeting room or video conference calls, and as you demonstrate the prototype, people respond to various aspects of the application's design. It is good practice to request attendees to suspend their feedback until you have a chance to complete an initial walkthrough of the proposed interaction. However, it is rare that people can hold off their comments and typically, the presentation flow is interrupted, with a risk of derailment due to tangential discussions.

Of course, experience and good facilitation skills play a major role in one's ability to drive a presentation forward in a productive way. However, regardless of the facilitation, it is objectively difficult for stakeholders to provide you with a thoughtful response because they have a relatively brief window of opportunity to view, digest, and respond to your presentation.

Axure's Discussion feature is meant to address this difficulty by providing stakeholders with the ability to respond in writing directly to the HTML prototype, which can be difficult and time consuming to do using traditional means. The **Discuss** tab is located on the prototype's left menu bar. Multiple stakeholders can initiate or respond to multiple discussions organized by topics for every individual page listed in the **Sitemap** pane. This feature is far from being robust, but it has been evolving over the past few years in the right direction.

Specifically, it is fairly easy for non-technical stakeholders to participate in feedback loops. Given Axure's track record of listening to the user community and enhancing features, the Discussion feature is likely to become an important value addition to users.

Discussions Hosted on axureShare

As was mentioned earlier in this chapter, in the context of using a third-party SVN hosting service for your shared repository, it is important that you get documented clearance to use axureShare from the relevant department in the organization for which you are working. It is also a good idea to test how the corporate firewall impacts access to the site since you want to provide a hassle-free experience to stakeholders.

With axureShare, you have two options to facilitate a discussion with stakeholders and users:

- Host the project on axureShare. This option is free and has very few limitations in terms of file size or the number of files you can host. Security concerns by the organization you are working for may pose the main reservation.
- Host the HTML on an internal server and enable the discussion feature.

The first option begins by uploading your file to axureShare, illustrated as follows:

1. Once you sign in, you can upload your `.rp` file by creating a new project. The **Create a New Project** dialog is straightforward (*Image 28*, **A**).
2. Select the RP file you wish to upload (**B**). If you want to share a team project, export the latest version of your RPPRJ file to an RP file. Check the file size to make sure that it is smaller than 100 MB and you are good to go.

3. Add the project's name and an optional password (**C**). If you add a password, it will be required from everyone who attempts to view or add feedback to your prototype. It is a good idea to use a password because it provides stakeholders with an added sense of confidence in the confidentiality of the work.

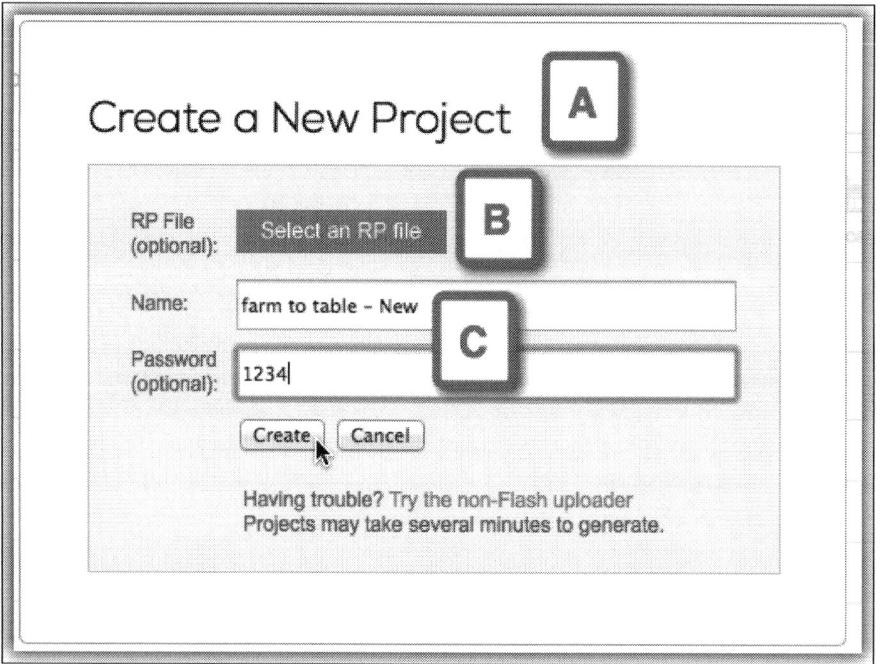

Image 28

Prototype ID and Other Features

Once the file is uploaded and generated on the axureShare server, it will be listed under the **My Projects** table, as shown in the following screenshot (*Image 29*, **A**):

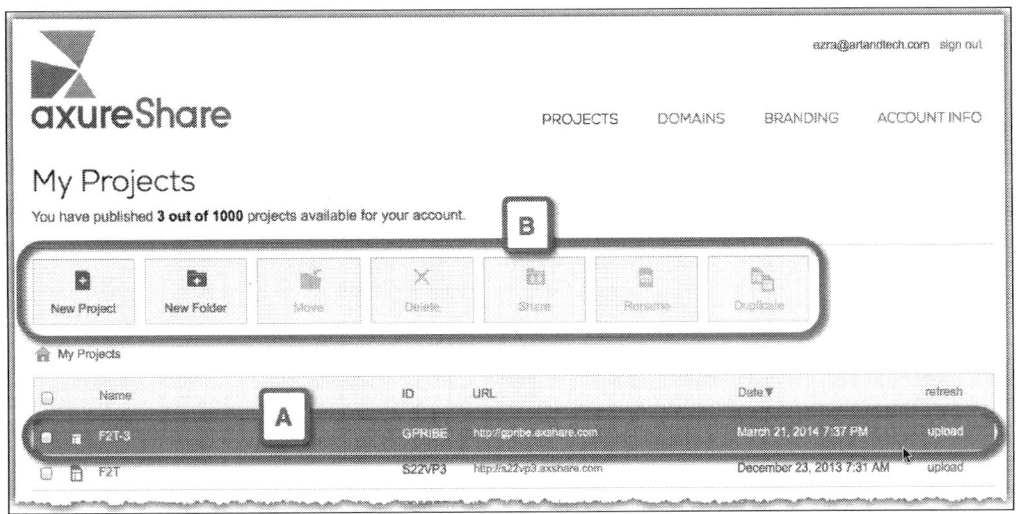

Image 29

Under **My Projects**, there is a row of buttons (**B**) for creating new projects and folders. Projects and folders can be moved for better organization.

By selecting a row in the **My Project** table (**A**), you can apply the following actions with the help of buttons in the button row:

- Move to a folder
- Delete
- Rename
- Duplicate

axureShare generates a prototype ID for each hosted prototype. This ID enables the **Discuss** tab in the generated prototype. Note that you do not need to upload the file to axureShare in order to generate the ID, which means that you can enable discussions on prototypes hosted internally.

In Axure, click on **Generate Prototype Files...** from the **Publish** menu or the **Publish** button to see the **Generate Prototype** dialog. Select the **Discuss** tab and paste the ID you copied from the axureShare website into the **Prototype ID** field (*Image 30*, **A**). This is how you enable the **Discuss** tab in the generated HTML prototype.

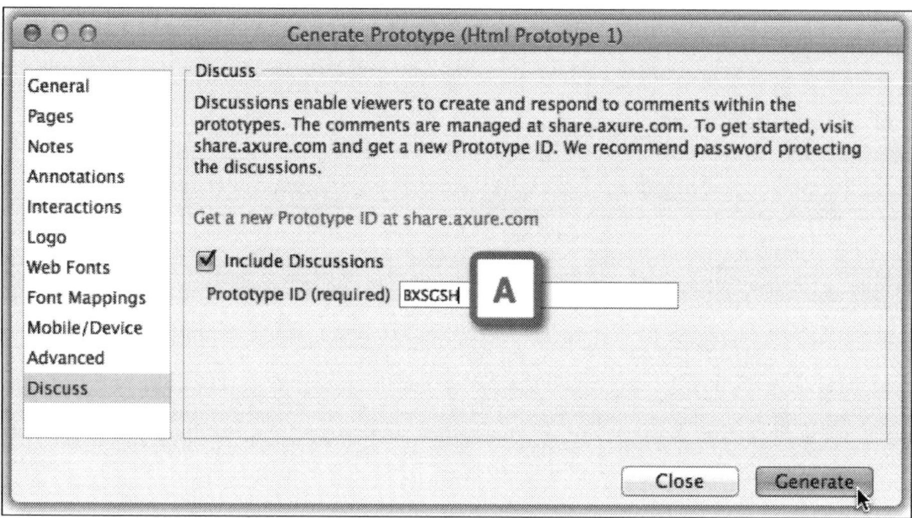

Image 30

We highly recommend that you provide some basic training to stakeholders on how to use the **Discuss** tab feature (*Image 31*, **A**) and include simple instruction each time you seek feedback. Organizing the discussion threads is important. The person who begins a thread should use the first entry just for the topic (**B**).

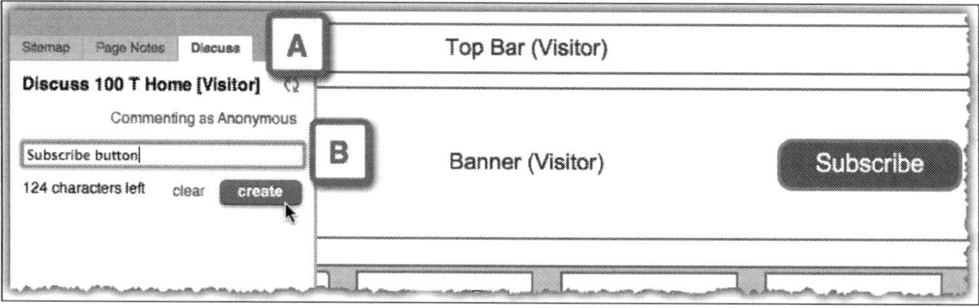

Image 31

The following is a use case:

- Susan is a stakeholder who has access to the prototype via the URL you provided. Depending on your subscription level and use of individual passwords, there might be minor variations in the flow, but essentially, it is very easy for every participant to associate their names with their entries (*Image 32*, **A**).

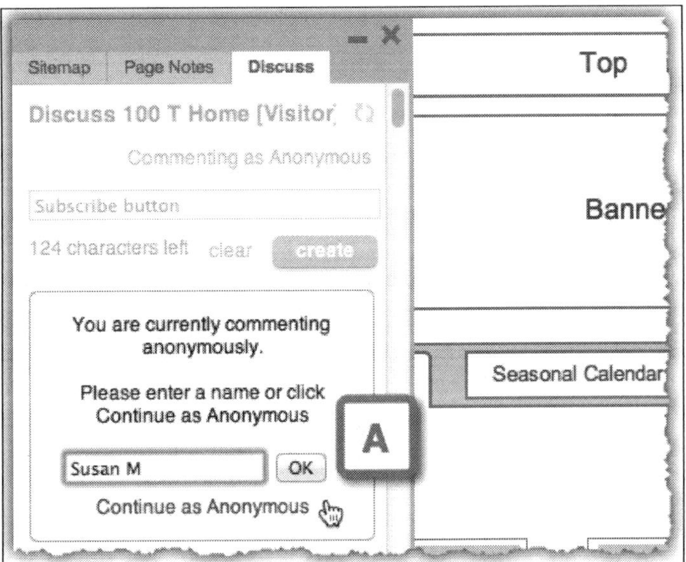

Image 32

The first discussion thread is made of a topic and a response; both are created by the first person to start the thread (*Image 33*, **A**). That's because at this point, there are no title or subject fields for the thread, which is unfortunate.

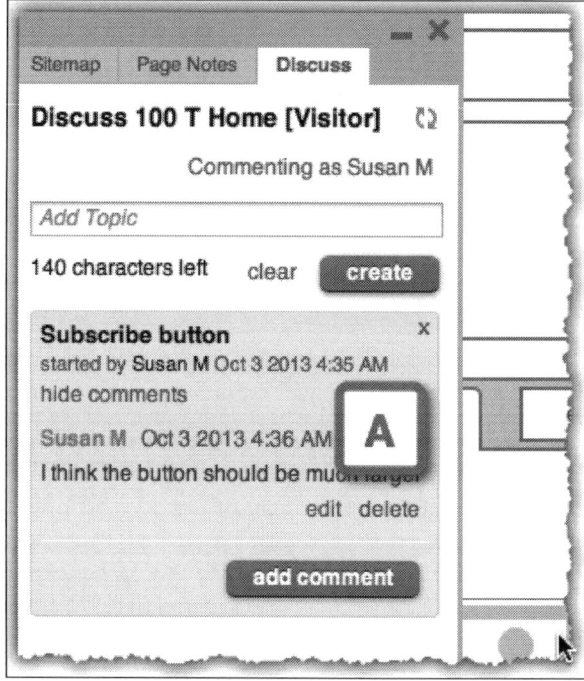

Image 33

When another stakeholder wants to post a response, begin by using the **Commenting as** field to associate their names with the response (*Image 34*, **A**) as shown in the following screenshot:

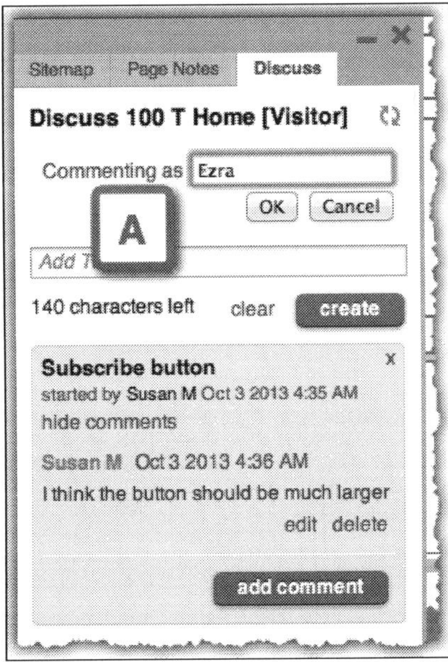

Image 34

The following screenshot shows how the thread handles the discussion between two or more stakeholders (*Image 35*, **A**).

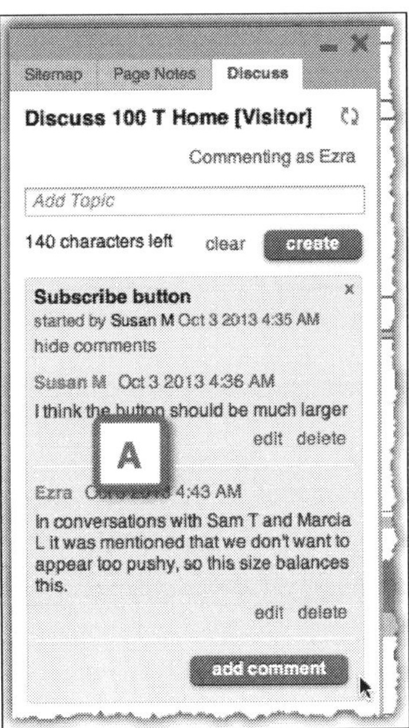

Image 35

So, for each page, it is possible to manage multiple conversations around multiple topics (*Image 36*, **A** and **B**). The timestamp helps with the timeline organization.

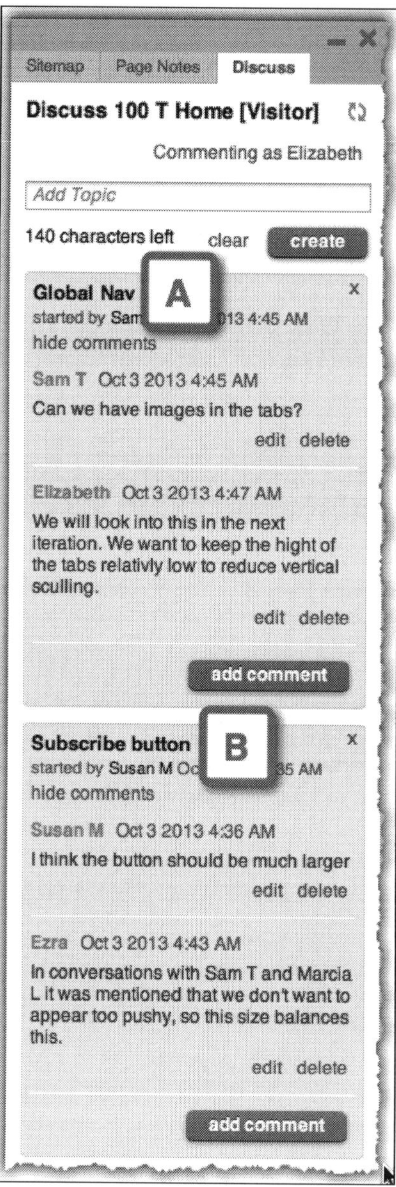

Image 36

Discussions Not Hosted on axureShare

Another option to facilitate a dialog in the prototype via the **Discuss** tab is to use axureShare to generate a special code which you enter in the HTML generator configuration. The actual prototype HTML files can be hosted on an internal server. The following are the steps:

1. From the **Discuss** section in the **Generate Prototype** dialog in Axure, click on the link **Get a new ID at share.axure.com** or point your browser directly to `share.axure.com`.
2. Log in and click on the **New Project** button (*Image 37*, **A**). There is no need to upload your project file. A new row will be added to the list of prototypes, with the code you need.

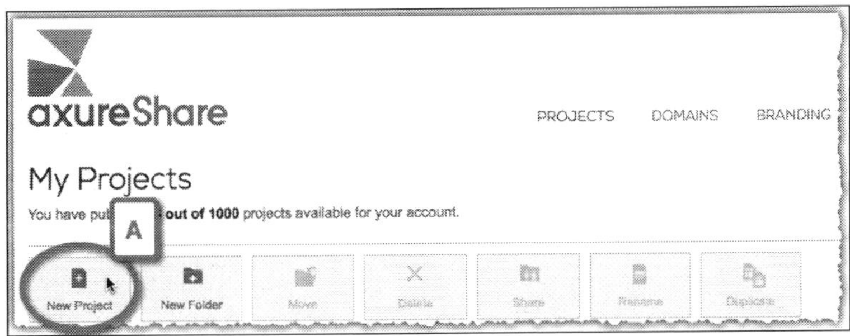

Image 37

3. Open the **Generate Prototype** dialog and click on the **Discuss** section.
4. Type or paste the prototype ID into the field (*Image 38*, **A**) and click on the **Generate** button as shown in the following screenshot:

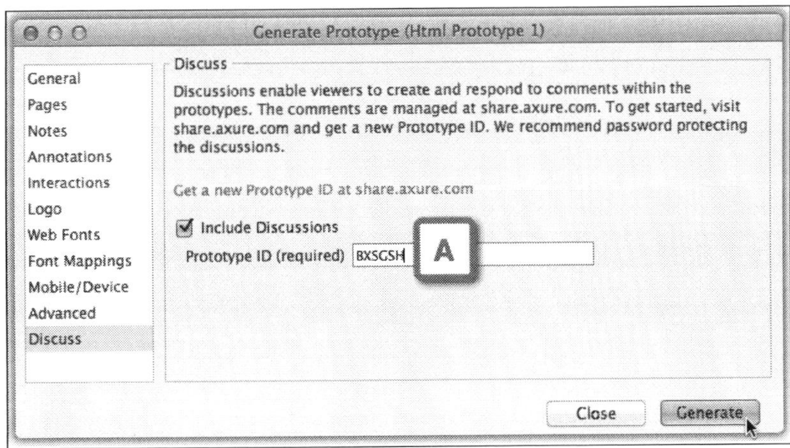

Image 38

5. Send an e-mail to anyone you want to have a discussion with, and provide them with the URL to prototype and the password to the **Discuss** tab.

Should you protect the discussion with a password? The truth is that it is a matter of control. By not sharing the password with everyone who has access to the prototype, you are controlling who can participate in the discussion and adding feedback. Consider the stakeholders that you want to get involved with. If the feedback is going to be of business strategy, perhaps it is not wise to have it exposed to contract developers and others who will also access the site, but from which you are not expecting feedback via the discussion option. If you are not sure, ask.

In conclusion, Axure's Discussion feature is promising because it is integrated in the product. The feature is not limited to the team project files. It can also be activated on the standard RP files.

It is important to make sure that stakeholders and users who are supposed to participate in the discussion can figure out how to navigate the prototype. Often, not all widgets have interactions assigned to them: some features work, and others do not. Let the user know in advance that upon moving the mouse over a certain area of the screen, a guide (constructed as a hidden dynamic panel) will appear, instructing them where to click on. This layer of instructions could also include letter or number tags over certain areas you want feedback on. These footnotes will make it easier to get a more structured feedback since all reviewers will refer to the same elements.

Publishing to Axure Share

Finally, another method to host your project on axureShare is from the **Publish** menu, which is illustrated as follows:

1. From the **Publish** menu (*Image 39*, **A**) or the **Publish** button (**B**), select the **Publish to Axure Share...** option (**C**), as shown in the following screenshot:

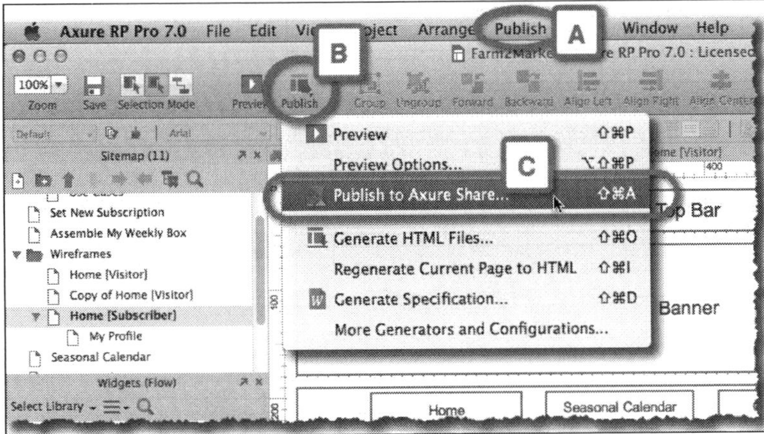

Image 39

2. The **Publish to Axure Share** dialog (*Image 40*, **A**) provides the option to a new axureShare account directly from the **Create Account** section (**B**) and spares you a trip to the website.

> Note that the following screenshot (*Image 40*) was taken at the end of March 2014; the actual Axure dialog still makes reference to AxShare, which has been renamed axureShare.

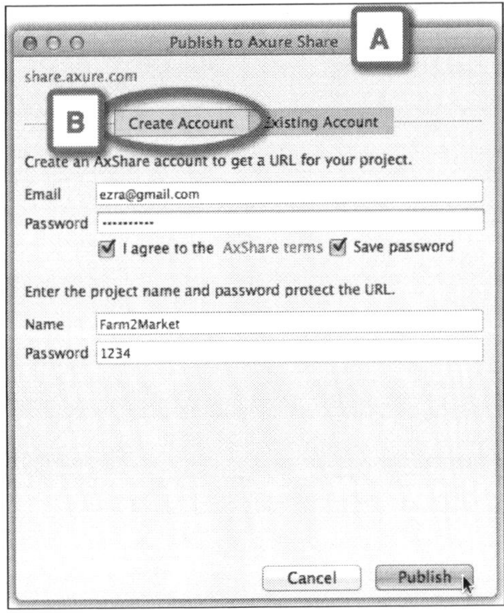

Image 40

3. If you already have an axureShare account, switch to the **Existing Account** section (*Image 41*, **A**).
4. The **Create a new project** option (**B**) is the default option.
5. The integration with the cloud works nicely. By using the **Folder** field (**C**), you can point the project directly to a folder located on axureShare (**D**). However, at this point, you still cannot create a folder from here.
6. Finally, you can select the **Replace an existing project** option (**E**). You will need to provide the code.

Note that the following screenshot (*Image 41*) was taken at the end of March 2014; the actual Axure dialog still makes reference to AxShare, which has been renamed axureShare.

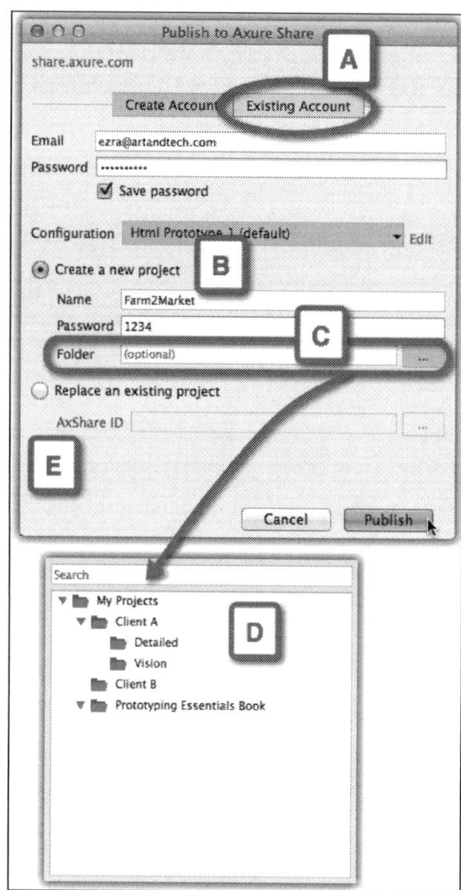

Image 41

Summary

Once you experience Axure's Team Projects features, you may wonder how UX teams managed projects before Axure Pro. Well, obviously you and others did, but at a premium cost of time and effort. Teams that are evaluating prototyping tools to support their work can reflect on their current workflow and methods, and then consider Axure's value proposition compared to other options in the market.

Axure's Team Projects feature adds real, measurable value by helping the UX team address head-on the following three major obstacles:

- It provides a controlled environment which facilitates work on the same prototype and specifications file by multiple team members.
- It maintains unlimited version control which is critical for disaster recovery or reverting to a previous revision.
- It facilitates dialog between the team and its stakeholders by providing a direct feedback in the Discussion pane, an Axure feature which is not limited just to Team Projects, and yet compliments the entire iterative process of teamwork.

These capabilities are built on top of the tool's rich, reliable, yet constantly evolving platform of UX-specific features set for prototyping and specifications.

- Closing the book is an appendix we hope you will find valuable. The *Appendix, Practitioners' Corner*, covers troubleshooting tips and provides interesting tutorials and case studies written by practitioners who share their expertise.

Practitioners' Corner

Axure enjoys one of the most vibrant, supportive, and sharing user communities. UX practitioners from all over the world generously share their expertise with others through various online meeting places such as the Axure Forum, AxureWorld.org, and so on. The overwhelming majority of this sharing is free.

For a tool that is used by so many consultants, the community culture of openness and collaboration is not necessarily a given, since expertise and know-how are often valued as a competitive advantage in the competition for work. So, we are fortunate to have a wealth of ever-evolving best practices and support.

Therefore, for this book, we approached the community and asked for contributions. In the following sections, you will find several entries written by fellow UX practitioners, which we hope you will find valuable since learning from the experience of others can be helpful.

Additionally, we included the results from a brief survey we conducted, which gives some insights into the users and use of Axure throughout the world, and also a brief set of troubleshooting tips.

Survey of Axure Users

In March 2014, a few weeks before this book went to press, we collected the responses of 123 UX practitioners who responded to an open invitation we published on the Axure forum and the LinkedIn groups AxureWorld and Ax-Stream. The following table shows the responses. We were surprised by the high number of respondents who use the Team Project (formally Shared Projects) feature, the high number of respondents who have experience with RWD, and the high number of respondents who use/d Axure to generate Word/PDF specifications.

The survey questions and responses are presented as follows:

Questions and options	Response percent
Q1. For how many years have you been using Axure?	
More than 6 years	20.3%
2-5 years	**58.5%**
1 year or less	20.3%
I'm evaluating Axure, have never used it	00.8%
Q2. Have you worked or are you working now on a project that involves RWD prototyping?	
Yes	**69.9%**
No	30.1%
Q3. Is Axure your exclusive prototyping tool?	
Yes	**64.2%**
No	35.8%
Q4. Have you ever used Axure Shared Projects (Team Projects in v7)?	
Yes	**52.0%**
No	48.0%
Q5. Have you ever used Axure to create Word/PDF specifications?	
Yes	**62.6%**
No	37.4%
Q6. Have you ever used Raised Events?	
Yes	45.5%
No	**54.5%**
Q7. Have you ever used variables?	
Yes	**86.2%**
No	13.8%
Q8. Is there a feature within Axure that you find hard to grasp?	
Raised Events	26.0%
Masters	04.9%
Dynamic panels	13.0%
Variables	22.0%
Functions	24.4%
Creating PDF/Word output that is easy to read	34.1%
Debugging when something does not work	49.6%
Repeater	29.3%

Questions and options	Response percent
Q9. Do you run into any performance issues with Axure 7?	
No issues	26.8%
The HTML runs slow after I generate a prototype	37.4%
Tabbing between pages is slow	31.7%
Clicking between tasks always takes time	26.8%
Axure crashes on me more than twice a day	15.4%

It is interesting to note that less than a half of respondents used Raised Events and about a quarter found the feature hard to grasp. We find Raised Events to be one of the most valuable actions in Axure (as explained in *Chapter 5, Advanced Interactions*). So, if over a half of respondents do not use Raised Events, it is logical to conclude that they are not creating the most effective and robust prototypes. We leave it to you to infer other insights from this survey. It was not meant to be scientific, but it is a nice sample.

Troubleshooting Interactions Checklists

Sometimes interactions in the prototype don't work as you expected—an experience that can be frustrating, and sometimes stressful, if you are under a tight deadline. Bugs happen: it is unavoidable, and you should build time into the project plan for testing and debugging. Of course, so many things can go wrong, but we found that there are a few common behaviors that lead to the creation of issues and other behaviors that help resolve them systematically and efficiently.

Experienced Axure users are often asked by colleagues for help in debugging their interactions. While sometimes, especially during looming deadlines, it is very tempting to just fix the problem for them and move on, we believe that taking the time to help team members adopt good troubleshooting habits pays off. It reduces the frequency of you being disrupted to help with a bug just to find a very basic error, which your colleague could have easily identified had they followed a basic troubleshooting checklist. Stress and annoyance can be reduced, which is very important for good teamwork.

The following sections are brief on purpose and meant to help you, if you are a novice user, quickly absorb and internalize core best practices, and reduce time spent and frustration built over bugs, as you enhance your skills in constructing interactions. For experienced users, we hope they will save the time needed to come up with such a list to hand out to less-experienced colleagues.

The General Approach

The following list combines common-sense and learned behaviors that we have adopted over the years, because they help us reduce bugs or tackle them more efficiently:

- Axure invokes events in the order listed in the **Interactions** tab. Therefore, make sure you order the events in the order you want them to play out.
- Assign unique names and IDs to widgets and dynamic panels. This will save you from accidentally assigning an action/event to the wrong widget or dynamic panel.
- If you have multiple bugs on one wireframe, fix one bug at a time. When you uncover a bug, isolate it, fix it, and then verify the fix before moving on.
- Read the code in the **Interaction** tab. For example, you may be 100 percent positive that you set the associated widget to **Show**, but when reading the code, you may find it is set to **Hide**.
- When relevant, add the **Bring to Front** and **Send to Back** actions to cases. Sometimes, the widget you are trying to have do something is simply covered up by other widgets.
- If you hit the wall trying to fix a particular bug and getting increasingly frustrated and stressed because of lost time, it is sometimes best to walk away from it for a bit, and then review it afresh.
- If you have spent a lot of time on an issue, and still cannot figure it out, try the following:
    - The first approach to isolate the issue could be: delete the case and start over, or make a copy, delete the original, and slowly rebuild it from the copy. Add one chunk at a time until something goes wrong.
    - The second approach to isolate the issue could be: start a new RP file, and recreate only the problematic cases from scratch. Don't copy or import anything from the production file. As you rebuild the integration step by step, consider the logic and order of operations.
    - Generally, the use of copy and paste is a great time saver, but often, it is a source of issues. Look at the original interaction, and see what makes it work. Then look at the pasted version and make sure that all the actions are pointing to the correct widgets.
    - Ask a colleague for help.
    - Send the Axure file to Axure support, as they are very helpful.
    - Axure additionally has a wonderful support forum which you can find at `http://www.axure.com/forum/forum.php`.

Questions to Ask when Debugging

This list reflects some of the common mistakes we keep repeating. Taking the liberty of assuming we are not significantly more stupid than the average Axure user, we think that the reason for repeating some of these mistakes can be attributed to fast pace of work, multitasking, and other very normal causes. So, when you run into a bug, ask yourself the following questions, just as we often do:

- Is the action assigned to the correct widget or dynamic panel?
- Are you using the correct action?
- Do you have the order of events correct?
- Do you have an action in your event that is cancelling out what you are trying to do? For example, did you set up a **Show** action, and then two lines later you have a **Hide** action? Since the **Hide** action is after the **Show** action, Axure will hide the widget or dynamic panel, so you will not be able to see what you are actually trying to show.
- Do you have a panel in front of the widget or dynamic panel from which you are trying to invoke an action, and thus, cannot click on it? Make sure the item you want to click on is in front, otherwise you will not be able to click on it.
- Have you reviewed the interaction you have set up at the page level and at the widget/dynamic panel level? You may have an action at the page or master level that is cancelling out your widget/dynamic panel events.
- Have you initialized global variables by setting their default value?
- Are the variables you are using working as intended? The generated HTML prototype includes the ability to observe how interactions change the values of variables. You should know the variable's initial value, and its expected values as the interaction progresses. Click through the prototype, and stop when the variable does not change as expected. Check the relevant case to make sure it includes an action that affects the variable.
- Do you have extra actions? As you add actions to a case, some of the initial actions may be conflicting with those added later, or causing some unexpected behavior.

Common Hurdles

This section is organized by core Axure features and is focused on basic sources of trouble which inexperienced users often face:

Category	Hurdles	Recommendations
Masters	I have the master on my wireframe but do not see how to create events for it.	Go to the master and create a raised event to it. To invoke an action in a master, use raised events. When creating a raised event, remember that its name cannot have spaces, and it must be checked in order to be associated with an action. To read more about raised events, refer to *Chapter 5, Advanced Interactions*.
Masters	I create the raised event but still do not see it on my wireframe.	Go to the master wireframe and make sure that the raised event that should be triggered by the action is checked.
Moving widgets and dynamic panels	Where did the widget/ dynamic panel go?	Check to see if you have it set to a **Move To** or **Move By** option. You may think you are moving is *to* 1200 pixels, but you may be moving it *by* 1200 pixels.
IF/THEN Statements	When do I use **All** versus **Any**?	When you use **All**, the interaction will work only if all the conditions are satisfied. In Axure, "AND" shows in the code. When you use **Any**, the interaction will happen as long as at least one condition is satisfied. In Axure, "OR" shows in the code.

Category	Hurdles	Recommendations
Adaptive Views	Why are my views changed when I do not want them to?	If you have the checkbox **Affect All Views** checked, all views will now be "tied" together. The checkbox should really only be used if you are in a child view and want your change to apply to the parent view. Be sure to check the checkbox before you make the changes, and uncheck when you are done making the desired changes.
Adaptive Views	What do I do when I generate the HTML (not preview) and the views do not change?	This is most likely a settings issue. Go to the generator you are using in the **Adaptive Views** tab, and click on **Generate ALL pages**.

Construction Tutorials

Axure has a thriving user community, and the sharing of know-how is quite wonderful. For this book, we approached a number of experienced Axure users and asked them to submit a tutorial that could be of use to the readers. These tutorials are quite descriptive, but they do assume familiarity with Axure and an ability to fill in possible gaps in the descriptions. Each of the RP files are available on AxShare for download and review, and like other tutorials in the book, we recommend you follow by constructing them yourself.

Shira Luk-Zilberman – Simulating a Type-ahead Search Experience

Tutorial level: Intermediate/advanced

Practitioner Profile

Shira Luk-Zilberman is currently a user experience designer at Sizmek, a leading campaign management platform. She previously worked at Netcraft, one of Israel's top UX consulting agencies. She completed her BSc and MSc in Computer Science, and she was on the path towards a career in software engineering before she realized that UX is far more interesting.

Shira brings her analytical and technical skills to the design process, and she specializes in creating usable solutions for complex domains. She is always excited to explore Axure's most advanced capabilities (and hacks) to achieve a truly realistic experience. She is an active user of the online Axure forums, and she is one of the admins of Israel's Axure community on Facebook, where she answers (and asks) questions daily.

When she is not building prototypes, she is busy mothering little baby Noga, who occupies most of her waking (and also most of her sleeping) hours. Her LinkedIn profile is `il.linkedin.com/in/shiraluk/`.

The Tutorial

In this tutorial, I would like to share with you some construction ideas for simulating the familiar search field using a new **repeater** widget of Axure 7. The interface comprises a search box and drop-down list of items. As the user types a search query, the values in the list change dynamically and display relevant suggestions according to the text entered.

Some familiar interfaces that use this pattern include Google (*Image 1*, **A**), Facebook (**B**), and LinkedIn (**C**), as shown in the following screenshot:

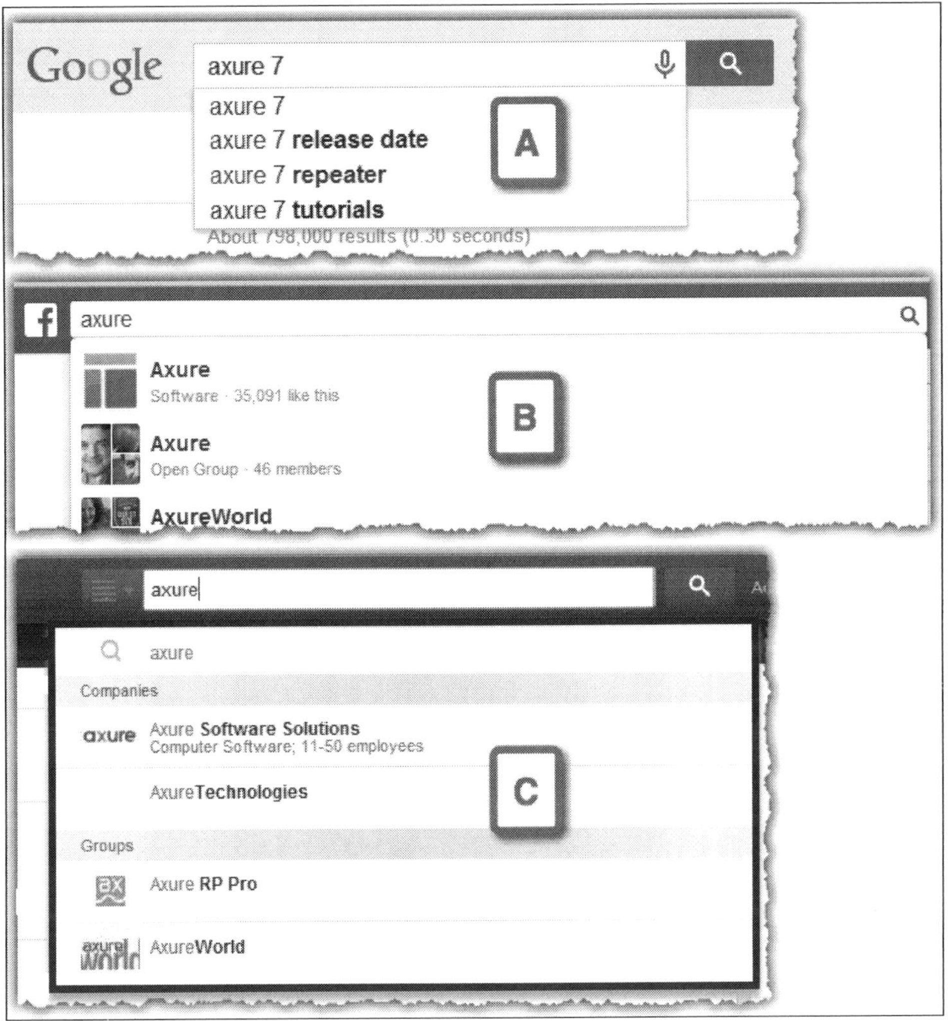

Image 1

We will cover the following topics in this tutorial:

- A simple implementation of type-ahead, similar to Google's search
- Adding images and summary text, as used by Facebook's search
- Adding category fields to simulate LinkedIn's example

In the previous versions of Axure, the simulation required use of a dynamic panel with several states that match only a single query string. Applying changes to the design was a tedious task.

The repeater widget allows us to create a generic, easy-to-maintain interface that works for any search query. Now that's powerful!

1. Creating a Google-like Type-ahead Search Interface

In addition to simulating the behavior of a type-ahead search, this section also covers handling the widget's borders and dealing with a use case where there is no text in the search field.

Start by creating a sandbox file and drag over a repeater widget to the default **Home** page. Label the repeater widget `RPTR_SearchOptions`.

1.1 Configuring the Repeater

Perform the following steps to configure the repeater:

1. Double-click on the widget.
2. In the new tab, **(RPTR_SearchOptions) Home** (*Image 2*, **A**), that opens, rename the first column in the **Repeater Dataset** tab (**B**) to `Search_Option` (**C**) and insert as many permutations as you can of search suggestions (**D**).

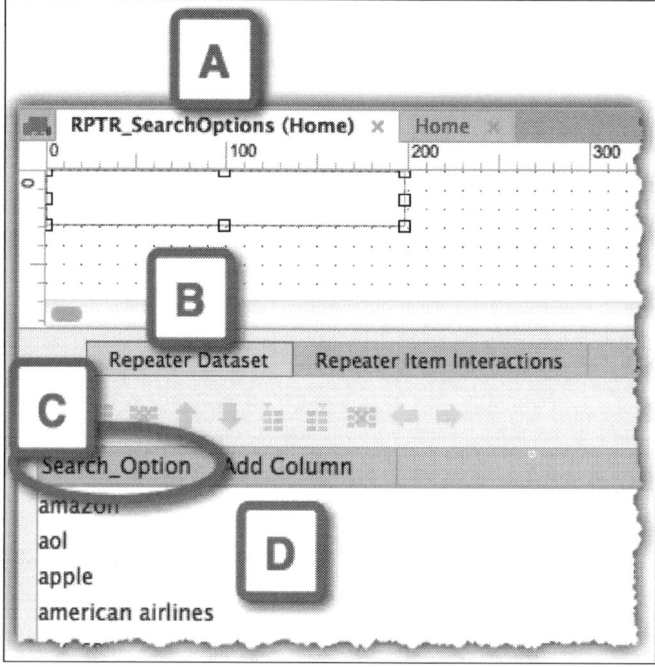

Image 2

Don't sweat over coming up with the list. You can copy the values that appear in a real Google type-ahead.

3. While still on the **(RPTR_SearchOptions) Home** tab (*Image 3*, **A**), rename the default repeater item shape (**B**) to `LBL_SearchOption` (**C**).
4. In the repeater pane below, switch to the **Repeater Item Interactions** tab (**D**), and double-click on the **OnItemLoad** interaction (**E**).

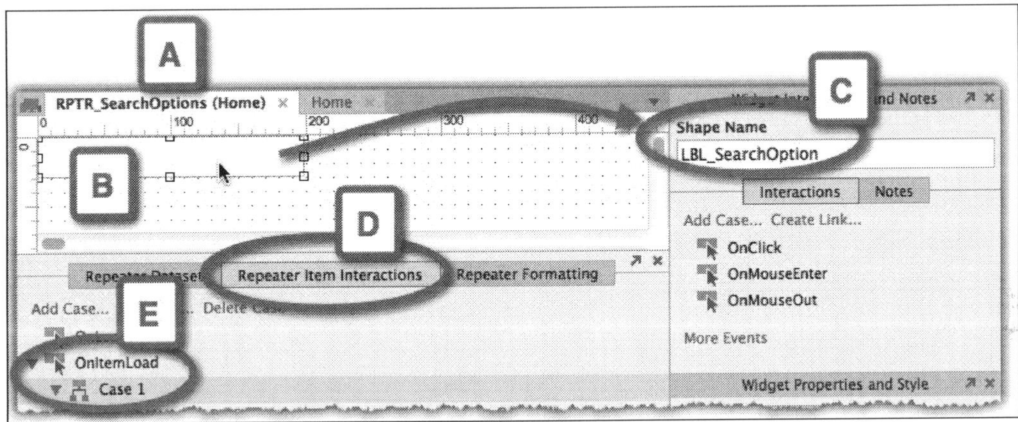

Image 3

5. In the **Case Editor** window (*Image 4*, **A**) that opens next, select the **Set Text** action (**B**) and click on the **fx** button (**C**) to set the values that will be displayed in the repeater.
6. In the **Edit Text** window (**D**) that opens, click on the **Insert Variable or Function...** link (**E**), and from the **Repeater/Dataset** category, select **Item. Search_Option** (**F**). This is where naming the item, an earlier step, helps.

7. Back in the **Case Editor** window, the configured action is displayed in the **Organize actions** as well as in the **Configure actions** columns (**G**).

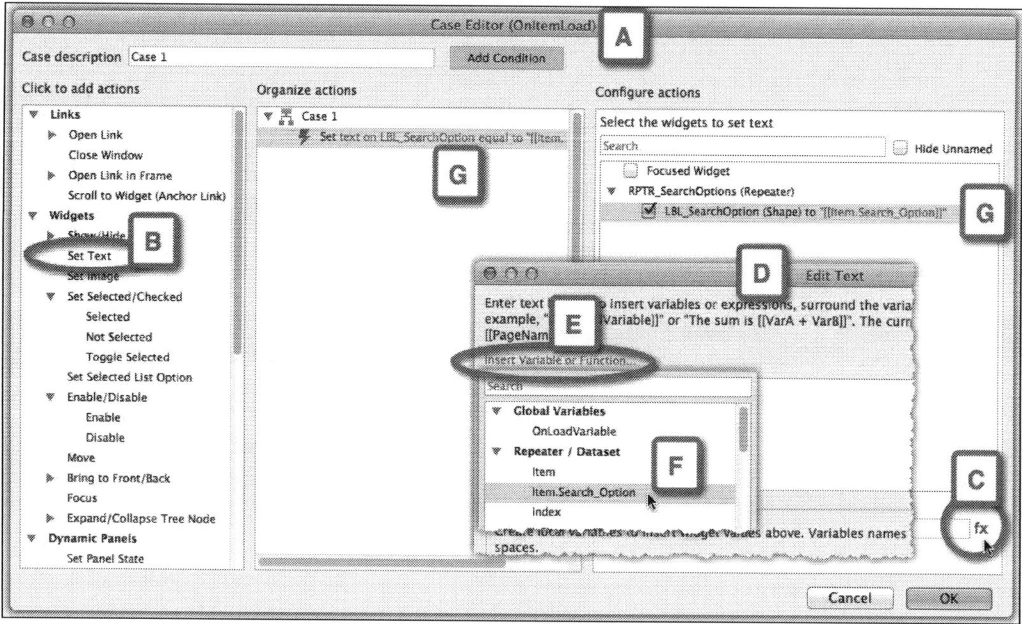

Image 4

8. When switching to the **Home** page tab (*Image 5*, **A**), the values entered in the dataset are visible (**B**). This preview helps with formatting, which is done back in the **RPTR_SearchOptions** tab (**C**) where you can apply formatting to the repeater item (**D**) such as, **Right Alignment** (**E**), and **Left Padding** (**G**).
9. View the results back in the **Home** tab (**G**) and tweak the repeater (**H**), as needed.

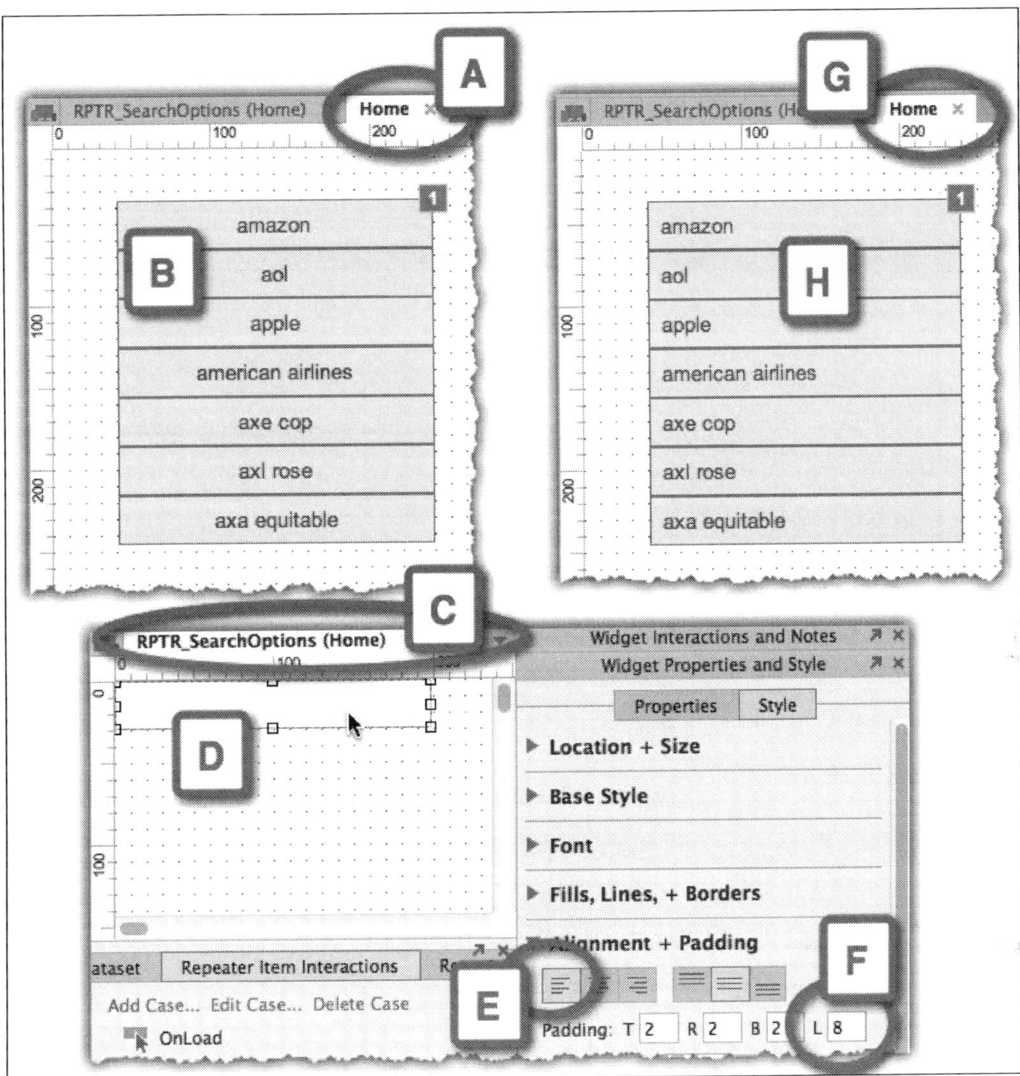

Image 5

1.2 Simulating Search

With the repeater widget in place, we continue with the construction by associating an input search field to the suggestions drop-down list.

While still on the **Home** page (*Image 6*, **A**) tab, add a **Text Field** widget (**B**) that will serve as the search box. Name it `TXT_Search` (**C**). We will use the **OnTextChange** (**D**) event to dynamically change the displayed repeater values according to the current content of the search box. Double-click on it to open the **Case Editor** window.

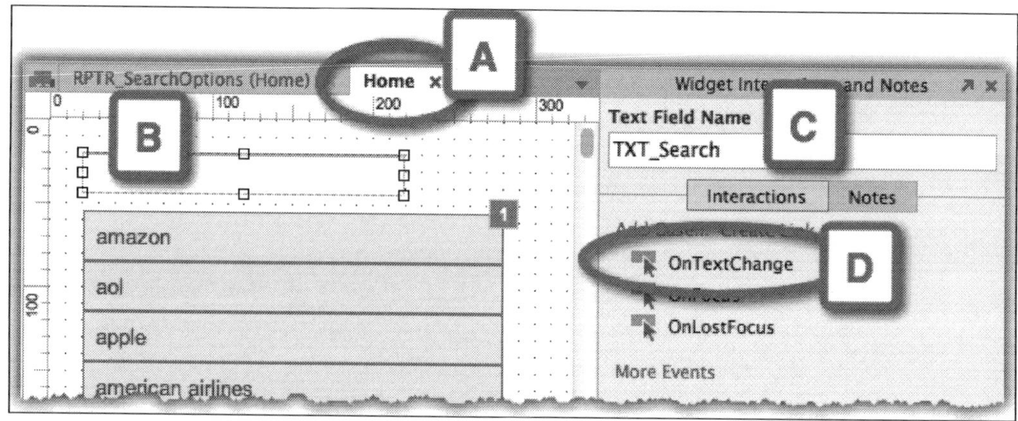

Image 6

A brief explanation before we continue with the step-by-step description: we will use the **Add Filter** action of the repeater so that every time the user changes the text in the search box, a new filter is applied to the repeater. The new filter uses the text in the search box for its input.

The tricky part is to filter only the search options that contain the search text. The **Add Filter** action works with a Boolean (true/false) expression that is applied to each item of the repeater. The items that evaluate to true are filtered and made visible. The items that evaluate to false are not visible. The goal is to build an expression that will only be "true" for items that contain the text in the search box.

In plain English, we are telling Axure: as the user types in the search field, look for a match in the list of search options we created in the repeater; if there is a match, show it.

The following is the step-by-step process:

1. In the **Case Editor** window (*Image 7*, **A**), select the **Add Filter** action (**B**) from the **Repeaters** category (**C**).
2. We want to filter the list of items in the repeater based on live input to the search box. Click on the **fx** button (**D**) to open the **Edit Value** window, as shown in the following screenshot:

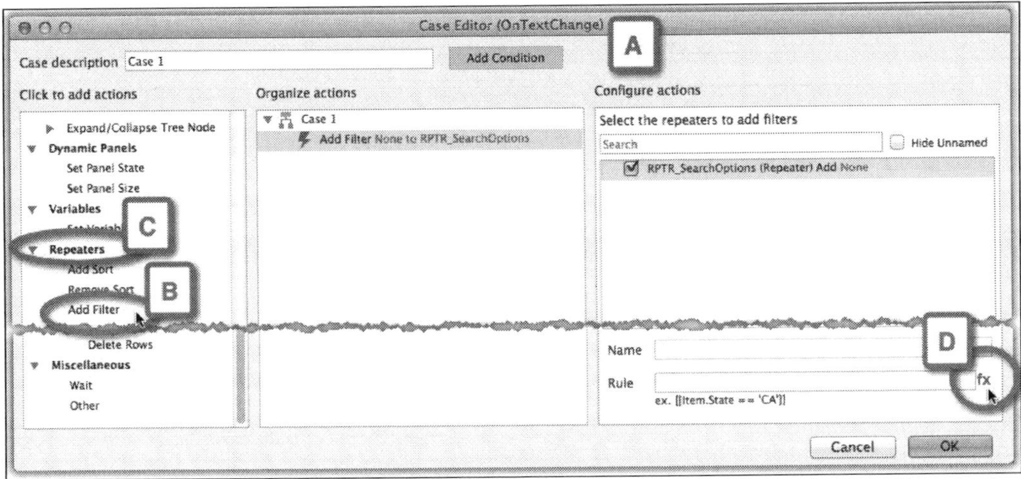

Image 7

3. First, we select the repeater column we want to filer. In our case, it is the **Search_Option** column we created in the repeater dataset in an earlier step.
4. In the **Edit Value** window (*Image 8*, **A**), click on the **Insert Variable or Function** link (**B**), and from the **Repeater / Dataset** group, select **Item. Search_Option** (**C**).

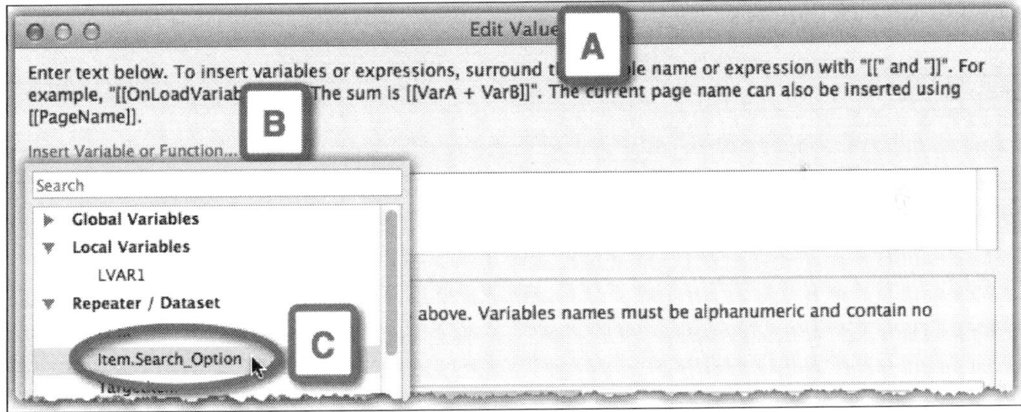

Image 8

5. **[[Item.Search_Option]]** will be pasted into the field. Place the mouse pointer in between **n** and **]]**, and move to the next step.
6. Next, still in the **Edit Value** window (*Image 9*, **A**), click on the **Insert Variable or Function...** link (**B**) again.

7. From the **String** category (C), select **indexOf('searchValue')** (D) as shown in the following screenshot:

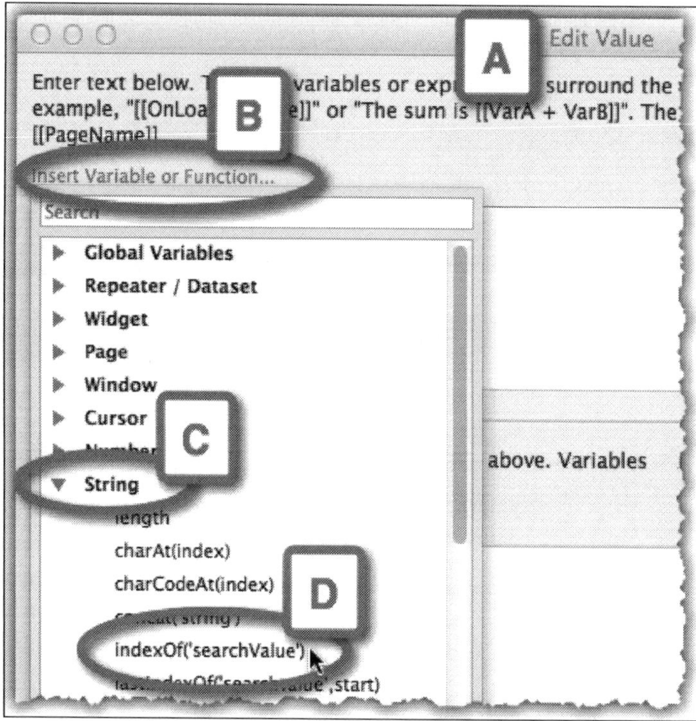

Image 9

8. The method **indexOf** returns the position of the first occurrence of the input value in a string, and in the next step, you will see how it is relevant to us.
9. Continue in the **Edit Value** dialog (*Image 10*, **A**), and click on the **Add Local Variable** link (**B**) to create a local variable of type **text on widget** (**D**) named **LVAR1** (C), which will reference the text in the textbox **TXT_Search** (E).

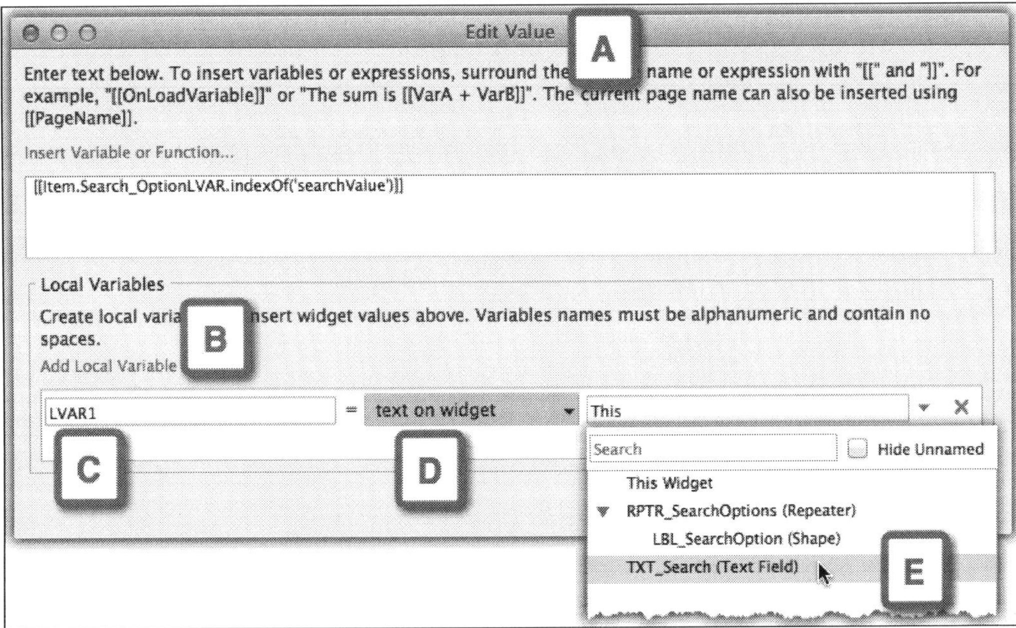

Image 10

Remember that we are using the string method **indexOf()**, which returns the position of the first occurrence of the input value in a string. In other words, if the expression **[[item.Search_Option.indexOf(LVAR1)]]** is larger than or equal to 0, there is some occurrence of **LVAR1** within **item.Search_Option**. Otherwise, if the expression returns -1, there is no occurrence.

In the formula **[[Item.Search_OptionLVAR.indexOf('searchValue')]]**, substitute **searchValue** with **LVAR1**, and evaluate it to be equal to or greater than 0. The final query string should be as follows:

[[item.Search_Option.indexOf(LVAR1) >= 0]]

This query string is case sensitive. To make it case insensitive, add the string method **toLowerCase()**, which converts a string to lowercase letters, as follows:

[[item.Search_Option.toLowerCase().indexOf(LVAR1.toLowerCase( )) >= 0]]

Preview the **Home** page in the browser (*Image 11*, **A**). As you type into the search field (**B**), the letters in the string that make up the word Axure and the type-ahead options in the list (**C**) refresh instantly, as shown in the following screenshot:

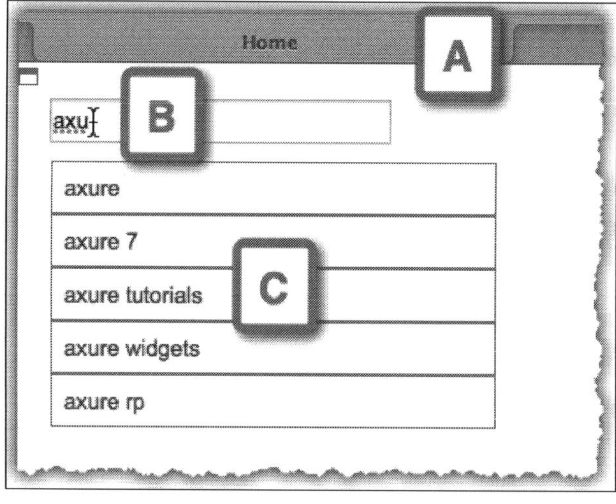

Image 11

We now have a search box that dynamically filters the search options according to the entered text. Yay!

1.3 Tweaking the Borders

Now, we want to achieve a Google-style pane with only an outline border. Here is the trick to do that.

Change the shape of the repeater item (*Image 12*, **A**) to a bottom border shape (**B**), and place it in location **Left**: `0`, **Top**: `-1` (**C**).

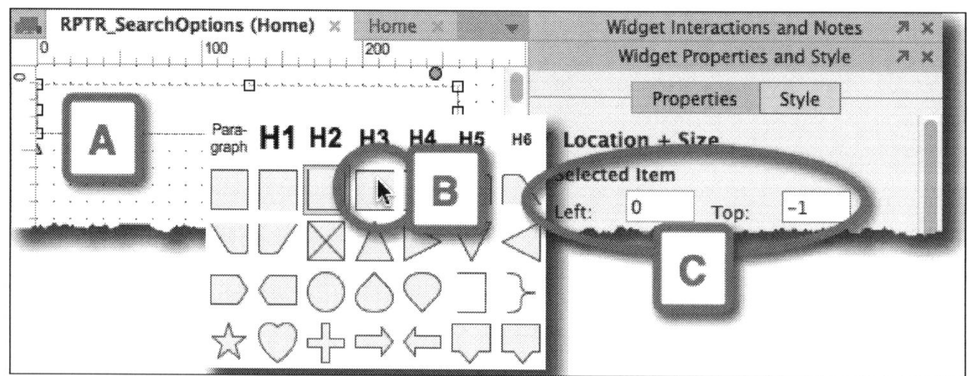

Image 12

Now, when the repeater is rendered, each item will hide the bottom border of the item before it, and the result will be a list with no horizontal borders, except for the last element (*Image 13*, **A**).

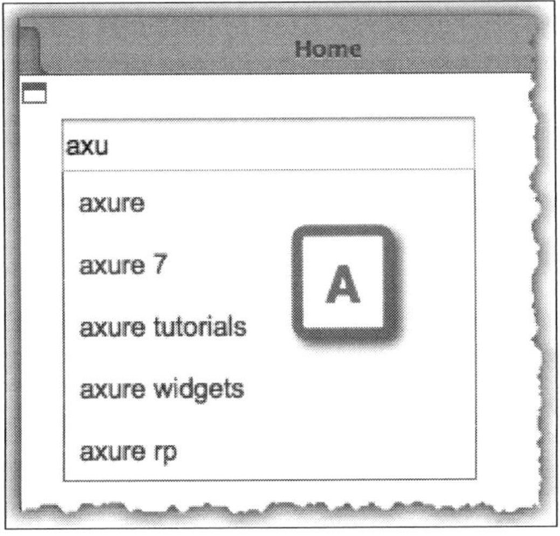

Image 13

We still need to account for the missing top border of the first element. Add a horizontal line named **HL_TopBorder** (*Image 14*, **A**) to the repeater item, and set it to **Hidden** (**B**).

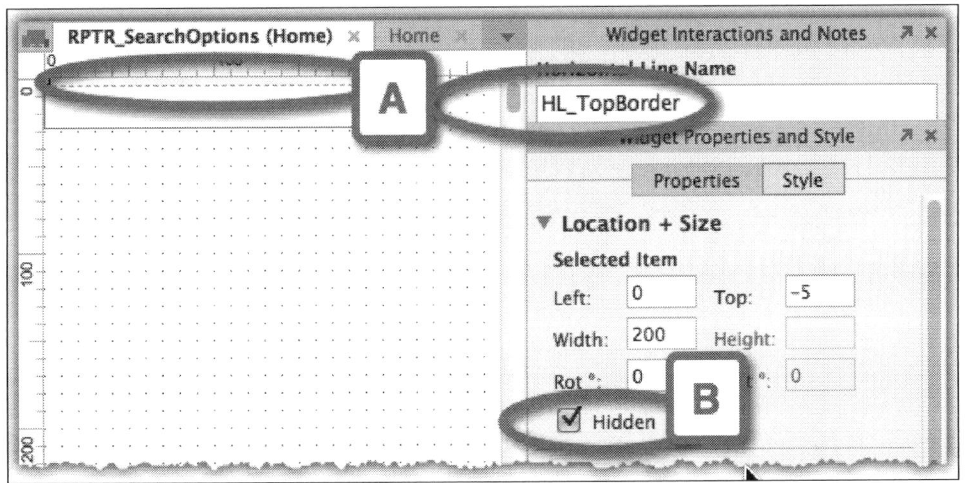

Image 14

The line will be visible only for the first rendered element. Here's how:

1. In the **RPTR_SearchOptions** tab (*Image 15*, **A**), we add a case to the **OnItemLoad** event (**B**).
2. Double-click on it to open the **Case Editor** window (**C**), and click on the **Add Condition** button (**D**).

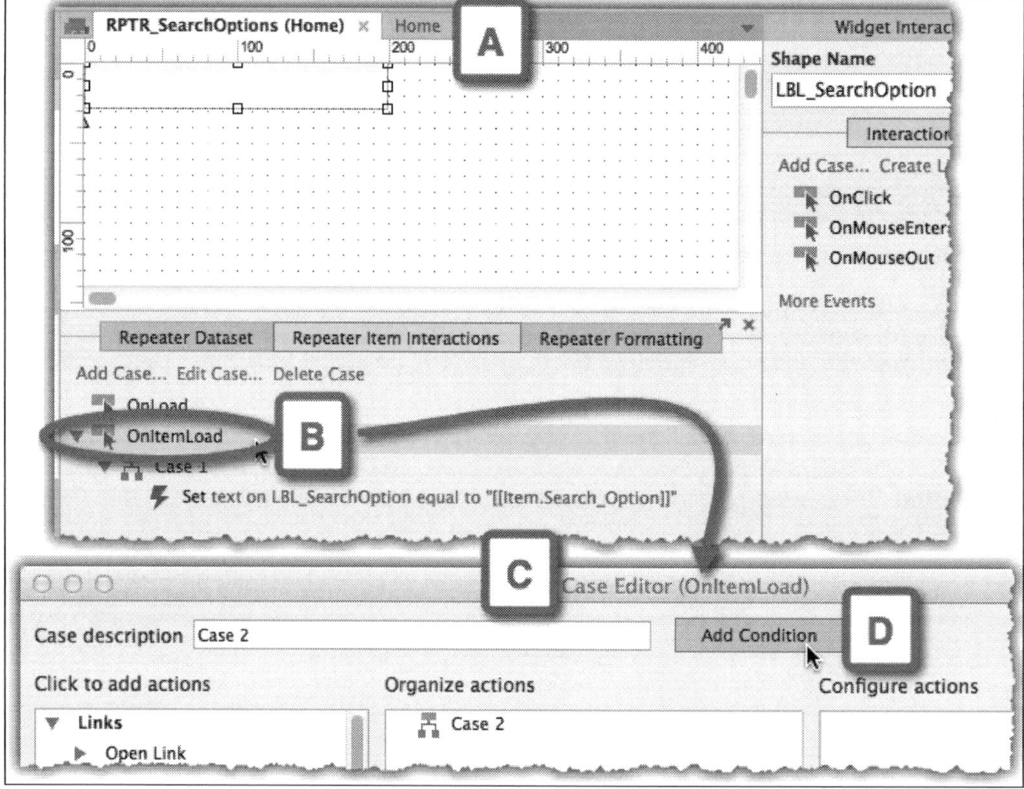

Image 15

3. We can figure out when the first element is rendered by using the built-in **isFirst** function. We do this by adding a condition to the **OnItemLoad** event, which evaluates to true for the first element the repeater is rendered on.
4. In the **Condition Builder** window (*Image 16*, **A**), set the first drop-down list to **value** (**B**), and click on the **fx** button on the next field (**C**) to launch the **Edit Text** window (**D**).

5. There, click on the **Insert Variable or Function...** link (E), and from the **Repeater / Dataset** group (F), select **IsFirst** (G).

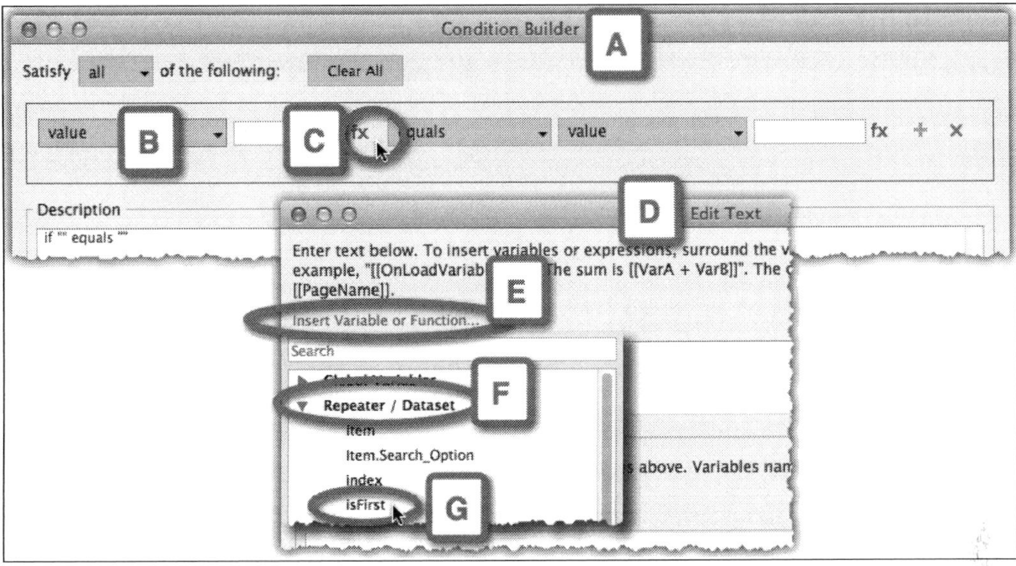

Image 16

6. Complete the condition to read as: **if "[[Item.isFirst]]" equals "true"** (*Image 17*, **A**) as shown in the following screenshot:

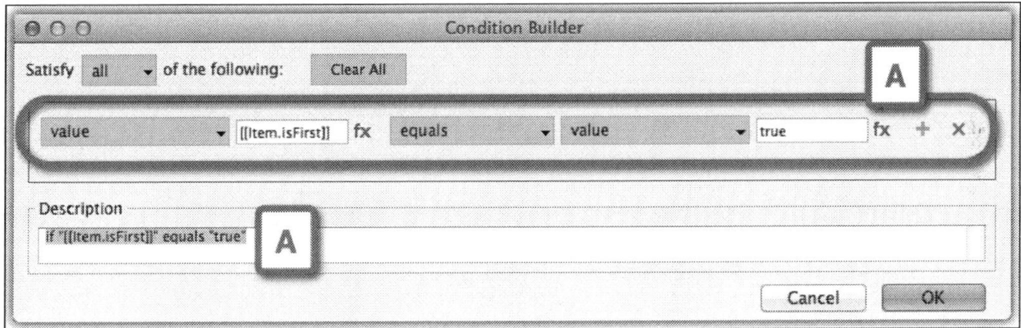

Image 17

7. Close the **Condition Builder** window.

8. Back in the **Case Editor** window (*Image 18*, **A**), use the **Show** action (**B**) to control the visibility of **HL_TopBorder** (**C**).

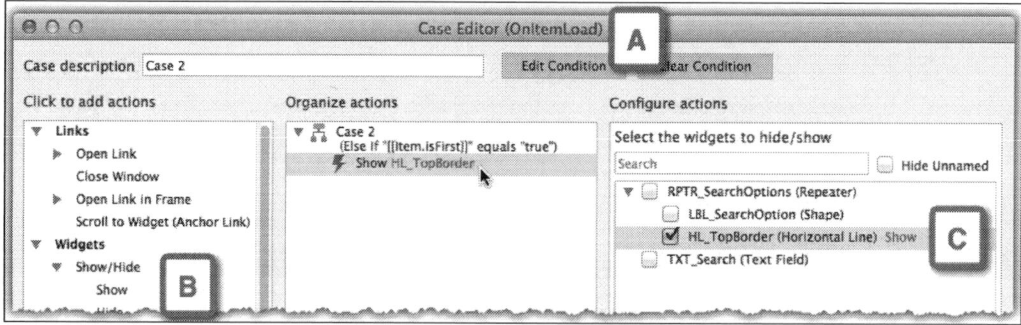

Image 18

9. Close the **Case Editor** window.

So, now we have two cases associated with the **OnItemLoad** event (*Image 19*, **A**). Remember that the cases are not associated with each other. The first controls the items that display in the list, the other deals with the display of the top line. Use the **Toggle IF/ELSE IF** option (**B**) to make the two IF conditions, instead of the default IF-ELSE.

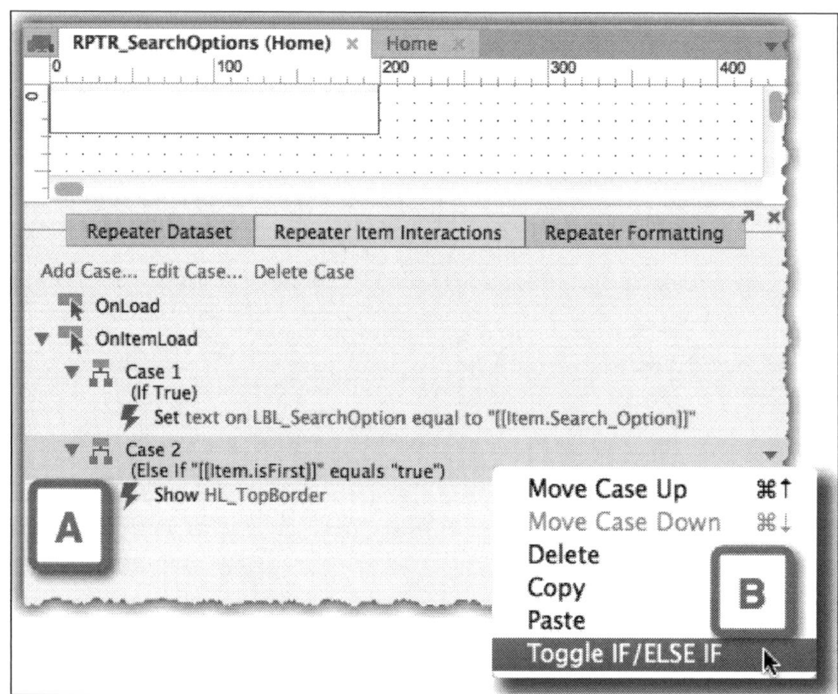

Image 19

The two cases should look as shown in the following screenshot (*Image 20*):

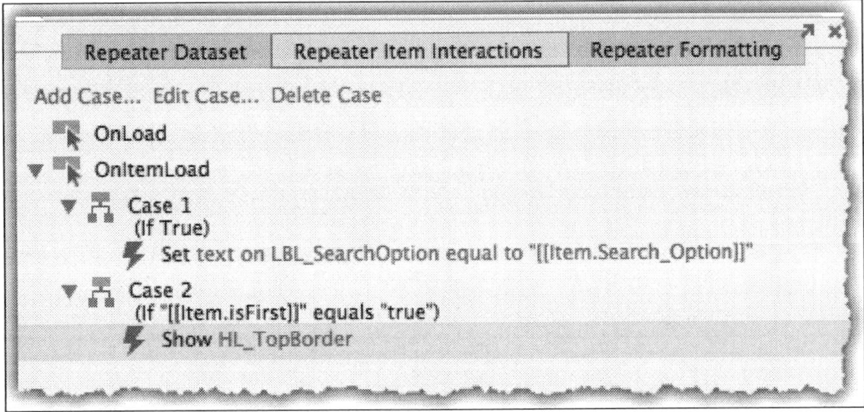

Image 20

Preview the **Home** page in the browser and voila - the top border is rendered only for the first element (*Image 21*, **A**).

To help you debug, make the line color red to better distinguish it.

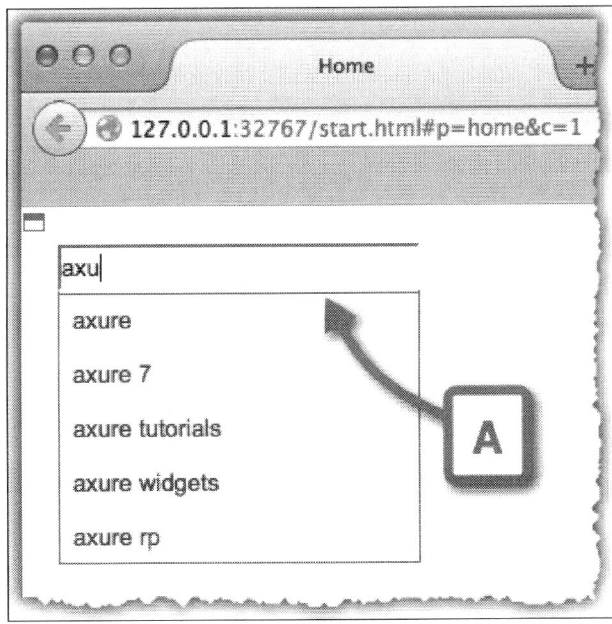

Image 21

1.4 Dealing with No Text

The following are the final refinements to complete the Google-like interaction:

1. First, hide the repeater widget (*Image 22*, **A**), as suggestions will not be visible until the user starts typing.
2. Then, we need to make sure that the repeater is not shown when the search box is empty. Add a condition to the **OnTextChange** event that hides the repeater if the text is empty (**B**), and add another condition that displays it when it is not empty (**C**).

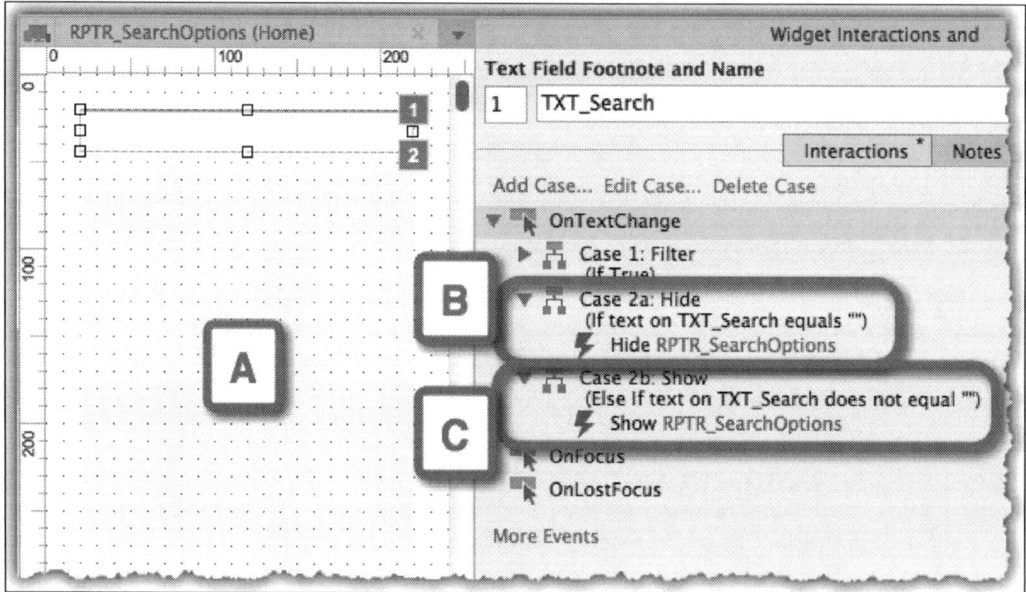

Image 22

With that, we are done! We have successfully simulated a Google-like type-ahead search interface. In the next part, we will see how we can convert this interface to resemble the Facebook interface.

2. Creating a Facebook-like Type-ahead Search Interface

The behavior of Facebook's type-ahead search pattern is similar to Google's, but it has a richer interface. Facebook's type-ahead drop-down list includes an image (*Image 23*, **A**), a title (**B**), and a summary line (**C**), as shown in the following screenshot:

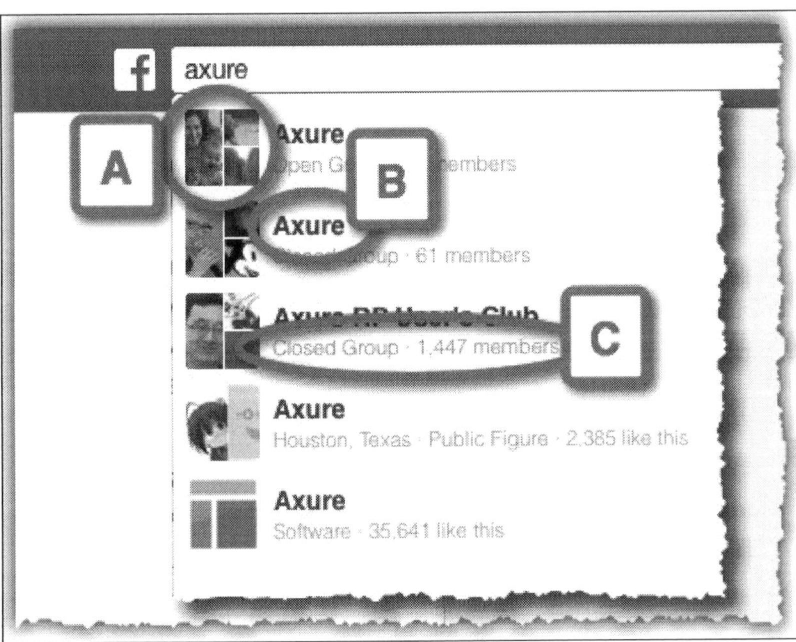

Image 23

It is fairly easy to tweak our Google example to the Facebook one. This is one of the major strengths of the repeater widget. Once you have an infrastructure of working patterns, it is easy to apply the changes:

1. Start by duplicating the **Home** page. Rename the **Home** page `Google Type Ahead` and the new page `Facebook Type Ahead`.
2. On the repeater item page's **RPTR_SearchOptions** tab (*Image 24*, **A**), update the **Repeater Dataset** tab (**B**).

3. Update the **Search_Option** column (**C**) with the company names.
4. Add a column named **Summary_Line** (**D**), which contains a short summary of the item.

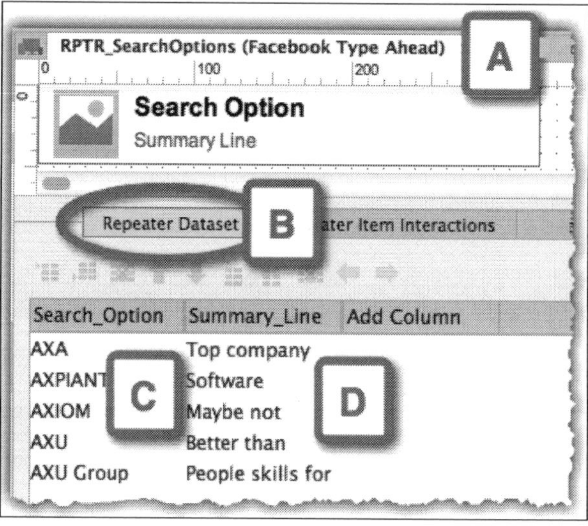

Image 24

5. Now, update the repeater to match the Facebook item layout with the following two label widgets:
   - **Search Options** (*Image 25*, **A**), named **LBL_Name**
   - **Summary Line** (**B**), named **LBL_SummaryLine**
6. Also, add an Image widget (**C**) and name it `Item_Image`.

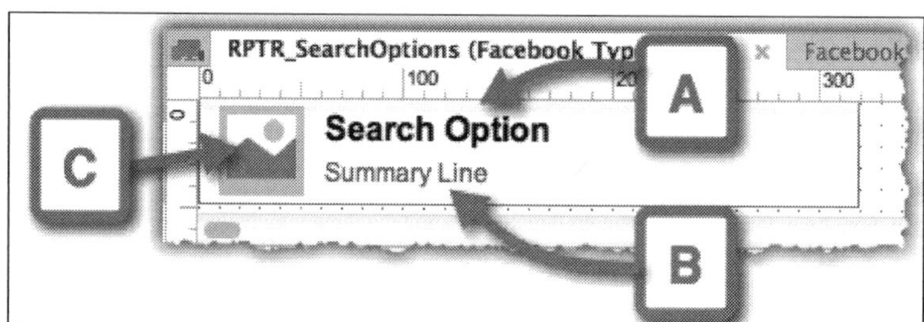

Image 25

7. Also, remember to adjust the width of the top horizontal rule, if needed.
8. In the **Repeater Item Interactions** tab (*Image 26*, **A**) associate the newly created labels, **LBL_Name** and **LBL_SummaryLine**, with the matching repeater item columns (**B**).

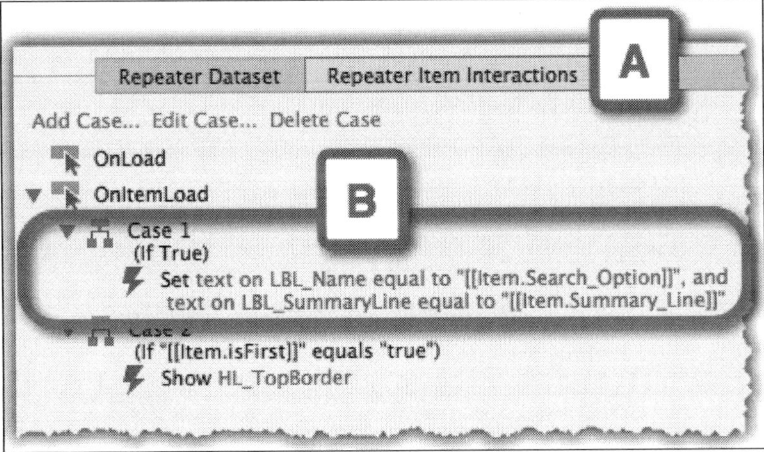

Image 26

9. Preview the page on the browser (*Image 27*). Tweaking the Google pattern to fit a Facebook type pattern required only a little effort, which involved updating the dataset and item layout.

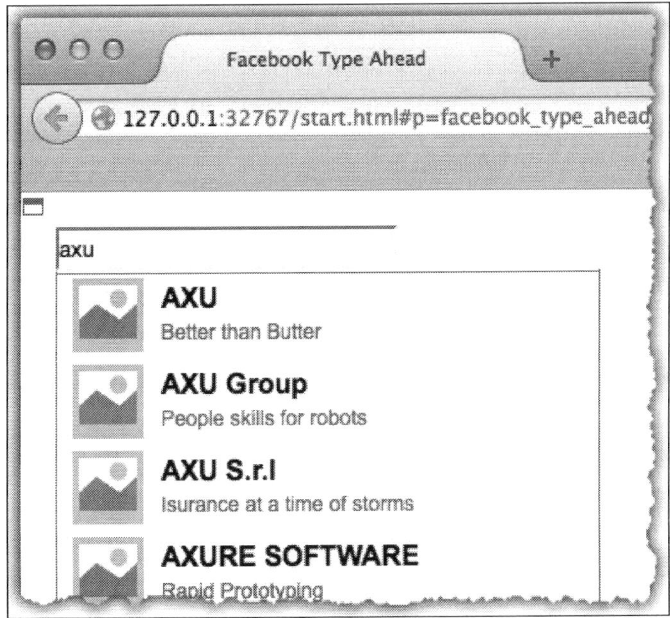

Image 27

Now let's take our tutorial to the next level and see how to create the LinkedIn interface.

3. Creating a LinkedIn-like Type-ahead Search Interface

The LinkedIn type-ahead search is a bit more complicated to simulate, as it contains two types of items: a category item (*Image 28*, **A**) and a result item (**B**). To simplify this, we will ignore the first item in the LinkedIn panel (**C**). This item is actually a link to the LinkedIn search result page, and it can be incorporated into the repeater in a technique that is similar to the one shown in the following screenshot:

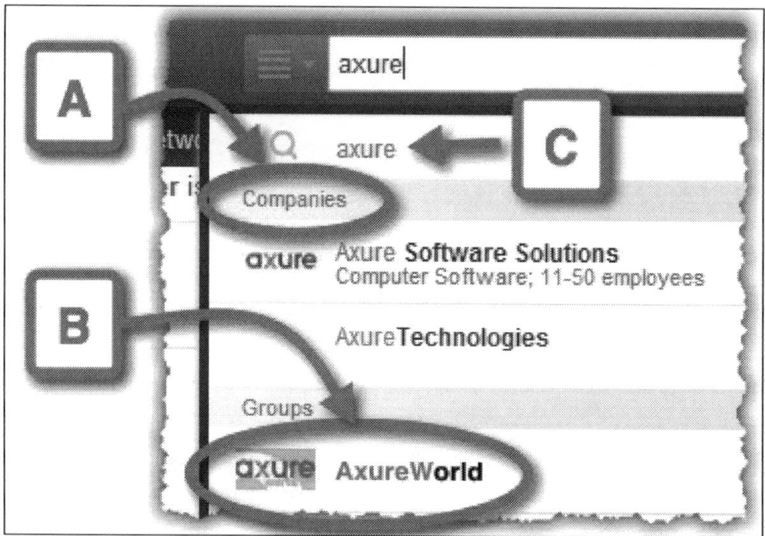

Image 28

3.1 Updating the Data

Perform the following steps to update the data:

1. Start by duplicating the **Facebook Type Ahead** page and rename it `LinkedIn Type Ahead`.

2. Tweak the **Repeater Dataset** tab (*Image 29*, **A**) by adding a column to the repeater named **Item_Type** (**B**). This column will later help you differentiate between a category item and a result item.

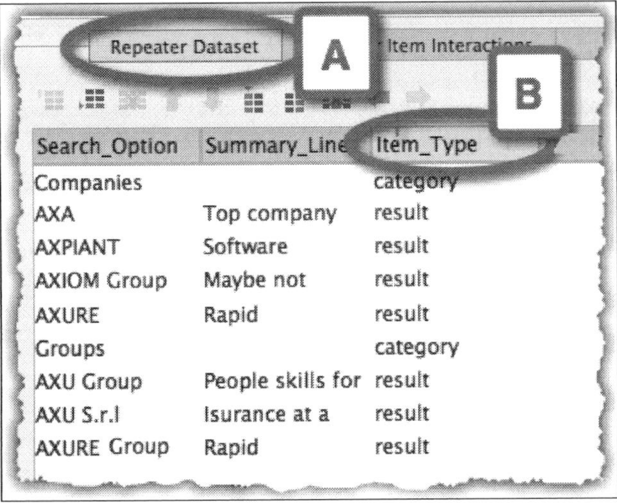

Image 29

3. Next, slightly tweak the design to resemble the LinkedIn pattern (*Image 30*) as shown in the following screenshot:

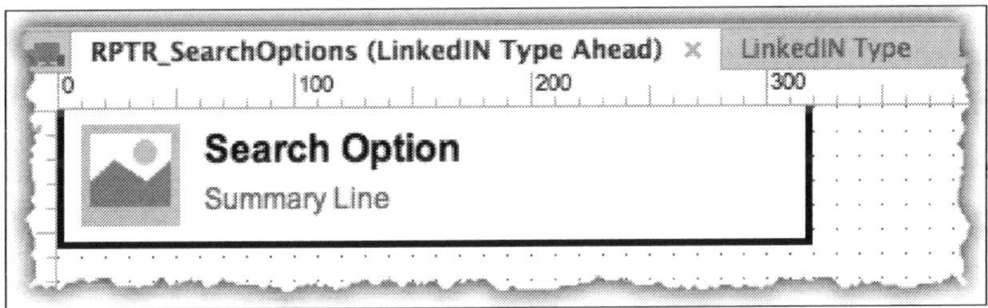

Image 30

The following screenshot (*Image 31*) shows you the interim result:

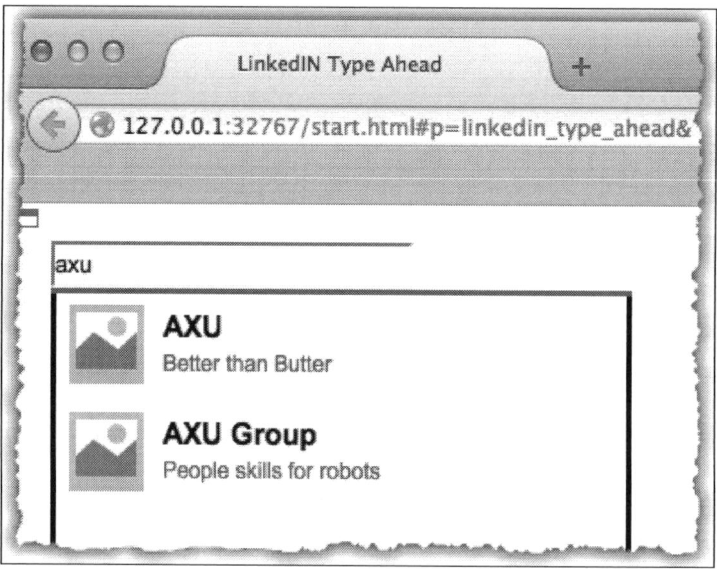

Image 31

Now, there are two problems to deal with regarding the category items' companies and groups:

- They still look like a result item
- They'll get filtered out when performing a search

We will deal with the latter problem first, because it's easier.

3.2 Ensuring that Category Items Always Show

To ensure that category items do not get filtered out, we add another condition to the query string associated with the **OnTextChange** event of the search field itself, which we created back in the Google example. We use the logical operator OR (which looks like two vertical lines, | |), which combines two expressions with an OR operator between them.

We used the following string for the Google and Facebook examples:

[[item.Search_Option.toLowerCase().indexOf(LVAR1.toLowerCase( )) >= 0]]

The following string is the additional expression that we want to evaluate:

item.Item_Type=='category'

The condition checks whether the **item.Item_Type** property is equal to the category. This condition will always be true for category fields, and as we are using an OR operator, the entire expression will always be true for category fields. This ensures that they will always be shown when filtering.

So the new query string should look like the following:

[[item.Search_Option.toLowerCase().indexOf(LVAR1.toLowerCase( )) >= 0 | | item.Item_Type=='category']]

Now the results will always contain the **Companies** and **Groups** categories (*Image 32*, **A**) regardless of the search query. This, of course, means that these categories will appear whether the results in these categories (**B**) match the query or not.

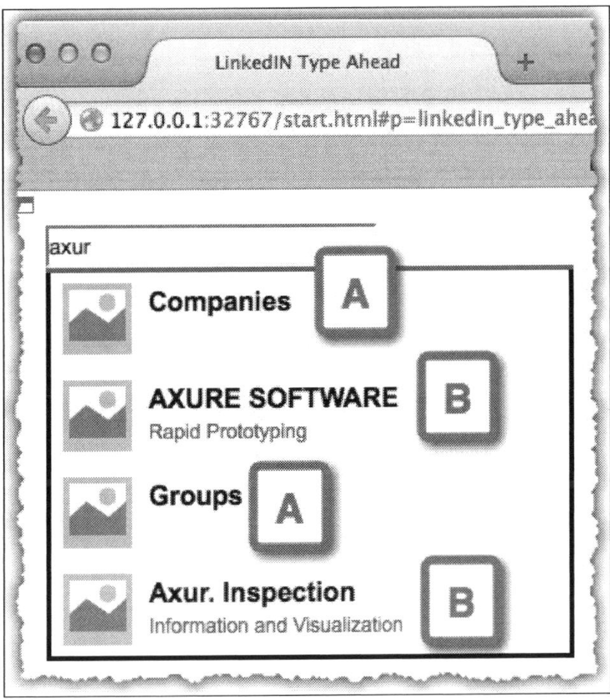

Image 32

> This problem can be fixed but the solution is beyond the scope of this tutorial.

3.3 Applying the Correct Design to Category Fields

Now, this is where it gets even trickier; we need to change the design for the **Companies** and **Groups** items, so they will look like a header for the category:

1. Convert the repeater item widget into a dynamic panel (*Image 33*, **A**) and name it `DP_List_Items` (**B**).
2. The dynamic panel should have two states (**C**):
    - The first state is for a result item. The design will not change. Label this state `Result_Item`.
    - The second state is for a category field. Duplicate the first state to create this state. We will change its design to be a category header. Label this state `Category_Item`.

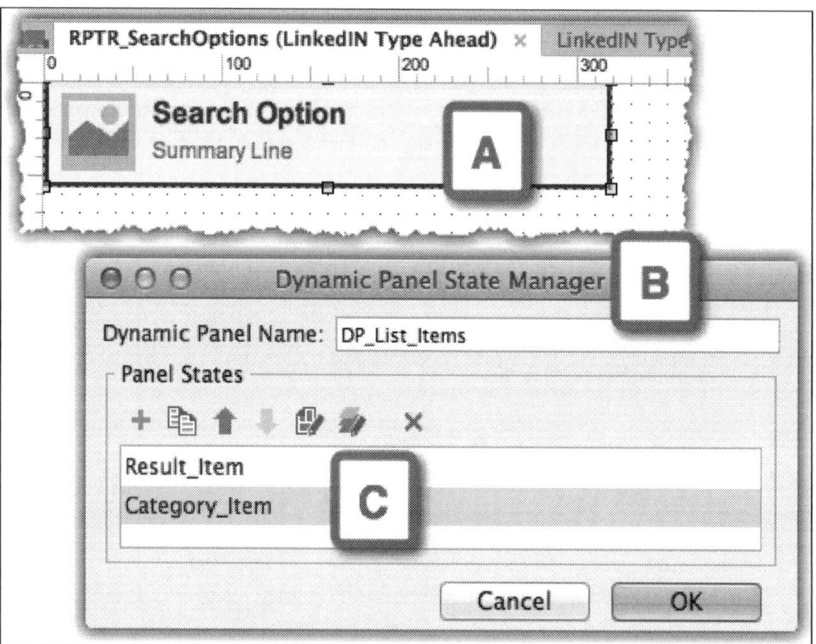

Image 33

3. Note that the horizontal line, **HL_TopBorder**, should stay outside of the dynamic panel and retain the visibility behavior that we created earlier.
4. Next is the design of the **Category_Item** state. As we duplicated the state from the original state, delete the image and the two labels, create a new label widget for the category name, and label it `LBL_Category-Name` as shown in the following screenshot (*Image 34*):

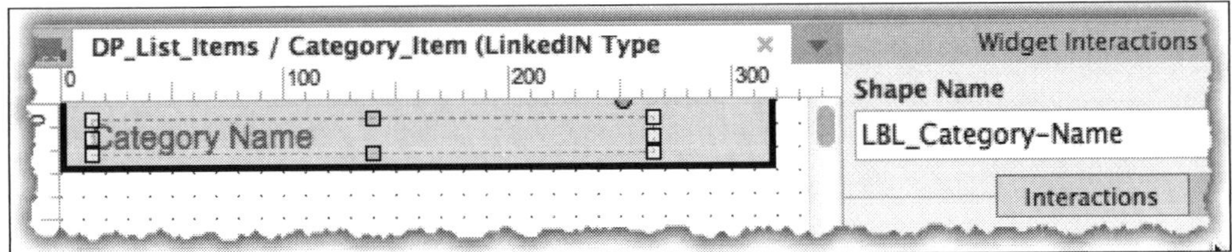

Image 34

5. Also, change the background color to gray and adjust the height of the rectangle. In the **Repeater Item Interactions** tab (*Image 35*, **A**), update the **OnItemLoad** actions (**B**) of the repeater. Associate **LBL_Category-Name** with the **Search_Option** column of the dataset (**C**).

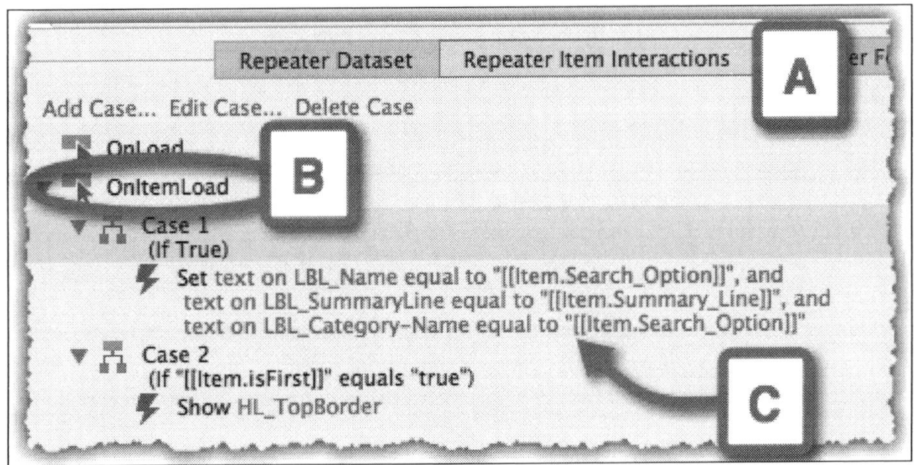

Image 35

6. Next, we will add a case to the **OnItemLoad** event, which will switch the state of the dynamic panel for all the categories.
7. To this case (the third case for this event), we add a condition that changes the state of the dynamic panel for all the category items.
8. In the **Condition Builder** window, select a value (*Image 36*, **A**) for the first drop-down list in the condition row. Click on the **fx** button (**B**) to launch the **Edit Text** window (**C**). There, click on the **Insert Variable or Function...** link (**D**), and from the **Repeater / Dataset** group (**E**), select **item.Item_Type** (**F**).

9. Close the **Edit Text** window and set the third drop-down list to **equals** (**G**), the fourth drop-down list to **value** (**H**), and type **category** (**I**) in the last field.

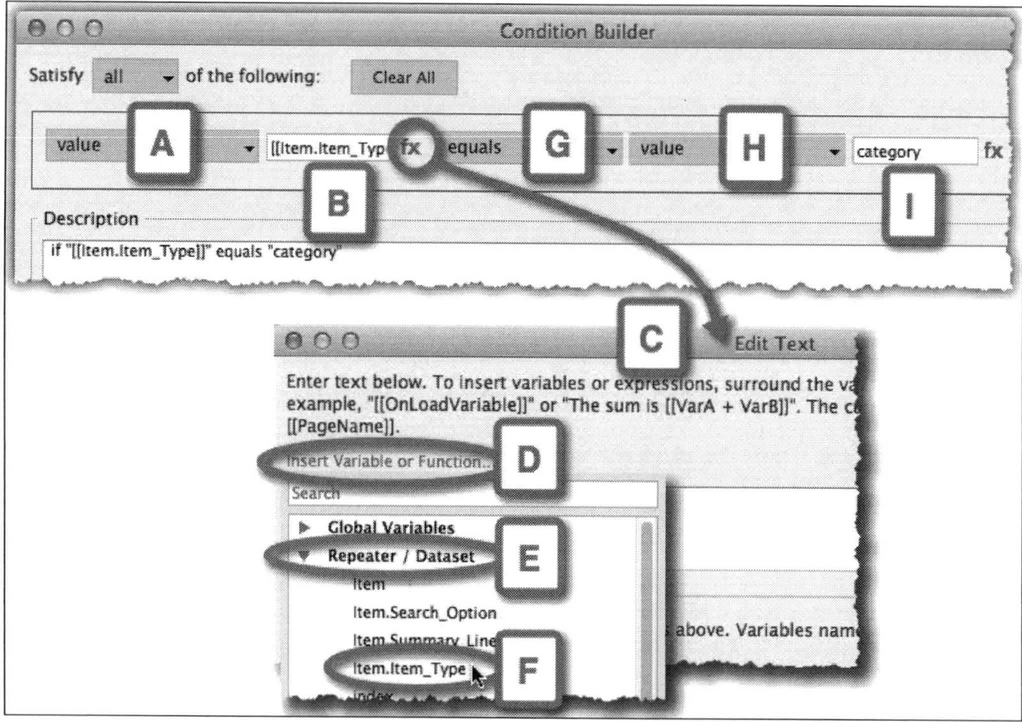

Image 36

10. Close the **Condition Builder** window and set an action to set the dynamic panel, **DP_List_Items**, to **Category_Item** (*Image 37*, **A**).

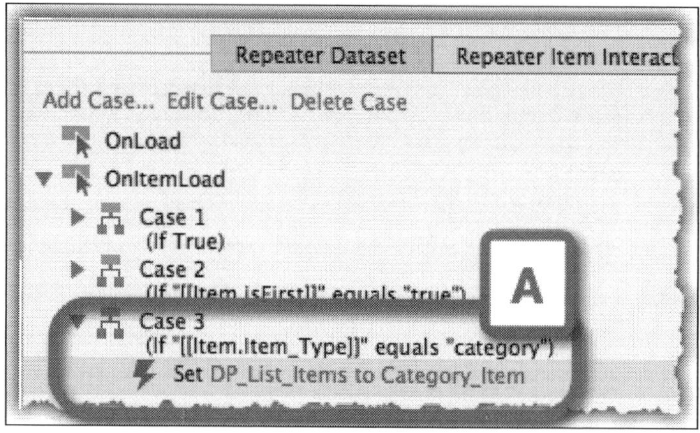

Image 37

11. Remember to toggle the case from **Else If** to **If**.
12. When viewing the resulting page, the category rows start to resemble the LinkedIn style. We encounter a new challenge now, which is the gap that comes after each category item (*Image 38*, **A**).

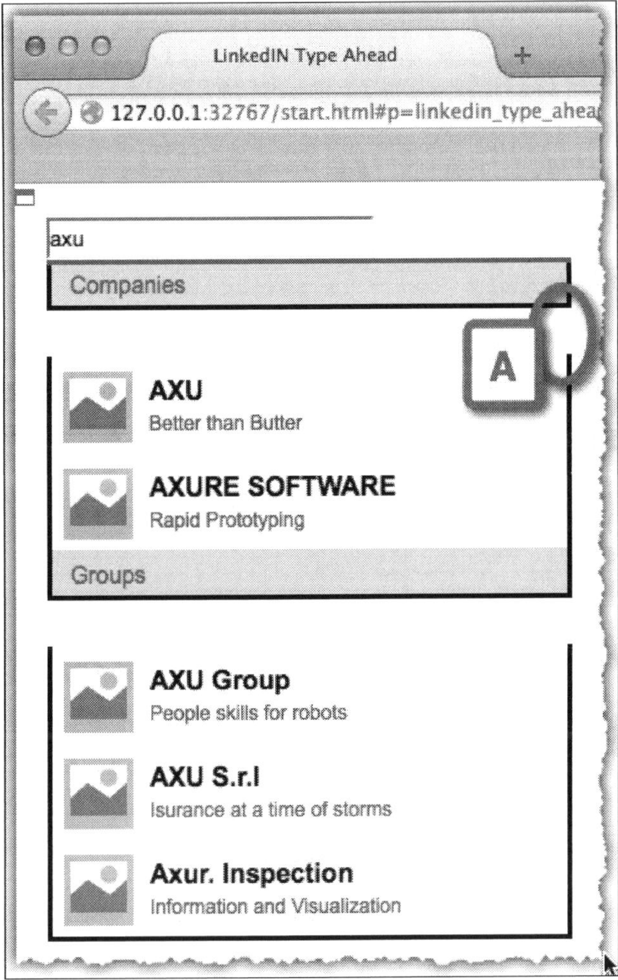

Image 38

This happens because the **Result_Item** rows are 60 pixels high and the **Category_Item** rows are 30 pixels high. The repeater doesn't know this because the panel state is changed dynamically. It allocates 60 pixels for each item regardless of the state of the dynamic panel.

Hopefully, this problem will be addressed in the newer versions of Axure. Until then, we use another trick.

3.4 Dealing with the Gaps

What we now have is a 30 pixels gap that needs to be closed. Basically, what we do is push each item up so that it will close the gap. This is a bit tricky because items in the first **Companies** category need to be moved by -30 pixels, and items in the **Groups** category need to be moved by -60 pixels, as they have to close both the gaps. When we add a third category later, the items there would need to close three gaps and move by -90 pixels. So, the trick is to figure out the number of pixels by which we need to move each item.

We do this by adding a new global variable named **ItemOffset**. This variable will store the current offset and will decrease by 30 pixels each time we meet a new category.

The following screenshot (*Image 39*) shows us the cases applied to the **OnItemLoad** event:

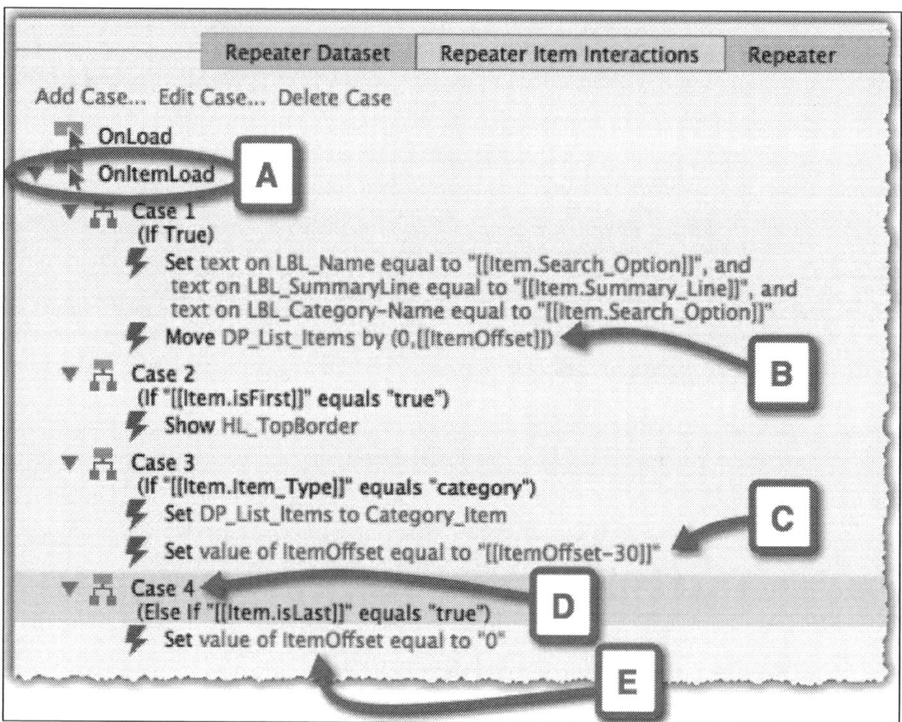

Image 39

Let's review what happens in the **OnItemLoad** event (*Image 39*, **A**):

1. The first item we meet when the repeater is rendered is the first category item, **Companies**.
2. The first case is triggered and **Companies** is moved by 0 pixels—since we are not looking to really move the widget, just to trigger an action (**B**).
3. As this is an item of the category type, the third case is executed and the **ItemOffset** variable is updated to 0-30 which is -30 (**C**).
4. The next items will be shifted by -30 pixels.
5. Once we meet the second category, the third case is executed again and **ItemOffset** is updated to -60.
6. Now the next items are shifted by -60 pixels. Mission accomplished!
7. When the last item is rendered, the **ItemOffest** global variable is reset to 0.

The following screenshot (*Image 40*) shows us the final result:

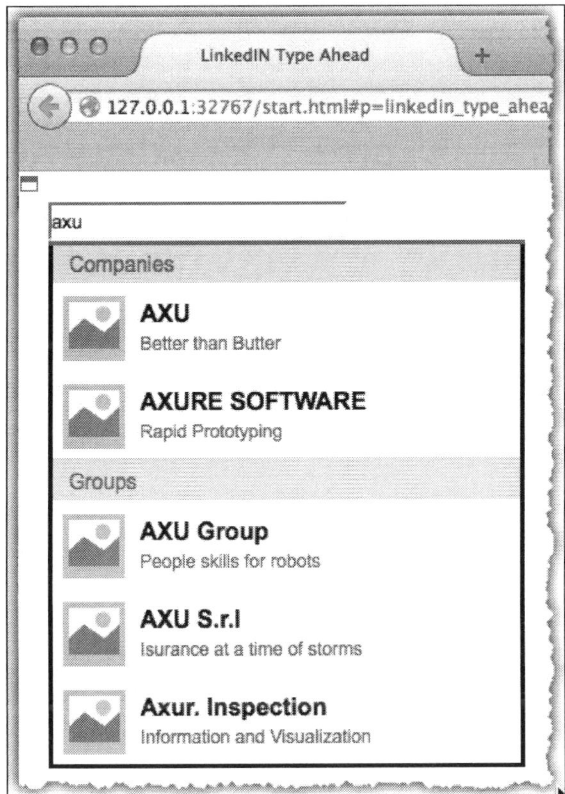

Image 40

To add an additional category to this example, all we need to do is add a few more category items and result items to the repeater dataset, and that's it!

Summary

This was an opportunity to demonstrate the repeater's powerful abilities to create a robust, generic interface that can be easily scaled with new data and/or a new design. Like many powerful features, mastering the repeater widget requires an investment of your time. However, once you do master it, you can achieve a realistic, high-fidelity interface on Axure like never before.

Svetlin Denkov – Building a Form-factor Viewer/Emulator to Support Effective RWD Demos on the Desktop

Tutorial level: Intermediate/advanced

Practitioner Profile

Svetlin Denkov is a UX Prototyper at GN ReSound in Chicago, where he builds highly interactive prototypes for mobile and tablet devices using different technologies. He has a masters degree in Human-Computer Interaction from DePaul University. Svetlin is also a leader at the Chicago chapter of IxDA, which introduces technology events to the local UX community on a monthly basis.

He has used Axure for several years now as his favorite prototyping tool and regularly contributes to the Chicago Axure Users Meetup. In his spare time, as a "Sifu" user, Svetlin helps others on the Axure forums under the name light_forger. You can also follow him on Twitter at `@svetlindenkov`, where he posts about UX, prototyping, and technology.

When he is not prototyping, Svetlin seeks creative inspiration for new ideas over a strong cup of oolong tea, unless he is mountain biking, which he enjoys immensely!

The Tutorial

Denkov is a User Experience Designer who seeks productive workflows to create **Responsive Web Designs (RWD)**. He was excited to learn about the inclusion of an Adaptive Views feature in Axure 7 Beta. Adopting the software during its Beta phase enabled him to test Mobile-First RWDs for iOS-specific breakpoints. Breakpoints identify device segmentations based on the resolution's width or height.

The electronic magazine *UXmatters*, accessible at `http://www.uxmatters.com`, inspired him to work on his early tests; therefore, he created a two-page RWD design for a *UXmatters* mobile site with a **Home** page linking to an **Article** page. He is not associated with the magazine in any way, but he enjoys their content and built the mobile site as an exercise. He shared many of his findings from these tests with other UXers at Axure Meetups in Chicago and Orlando.

However, an unexpected problem emerged during these presentations. To trigger designs at different breakpoints (*Image 41*, **A** and **C**) on the desktop, the browser (and therefore, the viewport) had to be resized by dragging the bottom-right window corner (*Image 41*, **B**). However, this confused the participating UX designers and other design professionals. Many asked for an explanation of what exactly was being done on the screen; they wanted to know what role the resizing of the browser played in the demonstration.

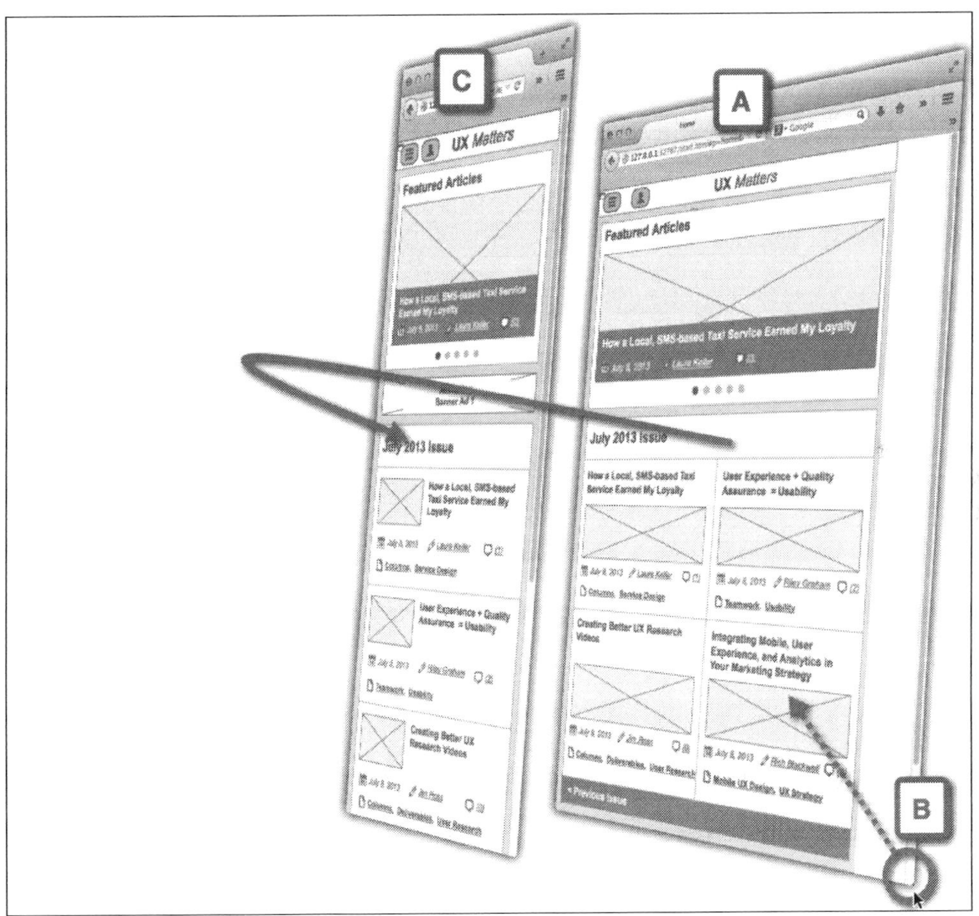

Image 41

Based on comments he received, it was obvious that the current approach to demonstrate RWDs communicated designs ineffectively, because the audience was distracted by the presentation method. The resizing of the browser and the consequent screen lag introduced an unfamiliar situation that confused the participants.

This can be very disruptive, especially when a user experience designer is making a presentation to stakeholders during design reviews; it sets up a scenario that can compromise a project's momentum and ultimately its timeline. A new approach to demonstrate RWD was needed.

1. Setup and Assumptions

Luckily, there is a relatively easy-to-implement solution that can be adopted by UX designers. Before diving into the explanation, we need to take note that several assumptions were made while designing this solution.

The breakpoints have been identified ahead of time. In this tutorial, I am using an iPhone 5S in portrait and landscape modes (*Image 42*, **A** and **B**), as shown in the following screenshot:

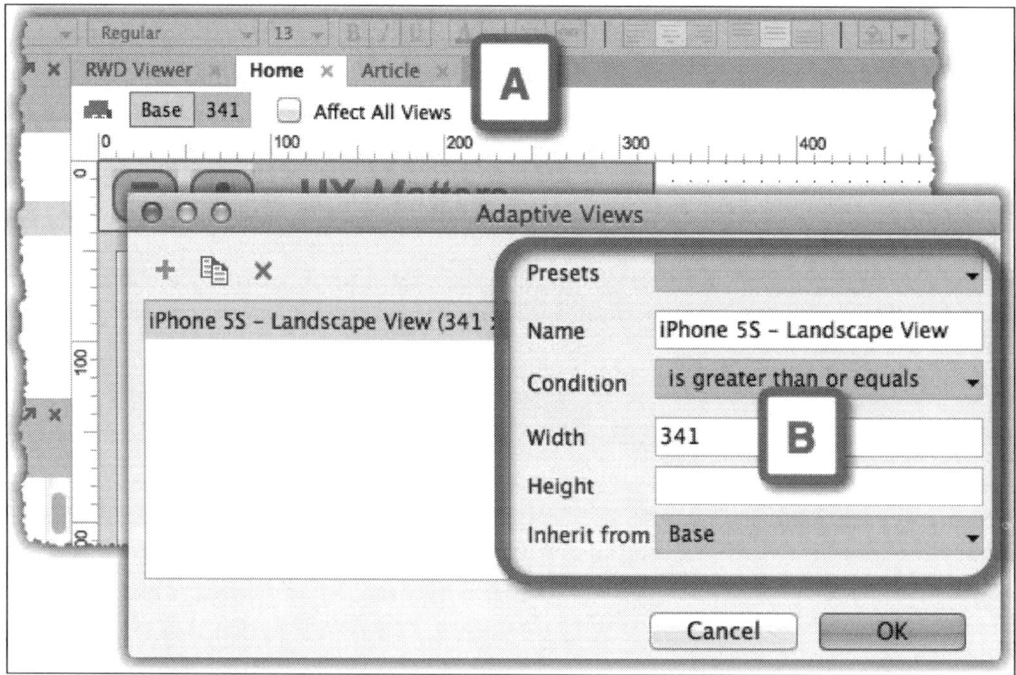

Image 42

The iPhone 5C has an identical retina resolution of 1136 pixels by 640 pixels. For more information on the mobile project setup, refer to the tutorials on iPhone at `http://www.Axure.com`. The initial RWD prototype is organized in discrete pages for **Home** (*Image 42*, **A**) and **Article** (**B**):

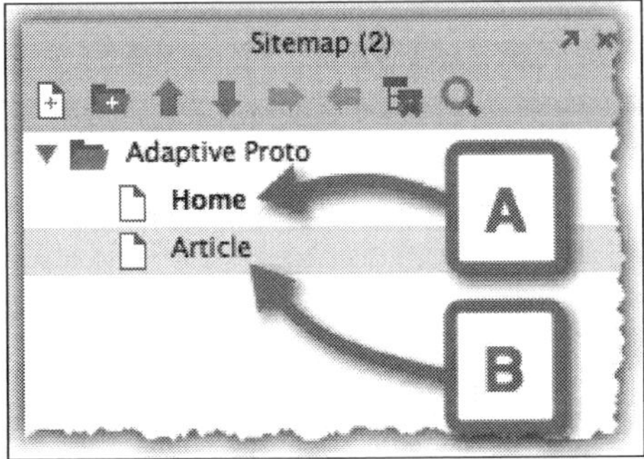

Image 43

Call to Action (**CTA**) allows for navigation between pages. For example, on the **Home** page, clicking on the article's title (*Image 44*, **A**) leads to an action (**B**) that opens the **Article** page, as shown in the following screenshot:

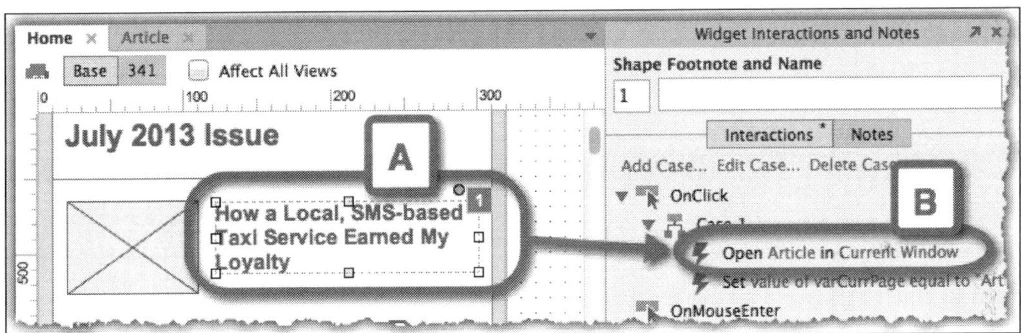

Image 44

2. Constructing the Representation

The solution includes a new page, **RWD Viewer** (*Image 45*, **A**), with a two-state dynamic panel (**C**), and controls for alternating between the states. Each state holds an iFrame that has been sized to match the appropriate breakpoint (**D**). A global variable keeps track of the current page that is being viewed, and its value is passed on, changing the dynamic panel to a different state, switching between breakpoints using the top-button navigation (**B**), as shown in the following screenshot:

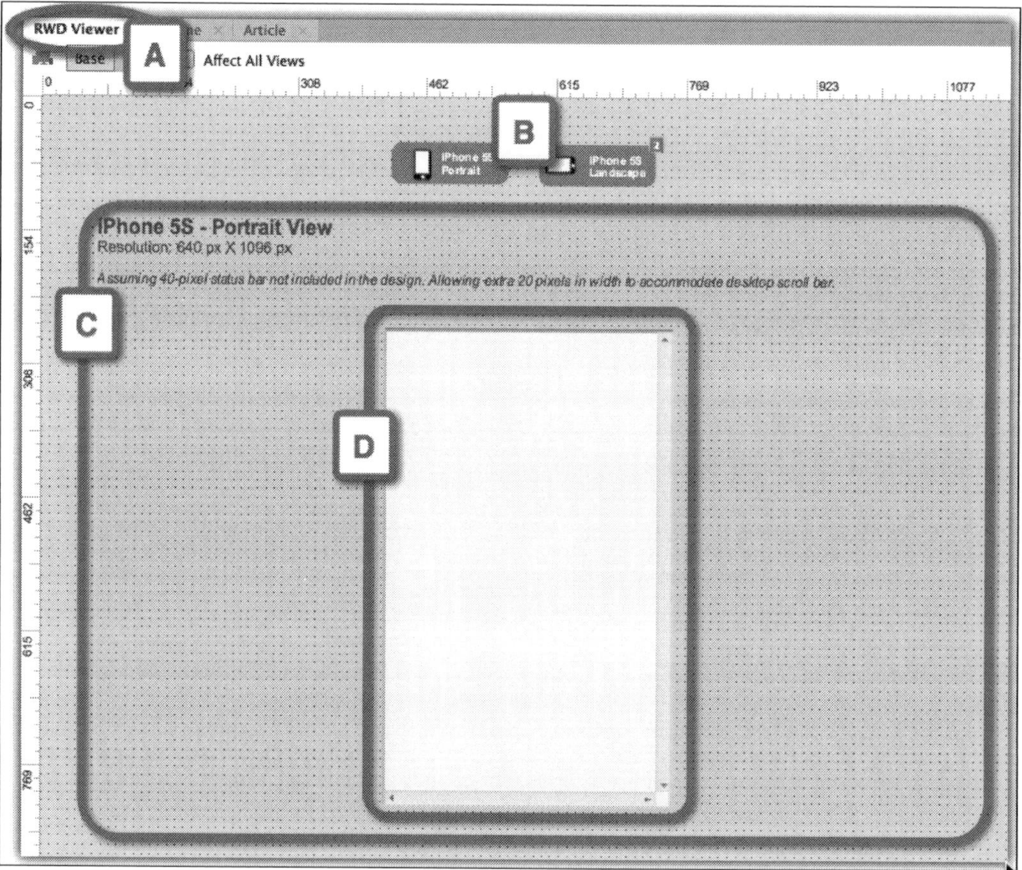

Image 45

2.1 Setting Up the View

The following are the steps to set up the view:

1. Create a new **RWD Viewer** page as the container for the viewer (*Image 46*, **A**), as shown in the following screenshot:

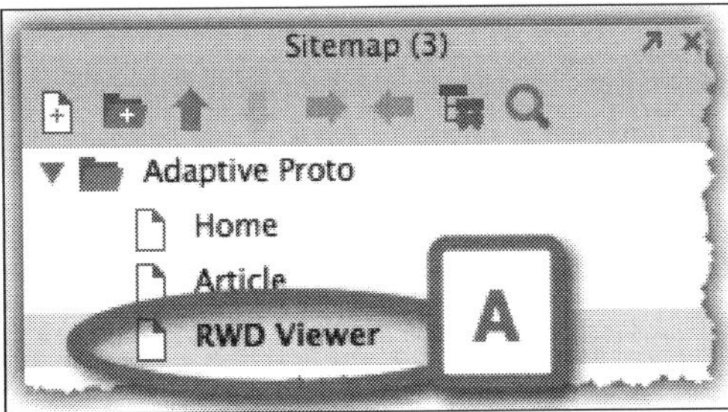

Image 46

2. Create two buttons that include a description of the breakpoint and a visual of its orientation. (*Image 47*, **A** and **B**). You can also opt for a much simpler treatment. The styling is up to you!
3. Group the buttons using the **Selection Group** pop up (C) in a group called **buttons**.

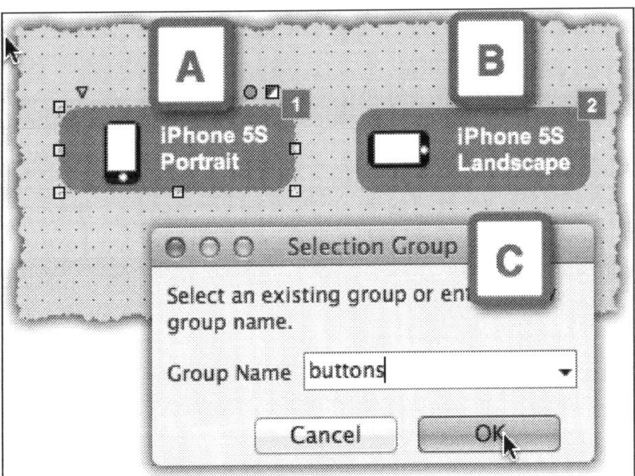

Image 47

4. Create a two-state dynamic panel and label it `dp_Viewer` (*Image 48*, **A**). Name each of the states to reflect the appropriate breakpoint, for example, `s1_iPhone5SPortrait` (**B**) and `s2_iPhone5SLandscape` (**C**).

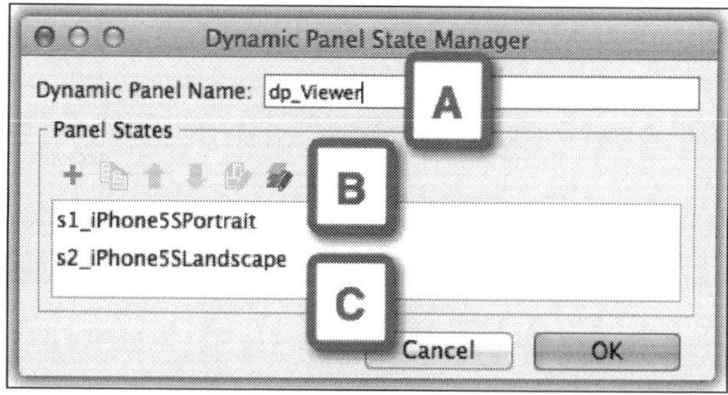

Image 48

5. Size the dynamic panel so it accommodates all the content. Adjust its height and width to be, at the very least, the height and width of the largest content across all views.

Next, in each state of the dynamic panel, create an iFrame sized to its breakpoint:

A 340 pixels by 548 pixels iFrame for portrait, which you label `if_iPhone5SPortrait` (*Image 49*, **A**) and 588 pixels by 320 pixels iFrame for landscape, which you label `if_iPhone5SLandscape`.

20 pixels are added to the width to accommodate the scroll bar so that it is shown in Firefox. If you're giving a demo in Chrome or Safari, the scroll bar is only 2 pixels wide. Additionally, 20 pixels are removed from the top to accommodate iPhone's status bar. For more information on handling the status bar in iOS 7, refer to the Axure Mobile forum at `http://forum.Axure.com`.

The following screenshot (*Image 49*) illustrates the vertical state (**A**) and the **Location + Size** panel (**B**):

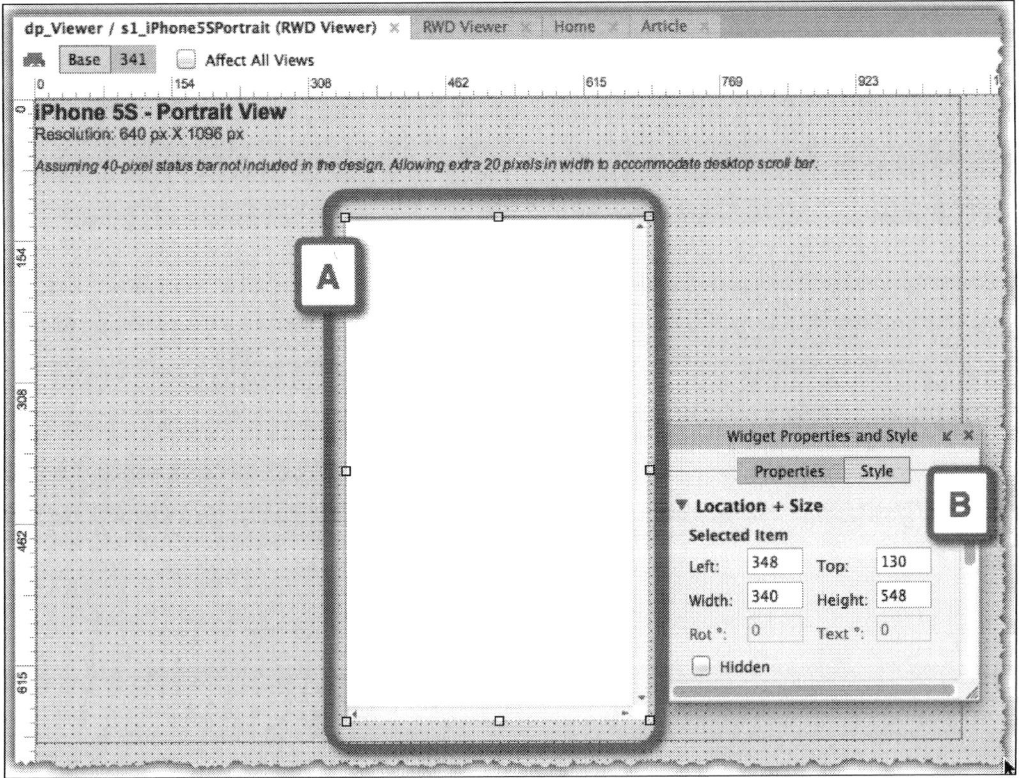

Image 49

The following screenshot (*Image 50*) illustrates the horizontal state (**A**) and the **Location + Size** panel (**B**):

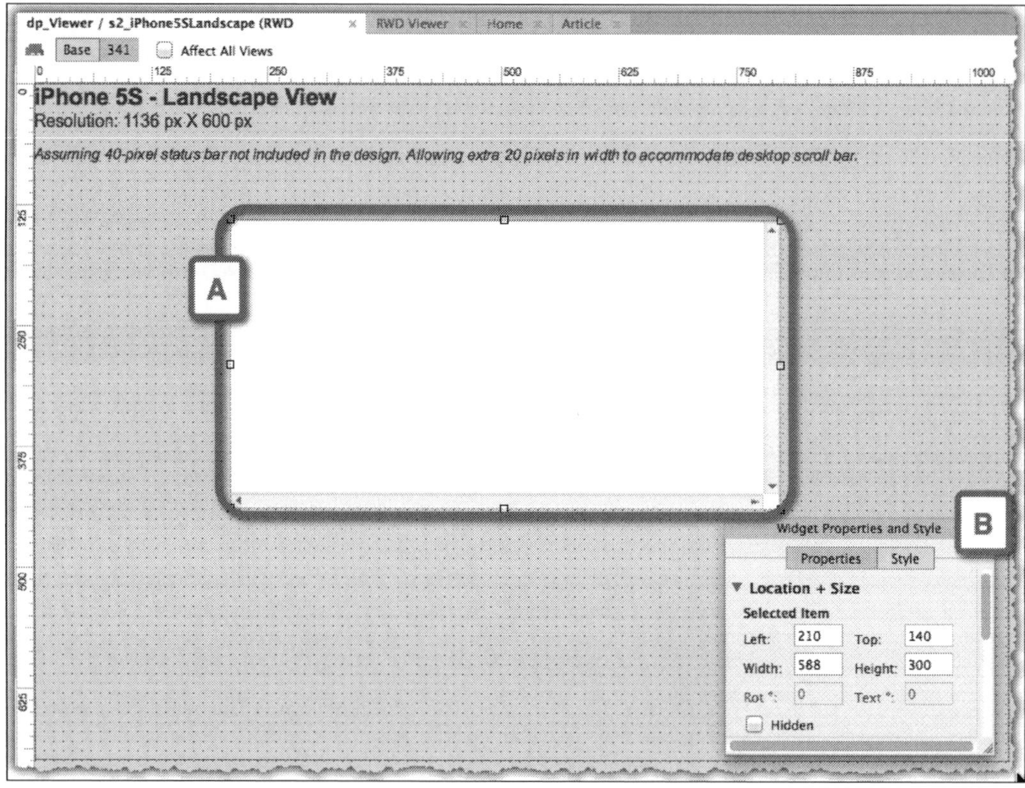

Image 50

Next, we will configure the iFrame. Set **Home** as the default target page for both the iFrames (*Image 51*, **A**). For a seamless experience, enable scrolling for both iFrames by selecting the **Show as Needed** option (**B**), as shown in the following screenshot:

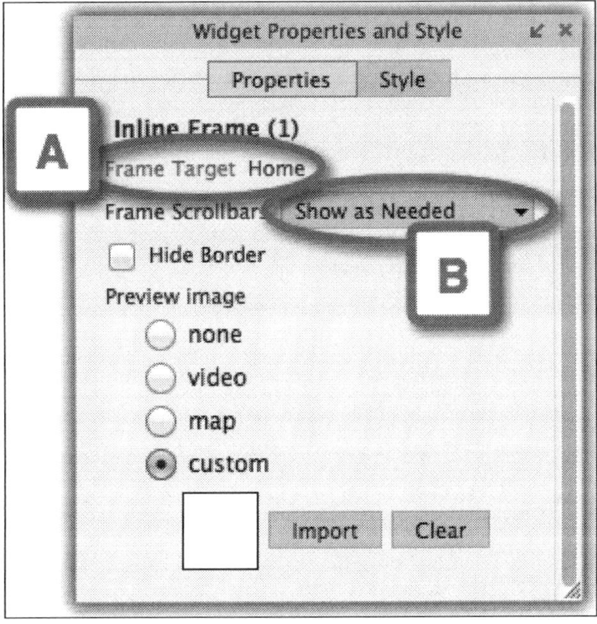

Image 51

2.2 Adding Interactivity

The next section details wiring interactions to the wireframes:

1. To pass context from one iFrame to another, a global variable must be used to store the currently opened Axure page as a text string. Create a global variable and name it `gVarCurrPage`. Set `Home` as the variable's default value.
2. Clicking on the article's link in the **Home** page (*Image 12*, **A**) sets the value of the global variable to **Article** (**B**) as shown in the following screenshot:

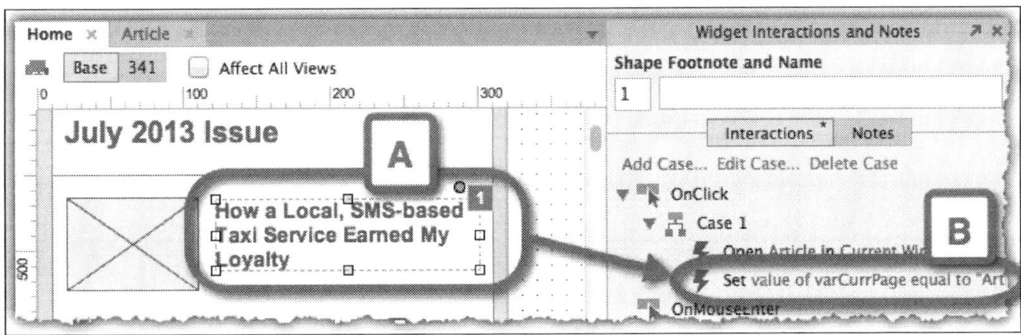

Image 52

3. Similarly, in the **Article** page, **gVarCurrPage** will be set to **Home** if the user clicks on the relevant navigation there. Essentially, for every CTA that triggers a page change, the value of the global variable has to be updated.
4. Lastly, for the two buttons we created in step *2.1 Setting Up the View*, the actions must be updated for every button.
5. Click on the first button to set the **dp_Viewer** to **s1_iPhone5SPortrait** state.
6. Add conditional statements to check the value of **gVarCurrPage** and open the appropriate page in the iFrame; for example, if the value is **Article**, open the **Article** page in **if_iPhone5SPortrait**.
7. The same applies for the second button, except this time **dp_Viewer** is set to **s2_iPhone5SLandscape**.
8. You must do this for every button depending on the number of breakpoints you have included in your design.

2.3 Testing the Prototype

Preview or generate the prototype in the browser to check the interaction and layout. Possible tweaks include toggling the iFrame borders and changing the captions above each layout option. Switching breakpoints via buttons (*Image 53*, **A** and **B**) is now elegant and seamless and resizing the browser window is no longer required. Presenting layouts in meetings has now been transformed to a polished experience.

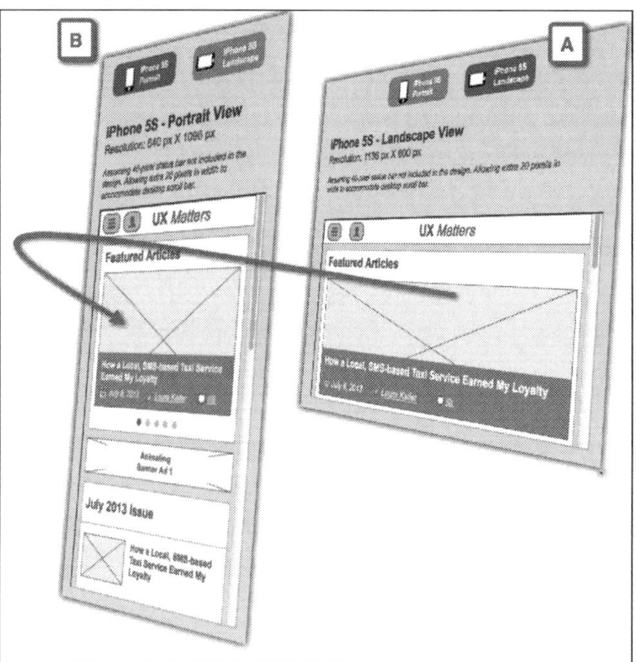

Image 53

3. Possible Limitations

While this organizational approach significantly improves the RWD presentation, it is not without limitations. The following is a list of the possible limitations:

- The RWD viewer assumes that all screens map across all breakpoints. If you have breakpoints for which some of the screens are combined/removed, this has to be reflected by updating the values in the conditional statements assigned to the buttons.
- Using nested dynamic panels to organize your screen content may break the RWD viewer. This is true when you try to pass context between iFrames because there is a single container page. Therefore, instead of checking for the page name, you must check for the state of the parent dynamic panel (the content container). Not only will you have to change the state of this panel, but you will also have to adjust the states of any other existing panels, for example, headers, footers, and so on. You can see how this easy task becomes quite a daunting task.

  The newly introduced **OnAdaptiveViewChange** event may help in handling custom interactions in dynamic panels (and possibly content, although Axure at this point does not provide actions for "Place in View" and "Unplace from View" of widgets), but this does not eliminate the need to use the resizing metaphor for triggering views.
- An inherent limitation of using a page-based design is that the content does not load immediately when opened in an iFrame. Each page loads separately, introducing a lag in updating the iFrame. This can be solved by using a transitional loading screen, which displays the content as the screen loads, but this is outside the scope of the tutorial.

With the Axure's 7.0 update and its cloud storage service AxureShare (`http://share.Axure.com`), it appears that the pages' speed for loading content has significantly improved, but this speed will vary depending on the amount and type of content (for example, rich visual assets versus vector Axure widgets) you have per page.

Takeaways

Despite the limitations, using this approach will benefit the communication of RWD by:

- Helping project members and stakeholders understand design views across devices
- Facilitating a discussion of the design during reviews
- Ensuring close team collaboration for iterating the design
- Separating the content from the viewer, which will allow prototype demos on a mobile device or on a desktop

In addition to the time and effort spent in creating the RWD design, a User Experience designer must put in more effort and work harder to adopt this presentation strategy; he/she must build the viewer before the design is ready for demonstration. For multiple projects that target the same number and type of platforms, building the viewer can be done once and consequently tweaked from one project to another.

Furthermore, just like any change management exercise, prototypers must be careful to reflect updates in page names and the overall flow of the prototype in order not to break the iFrame content loading.

Lastly, this technique may not be applicable to all types of project work. More specifically, maintaining deep, highly interactive prototypes using this approach may prove challenging. Ideally, the technique should be applied for click-through experiences. Regardless of the scope and goals of your projects, I hope what I presented here will be useful to many of you who engage in creating RWDs!

Reusing Cases Across Different Widgets and Events

Tutorial level: Intermediate/advanced

Practitioner Profile

Ritch is the CEO of Ax-Stream—the approved Axure RP training and support partners for Europe. He has worked in UX, UCD, and Usability since 1995 and has particular expertise in designing and usability testing of early conceptual prototypes (using Axure). Ritch has published numerous refereed papers in this field and was on the editorial board of the Encyclopedia of Human-Computer Interaction, published in the year 2007. He is a member of as well as a guest speaker for the User Experience Professionals Association (UXPA).

He has been using Axure, in lead UX roles, on multimillion dollar projects since 2008 and focuses on: highly complex Axure prototyping, developing intelligent widget libraries and strategic work around integrating Axure into UCD and Agile methods. He contributed a tutorial to the book *Axure RP 6 Prototyping Essentials, Ezra Schwartz, Packt Publishing*; he is "Sifu" on the Axure forum, owns the Axure RP Pro LinkedIn group, and is a regular panel speaker at AxureWorld.

He holds a PhD in Human-Computer Interaction (HCI) from Loughborough University's Human Sciences and Advanced Technology (HUSAT) research center and has delivered lectures at the masters level across five countries on UXD, UCD, Usability, IT Strategy, Business Analysis, and IT development methodology.

The Tutorial

In the training courses we conduct at Ax-Stream, our delegates often ask if it is possible to reuse cases across different events and widgets. The more technical of them frame this question, "Is it possible to define a library of subroutines in Axure that can be reused?"

This requirement can usefully be explained by considering the following screenshot (*Image 54*), where we have prototyped a very simple usability questionnaire using Axure 7:

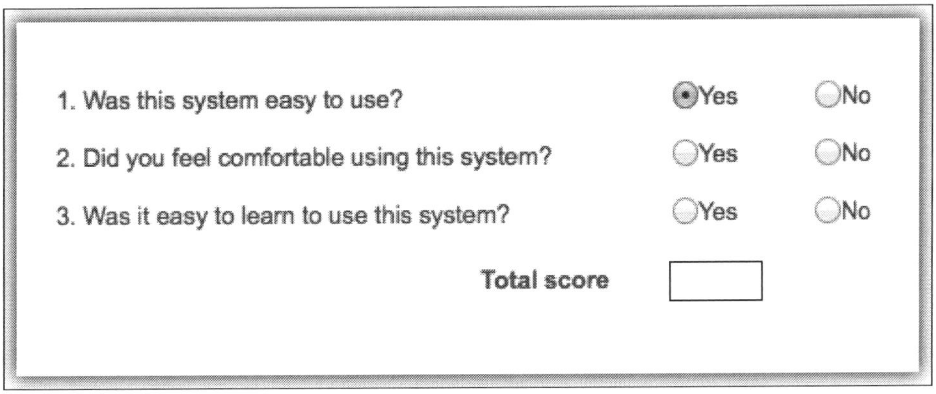

1. Was this system easy to use? Yes No
2. Did you feel comfortable using this system? Yes No
3. Was it easy to learn to use this system? Yes No

Total score

Image 54

There are three questions and a pair of radio buttons for answering each question. As the questions are answered by clicking on the radio buttons, we want the total score to be updated whereby one point is scored for each **Yes** answer. So, if the user answers **Yes** to all three questions, the total score is 3, and if the user answers **No** to all three questions, the total score is 0.

To prototype this in Axure 7, perform the following steps:

1. Create a page titled `questionnaire` (*Image 54*, **A**).
2. Add Label widgets for questions (**B**) and their corresponding pairs of **Yes** and **No** radio buttons (**C**).
3. Add a Rectangle widget to display the total score (**D**).

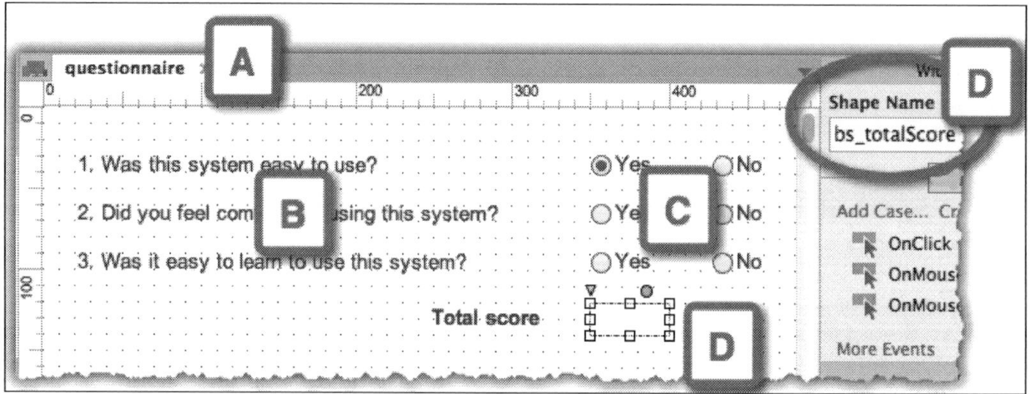

Image 55

4. Label all of the radio buttons and the total rectangle shape.
5. Assign each pair of radio buttons (*Image 56*, **A**) to a radio group (**B**), which will take care of the exclusivity of each answer.

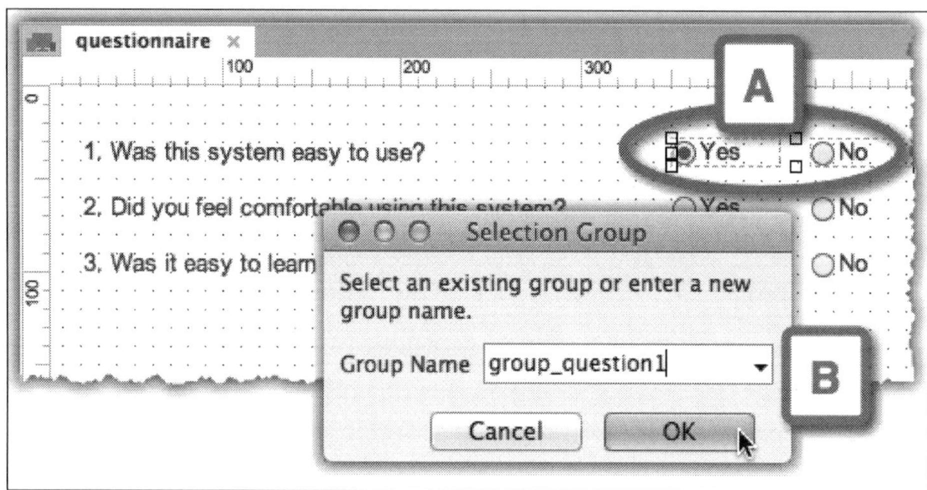

Image 56

6. Add a case to the **OnClick** event of the first radio button (*Image 57*, **A**) named **setTotalScore** (**B**). It calculates the total score based on the status of the radio buttons.
7. This is done with three local variables: **LVar_question1**, **LVar_question2**, and **LVar_question3**, which are mapped to the **is selected of** status of the three **Yes** radio buttons (**C**). When in the selected state, the value of their local variable will be `1`. The three values are added and placed in a global variable called **gVar_totalScore**.

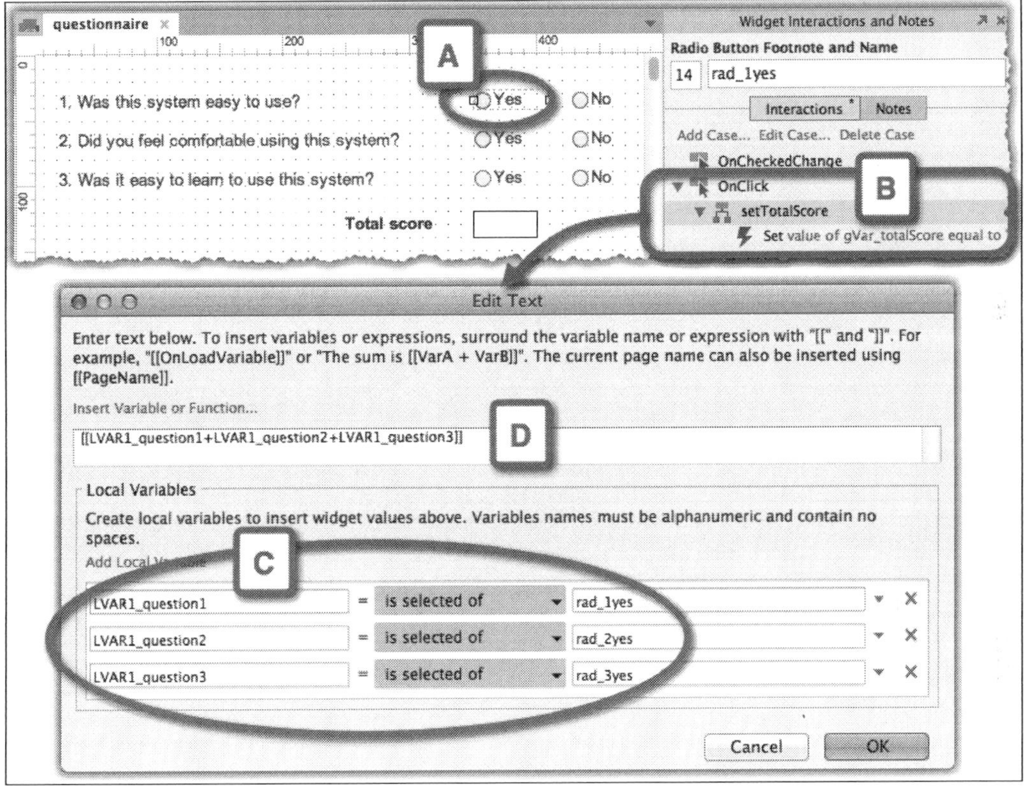

Image 57

8. For the same radio button (*Image 58*, **A**), add an action (**C**) to the **setTotalScore** case (**B**) that uses the **Set Text** action.

9. Place the value of the **gVar_totalScore** variable in the **bs_totalScore** (**D**) Rectangle widget.

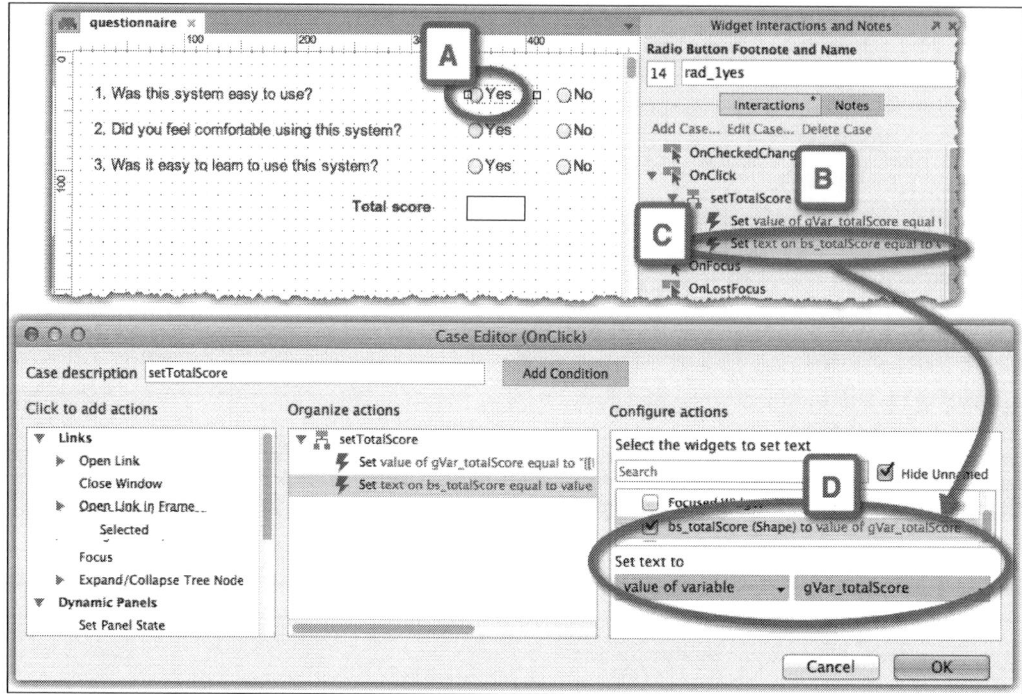

Image 58

10. Copy this case onto all the radio buttons so that the total score will be updated when the user clicks on any of the radio buttons.

The Problem

This example will work just fine, but the architecture of this Axure prototype has a significant problem that can cost us a lot of time later on! The problem comes when we want to add additional questions and an associated pair of radio buttons.

In addition to adding cases to the new radio buttons, we also need to update every case on each of the existing six radio buttons so that the total score is now calculated on the basis of all questions. This can be quite a lengthy and tedious task, and in real prototyping scenarios, we may have to update lots of cases this way! Remember, a key feature of prototyping is **speed**!

When there are many actions and conditions to be updated within each case, we can save some time by updating just one case, deleting any old cases, then copying and pasting the updated case as required. However, this is still quite lengthy and tedious. Its repetitive nature also means that it is error prone; for example, it is easy to forget to update one or more widgets if we are editing lots of them. In turn, bugs introduced by such errors can be quite difficult to track down, as we may be convinced that all the widgets have been correctly updated.

The Solution

Fortunately, there is a great solution to this problem. The approach involves a small dynamic panel, which has one empty state. This panel responds to an event triggered by the radio buttons, executing a case that contains all of the necessary actions to calculate and set the total score. The same cases that were present on each radio button in the previous version of our prototype are now concentrated at a single place.

Start by duplicating the **questionnaire** page to **questionnaire2** (*Image 59*, **A**). Add a fourth question (**B**). Due to the duplication, there is a bit of work—tweaking the widgets and the calculations that are based on the local variables. Try to do this yourself before looking at the file for answers. Add a small dynamic panel to the right of the **bs_totalScore** widget (*Image 59*, **C**) and label it `calculator`. There is nothing you need to do with its states.

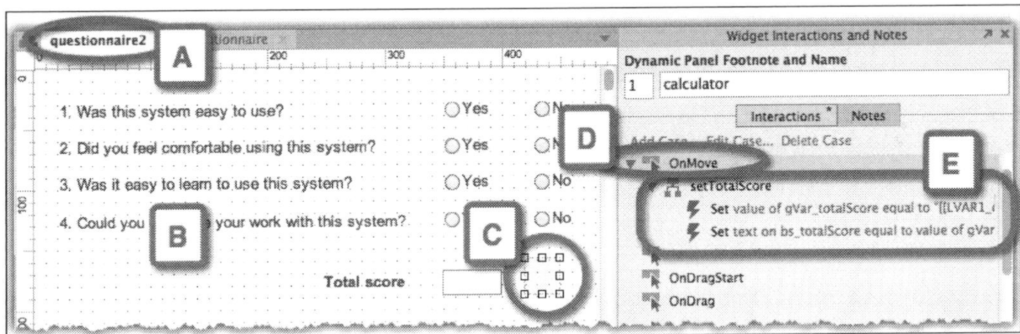

Image 59

Copy the **setTotalScore** action from any of the radio buttons in the **questionnaire** page and paste it to an **OnMove** event of the **calculator** dynamic panel. For the **rad1_yes** radio button (*Image 60,* **A**), create a **Move calculator by (0,0)** (**B**) case for an **OnClick** event.

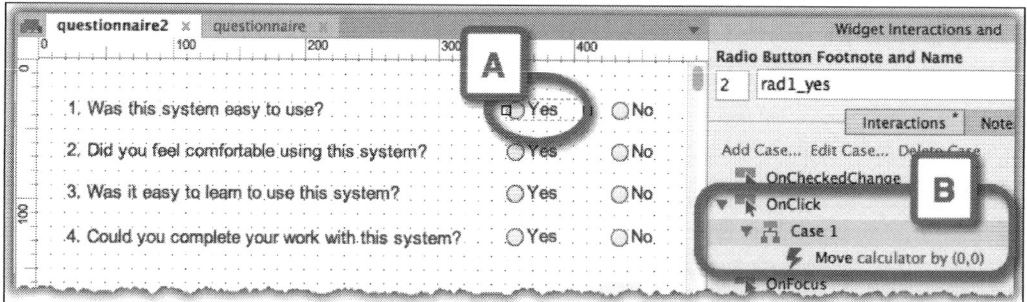

Image 60

This panel is obviously not intended to move. Rather, the action triggers the panel's **OnMove** event, which, in turn, performs the cases and sets the total score. Paste this action to all radio buttons.

This architecture means that if we add one more question, we simply have to update one case on the **OnMove** event of the dynamic panel and copy and paste some cases onto the *new* radio buttons—we do *not* have to update any of the cases on the exiting radio buttons!

Discussion, Takeaways, and Next Steps

Of course, the time-saving and error-prevention benefits of this architecture increase along with the number of times similar cases would otherwise need to be replicated across the prototype, but the architecture has another, less obvious, but key advantage! Keeping track of what interactions each widget/event is performing in a prototype can ultimately become the limiting factor in how complex an Axure prototype an individual can produce. This architecture, whereby we keep more complex cases in *one* place or *modularize* the interactive aspects of the prototype, makes the process of managing complex interactivity easier and more scalable; thus, this increases the potential complexity of the prototype.

The ultimate progression of this architecture is to set global variables prior to triggering a dynamic panel's **OnMove** event such that the panel then uses the value in the variables to determine (through the use of conditions) which case(s) to execute, and how this execution should be performed, in particular contexts. Indeed, some Axure experts, including myself, have pushed this architecture to the point whereby for very complex prototyping, we manage most, or even all, of the interactivity using a *single* control panel and a suitable set of variables to manage the behavior of this panel. In my experience, this makes it easier to keep the interaction model in mind and identify/correct any bugs. Indeed, an example of this can be found in the widget called menuPanDragSwipeRepeaterItems in Ax-Stream's `Drag, Swipes and Spins` widget library (which is available for free download at `www.ax-stream.com`).

The use of such architectures can be extended in Axure prototyping, whereby we set up a bunch of such control dynamic panels on a page that act like a subroutine library we can simply call upon from any widget or event to execute the cases we need.

Of course, as with all Axure functionality, we can place these control panels into masters if we want to reuse them across pages. Similarly, we can place them within custom widgets so that (complex) cases can be reused across different projects via widget libraries. I also hope that such libraries will eventually be produced for distribution across the Axure community. This will ensure the Axure prototyping speed can be increased in general—just as code subroutines and objects that solve common programing problems are freely available to developers (for a wide variety of development environments).

Clearly, these more sophisticated progressions will be best suited to those with a more technical background, who are capable of complex Axure prototyping. However, the basic technique of using the **OnMove** event on a dynamic panel to reduce redundancy in a prototype's interaction model is not particularly difficult to understand at its most basic level, and I hope it will be useful to the wider Axure community.

Marc-Oliver Gern – Using the Axure UI Kit, a Widget Library

Tutorial level: Beginner to advanced

Practitioner Profile

Inconsistencies of interactive components and UI elements in software products are a nightmare. Not only are they confusing to end users and developers, but they also drive up the development costs, since they are extremely hard to manage and difficult to update. The end goal always should be to bundle up all the functionalities your app needs with as few UI components as possible.

Marc has created a new interactive toolkit in Axure (`http://wearebridge.co/ux-tools`) to help UX, IX, and visual designers build better, more consistent prototypes faster. It consists of UI elements, page modules, and page templates. You can now easily build wireframes and flows or start your own library with some of the stencils he has provided. Libraries can be used not only to verify design assumptions on a component-by-component basis, but also to define and document design decisions. Libraries constructed in Axure can be easily shared, tested, and kept up to date.

This section will briefly walk you through the process of creating and adding a new page module to the library of interactive components. A page module consists of multiple UI elements and can initiate several view changes inside its own property. Dynamic modules are becoming increasingly important with the growing popularity of single-page applications.

1. Ideate and Define

Let's assume that you already set the stage for your library and used the widget, interaction, and page style panes to define a consistent form language for your components (colors, shapes, proportions, fonts, margin, padding, and so on). We can jump straight to the design of a new module. We are also clear about the context, function, and form of the new module.

The way I always approach the next stage is to look at best practices on the web or on mobile and search to find out if there are already established design patterns out there that I can adopt. Especially, when you design components for closed platforms, such as the iOS and Android, or XBOX, you want to make sure you "stick to existing frameworks" (Roman Nurik, Android Design team). This is basically your first, free usability test; if you see it in action on a major site or app, it probably has been tested already with users. You can also quickly google usability and performance tests and get answers on more specific questions around touch events, gestures, form creation, naming conventions, icons, legibility, and so on. The web is full of knowledge.

Feeling a bit more fancy and ready to raise the design bar? Check out the Web and you can draw some inspiration from `www.pattrns.com`, `www.littlebigdetails.com`, `www.behance.com`, `www.cssdesignawards.com`, and so on. There are some really interesting design visions out there that might add just the pixel piece you needed. After all, design is about imagination and experimentation, not just designing by numbers.

So finally, you think you are on a good path and maybe have even discovered two solutions along your design journey. Now, let's quickly talk to a front-end developer and see if there are some issues around performance. He should also give you a rough estimate for coding. Connect the dots: the goal of this first step is to come up with the most elegant solution to solve your design problem.

2. Build

You are equipped with a clear idea, notes, and raw sketches and can go back to Axure to craft the new page module. I hope you made use of the built-in Axure widget library and created a new library. If not, do so; it's much easier to manage, share, and distribute your components later on.

Ok, let's start clicking. First thing, look at the existing UI elements you already crafted and see what you can reuse. Remember the overarching design mantra for interaction designers: build more with less, more efficiently. Think as a front-end developer and what code she or he can reuse to achieve a specific outcome quickly. Look at what is on your website or your app already and what combination of existing elements might do the job as well.

Take the following page module for example (*Image 61*). It is a Welcome Module for first-time users. It elegantly wraps multiple functionalities into a dynamic widget and was built quickly by merging a few basic UI elements: an accordion, form fields, a button, the carousel, and the modal window itself. These basic elements might be already in your library, so you just need to stitch them together, which is easy since you built them based on a grid and global style attributes. The solution and adaptive view for small screen devices can be just the accordion itself—the grid shows us where the breakpoints are and how it can fit on a vertical view of a smartphone.

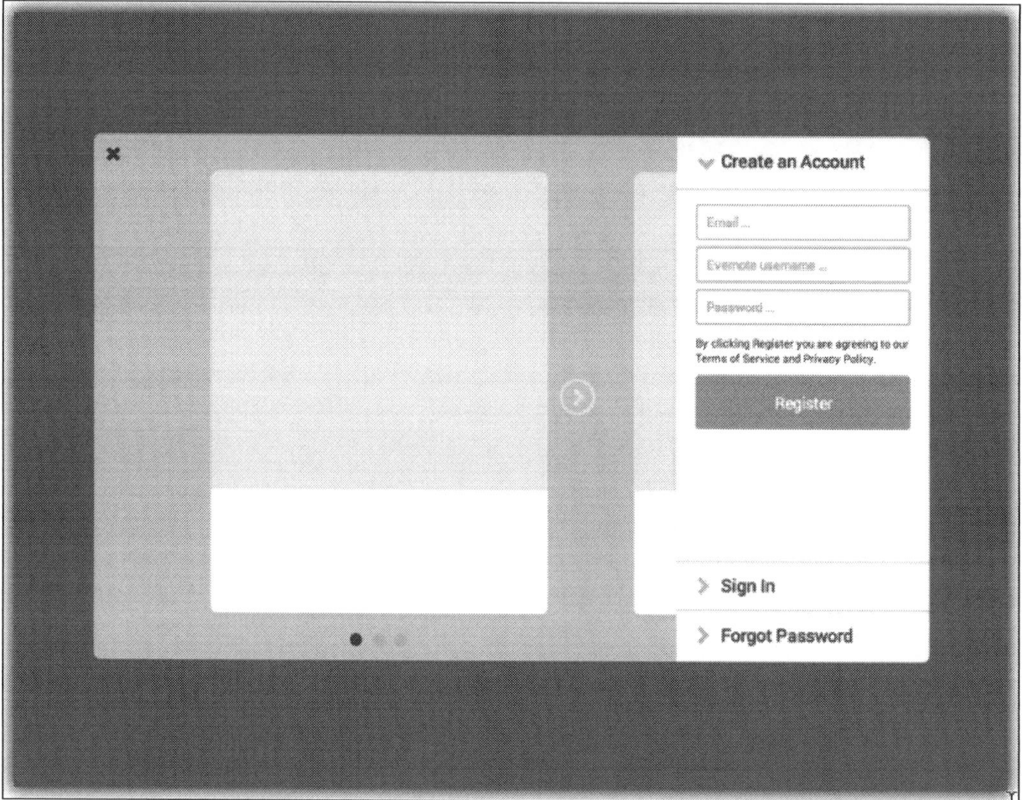

Image 61

The functionality for the individual components (the accordion, form fields, button, view controller, and so on) has been established earlier and should be available to you right away.

> You can use widget interactions and page interactions once you've created a master out of a single component. Page interactions are good for initializing **onPageLoad** events, such as setting a specific state for a dynamic widget. Be sure to name each and every component or group module. It will be easier for you to add interactions and reference the right widgets.

3. Contextualize

While building components, make sure you understand the context in which other designers, researchers, content strategists, or copywriters are going to use the library you created later. When you look at the previous example, I didn't define every single element, nor did I add all the content for the different states and views. I left it open and just provided the functional framework my colleagues can take and continue working on effectively. We will discuss one such case as an example: a UX researcher wants to test different images and alternative messaging on a welcome flow. You want to make it easy for him/her to change the content and quickly build several test cases. You might also have the chance to build products for different markets, and a library is an awesome tool to test localization. Give it a try: change English to the German or Russian version and see how the proportions of your components hold up. It is a good thing that you defined some global style attributes using the widget pane from Axure. Now, you can easily change the font size of all your green buttons in the UI library. Maybe the executive producer did not like the green color of the buttons either? If so, change it back to grey with a click of a button.

Think you are finished? Do the clean up: describe it, name it, and stitch it to an existing folder so people can find it easily later. I use categories that are more generic such as UI elements, page modules, and page components. Maybe it makes more sense to tie the components to your developer's naming conventions and how they refer to UI modules in the code. I also had good experiences with actual themes such as maps, forum, e-commerce, and so on. See what works best within your context.

4. Test

This is the beauty of Axure. Now that you've actually created your new module in a real prototyping tool, you can take it for a test ride. Go ahead, open a new document and drag your new module from the widget library onto your page. I often use the public folder of Dropbox, so I can share a link with the stakeholders too. Preview it in a browser and click on all the interactive components, change the views, and so on. Don't miss the opportunity to look it up on a tablet and/or small screen device, if you happen to optimize the view port in **Publish / Generate HTML Files**. You especially want to check where the copy breaks, readability, positioning, the timing for transitioning, and so on. Are you missing some interactions? While dragging your element from the library to your screen, Axure might have lost a reference to a specific widget. Go back to the interaction widget and see if there is an undefined piece of code. The goal of this state is to make it work rock solid so that it can be tested with real users, if needed.

5. Iterate

You have discovered some usability flaws or performance issues and might also have looked at some testing results from your UX researchers. It's time to implement the changes and put the official stamp on it: Version 1.0 of the software will change on a relatively frequent basis, so make sure to keep track of the changes. I usually add a change log page to each library. You can also use the Note widget from Axure to keep track of changes. With this, you keep the users of your library informed about the changes you made. Now, you might not be the only one working on this library, so it's good practice on how to log your work.

Here we go—you've added another page module with several UI elements to your widget library. Maybe you should inform your colleagues about it and introduce the new design snippet with a friendly "Welcome XYZ to the family" e-mail. I hope you crafted an e-mail template already. Get ready and start your own UI kit or even lay out an interactive style guide with Axure.

Collaboration

The following section includes contributions of Axure users who have experienced working in a team environment using Axure's Team Projects (previously known as Shared Projects). Some, like Ildikó's story, describe the experience of working in a small team. By reading about the challenges she describes, we hope that the readers who experience very similar issues will see that they are not alone. This entire book is filled with strategies which we hope can help readers, like they helped Ildikó, handle some of the issues. The case study from Orbitz, the global travel site, is at the opposite end of the spectrum. The team describes the meticulous process they let in transitioning the entire organization to Axure.

Ildikó Balla – Collaboration in Small Teams

The following section is based on a Skype interview with Ezra—one of the authors of this book.

Practitioner Profile

Ildikó Balla is a UX consultant currently living in Sydney, Australia. She has over six years of experience working on mobile, web, and desktop applications ranging from simple sites to complex back-office solutions and e-commerce platforms, and experience in establishing and leading a small team of junior interaction designers. Specializing in interaction design and medium-fidelity prototyping, Axure has been Ildikó's tool of choice for the past five years.

Ildikó is currently working for reInteractive (`www.reinteractive.net`), Australia's largest Ruby on Rails-focused development company. She is in charge of requirements analysis, information architecture, interaction design, and user testing for complex web applications and business intelligence solutions.

Some of Ildikó's short articles about UX, interaction design, and prototyping can be found on the company's blog. She is a regular attendee of AxureWorld and similar Axure- and UX-related events. She was the technical reviewer of *Axure RP Prototyping Cookbook, John Henry Krahenbuhl, Packt Publishing*.

In her spare time, Ildikó is often found taking pictures, travelling, riding, and learning new languages, though usually not all at the same time.

Reflections on Team Projects

On one of my projects, I was the lead of a small team of three additional junior interaction designers, who were also not familiar with Axure. So I had to quickly share from my experience in both UX and the tool. Another challenge was the limited ability of some members in the team to communicate in English when it came to writing clear annotations.

The team was required to annotate the wireframes, and these annotations were later consumed by **Business Analysts (BAs)**, who generated more extensive specification documents, and stakeholders through the HTML prototype.

Early on, we had to get to an agreement on how much to annotate, and who will write and review the annotations. It was important to provide the client with a consistent, fluid level of writing, and given the language challenge mentioned earlier, the majority of the task was assigned to one team member who was assigned the writing. As mentioned earlier, because BAs were assigned the task of writing the extensive specification documents, the agreement was that the team provides only light annotations, and the workload on the person was manageable.

To support team collaboration, we used the Shared Projects feature (renamed Team Projects in Version 7) from the get go. With help from the company's IT team, we were set up on the company's own SVN server, and we were supported by IT throughout.

I am a proponent of naming conventions and implement and use them. I encouraged my team to use the scheme, because it can save a lot of time in the long run, especially when trying to guess what things are or do. But, I ended up not enforcing it, just because it was difficult to govern on top of all the other things I had on my plate.

The prototype we were expected to deliver did include the visual design, but the interactions were in high fidelity. The way we split the work, each team member owned a set of pages in the file and was responsible for building the interactions on these pages.

We would have documented our code, if there was a way to do it in Axure, to add comments to interactions. Instead, we tried to use very descriptive names. But when it came to global variables, for example, we had a challenge. Because each team member was creating variables as needed, and because it is not possible to document variables (owner, purpose, and so on), the list of global variables mushroomed with redundancies and abandoned variables, but no one knew what they were and where they were used. Everyone was afraid to delete variables in case they broke something, somewhere in the prototype.

With each team member owning a chunk of the prototype pages, we had obvious style differences. Some were careful about alignment and measurements and some were more loose in their treatment of the layout, distorting images instead of fitting them, for example, use of line width, and so on. This created consistency issues. We did not initially have a widget library, but we quickly started using masters, as I wanted to ensure that consistency does not get out of control. We also incorporated the style guide, which was mostly textual, as a master in the file.

Susan Grossman – Enterprise Team Sharing

Susan's experience, while describing the challenges of large UX teams using Axure's collaboration features, shares many fundamentals with Ildikó's.

Practitioner Profile

Susan Grossman is a well-seasoned enterprise consultant who usually works under titles like Senior UX Analyst, Interaction Designer, or Technical Trainer. She has actively used Axure at a variety of corporations, working with their teams' nuances and processes, through many diverse projects: waterfall, agile, or lean. An avid all-inclusive web proponent, Susan volunteers to help nonprofits improve usability and meet accessibility. She works out of her California Gold Rush foothills home with a Rhodesian Ridgeback at her side.

Reflections on Team Projects

When using Axure in an enterprise environment, shared projects online and outside the firewall are a must. I can't imagine going back to working without one.

There are several repositories out there that allow you to set access permissions on different projects and maintain version control. One of them is Beanstalk, which keeps an activity log by project, supports grouping projects in separate repositories, has e-mail notifications, and prominently gives the subversion URL to use the first time you "Get and Open" a shared project. The ability to assign users to specific projects with separate URLs for retrieving is a must for busy UX teams. For me, it emphasizes teamwork, even when you're working remotely, and you see all those check-ins with comments in the main area and everyone with permissions in the right column.

Whatever repository you use, being able to add notes for every check in and downloading any past version are expected features. I like being able to get a past version, save it off locally as an `.rp` file and pull in older pages from it. When business asks for something that was removed in a previous release or an idea that wasn't used before, which could work now on a different screen, this comes in real handy.

Since Axure allows you to choose what pages to generate, some teams will set several cover pages in the prototype. There will be one cover page for the business that will always get published as the root or top-level page. This page explains what you're showing and gives details on what a wireframe is, what it does and doesn't include, and any disclaimers you may need about pages using screenshots from existing live sites, the look and feel of being in the comp part of the project, and what it means to be sketchy.

The second cover page is never published and is strictly for passing along information to someone who may pick up the project a year later. This is a significant time saver when looking up things, such as who was on the initial project, a summary of the main requirements, and nice-to-haves that are on unpublished pages for future releases, including in past versions, and so forth.

Why Have an Existing Online Product Outside the Firewall?

You don't have to create your own repository or install and maintain one. I'm a remote contractor for a large corporation, have been remotely contracting for quite a few years, and depend a lot on discussion.

A lot of companies use an online bug tracker, or put their knowledge base outside the firewall, and it makes sense to do the same for your shared Axure projects. They need to be accessible no matter where the team members are, and without relying on logging in and going through a network first. When well utilized in a collaborative team project, your files get pretty large, cumbersome, or completely unreachable if the network has issues. Even if the team is all onsite, there are often things that must be done in the evening or over the weekend when going back to the office isn't possible.

The repository must allow you to set different levels of permissions. Even when we're all pros, someone will accidently delete something, relocate to another project, or make some mistake wherever possible. And like Murphy's law, it will happen right before an important presentation of the work to business sponsors. At the minimum, you'll need roles for a limited number of team members who can administer (add/delete), an overall owner (or super admin) who can add users and assign administrators, and finally, users who can check in and out of a project once it is set up.

Process and Convention

It's important to have a process to use Axure-shared projects that the UX team follows. These include how they deal with the repository, how they add/remove pages in the site map, what masters must be used, when to create new masters, and how to display interactions and roles.

Always Get the Latest

Before starting work on an existing project, always get all the changes from the shared directory or there's a high probability of overwriting someone else's work. No exceptions.

Before generating a prototype, even if done to quickly show something, always get all the changes from the shared directory or there's a high probability that you may show work that's no longer valid. Again, no exceptions. I've seen this happen both with the site owner questioning why they're seeing something they thought was changed, or ended up showing something that has been scrapped.

Never use the **Check out Everything** option unless you change something on every page. Also, inform everyone else working on the project. There's nothing more frustrating than trying to fix something late at night and finding it checked out to an unreachable teammate who wasn't even working on that page. Pages should be checked out as determined. They then need to be edited in Axure using the option **Check Out**.

You need a process to check-in—some teams request that every night a check-in is done, both for versioning and a record of progress in the check-in notes. Others assign specific sections and request that they aren't checked in until the section is ready for its first review. This works fine as long as any new masters or changes to masters are coordinated. This is really a choice determined by the number of people working on the project, and how fast the turnaround is.

Size

One of the reasons why past versions should be saved and made easily available is file size. Often, multiple candidate wireframes exploring possible interpretations of the requirements are set up as root-level pages. Some of these pages are removed over time to reduce the file's size and its complexity. If all alternative interactions for all versions, including their notes, are retained on a large project, they become difficult to sync and pull down without crashing or not completing them on the standard issue company laptop.

Saved versions or past versions that can be easily fetched from the repository will allow you to import a style or concept down the line when the business remembers something they saw early on and think that the current requirements could use that treatment. It's also not best practice to leave all the pages in, even if they aren't published. A team member could unknowingly build the project and set pages that the business has decided against generating, causing invalid feedback, and making you look bad.

It's important to know and consider all your team mates' systems. If someone was issued with an older laptop, though you may have no problems uploading and retrieving a large project, if other members are unable to get the project running without errors, or crashing, timelines will slip. It's important to remember that this isn't an issue with Axure itself, but the systems using Axure and getting projects from a shared, external repository.

Enterprise Naming Conventions

As mentioned previously, initial versions of the wireframers' early interpretation of the requirements are set up as root-level pages. A lot of projects name their screens by the initial requirement feat, use case number, or user story name, depending on the company. Under each named version, there are sets of the same child pages (name and data) showcasing the style of the version.

For a simple example of initial concept versioning, one version may be a tabbed or panel experience, another maybe a dynamic version with a section of the page changing based on choices, the final version showing highlights of everything like a dashboard. It's important that each child of these different flows' names would reflect the parent version for easy referencing in remote meetings.

Names and Dynamics

For clear directions to those creating the comps and then relating the full experience to development, dynamics can sometimes add an unexpected kink. In a project that has several roles accessing the same pages that were shown different sections and/or possible data sets, we chose to display the role in Axure dynamic. When generated as HTML and demoed, we entered the screen as the core user, and there was a mini dashboard in the top corner that was not part of the flow. It allowed us to switch to the other roles by selecting the role name link. This changed areas on the screen using Axure variables with **OnClicks**. It was very clear to the business that we could include a bit of flow, keep the dashboard, and switch users at any time on any page. The business loved it.

Then, it was time to do the comps and many extra meetings had to be called. There wasn't a physical screen named with the company convention that they could tie directly to a comp and without this, a matrix had to be created so comps weren't missed. It also caused extra meetings with the development team on why there were comps that didn't appear to match up to a named page in the wires.

In this case, the dynamics could have been less fancy and utilized name screens from the dashboard so the business still had a feel of changing roles on the screen, but would be actually moving to another page. I'd recommend saving the in-page dynamics to represent data returns, or success and error messages for form submission.

Team Skillsets

Not all team members are equally skilled with Axure. You may have some team members who are highly skilled and will set up all the masters initially, while other team members work with the business doing the initial storyboarding, architecture, and rough wires. How interactive the wires are will be determined by the team's skill levels. If there's only one person who knows how to set panel states on page load, you'll want to keep your interactions basic so everyone can work on them and the final product is consistent.

There is also risk if you have a contractor come through that sets up fancy interactions and isn't there when you're doing updates/new releases. I had the chance to work with a very skilled Axure user on one of my contracts, and though he was brought in for one specific project, he ended up assisting with some complex flows and concepts on several projects. After he was gone, and some of these projects went to other UX people, there were some major requirement changes in the next release. Things were missed because the new team members didn't know how to update the wireframes and interactions correctly.

If your team has several members with strong Axure skills, then you should be taking advantage of the features available by adding cases to show different states, and using custom widgets along with your masters.

Most UX practitioners are skilled in storyboarding and information architecture and any team member should be able to set up the sitemap correctly and generate a flow diagram within Axure. Axure makes these tasks easy to use in order to display different options to the business, grouping the versions in the sitemap and rendering a flow for the business to visualize what you're proposing. Simple storyboards can be used at this stage, like we used to do in Visio, with the storyboard kept as the first page of the final version and the generated sitemap as the second.

Publishing and Prototyping Pages and Settings Updates

Several teams I've worked on have used password-secure AxShare outside the firewall, publishing space for their wireframes. AxShare allows each team to create their own unique URL and password—all administered from the same AxShare manage page.

Make sure before you demonstrate that only the pages that are a part of the discussion, or only the approved ones, are published, which means someone has to be responsible for making sure that only the agreed-upon pages are selected in the **Pages** tab of the **Generate Prototype** menu. Managing this tree correctly can become complex when multiple team members are working on the same file, but on different pages or versions.

Not all files created are for publishing, and yet making sure the ones that are to be published have been updated in this view correctly isn't as easy as it sounds. Someone always has this checked out. You can get around that locally, but when it's time to check in and publish, you need to check destination folders and make sure someone hasn't turned on anything you don't want published, or have checked annotations that were only meant to be published for the development team.

This is just another opportunity to process and make sure all the team members understand the publishing options and how they affect even team members who don't publish.

Setting Expectations

Starting a large website/web application project brings a lot of teams together, and each team has their own expectations on what deliverables they'll produce for what purpose. The teams that receive these deliverables have their own expectations on what they'll receive and how they'll use them. Often, there's a large chasm between these sets of expectations.

Axure has opened a lot of possibilities for higher-quality deliverables and has widened the gap between these expectations. Fortunately, expectations can be set early in the requirement process to help close the gap. The cover page discussed previously is part of setting expectations, and I have found it very helpful to read it out loud to the business before diving into the presentation.

So What Are You Boarding/Framing/Prototyping?

Teams need to determine how they're using Axure. Sometimes a project can be jumped into before there's a team together other than business analysts. Whoever is doing these early stage flows and story boards in Axure needs to know before they start how deep the final deliverables are for the UX team.

What are the architecture or design goals? Are they using the interactions for activity analysis or just to portray to the business? Will the business want to see the comps themselves added into the wires, or are they separate deliverables? What is the expected complexity level? All these factors affect the Axure skills you need for the project. Do you need all requirements, wire/comp/content in a comprehensive specification? If so, you many need team members who really understand how to coax Axure to generate a usable requirements document.

Is this being built off an existing look and feel? Is this an enhancement to an existing product that another team initially worked on? Then, you'll want to see what already exists and leverage any masters or other widgets available, base your team choices on the type of interactions, and set up.

I've seen very good UX people with basic Axure skills end up on pages that utilize a lot of the features they have no idea how to use. If paired with an Axure guru, they'll supply extremely high-quality deliverables, whereas alone they'd fail, with business and development both unhappy.

Look And Feel (L&F) in Wires

The following section addresses the impact and importance of wireframe fidelity.

High-fidelity Wireframes Really Get the Point Across!

I've had companies hire me for reviews and hand me their Axure project to use to see all the paths, what it should look like, and where each flow starts. They included full navigation that reflected the page you were on and all the content (final images and text). These projects made it possible to review the final project thoroughly and completely understand the kind of responses and when they should happen. Their high fidelity made it so we didn't need any clarification meetings, and enabled working remotely 100 percent, for a fast turnaround with more time available to produce a final quality analysis.

High-fidelity Wireframes Can Lead to Extreme Frustration

When working on a very large enterprise project, wireframes are not a living artifact. The framers don't expect to be updating them as the content people complete content, or the UI people create the final graphics. They are a stage in design that defines the interactions as well as the basic layout. Deliverables down the line, such as content matrices and comps, will refer to them by page names and someone will probably keep a mapping matrix too.

In this instance, the Axure project is a tool to help the business understand what they're asking for, what does and doesn't work, and show all the interactions. Once approved, the project is a tool for the UI to work up comps from, and content to see what they need to produce. Then this group of artifacts goes to development for coding, and quality assurance to write test scripts. At different stages of the wires, the teams all come together to discuss the path taken, voice their doubts, make suggestions, praise some ideas, and so forth.

If the wires are high fidelity, what happens is the business wants to see the content in the frames, not just placeholders, and wants to know what the image is going to look like. System admins will take apart pieces like your footer that may not exactly match the links they already have in production, and want you to match everything and change it with the next month's release. Then the developers start telling you that unless all the latest content and possible flows are covered, they can't start coding.

If you try to accommodate all these demands, you're changing content as it's altered and approved by legal, adjusting L&F as the live product changes and approvals for images come through, and so forth. The wireframe is suddenly the truth for everything, and you'll be updating it until the "end of life" of the live web application and never move onto another new and exciting project ever again. Everyone will be unhappy, the work will go way over budget, and the nuances you could have focused on will never get improved.

It's Kind of Sketchy

It's incredibly important to set the expectations for your Axure wireframes at the start of the project. Make sure stakeholders clearly understand exactly what deliverables to expect, when to expect them and their scope and fidelity level. On large projects, get all the teams to sign off on this statement of deliverables and remind stakeholders about the agreement when needed.

There are several methods of getting this point across, including visually in Axure itself. Things such as using color for emphasis only but keeping your pseudo headers and photos gray scale will clearly show that this is not about look and feel and/or turning up the level of sketchiness. So, it looks more like a story board than a prototype. And memorize your favorite "that's what the UI will do" phrase, because you'll be using it a lot.

Lorem Ipsum can be helpful as placeholders, though there's a fine line between when and how to use this. Combined with sketchiness, the initial content paragraphs are best in Lorem Ipsum, so business can concentrate on your interactions instead of the marketing language. This comes with a warning—in a recent project I saw some Lorem Ipsum getting into a few modal windows in the test environment. The development team left in the placeholder text, and the error was only discovered during testing.

Orbitz Worldwide – Axure As a Document Base

The following case study is a remarkable, detailed, and valuable description of transitioning an entire organization from Visio to Axure. The level of planning, risk-to-value assessment, and methodology echoes the general message of this book, which puts a premium on upfront investment in preplanning, strategy, and logistics, for winning long-term value and success with the tool.

The following case study includes feedback contributions from the following team members.

Practitioner Profiles

Adam C. Basey is currently an information architect at Orbitz Worldwide, one of the leading online travel agents with previous working experience at Accenture, User Centric, and Indiana University Alumni Association, all in IT- and HCI-related areas. He has a B.S. in Informatics and M.S. in Human-Computer Interaction/Design from the Indiana University School of Informatics and Computing. He has great passion for design and always looks for ways to make things simpler. He is an expert in having a bird's eye view of the problem and sets the vision clearly before stepping forward. Personal fitness is his hobby and passion and he is an ACE-certified trainer. In his free time, he passes out his bodybybasey.com business cards and flexes frequently. The cards usually end back on his desk. His LinkedIn profile is `http://www.linkedin.com/in/adambasey`.

Suresh Kandeeban is an information architect at Cognizant Interactive, User Experience division of Cognizant Technology Solutions, one of the top-tier services and consulting companies. He is an Axure enthusiast who actively looks for better ways to work with Axure and also loves to share his knowledge. He is an expert in using the Axure tool and has good knowledge (intermediate level) in using other popular prototyping tools, such as Balsamiq, Visio, and so on. He likes reading design books and those that are related to mobiles. Responsive design and SEO inspires him a lot. His personal website is `www.sureshkandeeban.com` and he can also be found on LinkedIn at `http://www.linkedin.com/pub/suresh-kandeeban/72/a3b/973`.

Melissa Sisco is currently the User Experience Lead at CA Technologies, a large independent software company. She has been working in the User Experience department for more than 16 years and is passionate about turning around failing product experiences into positive, simple, and intuitive designs. Previously, she worked at Orbitz where she helped the UX team make the transition from Visio to Axure for all their wireframing and prototyping needs. During her 12 plus years prior to Orbitz, Melissa was a member of the User Experience group at Accenture where she helped shape the design of several websites and products for a variety of Fortune 500 companies. Her LinkedIn profile can be found at `http://www.linkedin.com/in/melissasisco/`.

Vinoth Balu Gunasekaran is a Manager (Biz. Dev.) at Cognizant Interactive, User Experience division of Cognizant Technology Solutions, a global leader in business and information technology consulting. He started off his career in interaction design about 10 years ago, architecting user experience solutions for business applications, portals, and e-commerce sites across business domain, technology landscape, form factor, and geography. As part of a long-term consulting engagement, he has been jointly working with the in-house UX team of a leading US-based online travel agency where he helped the team make a business case, chart roadmap, and complete the transition to Axure, leaning down the wireframe specifications in the process. When not working on client projects, Vinoth is typically engaged in creating proof of concepts, conducting benchmarking studies, and crafting solution approaches for IT business proposals from Cognizant's global clientele.

Julie Harpring is a senior user experience architect for the travel website company, Orbitz Worldwide, where she recently created a custom Axure widget library for the UX team. Since she entered the field of interaction design in 2005, Julie has created mobile, tablet, and desktop experiences for organizations such as Orbitz, eBookers, HotelClub, CVS Caremark, Motorola Solutions, the University of Missouri, and Goodyear. She holds a master's degree in Science in Human-Computer Interaction from Indiana University, a bachelor's degree in Journalism, and a bachelor's degree in the field of Arts in English from the University of Missouri. Julie loves tapping into her journalistic sleuthing skills to gain user insights that lead to exciting new concepts. Her LinkedIn profile can be found at `www.linkedin.com/in/julieharpring/`.

Background

For years, Visio has been the documentation tool in our company for an extremely large document base/wireframes of our current set of platform pages. This is a comprehensive collection of all possible permutations, combinations, and conditions of every page that a customer can see on our e-commerce platform. We call these pages document masters.

A typical project process in the UX team of our company has been that every time someone works on a project, they create a copy of a document master page and update that page/module based on the project requirements. This copy of the document master for the project is referenced as a **Project Document (PD)**. The PD is what gets presented to the business for review and further iterations before implementing. Once the project goes live, the PD will be merged back with the document master file so that the document master stays up to date. We call this merging. The following diagram will give you a brief idea of the merging process:

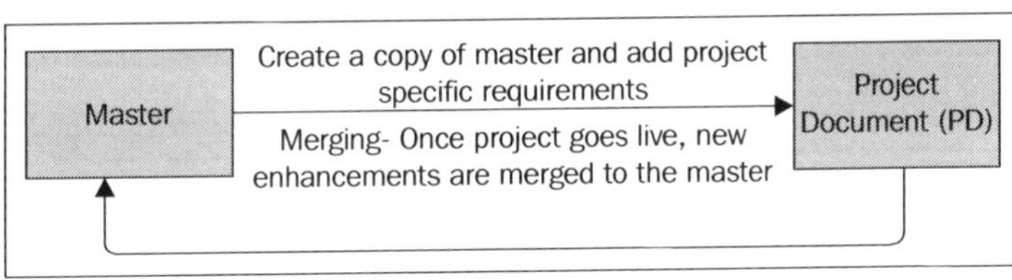

Image 62

Traditionally, this process as seen in the preceding diagram (*Image 62*) was done in Visio, which has served as a great wireframing and documentation tool, but was lacking in features as the UX industry evolved. At times, showing an interactive prototype/wireframe to stakeholders had a clear advantage in helping them understand the concept at hand. We needed a tool that allowed us to wireframe, annotate, capture functional specifications, as well as produce interactive prototypes for our PDs, and so we began to explore different tools outside of Visio to experiment with, during our PD phase.

Axure had become the go-to wireframing tool for our company for project work or PD but we still needed to justify recreating all of our Visio document masters in an Axure format. So, why Axure? From what we understood of the use of Axure during the PD phase, we felt, we could achieve the following for our document masters.

Why Axure

Following are the improvements Axure would have on our UX delivery process and how it maintains our current information architecture capabilities as well as enriches our interaction design capabilities:

Process Improvements

- Create a leaner doc base
- Simplify documenting
- Streamline delivery of doc base and project documents to stakeholders
- Simplify the merge process
- Project documents that are already being produced in Axure
- Majority of the team will be skilled in Axure
- Prototyping capabilities with less effort

Enriches Interaction Design (IxD)

Axure provides a rich canvas of prototyping and IxD-centric artifacts in its tool set:

- IxD is where we define system behaviors to answer the question, "How does a user take the action they want?".

  For example, the drop-downs lists, buttons, and checkboxes in a web e-mail application are defined in the IxD, so there I can find the answer to a question such as "How should I reply to the sender of this e-mail?".

Maintains Current Information Architecture (IA)

Axure is capable of maintaining current IA capabilities:

- In IA, we define the information structure to answer the question, "How does a user find the information they want?".

  For example, navigation links for a big corporate website are in IA and there we define the answer to a question like "Where can I find directions to the company's main headquarters?".

Investigation and Implementation of Axure as a Document Base

After reviewing multiple wireframing/prototyping tools in an agile environment during the PD phase, the team focused on Axure and its suitability in managing not only our PDs but our masters as well.

We created a working group of five people that met once or twice weekly over a course of six months, and used the following set of activities to investigate Axure's capabilities as a possible document base to hold our masters and determine the implementation strategy.

Proof of Concept

One of the first things we did in the working group was to begin building a skeleton/framework in the format of an **Axure Team Project** using one of our more complex document masters. It was necessary to test all the content and methods we used in Visio within the Axure environment and determine new ways to work.

Essentially, we began to create a **proof of concept** (**POC**) that was eventually shared with management and the UX team for buy in. While building the POC, we were able to determine why Axure would be a better tool for us, as shown in the following table:

Features	Description	Visio	Axure
Leverage doc base for PD creation	Exports a shared project to the mirror RP file for creation of PD.	5	1
Report creation	Uses annotations or page notes to create a report. For example, doc maintenance.	4	2
Masters	A container that can hold a collection of widgets that you can reuse throughout your doc base or RPPRJ (shared project).	5	1

Features	Description	Visio	Axure
Sharing doc base	Ability to generate an HTML link to share the doc base.	5	1
Doc base version control	Built-in version control that brings back the previous state of a master.	0	3
Merging	Ability to import from PD under certain circumstances (replaces an entire page or create a new page).	5	1
Doc base structure/nav	Provides the stakeholder and IA a hierarchy of document contents with active links.	5	2
Screen map	Provides the stakeholder and IA a screen map with active links to the associated pages.	4	1
File Management	Ability to see pages being worked on.	4	1
Widgets	Community of widgets and customization of widgets.	3	2

Project Document Improvements with Axure

The following table represents the improvements Axure would have on our PDs and UX delivery process with one being easy and five difficult:

Features	Description	Visio	Axure
Layering	Ability to cycle between annotations, wireframe, and design comp.	4	2
PD/deliverable consumption	Generate a single access point to PD with multiple pages and ensure stakeholders are viewing the most up-to-date PD.	4	2
PD version control	Self-contained versioning within the deliverable.	3	2
PD structure/nav	Provides the stakeholder and IA with a more clear hierarchy of document contents in a left rail.	5	2
Screen map	Provides the stakeholder and IA with a screen map with active links to the associated pages.	5	2
Widgets	Community of widgets and customization of widgets.	3	2
Prototyping	IA contents are already in a prototyping-ready environment.	5	1

Lean-down Documentation

Separate sessions were held where we identified and called out every type of documentation method and artifact used in our Visio document masters. The purpose of this activity was to allow our quality engineers, user interface engineers, product specialists, and developers raise a voice into what the future of the document base would be. More importantly, it was an opportunity to remove artifacts that no longer needed to be documented in our document masters. Essentially, we carried out a process to lean-down documentation to eliminate old or unnecessary documentation artifacts.

Effort/Estimation

The initiative to migrate the doc base from Visio to Axure started with an effort estimate. We considered two different approaches with the biggest assumption being "nothing will be dynamic" (as in, we will only move the masters over from Visio to Axure as static wireframes with no interactions) in the doc base document masters as follows:

- **Approach A**: Evolutionary (build the doc base in Axure by copying it from Visio or by taking a screenshot of it)
    - **Pros**: Communicate the vision by building the doc base in a lesser time span.
    - **Cons**: Not reusable from a project standpoint. This is one of the objectives for the migration.
- **Approach B**: Rebuild (start creating all the wireframe views/conditions in Axure)
    - **Pros**: Completely reusable from both a project document creation perspective and merging perspective.
    - **Cons**: Requires a longer time span.

To align with UX team's Vision for an efficient use of the doc base, we started with the rebuild approach to construct the entire doc base in Axure, though it took longer.

Effort Calculation

The following are the estimates for the effort required to migrate the document base:

- Conducted a quick audit of the existing document masters documented in Visio.
- Categorized those into three buckets—small, medium, and high complexity.

- Rebuilt a sample of each document master per complexity level (small, medium, and high) for an estimate of the time it would take to document the master into Axure based on approaches A and B.
- Split the team—one group focused on the evolutionary approach and the other on the rebuild approach.
- After completing the tasks, armed with the figures, we calculated the overall migration estimates/efforts.

The following table shows our estimates for the two approaches:

Hours for high complexity views/ conditions	Hours for medium complexity views/ conditions	Hours for low complexity views/ conditions	# of files	Total effort	Resource	Duration
Evolutionary approach—1.5 hours per Visio doc (average)						
0.5	0.5	0.5	305	305 x 1.5 = 457.5 hrs.	1	57 days
Rebuild approach—12 hours per Visio doc (average)						
6	4.5	1.5	305	305 x 12 = 3660 hrs.	1	457 days

Assuming a single resource was working 20 days a month, we estimated the Evolutionary approach will require three months compared to 23 months for the Rebuild approach.

To align with X team's vision to make an efficient use of the doc base, we started with the Rebuild approach to build the entire doc base in Axure, though it took longer. More about that in the *Axure Migration* section.

Internal Documentation Process

The following workflow table represents the collaborative working model of UXAs and UXDs at various stages of the design process/activities:

Step 1	Step 2	Step 3	Step 4	Next Stage:	Artifact/s
Process A. Project Kick-off					
Get all the changes from the shared directory	Quick check-in/ out to identify/ annotate the impacted pages	Export as an RP file	Retain only relevant pages	B. Project Updates	Project RP file
Process B. Project Updates					
User Research/ Concepting	Create a shared project from the current file	Share UXA/UXD artifacts with stakeholders		C. Usability Testing (Optional)	Project RPPRJ file – UXA/UXD solutions
Process C. Usability Testing (Optional)					
Prepare usability test artifacts	Create linked comps (if needed) or rich, interactive prototype	Test with users		D. Merging (Once the project goes live)	Highly Interactive RP/RPPRJ file
Process D. Merging (Once the project goes live)					
Get all changes from the shared directory	Archive the doc base	Check out all the master pages and merge project updates into it	Quick check in/out to remove annotations		Document master RPPRJ file

Workflow Details

The following sections will give you a detailed description of different stages in workflow.

Process A – Project Kick-off

This phase starts with getting all the changes from the shared directory so as to ensure we have the latest version of the document master to get started with the new project.

There have been conflicts in the past where two UXAs/UXDs work on the same page (for example, the search results page) later realizing/understanding the conflicts. Traditionally, Excel was used to resolve these conflicts; however, we identified a potential solution in Axure that we started using by annotating the site map under a user's name with intended page changes.

The following screenshot (*Image 63*) shows how Axure's annotation capability was used for a page tracker (content was scrubbed for confidentiality reasons):

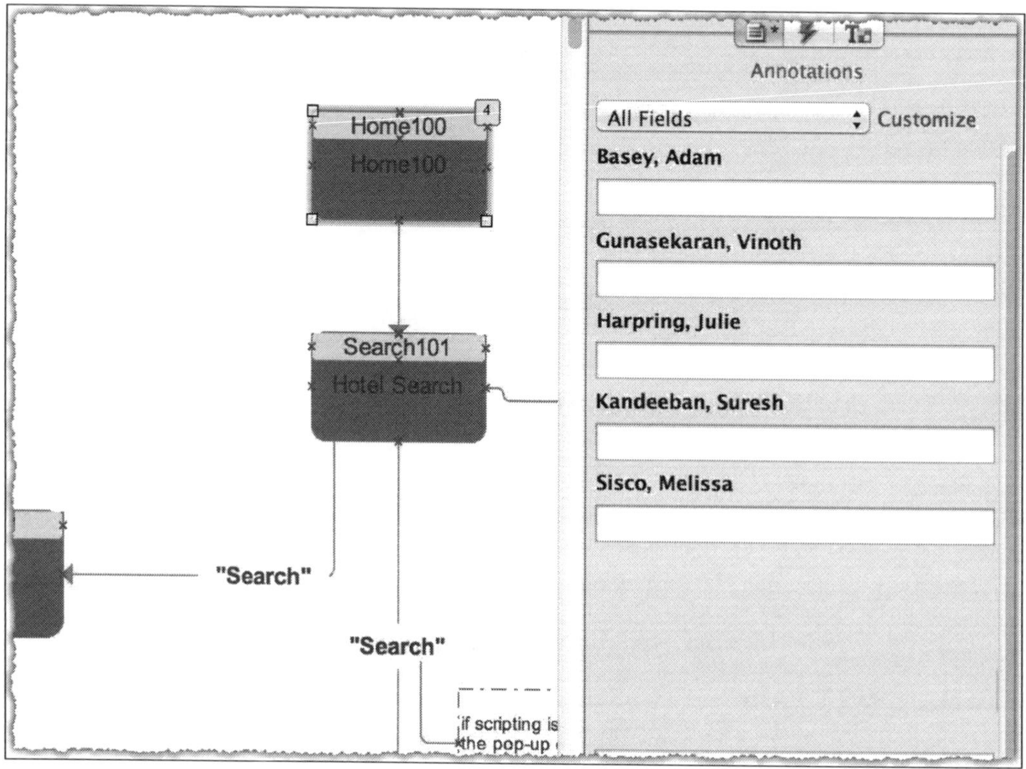

Image 63

A quick check in/out mentioned in the workflow table is the step to inform users to annotate pages that are getting impacted, so everyone on the team has visibility of the document masters that are being used for PDs, along with some high-level details of document master changes.

Next, a UX team member exports the document masters that have been identified from the document base shared file `.rppj` to a `.rp` file. The objective is to retain only those pages that are necessary or relevant to their project. It's important that no actual changes to the document base are made until a merge takes place.

Any work created on a PD should not be represented in the document base until the project goes live. Because team members may be working on the document master at the same time for different projects in different PDs, we used Axure's annotation feature to create an integrated file tracker, which allows team members to chat with one another on potential feature team/project overlaps.

Process B – Project Updates

This is the phase where most design explorations occur. UXAs/UXDs will set the exported (.rp) file as a shared project file (.rpprj) among themselves to work on collaboratively, which is now their shared PD. Based on reviews and iterations, the designs will be updated / changed and the final version will be shared with the stakeholders as detailed in the *Storing/Sharing Files* section. To iterate, the deliverable will host both UXA/UXD artifacts in the same location without having to go to different targets, which is one of the main advantages of using a shared project delivery. Another main advantage is to ensure there is communication between the UXA and UXD so that the designs/wires presented are in sync.

Process C – Usability Testing

As mentioned, this phase doesn't apply to all projects. For those applicable, interactive wireframes are created using the linked comps approach or Axure's interactive capability.

Process D – Merging

This phase starts only when the project goes live. As the first step, a team member would get all the changes from the shared directory for the latest version of the document base. In our company, there is a traditional process of archiving the old version of the documents whenever you make updates and we leveraged the same approach while using Axure by exporting a version of the document base `.rpprj` to a `.rp` file. Axure's built-in shared version history didn't work out to our specific needs, since it handles each and every update as a version.

Once a team member has the latest version of the doc base, they export it as a `.rp` file and archive it. Then, they will check out those pages that they want to update with the new project-specific changes from their PD, which is in the `.rpprj` or `.rp` format. They can either copy and paste or choose to import with Axure's import feature from the PD.

Once a team member completes the merge, they will remove any annotations/notes, from the screen map we are leveraging as the file tracker, to indicate that they are done with the project. The document base is now updated from the PD, and the PD is also archived in the `UX_Projects` file location mentioned in the following section, in a directory labeled `merged`.

Storing/Sharing Files

We created three file locations for people to manage their artifact throughout the design process; they are as follows:

- `UX_Doc Base`: This is the folder where the document base master configuration file resides.
- `UX_Projects`: This is the folder where the project-specific documents (project RP file, project RPPRJ file, design comps, assets, and so on) reside.
- `Design_Server`: This is the space where the shared prototype (`.rprj`) is published and shared with the stakeholders. Stakeholders can only see the readable version of the wireframes / design comps. By only sharing the generated HTML with stakeholders, we can take down PD anytime the project or UX standards used within that PD are out of date.

Demo to UX Team and Management

Another activity was presenting and demonstrating findings to the management and the UX team. We had many iterations of our POC, internal process documentation, training material, and other artifacts mentioned in this case study. Our approach was very iterative and eventually we landed on a version of the document base in Axure that was acceptable to the team, and we were given approval to migrate from Visio to Axure.

Training/Change Management

The activities that were used to bring our team up to speed on the Axure document base and delivery process of PDs are as follows:

- **Video / Audio training**: This activity is used to get the team excited with a fun video of how the POC worked.
- **Wiki pages**: This is the location for all internal process documentation to use Axure as the document base.
- **Open hours**: Open-door policy for questions and continued education.
- **Working sessions**: Sessions with smaller groups of the UX Team with their specific project needs and PDs.
- **Team meetings**: Meetings to show findings and updates to process changes when needed.
- **Retros**: Meetings where the UX team has the opportunity to give a design-and-process critique of the document base and process where we collect action items to make fixes.

Axure Migration

Our proof of concept finally worked well with all the investigations and explorations that we did. With multiple rounds of presentations and discussions, we got a buy-in from the management team to move on with the huge effort of document base migration from Vision to Axure.

We identified a resource by the name of Jessintha Jeyaraj who worked out of the southern part of India to help us in completing this migration. She did justice to this to a point where we can say, "The Axure doc base is up and running for use".

Afterword

Writing a book about software can often feel like attempting to build a skyscraper on quicksand and it certainly feels like it at times. We started writing this book about a year ago when Axure 7 was in its infancy. Back then, we thought that this project would be fast and relatively straightforward—merely an update to the Version 6 book. However, this was when we knew very little about the new stuff Axure was "cooking" such as the Repeater and Adaptive Views features meant to tackle head-on simulating data-driven applications and Responsive Web Design (RWD).

When we started writing, RWD has not been very common yet. Nonetheless, we had already noticed the trend among employers and recruiters to demand, in addition to UX mastery, also HTML/CSS and JavaScript proficiency for prototype coding—a frustrating demand that underscores how deeply UX is misunderstood in the software industry. The introduction of Adaptive Views and Repeater meant a chance to revert the trend and let UX designers regain control over rapid prototyping.

Axure's new capabilities meant that we, the authors, had to rethink the strategies around wireframe and prototype construction as well as the generation of specification documents. We also had to examine the impact of these new capabilities on collaboration. And another thing: when Ezra wrote *Axure RP 6 Prototyping Essentials*, and Elizabeth was one of his technical reviewers, we both had a wealth of experience with the tool; we were the experts. However, when we started working on this book, our challenge was to synthesize, fuse, and extrapolate the old and the new.

We quickly realized that in addition to Axure's new capabilities, Axure 7 will include numerous enhancements and improvements that also impact the entire process of prototyping with the tool. For example, you no longer need to create a dynamic panel just to control the visibility of a widget because visibility is now part of the style settings of widgets and can be controlled directly. This may look like a trivial tweak, but for any user working with Axure since Version 4, this is a major improvement to wireframing construction efficiency and quality. It also means having to unlearn, adapt, and remaster one's Axure skills.

To make the challenge a little more interesting, new features were formed and matured over many months. Through a succession of Alpha and Beta versions and regular conversations with Victor, Paul, and others at the company, we found ourselves rewriting and tweaking earlier drafts that became obsolete, or because we found better ways to get things done.

With a wealth of video tutorials available on the Internet, we decided to reduce the amount of step-by-step instructions that are so common to software books, including the previous version of this one. Where such detailed walkthrough is used, we tried to describe more of the "why" and less of the "what". As UX designers, we regret, however, that the usability of these instructions is sometimes poor; although, our original drafts had images and text side by side for improved readability, we had to revert to the final layout largely due to the requirements of Amazon's Kindle platform.

When Axure 7 was released in December 2013, the pressure to finish the book intensified for many good reasons. However, we felt that we needed more time to digest the tool before we could finish the writing. Our editors at Packt Publishing were fully supportive despite the loss of revenue.

In conclusion, despite the challenges, and the need to negotiate full-capacity workloads and personal life, we have focused on writing a book that both of us would want to read: a book about the continual process of getting better at controlling communication with stakeholders, managing expectations throughout the design process, and mastering the planning, estimation, and production of world-class artifacts.

We hope you find value in this book. We are looking forward to hear your comments and suggestions for improvement.

Ezra Schwartz and Elizabeth Srail

Index

A

H

I

L

M

Q

R

S

T

U

V

W

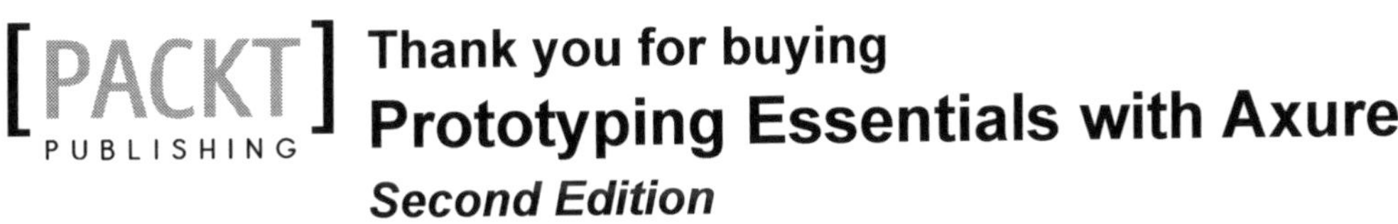

About Packt Publishing

Packt, pronounced 'packed', published its first book "*Mastering phpMyAdmin for Effective MySQL Management*" in April 2004 and subsequently continued to specialize in publishing highly focused books on specific technologies and solutions.

Our books and publications share the experiences of your fellow IT professionals in adapting and customizing today's systems, applications, and frameworks. Our solution based books give you the knowledge and power to customize the software and technologies you're using to get the job done. Packt books are more specific and less general than the IT books you have seen in the past. Our unique business model allows us to bring you more focused information, giving you more of what you need to know, and less of what you don't.

Packt is a modern, yet unique publishing company, which focuses on producing quality, cutting-edge books for communities of developers, administrators, and newbies alike. For more information, please visit our website: `www.packtpub.com`.

Writing for Packt

We welcome all inquiries from people who are interested in authoring. Book proposals should be sent to `author@packtpub.com`. If your book idea is still at an early stage and you would like to discuss it first before writing a formal book proposal, contact us; one of our commissioning editors will get in touch with you.

We're not just looking for published authors; if you have strong technical skills but no writing experience, our experienced editors can help you develop a writing career, or simply get some additional reward for your expertise.

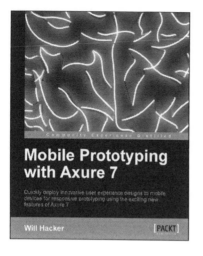

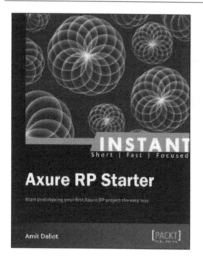

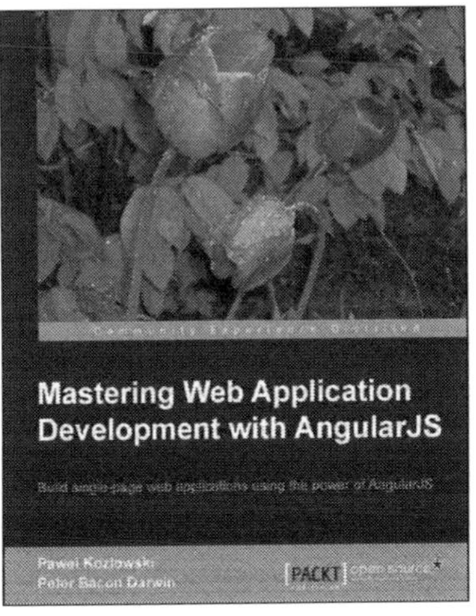

Mastering Web Application Development with AngularJS

ISBN: 978-1-78216-182-0 Paperback: 372 pages

Build single-page web applications using the power of AngularJS

1. Make the most out of AngularJS by understanding the AngularJS philosophy and applying it to real life development tasks.
2. Effectively structure, write, test, and finally deploy your application.
3. Add security and optimization features to your AngularJS applications.
4. Harness the full power of AngularJS by creating your own directives.

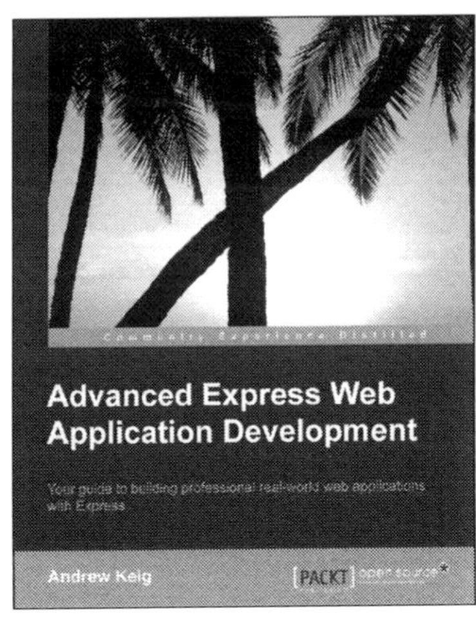

Advanced Express Web Application Development

ISBN: 978-1-78328-249-4 Paperback: 148 pages

Your guide to building professional real-world web applications with Express

1. Learn how to build scalable, robust, and reliable web applications with Express using a test-first, feature-driven approach.
2. Full of practical tips and real world examples, and delivered in an easy-to-read format.
3. Explore and tackle the issues you encounter in commercially developing and deploying an Express application.

Made in the USA
Lexington, KY
23 May 2015